W9-BBP-707

The Book Trade of the World

Volume I
Europe and International Section

The Book Trade of the World

Volume I

Europe and

International Section

Volume II

The Americas

Australia, New Zealand

Volume III

Africa, Asia

The Book Trade of the World

Edited by
Sigfred Taubert

Volume I
Europe and
International Section

Hamburg / London / New York
Verlag für
Buchmarkt-Forschung
André Deutsch
R. R. Bowker

English versions:
Frederick Plaat, London
Typography:
Hans P. Willberg, Frankfurt a. M.

Gesamtherstellung: Mohndruck
Reinhard Mohn OHG, Gütersloh
ISBN 3-578-06596-x
Printed in Germany

Distribution rights for North, Central and
South America: R. R. Bowker Company,
New York

Distribution rights for United Kingdom
and Commonwealth Countries (except Canada):
André Deutsch Ltd, London

Dedicated to the Memory of
Sir Stanley Unwin
19 December 1884 – 13 October 1968

Contents

III Europe — 77

IV Annex — 535

Publishing and trading in books is an act of bridge-building between author and reader, country and country, continent and continent. Never before have all branches of the book trade had so great and promising a mission in uniting the nations as they have today. Books stream daily across hundreds of frontiers. They bridge the oceans to reach the remotest parts of the earth.

This task, with which the book trade is faced—of promoting peaceful encounters between countries and of establishing the presence of books in every conceivable place—demands from the publisher and the bookseller not only a knowledge of conditions in his own country but equally of circumstances in other lands. Even the "small" publisher and bookseller can no longer afford to limit his horizon. The book trade has drawn the inevitable consequences. There are numerous forms of international cooperation, both on an individual and an institutional basis; but in both cases experience often shows that negotiating partners know too little of the book trade in other countries. Useless repetition, consuming time and energy, in international discussions is often the result of a wrong or totally inadequate conception of the structure of the book trade in other countries.

The Book Trade of the World offers such assistance, and at the same time presents in comprehensible form information which, experience has shown again and again, is required in book-trade work at international level.

In order to present material that is reliable and up to date, the editor has been at pains to obtain well-known experts as authors for the chapters on their countries. He wishes to express his thanks to all collaborators for their contributions to this work.

Contributors were asked to present the information under 35 headings laid down by the editor, and each author is responsible for his own contribution. Only in unavoidable cases has the editor discussed technical alterations and additions with authors. It must be expressly stated that these never referred to fundamental passages connected with the book trade or with politics or ideologies. On the other hand, the individual authors are not necessarily expected to identify themselves with the editor's chapter entitled "International Section".

The space at the disposal of the various countries was related to the number of book-titles produced annually. As a result countries fell into one of three groups, and this meant that by and large the space offered was sufficient to cover individual demands. Some authors exploited their space to the full, others were more modest. Where there was nothing to report under some of the individual 35 headings, these have been omitted.

Only the most important items could be quoted under Bibliography. Where a work is not printed in the language(s) of the particular country, a note to this effect has been added. As far as possible an English translation of titles has been placed in parentheses after the original, as with the names of associations and institutions.

This volume is dedicated to the memory of Sir Stanley Unwin, the "Grand Old Man" of the international book trade, who died in 1968 at the age of 83. More than any other publisher of his generation, Sir Stanley devoted his inexhaustible and exemplary energy, both in deed and word, to the free flow of books, and thus created a precedent which this book has tried to emulate.

6451 Hochstadt
Federal Republic of Germany

Sigfred Taubert

International Section

1 General Information

This chapter will give basic figures that are of interest in connection with the cultural and economic life of each country. This information will intimate in various ways the scope of books within a particular country and its connection with the rest of the world.

Source:

UNESCO *Statistical Yearbook, Paris,* UNESCO. *Since 1962.*

This yearbook is the main international source for cultural statistical information. But since the responsibility for national data lies with the respective contributors to BTW, other sources may have been used.

2 Past and Present

A manual intended to supply up-to-date information on conditions in the book trade throughout the world cannot be expected to present detailed historical surveys. Under this heading, therefore, the editor asked his collaborators to include only such historical material as would lead to a better and deeper understanding of the trade's situation today.

From this point of view certain comparative standards for the European book trade in general can be deduced from the past, e.g. the internal order achieved by the German book trade at the beginning of the nineteenth century, which became a model for other countries (Northern Europe, parts of Eastern Europe and the German-speaking countries of Central Europe) but has lost much of its binding force during the past decades.

Or again, the structure of the British book trade and its influence overseas, with its very individual tendencies on the one hand, but its coordination in a tightly regulated guild-like organization (The Stationers' Company) whose influence can be traced up to the end of the eighteenth century.

Both systems, however, support the view gained from experience that the book trade can only fulfil its duties and obligations to the public in the framework of certain rules (fixed retail price, Net Book Agreement, etc.).

For people today the most interesting stage in the historical development of the European book trade began with the Russian October Revolution of 1917. In the USSR a new structure in the book trade replaced individual, private initiative with the collective responsibility of the State. After 1945 the system derived from this was taken over by the majority of the socialist countries of Eastern and South-Eastern Europe, adapted to their own conditions and modified in one direction or another in the course of the years.

Apart from all the ascertainable national differences it can, however, be stated that the current picture presented by the book trade in Europe is determined decisively by the close proximity of forms based on private economy and socialism. In other parts of the world (Africa, America and Asia), similar circumstances prevail though as yet they are not so influential. Without a doubt, world trade is being increasingly affected by this.

Bibliography

G. MENZ, *Der europäische Buchhandel seit dem Wiener Kongress.* (The European book trade since the Congress of Vienna). Würzburg, K. Triltsch 1941. VIII, VI, 164 pp.

Y. JÄNTTI, *Kirjakaupan ja kustannustoiminnan historia. Vol. 1: Aika noin vuoteen 1789.* (History of bookselling and publishing. Vol. 1: The period up to *c.* 1789). Helsinki, W. Söderström 1950. XXV, 315 pp.

This is the first general book dealing with the international history of our subject. A second volume bringing the description up to our time was announced, but has not yet appeared. Unfortunately the work has not been translated into one of the world languages. Pp. XVI–XXV contain an important bibliography.

S. Taubert, *Bibliopola. Pictures and texts about the book trade—Bilder und Texte aus der Welt des Buchhandels—Images et textes sur la librairie.* 2 vols. Hamburg (Hauswedell), London (Allen Lane The Penguin Press) and New York (R. R. Bowker) 1966. 150, 534 pp.
The first iconography of the book trade covering Africa, America, Asia and Europe from the oldest times to the twentieth century. The 258 plates and the additional 300 illustrations are accompanied by descriptions and interpretations in English, French and German. An international anthology with literary and other expressions about the various aspects of publishing and bookselling is added to the plates, some of which are in colour.

Further bibliographical information may be obtained from the catalogues of the special libraries "Books about Books" (pp. 67–75) and from national book-trade histories.

Two Unesco publications deal with present-day problems and situations in modern publishing and the book trade.

R. Barker, *Books for all.* Paris, Unesco 1956. 102 pp.
This book also appeared in 1957 in French under the title *Le Livre dans le monde.*

R. Escarpit, *The book revolution.* Paris, Unesco, 1966. 160 pp. (Rev. ed. 1969).
This book also appeared in 1965 in German under the title *Die Revolution des Buches,* based on the French original, *La revolution du livre,* published by Unesco in 1965.
Both publications contain an extensive bibliography.

As part of a series published by the "Börsenverein des Deutschen Buchhandels" Frankfurt a. M. (→ Germany, F. R., 4) there has appeared:

A. U. Martens (ed.), *Das Buch als Mittler zwischen West und Ost.* (The book as mediator between West and East). Frankfurt a. M., Börsenverein 1967. 93 pp.

Since the history of the book trade in earlier times is in many respects identical or closely associated with that of printing, there is a great temptation to make bibliographical references to the latter. But, in view of the amount of such literature, this would lead to a list of unjustifiable proportions. We will therefore quote only one title as an excellent introduction to the history of European printing:

S. H. Steinberg, *Five hundred years of printing.* Harmondsworth, Penguin Books, 1955 (and later editions). 277 pp. Contains a bibliography on pp. 263–269.
A hard-cover edition of this work was published by Faber & Faber, London, in 1959 and a German edition by the Prestel Verlag, München, in 1958 under the title *Die schwarze Kunst.* Translations in other languages exist.

In all world languages there exists a vast literature on the history of printing and publishing, on relevant individual problems and associated subjects, and on the importance of books in the life of man. The best introductions to this literature among English publications are:

N. E. Binn, *An introduction to historical bibliography.* 2nd ed. London, Association of Assistant Librarians 1962. VI, 388 pp.
Included in this work are the following chapters: Early writing materials, paper, the history of papermaking; bookbinding, its evolution and history; publishing and bookselling, book auctions; the development of book-trade bibliography.

Esdaile, *Manual of bibliography.* 4th ed.,

revised by R. Stokes. London, Allen & Unwin 1967. 336 pp.
Contains the following chapters: The parts of a book; papyrus, parchment, vellum, paper; typography; composition and press work; illustration; binding; landmarks in the development of the book; the collation of books; the description of books; the arrangement of bibliographies; bibliographical tools.

Two chronologically arranged works deserve mention on account of their international character:

W. T. Berry and H. E. Poole, *Annals of printing. A chronological encyclopedia from the earliest times to 1950*. London, Blandford Press 1960. XIX, 315 pp.
and
C. Clair, *A chronology of printing*. London, Cassell 1969. 288 pp.

Those interested in the interrelations between the printing and paper trades of Eastern Asia and Europe will find the required information in the following two works:

Th. Fr. Carter and L. C. Goodrich, *The invention of printing in China and its spread westward*. 2nd ed. New York, Ronald Press 1955. XXIV, 293 pp.

D. Hunter, *Papermaking. The history and technique of an ancient craft*. 2nd ed. New York, A. A. Knopf 1957. XXIV, 611, XXXVII pp.

During the exhibition *Printing and the Mind of Man,* organized in connection with the "Eleventh International Printing and Machinery and Allied Trades Exhibition" (IPEX, → International Section, 34), a catalogue with the same title was produced (British Museum, London), a magnificent account in words and pictures of the most important periods in the technical and artistic development of book production, and of the effect and significance of individual books in the development of humanity. A book edition of this catalogue appeared in 1967, edited by John Carter and Percy H. Muir, and published by Cassell, London, under the same title. A German edition published by the Prestel Verlag, Munich, appeared in 1968 under the title *Bücher, die die Welt verändern* ("Books that change the world").

For those interested in the modern art of books and its historical foundations, mention should be made of the volume:

K. Day (ed.), *Book typography 1815–1965 in Europe and the United States of America*. London (E. Benn) and Chicago (University of Chicago Press) 1966. XXIII, 401 pp.

The history of the book trade in ancient Greece and Rome is covered by the following publications:

F. G. Kenyon, *Books and readers in ancient Greece and Rome*. 2nd. ed. Oxford, Oxford University Press 1951.

T. Kleberg, *Buchhandel und Verlagswesen in der Antike*. (Publishing and the book trade in ancient Greece and Rome). Translation from Swedish by E. Junker. Darmstadt, Wissenschaftliche Buchgesellschaft 1967. XII, 121 pp.—Selective bibliography, partly annotated on pp. 108–112.

W. Schubert, *Das Buch bei den Griechen und Römern*. (Books in ancient Greece and Rome). 3rd ed. Heidelberg, L. Schneider 1962. 158 pp.

H. Widmann, *Herstellung und Vertrieb des Buches in der griechisch-römischen Welt*. (The production and distribution of books in the world of ancient Greece and Rome). In: Archiv für Geschichte des Buchwesens, VIII, pp. 545–640. Frankfurt a. M., Buchhändler-Vereinigung 1967.

3 Retail Prices

One of the great historical achievements of the European book trade, which also influenced other parts of the world, was the creation of a generally binding price system for books, which could thus be ac-

quired by everyone and at every place for the same amount. The beginning of this process can be found in the eighteenth century.
In the modern book-trade structure of Eastern and South-Eastern Europe the retail price, which is frequently stamped on a book or mentioned in the imprint, is an indisputable part of their book-marketing system. Outside the socialist countries, and therefore in the greater part of the western world, things are similar, even though from a different point of view. The economic policy in most of these countries is clearly against price fixing; therefore—especially after 1945—appropriate legislation has been passed in these countries. If within a system favouring free competition the book proves in almost every case to be an exception as a result of the recognition of a fixed retail price, this has happened from the admission that perhaps only in this way a variegated, prosperous book production and an appropriate and qualified retail book trade can be guaranteed. Further, even with a system of fixed retail prices, the principles of a competitive economy are fully guaranteed by the strong competition between different publishers.

Bibliography

FR. GEORGI, *The economic and cultural aspects of price-maintenance for publications*. Delft, ICBA 1967. 64 pp.—In English, German, French.
Discusses on a broad level the main reasons for price-maintenance in the book trade.

O. G. PRACHNER (ed.), *The necessity of price maintenance to ensure the free flow of books*. Delft, ICBA 1964. 132 pp.—In English, French, German.
Contents: book and bookseller in modern society; the maintained price of books; history and significance; books as goods; national and international resolutions and recommendations concerning the price maintenance of books.

4 Organization

Organizations are a means to an end and not an end in themselves. This is true of the book trade too; its appearance is not determined in the first place by forms of organization. It is characterized by the performance of publishing houses and the various forms of the wholesale and retail book trade. A look at the history, present and past, of book-trade organizations in Europe makes it clear, however, that their collective behaviour and forms of organization generally reflect the individual achievements of the book-trade family. At least this is true for the West European book trade. In the form to be found in Eastern Europe, organization as an element of a state book trade assumes a directive role that would be impossible on the other side. To this extent the book-trade organizations of most countries of East and South-East Europe must be viewed from a totally different angle from the private associations in the other part of Europe. It must however be noted that even in East and South-East Europe differences exist—or, at least, tendencies towards this are perceptible.
From the very beginning the book trade has possessed an international character. Almost all its present-day tasks and problems require an openmindedness and readiness to discuss that transcends national frontiers. This applies to the individual publisher and retail bookseller as much as it does to the trade associations whose international alliances and meetings will be briefly sketched here. Many of these institutions are of a world-wide nature. The oldest of these organizations is the

International Publishers' Association (IPA)
Avenue Miremont 3
CH 1206 Genève

which goes back to 1896. Its congresses have met as follows: 1896 Paris; 1897 Brussels; 1899 London; 1901 Leipzig; 1906 Milan; 1908 Madrid; 1910 Amsterdam; 1913 Budapest; 1931 Paris; 1933 Brussels; 1936 London; 1938 Leipzig–Berlin; 1954 Zurich; 1956 Florence–Rome; 1959 Vienna; 1962 Barcelona; 1965 Washington; 1968 Amsterdam. The 1972 congress will be held in France after a "mini-congress" has been held in London (1970).

Articles 1 to 3 in the "Rules and Regulations of the International Publishers' Association" (25 June 1954) read as follows:

Article 1

Freedom of thought, expressed both in speech and in print, is the nerve-centre of the spiritual life of man and of his mental activity. Without that freedom the whole of literature—the recorded fruits of that activity—would suffer to the detriment of human growth in character and in knowledge. All, therefore, who understand the value of freedom of thought, speech and writing, and especially publishers and distributors of books, should unite to maintain that freedom, and firmly to oppose any attempts to restrict it.

Article 2

The International Publishers' Association has the essential task of upholding and defending the right of publishers to publish and distribute the works of the mind in complete freedom provided they respect all legal rights attached to these works both within the frontiers of each country and among nations. Its duty is to oppose steadfastly any attempt or threat to restrict that freedom.

Article 3

To accomplish these tasks the International Publishers' Association organizes international Congresses and establishes such other bodies as are necessary on the one hand to give effect to the resolutions passed at the Congresses and on the other to deal continuously with all problems affecting publishing in general.

The members of the IPA are generally the national publishers' associations. The following countries are at present (1970) members: Argentina, Austria, Belgium, Brazil, Canada, Ceylon, Denmark, Finland, France, the Federal Republic of Germany, Iceland, India, Israel, Italy, Japan, South Korea, Mexico, the Netherlands, Nigeria, Norway, Pakistan, Peru, Portugal, Spain, Sweden, Switzerland, the United Kingdom, the United States of America, Venezuela.

The "Music Section" has the following special associations of their countries as members: Austria, Belgium, Canada, Denmark, Finland, France, the Federal Republic of Germany, Greece, Israel, Italy, the Netherlands, Norway, Spain, Sweden, Switzerland, the United Kingdom, the United States of America.

The work of the IPA is arranged in sections

- A Copyright
- B General publishing
- C Educational publishing
- D Technical, scientific, medical and reference-book publishing
- E Music

In addition the following groups have been created: In 1964 a special "Educational Group", in 1966 a "Common Market Group", and in 1969, as an autonomous group, the

International Group of Scientific,
Technical and Medical Publishers (STM)
Secretary: Mr. P. N. Asser
Keizersgracht 462
NL Amsterdam 1002

with the following sections: copyright; preservation and protection of intellectual property; new printing techniques; sales and promotion.

The section "Music" of the IPA maintains the secretariat:

IPA—Section "Music"
4, Place de la Madeleine
F 75 Paris 8e

Whereas at one time only publishing in

the western world was represented in the IPA, there has recently been a tendency for the other side to be represented too, especially in the "Groups".

At the Congresses of the IPA and the meetings of the "Executive Committee" and of the "International Committee" publishing problems on an international level are discussed. Publications arising from these congresses are among the most interesting international documents in the professional literature of the publishing and bookselling trades.

There is no counterpart to the IPA among publishers in Eastern Europe, unless the *Publishers' Conference of the Socialist Countries* be regarded as such. In the report published in Leipzig (1957) on the first of these conferences the following countries are quoted as having participated: Albania, Bulgaria, China, Hungary, Mongolia, Poland, Romania, the USSR, the Korean Peoples' Democratic Republic, the Czechoslovakian Socialist Republic, the Democratic Republic of Vietnam and the German Democratic Republic.

The aims of this conference include the following:

> The calling of the conference is an expression of the close ties between the Socialist Countries in the field of ideological and cultural work, ties that are based on the common interests and aims of the Socialist Countries.

The report mentions among the practical tasks:

The creation of direct relations between publishers in the same field, with precedence for party and trade-union literature, scientific and technical writing, but also including almost all other prominent categories of book production. This cooperation shall also deal with the exchange of subject plans, advance information on intended titles and also the basis for prompt translations etc.; greater encouragement of personal contacts; common planning of important books; exchange of experience on the international book markets; the promotion of the art of book production through national and international competitions.

These and other announcements form an important foundation for information on the theory and practice of Socialist publishing and book-trade activities. Its forms of international cooperation, here to be understood as meaning most of the countries of Eastern and South-Eastern Europe, are based to a very large extent on the appropriate sections of bilateral cultural agreements and cooperation arrangements between publishers of the same or similar literatures. Strong thematic concentration on relatively few, but very productive, publishing firms emphasizes the importance of such agreements.

The most recent example of cooperation in socialist countries is the *Meeting of the State and Social Directorates for Publishing in Socialist Countries* which took place in East Berlin at the end of 1969. It was attended by Bulgaria, Czechoslovakia, the German Democratic Republic, Hungary, Mongolia, Poland, Romania and the USSR.

Due to Dutch initiative the

International Community of Booksellers Associations (ICBA)
Grünangergasse 4
A 1010 Wien I

was founded at the "Frankfurt Book Fair" in 1950 (→ International Section, 29) "to realize a close cooperation between booksellers with the purpose of discussing common problems and of exchanging experience".

The "Rules of the ICBA" include the paragraph:

In the interest of close cooperation, and with the purpose of exchanging experience and discussing common problems in the trade, the International Community of Booksellers' Associations is founded by the representative organization of booksellers of those countries in which freedom of mind, both spoken and written, is guaranteed.

The ICBA consists of the representative national booksellers' organizations and groups of the member countries.
Each representative national organization is autonomous and independent with regard to its internal affairs. With the consent of the national association(s) of the country concerned, the Executive Committee can admit an individual bookseller as an "associate member". "Associate members" receive the most important information and can attend the meetings of ICBA, but without right of vote.
The retail book-trade associations of the following countries are at present (1970) members of ICBA: Austria, Australia, Belgium, Canada, Denmark, Finland, France, the Federal Republic of Germany, Italy, Japan, the Netherlands, New Zealand, Norway, Spain, Sweden, Switzerland, the United Kingdom and the United States of America.
A plenary session of the delegates is held annually, and an International Booksellers' Congress takes place every five years; the first was in London (1959), followed by Paris (1964) and Rome (1969). The "International Congresses of Young Booksellers" reflect the great interest shown by the ICBA in all problems concerning the rising generation in the book trade (→ International Section, 11).
The ICBA has issued several publications dealing with matters from an international point if view. They have been quoted in the sections concerned (→ International Section, 3, 24).
General information on the ICBA can be found in:

What is ICBA? (Qu'est-ce que CIAL est? Was ist IASV?). 2nd ed. Delft 1970. 48 pp.

Although it is not a book-trade organization, the

*United Nations Educational, Scientific and Cultural Organization (*UNESCO*)*
Place de Fontenoy
F 75 Paris 7e

which was founded in 1946, is so strongly associated with books and their presence internationally, that a brief description of its programmes and activities concerning books should not be omitted. Information will be largely confined to the most recent developments, but reference must be made initially to the *Agreement on the Importation of Educational, Scientific and Cultural Materials* (the "Florence Agreement", adopted in 1959) under which books, newspapers, periodicals and many other categories of printed matter, whatever the language, are granted duty-free entry. The Agreement was ratified by many countries, but there will be a long way to go before it is fully practised (→ International Section, 27, 28). An *International Book Coupon Scheme* has been started in 1949, and a *Convention concerning the International Exchange of Publications* has been agreed in 1958.
Apart from giving strong support to the free flow of books, UNESCO's efforts at present are aimed at promoting the production and distribution of books in the developing countries. For this purpose several regional meetings were held in Asia, Africa and South America. Reports on these will be included in later volumes of BTW (→ International Section, 35 b). This also applies to the regional centres of UNESCO outside Europe. The activities of experts in developing countries is greatly promoted by UNESCO. Much emphasis is placed on everything concerning books for education within the

book development programmes. Numerous meetings in connection with this special subject were held. UNESCO assists in improving public and school libraries. For UNESCO's role in international copyright, → International Section, 14.

Emphasis must also be placed on the considerable publishing activity of UNESCO. In so far as this concerns subjects dealt with in this work, → International Section, 1, 2, 5, 6, 12, 14, 15, 16, 17, 27, 28, and 35. The addresses of the national distributors of UNESCO publications are a regular feature of the *Unesco Bulletin for Libraries*. For the *Unesco translation programme* → 17.

Bibliography

Unesco's activities in the book field. A report by Unesco to the 18th Congress of the International Publishers' Association. Amsterdam 1968. 22 pp.
Covers: book development; free flow of books; books for education; libraries; copyright, authors and translations; UNESCO publications; professional organizations.

A Summary of Unesco's activities in the fields of libraries, documentations and archives, 1946–1966. In: UNESCO Bulletin for Libraries, vol. XX, no. 5, Paris 1966. For *1967–8* in: UBL, vol. XXIII, no. 3, Paris 1969.

Among other international institutions of importance for sections of the publishing and book-trade industries are:

International Federation of the Periodical Press
129 Kingsway
GB London WC 2

Fédération Internationale des Editeurs de Journaux et Publications
(International Federation of Publishers of Newspapers and Periodicals)
6 bis, Rue Gabriel-Laumain
F 75 Paris 10e

International Association of Railway Bookstall and Kiosk Concessionnaires (IBA)
c/o A/S Narvesens Kioskkompani
Bertrand Narvesens Vei 2
N Oslo 6

European Association of Manufacturers and Distributors of Educational Materials
Kartäuserstraße 4
D 7806 Freiburg-Ebenet

International Association of Wholesale Newspapers, Periodical and Book Distributors (Distripress)
Beethovenstraße 20
CH 8002 Zürich

Founded in 1895 as the "Institut International de Bibliographie", the
International Federation for Documentation (IFD)
General Secretariat
7 Hofweg
NL 's-Gravenhage
has at present (1970) 46 member states. It concerns itself with many problems which are also of importance to the book trade, such as: research on the theoretical basis of information, classification, research, Universal Decimal Classification (→ International Section, 16), scientific and technical information for industry, training of documentalists, needs of developing countries. It cooperates closely with UNESCO. The official publication of the IFD is the *IFD News Bulletin* (monthly). The following should be mentioned from among its many publications:

Bibliography of directories and sources of information. 2nd ed. 's-Gravenhage 1968.

The
International Text Book Institute
(Internationales Schulbuchinstitut)
Rebenring 53
D 33 Braunschweig
is the documentary centre for all school textbooks, educational aids, etc. that are

used in the teaching of history and geography in the member countries of the "Council of Europe". The Institute attached to the *Pädagogische Hochschule* (College of Education) in Brunswick endeavours to improve the teaching of history and geography in a way to bring the nations closer together, and in this respect acts as an international clearing-house.

Apart from these general international bodies there are numerous ones of a similar nature that are limited to regions. For example, since 1951 questions of the German book trade in Europe are dealt with at so-called *Dreiländertreffen* ("Meetings of the Three Countries") which are attended by representatives of Austria, Germany (F. R.) and Switzerland. The *Dreiländertreffen der katholischen Buchhändler und Verleger* ("Meetings of Catholic Publishers and Booksellers of the Three Countries") are similar. These too are attended by representatives from the above three countries.

The French book trade of all categories has had the opportunity of dealing with problems of the book in French (since 1964) in the *Union des Editeurs de Langue Française* ("Union of French-Speaking Publishers"). Members are Belgium, Canada, France and Switzerland.

Special questions on publishing matters in the European Economic Community are dealt with by the

Group of Book Publishers in the EEC
12 Avenue Louise
B Bruxelles 5

A parallel body exists in the

Community of Periodical Publishers' Associations in the EEC
18, Rue Duphot
F 75 Paris 1e

In Scandinavia a *Nordic Publishers' Council* has been in existence since 1935.

For the *Association Typographique Internationale* → International Section, 34. For the *International League of Antiquarian Booksellers* → International Section, 26. For the *International Board on Books for Young People* → International Section, 10.

5 Trade Press

The trade publications quoted in the sections dealing with the various countries are mostly of an international character. Their sphere of influence often extends over large linguistic areas; they therefore have an importance in the publishing and book trades far beyond their countries of origin. Such publications are, for example, *The Bookseller* (London; → United Kingdom, 5) and *Publishers' Weekly* (New York; → vol. 2, USA, 5) in the English-speaking world; *Bibliographie de la France* (Paris; → France, 5) for the French-speaking world; both editions of the *Börsenblatt für den Deutschen Buchhandel* (Frankfurt a.M. and Leipzig; → Germany: Federal Republic of Germany, 5 and German Democratic Republic, 5) for the German-speaking world; and for the Spanish-speaking world *El Libro Español* (Madrid; → Spain, 5) and *El Fichero Latino-Americano* (Buenos Aires; → vol. 2, Argentina, 5). It may well be due to the international importance of such national trade publications that no purely international organ of any influence has appeared up to now in the book trade. Existing attempts have been ineffective.

For the journal *Fellow* → International Section, 11.

A publication meant for libraries, but also of importance to publishers and retail booksellers, is the

Unesco Bulletin for Libraries
Place de Fontenoy
F Paris 7e

It appears six times a year and, apart from extensive essays, contains much bibliographical material.

For further bibliographical references to

the subject "Trade press" → International Section, 6, 35 e.

6 Book-Trade Literature

Since specialist publications on subjects treated in this work are quoted in the section dealing with the various countries, it will suffice for this chapter to refer to international bibliographical compilations. Attention is, however, also drawn to the bibliographical information under International Section 2 and 7.

An international bibliography of specialist literature on the world of books, which has been revised over the years, is:

Die Fachliteratur zum Buch- und Bibliothekswesen. (Specialist literature on books and libraries). München, Verlag Dokumentation.

It is an attempt to include all modern specialist literature on this subject under the three headings: book trade, the library, book production. All monographs and periodicals connected in any manner with the world of books are considered.

Under the caption "Book Trade" this bibliography uses the following classifications: the history of the book trade in general; commemorative writings, biographies, jubilee catalogues; almanachs, periodicals; the book trade in general; address books, associations; dictionaries, reference books; training, general textbooks; book-trade traffic; export and international book trade; periodicals; publishing in general; organization, accountancy; publishing production; sales and publicity; union catalogues (including periodical ones); books and reading; distributive book trade in general; wholesale book trade, catalogues of books in print; retail book trade; mail-order book trade; book clubs; antiquarian book trade; lending libraries and other forms of distribution; organization, accountancy; publicity, shop, sale; bibliographical technique in the book trade; journalism in general; writing and translation; authors' periodicals; the press; periodicals on journalism; taxes and the law in general; copyright and publishing rights; periodicals. Under "Production" some of the groupings to be found are: history of the book; commemorative writings; graphic production in general; address books, associations; dictionaries, reference books; training, general textbooks; periodicals; the art of the book, bibliophily; periodicals; paper; paper production; the processing of paper; periodicals; printing techniques.

Issued by the National Book League (→ United Kingdom, 7) *A bibliography of books about books* (London, A. Deutsch 1970) gives details of available special literature.

A selective index, related to British and American conditions, is to be found in the section "Books about books" in *Reader's Adviser* (11th ed. 2 vols. New York, R. R. Bowker 1968–9).

In addition there is a series of bibliographies appearing more or less regularly, about new editions of "books about books". But they are predominantly of a national or limited international character. For example: *Nordisk bibliografi och biblioteks-litteratur* (part of the "Nordisk Tidskrift för Bok- och Biblioteksväsen") includes the following captions: book collecting; book plates; history of the book; paper; history of printing; the art of the modern book; book illustration; publishing and bookselling; bibliography. *Bibliographical Scholarship* in the annual volumes of "Studies in Bibliography" (Charlottesville, University Press of Virginia). The *Bibliographische Berichte* ("Bibliographical Bulletin", Frankfurt a.M., Vittorio Klostermann), which had its 12th year of publication in 1970, contains the section "Generalia, bibliography, library science", which it treats from an international point of view. A *Bibliography of dictionaries in the field of library science and related subjects*, which names some 170 titles, appeared in 1964 in the "UNESCO Bulletin for Libraries" (vol. XVIII, no. 6, pp. 277–84; → International Section, 5). The range of this specialist literature is very large. We can only make a limited choice, by referring to those dictionaries that have proved themselves well in book-trade practice. The latest bibliographical index on this subject is:

Books, libraries and documentation, journalism. München, Verlag Dokumentation (New York, R. R. Bowker) 1969. 24 pp.

A. THOMPSON, *Vocabularium bibliothecarii.* 2nd ed. Paris, UNESCO 1962. 627 pp.
The material, arranged according to the Decimal Classification, deals with the following languages: English, French, German, Spanish and Russian. About 2,800 technical terms from the whole book world are included. In 1965 an edition appeared in Cairo (United Arab Republic, National Commission for UNESCO) which included the Arab versions as well. The key language of the "Vocabularium bibliothecarii" is English.

J. SCHLEMMINGER, *Fachwörterbuch des Buchwesens.* (Dictionary of technical terms used in the book world). 2nd ed. Darmstadt, Stoytscheff 1954. 367 pp.
Arranged alphabetically in German, English and French, with German as the key language.

R. HOSTETTLER, *Technical terms of the printing industry.* 4th ed. St. Gallen, R. Hostettler 1963. 195 pp.
In English (key language), French, German, Italian and Dutch.

F. J. M. WIJNEKUS, *Elsevier's dictionary of the printing and allied industries.* Amsterdam, Elsevier 1967. X, 583 pp.
In English (key language), French, German and Dutch.

Since it is highly informative on technical terms used at the turn of the century and still of interest today, we mention:

Vocabulaire technique de l'éditeur en sept langues. (The publisher's technical vocabulary in seven languages). Bern, Congrès International des Editeurs 1913. IX, 365 pp.
In French (key language), German, English, Spanish, Dutch, Italien and Hungarian.

For a special dictionary concerning the antiquarian book trade → International Section, 26.

7 Sources of Information, Address Services

A number of yearbooks of an international character provide up-to-date and permanently valid information on important problems in the international book trade.

Publisher's World. New York, R. R. Bowker.
With its contents relating to practical work of the international book market, this annual, which has appeared for 5 years since 1965, was an important book in the technical library of the book trade. It is replaced by "International Editions", of "Publishers' Weekly", New York (R. R. Bowker).

Since 1966 a counterpart to the North American "Literary Market Place" has been issued as an "European edition" under the title:

International Literary Market Place. This also comes from R. R. Bowker, New York, and provides information from all parts of the publishing and book trade world in Europe.

These publications include a large number of addresses. More extensive, and endeavouring to attain world-wide completeness, is the

Internationales Verlagsadressbuch. (Publisher's international directory). München, Verlag Dokumentation (New York, R. R. Bowker). This directory has been revised several times since 1964. With its geographical classification and information on subjects covered by various publishers it represents an important part of international work.

In the practical field the annual *Catalogue* of the *Frankfurt Book Fair,* with its publishers' addresses and subjects covered by them, is much used as an international directory. A supplement to this, entitled *Who's who at the Frankfurt Book Fair,* appeared for the first time in 1970. Apart from these international reference books there are directories concerned with particular linguistic or geographical areas, e.g. *Cassell's directory of publishing* (Cassell, London), *African book trade directory* (Verlag Dokumentation, München), *Asian book trade directory* (Nirmala Sadanand, Bombay) and *American book trade directory* (R. R. Bowker, New York). These works are dealt with either in the national chapters or in the concluding volumes of this work.

A *World directory of booksellers* (London, A. P. Wales) provides many addresses in the retail book trade.

In 1962 UNESCO, Paris, published *International directories of education: educational publishers.* The introduction lists the national and international associations of publishers, booksellers and producers of teaching materials, and then provides in alphabetical order of the countries the addresses of the national publishers of school books. Each entry contains additional information. The supplement contains a bibliography of works on textbooks plus a list of some important publishers' directories. The bibliography is subdivided into: general; preparation and publication; evaluation and selection; technical processes; copyright and translation questions.

Various national address services in the book trade are also worth mentioning from the international angle. For this and for address books → the information under Section 7 in the different national chapters. R. R. Bowker, publishers, New York, maintain an international address service.

Information can also be obtained from the international associations (→ International Section, 4) and the national organizations (→ Section 4 in the various national chapters).

8 International Membership

Under this heading reference is made in the various national chapters to membership by the particular country's book trade of international book trade organizations. These have been limited to IPA (→ International Section, 4), ICBA (→ International Section, 4), ILAB (→ International Section, 26) and UNESCO (→ International Section, 4). It must, however, be remembered that the socialist countries of East and South-East Europe are in a different way served by a very efficient form of cooperation beyond firm organizations like associations, and their influence frequently goes much further than the loose associations of the western world.

9 Market Research

A dynamic age like ours demands that the book trade too must continually come to terms with changing situations. In earlier and calmer times whatever was new could everywhere be taken in and mastered through traditional attitudes and methods of work in the book trade. Today, however, new problems can frequently be recognized and mastered only by extensive and profound systematic research. The modern book trade can no longer exist without market research: "The aim of book-market research is objective information about economic and sociological facts of the book market as a field of action for the book trade" (Fr. Hinze, 1966).

The activities by national institutions engaged in book-market research led logically and of necessity to international contacts and activities.

The first conference of this kind took place in Amsterdam in 1963. The second was in Paris in 1965, followed by West Berlin in 1966, London in 1968 and Vienna in 1971. The

Secretariat for International
Book Market Research
Stichting Speurwerk
Jan Toorop Straat 109
NL Amsterdam

was set up experimentally.

Bibliography

FR. HINZE, *Ansätze europäischer Buchmarkt-Forschung*. (The beginnings of European book-market research). Hamburg, Verlag für Buchmarkt-Forschung 1966. 47 pp.

An English version of this book appeared in 1966 under the title *Book market research in Europe* by the same publishing house. This international survey covers general questions, problems and methods and research work in this field in the Netherlands, Belgium, Switzerland and Germany (F. R.).

Lesen, Leihen und Kaufen von Büchern. Ein internationaler Vergleich. (Reading, lending and buying of books. An international comparison). Hamburg, Verlag für Buchmarkt-Forschung 1968. 63 pp.—Bulletin of the Institute for Book Market Research, 41.

Covers the following nine countries: USA, Belgium, France, Germany (F.R.), the Netherlands, the United Kingdom, Turkey, India and Pakistan.

10 Books and Young People

Even a superficial perusal of developments in international book production and its contents during the course of the twentieth century shows a great increase in the volume of books for children and young people. This confirms the great importance achieved by this kind of book in the recent past. But it is only in our day that such books have begun to play their appropriate role. Admittedly, as far as the world as a whole is concerned, this is only true in theory. Where forms of education are still being built up and illiteracy lies like a cloud over countries and continents, the golden age for children's and young people's literature remains a hope for the future, which is being assisted and promoted by world-wide efforts, whether it be in the form of cooperation between the publishing houses of many nations or the endeavours of international institutions. In this respect mention must be made in the first place of the

International Board of Books
for Young People (IBBY)
Kaulbachstr. 11
D 8 München 22

which was founded in 1951 with headquarters in Zürich. IBBY has at present a membership of 33 sections in all parts of the world. This Board is concerned with the coordination of all endeavours towards the creation, distribution and reading of books for children and young people. Questions on these matters are discussed at biennial international congresses. An international jury, selected by the governing body of the board and guided by the suggestions of national sections, awards the *Hans Christian Andersen Medal* biennially to a living author and to an illustrator of children's and young people's books. The *International Children's Book Day* initiated by IBBY has also been associated with the great Danish fairy-tale writer since 1967, in that it is intended to be held whenever possible throughout the world on 2 April, the birthday of Hans Christian Andersen. All these endeavours are intended to promote international understanding and tolerance among nations through the medium of children's and young people's books.

Since 1963 IBBY has issued the quarterly

Bookbird
Verlag für Jugend und Volk
Tiefer Graben 7–9
A 1080 Wien 1
It bears the sub-title "Literature for children and young people. News from all over the world. Recommendations for translation".
IBBY shares the collective responsibility for "Bookbird" with the
Internationales Institut für Kinder-, Jugend- und Volksliteratur
(International Institute for Children's, Juvenile and Popular Literature)
Fuhrmannsgasse 18a
A 1080 Wien
This institute represents on a world-wide basis an attempt at a working, coordinating and documentation centre for the special fields of discussion here mentioned. In addition to its co-responsibility for "Bookbird", the Institute cooperates with the "Österreichischer Buchklub der Jugend" ("Austrian Youth Book Club") in the publication of the quarterly journal "Jugend und Buch" ("Youth and Books").
In many cases the initiative for all these international endeavours came from the
Internationale Jugendbibliothek (IJB)
International Youth Library (IYL)
Kaulbachstr. 11
D 8 München 22
which was founded with the support of UNESCO in 1945, but owes its origin chiefly to the personal initiative of Jella Lepman. The collection of some 100,000 children's and young people's books from all over the world is the largest and most interesting of its kind, including the literature on this subject. Through a generous act in 1969, the International Youth Library was enlarged by the 25,000 titles or so of the "Bureau International d'Education" collection ("International Office of Education"), which had existed in Geneva since 1925. The story of the birth of the International Youth Library is told by Jella Lepman in her book "Die Kinderbuchbrücke", published in 1964 in Frankfurt a. M. by S. Fischer Verlag. An American translation appeared in 1969 under the title "A bridge for children's books" (Chicago, American Library Association).
Every year in December IYL arranges an international exhibition of the most interesting children's and young people's books.
Founded in 1970, the
Internationale Forschungsgesellschaft für Kinder- und Jugendliteratur
(International Research Society for Children's and Juvenile Literature)
Georg-Voigt-Str. 10
D 6 Frankfurt a. M.
combines and coordinates the scientific research work in this special field with members of several countries.
The number of other international ventures in this sphere is great. As examples we quote the *Internationale Jugendbuchtagung* ("International Youth Book Conference"), which met in Europe for the fifteenth time in 1969, and the *Primer Seminario Centro-Americano de Literatura Infantil* ("First Central-American Seminary on Youth Literature), which was held in Costa Rica in 1969.
For the International Children's Book Fair, Bologna, → International Section, 29, and for the Biennale of Illustrations, Bratislava, → International Section, 20.

Bibliography

A. PELLOWSKI, *The world of children's literature*. New York, R. R. Bowker 1968. X, 538 pp.
The literature on this subject has become so vast that we can only refer to four books. The work of Anne Pellowski has a special place in that it is a report in the form of a global study on the condition of children's and young people's book literature throughout the world, and also contains a descriptive and annotated bibliography divided according to inter-

national conceptions, continents and countries.

V. Haviland (ed.), *Children's literature. A guide to reference sources.* Washington, Library of Congress 1960. X, 341 pp.
This too is an international study, but the subject matter is more limited and refers more to the English-speaking world.

J. Lichtenstein-Rother (ed.), *Jugend und Buch in Europa. Untersuchungen und Berichte.* (Youth and books in Europe. Investigations and reports). Hamburg, Verlag für Buchmarkt-Forschung 1967. 305 pp.
A summary of modern European research work on children's and young people's books. Including numerous studies of a sociological and market-research nature, this work presents a noteworthy cross-section of theory and practice in the present-day interpretation of this subject.

W. Scherf (ed.), *Children's prize books.* München, Verlag Dokumentation (New York, R. R. Bowker) 1969. XVI, 238 pp.
Deals with book awards for children's and young people's books on a national basis in 25 countries (Africa, America, Asia and Europe). The international prizes awarded in this connection are also included.

11 Training

A bookseller, in whatever branch, can only do justice to his occupation if he possesses sound general and specialized knowledge, guaranteed by an appropriate system of training. In many places this is still lacking in an alarming manner, which is detrimental both to the trade and to the general public. However, in recent times the belief in the need for training is gaining ground where at one time it was thought to be superfluous.

Specialist training means two things: firstly, a practical apprenticeship of several years undertaken according to definite and generally binding regulations in a suitable book-trade firm; and secondly a contemporaneous or subsequent theoretical training in book-trade classes and specialist schools. It will be seen from the various national chapters how far individual countries comply with this principle.

Here we will merely add a few general remarks on the state of the efforts being made internationally for the training of booksellers. Unfortunately there is not much of a positive nature to tell. Although anyone informed about the general development of world book trade is aware that it has entered a new phase of global communication, and that at the same time problems of training have arisen that cannot be solved from the usual national point of view, these problems remain so considerable that they bar the way to necessary new experiments. A number of welcome efforts, like the *International Congresses of Young Booksellers,* which have been taking place since 1957, are proof that the circle of far-sighted people is increasing, particularly among younger members; but this process is very slow, and both ideally and materially it is not sufficiently supported by the national book-trade organizations and individual representatives of the book trade.

The above-mentioned International Congresses of Young Booksellers are organized by the Committee IV Training and Exchange of Assistants of the ICBA (→ International Section, 4). These congresses, each of which deals with a general subject and lasts a week, are attended by booksellers from many countries. Guests are welcome. The group publishes the annual journal

Fellow
Grünangergasse 4
A 1010 Wien I

which reports on the activities of the congresses for that particular year.
Other international associations have also become active in this direction, but seldom with continuing success. Mention can be made of an *International Meeting of Young Antiquarian Booksellers* (1968 in Amsterdam) under the aegis of the ILAB (→ International Section, 26). Other efforts are of a limited international character, for example the traditional Scandinavian meetings.
Introductory and informatory courses offered by countries with a large book trade to foreign members of the book-trade family must be viewed as part of their national export efforts and similar aims; these therefore only do partial justice to the fundamental tasks under discussion here. Opportunities offered to foreigners in many countries' book-trade schools must also be viewed predominantly under the same aspect.
The training efforts undertaken by UNESCO are different (→ International Section, 4). These are related exclusively to the developing countries and are in operation there. They will therefore be treated in the concluding volumes of BTW (→ International Section, 35 b).
The caption "Developing Countries" also calls for some general observations. Here too the impression will be gained that the performance of the classical book-trading countries in the training of book-trade personnel in the developing countries has been completely insufficient to date. Help and support have been regarded more or less as national tasks, combined with corresponding conceptions and hopes; yet even the most modest knowledge of book-trading conditions in the majority of the developing countries shows how essential it is for the older nations to have a common sense of responsibility. The aim should be an altruistic solution undertaken by all. This, among other things, would have the advantage of being free from the suspicion of national self-interest or worse. Emphasis should be placed on the training of retail booksellers. These more than anything else are lacking in the developing countries. It is conceivable that such tasks could best be solved in connection with continental book-trade training centres. The national book-trade associations ought to show more understanding and enthusiasm, without which such centres cannot come about.
In the concluding volumes of BTW we shall deal with the

Tokyo Book Development Centre
6, Fukuro-machi
Shinjuku-ku
J Tokyo

founded in 1969 by Japanese publishers in association with UNESCO as a training centre for qualified personnel in the South-East-Asian book trade, and also with the

Unesco Regional Centre for Book Development
26/A–P.E.C.H.Society
PAK Karachi 29

→ International Section, 35b.

12 Taxes

Only a special investigation can attempt a comparative international survey of the existing tax situation in all branches of the book trade. Here we shall have to be content with references to the more or less exhaustive information contained in the various national chapters and with some general observations.
In many countries there exists a tendency to treat the printed word as an exception on account of its cultural and educational associations. This takes the form of total or partial freedom from taxation. Such favourable signs frequently indicate a variable state of affairs that underlines the dependency of the existing situation on the poltical structure of the particular country.

The fact, however, that it is in a nation's own interest to keep book prices low and, among other things, free from additional burdens of taxation, invites the taxation authorities to be continually aware of these matters.

In spite of intensive international efforts and the theoretical understanding of all far-sighted institutions and individuals, the printed word is still subject to serious impediments, sometimes restrictive and even prohibitive, when crossing frontiers. The *Agreement on the Importation of Educational, Scientific and Cultural Materials* (→ International Section, 27/28) is still far removed from the international aim of the free flow of the cultural wealth of the human race. But even here can be seen the beginnings of a fundamental transformation, for example in economic communities like the Organization of the European Economic Community and other international federations which, with reciprocal removal of customs and import charges, are contributing to a gradual abolition of barriers in the international traffic in books and periodicals.

Bibliography

Trade barriers to knowledge. A manual of regulatons affecting educational scientific and cultural materials. 2nd ed. Paris, UNESCO 1955. 364 pp.

Although the information is in part out of date, this book provides a good picture of the barriers still confronting international trade in books.

(F. K. LIEBICH), *Removing taxes on knowledge.* Paris, UNESCO 1969. 43 pp.

The Paris version has not yet come into effect. Once it will be ratified (by 5 associate countries which must accept also the appendix providing for the developing countries' privileges, plus ratification of the UCC Paris version by France, the United Kingdom, Spain and the USA), ratification of or joinders to all previous versions, such as the Stockholm texts, will be barred.

An up-to-date study of such international trade patterns concerning the free flow of books.

13 Clearing Houses

Establishments for the settlement of accounts in the book trade exist at present only on a national baxis. But here too new forms of international cooperation will take place in the near future.

14 Copyright*

International copyright is guaranteed by international agreements concluded bilaterally or multilaterally. These agreements usually rest on the principle of "national treatment", i.e. the foreigner or foreign work are afforded the same protection as a native or native work. Only after further progress in unification of the legal situation within the various Conventions will it be possible to agree on a text of a law that could be the same for all countries or as many as possible.

I

The two most important world-wide Conventions are:

The Revised Berne Convention for the Protection of Literary and Artistic Works (RBC)

and

The Universal Copyright Convention (UCC)

also called

The Geneva Copyright Convention.

The member countries of the Berne Convention and the treaty states of the UCC are enumerated in special lists (→ Annex

* This chapter has been compiled by RA Dr Heinz Kleine, Frankfurt a. M. The Editor takes the opportunity of thanking him for his cooperation.

6), where the signatory countries of the Paris version of the international conventions are indicated by a P (Paris, July 24, 1971).

1. The most comprehensive protection is guaranteed by the *RBC*. It has been improved at several Revisionary Conferences, of which those in Rome (1928), Brussels (1948), Stockholm (1967), and Paris (1971) deserve special mentioning. The Paris version has not yet come into effect. Once it will be ratified (by 5 associate countries which must accept also the appendix providing for the developing countries' privileges, plus ratification of the UCC Paris version by France, the United Kingdom, Spain and the USA), ratification of or joinders to all previous versions, such as the Stockholm texts, will be barred.

The principle of "national treatment" is supplemented by rules on points of contact which decide when national treatment shall be given. According to the Brussels version the author must be a national of one of the member countries, and the first publication of the work must have taken place in a member country. According to the Stockholm version only the nationality is decisive. For works associated in this way with the Convention (also called convention works) the author enjoys the same rights as a native author in all the associated countries, with the exception of the country of origin (where the work was first published); here he is directly protected by the laws of that country. Protection by the RBC is free from formalities. The period of protection is 50 years after the death of the author. However, no author can claim in another country a longer period of protection than that granted by the country of origin (reciprocity). Accordingly, in the Federal Republic of Germany, where a period of protection of 70 years operates, the work of a foreigner who is a member of the association is generally protected for only 50 years. On the other hand, the RBC guarantees certain minimum rights to authors of convention works even when the laws of a country do not guarantee these rights to its own citizens: these or the right of translation to new member states imposes the possibility of certain limitations; the right of recital, performance and broadcasting; broadcasting comprises television as well as sound broadcasts. This includes, according to the Stockholm version, the author's right to permit the public transmission of a lecture, performance or a radio or television programme through any technical device (public communication of a performance in hotels, restaurants, places of amusement or educational institutions), as well as the right of reproduction. But there is a reservation for the legislation of the member countries to permit exceptions within certain limits. The right of reproduction comprises also the author's right to permit mechanical recordings (discs or other sound recorders); this right had been dealt with separately in the former version of the RBC. The moral rights of the author to protection is expressly recognized.

At the Stockholm Conference a "Protocol for Developing Countries" was added to the RBC as an integral part, and this grants extraordinarily far-reaching special privileges, in so far as these countries are recognized as developing countries by the UNO.

It became apparent early that the industrial countries were unwilling to ratify the Stockholm version because of that protocol, and that the United States were not prepared to sign the Berne Convention. As a consequence, a revisionary conference was called to meet in Paris during July 1971 while another conference, also in Paris, went on to revise the UCC. It was resolved at that conference that the Stockholm version should be amended and that

the protocol outlining the position of the developing countries should be replaced by an appendix which in turn was to be part of the Paris Act. Contrary to the Stockholm protocol, the Paris Act greatly curbed the nearly unlimited rights of the developing countries to publish translations and reproductions; it provided for mere Compulsory Licenses in the event that certain conditions were met (e.g., lapse of time, pursuit of privileged aims, guaranty of reasonable compensation). C.L. are granted only once it has been shown that negotiations to arrange for a license by agreement was attempted and failed. The methods of how contacts must have been made are described in detail. There are plans to facilitate the required contacts by installing information centers throughout the industrial countries.
C.L. cover translations and reproductions. Translations must be intended for purposes of teaching, scholarships and research. Reproductions may be used for systematic teaching only. C.L. for radio stations are subject to even more stringent requirements; broadcasts in which translations may be used must either be labeled educative or must serve as information to members of certain professions on the most recent results of scientific research. This includes texts contained in audiovisual publications as well. Also, 3 years must have gone by since the publication date if a C. L. is sought for a translation into either English, French or Spanish. The time is shortened to one year in the case of translations into a language spoken nowhere but in developing countries. For translations into other languages, there is a basic waiting period of 3 years. The time is generally five years for reproductions, but there are exceptions: reproduction of scientific and technological texts may be licensed after only 3 years, while novels, art books and music publications must wait 7 years. C.L. become null and void whenever copyrighted copies are available at prices comparable to those normally charged for works of that nature within the developing country concerned. Contrary to the provisions of the Stockholm protocol, all exports of copies produced under C.L. are prohibited, and each copy so produced must carry a warning stating that distribution is allowed only throughout the country granting the C.L. Instead, developing countries may use a different privilege which they share with the non-developing ones to the effect that translation rights will be granted for 10 years, provided that all other privileges as to translation rights are waived.
2. The UCC, contrary to the RBC, does not create an autonomous federation of countries; it merely obligates the individual signatory countries to enact all rules required for to provide all necessary regulations to safeguard effectively the rights of authors. Minimum rules are set up for the fulfilment of formalities that are fundamentally admissible, for the length of the protection and for translation rights (copyright reservation on works; no deposition on principle, duration of copyright at least 25 years, translation rights at least 7 years after the first publication). In addition, the principle of "national treatment" (see above) prevails. As new minimum rights to be guaranteed by the signatary countries, the Paris Conference 1971 (vide 1, supra) included in the Act the right to reproduce and to edit works as well as the right to publicly perform and broadcast them, however, it empowered the member countries to legislate exceptions as long as such exceptions violate neither the spirit nor any express rules of the agreement. Furthermore, the revised UCC includes the appendix mentioned before (vide 1) that was resolved in Paris, which guarantees the developing countries' access to copyrighted works for purposes of teaching, scholarships and research. The provisions

of the RBC are not affected by the UCC. In the relationship between the countries of the Berne Union who are at the same time member countries of the UCC this convention cannot be applied to the protection of works whose country of origin is a Union country according to the regulations of the RBC. This precedence of the RBC is further strengthened by the fact that any country that is a member of both Conventions and leaves the Berne Convention loses the protection of the UCC for works of which it is the country of origin in all signatory countries of the Berne Convention. This clause, according to the Paris revision, is suspended in favour of the developing countries which may leave RBC while continuing their membership in (or joining) UCC, without negative consequences for as long as their status as developing countries remains unchanged.

II

In addition to the two world-wide Conventions dealt with, there is also the group of *Inter-American Conventions*. They have largely lost their importance as far as the relationship between those countries is concerned that at the same time are members of the RBC or the UCC. This is particularly so in the case of the Convention of Montevideo, which was the only one also open to European countries. Individually they are concerned with the following international agreements:

1. Treaty on Literary and Artistic Property, signed at the First South American Congress on Private International Law. Montevideo, 1888–9.

   Parties: Argentina, Bolivia, Paraguay, Peru, Uruguay. Adherences by European countries: France, Spain, Belgium, Italy, Hungary, Germany and Austria. Argentina and Paraguay accepted the adherence of all countries named; Bolivia those of Austria, Germany and Hungary.

This treaty was replaced by a treaty of the same name signed at the Second South American Congress on Private International Law, held at Montevideo in 1939–40. However, the new agreement has been ratified only by Paraguay and Uruguay, and these countries are governed by the 1946 Convention of Washington (cf. no. 7).

2. Convention on Literary and Artistic Copyright, signed at the Second International Conferences of American States, Mexico City, 1901–2.

   Parties: Costa Rica, Dominican Republic, El Salvador, Guatemala, Honduras, Nicaragua, and the United States.

   (Modified by 3 and replaced by 4 and 7).

3. Convention on Patents of Invention, Drawings and Industrial Models, Trade Marks, and Literary and Artistic Property, signed at the Third International Conference of American States, Rio de Janeiro, 1906.

   Parties: Brazil, Chile, Costa Rica, Ecuador, El Salvador, Guatemala, Honduras, Nicaragua, and Panama.

   (Replaced by 4 and 7)

4. Convention on the Protection of Literary and Artistic Copyright, signed at the Fourth International Conference of American States, Buenos Aires, 1910.

   Parties: Argentina, Bolivia, Brazil, Chile, Columbia, Costa Rica, Dominican Republic, Ecuador, Guatemala, Haiti, Honduras, Mexico, Nicaragua, Panama, Paraguay, Peru, United States, and Uruguay.

   (Revised by 6 and replaced by 7)

5. Agreement on Literary and Artistic Property, signed at the Bolivian Congress, Caracas, 1911.

   Parties: Bolivia, Ecuador, Peru, and Venezuela. (Replaced by 7)

6. Convention of Buenos Aires on the Protection of Literary and Artistic Copyright, as revised by the Sixth International Conference of American States, Havana, 1928.

Parties: Costa Rica, Ecuador, Guatemala, Nicaragua, and Panama.
(Replaced by 7)

7. Inter-American Convention on the Rights of the Author in Literary, Scientific, and Artistic Works, signed at the Inter-American Conference of Experts on Copyright, Pan American Union, Washington, June 22, 1946.
Parties: Argentina, Bolivia, Brazil, Chile, Costa Rica, Cuba, Dominican Republic, Ecuador, Guatemala, Haiti, Honduras, Mexico, Nicaragua and Paraguay.
(As between the parties, this Convention replaces all previous Inter-American conventions on copyright.)

Apart from the Convention of Montevideo, all these Conventions are based on the principle of "national treatment" (cf. introductory remark). The Montevideo Convention lays down the application of the law of the country in which the work was first published or produced.

As far as the duration of copyright is concerned, the principle of national treatment is replaced by the principle of reciprocity—no period of protection longer than that of the country of origin is granted (cf. I, 1 above). Formalities must be observed. Only since the last Convention (Washington, 1946), which provides the highest degree of protection of all the Pan-American Conventions, a guarantee of protection does not here to be made to depend on the fulfilment of formalities. In addition, this Convention, like the RBC, prescribes as minimum rights all essential rights of disposal which pertain to the members of the Convention independently of the national legislation. It also recognizes the right of an author's moral rights (i.e. protection against alternations or exploitation that could damage the author's reputation).

In the case of contradictions between the afore mentioned Conventions and the provisions of the UCC, or between the UCC and the regulations of any future Inter-American Conventions, the agreement last signed by the parties shall have precedence.

III

Until 27 April 1970 the everyday business of the Berne Convention was dealt with by an international office which for simplicity of administration was linked under a single management with the office for the management of the Paris Association Agreement for the Protection of Industrial Property (patents, registered designs, distinguished marks, unfair competition, etc.). At the Stockholm Conference for Intellectual Property in 1967 a new *World Intellectual Property Organization* (WIPO) was founded. This left the independence and sovereignty of the two Conventions untouched, but their administrative structure has been greatly altered. While the *United International Bureaux for the Protection of Intellectual Property* (BIRPI) merely represented an international secretariat under the supervision of the Swiss government, the Convention for the establishment of a world organization for intellectual property has for the first time created an international organization which is a subject of international law. The offices of the two Conventions and the office of the WIPO now form the *International Office for Intellectual Property* under a general director who represents the organizations and the Conventions in all international affairs. The official name of the new internatonal authority is:

World Intellectual Property Organisation
Bureaux for the Protection of
Intellectual Property
(WIPO)
32 Chemin des Colombettes
CH 1211 Genève 20

The supreme authority for each of the two Conventions is the Assembly of Member States which has assumed all the administrative and supervisory powers exercised till now by the Swiss Government. The WIPO is responsible for the coordination of the activities of the Conventions; it also devotes its activities to furthering the protection of intellectual property. Its supreme authority is the General Assembly, in which all member states of the Paris and Berne Conventions are represented.

Not only member states of the Conventions can be members of the WIPO, but also other states belonging to the UN or to one of its special organizations, to the International Commission of Atomic Energy, or to the Statute of the International Court of Justice or that are invited to become members by the General Assembly. The advisory body of the member states of both Conventions and the members of the WIPO not belonging to the Conventions is the socalled "Conference".

The business of the UCC is dealt with by

Unesco
Copyright Division
Place de Fontenoy
F 75 Paris 7e

The business of the Inter-American Conventions is dealt with by the

Pan-American Union
General Secretariate
USA Washington D.C.

Bibliography

a) The Conventions and National Copyright Laws

These are printed in English in:

Copyright laws and treaties of the world. Paris, Unesco, since 1956. Loose-leaf collection.

In French in:

Lois et traités sur le droit d'auteur. (Laws and treaties on copyright). Paris (Unesco) and Geneva (BIRPI) 1962.

In German (and English) in:

Quellen des Urheberrechts. Gesetzestexte aller Länder und Tabellen über internationale Verträge. Mit systematischen Einführungen. (Sources of copyright. Texts of the laws of all countries and tables on international treaties. With systematic introductions). Frankfurt a.M., A. Metzner, since 1961. Loose-leaf collection.

The Inter-American Conventions and UCC are also printed in:

Copyright protection in the Americas. 3rd ed. Washington D.C.

In Spanish in:

RUDA. Repertorio universal de legislación y convenios sobre derecho de autor. (Universal repertory of legislation and conventions on copyright). Paris, Unesco 1960.

In Italian in:

Bonasi, Benucci and Fabiani, *Codice della proprietà industriale e del diritto d'autore.* (Code of industrial property and copyright). Milan, Ginoffrè 1969. 2,280 pp.

b) Literature

W. Bappert and E. Wagner, *Internationales Urheberrecht, Kommentar zur RBC Brüsseler Fassung und WUA.* (International copyright. A commentary on the Brussels version of the RBC and UCC). München–Berlin, C. H. Beck 1956.

A. Bogsch, *The law of copyright under the Universal Copyright Convention.* 3rd ed. Leyden, Sijthoff (New York, R. R. Bowker) 1968.

M. Boutet and M. Plaisant, *Le régime international du droit d'auteur: La convention de Berne rév. à Bruxelles.* (International operation of copyright: The Berne Convention as revised at Brussels). Paris 1959. Reprinted from Juris-Classeur Civil, Annexes.

P. F. Carter-Ruck and E. P. Skone James, *Copyright. Modern law and practice.* London, Faber & Faber 1965. 640 pp.

Copyright International Conventions Handbook. New Delhi, Government of India—Ministry of Education—Copyright Office 1967.

W. Goldbaum, *Welturheberrechtsabkommen. Kommentar.* (Universal Copyright Convention. A commentary). Berlin–Frankfurt, Fr. Vahlen 1956.

W. Goldbaum, *Convención de Washington sobre el derecho de autor*. (The Washington Convention on copyright). In: Obras literarias scientificas y artisticas. Quito, Liebmann, n. d.

W. Hoffmann, *Die Berner Übereinkunft zum Schutze von Werken der Literatur und Kunst*. (The Berne Convention for the Protection of Literary and Artistic Property). Berlin, J. Springer 1935.

St. Ladas, *The international protection of literary and artistic property*. New York, Macmillan 1938.

Fr. W. Peter, *Das Stockholmer Protokoll für die Entwicklungsländer*. (The Stockholm Protocol for the Developing Countries). Frankfurt a.M., Börsenverein 1970. 88 pp.—Schriften des Börsenvereins, 5.

H. L. Pinner, *World copyright. An encyclopaedia*. 5 vols. Leyden, Sijthoff 1953–60.

G. Roeber (ed.), *Das Stockholmer Vertragswerk zum internationalen Urheberrecht*. (The Stockholm Convention and international copyright). München, Verlag Dokumentation, 1969.—Schriftenreihe der Ufita, 35.

V. de Sanctis, *La convenzione universale del* V.*diritto di autore*. (The universal copyright convention). Rome, S.A.I.E. 1949.

de Sanctis, *La convenzione internationale di Berna per la protezione delle opere letterarie et artistiche*. (The International Berne Convention for the Protection of Literary and Artistic Works). Rome, S.A.I.E. 1949.

Die Stockholmer Konferenz für geistiges Eigentum und gewerblichen Rechtsschutz und Urheberrecht. Internationaler Teil. (The Stockholm Conference on Intellectual Property and Industrial Property and Copyright. International section). In: Zeitschrift "Gewerblicher Rechtsschutz und Urheberrecht", 1967, No. 12. Weinheim, Verlag Chemie 1967.

A. Troller, *Die mehrseitigen völkerrechtlichen Verträge im internationalen gewerbli-* Lemoine. *chen Rechtsschutz und Urheberrecht*. (The multilateral international treaties of international property and copyright). Basel, Verlag für Recht und Gesellschaft 1965.

c) Periodicals

Le Droit d'Auteur. Ed. by BIRPI, Genève. Two editions (English and French).

Copyright Bulletin. Paris, Unesco.

Revue Internationale du Droit d'Auteur. (International Copyright Review). Paris, Lemoine
Texts in French, English and Spanish.

15 National Bibliography, National Library

Reliable national bibliographies are among the most important sources for national and international book-trade work. Where such bibliographies do not exist, or for one reason or another appear irregularly, and then incomplete, it is impossible for the book trade to develop in such a way as to fulfil its obligations to society. In spite of this platitude there are still enough negative examples for which in part an apathetic book trade may also bear some of the responsibility.

In view of the close connections existing in most countries of the world between National Bibliography and National Library, which is frequently an important centre of bibliographical information for the book trade too, we have also included this subject in the national chapters.

Bibliography

P. Avicenne, *Bibliographical services throughout the world, 1960–1964*. Paris, Unesco 1969. 228 pp.
Continues the series of reports prepared by L. N. Malclès (1951–2 and 1952–3) and R. L. Collison (1950–59). The first part contains an over-all survey of the evolution of bibliographical services during the period 1960–64. The second part, arranged alphabetically by

country, describes bibliographical achievements in eighty-three countries under the following headings: national bibliographical commission; inter-library co-operation; national bibliographies; special categories; teaching bibliography; archives. Furthermore it includes a comparative table showing the present state of bibliographical activities in each country. A French edition appeared in 1967.

Present-day problems and conditions in the national bibliographies in many parts of the world are dealt with in

R. C. GREER, *Bibliography. Current state and future trends.* Urbana, University of Illinois Press 1967. VII, 611 pp.

The international catalogue card service, which is of interest to certain branches of the book trade, is dealt with in

R. S. GILJAREVSKIJ, *International distribution of catalogue cards. Present situation and future prospects.* Paris, UNESCO 1969. 84 pp

Guide to national bibliographical information centres. 3rd ed. Paris, UNESCO 1970. 195 pp.

Lists the main national bibliographical centres of general scope or specializing in some fields of the humanities. 186 centres from 77 countries have been selected.

The journal

Bibliography, Documentation, Terminology

which is published twice a month by the Division of Libraries, Documentation and Archives of UNESCO, deals continuously with the problems of national bibliographies. It also appears in French, Russian and Spanish.

16 Book Production

The range of book production in a country is, of course, not the only indication, but certainly an important one of the book situation in the life of a nation. However, in order to obtain a comparative and to some extent standardized picture it is necessary, and independently of that, to consider also national book imports, which are of great importance for many countries and strongly influence the total picture. But since there are still no standards for book production, import or export that are internationally practised and comparable one with another, the foundations for this interesting part of our global statistics on culture remain weak.

There is no uniform foundation on which the national statistics on book production are based: the Recommendations worked out by UNESCO in 1961 and 1964 (Document 13 C/PRG/11) have to date been followed very little in practice. As far as book-production statistics are concerned (the Recommendations also deal with printed periodical publications), they contain among other things the following definitions:

a) a *book* is a non-periodical printed publication of at least 49 pages, exclusive of the cover pages, published in the country and made available to the public;
b) a *pamphlet* is a non-periodical printed publication of at least 5 but not more than 48 pages, exclusive of the cover pages, published in a particular country and made available to the public;
c) a *first edition* is the first publication of an original or translated manuscript;
d) a *re-edition* is a publication distinguished from the previous editions by changes made in the contents (revised edition) or layout (new edition);
e) a *reprint* is unchanged in contents and layout, apart from correction of typographical errors in the previous edition. A reprint by any publisher other than the original publisher is regarded as a re-edition;
f) a *translation* is a publication which reproduces a work in a language other than the original language;
g) a *title* is a term used to designate a

printed publication which forms a separate whole, whether issued in one or several volumes.
The following is also emphasized:
Book-production statistics should indicate the number of titles and, if possible, the number of copies of published works. Countries not able to supply information on the number of copies produced may, as an interim measure, supply information on the number of copies sold or otherwise distributed.
The General Conference of UNESCO adopted in 1967 the following classification by subject:
Book-production statistics should, in the first place, be classified by subject groups. Until another classification system has been evolved and adopted, the classification given below, which is based upon the Universal Decimal Classification (UDC) and has 23 groups (the figures given in parentheses refer to the corresponding UDC headings) is the one which should be used:
1. Generalities (0); 2. Philosophy, psychology (1); 3. Religion, theology (2); 4. Sociology, statistics (30–31); 5. Political science, political economy (32–33); 6. Law, public administration, welfare, social relief, insurance (34, 351–354, 36); 7. Military art and science (355–359); 8. Education (37); 9. Trade, communications, transport (38); 10. Ethnography, manners and customs, folklore (39); 11. Linguistics, philology (4); 12. Mathematics (51); 13. Natural sciences (52–59); 14. Medical sciences, public health (61); 15. Technology, industries, trades and crafts (62, 66–69); 16. Agriculture, forestry, stockbreeding, hunting, fishing (63); 17. Domestic science (64); 18. Commercial and business management techniques, communications, transports (65); 19. Town planning, architecture, plastic arts, minor arts, photography, music, film, cinema, theatre, radio, television (70–78, 791–792); 20. Entertainment, pastimes, games, sports (790, 793–799); 21. Literature (8): a) History of literature and literary criticism, b) Literary texts; 22. Geography, travel (91); 23. History, biography (92–99).
Almost all national book-production statistics differ from each other in many important details. Comparisons should therefore be regarded with caution. Since in only a few socialist countries numbers of copies printed are named—in these cases they belong to the component of production statistics—comparisons of this kind are completely out of the question. Added to this, the equating of books produced

Continent	Percentage of world population	Number of titles	Number of titles per million inhabitants	Percentage of book production
Africa	9.6	8,000	24	1.6
America, North	8.9	70,000	227	14.4
America, South	5.1	13,000	72	2.7
Asia	55.9	100,000	51	20.5
Europe	13.1	216,000	475	44.4
Oceania	0.5	4,000	216	0.8
USSR	6.8	76,000	319	15.6
World	100.0	487,000	140	100.0

with books sold or read can be very misleading. The greatest uncertainties in international comparisons arise from divergent classifications, different definitions of books as regards size and the principles of new edition and reprint, and finally, hazy boundaries between what constitutes a book meant for the public and one for some other purpose.

ON p. 34 is a global survey according to "Unesco Statistical Yearbook 1969" covering estimated world book production for 1968.

For translations → International Section, 17.

Bibliography

Preliminary statistical report on book production in various countries. Paris, Unesco 1951. 81 pp.—Unesco /ST/R/2.

Book production 1937–1954 and translations 1950–1954. Paris, Unesco 1955. 83 pp.—Unesco ST/S/2.

Unesco statistical yearbook. Paris, Unesco. Since 1963.

Contains a detailed chapter, "Book production", as the most important international source of information.

The Bowker annual of library and book trade information. New York, R. R. Bowker. Annually since 1955.

Regularly contains international book-production statistics.

Buch und Buchhandel in Zahlen. (Books and the book trade in figures). Frankfurt a. M., Börsenverein. Annually since 1952.

In addition to German information, it regularly offers international book-production statistics.

Publishers' World. New York, R. R. Bowker. From 1965 to 1969.

Includes statistical data on international book production.

A. J. Richter (ed.), *Compiling book publishing statistics.* 2nd ed. New York, Standards Institute 1969.

17 Translations

In the modern book world translations play a considerable role in national book production.

About 8% of the world's annual book production is based on translations. The percentage share of translations, however, varies a great deal between individual countries. Others, again, have only a small proportion of translations in spite of their large book production.

According to "Index Translationum" (vol. 21) 36,808 translations appeared in 1968 throughout the world, divided into subjects as follows:

Subject group	Titles
0 General	263
1 Philosophy	1,565
2 Religion, Theology	2,484
3 Law, Social Sciences, Education	4,208
4 Philology and Linguistics	176
5 Natural and Exact Sciences	2,340
6 Applied Sciences	3,047
7 Arts, Games, Sports	1,659
8 Literature	17,910
9 History, Geography, Biography	3,156
Total	36,808

According to the same source the countries publishing the greatest number of translations were as follows (1,000 titles and more):

Countries	Titles
USSR	3,607
Germany (F. R.–G. D. R.)	3,026
Spain	2,538
USA	2,182
Japan	2,145
France	2,035
Netherlands	1,942
Italy	1,688
Sweden	1,479
Denmark	1,419
Yugoslavia	1,294
Hungary	1,043

By far the largest number of translations are made from English or American sources. A middle group consists of translations from French, Russian and German. There is a considerable gap between these groups and all other languages.

As an international association the

International Federation of Translators
(Fédération Internationale des Traducteurs)
Dr. De Reusestraat 15
B Sint-Amandsberg

publishes the quarterly

Babel
16, Rue A.-de-Pontmartin
F 84 Avignon

The association has been in existence since 1953 and has dealt with fundamental questions on the work of translation at several large Congresses (Paris—1913; Rome—1956; Bad Godesberg—1959; Dubrovnik—1963; Lahti—1966; Prague—1970).

Bibliography

Index translationum. International bibliography of translations. Paris, UNESCO, since 1949, annually. Vol. 21 (1970) for 1968.

This most widespread international bibliography of translations continues the "Répertoire international des traductions" which was started in 1932 by the "Institut International de Coopération Intellectuel". The material is divided up according to countries, and within these according to the UDC (→ above). The bibliographical entries also give the translator, the publisher of the translation and the original title, but unfortunately not the publisher of the original. Brief statistics will be found at the end of each volume after the alphabetical list of authors.

Detailed information can be found in the "Statistical yearbooks" of UNESCO (→ International Section, 16).

Great literature East and West. The Unesco translation programme. Washington D.C., USA. National Commission for UNESCO 1969.

Since 1948 UNESCO has maintained a special translation programme. More than 200 titles have been published to date. This booklet reports on translations into English. A bibliography is included, mentioning also the names of the respective private and institutional publishers.

Unesco literature translation programme. Paris, UNESCO 1966. 43 pp.

Presents a general introduction to this programme.

Chartotheca translationum alphabetica. Frankfurt a.M., Hans W. Bentz.

This card catalogue has appeared since 1954 with supplements from 1945 onwards. Its particular value lies in bibliographical information on original editions; evidence of new translations in the shortest time; separation of English and North American authors; information on the contents of collected works and anthologies; uniform use of the English language for technical expressions and descriptions; every language combination possible.

18 Book Clubs

Anyone referring to the "Vocabulaire technique de l'éditeur" ("Publisher's technical vocabulary" → International Section, 6—published by the "Congrès International des Editeurs" in 1913, Berne, Switzerland) will look in vain for the caption "book club" or anything corresponding to it in English or any other language. Book clubs, so important these days for the book market in many countries, did not exist at that time. Beginning with Germany, they did not become noticeable till the 1920s, and their break-through into the general market is part of the recent history of the book trade. The main centres are Europe (with the largest number of

members in Germany—F. R.) and North America (USA). However, information given in the various national chapters reveals how great a foothold this form of book distribution has gained almost everywhere.
The following is taken from G. A. Glaister, *Glossary of the book* (London, Allen & Unwin 1960; p. 38) in reference to the, in some parts, controversial term "book club":

book club: 1. a business organization which selects from current books a monthly choice for its subscribers...
2. a similar organization which publishes limited de luxe or cheap editions for members...

The following definition in German is taken from the *Lexikon des Buchwesens* ("Encyclopedia of the book world"), vol. 1, Stuttgart, Hiersemann 1952; p. 115:

book clubs: enterprises selling selected productions of their own or other publishing houses produced in very large editions at a cheap price in the following special form, that the recipients commit themselves in the form of a subscription to take regularly a definite number of volumes at regular intervals...

From North America comes the following interpretation (M. C. Turner, *The bookman's glossary*, 4th ed., New York, Bowker 1961; p. 23):

book club. A member of a book club usually receives an expensive book premium for joining, and agrees to purchase a minimum of four books during the year. The monthly selection is a special "book club edition" of a current book, produced in such a large printing that the club can afford to give its members a special price...

Apart from the large book clubs, with a membership of several millions, there arose in the fifties and sixties special book clubs in many countries with specific subjects or aimed at specific sections or age groups in the population.
No thorough investigation of the past and present history of book clubs throughout the world has as yet been made. Reference to individual investigations is made in the national chapters (→ Section 18).

19 Paperbacks

The appearance of "Penguin Books" in Britain (1935) and "Pocket Books" in the USA (1939) started a development that has assured paperbacks of all categories a large share in almost all book productions throughout the world. The mass distribution of cheap, paper-bound books and the offer of a wide range of subjects as it exists in this form are among the most striking features of present-day book production, and therefore contribute to the still evolving process of democratization to assure everywhere the presence of books that are good value for money and within everyone's reach.
Penguin Books and Pocket Books, which started off the modern paperback development, had notable predecessors that have had an effect on later developments; for example: "Tauchnitz Edition" (Leipzig, founded in 1841) and "Albatross Modern Continental Library" (Hamburg, founded in 1932).
Since information from national sources is for the most part incomplete and often totally lacking, it is not possible to gain a reliable picture of the share that paperbacks have in international book production. Moreover, the number of copies printed and the relation between editions produced and sold should here be taken into account. It is estimated that about 20% of world book production is in the form of paperbacks, under which are included all forms of the modern, lightly bound book meant for bulk sale and in large editions, whether it be the popular paperback with an average edition of 50,000 copies, occasionally reaching the hundred thousands or millions, or the

paper-bound editions of highly qualified titles catering for special interests and printed in much smaller quantities.
The idea of a self-service system, which is fundamental to all paperbacks, has led among other things to very creative cover design, which in turn has become an invigorating influence on traditional fields of book production.

Bibliography

P. I. Gedin, *Den nya boken*. (The new book). Stockholm, Prisma 1966. 116 pp.—In Swedish.
The international paperback situation and its historical background is described here, as well as that in Sweden. pp. 110–14: bibliography (General, United Kingdom, USA, Germany, France, Netherlands, Denmark, Sweden).

Fr. L. Schick, *The paperbound book in America*. New York, R. R. Bowker 1968. XVIII, 262 pp.
Although the author is largely concerned with developments in North America, he has attempted to deal with the subject against a large historical and contemporary background in two chapters entitled "The inexpensive book in Great Britain" and "European Continental publications". For this reason the book deserves mention here. pp. 245–50: selected bibliography.

20 Book Design

Starting in Central Europe, where such competitions have existed (in Germany) since 1929, the idea of awarding prizes annually for the best-designed books has now spread to many countries. They vary a good deal in their conditions and guiding principles, but fundamentally they endeavour to draw the attention of all those interested in the production, distribution and reading of books to exemplary forms of book production. All the material and aesthetic elements that contribute to the appearance and impression of a book, from the choice of paper to the binding, are taken into consideration. The ever-increasing demand for books that are good value for money and within the reach of all encourages the endeavour to include this kind of book in these national competitions, assuming that even a cheap book can be well designed.
The competitions for the best-designed books, usually drawn from a country's annual book production and judged by a jury consisting of expert representatives of the trade and artistic circles concerned in book production, sharpen the ability to distinguish between outstanding work and the rest, and so they encourage the printing industry, the book trade in general, illustrators, book designers and publishers to take part in fruitful competition, in which the aesthetically sensitive public is the beneficiary.
International exhibitions of the art of the book, based on the best-designed and prize-winning books of the participating countries, were held in Leipzig (German Democratic Republic) in 1959, 1965 and the latest in 1971. At the Leipzig Autumn Fair (→ International Section, 29) an up-to-date exhibition of the "Best-designed Books" of many countries has been regularly held since 1963. A special international exhibition, "Best-designed Books", is annually held at the Frankfurt Book Fair (→ International Section, 29). In 1971 twenty-five countries were represented. The "National Book League", London (→ United Kingdom, 20) holds an annual "International Book Production Exhibition".
As an example of fruitful international co-operation in this field, mention should be made of "Nordisk bokkunst" ("Nordic Art of the Book"), which was founded in 1946 by "Nordiska Boktryckarrådet" ("The

Nordic Bookprinters' Council"). Denmark, Finland, Norway and Sweden have created a common platform which, among other things, guarantees the exhibition of the best-designed books of these Scandinavian countries.

Associated with the idea of "best-designed books", but restricted to special subjects, are two great international events. The

Biennale of Illustrations
Námestie SNP 11
CS Bratislava

first took place in 1967 and was repeated with great success in 1969. At this Biennale modern original illustrations are exhibited with the books resulting from them. Children's books have a particularly strong representation. An international jury awards prizes for the best examples.

Thanks to the initiative of "The Scotsman" newspaper, an annual

International Book Jacket Exhibition
c/o Publicity Manager "The Scotsman"
North Bridge
GB Edinburgh 1

has been organized since 1962. It is divided into 18 groups. A prize is awarded in each group, and the best-designed book jacket in the whole exhibition is awarded a gold medal.

In 1967 for the first time a "Salon" devoted to books for bibliophiles was held in Paris. It will be repeated in 1971 as the

2nd International Salon for Art Books
and Bibliophily
Palais de Beaulieu
CH 1002 Lausanne

Bibliography

Internationale Buchkunst-Ausstellung. Leipzig 1959 and 1965. (International Book Design Exhibition. Leipzig 1959 and 1965). Leipzig 1959, 1965 and 1971. 478 pp.; 518 pp.; 440 pp.

These volumes contain numerous contributions to the subject "best-designed books" in many parts of the world, especially the socialist countries of East and South-East Europe. An extensive illustration section.

21 Publishing

In modern international publishing—here is meant only the publishing of books and of professional, scientific and technical journals—three groups can be identified, and these differ clearly from one another:

a) private publishing of the Western kind
b) nationalized publishing of the Eastern (socialist) kind
c) mixed forms of a) and b).

There are numerous variants in each of these groups:

in private publishing, from firms owned exclusively by individuals to enterprises governed by collective responsibility and management, in both of which recent experiments in socialization can be found;

in nationalized publishing, from strict, exclusive centralization to undertakings that almost smack of private economy with emphasis on regional or local responsibility, and taking account of demands of the market;

in mixed forms there are those which hold themselves aloof from the two forms that are conditioned by political circumstances, but see no obstacle in taking features from one or the other, or operating simultaneously with both systems.

The publishing structure in Europe is sufficiently, even if rather broadly, characterized in this threefold division. This is also true on the whole for other parts of the world, but it must be realized that there are examples here that display the extreme forms of private and nationalized publishing under one roof. These will be dealt with in the closing volumes of BTW.

All cultural statistics, international comparisons and information on the number of existing publishers must be seen from the above point of view. Only thus can wrong interpretations be avoided. A strongly centralized, nationalized publishing system, divided up according to subjects, will have far fewer publishing houses than the number of firms in a comparable country under private enterprise, in spite of its greater or very great production. For example, the Federal Republic of Germany, with an average annual production of 30,000 titles, has about 2,000 publishing houses; the average per publisher is therefore 15 titles. The German Democratic Republic has an average annual production of about 6,000 titles, published by some 60 publishing houses, i.e. 100 titles per publisher. Many similar examples could be quoted.

The different ideas on publishing, revealed in the first place by their external features, are basicly derived from fundamental differences in conception and attitude to problems.

They affect all aspects of publishing and the book trade. For this reason they present one of the most interesting sides of modern international publishing which as a result of competition between these two large groups differs essentially from earlier traditional conditions; and this situation will play a decisive role in determining future developments. At the same time this competition will exercise a great influence on the structure and tendencies in the third group.

For organizations → International Section, 4.

Bibliography

The best book about publishing is still the classical work by the Grand Old Man of the international book trade, who died in 1968:

Sir Stanley Unwin, *The truth about publishing.* 7th rev. ed. London, Allen & Unwin (New York, Macmillan) 1960. 348 pp.
In this book, which has been translated into many languages, a great publisher tells of his experiences and knowledge, which for all the subjective manner of expression can be regarded as objective truth. The book is a convincing document of an individual publisher from the Western World. Unfortunately there exists no equivalent in the nationalized publishing world of East and South-East Europe. Only then would the picture be to some extent complete.

There is an extensive literature on publishing in general, and on production, distribution, promotion and publishers' readers. A good general survey is to be found in *Die Fachliteratur zum Buch- und Bibliotheks-wesen* ("Specialist literature on books and libraries," → International Section, 6). An interesting survey in English will be found in *The reader's adviser* (→ International Section, 6), in which the first chapter "Books about books" contains a bibliography with comments that also include the subjects "The practice of publishing" (bestsellers, censorship, editing, tools for editing), and "Books about book-making".

A work providing an introduction to the fundamentals of publishing which is particularly interesting for developing countries is:

D. C. Smith, Jr., *A guide to book-publishing.* New York, R. R. Bowker 1966. XI, 244 pp.
Bibliography: pp 229–233.—The author refers in particular to the experience gained by the "Franklin Programs", New York, in many developing countries. (→ BTW vol. 2, International Section, 4 and USA, 4 and 28).

22 Literary Agents

Literary agents, who play such an important part in large areas of book supply in the United Kingdom and the United States, are in a relatively weak position in

most other countries, or, as in the socialist countries of East and South-East Europe, do not exist at all as individual private institutions. In these latter countries they are replaced by centralized nationalized or cooperative enterprises, which will be treated in the various national chapters.
Names and addresses of literary agents can be found in some of the national directories of the book trade. Many agencies are represented every year at the Frankfurt Book Fair (→ International Section, 29), which also includes a list of such agencies (1969: 55 agencies from 21 countries) in the official catalogue of the Fair.

23 Wholesale Trade

In the highly developed book nations the wholesale trade is one of the most important features in book distribution. This service is performed in private or cooperative firms, or by nationalized or semi-official institutions. In all cases the functioning of the book trade, i.e. the fulfilment of its material and idealistic tasks, is as dependent on the existence of a highly efficient wholesale trade as on first-class publishing and retailing. Many wholesale firms are also engaged in import and export. In this respect they play an important role internationally.

24 Retail Trade

Presumably there will never be a conclusive answer to the old question as to who is responsible for the fate of a book. Is it the publisher or, as others assert, the retail bookseller? Successful cooperation between the two is perhaps nearer the true answer, and with that the fundamental importance of the retail book trade receives its due emphasis. Without it, without a network of good retail bookshops catering for a large range of subjects, contact between book and reader would be poor. The closer the network and the better the quality of the shops, the greater will be the prospects for a book and its publisher, let alone the author. This statement is not contradicted by the existence of book clubs, direct sale by publishers, and other modern phenomena. These supplement the general scene in the book trade, but do not determine it. In the international field it can be observed that in the development of their own book trade, countries are not often aware of the key position played by book distribution. Planning and wishes are in such cases biased in favour of publishing. It is forgotten that the sale of books is as important as their production, and surprise is then expressed when in effect books and their potential readers remain as remote from each other as before. It is necessary to realize the urgent need for this in many developing countries. To this must be added the frequent lack of understanding by publishers in such countries as to what are the material prerequisites for a healthy retail book trade.
A generally applicable definition of an efficient retail book trade does not and cannot exist, in view of the varying conditions from one country to another, but the following points might be acceptable in forming a judgement: the existence of a well-assorted stock; qualified management and staff; the presence of a bibliographical reference library sufficient to act as a foundation for providing first-class information.
The bookshop as a centre of information, as one of the intellectual centres of its locality this is indeed only one of the many aspects of the retail book trade, which also has the task of adjusting itself to any new demands of the time and of boldly entering new territories on its own initiative. In this respect self-service systems play an ever-increasing role. Association with the mail-order business is also becoming more

and more marked. In so far as book distribution allied to a nationalized form of publishing is also in cooperative hands, the same standards fundamentally apply as in the private sector, despite appearances to the contrary. After all the planning there still remains the demand for first-class personnel as the most important guarantee for an effective book trade.

Bibliography

Since the differences in the retail book trade are usually very great from one country to another, there are no books describing the work of this branch of the book trade from an international point of view. Reference is made below, however, to the bibliography in the various national chapters (→ 24), which in the case of large book nations is often valid for the whole of their linguistic area.

International problems of bookselling are discussed in:

Bookselling. A way to international understanding. Delft, ICBA 1959. 102 pp.
This tri-lingual brochure (English, French, German) deals with the lectures given at the First International Congress of ICBA (→ International Section, 4).

H. Grundmann (ed.), *Das Bild des Buchhändlers*. (The image of the bookseller). Delft, ICBA 1966. 54 pp.
An anthology covering books and the book trade.

25 Mail-Order Bookselling

Book sales through the post play a great part in the book trade today. Therefore it was deemed necessary to make reference to this and provide information in the various national chapters. From these it will be recognized how many different activities lie hidden behind this term. They extend from direct sale by the publisher via the mail-order business of the traditional retail book trade to specialized undertakings that work exclusively in this way, frequently in association with the remainder business. Large international economic communities provide this trend with new impulses.

26 Antiquarian Book Trade, Auctions

The bibliophilic, scholarly antiquarian book trade in its international aspect is among the essential media for world-wide book exchange. The contributions made by this special branch of the book trade are as essential for the libraries in all countries of the world as they are for the private collector. The most recent tendencies in this market have been a fundamental gap between demand and supply of rare works, and as a result a steep rise in prices.

In the international antiquarian book trade there have always existed numerous forms of cooperation on an individual basis. But not until 1947 did there exist an international association of national antiquarian booksellers' associations in the form of the

International League of
Antiquarian Booksellers (ILAB)
35 Rue Bonaparte
F 75 Paris 6e

At present (1970) the following 16 countries are members of the ILAB: Austria, Belgium, Brazil, Canada, Denmark, Finland, France, Germany (F.R.), Italy, Japan, Netherlands, Norway, Sweden, United Kingdom, and the USA.

Since 1948 the ILAB has held annual congresses. These are meant to foster international contact and the discussion of mutual problems. By this means a "code of usages and customs" was drawn up as a guide for the basic procedure in the antiquarian book trade. International antiquarian book-trade fairs were promoted (twice in Amsterdam and once in Los Angeles since 1965), questions of specialized training were discussed and a "Triennial Prize for Bibliography" was created.

Bibliography

The following directory was published on the initiative of the ILAB:

International directory of antiquarian booksellers. 4th ed. Paris, ILAB 1968. 672 pp.
The directory, obtainable through the secretaries of the national associations, is divided according to countries; within these divisions according to places, and finally in alphabetical order of firms. The index section is classified according to specialized fields and contains an alphabetical list of names.

The ILAB has also published:

M. Hertzberger (ed.), *Dictionary of the antiquarian book trade in French, English, German, Swedish, Danish, Italian, Spanish and Dutch.* Paris, ILAB 1956. 190 pp.
The first and only work of its kind, it contains the technical terms used by antiquarian booksellers throughout the world. English is the key language.

Apart from these handbooks meant for everyday use, there is little in the way of international literature on the antiquarian book trade and auctions. There are only a few works written from a historical point of view. The following may be mentioned:

T. Kleberg, *Antiquarischer Buchhandel im alten Rom.* (Antiquarian book trade in ancient Rome). In: Annales Academiae Regiae Scient. Upsalensis, 8/1964, pp. 21–32. Stockholm, Almqvist & Wiksell 1964.

B. Wendt, *Der Versteigerungs- und Antiquariats-Katalog im Wandel von vier Jahrhunderten.* (The auction and antiquarian catalogue during four centuries). In: Archiv für Geschichte des Buchwesens, IX, 1–88. Frankfurt a. M., Buchhändler-Vereinigung 1969.
Describes some basic European trends and examples from the end of the 16th century onwards.

Since 1949 the editors of "AB Bookman's Weekly" (earlier "Antiquarian Bookman") have been publishing a yearbook which since 1967 has borne the title "AB Bookman's Yearbook". In the editorial section in each volume it includes a great deal of material on the past and present in the national and international antiquarian book trade and auctions. The 1969 edition deserves special mention:

AB bookman's yearbook, 1969. 2 parts. Newark, N.J., Bookman's Weekly, 1969.
Part 2 contains articles on the antiquarian book trade in the 20th century and on the past and present situation in the antiquarian book trade in various countries of the Old and New World, partly with bibliographical references.

At present there is no journal dealing with the subject of the antiquarian book trade internationally. But the specialist journals appearing in the countries with the most important antiquarian book trade are almost all aimed at an international reading circle associated with the particular linguistic area. This is particularly so in the case of Germany (F.R.), the United Kingdom and the USA (→ 26 in the national chapters). Under this reference will also be found journals advertising "books wanted and offered".

For the sake of completeness we will include the "modern antiquarian book trade", which can be of considerable importance as "remainder business" for the sale of large sets of books left lying at the publishers', often with valuable titles among them.

International auctions are patronized by a fairly large number of firms, but the number of those that are of international importance is relatively small. The most important centres are London and New York. Information on firms is obtainable from the above-mentioned directory or from the national reference books (→ Sections 7 and 26 in the national chapters).

Several publications give information on the results of auctions. These will be found in Section 26 of the national chapters.
Problems concerned with the restoration and repair of books, periodicals and printed illustrations are dealt with in the journal

Restaurator
P.O.B. 96
DK 1004 København

which has been appearing since 1969.
→ International Section, p. 62.

27 Book Imports
28 Book Exports

During these last decades the flow of books from country to country and from continent to continent has increased in a hitherto inconceivable manner. After the terrible losses and damage caused by the Second World War the rate of international book exchange multiplied many times compared with that in the preceding years of peace. Owing to the huge number of interwoven channels used for this trade it is impossible to quote the exact volume, but a glance at the import and export figures of the great book nations is sufficient to show how immense the quantity of books is.
Particularly in the case of the book markets of countries encouraging and favouring exports, the export figures form almost half the total turnover. But even lower percentages, related to the books concerned, are impressive enough.
It is obvious that a comparison of the export and import figures of the important countries in these two activities is relevant for obtaining an international survey, but as things stand at present it would not be of great significance. Official and institutional figures on foreign trade in books and periodicals cannot be reduced to a common denominator, which means that an essential prerequisite is missing for comparisons of this kind to be made. Moreover, many books crossing the frontiers escape the interested observer (book exchange, free informatory literature, etc., etc.) It is to be hoped that UNESCO will some day show an interest in these statistics and, by developing guiding ideas, contribute to thinning out this jungle and make it more easily surveyable. Those countries which regard information on their book exports and imports as a secret to be closely guarded, should realize that by doing so they damage rather than enhance their international reputation. Those who are seriously interested will always manage to obtain by devious ways whatever they have the urge to discover. It should be everybody's aim to create an annual comparative survey of the book imports and exports of all countries in line with international statistics on book production.
Foreign trade in books is becoming more and more important for a growing number of countries. In many cases this can be recognized from the support, both material and ideal, being given within a country to book exports, officially, semiofficially, and by various institutions. Here too we can only speak in general terms. The inclination to support book exports one way or another is most noticeable in those countries that are conscious of the positive relationship between the books being exported and the reputation of the country.
But apart from any desired national advantages, an intensive exchange of books on as large a scale as possible is in the interest of human beings tuned to peaceful competition and human cooperation. This thought, so important for world development and offering the world of books so many good prospects, is to be found in the *Agreement on the Importation of Educational, Scientific and Cultural Materials.* It was adopted at the fifth session of the General Conference of UNESCO in Florence (→ Annex 4).
But here too there are considerable differences between theoretical acknowledge-

ment and practice. The best illustrative material for this is "Trade barriers to knowledge", mentioned lower down.

To coordinate the efforts towards the free flow of books throughout the world and to discuss ways in which UNESCO might promote the international circulation of books, there exists cooperation between the major international organizations in the book world and UNESCO.

By the end of 1970 the two multilateral conventions on the international exchange of publications adopted by the general conference of UNESCO in December 1958 had been ratified or accepted by 30 states. These conventions were: the "Convention concerning the International Exchange of Publications" and the "Convention concerning the Exchange of Official Publications and Government Documents between States".

These agreements provide in particular for the free exchange of institutional, official and semi-official publications. "National Exchange Centres" exist in the participant countries.

The "UNESCO Book Coupons" provide a further contribution by UNESCO to the promotion of international book exchange. → International Section, 4.

Bibliography

Agreement on the Importation of Educational, Scientific and Cultural Materials. A guide to its operation. Paris, 2nd ed. Paris, UNESCO 1958. 32 pp.

Handbook on the international exchange of publications. 3rd ed. Paris, UNESCO 1964. 768 pp.—In English, French, Spanish and Russian.

Chapters on: the different types of exchange; the organization of national and international exchange services; conventions and agreements for the exchange of publications; transport and customs; summary recommendations of regional meetings on the international exchange of publications; a list of exchange offers of international organizations; details on the development of national exchange. A select list of current international directories, a subject index and an index to countries are also provided.

F. K. LIEBICH, *Removing taxes on knowledge.* Paris, UNESCO 1970. 43 pp.

An analysis of the transformation of international trade patterns in the 50s and 60s covering the cultural field and including "products of printing and writing".

Trade barriers to knowledge. A manual of regulations affecting educational, scientific and cultural materials. 2nd ed. Paris, UNESCO 1955. 364 pp.

This book, arranged according to countries, gives detailed information on the charges on and obstacles to imports which fall within the scope of the "Florence Agreement" (→ above).

29 Book Fairs

The term "book fair" can stand for many things: local, regional and national events devoted to general promotion on behalf of books and to increased book sales, and more or less consciously bearing the character of an annual fair. Where such events play a fairly large part in the book trade of a country they are mentioned in the chapter devoted to that country. Here, however, we are interested in a different interpretation, namely, the book fair as a means for international book exchange.

Book fairs of this nature can in Europe be traced back to the end of the fifteenth century (Frankfurt a. M.). Their role as important centres for the exchange of books in Europa represents an interesting chapter in the intellectual, cultural and economic history of the Old World. Leipzig, as well as Frankfurt a. M., assumed a leading role in this development.

Interesting, however, as this historical process may be, it must be distinctly appreciated that modern international book fairs are almost exclusively a product of our time. The need for book fairs of this kind grew as the nations were brought more closely together and as modern techniques in transport and news created new provisions for swift international communication.

Their number has grown considerably in recent years and it seems that this development will continue. The first book fair after the Second World War bearing the stamp of our age and the greatest and most influential on an international scale is the

Frankfurter Buchmesse
(Frankfurt Book Fair)
Postfach 3914
D 6 Frankfurt a. M.

It came into being in 1949 and has assumed international importance on a broad basis. With the participation of every continent, this book fair, which is held annually in the autumn (September or October), presents an almost complete survey of recent book production throughout the world. This book fair also holds a key position in international agreements on co-productions, translation rights and other forms of cooperation in the publishing and book trades throughout the world. The Frankfurt Book Fair offers the developing nations unique pictorial instruction and the opportunity of presenting to the world the results of their own published work. On the occasion of the FBF the annual "Peace Prize of the German Book Trade" is awarded to a person who has contributed in an outstanding way to a peaceful world.

There is a very extensive literature on the old Frankfurt and Leipzig Book Fairs. It will be found in the works mentioned under Sections 2 and 6 in the chapters "Germany—Federal Republic of Germany" and "Germany—German Democratic Republic". The following publication gives a brief description of the old and modern Frankfurt Book Fairs:

Henricus Stephanus (Henri Estienne), *Francofordiense emporium. Der Frankfurter Markt. La Foire de Francfort. The Frankfurt Fair.* Ed. by S. Taubert, Frankfurt a. M., Frankfurt Book Fair 1968. 181 pp.

An annual

International Book Exhibition
Winterfeldstr. 3
D 1 Berlin (West)

has been held in Berlin since 1952.

The

International Warszawa Book Fair
Krakowskie Przedieście 7
PL Warszawa

has been held in Warsaw since 1956. With its international character it plays a leading role in this field among the socialist countries of East and South-East Europe. The Western World and the neutral countries see in it primarily a means of engaging in import and export in this part of Europe. The "Warsaw Book Fair" takes place annually in May.

Other international book fairs can also be viewed from the same angle. Mention may be made of the

International Beograd Book Fair
P.O.B. 883
YU Beograd

which has been in existence since 1955 and always takes place after the Frankfurt Book Fair.

The first annual

International Sofia Book Fair
DSP "Hemus"
Russkij Bulwar 6
BG Sofia

was held in October 1968. It regularly takes place in autumn.

The

Leipzig Book Fair
c/o Leipziger Messeamt

Markt 11–15
DDR 701 Leipzig
holds an eminent position in the history of the German and international book trade. Following an old custom, it is part of the international general spring and autumn fairs. Foreign publishers are most strongly represented in the spring.
The
Mostra del Libro
(Book Fair)
which from 1961 onwards was originally held annually in Milan, but has recently been associated with other Italian book centres, is organized jointly by the Italian Publishers' Association (→ Italy, 4) and the
A.P. Wales Organization
18 Charing Cross Rd.
GB London WC 2
The latter also cooperates with the appropriate national bodies in organizing the annual
USA International Book Exhibition
and the
International Book Exhibition, Madrid
The
International Book Biennial
Caixa Postal 7832
B São Paulo
held for the first time in 1970, offers special advantages for contact between the Latin-American book world and other continents.
The most influential special book fair is the
International Children's Book Fair
Via G. Ciamician 4
I 40127 Bologna
which has existed since 1964 and is assuming an ever-increasing importance internationally in the matter of books for children and youth. It takes place in April, and connected with it is an "International Exhibition of Illustrators".
The same can be said of the
Salon international du Livre et de la Presse Scientifique et Technique
(International Exhibition of Books and of the Scientific and Technological Press)
117, Boulevard Saint-Germain
F 75 Paris 6e
for scientific and technological books. It has existed since 1964 and is held every two years in the early summer.
The
International Book Fair Brussels
111 avenue du Parc
B 1060 Bruxelles
has been among the large international book fairs since 1968. It is held in the spring.
The
International Nizza Book Festival
c/o Promotion Commerciale
Public Editions
12, Avenue de la Grande Armée
F 75 Paris 17e
was held for the first time in 1969 and changed the idea of a book fair in the direction of a festival with many additional programmes.
Two international book fairs exist in the Middle East. Both the
Cairo Book Fair
1117, Corniche El Nile Street
ET Cairo
and the
International Jerusalem Book Fair
P.O.B. 1508
IL Jerusalem
enjoy a great reputation internationally. The Cairo Book Fair is held annually, and the International Jerusalem Book Fair every two years.
Although primarily for educational publications, the
Didacta
(European Educational Materials Fair)
Kartäuserstr. 4
D 7806 Freiburg-Ebnet
is of great importance for publishers of textbooks and multi-media materials. It takes place every two years in June at varying centres.

International Section

The latest newcomer to the vast field of international book fairs is

World Book Fair
A 5, Green Park
IND New Delhi 16

which will be held in 1972. → Hungary, 29 → International Section, 20.

30 Public Relations

As we consider the image of the publisher and bookseller in the public mind, the whole question of public relations in all branches and institutions becomes more and more important and topical. But since any inclination or demand for this has only assumed any real shape in the recent past, the efforts at public relations by the book trade are almost everywhere still in their initial stages. Under these circumstances it is hardly possible to speak of any desirable international cooperation commensurate with the spirit of our times.

In many countries of the world not a single thought has been given to this interesting question, which may one day be vital to the book trade. In others collective publicity, i.e. one part of public relations, is continually confused with the latter itself. Elsewhere a bold but fruitless appeal is made to the long and great traditions of the book trade, and surprise is shown when dignity and grandeur meet with no response today, and the achievements of the past are not considered with the merits of our days.

The situation with regard to public relations in the modern book world can be gathered from the individual national chapters. They show starting-points and aims differing widely from one another. Often they come under the subordinate heading of book promotion. There are only meagre analyses which would lead to a thoroughly thought out conception, which goes to the root of the matter and unites all relevant fields of activity, and there is little enthusiasm for fundamental work on principles, for consideration of modern market research, and for the analysis of readers and leisure hours. Correspondingly, there is hardly any source from which the material can be obtained from any national book trade in order to make such a task possible in its totality.

Only occasionaly is there any international exchange of experience, and then only among a few nations. Efforts by international bodies to improve the climate between book and reader are usually no more than ineffectual obligatory exercises. Such experience also shows the great national and international tasks awaiting the book trade.

At present there are only a few events that can be described as distinct contributions to public relations in the international book trade. Among these could be named the congresses of the international organizations (→ International Section, 4), the meetings of UNESCO devoted to books (→ International Section, 4), and the leading international book fairs (→ International Section, 29). Among the last the Frankfurt Book Fair makes a special contribution in this connection with its "International Book Poster Exhibition", which was first held in 1968. In 1970 contributions were made by 16 countries with 150 posters from the year 1969–70.

Public-relations work without reference to market, readers and leisure-time research becomes in the long run a fruitless labour of love, and so particular attention is drawn to International Section, 9.

Bibliography

There is no book dealing with public relations in the book trade on an international scale. Attention is drawn to the bibliography in the respective national chapters and to International Sections, 6 and 9.—A new contribution on this field will be the "International Book Year 1972".

31 Bibliophily

Apart from the numerous bibliophile associations mentioned in the national chapters under Section 31, the
International Association of Bibliophily
58 Rue de Richelieu
F 75 Paris 2e
has been in existence since 1959 and holds an "International Congress of Bibliophiles" every two years (Munich 1959, Paris 1961, Barcelona and Madrid 1963, London 1965, Venice 1967 and Vienna 1969). "Transactions" inform IAB members of events and the results of congresses.

This Association publishes the journal:
Bulletin de l'Association Internationale de Bibliophilie
(Bulletin of the International Association of Bibliophily)
58, Rue de Richelieu
F 75 Paris 2e

As international journal for the preservation of library and archival material appears three times a year
Restaurator
P.O.B. 96
DK 1004 København

For special problems of book pathology and therapy → International Section, Book Museums: Italy.

Paper historians exchange their findings and ideas in the
International Community of Paper Historians
(Internationale Arbeitsgemeinschaft der Papierhistoriker)
Liebfrauenplatz 5
D 65 Mainz

This association has 166 members in 23 nations (1971).

For the International Salon for Art Books and Bibliophily, → International Section, 20.

Many of the national associations have an international inclination.

Bibliography

There is an extensive literature on book collecting and bibliophily, particularly in English, including:

J. Carter, *ABC for book collectors.* London, R. Hart-Davis 1952 and later revised editions.
In this book, arranged alphabetically, an expert has explained the terms most important to the bibliophile in the field of books.

32 Literary Prizes

The number of national and international literary prizes has increased so much that not even a work endeavouring to give a world-wide survey (→ below in the bibliography) can claim to be complete. The information in the national chapters under Section 32 is in the majority of cases only a selection. Even in the socialist countries, with their prevailing inclination to concentrate literary prizes, inflationary tendencies will be found here and there.

An exact definition of a literary prize is hardly possible. There is obvious overlapping with general cultural distinctions or awards in other categories. This is also true of the distinction between national and international prizes. Here too the frontiers are hazy. Last but not least, the effect and significance of literary prizes vary considerably. There are prizes that have a direct effect on the reputation and sale of a book, as, for example, the great literary prizes in France, while others do not influence the fate of a book in any way whatsoever.

The only literary prize of an indisputably international character, i.e. a prize that has taken into account total world production in literature, is the *Nobel Prize for Literature,* founded in 1901 by the Nobel bequest. It is awarded by the "Swedish Academy", Stockholm, for the complete literary work of an internationally recognized author. It was awarded for the first time in 1901 and is one of five Nobel Prizes. The others are for outstanding achievements in Physics, Chemistry, Physiology or Medicine, and Peace. The Norwegian Parliament (Storting) in Oslo is responsible for the "Nobel Peace Prize".

Private literary awards like the *Selección Formentor* (a "discovery" award) and the *International Publishers' Prize* (a "confirmation" award) both offered by a group of publishers from various countries since 1961, gained an outstanding international reputation.

For international prizes associated with the subjects of this book → International Section, 10, 26, 29.

Bibliography

H. Schück and others, *Nobel, the man and his prizes*. Amsterdam, Elsevier 1962. X, 690 pp.

This comprehensive work gives extensive information on all aspects of the five Nobel Prizes and includes a biography of Alfred Nobel.

J. Clapp, *International dictionary of literary awards*. New York, Scarecrow Press 1963. 545 pp.

Deals with all literary prizes that in one way or another deserve attention beyond the frontiers of their country of origin. They are arranged in alphabetical order of prizes, which are described in broad outline. The names of recipients are included. There is an index of countries and authors; pp. 347–74 contain sources of information on literary awards. Selected bibliography.

33 The Reviewing of Books

In view of the great importance that book reviews have for the national and international distribution of many books, we considered it appropriate to give at least some information in the national chapters. However, the number of publications containing reviews being so very large, only brief references can be made. In addition, we have to confine ourselves to reviews of general literature while bearing in mind divergent data for special fields (science, technology, etc.). As far as reviews of specialized literature for the book trade are concerned, the national book-trade journals frequently do good service in this cause. These reviews also have great importance internationally, in so far as the journals are distributed beyond their national frontiers.

Some of the periodicals mentioned under Section 33 in the national chapters have a reputation beyond the frontiers of their own country or linguistic area. The best and most influential example of this is

The Times Literary Supplement
Printing House Square
GB London EC 4

TLS appears weekly, with special editions dealing with various aspects of modern cultural life, including the Frankfurt Book Fair (→ International Section, 29). It is one of the few general international periodicals that regularly deal with books for children and youth (in special editions).

A work on book reviews worth mentioning on an international scale does not exist. It would have to refer to the great part played by the review sections of general periodicals, political weeklies and other magazines that are widely read in our modern society, and—a fact that must be particularly emphasized—it would have to take note of the range and influence of book reviews in radio and television.

The

International Association
of Literary Critics
(Association des Critiques Littéraires)
38 rue de Faubourg St. Jacques
F Paris 14e

has existed as an organization since 1969. Critics from 22 countries are among its members. It held its first Congress in Parma, Italy, in 1969.

34 Graphic Arts

Between the graphic arts and the book trade there are so many points of contact that it would be presumptuous to expect exhaustive information at this point or in Section 34 of the national chapters. We had to be content with information that could further assist those interested, at least at the initial stages. This would be guaranteed most readily through the graphic associations.
From an international point of view, attention must be drawn to two institutions of this kind.

International Typographic Association
(Association Typographique Internationale—A. TYP. I)
Secretariat
43 Fetter Lane
GB London EC 4

A. TYP. I was founded in 1957 and has over 300 members from 16 countries (1970). The aim of the Association, according to its statutes, is "to unite and harmonize the efforts of all who practise or are interested in the graphic arts". At large international Congresses (the seventh in London, in 1971) the A. TYP. I has predominantly dealt with questions on the following subjects: type and the use of type in typography; legal protection of type; work in developing countries; legibility of type; computers and aesthetic problems of type.
The Association publishes a series of writings. From 1971 onwards an A. TYP. I Year Book is to be published.

International Centre for the
Typographic Arts (ICTA)
Postfach 349
D 7 Stuttgart-Untertürkheim

was founded in 1961 and acts as an educational organization for the exchange of ideas, information and examples concerned with all fields of communication. ICTA promotes experimental working projects, gives assistance in the field of communications, increases the understanding of the public by exchanging exhibitions and organizing contacts, and sets standards for the occupational level in training and practice. ICTA is responsible for the international competition "Typomundus". It also works in close cooperation with A. TYP. I (→ above).
In September 1969 this organization had over 800 members in 28 countries in Africa, America, Asia, Australia and Europe.
Technical development in printing and, to some extent, in paper manufacture, is reflected in special great international events. The most important of these are

Drupa
Düsseldorfer Messegesellschaft
Postfach 10203
D 4 Düsseldorf

IPEX
F. W. Bridges & Sons Ltd
Commonwealth House
1–19 New Oxford Street
GB London WC 1

and

Congresso e Mostra Internazionale Grafica Editoriale e Cartaria (GEC)
(International Congress and Fair of the Graphic, Publishing and Stationary Industry – GEC)
Lungo Po Antonelli 49
I Torino
Salon International des Techniques, Papetières et Graphiques (TPG)
(International Exhibition of Paper and Graphic Techniques – TPG)
40, rue du Colisée
F 75 Paris 8e

In cooperation of those four institutions it is planned to have exhibitions and fairs of this character every two years. The follow-

ing rhythm is to be expected: 1971 IPEX, 1973 Drupa, 1975 GEC, 1977 TPG.
The periodical
Graphis
45 Nüschelerstr., CH 8001 Zürich
in three languages (English, German, French) offers as "International Journal of Graphic Art and Applied Art", world-wide documentation and information of a high standard and with first-class illustrations. It also covers relevant questions of book-layout, publicity, etc.
The monthly magazine
Gebrauchsgraphik
(Applied Art)
Nymphenburger Str. 86, D 8 München 2
deals from an international standpoint with subjects of visual communication and artistic advertising, and so with matters that are closely related to publishing and the book trade. It too is trilingual (English, German, French).
An international quarterly of graphic design is
Interpressgrafik
Szarvas Gábor utca 20
H Budapest XII

35 Miscellaneous

a) Authors

The life of a book begins with its author, its creator. In the hierarchy of the book world the author reigns over all. If, then, he hardly appears in this book, the reason lies in the necessary limitation of our subject.
However, having paid due homage to the author, we also wish to facilitate the acquisition of information from one source or anothers. From the headquarters of International P.E.N. information can be obtained on all matters concerning the problems of world-wide authorship. An up to date list with the names and addresses of the secretariats of national member associations is available from:
International P.E.N.
Glebe House
62/63 Glebe Place
Chelsea
GB London SW 3
This institution was founded in 1921. Relevant problems are discussed at large congresses attended by authors from many countries.

b) Development Aid

Since individual and institutional efforts in development aid in the book world are aimed at countries and territories outside Europe, this subject will be treated in detail in the concluding volumes of BTW. Here it will suffice to say in general that the countries with an established book trade are conscious of the tasks presented, even if the paths of common action and the intensity of those actions leave much to be desired. Efforts by national and international institutions, and by individual publishers and groups of publishers are to date not sufficient to meet moral and technical obligations towards the developing countries.
→ International Section, 11, 14.

Bibliography

The following publications deal with general and special problems of development aid in the book world:

Book development in Africa. Problems and perspectives. Paris, UNESCO 1969. 37 pp.
Book development in Asia. A report on the production and distribution of books in the region. Paris, UNESCO 1967. 70 pp. Part I: Report of the meeting of experts on book production and distribution in Asia (Tokyo, May 1966). Part II: Asia's book needs; facts and figures.
O. PRAKASH and CL. M. FYLE, *Books for the developing countries.* Paris, UNESCO 1965. 31 pp.
Contains: The production and flow of books in South-East Asia and the pro-

duction and flow of books in Africa.

N. Sankaranarayanan (ed)., *Book distribution and promotion problems in South Asia.* Paris, Unesco (Madras, Higginbothams) 1964. 278 pp.

c) International Standard Book Numbering

The compulsion towards increased rationalization is also playing an important part in the international book trade. With the ever-growing use of modern computer systems comes the necessity of having to make use of them individually and collectively. As a result of this development, and first of all at national level (United Kingdom), then in the course of international meetings and agreements in the form of the International Standard Book Numbering System (ISBN), a system has been developed that will be of great importance for book-trade activities of the future—whether it be publishing, wholesale, or retail bookselling. It will also assist rational cooperation between the book trade and other branches of the book world, particularly libraries.

By using numerical marking, each book title is given a number which provides considerable information and can claim to be of international application.

The fundamentals of this system can be seen from the following example:

ISBN 3 632 07313 4

These mean

3: group identifier (countries or linguistic group)

632: publisher identifier (number of the publishing house in this group)

07313: title number

4: check digit

The "British Standards Institute" is to be responsible for the determination and registration of the group identifier.

The following 15 countries have taken part in the basic discussions on such an international system under the observation of Unesco (October 1969): Austria, Belgium, Denmark, France, Germany (F. R.), Hungary, Ireland, Italy, Japan, Netherlands, Norway, Portugal, Romania, Sweden, United Kingdom, USA.

Experts from 12 countries discussed at an Oslo meeting (June 1970), the possibilities for an international standard serial numbering system (ISSN) covering periodicals and serial publications.

Bibliography

Standard book numbering. New York, R. R. Bowker 1968. 13 pp.

d) Reprints

The great loss of books during the Second World War and the huge demand for literary works of former centuries as a result of the expansion of universities and other cultural institutions throughout the world have combined with progress in modern techniques of reproduction to invigorate facsimile reprinting, and to give to the book trade of our day new impulses in the form of reprints. There is no information to hand on the number of these reprints available. Estimates vary between 30,000 and 70,000 titles.

Bibliography

The following titles offer a guide to this difficult estimate of reprints available:

Announced reprints. Washington, D.C., Microcard Editions. Since 1969, 4 numbers annually.

Bibliographia anastatica. Amsterdam, Bonset-Gruner-Schippers-Hakkert. Since 1964, 6 numbers annually.

Börsenblatt für den Deutschen Buchhandel, Frankfurt edition, (→ Germany, Federal Republic of Germany, 4 and 5), *Reprint special number.* Frankfurt a.M., Buchhändler-Vereinigung. Annually since 1967. Apart from the bibliography, this publication also contains an editorial section with contributions on the subject "Reprint".

Diaz-Ponce, *Guide to reprints*. Washington D.C., Microcard Editions. Since 1967, annually.

R. Ostwald, *Nachdruckverzeichnis von Einzelwerken, Serien und Zeitschriften aus allen Wissensgebieten*. (Index of reprints of individual works, series and periodicals in all branches of knowledge). Wiesbaden, Nobis. Vol. 1 appeared in 1965, vol. 2 in 1969.

e) Periodicals

Never before has the periodicals business played such a large part in publishing and the retail book trade, whether it be technical, scientific or professional periodicals, or popular entertainment magazines. Whereas serious periodicals are almost exclusively products of the book trade, the latter only partially participates in the lighter magazines. But the sale of this category is important for the existence of many bookshops and book outlets, even in the classical book-trading countries.

There are no exact figures on the size of the international production of periodicals. Figures such as about 50–60,000 (in 1970) are only very rough estimates. It must be noted that the swift development of modern research into professional, scientific and technical periodicals has opened up new prospects.

Bibliography

G. Duprat, K. Liutova and M. L. Bossuat, *Bibliographie des répertoires nationaux de périodiques en cours*. (Bibliography of the national bibliographies covering current periodicals). Paris, Unesco 1969. 141 pp.
Lists national directories of current periodicals published in 183 countries or territories. Entries are arranged alphabetically by names of countries or territories. Text in French.

Internationale Bibliographie der Fachzeitschriften. (International bibliography of professional and scientific periodicals). 5th ed. 3 vols. München, Verlag Dokumentation 1967. 2,316 pp.
More than 30,000 periodicals in all scientific and professional fields are registered, arranged under subjects, with extensive indexes.

Ulrich's international periodicals directory. 13th ed. 2 vols. New York, R. R. Bowker 1969. XXIV, 1,659 pp.
Lists more than 40,000 periodicals currently published throughout the world. Arranged by subjects with title and subject index. Vol. 1, pp. 162–76: bibliography; vol. 1, pp. 224–34: books and the book trade.

The establishment of book museums has been greatly furthered by the rapid change of traditional forms in the book world in our day and age and by the certainty that many past and passing features are not only worth remembering but also indispensable for a full understanding of the present and the future. Originally it was mainly those who studied the history of printing and writing who took care that the inheritance of the great masters of the art of printing and typography was preserved in museums. That applies, for example, to such excellent, relatively early establishments as the *Museum Plantin Moretus,* Antwerp, the *Deutsches Buch- und Schriftmuseum* ("German Museum for Books and Writing"), Leipzig, and the *Gutenberg Museum* in Mainz. Recently many similar museums have come into existence. These too try to combine tradition and modern work, but with more emphasis on the books of our time. As these museums are all stimulating, necessary and interesting for those who study the book, we shall give a brief survey of the most notable establishments in this field. In doing so, we refer to the information provided by these institutions. Some have not been mentioned, in compliance with their own wishes.

Belgium

Museum Plantin Moretus (The Plantin-Moretus Museum)

History Its origin goes back to the Plantin printing office, which was founded in 1555 and continued by the Moretus family until 1876, when it was sold to the city of Antwerp.

Sponsor The city of Antwerp.

Address
Museum Plantin Moretus
(The Plantin-Moretus Museum)
Vrijdagmarkt, 22
B Antwerpen

Times of opening Daily (except Mondays), 10.00–17.00 hrs.

Functions Care of the workshops, rooms and buildings handed down from the printing dynasties of Plantin and Moretus.

Behind the typical eighteenth-century gable in Louis XV style is one of the finest examples of patrician Renaissance building in Belgium; the courtyard alone would be well worth a visit. A great number of rooms have retained their ancient character and with their period furniture show how rich patricians of Antwerp used to live in the sixteenth, seventeenth and eighteenth centuries.

Although other museums and historical buildings have similar period rooms, this is not the case with those rooms in the museum which are a reminder of its real purpose—the original workshop character of the old Plantin house: the printer's, the foundry, the correctors' room and the bookshop are unique.

In addition the Plantin-Moretus Museum possesses three well-stocked libraries numbering some 20,000 volumes: most of them are editions of Plantin and the Moretus family, and a magnificent collection of Antwerp prints, as well as a rich selection of works by other typographers, among them about 150 incunabula, the most precious being the only 36-line Gutenberg Bible in Belgium.

The archives of the Museum contain the indexes, letters and other documents of Plantin and the Moretus family. It is a rich source for the history of the Plantin printing shop, and of printing in general.

The Museum has also about 500 manuscripts; many of them are of great interest to historians and art historians. About 650 drawings, of interest to the expert, are mainly sketches for book illustrations. There are about 15,000 carved wooden blocks and about 3,000 copper engravings which have illustrated the works of Plantin and the Moretus family. Among the many instruments for type-casting are also about 15,000 matrixes and about 5,000 punches.

Special fields Old prints (sixteenth – seventeenth centuries), old printing presses.

Stock 650 drawings, 15,000 carved wooden blocks, 3,000 copper engravings, 15,000 matrices, 5,000 punches, 150 paintings, 20,000 books (almost all editions of Plantin and the Moretus family and a magnificent collection of Antwerp editions, as well as a rich selection of works by the other typographers).

Bibliography

L. VOET, *The Plantin-Moretus Museum.* 3rd ed. Antwerpen 1965.—Other editions in Dutch, French and German available.

L. VOET, *The golden compasses. A history and evaluation of the printing and publishing activities of the Officina Plantiniana.* vol. 1. Amsterdam, Vangendt 1969. XXII, 501 pp.
This fundamental study is primarily based upon the collections of the Museum.

Czechoslovakia

Muzeum knihy Žďár nad Sázavou, Expozice Knihovny Národního Muzea v Praze (Book Museum Žďar nad Sázavou, Exhibition of the National Museum Library, Prague)

History Founded in 1957, extended in 1962; today the permanent exhibition has 24 rooms with stock-rooms and a reading-room.

Sponsor Library of the National Museum, Prague.

Address
Muzeum knihy Žďár nad Sázavou
Expozice Knihovny Národního Muzea v Praze
(Book Museum Žďár nad Sázavou
Exhibition of the National Museum Library, Prague)
CS Žďár nad Sázavou

Times of opening 1 April to 30 September daily, from 8.00–17.00 hrs, except Mondays. In winter by previous appointment at the Castle's administrative office.

Functions Permanent exhibition about the development of writing and the book. Special exhibitions about important people and features in the history of writing and the book.

Special fields Manuscripts, old prints, artistic prints, bibliophilic prints, book illustrations, designs of printing types, publishers' advertisements, typographic machinery and tools, correspondence of book artists and designers, personal souvenirs, book-covers, ex-libris, writing equipment, etc. The entire stock of the library of the National Museum of Prague is available to the Book Museum.

Bibliography

Muzeum knihy Žďár nad Sázavou Katalog. Národní muzeum v Praze 1958. (Catalogue of the Book Museum Žďár nad Sázavou. National Museum of Prague 1958). With summaries in Russian, English, French, German and Italian.

Muzeum knihy. Expozice Národního Muzea v Praze. (The Book Museum. Exhibition of the National Museum of Prague). 1965.

Knihovna Národního Muzea v Praze. (The National Museum Library of Prague). 1959.

Sborník Národního Muzea. Acta Musei Nationalis Pragae. Řada C—literární historie. Sectio C Historia litterarum. (Catalogue of the National Museum of Prague. Section C—History of literature). Published five times a year.

Památník národního písemnictví (Museum of Czech Literature)

History "PNP" was founded in 1953 in the buildings of the former Strahov Premonstratensian Monastery.

Address
Památník národního písemnictví
(Museum of Czech Literature)
Strahovské nádvoří 132
CS Praha I—Hradčany

Times of opening Tuesdays—Sundays, 9.00–17.00 hrs.

Functions Central museum of Czech literature: permanent exhibition of the development of Czech literature from the earliest times to the present. This subject is further illustrated by exhibitions and lectures.

Special fields Czech literature and its relation to world literature, the culture of the book, fine arts inspired by literature. The Strahov library and other monastic libraries, Karásek's gallery and library, central literary archives; the Strahov library, department for the collections of fine art in relation to literature.

Stock Manuscripts: 4,000 volumes (ninth–nineteenth centuries), incunabula: 3,500 volumes, old prints till 1800: about 250,000 items, graphic prints 80,000 items.

Bibliography

The Museum of Czech Literature, Prague 1956.—Also printed in Russian, Polish, Bulgarian, Croatian, Serbian, Hungarian, Italian, French and German.

France

Musée de l'Imprimerie et de la Banque (The Museum of Printing and Banking)

History The Museum of Printing and Banking, founded by Maurice Audin, was opened in December 1964, in the former "Hôtel des Echevins", which was entirely restored.

Sponsor Ville de Lyon (The City of Lyon).

Address
Musée de l'Imprimerie et de la Banque
(Museum of Printing and Banking)
13 Rue de la Poulaillerie
F Lyon 2e

Times of opening Wednesdays–Sundays, 9.30–12.00 hrs, 15.00–18.00 hrs, Tuesdays 15.–18.00 hrs.

Functions A didactic presentation of the book and engraving, of use to the general public and the specialist.

Special fields Invention of printing, an aesthetic and technical history of the book and engraving, machine rooms, the technique of wood-engraving, the technique of copperplate engraving, lithography; important stock of engravings, old books, paper samples of all ages.

Affiliated institutions In preparation: Société des Amis du Musée de l'Imprimerie ("The Society of Friends of the Printing Museum").

Bibliography

Guide raisonné du Musée de l'Imprimerie et de la Banque. (Systematic guide-book of the Museum of Printing and Banking). Lyon, n.d., 64 pp.

M. Audin and A. Jammes, *L'estampe — cinq siècles de recherches et de technique*. (Engraving—five centuries of research and techniques). Lyon 1965. 50 pp.

M. Audin and A. Jammes, Essai sur la lettre d'imprimerie. (An essay on printed characters). Lyon n.d., 69 pp.

M. Audin, *Les peintres en bois et les tailleurs d'histoires*. (Woodcut illustrators and story cutters). Lyon n.d., 44 pp.

Book Museums

Germany: Federal Republic of Germany

Deutsches Museum, Abteilung Schreib- und Drucktechnik (German Museum, Department of Writing and Printing)

History 1903: founded by Oskar von Miller; 1906: opening of the provisional collections; 1925: opening of the building on an island in the river Isar; 1932: opening of the library; 1944: destruction by bombing; from 1948: rebuilt; 1965: the Department of Writing and Printing reopened.

Sponsor Deutsches Museum.

Address

Deutsches Museum
Abteilung Schreib- und Drucktechnik
(German Museum, Department of Writing and Printing)
Museumsinsel I
D 8 München 26

Times of opening Daily, 9.00–17.00 hrs. (closed 1 January, Good Friday, Easter Sunday, 1 May, Whit Sunday, the 2nd Monday in June, Corpus Christi, 17 June, 1 November, 24 December, 25 December, 31 December; open from 9.00–13.00 hrs: the Sunday before Ash Wednesday and Shrove Tuesday; open from 10.30–17.00 hrs: 19 March, 29 June, 'Buss- und Bettag', and 8 December.

Functions The Museum in general: the history of science and technology.

Special fields Historical examples show the development of writing and printing. A few historical books in the Department of Writing and Printing demonstrate the art of writing and the techniques of book printing.

Bibliography

R. Ranc, *La section des techniques de l'écriture et de l'impression au "Deutsches Museum" de Munich.* (The Department of Writing and Printing in the "Deutsches Museum" München). In: Techniques Graphiques, Paris, No. 63. June 1966.

H. K. Scholl, *Wegmarken der Entwicklung der Schreib- und Drucktechnik.* (Landmarks in the development of writing and printing). München, Deutsches Museum 1965. 70 pp.

Wiederaufbau im Deutschen Museum, München: Abteilung Schreib- und Drucktechnik. (The reconstruction of the German Museum, München: Department of Writing and Printing). München, Deutsches Museum 1965. 36 pp.

Forschungsstelle Papiergeschichte (Research Institute for the History of Paper)

History Founded 1938. Housed in the Gutenberg Museum in Mainz. Reopened together with the latter in 1962.

Sponsor Verein der Zellstoff- und Papier-Chemiker und -Ingenieure, Darmstadt. (Association of Pulp and Paper Chemists and Engineers, Darmstadt).

Address

Forschungsstelle Papiergeschichte
(Research Institute for the History of Paper)
Liebfrauenplatz 5
D 65 Mainz

Times of opening Exhibition: Tuesdays to Saturdays 10.00–13.00 hrs and 15.00–18.00 hrs. Sundays 10.00–13.00 hrs. Library and Archives: Mondays to Fridays 9.00–12.00 hrs and 14.00–17.00 hrs.

Functions To record and promote research in the history of paper of all times and nations; collection of publications on the history of paper; paper-mill research.

Special fields Extensive international reference library about the history of paper and other materials used for writing. National and foreign periodicals of the paper industry and related fields. Moulds and similar objects from the times of hand papermaking; models of old and present-day paper manufacture.

A Japanese papermaker's workshop, etc. Various materials used for writing throughout the ages in all countries. Collection of watermarks. Ream covers and similar objects.

Bibliography

Papiergeschichte. (The history of paper). 6 issues a year at irregular intervals. Darmstadt, Eduard Roether Verlag.

Gutenberg-Museum (Gutenberg-Museum)

History Founded in 1900 in connection with the great Gutenberg anniversary of that year. The aim of the museum has always been "to collect, classify, record and exhibit everything that bears witness to Gutenberg's invention as well as everything concerning the history of the whole art of printing in all civilized nations of the world and to make it known to as many people as possible in scientific publications". The museum was destroyed during the Second World War, but reopened in 1962 in a new building, during the 2000th anniversary of the City of Mainz. The museum, with its extensive stock, large library and modern working methods, is a unique memorial place to Johannes Gutenberg and to all decisive phases of book culture throughout the world.

Sponsor Stadt Mainz (The City of Mainz)

Address

Gutenberg-Museum – Weltmuseum der Druckkunst
(Gutenberg-Museum—The World Museum of the Art of Printing)
Liebfrauenplatz 5
D 65 Mainz

Times of opening Tuesdays to Saturdays, 10.00–13.00 hrs, and 15.00–18.00 hrs, Sundays, 10.00–13.00 hrs.

Functions Gutenberg research, everything concerning the art of writing, printing and books.

Special fields The history of writing and printing, book illustrations, book covers, ex-libris, William Morris, samples of writing, prints made from plants, posters.

Stock Reference library free of charge, specialized library, 24,000 volumes; exhibition pieces—particularly 2,360 incunabula on permanent loan from the City Library; graphic collection (loose-leaf prints, woodcuts, copper engravings, lithographs).

Affiliated institution Research Institute for the History of Paper (see above). Gutenberg Gesellschaft → Germany, Federal Republic of Germany, 31.

Bibliography

(H. Presser), *Gutenberg-Museum der Stadt Mainz. Weltmuseum der Druckkunst.* (Gutenberg-Museum of the City of Mainz, The World Museum of the Art of Printing). Mainz 1968. 108 pp.

Gutenberg-Jahrbuch. (Gutenberg Year Book). Since 1926.

Klingspor-Museum der Stadt Offenbach a.M. Internationale moderne Buch- und Schriftkunst (Klingspor Museum of the City of Offenbach a.M. International Modern Book Design)

History Founded November 1953 by the City of Offenbach a. M., after the heirs of the typefounder Karl Klingspor had donated his private collection to the City.

Sponsor Stadt Offenbach a. M. (The City of Offenbach a. M.).

Address

Klingspor-Museum der Stadt Offenbach a. M.
Internationale moderne Buch- und Schriftkunst
(Klingspor Museum of the City of Offenbach a. M.
International Modern Book Design)
Herrnstr. 80
D 605 Offenbach a. M.

Times of opening Daily, 10.00–12.00 hrs, Mondays to Fridays also 15.00–17.00 hrs.

Functions To collect, exhibit and edit the masterpieces of modern calligraphy, typography, book design, illustrations and original prints, the art of bookbinding, the illustration of children's books.

Special fields Modern calligraphy: handwritten books and folios; typography; the art of the book (press-prints and private prints, illustrated books and prints with original illustrations); the art of bookbinding (publishers' bindings and hand-bindings); posthumous collection of the calligrapher Spemann; the Guggenheim collection (manuscripts, prints and liturgical implements for the private Seder celebration); posthumous collection of the calligrapher F. H. E. Schneidler; posthumous collection of the calligrapher Otto Reichert; the Ignatz Wiemeler collection (100 handbindings, created by Ignatz Wiemeler at the request of Karl Klingspor); in preparation: the Walter Tiemann collection (calligraphy and book design) and the F. H. Ehmcke collection (acquisition of his posthumous works in the fields of book design and calligraphy); international archives of the finest children's books.

Stock December 1970: 18,000 items.

Affiliated institution Association Freunde des Klingspor-Museums ("Friends of the Klingspor Museum"), founded 1958 (1970: 700 members from 9 countries). Secretariat of the Bund Deutscher Buchkünstler ("Association of German Book Designers").

Bibliography

Drucke des Klingspor-Museums, ("Prints of the Klingspor Museum".), edited by the Association "Friends of the Klingspor Museum": 1957 *Georg Alexander Mathéy; Gunter Böhmer;* 1959: *Hannes Gaab;* 1961: *Hans Schmidt;* 1963: *Gerhard Oberländer; Karlgeorg Hoefer;* 1966: *Kurt Londenberger;* 1967: *Ernst Engel.*

H. A. Halbey, *Zehn Jahre Klingspor-Museum* (The first ten years of the Klingspor-Museum). In: Imprimatur, N.F., vol. 4, pp. 128–32. Frankfurt a. M. 1964.

Modern German book design. (Catalogue published for an exhibition of the German Publishers' and Booksellers' Association, Frankfurt a. M., together with the Klingspor-Museum), Frankfurt a.M. 1959.

Stiftung Buchkunst (Foundation 'The Art of the Book')

History Founded October 1965. It has developed from the "Art of the Book Collection" in the Deutsche Bibliothek ("German Library"), Frankfurt a. M.

Sponsors Börsenverein des Deutschen Buchhandels; Bundesverband Druck; Deutsche Bibliothek (German Publishers' and Booksellers' Association; Federal Association of Printing; German Library).

Address
Stiftung Buchkunst
(Foundation 'The Art of the Book')
Sophienstrasse 8, D 6 Frankfurt a. M.

Times of opening Mondays to Fridays, 10.00–13.00 hrs, 15.00–18.00 hrs.

Functions The annual competition "The best-designed books of the Federal Republic of Germany". Travelling exhibitions and temporary exhibitions on the Foundation's premises. History of the art of the book in the twentieth century.

Special fields The archives of the abovementioned competition, the art of the book in the twentieth century, official prints (industry, schools, museums, etc.), book covers.

Bibliography

The annual catalogue of the competition

Die schönsten Bücher ("The best-designed books"), F. R. G.

Germany: German Democratic Republic

Deutsches Buch- und Schriftmuseum der Deutschen Bücherei (German Museum of Books and Writing in the German Library)

History Founded 1884 by the German book-trade association; in 1914, the stock of the "BUGRA 1914", international in scope, was taken over. 1911–26: publication of the "Zeitschrift des Deutschen Vereins für Buchwesen und Schrifttum" ("Journal of the German Association for Bibliology and Writing"), together with a literary supplement 1924–35. 1928–43/44: publication of the year book "Buch und Schrift" ("Book and writing"). 1940: transferred to the extended exhibition rooms in the new buildings of the German Book Trade Centre. 1943: destroyed by bombing. 1950: affiliated to the Deutsche Bücherei ("German Library"). 1954: opening of a provisional permanent exhibition. 1963: transferred to the new building of the "German Library", with the establishment of a new permanent exhibition.

Sponsor Ministerium für Hoch- und Fachschulwesen der Deutschen Demokratischen Republik, Berlin. (Ministry for Higher Education in the German Democratic Republic, Berlin.)

Address
Deutsches Buch- und Schriftmuseum der Deutschen Bücherei
(German Museum for Books and Writing in the 'German Library')
Deutscher Platz, DDR Leipzig

Times of opening Exhibitions: Mondays to Saturdays 9.00–18.00 hrs. Library: Mondays to Fridays 8.00–16.00 hrs, Saturdays 9.00–18.00 hrs.

Functions Collecting and making accessible past records of the history of books, writing, printing and paper of all nations and ages; information and research; exhibitions.

Special fields Specialized literature, pertaining to the book, illustrations of the culture of the book on an international scale, manuscripts, incunabula, old prints, modern book design, dust covers, script designs and samples, ex-libris, antiquarians' and publishers' catalogues, water-marks, samples of paper, objects and documents concerning the history of paper. Heinrich Klemm's collection of the history of printing (the Klemm collection), collection of artistic prints, Deutsches Papier Museum ("German Paper Museum"), the former library of the Leipzig Börsenverein (German Publishers' and Booksellers' Association), Deutsche Buchkunststiftung ("German Foundation for the Art of the Book").

Stock Specialized literature: 39,312 volumes; rare books: 23,512 volumes; bibliological folio collection: 31,225 leaves; water-marks: 210,325 items; "German Foundation for the Art of the Book": 2,361 volumes.

Bibliography

Fr. Funke, *Tradition und Gegenwartsaufgaben des Deutschen Buch- und Schriftmuseums.* (Tradition and present functions of the German Museum for Books and Writing.) In: Neue Museumskunde, vol. 464, No. 6, pp. 279–88.

Fr. Funke, *Originales Sammelgut im Deutschen Buch- und Schriftmuseum.* (Original documents in the German Museum for Books and Writing.) In: Deutsche Bücherei 1912–1962. Leipzig 1962, pp. 219–41.

Fr. Funke, *Bibliothek und Museum.* (Library and Museum). In: Jahrbuch der Deutschen Bücherei, vol. I, 1965, pp. 37–58.

Fr. Funke, *Buchmuseale Fragen aus der Sicht des Deutschen Buch- und Schriftmuseums der*

Deutschen Bücherei Leipzig. (Issues connected with a book museum as presented in the German Museum for Books and Writing in the German Library, Leipzig). In: Sborník Národního Muzea v Praze. (Catalogue of the National Museum of Prague). Series C. vol II, 1966, No. 2, pp. 41–55.

FR. FUNKE, *Buch und Schrift von der Frühzeit bis zur Gegenwart.* (Books and writing from the earliest times to the present day). Leipzig, Deutsche Bücherei 1968. 116 pp.

Israel

The Alphabet Museum

History Founded in 1965. The bulk of the exhibits was donated by Prof. David Diringer of the University of Cambridge (England).

Address
The Alphabet Museum
26, Bialik Street
IL Tel Aviv

Times of opening Daily, 9.00–12.30 hrs.

Function To build up an "International Institute for the Study of Writing".

Bibliography

I. SOIFER, *Dr David Diringer and the Alphabet Museum.* In: Publishers' Weekly, New York, 7 Sept. 1970, pp. 48 and 50.

Italy

Istituto di Patologia del Libro (Institute for the Pathology of Books)

History Founded 1938 as a research centre with an additional special library, a museum and a documentation office.

Sponsor Ministero della Pubblica Istruzione (Ministry of Public Education).

Address
Istituto di Patologia del Libro
(Institute for the Pathology of Books)
Via Milano 76
I Roma

Times of opening Not open to the public. Visits by appointment.

Functions The leading institute in the world for book pathology and therapy. Research studies concerning the preservation and restoration of written and printed material.

Special fields Everything concerning damaged books and their repair.

Bibliography

Bollettino dell'Istituto di Patologia del Libro. (Bulletin of the Institute for the Pathology of Books).

E. VACCARO, *Restoration laboratory of the Alfonso Gallo Institute of book pathology, Rome.* In: UNESCO Bulletin for Libraries, vol. XX, No. 2, 1966. Paris 1966.

Museo Bodoniano (The Bodoni Museum)

History Established in July 1960 and unveiled in November 1963. It is the only Italian Museum specializing in the history and the art of printing.

Address
Museo Bodoniano
(The Bodoni Museum)
Palazzo Pilotta
I Parma

Times of opening 9.00–12.00 hrs, 15.00 to 20.00 hrs (Summer: 9.00–13.00 hrs).

Functions History and art of printing.

Special fields Classic books printed from the middle of the seventeenth century to the eighteenth century; Bodoni's life and collections of his works, Bodoni's books, tools, matrices and types; graphic art, binding in boards, de-luxe editions on silk and vellum.

Bibliography

Catalogo del Museo Bodoniano di Parma. (Catalogue of the Museo Bodoniano in Parma). Parma 1968.

Bodoni celebrato a Parma. (Bodoni celebration in Parma). Parma 1963.

Japan

Paper Museum

History This museum was established in 1949 and opened in 1950.
Sponsor Foundational juridical person.
Address
Paper Museum
1-1 Horifune, Kitaku
J Tokyo
Times of opening March – October, 9.00 to 17.00 hrs, November–February, 9.30–16.30 hrs.
Functions Display materials are mostly samples of old paper and its products such as paper kimonos. Display of machine papers, paper toys, etc. 17,000 display materials, 5,000 books about paper and related industries. The most important collection of this character in Japan.

Netherlands

Rijksmuseum Meermanno-Westreenianum; Museum van het Boek (National Museum Meermanno-Westreenianum; Museum of the Book)

History In 1848 the collector and bibliophile, Willem Hendrik Jacob Baron of Westreenen bequeathed his house and collections to the Netherlands, which in turn put them in the charge of the Royal Library. The property was converted into a museum, and by the provision of special exhibition rooms in 1960 it also acquired the character of a book museum. The large stock of valuable manuscripts and old prints partly belonged to the collector Johan Meerman (1753–1815).
Sponsor Koninklijke Bibliotheek, Amsterdam (Royal Library, Amsterdam).
Address
Rijksmuseum Meermanno-Westreenianum
Museum van het Boek (National Museum Meermanno-Westreenianum;
Museum of the Book)
Prinsessegracht 30
NL Den Haag
Times of opening Mondays – Saturdays, 13.00–17.00 hrs.
Functions The administration and care of the Van Westreenen foundation, especially of its treasures of manuscripts and early prints. Cultivation of contemporary book design by special exhibitions.
Stock 20,000 volumes, containing more than 300 manuscripts, 1,233 incunabula, 415 Elzevirs. Modern private-press books.

Bibliography

A. J. de Mare, *Catalogus der gedrukte werken van het Museum Meermanno-Westreenianum.* (Catalogue of the printed works in the Meermanno-Westreenianum Museum). Den Haag 1937–38.
Rijksmuseum Meermanno-Westreenianum, Museum van het Boek. A general guide. Den Haag n.d.
D. van Velden, *Het Museum von het Boek.* (The Museum of the Book). In: Bibliotheekleven, 1965, pp. 442–444. Den Haag 1967.
P. J. H. Vermeeren and A. F. Dekker, *Inventaris van de handschriften Museum Meermanno-Westreenianum.* (Catalogue of the manuscripts in the Meermanno-Westreenianum Museum). Den Haag 1960.

Stichting 'Museum Enschedé' (Foundation 'Museum Enschedé')

History Since 1914 the typographic collection of the firm of Enschedé has been designated a museum. The Foundation "Museum Enschedé" was established in 1946.
Sponsor Although the museum is legally a

foundation, it is sponsored in every respect by Joh. Enschedé en Zonen Grafische Inrichting N.V. The work rooms and exhibition rooms are situated on the Enschedé business premises. Because of limited space, the conference room and exhibition room have had to be combined.

Address
Stichting 'Museum Enschedé'
(Foundation 'Museum Enschedé')
Klokhuisplein 5
NL Haarlem

Times of opening Mondays – Fridays, 10.00 to 12.00 hrs, 14.00–16.00 hrs (subject to alteration).

Functions The "Enschedé Museum" is not a comprehensive book museum. Apart from the history of the Enschedé firm, it deals with the history of type-founding and printing.

Special fields History of type-founding and printing in general and especially in connection with the Enschedé firm. Script samples; "Oprechte Haarlemse Courant" (from 1656 to the present day, almost complete).

Affiliated institution Joh. Enschedé en Zonen Grafische Inrichting N.V.: Afdeling Technische Bibliotheek (Department Technical library).
Not open to the public; no loans to non-members.

Bibliography

Catalogus van de technische Bibliotheek. (Catalogue of the technical library). Haarlem 1953. Describes the stock of this comprehensive special library.

Switzerland

Schweizerisches Gutenbergmuseum (Swiss Gutenberg Museum)

History The Swiss Gutenberg Museum was founded in 1900 by the printers of Berne (journeymen and employers). In 1910 the Verein des Schweizerischen Gutenbergmuseums ("Society of the Swiss Gutenberg Museum") took it over, and has since developed it. It collects prints, presses and utensils from early times to the present, and makes them available to science and professional interests by means of exhibitions, conducted visits and conferences. Everybody interested in the art of printing can join this society.

Sponsor Verein des Schweizerischen Gutenbergmuseums ("Society of the Swiss Gutenberg Museum").

Address
Schweizerisches Gutenbergmuseum
(Swiss Gutenberg Museum)
Zeughausgasse 2
CH Bern

Times of opening Tuesdays – Saturdays, 10.00–12.00 hrs, and 14.00–17.00 hrs. Sundays: 10.00–12.00 hrs.

Functions Specialized library; collection of specimens produced in famous places of printing; exhibitions concerning the book trade, the graphic arts and printing techniques; collection of type-setting and printing machines; bookbinding.

Special fields Incunabula, examples of movable type through the centuries to the present day, type-setting and printing machines and equipment, bookbinding machines and implements.

Stock About 6,000 volumes (1970).

Affiliated institutions Schweizerisches Berufsmuseum für Buchbinderei. ("Swiss Professional Museum for Bookbinding").

Bibliography

The Museum publishes quarterly the periodical *Schweizerisches Gutenbergmuseum* ("Swiss Gutenberg Museum").

United Kingdom

Victoria and Albert Museum

History Founded in 1857, with the Museum of Ornamental Art (opened in Marlborough House, 1852) its true ancestor.

Sponsor The museum is a branch of the Department of Education and Science.

Address
Victoria and Albert Museum
South Kensington
GB London S.W. 7

Times of opening Mondays – Saturdays, 10.00–18.00 hrs; Sundays, 14.30 to 18.00 hrs.

Functions Museum of fine and applied art, covering mainly post-classical art in Europe, as well as Islamic, Indian, and Far Eastern art.

Special fields Among many other categories the museum includes the following categories of objects: the art of the book, calligraphy, engravings, lithographs, manuscripts, miniatures, prints.

Stock The museum includes the National Art Library, with a reference collection of some 300,000 books, pamphlets and periodicals. It is the largest art library in the world. In room 74 of the museum are specially selected exhibits from the library, including illuminated manuscripts, book illustration, typography, calligraphy, and bookbindings. There is a printed catalogue about the collection of the National Art Library.

Bibliography

Brief Guide to the Museum. 2nd ed. London 1964.

Many publications covering the book field, listed in: *Victoria and Albert Museum,* London, H.M.S.O.

United States of America

The Dard Hunter Paper Museum at the Institute of Paper Chemistry

History Established at the Massachusetts Institute of Technology in 1939. Moved to the Institute of Paper Chemistry as a permanent home in 1954. Majority of items collected by Dard Hunter in travels to countries of early papermaking history.

Sponsor The Institute of Paper Chemistry.

Address
The Dard Hunter Paper Museum
at the Institute of Paper Chemistry
1043 East South River Street
P.O.B. 1048
USA Appleton, Wisc. 54911

Times of opening Mondays – Fridays, 8.30 to 16.30 hrs.

Functions A general and specialized representation of all aspects of early paper history.

Special fields Hand papermaking, watermarks, handmade books. Stock: 1,000 books, undetermined number of periodical reprints, old letters.

The Grolier Club, Library, New York

History The Grolier Club was founded in 1884 for "the literary study and promotion of arts pertaining to the production of books". Present house erected in 1917, members: 625.

Address
The Grolier Club
47 East 60th Street
USA New York, N.Y. 10022

Times of opening Mondays–Fridays, 10.00 to 17.00 hrs., Saturdays (September to June) 10.00–15.00 hrs.

Functions 4 major and 6 small exhibitions per season, free to the public; reference library available to qualified persons. Lectures for members and guests.

Special fields Main subjects of the library: bibliography, history of printing, graphic arts. Large collection of booksellers' and auction catalogues back to the seventeenth century.

Own publications Important, finely printed works on subjects of interest to the Club.

The Shakespeare Press Museum

History The museum was established in 1939 by Charles L. Palmer.

Sponsor California State Polytechnic College, Printing Technology and Management Department.

Address
The Shakespeare Press Museum
California State Polytechnic College
USA San Luis Obispo, Cal. 93401

Times of opening September 15 through June 14: Tuesdays, Thursdays 11.00 to 14.00 hrs. June 15 through September 14: Tuesdays, Thursdays 10.00 to 12.00 hrs, Saturdays 10.00 to 14.00 hrs.

Functions The museum portrays an old-fashioned print shop, complete with an office, composing room, press room, and a bindery.

Bibliography

G. Shaw, V. Strandskov and A. Yaras, *Faces of antiquity*. San Luis Obispo 1969. XI, 35 pp.

The United States of America—Puerto Rico

La Casa del Libro (The House of the Book)

History In 1955 Elmer Adler was invited by the Puerto Rican government to create with funds appropriated by the legislature a typographical library. Funds were provided also for the restoration of an eighteenth-century colonial townhouse to hold the collection and to afford space for exhibitions. Two years later the sponsoring organization, Amigos de Calle del Cristo 255, was incorporated. The collection that had been acquired by that time was moved in January 1959 into the restored house at Calle del Cristo 255. Since then, nver thirty exhibitions have been presented there and considerably more than that number have been lent to librarieos i Puerto Rico. Since Elmer Adler's death in January of 1962, La Casa del Libro has been under the direction of David Jackson McWilliams. Recently a house adjoining Calle del Cristo 255 has been acquired to permit physical expansion of the library.

Sponsor The Institute of Puerto Rican Culture. There is also an organization of patrons: Amigos de Calle del Cristo 255 ("Friends of Christ Street 255").

Address
La Casa del Libro (The House of the Book)
Calle del Cristo 255
P.O. Box 2265
USA Old San Juan, Puerto Rico

Times of opening Mondays – Fridays, 11.00 to 17.00 hrs; Saturdays, 13.–17.00 hrs.

Functions Reference library and museum devoted to the history and art of printing and the related arts and crafts. Exhibitions at "La Casa del Libro" and shows lent to libraries in Puerto Rico.

Special fields Incunabula, especially Spanish; modern private-press books; calligraphy and lettering; manuscripts; typography and book design; book illustration; bookbinding; papermaking.

Affiliated Institution Amigos de Calle del Cristo 255 (Friends of Christ Street 255).

Bibliography

Amigos de Calle del Cristo 255. (Friends of Christ Street 255). San Juan, Puerto Rico. Designed by Jan van Krimpen and printed in Haarlem by Joh. Enschedé en Zonen, 1958.

D. J. McWilliams, *La Casa del Libro.* In: Inland Printer/American Lithography, June 1967.

Special Libraries: "Books about Books"

These special collections are to be understood as an active element of the modern world of publishing and bookselling. They afford a retrospective glance into the varied aspects of the history of the book trade in all ages and among all nations, and enable us to understand the present-day situation and so clarify the phenomenon of the book trade in its organic connection with culture, economy and politics.

Our list refers only to those libraries which are known to us as individual special collections. It should be mentioned that within the large public and scientific libraries there are important stocks on the theme "Books about Books", which are frequently larger than the special collections. In addition, attention is drawn to the libraries of book museums.

Austria

Bibliothek des Österreichischen Buchgewerbehauses (Library of the Austrian Book Trade Centre)

History Founded in 1862 on the initiative of Rudolf Lechner. Extension and indexing in 1886; increased to 2,000 volumes in 1901. Transferred to the former Palace of Cardinal Fürstenberg in 1933, new indexing 1946/7.

Sponsor Hauptverband des österreichischen Buchhandels (Head Association of the Austrian Book Trade).

Address
Bibliothek des Österreichischen Buchgewerbehauses
(Library of the Austrian Book Trade Centre)
Grünangergasse 4
A Wien 1

Times of opening On appointment during the office hours of the Association.

Functions Collection of literature on the history and practice of the trade in books, art and music in Austria, as well as of the entire graphic trade.

Special fields History of the trade in books, art and music, as well as of the graphic trade, especially in Austria; older literature in these branches. Archives of the Austrian book trade ("Wiener Buchhandelsarchiv", "Viennese Book Trade Archives"). Approximately 12,000 volumes.

Bibliography

K. Pleyer, *Die Bibliothek des Österreichischen Buchgewerbehauses.* (The Library of the Austrian Book Trade Centre). In: Das Österreichische graphische Gewerbe, Wien, November 1949, p. 175ff.

K. Pleyer, *Das Österreichische Buchgewerbehaus.* (The Austrian Book Trade Centre). In: Das Antiquariat, Wien, vol. VII, 1951, p. 94ff.—(Memorial Volume for Walter Krieg).

K. Pleyer, *100 Jahre Bibliothek des Hauptverbandes.* (Centenary of the library of the Head Association). In: Anzeiger des österreichischen Buch-, Kunst- und Musikalienhandels. Wien, 1962, p. 95ff.

Denmark

Boghandler-Medhjaelper Biblioteket (Library of the Association of Bookseller Assistants)

History The Library was founded on 28 January 1873 as an independent institution. In 1898 it was institutionalized under the "Booksellers' Association"; in 1937 the Library was given premises in "Booksellers House". In 1967 it moved again, this time to entirely new surroundings.

Sponsor Boghandler-Medhjælper Forening (Association of Bookseller Assistants).

Address
Boghandler-Medhjælper Biblioteket
(Library of the Association of Bookseller

Assistants)
Boghandlernes Hus
Siljansgade 6–8
DK København

Times of opening Thursdays, 19.00 to 21.00 hrs.

Functions To possess as many books as possible concerning bookselling, publishing, printing, etc.

Special fields Biographies of famous Danish booksellers, Danish history of literature. Books dealing with the commercial aspects of bookselling. Book catalogues dating from the earliest book fairs in Germany to the present. Stock: 3,000 volumes plus periodicals, etc.

Bibliography

Katalog over Boghandler-Medhjælper-Biblioteket. (Catalogue of the Library of the Association of Bookseller Assistants). København 1944.

France

Bibliothèque Technique (Technical Library)

History Founded in 1884 by Paul Delalain, Louis Polain and Philippe Renouard. Started largely by donations and completed by purchases.

Sponsor Cercle de la Librairie, Syndicat des Industries du Livre (Association of Publishers and Booksellers, Syndicate of the Book Industry).

Address
Bibliothèque Technique
(Technical Library)
117, Bd. St.-Germain
F Paris 6e

Times of opening Tuesdays – Saturdays, 14.30–18.30 hrs.

Functions To offer everyone connected with the book trade documented information about the past and present of their industry and the various fields of research.

Special fields Librarianship, history of printing and the book, the book trade, book production, and the art of the book. Collection of the bibliography of France since 1811, collection of printers' marks, ex-libris and publisher's correspondence.

Bibliography

Catalogue, printed 1894.

PH. RENOUARD, *Bibliothèque technique du Cercle de la Librairie. Ouverture des nouvelles salles.* (The Technical Library of the Association of Publishers and Booksellers. Opening of the New Rooms). Bibliographie de la France, Chronicle, 1926.

A. ROUART, *La Bibliothèque technique du Cercle de la Librairie* (The Technical Library of the Association of Publishers and Booksellers). Bibliographie de la France (Bibliography of France). Chronicle of 26 April 1935.

Unesco – Library

History Established in 1946.

Sponsor United Nations Educational, Scientific and Cultural Organization.

Address
Unesco-Library
Place de Fontenoy
F 75 Paris 7e

Times of opening Not open to the public.

Functions Responsible for serving the members of the UNESCO Secretariat, permanent delegations of member states and personnel accredited of non-governmental organizations domiciled in Paris.

Special fields Education, natural and social sciences, communication, humanities and culture, bibliography, documentation. Stock: 55,000 books.

Bibliography

New publications in the UNESCO *Library* (Nouvelles publications acquises par la Bibliothèque de l'UNESCO). Monthly.

Check list of periodicals. Issued every 2 or 3 years.

Germany—Federal Republic of Germany

Bibliothek des Börsenvereins des Deutschen Buchhandels e. V., Frankfurt am Main (Library of the German Publishers' and Booksellers' Association, Frankfurt am Main)

History The division of Germany into East and West, together with the resultant loss of Leipzig for the book trade of the Federal Republic, has deprived West Germany of the collections which the old Börsenverein of Leipzig had started, and which were by far the most comprehensive in the world on the book trade and its history (for the present Leipzig collection, see the next entry). As a result, in 1953 the Frankfurt Börsenverein established a new library, which has since developed into a collection of international repute. A large extension is envisaged in the further plans of this library.

Sponsor Börsenverein des Deutschen Buchhandels e. V., Frankfurt a. M. (German Publishers' and Booksellers' Association, Frankfurt a. M.).

Address
Bibliothek des Börsenvereins des
Deutschen Buchhandels e. V.
(Library of the German Publishers' and
Booksellers' Association)
Großer Hirschgraben 17–21
D Frankfurt a. M.

Times of opening Mondays – Fridays, 8.00 to 16.45 hrs.

Functions To collect special literature on the book trade at home and abroad.

Special fields The book and the book trade; antiquarian-booksellers' catalogues.

Bibliography

Quarterly publication of *accessions* in the *Börsenblatt* (→ Germany, F.R.G. 5).

Archiv für Geschichte des Buchwesens (Archives for the history of the book), edited by the "Historical Commission" of the "German Publishers' and Booksellers' Association". Vol. I and ff. Ten volumes appeared by the end of 1970. By international standards this series is one of the most comprehensive in the field of research into the history of the book. Thematically it also touches on foreign bibliology. It continues the "Archiv für Geschichte des Deutschen Buchhandels" ("Archives for the history of the book trade", Leipzig 1878–1898).

Germany—German Democratic Republic

Bibliothek des Börsenvereins der Deutschen Buchhändler zu Leipzig (Library of the German Publishers' and Booksellers' Association, Leipzig)

History In 1843 W. A. Barth initiated the foundation of a library for the "German Publishers' and Booksellers' Association". From 1844 the project was realized by developing the library of the "Association of Leipzig Booksellers". From 1861 A. Kirchhoff was the first full-time librarian; the library was extended systematically. 1869/70: first printed edition of the catalogue. 1885–1920: revised edition of the catalogue in 2 volumes, together with 20 supplements. 1943: partly destroyed in the war. After the Second World War the remaining stock was transferred to the Deutsche Bücherei, Leipzig. Since 1960 the Library is administered by the "German Museum for Books and Writing in the German Library", classification and cataloguing have been systematically revised.

Sponsor Ministerium für Hoch- und Fachschulwesen in der Deutschen Demokratischen Republik, Berlin (Ministry for

Higher Education in the German Democratic Republic, Berlin).

Address
Bibliothek des Börsenvereins der Deutschen Buchhändler zu Leipzig (Library of the German Publishers' and Booksellers' Association in Leipzig)
Deutsche Bücherei (German Library)
Deutscher Platz
DDR Leipzig

Times of opening → "Deutsches Buch- und Schriftmuseum, in der Deutschen Bücherei" ("German Museum of Books and Writing in the German Library") p. 61.

Functions Although reduced by war damage, the library offers a comprehensive stock of specialized literature on the book and bookselling, rare books, business circulars, archives and a collection of pamphlets on the book.

Special fields Specialized literature on books and bookselling, archives of the book trade. Booksellers' business circulars, catalogues of publishing firms and antiquarian bookshops, portraits of booksellers, collections of the letters of Göschen and Dürr. Stock (1970) over volumes, about 17,000 folios, and about 60,000 business circulars.

Bibliography

M. Debes and L. Reuschel, Die ehemalige Bibliothek des Börsenvereins der deutschen Buchhändler in Leipzig. (The former library of the German Publishers' and Booksellers' Association in Leipzig). In: Deutsche Bücherei 1912–1962, pp. 243–57. Leipzig 1962.

Katalog der Bibliothek des Börsenvereins der Deutschen Buchhändler. (Catalogue of the German Publishers' and Booksellers' Association). 4 volumes. Leipzig 1885 to 1920.

Schätze der ehemaligen Bibliothek des Börsenvereins der deutschen Buchhändler zu Leipzig. (Treasures of the former library of the German Publishers' and Booksellers' Association in Leipzig). Leipzig 1961. 59 pp.

Netherlands

Bibliotheek van de Vereeniging ter bevordering van de belangen des Boekhandels (Library of the Dutch Publishers' and Booksellers' Association)

History Founded in 1845 by Fred. Muller. Since 1960 transferred on loan to the University Library, Amsterdam. Since the partial destruction of the Leipzig collection in the Second World War, the largest specialized library of its kind in the world.

Sponsor Vereeniging ter bevordering van de belangen des Boekhandels, Amsterdam (Dutch Publishers' and Booksellers' Association, Amsterdam).

Address
Bibliothek van de Vereeniging ter bevordering van de belangen des Boekhandels (Library of the Dutch Publishers' and Booksellers' Association)
Nieuwe Prinsengracht 57
NL Amsterdam C

Times of opening Daily, 9.30–13.00 hrs, 14.00–17.00 hrs, except on Saturdays.

Functions The collection and compilation of all literature dealing with the book and its circulation.

Special fields Bibliography; history of the techniques, circulation, protection and preservation of the book; the field of periodicals and newspapers; booksellers' catalogues; archives of the book trade. Stock (1970): 35,000 books, 700 periodicals. Catalogues.

Bibliography

Catalogus der Bibliotheek van de Vereeniging ter bevordering van de belangen des Boekhandels. (Catalogue of the Library of the Dutch Publishers' and Booksellers' Association).

7 volumes so far. 's-Gravenhage, Nijhoff 1920–65.

Spain

Instituto Nacional del Libro Español, Biblioteca (National Institute of the Spanish Book, Library)

History Founded in 1930.
Sponsor Instituto Nacional del Libro Español (National Institute of the Spanish Book).
Address
Instituto Nacional del Libro Español,
Biblioteca
(National Institute of the Spanish Book, Library)
Mallorca, 274
E Barcelona 9
Times of opening Mondays to Saturdays, 8.15–14.00 hrs, 19.00–21.30 hrs.
Function Documentation about all aspects of the book.
Special fields Bibliography, copyright, the art of the book. Stock: 15,700 titles (books and brochures) and approx. 100,000 catalogues of publishers and booksellers. Catalogue by authors and subjects.

Sweden

Biblioteket Grafiska Institutet (The Graphic Institute Library)

History The Library was established as part of the "Grafiska Institutet. Institutet för Högre Kommunikations- och Reklamutbildning—IHR" ("The Graphic Institute. The Graduate School of Communications") which was founded in 1944.
Sponsor Grafiska Institutet, Stockholm (The Graphic Institute, Stockholm).
Address
Biblioteket Grafiska Institutet
(The Graphic Institute Library)
Box 27094
S 102 51 Stockholm 27
Times of opening Mondays – Fridays, 9.00 to 16.00 hrs.
Special fields The field of writing, the book trade, printing, organization of trade and industry, business administration, advertising, photo-mechanical processengraving. Stock (January 1969): 6,725 books.

Bibliography

Published by the "Institute":
Grafiska uppsatser. (Graphic essays). 2 volumes so far, 1956 and 1964).

Switzerland

Bibliotheca Bodmeriana (Bodmer Library)

History Founded by Martin Bodmer shortly after the First World War; since then it has been continuously developed and enlarged.
Sponsor In the possession of the family.
Address
Bibliotheca Bodmeriana
(Bodmer Library)
Cologny
CH Genève
Times of opening Visits by appointment only.
Functions Collection and cultivation of all the important works of world literature throughout the ages and in all languages, in the original and in translation, in very early or famous editions, critical editions and collectors' editions; papyri, manuscripts from the High and Late Middle Ages and from the Renaissance; incunabula, first impressions from the 16th–20th centuries and autographs.
Special fields Goethe, Shakespeare, Homer, the Bible, papyrology, autographs. Stock (1970): over 100,000 items, i.e. volumes pamphlets and loose-leaves.

Bibliography

M. Bodmer, *Eine Bibliothek der Weltliteratur.* (A library of world literature). Zürich 1947.

M. Bodmer, *Variationen zum Thema Weltliteratur.* (Variations on the theme of world literature). Frankfurt a. M. 1956.

Bibliothek des Angestelltenvereins des Schweizer Buchhandels (Library of the Employees' Society of the Swiss Book Trade)

History Originally this library, founded in 1920, was devoted predominantly to literature and cultural history. In 1925 it was converted into a completely specialized library with an initial stock of about 60 volumes. The first catalogue was published in 1943; supplements appeared in 1948 and 1956. The annual list of accessions is published in the society's journal, 'Der Buchhändler'. As its budget is very modest, the library still relies on donations.

Sponsor Angestelltenverein des Schweizer Buchhandels (Employees' Society of the Swiss Book Trade).

Address
Bibliothek des Angestelltenvereins
des Schweizer Buchhandels
(Library of the Employees' Society
of the Swiss Book Trade)
c/o Schweizerisches Buchzentrum
CH Olten

Times of opening During office hours.

Functions To make literature on the book trade accessible to the members of the Employees' Society of the Swiss Book Trade and other interested parties.

Special fields Books about books and writing, book-craft and the art of the book, the book trade, the history of literature, and the science of literature. Stock: (on May 1968): 1,489 books, 3 periodicals totalling 32 volumes, almanacs from 56 firms totalling 159 volumes, 8 magazines totalling 108 annual volumes, 73 issues from incomplete annual volumes.

Bibliography

Verzeichnis der Bibliothek des Schweizerischen Buchhandlungs-Gehilfen und -Angestellten-Vereins. (Catalogue of the Library of the Employees' Society of the Swiss Book Trade). Zürich 1943. Supplements 1948 and 1956.

United Kingdom

Aslib Library

History Founded in 1924.

Sponsor Council of Aslib (= Association of Special Libraries and Information Bureaux).

Address
Aslib Library
3 Belgrave Square
GB London S.W. I

Times of opening 9.00–17.15 hrs.

Functions Special librarianship.

Special fields All forms of selected world literature on special library science and documentation techniques. 15,000 books and pamphlets, 350 current and retrospective journal titles, trade literature relative to librarianship.

Bibliography

P. L. Erskine, *Coordinate indexing: a bibliography based on material in the Aslib Library in December 1962.* In: Aslib Proceedings, vol. 15, no. 2, February 1963, pp. 41–61.

Y. Foy, *Periodicals held in the Aslib Library as at 15th July 1967.* In: Aslib Proceedings, vol. 19, no. 8, August 1967, pp. 260–71.

K. Gaster, *Thesaurus construction and use: a selective bibliography based on material in the Aslib Library in July 1967.* In: Aslib Proceedings, vol. 19, no. 9, September 1967, pp. 310–17.

British Library of Political and Economic Science

History The nucleus of a special collection, "Publishing and Bookselling", was formed by the late A. D. Power, who presented it in 1934 to the Library and who supported it with additional gifts up to his death in 1959. Another important part of the collection consists of the library of G.S. Williams, which came to the Library via the Publishers' Association, London.

Sponsor London School of Economics and Political Science.

Address
British Library of Political and
Economic Science
Houghton Street, Aldwych
GB London W.C. 2

Times of opening Daily, 10.00–21.20 hrs, Saturdays, 10.00–17.50 hrs. In August daily from 10.00–17.00 hrs.

Functions The Library contains a special collection of works on publishing and bookselling.

Special fields Publishing, bookselling. About 4,000 titles (1970).

Bibliography

Classified catalogue of a collection of works on publishing and bookselling in the British Library of Political and Economic Science. London 1969. 186 pp.

Library Association, Library and Information Bureau

History Library Association founded 1877, Royal Charter 1898. Permanent headquarters, Chaucer House 1933–65. Present address (new building), 1965.

Sponsor Library Association.

Address
Library Association Library
and Information Bureau
7 Ridgmount Street
GB London W.C. I

Times of opening 9.00–18.00 hrs.

Functions Special collection about librarianship and all connected aspects of the book world.

Special fields Library science and techniques of bibliography, documentation, information retrieval, publishing, bookselling. 25,000 books, 650 current periodicals.

Bibliography

D. C. H. Jones, *The Library Association: Catalogue of the library.* London 1958. 519 pp.

L. J. Taylor, *The Library Association Library.* In: Library Association Record. April 1966, pp. 123–129, 145.

Library of the Antiquarian Booksellers' Association of Great Britain

History The Library was founded in 1956 based on a large gift from Arthur Swann of the Parke-Bernet Galleries of New York.

Sponsor Antiquarian Booksellers' Association of Great Britain.

Address
Library of the Antiquarian Booksellers'
Association of Great Britain
c/o Howes Bookshop Ltd
3, Trinity Street
GB Hastings, Sussex

Times of opening Not open to the general public.

Special fields Bibliography. Stock: 600–700 volumes.

Library of the National Book League

History Personal collection of books about books donated by Maurice Marston, 1924. Moved to present premises 1945. Renamed "Winterbottom Book Production Library" 1959. May Lamberton Reading Room opened 1960.

Sponsor National Book League.

Address
Library of the National Book League
7 Albemarle Street
GB London W 1

Times of opening Mondays–Fridays, 9.30 to 17.30 hrs, Saturdays, 11.00–16.00 hrs.

Functions All aspects of the world of the book.

Special fields Books about books and their authors, publishing, printing, illustration, binding, bookselling, collecting, care and preservation, bibliography, children's books, reading techniques, librarianship, critical studies of literature. Special collections: Harriet Weaver bequest of James Joyce first editions, 1955. Marino Perez collection of bookplates, 1963. Visual register of illustrators' section of "Society of Industrial Artists", 1956. Pamphlets and press cuttings relating to the book trade. Stock: 9,000 books, 100 periodicals.

Special Service The library maintains a highly effective book-inquiry service for the members of the NBL.

Bibliography

Books about books. Catalogue of the library of the National Book League. 5th ed. London 1955. 126 pp. – New ed. → International Section, 6.

London College of Printing

Sponsor Inner London Education Authority.

Address
London College of Printing,
Elephant and Castle
GB London S.E. 1

Times of opening Mondays–Fridays, 9.00 to 19.15 hrs.

Functions Printing history and technique.

Special fields Printing and graphic design: modern printing techniques in the world. 30,000 books, 500 current periodicals.

St Bride Institute

History Established 1891 as the library of the printing school of the St Bride Foundation Institute. Includes collections of William Blades, Talbot Baines Reed, John Southward. Administered since 1966 as one of the City of London libraries.

Sponsor Corporation of London.

Address
St Bride Printing Libarry
St Bride Institute
Bride Lane
Fleet Street
GB London EC 4

Times of opening Monday to Friday, 09.30–17.30 hrs.

Functions Public reference library of books and periodicals on the technique, design and history of printing and related subjects. 30,000 titles. 700 periodicals. Photograph and slide loan collection.

Special fields Technical handbooks, typefounders' specimens, trade union documents. Small museum of printing equipment.

Bibliography

Catalogue of the technical reference library of works on printing and the allied arts. London 1919.

Catalogue of the periodicals relating to printing and allied subjects in the technical library of St Bride Institute. London 1951.

United States of America

AB Reference Library

History Founded 1948 as Antiquarian Bookman Reference Library, based on the personal collection of Sol. M. Malkin.

Sponsor Antiquarian Bookman (AB Bookman's Weekly and AB Bookman's Yearbook).

Address
AB Reference Library
240 Mulberry Street

USA Newark, N.J. 07101
Times of opening By appointment only.
Functions Reference use by book-trade specialists.
Special fields Auction book records, bibliography, book-trade fiction, bookseller catalogues, books about books, books about collectors, books about libraries, ephemera, exhibit catalogues, printing and typography.

Frederic G. Melcher Library, R. R. Bowker Company

History The library was founded in 1962. Frederic G. Melcher's lifelong personal collection of books about books was the nucleus of the library, to which was added a general reference collection.
Sponsor R. R. Bowker Company, New York
Address
Frederic G. Melcher Library
R. R. Bowker Company
1180 Avenue of the Americas
USA New York, N.Y. 10036
Times of opening Monday through Friday, 9.15–17.15 hrs.
Functions Provides reference and general library services for the Bowker staff and is open, by appointment, to members of the book trade for research.
Special fields Books about books (includes printing, publishing, censorship, bookmaking, copyright, illustrations, typography); library science, Growoll scrapbooks of early book-trade history. 7,000 volumes, 100 vertical file drawers, 300 periodical titles. The collection is completely catalogued, on cards, with author, subject, title entries.

Bibliography

A. J. Richter, *The Frederic Melcher Library of books about books*. In: School Library Journal, vol. 11, 1964, pp. 126–128.

The Grolier Club Library

History Founded in 1884 as part of the Grolier Club to support its exhibitions and publications.
Sponsor The Grolier Club.
Address
The Grolier Club Library
47 East 60th Street
USA New York, N.Y. 10022
Times of opening 9.00–18.00 hrs.
Functions Bibliography and book-collecting, printing history.
Special fields Catalogues of libraries, descriptive bibliographies, history of printing, binding and ex-libris. Special collections: miniature books, silver bindings. Present collection about 60,000 volumes.

Bibliography

G. Austin, *Der Grolier-Klub*. (The Grolier Club). In: Librarium, vol. I, 1967, pp. 54–56: *Die Bibliothek des Grolier-Klubs* (The Grolier Club Library). Zürich 1967.

Europe

Greenland
Iceland
Faeroe Islands
Norway
Sweden
Finland
Ireland
United Kingdom
Denmark
Union of Soviet Socialist Republics
Netherlands
Belgium
Luxembourg
Federal Republic of Germany
German Demo-cratic Republic
Poland
Czechoslovakia
France
Switzerland
Liechtenstein
Austria
Hungary
Romania
Andorra
Monaco
San Marino
Yugoslavia
Portugal
Spain
Italy
Bulgaria
Albania
Turkey
Greece
Gibraltar
Malta
Cyprus
1:40 000 000

Albania

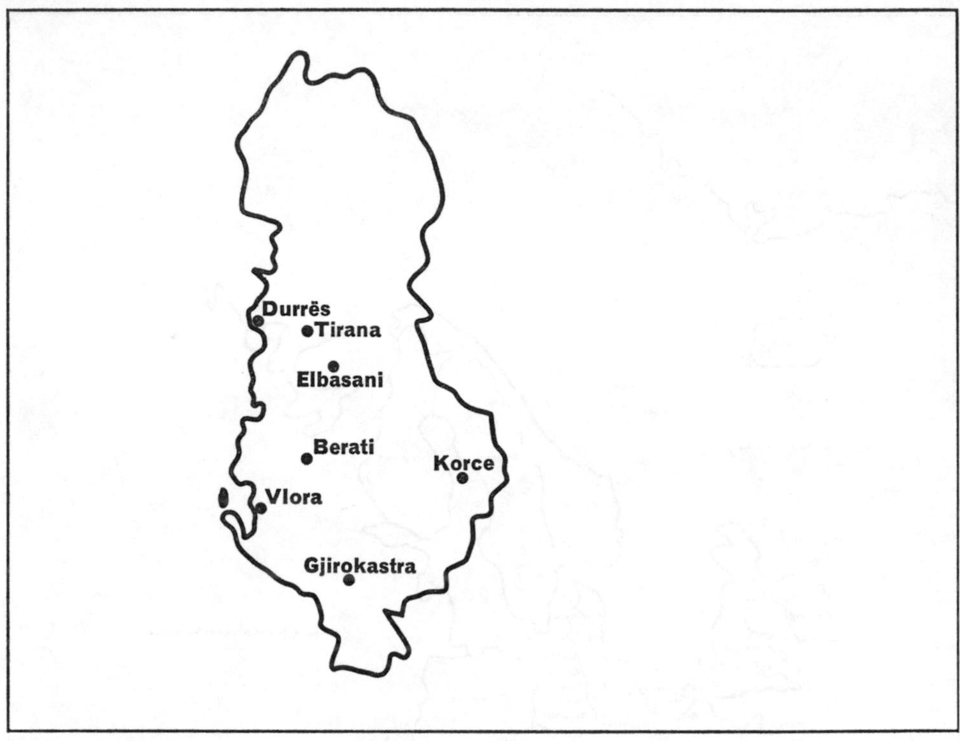

Important Book Centres

1 General Information

Area 28,748 km²
Population 2,018,000 (70.8 per km²)
Capital Tirana (174,900)
Largest towns Tirana (174,900); Durrës (81,500); Vlora (59,100); Korça (54,100); Shkodra (50,800)
Government People's Republic. The supreme organ of the PR of Albania is the Popular Assembly and the Presidium of the Popular Assembly elected by it. In Albania state power stems from the people and belongs to the people. Albania is a socialist country
National language Albanian. A small minority in the south speak Greek (books and the "Laiko Vima" newspaper are published in this language, too)
Leading foreign languages Russian, French, English, Italian, German
Religion After 1966 there is no officially recognized religion in Albania. The Albanian people are atheists
Weights, measures Metric system
Currency unit Lek (= 100 qindarka)
Education Compulsory. 17,000 students (3rd level)
Membership UNESCO

2 Past and Present

One cannot have a clear idea about the history of the book trade in Albania without taking into account some facts from the past of the country.

The Albanians are successors of the Illyrians, an autochthonous and one of the oldest peoples in south-eastern Europe and in the Balkans. Successive invasions have badly damaged the production forces and have paralysed the economy of the country for centuries at a stretch. At a time when the countries of Europe entered the road of progress and economic development Albania languished under the Ottoman yoke which oppressed Albania for about five centuries until she regained her independence in 1912. But even after this period and until November 1944 Albania remained a semi-feudal country because of the antipopular regimes and foreign invasions.

The year 1944 marked a turning point in the history of the Albanian people. On November 29, 1944 they won their national independence and genuine freedom. Since then Albania is marching along the road of its free economic and cultural development, along the road of socialism.

In everything Albania had to start from scratch. The country inherited a terrible economic backwardness, its population was about 90% illiterate. From a backward agrarian country it has now been turned into an advanced agrarian-industrial country. Now Albania boasts of a developed national industry. It was during these years that the printing industry assumed a vigorous development, too. Its specific weight in general industrial production was 1% in 1968, or 183.6 times as much as in 1938.

The deep social and economic transformations, the development of education and culture, led to the disappearance of illiteracy. At present, there is no illiterate man or woman under 50 years of age in Albania. In the 1967-8 school year one out of four inhabitants of the country studied at general education, vocational or high schools.

The first book up to now known to be published in Albanian is a missal (1555). Its place of publication has not been found as yet, but as there are books printed at Shkodra as early as 1563, we may assume that the first book in Albanian was also printed in that city.

The long period of foreign domination could not help being reflected in book printing as well. Books were very rare and, due to the lack of a national alphabet, until 1908 books were published with varying characters. Likewise, during this period and until the achievement of national independence, one cannot speak of a book trade worthy of its name. During that time there were published books of a patriotic character as well as books whose chief purpose was the preservation of Albanian language and culture. These books were printed in foreign countries and introduced afterwards with great peril into Albania. Especially fruitful is the period of the national revival. Bibliographical data over this period (1800–1910) give the titles of 282 Albanian books.

The first bookshops were opened before the First World War. In 1908 there was a bookshop in Tirana, too. Nevertheless bookshops were very rare and in 1938 their number did not exceed 15 firms. They sold chiefly foreign books and newspapers and only now and then an Albanian book. And it could not be otherwise, because the overwhelming majority of the population was illiterate and extremely poor while, on the other hand, publications were very scarce. Only 61 book titles were printed in 1938. Publishers, booksellers and writers had to struggle against heavy odds. The book trade, for the same reasons, was at a very low level of development.

For this period one cannot even mention societies of booksellers or publishers. Authors had to pay printers for all the expenses incurred for the publication of their books and were obliged to look after their sale themselves. Only some booksellers agreed to embark on the sale of a given book provided that the author was to be paid only after it was sold out. There were only a few cases in which printers engaged in publishing original or translated books on their own. The publication of Albanian books was hampered also by the inflow of foreign books and the lack of state care.

3 Retail Prices

Before 1944 book prices were fixed according to the whim of printers, booksellers and authors. There were no single and fixed prices. Prices went up with the devaluation of currency or with the lapse of time.

Today prices are fixed by the Central Administration (→ 4), with the exception of school-text prices, which are fixed by the publishers themselves. In fixing prices the expenses incurred in the sphere of production and circulation are taken into account, always abiding by the principal criterion that prices should cover expenses without gain or loss. It is for this reason that these enterprises are not commercial organs. Their sole mission is to spread the book and serve the cultural development of the country.

Book prices are the same throughout the territory of the People's Republic of Albania. Book prices are fixed and do not undergo any changes with the passing of time or when books become rare.

Alongside with the development of the national economy as a whole prices in Albania go down constantly. This is felt also in the book trade. Prices for special and indispensable books have gone down to 50%.

As is known, books with a low circulation or with special difficulties of composition, printing, etc. are sold at higher prices. But even in such cases their prices are cut down 30–40% so that too high a price should not make acquisition difficult for readers.

Book prices also reflect the attitude of our state organs towards this question. According to a general principle, book prices should be fixed so as to serve the material well-being and the cultural level of the population.

4 Organization

Book distribution worth mentioning begins only after liberation (1944) and is an essential part of socialist culture.

In compliance with the conditions of the economic and cultural development of the country the book trade also went through some transitory stages until it reached the present stage. After the liberation all printing shops were nationalized and a General Press Centre (1945) was set up which was engaged in publishing, distributing and selling books and other press materials; then the State Publishing and Distributing Enterprise (now the "Naim Frashëri" Publishing House) was founded. During this period were set up and enlarged various organs charged with the distribution and trade of books within the country and abroad, to all those interested in Albanian publications. 1951, too, witnessed the start of an organized advertisement service through catalogues and other means, attached to the aforesaid enterprise.

The year 1965 marks the establishment of the first State Enterprise of Book Trade—"N. SH. T. Librit" which was detached as an independent entity from the State Publishing Enterprise "Naim Frashëri" (now the "Naim Frashëri" Publishing House).

During the last four years the book trade underwent a further development; new bookshops were opened in small towns and villages. The spread of bookselling centres continues even today, and by 1971 all the villages of the country should have their bookshops. Thus, within a short lapse of time, a new situation was created which led to the founding of 26 bookselling enterprises in the 26 administrative centres of the territory of the PR of Albania. These enterprises are named Enterprises for the Distribution and Propagation of Books (in Albanian: "NPP Librit").
Starting from July 1969 the former State Enterprise of Book Trade was abolished and was replaced with

Drejtoria Qendrore e Perhapjes dhe Propagandimit te Librit
(The Central Administration for the Distribution and Propagation of Books)
Rruga Konferenca e Pezës
AL Tirana

which is directly dependent on the Ministry for Education and Culture.
The organizational structure of the Central Administration for the Distribution and Propagation of Books is as follows:
The Director, the Planning and Distribution Branch, the Advertisement Branch, the Export-Import Branch, the Finance and Administration Branch.
The principal functions of these branches:
The Planning and Distribution Branch draws up, supervises and looks after the implementation of the turnover plans of the enterprises for the distribution and the propagation of books in administrative centres, organizes the distribution of all sorts of books in administrative centres, fixes book prices, etc.
The Advertisement Branch: is engaged in the organization of the propagation of books. It periodically compiles catalogues and other materials through which readers are kept in touch with the various publications of the month, the semester and the year (with the exception of textbooks). Every month foreign firms receive a pamphlet in French with the list of books to be published during the following month. There is also a short summary of every book.
The Export-Import Branch is principally engaged in the export and import of books, newspapers and magazines.
The Financial Branch carries out all the operations connected with the financial aspect both with the enterprises for the distribution and the propagation of books within the country and with foreign firms abroad.
All the work for the sale of books within the country and for the export and import of books, newspapers and magazines from and to various countries of the world is centred in the Central Administration. In fact, the sale of books within the country is carried out by the enterprises for the distribution and propagation of books in the different administrative centres, and the Central Administration is their sole supplier for all sorts of books, newspapers, magazines and school materials.
As a rule, books are allotted to the enterprises for the distribution and propagation of books in the different administrative centres according to a ratio between book circulation and the population of each district.
This is the best way to fulfil the needs of readers throughout the country.

5 Trade Press

The special magazine for the Albanian book trade is

Libri
(The Book)
Rruga Konferenca e Pezës
AL Tirana

published by the Central Administration (→ 4).

7 Sources of Information

Questions concerning the Albanian publishing and book-trade world are answered by

Drejtoria Qendrore e Perhapjes dhe Propagandimit te Librit
(The Central Administration for the Distribution and Propagation of Books)
Rruga Konferenca e Pezës
AL Tirana

(→ 15).

10 Books and Young People

Special care is taken of children and young people. Books and other publications should serve to educate them and widen their horizons of knowledge. A simple comparison with the recent past gives ample proof for this. In 7 years before Liberation (1938–44) a total of 1,245,000 copies of all categories of books were printed. This figure is lower than the total circulation of books for young people in the two-year period 1966–7, which amounted to 1,417,000 copies. On the other hand, books were selected more carefully and according to sounder criteria. At present in Albania no book is published which could in any way offend the morality of minors. This is the most important and positive aspect of this problem.

The stock of books for children and young people has greatly increased, too. Alongside with original literature, they can now read in their mother tongue the works of well-known foreign writers.

11 Training

In Albania constant care is taken for the professional qualification of booksellers. This is achieved through lessons or talks as well as various materials published by the Central Administration (→4). For this purpose are also organized special courses and meetings, in particular, national gatherings convened between certain periods of time.

Of great help to booksellers is the magazine "Libri" (→ 5), which is published for more than 11 years now by the Central Administration. This newspaper publishes special articles on the professional qualification of booksellers, on the exchange of experience among them, as well as various materials about the problems of the distribution and propagation of books, etc. The magazine gives also a brief summary of the contents of the books put into circulation.

14 Copyright

Copyright was enforced by law for the first time only after liberation (1944). Prior to liberation there was no law to defend the rights of the author. On the other hand, there were only a few authors who succeeded in publishing their works. Authors suffered heavy losses, as they were obliged to pay as much as they were requested whereas they could almost never get back the money they had invested in their books.

The copyright law now regulates the situation in the field of publications. According to this law, authors are entitled to special remuneration for their work. All expenses incurred by the author and for the publishing of the book are calculated in the cost of the book itself.

15 National Bibliography, National Library

Based upon compulsory deposit of all printed matter the

Biblioteka Kombîtare
(National Library)
AL Tirana

is one of the most important cultural centers of the country. It now possesses the biggest albanological stock in the world. Beginning from 1961 the National Library has systematically issued the *Bibliografija e Republikës Popullore të Shqipërise* (National Bibliography of the People's Republic of Albania). It is divided into two parts:

1. The National Bibliography of the PR of Albania. Albanian Books (published once in three months) and
2. The National Bibliography of the PR of Albania. Articles of Albanian periodicals (it is published monthly).

The National Library has exchange and lease relations with numerous other libraries throughout the world. In the framework of these relations, which are developed on a basis of equality and mutual utility, the National Library in 1970 has exchanged Albanian periodicals with 83 other libraries in foreign countries. According to these agreements, the National Library receives 746 press organs from different countries. The National Library also leases books from other libraries. These are chiefly rare scientific, technical and linguistic works.

The National Library gives every datum of bibliographic character about Albanian books.

16 Book Production

Special attention is paid to the production of books because they are a powerful lever for the political and cultural education of the popular masses. That is why their circulation is increasing more and more with each passing year. If in 1938 there was only one book per 6 persons, in 1968 there were on average 3 books per inhabitant. Such a ratio demonstrates a very high book production in our country. But this is not a distinctive feature of our publications either. They are characterized by the high quality of their ideological and artistic content, which influences the all-sided education of the working masses.

The main place in book production is taken by political, ideological, social and cultural, and social and economic literature. In the period 1959–69 they made up 40% of all Albanian publications. The most valuable books published during this decade are The History of the Party of Labour of Albania and the Works of Comrade Enver Hoxha, which represent the most important event in the field of Albanian publications. (Selections of the Works of Comrade Enver Hoxha and the History of the Party of Labour of Albania have also been published in English, French and Spanish.)

During the same period, to the Selected Works of Karl Marx and Friedrich Engels (1968) was added the first volume of "Capital"—the monumental work of Karl Marx. Publication of the Complete Works of V. I. Lenin and J. V. Stalin as well as the Selected Works of Mao Tse-tung has been completed. For the first time in the world, Albania, in 1969, published the 14th volume of the Complete Works of Stalin.

Other important publications of this period were the "History of Albania", the "History of Albanian Literature", and many other books.

→ 21.

17 Translations

For a period of time (even after liberation) translations took an important place in Albanian publications. Thus, in 1960, 86 out of 124 literary works were translations (67% of all fiction and poetry published in Albania).

Such a ratio, of course, was not to the liking of the readers but time was required to redress it. The new literary talents in their bloom had to fill as swiftly as possible this yawning gap in the development of national literature. So with each passing year the number of original works began to increase. In 1969 original

fiction and poetry made up 91% of all literary works published in Albania—or 7 times as much as in 1960.
In the field of translations, too, publishers proceed from the principle that all valuable and worthy works of international literature should be made accessible to the readers. For this reason in the future, too, translations shall hold the place appertaining to them in the field of Albanian publications.

21 Publishing

The main institution engaged in the preparation and publication of books in Albania is the "Naim Frashëri" Publishing House. In 1968 this institution issued 368 out of 644 titles, or 57% of all the book production of the country.
The "Naim Frashëri" Publishing House publishes political, social, economic, technical and scientific literature as well as various works of fiction and poetry.
Its book production is constantly on the rise. If in 1960 it published 227 books with a total number of 718,300 copies, in 1969 it turned out 295 books with a total number of 2,293,000 copies.
Besides the "Naim Frashëri" Publishing House, in book publishing are also engaged the State University of Tirana and the High Institute of Agriculture, which have special publishing administrations. Alongside textbooks for higher schools, the State University of Tirana and the High Institute of Agriculture publish books of a scientific character, studies, monographs, etc. The former in the field of political, economic, juridical, historical, social, linguistic and other sciences and the latter in the field of agriculture, livestock and forestry. The Schoolbooks Publishing House is engaged in the publication of textbooks for the general education and vocational schools.
All these institutions taken together published 644 titles with a total number of 6,915,000 copies in 1968. The "Naim Frashëri" Publishing House published within a period of ten years (1957–1967) more books than it did within a period of 23 years before liberation (1917–1940).
Book circulations in Albania, although very high according to the standards of advanced countries, often do not meet the requirements of the numerous readers.
Contacts between the publishers and the Central Administration (→ 4) have to do with the circulation and reprinting of books as well as with other questions connected with their sale and distribution.
As a rule, circulations are laid down by the publishers themselves in agreement with the Central Administration about their reprints as well. On its part, the Central Administration proposes the reprint of books much in demand.
At the end of each year the publishers contact the Central Administration in connection with their perspective publishing plans.
→ 4.

23 Wholesale Trade

→ 4, 24.

24 Retail Trade

Within the country books are distributed by the enterprises for the distribution and propagation of books which exercise their functions in 26 administrative centres (→ 4). They are independent economic organs and render account only to the Executive Committee of the District People's Councils (administrative centres). These enterprises carry on their activity through the bookshops. The latter engage in the sale of all sorts of books, newspapers, magazines, as well as school texts and other school materials.
The number of bookshops is rising with each passing year. In 1938 there were only

15 bookshops throughout the country, whereas in the first trimester of 1970 their number rose to 168, or about 11 times as much as in 1938.

The number of bookshops according to the enterprises:

Enterprises of the first category have 95 bookshops

Enterprises of the second category have 26 bookshops

Enterprises of the third category have 47 bookshops

Total: 168 bookshops in all Albania.

A bookshop usually has only one bookseller, but there are also bigger bookstores with two and more booksellers. All booksellers should have graduated from a middle school of general education.

A special subscription system has been established with the purpose of helping the libraries, especially those of the villages, to have in their book stocks all the important books on sale.

According to this system, each library reserves a sum of money which goes to the local bookshop. After that the bookshop is obliged to reserve for its subscriber every important publication put into circulation (at least one copy).

Although all bookselling enterprises are organized on an independent basis, they keep close contact with the Central Administration, because it is from it that they receive all the books, newspapers and materials to meet the needs of their clients, including their subscriptions for foreign newspapers and magazines.

The enterprises report to the Administrative Centre on all problems connected with the distribution and propagation of books, on their circulation and other questions. They inform the Central Administration (→ 4) about the fulfilment of their turnover, labour force and wage plans.

For all articles supplied the accounts are liquidated by the State Bank and its branches throughout the country.

The Central Administration (→ 4) is obliged to help and supervise the various bookselling enterprises in order to have them improve their work for the distribution and propagation of books.

Likewise, the Central Administration (→ 4) helps the local enterprises with different advertisement materials so as to keep readers informed about the books that will be put on sale.

27 Book Imports

28 Book Exports

The Administrative Centre (→ 4) is the sole organ in Albania engaged in the export and import of books and periodicals.

The Central Administrations is in touch with *c.* 100 commercial firms and different individuals throughout the world.

The interest shown for Albanian books and periodicals, or for Albanian books translated into foreign languages, is becoming deeper and deeper with each passing day. During just the period 1967–9 the export of Albanian books rose three times.

Of particular importance is the growth of the export of original Albanian literature. In 1969 13 times as many Albanian books were exported as in 1967.

The export of books and periodicals is regulated through special agreements with foreign firms.

The import of books is made from numerous countries of the East and West to meet, in the first place, the needs of central libraries and administrative centres and, in the second place, of individuals. In 1969 the import of books and periodicals from foreign countries rose 179% in comparison to 1967.

The export of Albanian books and periodicals is carried out directly by the Central Administration, but cases of intermediary transactions are not excluded. Thus, for instance, a firm in West Germany carries on transactions for the export of Albanian books and periodicals to some foreign countries.

30 Public Relations

Special attention is devoted to this aspect of the book trade. All the mass organizations render an important help for the propagation of the books among the broad working masses. The press, radio and television carry on a consistent advertisement work to keep readers abreast of all the new books published.

Anyone can give his contribution to the propagation of books on a voluntary basis. The citizens of the People's Republic of Albania consider it a question of honour and do not demand any remuneration for their efforts in this field.

Usually every local enterprise for the distribution and propagation of books has a broad circle of activists who volunteer to sell and propagate books in remote places outside the sphere of activity of bookshops. Particularly valuable help is rendered by teachers and young people.

Other methods used by the enterprises to sell their books are book fairs organized at work and administrative centres, villages and towns. Reviews, talks, etc. are other means of spreading among the people the love of and the desire for books.

In this respect, an important role is played by the state libraries in the districts and, particularly, by the National Library in Tirana (→ 15).

32 Literary Prizes

In the People's Republic of Albania great care is taken of books and constant efforts are made to encourage those engaged in creative activities. To this purpose are subordinated the Prizes of the Republic which are awarded at intervals of some years.

The Prizes of the Republic are awarded by the Council of Ministers on the recommendation of the Commission for the Prizes of the Republic attached to the Council of Ministers for eminent works of science, for inventions, rationalizations and literary and artistic works. The Prizes of the Republic were last awarded on 21 May 1970. Among the laureates were also 13 writers who have distinguished themselves through works published after 1965.

The Prizes of the Republic are the supreme honour to be given to an Albanian writer. They inspire and encourage them to write other still worthier literary works.

33 The Reviewing of Books

→ 30.

Austria

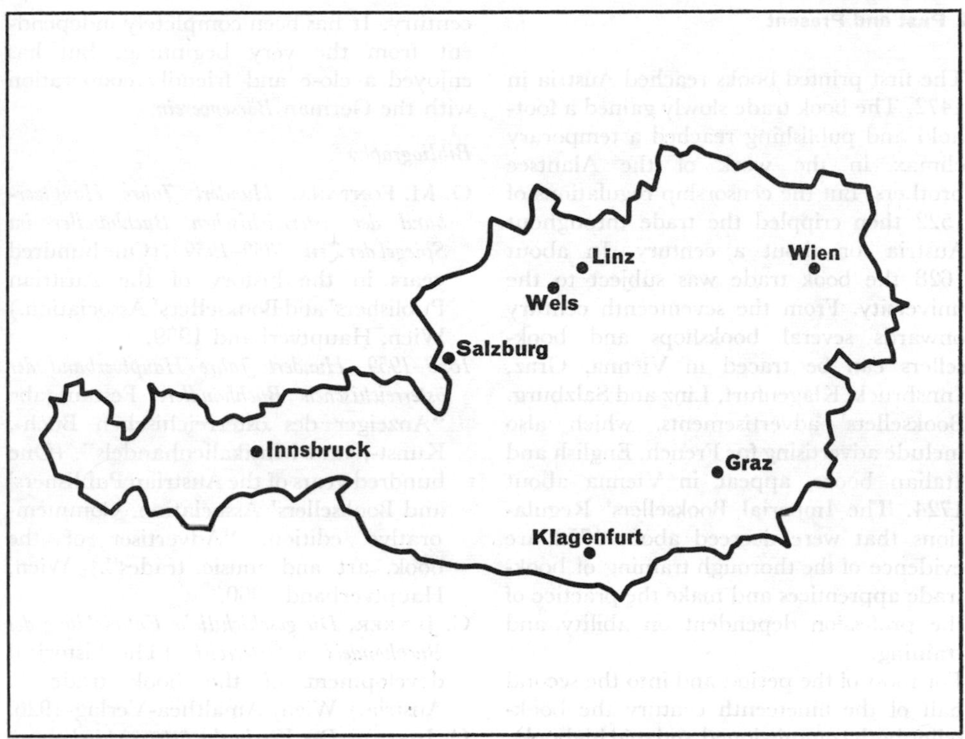

Important Book Centres

1 General Information

Area 83,849 km²
Population 7,373,000 (88 per km²)
Capital Wien (1,644,900)
Largest towns Wien (1,644,900); Graz (253,800); Linz (205,808); Salzburg (121,306); Innsbruck (112,824)
Government Federal Republic comprising 9 states
Religion Roman Catholic 89.0%
Protestant 6.1%
No denomination 3.8%
Small religious bodies 1.1%
National language German
Leading foreign language English
Weights and measures Metric system
Currency unit Austrian shilling (öS)
Education Compulsory. 53,765 third-level students (in 1969), 21.0% being women and 18.0% being foreigners, at university, technical and other colleges
Illiteracy Nil
Paper consumption a) Newsprint 9.7 kg per inhabitant (1967)
b) Printing paper (other than newsprint) 17.3 kg per inhabitant (1967)
Membership UNESCO; IPA, ICBA, ILAB

2 Past and Present

The first printed books reached Austria in 1472. The book trade slowly gained a foothold and publishing reached a temporary climax in the work of the Alantsee brothers. But the censorship regulations of 1522 then crippled the trade throughout Austria for about a century. In about 1628 the book trade was subject to the university. From the seventeenth century onwards several bookshops and booksellers can be traced in Vienna, Graz, Innsbruck, Klagenfurt, Linz and Salzburg. Booksellers' advertisements, which also include advertising for French, English and Italian books, appear in Vienna about 1724. The Imperial Booksellers' Regulations that were decreed about 1772 are evidence of the thorough training of book-trade apprentices and make the practice of the profession dependent on ability and training.

For most of the period and into the second half of the nineteenth century the bookseller both commissioned and sold his books. Although various combinations have been maintained to the present time, the general rule today is a strictly defined and economic separation between publisher and retail bookseller. An effective wholesale book trade with its main centre in Vienna has been created as an intermediary between publisher—both Austrian and foreign—and retail bookshop.

Vienna's booksellers met in 1807 under the name of *Gremium der Bürgerlichen Buchhändler* ("Board of Booksellers") in order to organize matters concerning their profession. The "Association of Austrian Booksellers" was founded in Vienna 1859. The Association, which today is called *Hauptverband des österreichischen Buchhandels* ("Austrian Publishers' and Booksellers' Association") (→ 4), has included all branches of the book trade, wholesale and publishing, during its existence over more than a century. It has been completely independent from the very beginning, but has enjoyed a close and friendly cooperation with the German *Börsenverein.*

Bibliography

O. M. Fontana, *Hundert Jahre Hauptverband der österreichischen Buchhändler im Spiegel der Zeit (1859–1959).* (One hundred years in the history of the Austrian Publishers' and Booksellers' Association.) Wien, Hauptverband 1959.

1859–1959. Hundert Jahre Hauptverband der österreichischen Buchhändler. Festausgabe "Anzeiger des österreichischen Buch-, Kunst-, und Musikalienhandels". (One hundred years of the Austrian Publishers' and Booksellers' Association. Commemorative edition, "Advertiser of the book, art and music trades".) Wien, Hauptverband 1960.

C. Junker, *Die geschichtliche Entwicklung des Buchhandels in Österreich.* (The historical development of the book trade in Austria.) Wien, Amalthea-Verlag 1926.

C. Junker, *Der Verein der österreichisch-ungarischen Buchhändler 1859–1899. Ein Beitrag zur Geschichte des österreichischen Buchhandels.* (The Association of Austrian and Hungarian Booksellers 1859–1899. A contribution to the history of the Austrian book trade.) Wien, R. Lechner 1899.

C. Junker, *Korporation der Wiener Buch-, Kunst-, und Musikalienhändler 1807–1907.* Festschrift. (Corporation of the Viennese Book, Art and Music Trades 1807–1907. Commemorative publication.) Wien, Deuticke 1907.

Fr. Kapp and J. Goldfriedrich, *Geschichte des Deutschen Buchhandels.* (History of the German book trade.) 4 vols and index. Leipzig, Börsenverein 1886–1923.

3 Retail Prices

The obligation to maintain fixed retail prices was included in the statutes of the

"Austrian Booksellers' Association" in 1888. A *Verkehrs- und Verkaufsordnung* (Regulations concerning business and sale) was published in 1889, and in a revised and expanded form this governs the conditions of sale to the public until today as well as business practice between publishers and retail bookshops. The most recent edition appeared in 1947.

The fixed retail price is established by law in Austria insofar as agreements concerning the obligation of retail salesmen in the book, magazine and music trades to maintain the selling price fixed by the publisher are not subject to the Austrian Cartel Law of 1951.

The obligation to maintain fixed retail prices also operates in the sale of foreign publications. In accordance with the "Regulations concerning business and sale" the "Hauptverband" lays down conversion tables for the currencies of the most important supplying countries.

Bibliography

Federal Law of 4 July 1951, Book of Federal Law no. 173 on the regulation of cartels (Cartel Law), § 2 figure 2, letter e.

Verkehrs- und Verkaufsordnung für den Buch-, Kunst-, Musikalien- und Zeitschriftenhandel in Österreich. (Regulations concerning business and sale for the book, art, music and periodical trades in Austria.) Wien, Hauptverband 1961 and 1966.

H. Franzen and G. Schwartz, *Preisbindungsfibel für den Buchhandel.* (Handbook for price maintenance in the book trade.) München, C. H. Beck 1966. XIII, 99 pp.

H. Falter, *Buch und Buchhandel im Rahmen der Wirtschaftspolitik verschiedener Länder unter besonderer Berücksichtigung der vertikalen Preisbindung.* (Books and the book trade in the economic framework of various countries, with special reference to vertical price maintenance.) Aachen, J. A. Mayer 1965. 135 pp.

4 Organization

Founded in 1859, the independent body representing the interests of all branches of the book trade is the

Hauptverband des österreichischen Buchhandels
(Austrian Publishers' and Booksellers' Association)
Grünangergasse 4,
A 1010 Wien I

To this belong the following subsidiary associations:

Österreichischer Verlegerverband
(Association of Austrian Publishers)
Österreichischer Buchhändlerverband
(Association of Austrian Booksellers)
Verband der österreichischen Kommissionäre, Grossobuchhändler und Auslieferer
(Association of Austrian Commission Agents, Wholesale Booksellers and Deliverers)
Verband der Antiquare Österreichs
(Association of Austrian Antiquarian Booksellers)
Verband der österreichischen Zeitungs- und Zeitschriften-Grossisten und der Werbenden Zeitschriftenhändler
(Association of Newspaper and Magazine Wholesalers and Magazine Salesmen)

The main tasks of the "Hauptverband" are: to guard the interests of the book trade, to foster and codify the practices in the trade, to facilitate business procedure, to cooperate in book promotion, including exhibitions and the organization and support of exhibitions of Austrian publications abroad, to encourage young recruits for the trade, to further training and social benefits, and to promote contact with trade associations abroad.

The governing body, which is elected for a period of three years, consists of representatives of the governing bodies of all the subsidiary associations. From among its members the governing body chooses a president and two vice-presidents. To facilitate its work the governing body has at the moment set up the following special committees: the tax committee, the advertising committee, the committee for rationalization, the committee for market research, the committee for exhibitions abroad, the committee for contact with the "Austrian Youth Book Club" (→ 10), the Branch Group of the Austrian Schoolbook Publishers.

The Association's office with the secretariat and press and advertising department is to be found in the *Österreichisches Buchgewerbehaus* ("Austrian Book Trade House"). Here are also archives of the Association and firms and the *Library of the Austrian Book Trade Centre* (→ Books about Books, p. 67).

The most important publications are: *Anzeiger des österreichischen Buchhandels* (→ 5), *Adressbuch des österreichischen Buch-, Kunst-, Musikalien- und Zeitschriftenhandels*, *Verzeichnis der österreichischen Auslieferungsstellen in- und ausländischer Verlage* (→ 23), *Verkehrsnummern-Verzeichnis* ("Index of delivery numbers"), "Currency conversion tables for books and music" (German Marks and Swiss Francs) and catalogues "Aus der Schatzkammer der Bücher" ("The treasury of books") and "Das österreichische Buch" ("The Austrian book").

The statutory organization for all book-trade firms is the *Gremium des Handels mit Büchern, Kunstblättern, Musikalien, Zeitungen und Zeitschriften* ("Board for Trade in Books, Art Publications, Music, Newspapers and Magazines") in the *Kammern der gewerblichen Wirtschaft* ("Chambers of Commerce"). The chambers take care of training and confer licences for engaging in publishing and the retail book trade. They also have the right to pass judgement on laws and decrees.

Bibliography

O. M. Fontana, *Hundert Jahre Hauptverband der österreichischen Buchhändler im Spiegel der Zeit (1859–1959)*. (One hundred years in the history of the Austrian Publishers' and Booksellers' Association.) Wien, Hauptverband 1959.

1859–1959. Hundert Jahre Hauptverband der österreichischen Buchhändler. Festausgabe des Anzeigers des österreichischen Buch-, Kunst- und Musikalienhandels. (One hundred years of the Austrian Publishers' and Booksellers' Association. Commemorative edition, "Advertiser of the book, art and music trades".) Wien, Hauptverband 1960.

C. Junker, *Der Verein der österreichisch-ungarischen Buchhändler 1859–1899. Ein Beitrag zur Geschichte des österreichischen Buchhandels.* (The Association of Austrian and Hungarian Booksellers 1859–1899. A contribution to the history of the Austrian book trade.) Wien, R. Lechner 1899.

Adressbuch des österreichischen Buch-, Kunst, Musikalien- und Zeitschriftenhandels, Organisationsteil (Directory of the Austrian book, art, music and magazine trades, organization section). Wien, Hauptverband 1967.

5 Trade Press

The trade paper for the Austrian book trade is the

Anzeiger des österreichischen Buchhandels
(Advertiser of the Austrian Book Trade)
Grünangergasse 4
A 1010 Wien I

appears on the first and fifteenth of every month. 1970 was the 105th year of publication. It is the channel of communication for the *Hauptverband des österreichischen Buchhandels* (→ 4), and contains notices from the federal and provincial "Boards" (→ 4). The contents are divided into editorial and advertising sections. The editorial section is primarily devoted to problems in the Austrian book and publishing trades and also contains important news from abroad and information

on work in international trade organizations. The advertising section contains advertisements from Austrian and also from German and Swiss publishers on their latest publications, new editions, retail price changes, etc.
The following special numbers appear annually: Spring (March), Travel (April), Austria (May), technical and scientifical books (August) and the Frankfurt Book Fair (September). The special numbers contain an index of titles and authors.
A regular supplement to the above is the official *Anzeiger des Verbandes der Antiquare Österreichs* ("Advertiser of the Austrian Antiquarian Booksellers' Association). It contains an editorial section, advertisements for wanted items and offers (→ 26).

6 Book-Trade Literature

Modern trading methods in the Austrian book trade have developed on similar lines to those in Germany. A lively exchange of books and close business connections has led to a far-reaching similarity in commercial methods and trade customs. The works quoted under "Bibliography" in the various sections of the Austrian and German (F. R.) chapters of this work provide information on any peculiarities or variations. Austrian material is contained in:

H. Kliemann and P. Meyer-Dohm, *Buchhandel. Eine Bibliographie.* (The book trade. A bibliography) Hamburg, Verlag für Buchmarkt-Forschung 1963. 160 pp. – Schriften zur Buchmarkt-Forschung, 1.

The selective and descriptive bibliography of

G. K. Schauer (ed.), *Eine Fachbibliothek für Buchhändler* (A special library for booksellers). 4th ed. Frankfurt a. M., Buchhändler-Vereinigung 1970. 63 pp.

is also applicable to conditions in Austria.
Text and reference books on the book trade that are used in Germany are generally also in use in Austria.

Information on the structure of the "Hauptverband" (→ 4) and related societies and organizations can be found in the organization section of the *Adressbuch des österreichischen Buch-, Kunst-, Musikalien- und Zeitschriftenhandels* (→ 4, under "Bibliography").

7 Sources of Information, Address Services

All information concerning the Austrian book trade is disseminated by and obtainable from the "Hauptverband" (→ 4).

8 International Membership

The "Hauptverband" has been a member of the "International Publishers' Association" since 1899. It is a member of the "International Community of Booksellers' Associations". The "Verband der Antiquare Österreichs" (→ 26) belongs to the "International League of Antiquarian Booksellers".
A regular exchange of experience on all matters concerning the bookselling business, bibliographical cooperation, problems of price-fixing, joint advertising, etc. takes place between the Federal Republic of Germany, Switzerland and Austria annually at the *Dreiländertreffen* ("Three Countries' Meeting").
Austria is a member of Unesco.

9 Market Research

The history and practice of publishing has been the subject of a lecture at the university of Vienna since the winter semester of 1964/65.
A series of statistics, such as annual book production and the results of foreign trade with goods from the book trade, are collected by the "Hauptverband" (→ 4).

In connection with a comparison being made among various businesses, the development in turnover in the retail book trade has been evaluated since 1955 by the

Arbeitsgemeinschaft für Handelsforschung an der Hochschule für Welthandel
(Working Group for Trade Research at the University of Economics and Business Administration)
Franz Kleingasse 1
A 1190 Wien

After a lengthy pause the cost, profit and turnover situation in the retail book trade for the years 1959, 1960 and 1965 were investigated in 1967, and compared with developments in the Federal Republic of Germany. A comparison of the cost and profit for the years 1966 and 1967 was published in 1969.

Since 1954 an index of the turnover in the retail book trade has been evaluated by the

Österreichisches Institut für Wirtschaftsforschung
(Austrian Institute for Economic Research)
Arsenal
A 1030 Wien

Bibliography

R. Rehberger, *Statistik der österreichischen Buchproduktion 1969*. (Statistics on Austrian book production 1969.) In: *Anzeiger des österreichischen Buchhandels*, no. 2, Wien, Hauptverband 1970.

H. Lexa, *Erfahrungen aus Betriebsvergleichen und ihre Anwendung im Betrieb*. (Experience gained from comparing trade firms and its use in business.) In: *Anzeiger des österreichischen Buch-, Kunst- und Musikalienhandels*, no. 17 and 18, 1967. Wien, Hauptverband 1967.

Die Kosten-, Ertrags- und Umsatzlage im österreichischen Einzelhandel 1965/66 bzw. 1967/68. (The cost, profit and turnover situation in the Austrian retail trade 1965/66 respectively 1967/68.) In: *Der österreichische Betriebswirt*, no. 3, p. 179ff., and no. 3, p. 162ff. and p. 179ff., Wien, Manz 1969.

Die Situation im österreichischen und westdeutschen Sortimentsbuchhandel im Jahre 1965. (The situation in the Austrian and West German retail book trades in 1965.) Wien, Hauptverband 1966.

10 Books and Young People

The Federal Ministry for Education has promoted the writing of literature for youth since 1947 through the

Österreichische Jugendschriftenkommission
(Austrian Commission on Literature for Youth)
Bundesministerium für Unterricht
Minoritenplatz 5
A 1010 Wien

The Commission's task is to give its opinion on printed works and manuscripts suitable or intended for adolescents. After scrutiny a book can be placed on the "List of recommended books for adolescents of the Austrian Commission on Literature for Youth". In addition it can receive the distinction "highly recommended for adolescents", or be refused a position on the list. Books so recommended are discussed in the youth-book advisory section of *Die Jugend* (Youth), a magazine published by the Ministry of Education.

An encouragement to authors and publishers is to be found in the "Austrian state prize for small children's books and for literature for children and adolescents" and in the "Youth book prize of the City of Vienna".

In 1947 the

Österreichische Buchklub der Jugend
(Austrian Youth Book Club)
Fuhrmannsgasse 18a
A 1080 Wien VIII

was founded as a public association to encourage good books for adolescents. Its membership of about 800,000 includes the majority of all children of compulsory school age. Honorary book club advisers work in 6,000 elementary and central schools. The department of the book club responsible for initial readings cooperates with the "Austrian Commission on Literature for Youth" at the Federal Ministry of Education. Lively and enlightening discussions are promoted in the parents' organizations. In the work of the book club particular notice is being taken of the tranformation of centrally controlled school libraries into class libraries. In the "Youth Book Club" there is also a central point where applications can be made to limit the distribution of printed matter unsuitable for adolescents.

The most important Catholic organization dealing with literature for adolescents is the

Studien- und Beratungsstelle für Kinder- und Jugendschrifttum am Katholischen Jugendwerk Österreichs
(The Study and Advisory Centre for Literature for Children and Adolescents with the Catholic Youth Organization of Austria)
Nibelungengasse 1
A 1010 Wien I

Its deliberations are published in a catalogue that appears annually. Very thorough reviews can also be found in the Catholic magazine

Die Zeit im Buch
Stefansplatz 3
A 1010 Wien I

The particular task of the

Österreichische Kinderfreunde
(Austrian Friends of Children)
Rauhensteingasse 5
A 1010 Wien I

is the distribution of a large number of books to their members' children.

In addition to the above the

Internationales Institut für Kinder-, Jugend- und Volksliteratur
(International Institute for Children's, Juvenile and Popular Literature)
Fuhrmannsgasse 18a
A 1080 Wien VIII

also has its centre in Austria (→ International Section, 10).

Bibliography

R. Bamberger, *Jugendlektüre.* (Youth literature.) 2nd ed. Wien, Verlag für Jugend und Volk 1965. 848 pp.

Schriftenreihe des Buchklubs der Jugend. (Series of Works of the Youth Book Club.) Vols. I–XX. Wien, Buchklub der Jugend, no date.

Schriftenreihe zur Jugendlektüre. (Series of works for youth literature), Wien, Internationales Institut für Kinder-, Jugend- und Volksliteratur und Österreichischer Buchklub der Jugend (International Institute for Children, Youth and Popular Literature and Austrian Youth Book Club), published continuously since 1969.

11 Training

In Austria a licence is required to publish and sell books. The acquisition of this licence is subject, among other things, to possession of the necessary qualifications. For a publishing licence, proof of three years' practice with a publisher is sufficient, together with certain academic training. Proof of ability to work in the book trade presupposes not only certain training at school and three years' practice, but also passing an examination at the end of a one to three years' apprenticeship, depending on previous training. Thus in Austria there is no special apprenticeship training for publishers, but only for the retail book trade.

Depending on previous training, an apprentice in the book trade enters into an apprentice's agreement with a book-trade firm for a period of one to three years, and that is done with the participation of the apprentices section of the *Chambers of Commerce* (→ 4). During his apprenticeship the apprentice must attend a trade school. Where the number of book-trade apprentices is sufficient, special book-trade classes are provided.

In 1969 there were 341 book-trade apprentices in Austria, of whom 121 were male and 220 female.
Young booksellers' study groups provide further training outside the school and the firm. A central event every year is the "Austrian Young Booksellers' Week". Financial support for such events and for participation in international meetings, foreign booksellers' seminars, etc., comes from the *Rudolf-Lechner-Fonds für die Aus- und Weiterbildung des buchhändlerischen und verlegerischen Nachwuchses* ("Rudolf Lechner Fund for the Training and Further Training of Young People in the Publishing and Book Trades"). The fund was founded by the "Hauptverband" (→ 4).

12 Taxes

Books and pamphlets are subject to turnover tax. Goods and services are subject to it, and in principle it is levied on every individual sale in all branches of the economy. A reduced rate of 1.7% is fixed for books and pamphlets. All other goods of the book trade (music, newspapers, magazines, cartographical products, etc.) are levied at the general rate of 5.5%, which is reduced to 2% on deliveries in the wholesale trade.
The adjustment tax on imported books, brochures and similar printed items as well as loose sheets (custom tariff no. 49.01) was abolished on 1 December 1969. Magazines (with the exception of fashion magazines) and newspapers imported from abroad are subject to 10.6% and illustrated books, music and cartographical items to 13% adjustment tax.

13 Clearing Institutions
None.

14 Copyright

Copyright is governed in Austria by the law of 9 April 1936, Book of Federal Law No. 111 concerning "Copyright on works of literature and art and related safeguarding rights (Copyright Law)" in the version of the Federal Laws of 14 July 1949, Book of Federal Law No. 206 and of 8 July 1953, Book of Federal Law No. 106, which effected changes in the Copyright Law (Amendment to the Copyright Law 1953).
Apart from copyright on works of literature and art, including the film, the law also includes regulations on the protection of lectures and performances of works of literature and music, of photographs and sound productions, of letters and portraits, of news, and of titles of works of literature and art.
Austria is a signatory to the Berne Convention of 9 September 1886 in the Brussels version of 26 June 1948.
She is also a member of the Universal Copyright Convention of 6 September 1952 and the Agreement of Montevideo of 11 January 1889. Bilateral agreements exist with Belgium, Denmark, Germany, Norway, Romania, Spain, Czechoslovakia and the USA.
Copyright ceases 57 years after the death of the author. Where the author has not been noted in a manner that could presume authorship according to paragraph 12 of the Copyright Law, copyright on works of literature, music and the fine arts ceases 57 years after publication, unless an earlier date is arrived at from paragraph 60 of the Copyright Law, according to which copyright ceases 57 years after the death of the author.

Bibliopgraphy

a) Periodicals

Österreichische Blätter für gewerblichen Rechtsschutz und Urheberrecht. (Austrian Journal for Legal Protection and Copyright.) Wien, Manz.
Österreichische Autorenzeitung. (Austrian Authors' Journal.) Wien.

b) Books

R. DITTRICH: *Das österreichische Verlagsrecht.* (Austrian copyright.) Wien, Manz 1969.

W. PETER, *Das österreichische Urheberrecht samt den Bestimmungen über die Verwertungsgesellschaften und die zwischenstaatlichen Urheberrechtsverhältnisse Österreichs.* (Austrian laws of copyright together with the regulations on performing right societies and international copyright arrangements with Austria). Wien, Manz 1954.

M. RINTELEN, *Urheber- und Urhebervertragsrecht nach österreichischem, deutschem und schweizerischem Recht.* (Copyright and contractual rights in Austrian, German and Swiss law.) Wien, Springer 1958.

15 National Bibliography, National Library

There is proof that as early as the fourteenth century there existed a stock of manuscripts in the Viennese "Court Library". The present library building was completed in 1726 and additional accommodation was added in 1966. The library was taken over by the State in 1920, and since 1945 it has borne the name

Österreichische Nationalbibliothek
(Austrian National Library)
Josefsplatz 1
A 1010 Wien I

Apart from the main collection, which includes magazines and journals, it has various special collections. In view of the tendency towards collecting, it shares functions with the Viennese University Library, which deals with the sciences, etc., whereas the National Library concentrates its collecting activities on the arts, and is above all the central collecting centre for Austriaca.

The collection of works appearing in Austria is compiled from two copies of each work which every publisher must by law deliver to the National Library. Further compulsory copies are received by the provincial libraries of the Austrian provinces and by the "Administrative Library" of the Federal Chancellery.

After the delivery of compulsory copies had been regulated by the Press Law of 27 May 1852, an Austrian bibliography existed under various names, but all these were of short duration and do not give an unbroken picture of new publications in Austria in those days.

Austrian writing has been recorded in the *Österreichische Bibliographie* ("Austrian Bibliography") since 1946. It appears bimonthly, with the addition of three quarterly indexes, an annual index, and a publication devoted to music. An annual index of official publications is planned.

Apart from the "Austrian Bibliography" and the relevant German and Swiss bibliographies, the catalogues of wholesale firms are of practical importance for the bibliographical work of the book trade.

Bibliography

Festschrift der Nationalbibliothek in Wien. (Commemorative publication of the National Library, Vienna.) Wien, Staatsdruckerei 1926. VII, 870 pp.

Die österreichische Nationalbibliothek. (The Austrian National Library.) Commemorative publication. Wien, H. Bauer 1948. XII, 693 pp.

G. PRACHNER, *Zur Geschichte der österreichischen Bibliographie* (History of Austrian bibliography). In: Biblos 4, pp. 108–117. Wien, Gesellschaft der Freunde der ÖsterreichischenNationalbibliothek1955.

Handbuch österreichischer Bibliotheken. (Handbook of Austrian libraries.) 2 vols. Wien, Österreichische Nationalbibliothek 1961. XXVI, 333 and XIV, 139 pp.

R. WEITZEL, *Die deutschen nationalen Bibliographien.* (The German national bibliographies.) 3rd edition, Frankfurt a. M., Buchhändler-Vereinigung 1963. 92 pp.

Die Österreichische Nationalbibliothek. Geschichte, Bestände. Aufgaben. (The Austrian

National Library, its history, stock and task.) 3rd ed. Wien, Österreichische Nationalbibliothek 1964. 80pp.

Handbuch der österreichischen Wissenschaft. (Handbook of Austrian scholarship.) 5th year of publication, 1964, pp. 351–4. Wien, Österreichischer Bundesverlag 1965.

Die Österreichische Nationalbibliothek in der Neuen Hofburg. Lesesäle, Kataloge und Magazine der Druckschriftensammlung. (The Austrian National Library in the Neue Hofburg. Reading rooms, catalogues and magazines of the collection of Printed Work.) Wien, Österreichische Nationalbibliothek, no date. 65 pp. illustrations and plan.

16 Book Production

In 1969 Austrian book production amounted to 6.808 titles. First editions were, in proportion to new editions about 8 to 2. 13% of the new editions were translations from foreign languages.

The five most important categories of books obtainable through the book trade were as follows:

Subject group	Titles	Percentage of total production
Belles-lettres	463	13.0
History, history of civilization, folklore	291	8.2
Economics, sociology, statistics	261	7.3
Youth publications	234	6.6
Religion, theology	189	5.3

Bibliography

R. Rehberger, *Statistik der österreichischen Buchproduktion 1969.* (Statistics of Austrian book production in 1969.) In: Anzeiger des österreichischen Buchhandels, no. 2, 1970, Wien, Hauptverband 1970.

17 Translations

In 1969 there appeared in Austria 584 translations, 30% more than in the previous year. Heading the list again with a share of 58% were translations from English, followed by works from French with 20% and Dutch. 37% of the translations were literary works, 19% were books for youth.

Bibliography

→ 16, Bibliography.

18 Book Clubs

Book subscriptions were known in Austria before 1900. They can be regarded as forerunners of the book-club idea. Several book clubs were already active in Austria between the two World Wars, including two well-known German book clubs. The situation since 1945 is characterized by the establishment of new Austrian book clubs in the provinces too, and the influence of German firms. At one time there were some 15 book clubs in Austria. At the present time the number has sunk to about 8.

Modern advertising methods brought the book clubs new readers in Austria too, which led to a worsening of relations with the retail book trade. From the very beginning the trade organization tried to mediate, but years passed before tension was reduced and gave way to reason and the realization that both forms of sale have their specific tasks in furthering the distribution of books.

19 Paperbacks

A single series of paperbacks has appeared in recent years with emphasis on the publication of works by Austrian authors. Before its suspension the series comprised more than 100 available titles.

20 Book Design

The competition for the "Best-designed Austrian Books" was started by the "Hauptverband" (→ 4) in 1953. Thanks to the support given it since 1956 by the

Federal Ministry of Trade, Commerce and Industry, the competition now has State prizes to confer. The jury, mostly independent specialists in bibliology and typography and representatives of the trade associations concerned, annually select about 20 best-designed books, with particular attention to the quality of content, printing, illustration and binding.

All publications appearing in book form that have been printed and published in Austria are eligible to enter the competition. This competition has advantageously influenced the sense of quality among publishers and booksellers and has contributed to the spread of well-designed books. The "Hauptverband" (→ 4) undertakes to display the "Best-designed Austrian Books" at all general exhibitions at home and abroad and at the most important book-art exhibitions.

Bibliography

The illustrated catalogue *Die schönsten Bücher Österreichs* (The best-designed Austrian books) appears annually and reports on the selection made.

Articles on the "Best-designed Austrian Books" and the annual presentation of the State prizes appear in the *Anzeiger* (→ 5).

21 Publishing

The number of Austrian publishing houses whose activities go back without interruption to the 19th and 18th centuries, and even further, is by no means small. This is particularly so in the publishing of scientific and technical works. A publishing house of European importance for literary works, however, did not appear until after the First World War. Not until after 1945, as a result of the setbacks due to the economic and political situation, did a gradual but continuous development begin, with the participation of both traditional firms and newly founded publishing enterprises. An official census of 1967 showed the existence of 376 publishers in Austria, with 5,238 employees. The majority are small firms. Only 33 firms have more than 20 dependent employees.

Most firms are based in Vienna, but influential publishers are also to be found outside Vienna:

	Firms
Wien	243
Steiermark	27
Salzburg	25
Oberösterreich	24
Niederösterreich	23
Tirol	20
Kärnten	8
Vorarlberg	4
Burgenland	2

No official statistics are available for the sale of books and scientific and technical journals by publishers.

Bibliography

O. M. Fontana, *Hundert Jahre Hauptverband der österreichischen Buchhändler im Spiegel der Zeit (1859–1959).* (→ 4 Bibliography.)

H. Rieder, *Verlagsbuchhandel in Österreich. Ein Beitrag zur Entwicklung ab Mitte des 19. Jahrhunderts.* (The publishing trade in Austria. A contribution to its development since the middle of the 19th century.) In: Anzeiger des österreichischen Buch-, Kunst- und Musikalienhandels, Österreich-Sondernummer Juli 1967 (Austrian special edition, July 1967). Wien, Hauptverband 1967.

22 Literary Agents

These are rare in Austria. For a long time now there has been direct contact between author and publisher. Foreign agents, on the other hand, assume a certain importance in international dealings.

23 Wholesale Trade

The development of the Austrian wholesale trade began in the second half of the 19th century. The wholesale trade has contributed decisively to the forms of book sales still valid today as well as to the efficient distribution of books. It had already assumed its special role as intermediary between the home and foreign publisher and the Austrian retail book trade, and as an importer of books predominantly in German, at a time when Leipzig was still the old centre of the book trade. The importance of the wholesale trade as a stockholder who has to bear the risks and take care of promotion, as well as intermediary of information also in view of the high proportion of foreign books on the Austrian market, has increased since 1945.
Today there are more than 10 firms occupied in just this business. In addition there are a huge number of delivery firms. Most of these wholesale and delivery firms have their headquarters in Vienna, Salzburg and Innsbruck.

Bibliography

Österreichische Auslieferungsstellen in- und ausländischer Verlage. (Austrian delivery centres for Austrian and foreign publishers.) Wien, Hauptverband, annual.

24 Retail Trade

Although independent nationally, the Austrian retail book trade developed almost parallel to that in Germany.
In Austria a licence is required to carry on the book, art and music trades, i. e. proof of the appropriate ability must be produced (→ 11).
An official census of 1967 showed the existence of 918 retail book firms in Austria with altogether 4,286 employees. Small firms with up to about 10 employees formed the majority. The distribution of the firms in the most important towns can be seen in the following table:

	Firms
Wien	384
Niederösterreich	117
Steiermark	105
Oberösterreich	85
Kärnten	68
Salzburg	61
Tirol	53
Vorarlberg	28
Burgenland	17

No offical statistics are available for the turnover in the retail book trade.

Bibliography

O. M. Fontana, *Hundert Jahre Hauptverband der österreichischen Buchhändler im Spiegel der Zeit (1859–1959).* (→ 4, Bibliography.)

H. Lexa, *Erfahrungen aus Betriebsvergleichen und ihre Anwendung im Betrieb.* (→ 9, Bibliography.)

25 Mail-Order Bookselling

This branch of the bookselling trade has also continued to develop in Austria. Particular published works, such as encyclopedias and comprehensive series, are being systematically sold throughout the country by large and small firms. These also sometimes work beyond the frontiers of Austria.

26 Antiquarian Book Trade, Auctions

Austria's antiquarian book trade has suffered serious reverses as a result of political developments and the consequences of the Second World War. It owes its present position to the reputation of a few firms that have re-established relations with the international market. A large proportion of Austrian antiquarian booksellers are members of the

Verband der Antiquare Österreichs (Association of Austrian Antiquarian Booksellers)
Grünangerstraße 4
A 1010 Wien I

This Association is a subsidiary to the "Hauptverband" (→ 4). It has 42 members at the present time and has drawn up its "Principles for business practice", which adhere to international usage. The Association is a member of the "International League of Antiquarian Booksellers".

Bibliography

a) Periodicals

Anzeiger des Verbandes der Antiquare Österreichs. (Advertiser of the Association of Austrian Antiquarian Booksellers.) Wien, Hauptverband.

Antiquariat. (Antiquarian Book Trade.) → Germany (F. R.), 26.

b) Search lists

Gesuchte Bücher. (Wanted books.) In: Anzeiger. Wien, Hauptverband.

c) Books

Verband der Antiquare Österreichs: Verzeichnis der Mitgliedsfirmen. (List of member firms.) Wien, Hauptverband 1968.

I. Nebehay, *Das bibliophile und das moderne Antiquariat.* (The bibliophile's and modern antiquarian bookshop.) In: Berichte und Informationen, no. 1040. Salzburg, Österreichisches Forschungsinstitut für Wirtschaft und Politik.

27 Book Imports

Between 1950 and 1969 imports of goods from the book trade have increased forty-seven-fold. (15,400,000 öS in 1950 as against 717,400,000 in 1969.)

The real figures in the case of book imports may well be greater than this, since, as compared with export figures, the amount for imports quoted in the official foreign trade statistics should be regarded as too low.

The figures for 1969 are as follows:

Category	Amount m. öS
Books	309.6
Periodicals	390.0
Illustrated books for children	3.8
Music	2.5
Cartographical productions	11.5
Total	717.4

The most important countries of origin for book imports in 1969 were:

	Amount öS 1,000	Percentage of total
Federal Republic of Germany	251,636	81.3
Switzerland	12,484	4.0
Netherlands	11,531	3.7
USA	7,442	2.4
Yugoslavia	6,516	2.1
United Kingdom	5,878	1.9
German Democratic Republic	4,131	1.3
Italy	2,650	0.9
Belgium and Luxembourg	2,628	0.8
Czechoslovakia	1,818	0.6

The Federal Republic of Germany and Switzerland together account for nearly 85% of total imports.

The figures for the import of periodicals are similar. The most important countries of origin for the import of periodicals in 1969 were:

Country	Amount öS 1,000	Percentage of total
Federal Republic of Germany	371,077	95.1
France	5,096	1.3
United Kingdom	4,787	1.2
Netherlands	3,064	0.8
Switzerland	2,609	0.7
Italy	1,365	0.3
USA	1,306	0.3

The import of goods of the book trade is completely liberalized and in general duty-free. Only picture albums, cartographical productions for advertising purposes, post cards and calendars are subject to custom. Books, brochures and similar printing items (loose sheets too) do not bear an adjustment tax when imported. Newspapers and magazines are subject to an adjustment tax of 10.6%. Illustrated books, painting books, music and cartographical products are charged with an adjustment tax of 13% when imported.

28 Book Exports

During the period 1950–1969 the export of goods from the book trade increased about four and a half-fold (75,500,000 öS in 1950 as against 329,800,000 öS in 1969).

Category	Amount m. öS
Books	291.0
Periodicals	25.8
Illustrated books for children	1.2
Music	4.0
Cartographical productions	7.8
Total	329.8

In 1969 books and periodicals were exported to 25 European and 27 non-European countries, the most important of which were as follows:

Country	Amount öS 1,000	Percentage of total
Federal Republic of Germany	232,482	79.4
Switzerland	20,817	7.2
USA	10,571	3.6
United Kingdom	4,481	1.5
USSR	3,907	1.3
Italy	2,945	1.0
France	2,878	0.9
German Democratic Republic	2,440	0.8
Netherlands	1,729	0.6
South African Republic	1,465	0.5

The most important purchasers of Austrian books are the Federal Republic of Germany and Switzerland; together they account for about 87% of total book exports. The corresponding amounts for the remaining countries are very much smaller. Periodicals were exported in 1969 to the following countries:

Country	Amount öS 1,000	Percentage of total
Federal Republic of G.	10,947	42.2
Italy	4.592	17.8
Czechoslovakia	2,302	8.9
France	1,973	7.6
Hungary	756	2.9
Netherlands	715	2.7
Yugoslavia	678	2.6
Spain	613	2.3
Switzerland	590	2.3
Poland	588	2.2

Austrian exports with respect to goods of the book trade are completely liberalized. Exporting firms receive an export allowance of 5.78% of the invoice amount to compensate for the turnover tax (→ 12). The export dealer's allowance amounts to 1.61% of the value at the frontier (invoice amount).

The present level of Austrian book exports, which had to be started up again after the war, and often with the greatest difficulty, represents a success for the individual efforts of publishers, wholesale and retail booksellers. The "Hauptverband" (→ 4) encouraged these exertions at an early date by organizing Austrian book exhibitions abroad; 105 general and 68 special exhibitions have been held since 1949 in 60 European and 19 non-European towns.

The exertions of the booksellers' trade organization were supported from the very beginning by the Federal Ministry of Commerce, Trade and Industry, by the Federal Ministry of Education, and subsequently by the Institute for the

Economic Development at the Federal Chamber of Commerce. Generally speaking, exhibitions abroad are planned and carried out with the cooperation of the last of these three bodies. In addition, close contact is maintained with the Austrian cultural institutes abroad as regards projects for exhibitions.

30 Public Relations

The ever-repeated question as to the importance of books and the book trade in the public mind has led to increasing efforts by the "Hauptverband" (→ 4) in encouraging contact with the public and the various mass media. This work extends, of course, beyond the field of publicity, especially when it is concerned with giving the book its rightful place as a means of education and communication in the educational and fiscal policy of the state. One example of this work can be mentioned: the "Hauptverband" is represented on the "Committee for Cultural Home Defence" in the Federal Ministry of Education, and also took part in a cultural inquiry into the aims and nature of Austrian cultural policy abroad.

A similar broad task is the encouragement of positive reading habits among young people; in this matter the "Hauptverband" among other bodies continually cooperates with the "Austrian Youth Book Club" (→ 10).

The annual *Österreichische Buchwoche* ("Austrian Book Week"), which is held throughout Austria by the "Hauptverband", advertises the work of Austrian publishers and distributes information on present-day Austrian literature. One of the tasks of the "Press and Advertising Section" of the "Hauptverband" is the creation of posters, catalogues and similar publicity material. Whenever the occasion requires it, a press service is available to maintain contact with local and foreign newspapers.

Recent years have seen the beginning of close cooperation with radio and television. Both of these broadcast extensive cultural programmes in which literature, books and the book trade assume a special place.

31 Bibliophily

A small circle of Viennese bibliophiles has existed since 1908. Four years later—in 1912—a number of bibliophiles formed an association, the

Wiener Bibliophilen-Gesellschaft
(Viennese Bibliophiles' Society)
Liechtensteinstraße 61
A 1090 Wien 9

to protect their interests in Vienna and in a wider sense throughout the whole of Austria. The society has taken on the task of bringing together connoisseurs and those who appreciate books that are significant and valuable in any way, to promote this interest by the publication of rare works in modern editions and facsimiles with elucidations for a closed community whose number may not exceed 300 by its statutes, and finally to canvass for their culturally valuable mission in wider circles.

The "Viennese Bibliophiles' Society" has distributed 60 publications (annual gifts) to its members since its foundation.

A task closely allied to the art of the book is undertaken by the

Österreichische Exlibris-Gesellschaft
(Austrian Ex-Libris Society)
Türkenstraße 17/4
A 1090 Wien 9

This society encourages the artistically valuable bookplate and in addition high-class graphic art of small proportions, especially copperplate engraving, etching, wood engraving and lithography.

32 Literary Prizes

Apart from State prizes there is a whole series of literary prizes in Austria, awarded by the provinces, towns, associations, literary societies, and also by publishers.
Both at home and abroad the "Great Austrian State Prize for Literature", which has been awarded annually since 1950 by the Federal Ministry for Education, has acquired a considerable reputation. On a motion passed by an arts council this prize is awarded for an important life's work in literature. There is also a State "Förderungspreis" ("Encouragement Prize"), which is awarded annually by the Federal Ministry of Education following a competition, and over a period of five years it is awarded for poetry, novels, stories, drama and radio drama in turn.
The "Austrian State Prize for Small Children's Books and for Literature for Children and Youth" and the "Youth Book Prize of the City of Vienna" offer further encouragement for authors and publishers. (→ 10 above.)
The following list of literary prizes makes no pretence of completeness:

Albert Stifter Prize for Literature (Upper Austrian Provincial Government), Linz.
Anton Wildgans Prize of Austrian Industry (Association of Austrian Industrialists), Wien.
Literary Prize of the Province of Upper Austria, Linz.
Georg Trakl Prize (awarded alternately by the Provincial Government of Salzburg and the Federal Ministry for Education).
Grillparzer Prize (Austrian Academy of Sciences), Wien.
International Nikolaus Lenau Prize (Federal Ministry for Education), Wien.
Cultural Prize for Poetry of the Provinces of Lower Austria, Wien.
Peter Rosegger Prize (Provincial Government of Steiermark), Graz.

33 The Reviewing of Books

The Austrian press, radio and television contribute to the spread of books through their reviews.
All daily papers and almost all magazines print book discussions, usually at regular intervals. First among the publications containing reviews are the daily papers, with a wide circulation and a qualified literary section, e.g.: *Die Presse*, *Kurier*, *Arbeiter Zeitung* (all in Vienna), *Salzburger Nachrichten*, *Linzer Tagblatt*, *Kleine Zeitung* (Graz), *Kronenzeitung* (Vienna), *Wochenpresse* (Vienna), *Kärntner Tageszeitung* (Klagenfurt) and others. Individual papers publish book supplements written by reputable critics when spring and autumn book productions appear. The books reviewed are almost exclusively in German.
At least once a month there is a television programme in which several new works are introduced both from the literary and publishing points of view ("Welt des Buches", "Das Buch des Monats"), ("World of the Book", "The Book of the Month"). The most important weekly review of books in the radio has the title "Ex-Libris".
Apart from announcements of new publications in the advertisement section, the
Anzeiger des österreichischen Buchhandels
Grünangergasse 4
A 1010 Wien I
prints reviews of works on book science and publishing at irregular intervals in its editional section.

Bibliography

Handbuch Österreichs Presse—Werbung—Graphik. (Handbook of Austria's press, publicity, graphic arts.) Wien, Verband österreichischer Zeitungsherausgeber, annually.

Handbuch der Werbung. (Handbook of publicity). Ludwig Schneller, annually.

34 Graphic Arts

Firms connected with the graphic arts have formed the

Hauptverband der graphischen Unternehmungen Österreichs
(Association of Austrian Graphic Firms)
Grünangergasse 4
A 1010 Wien I

The Association can provide all relevant information on the Austrian graphic industry.

Belgium

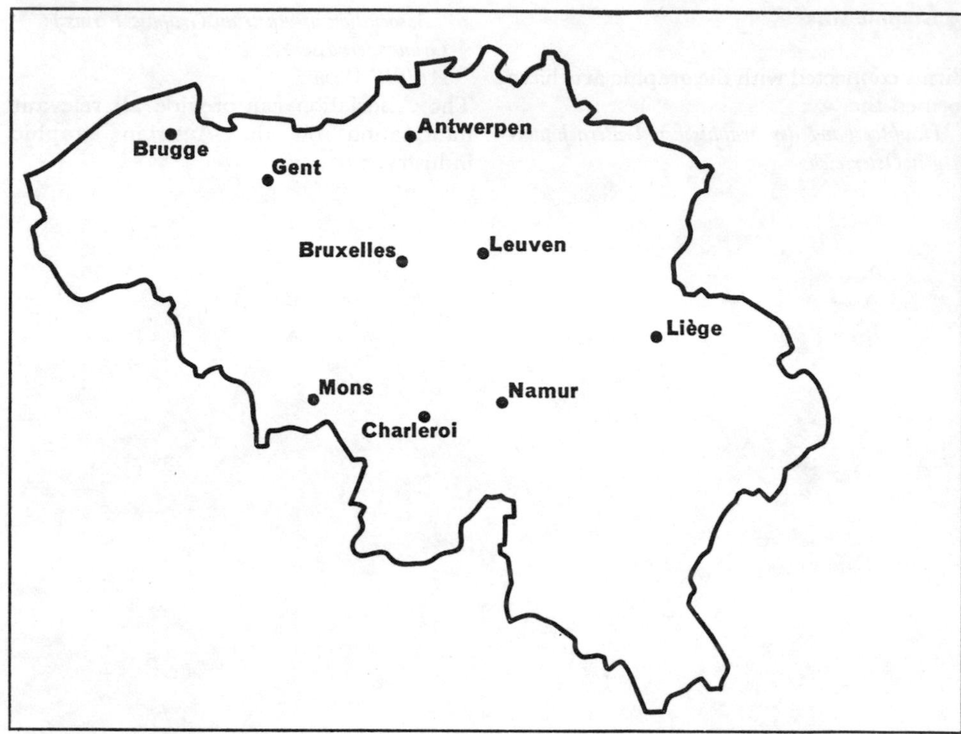

Important Book Centres

1 General Information

Area 30,513 km²
Population 9,500,000 (311 per km²)
Capital Bruxelles/Brussels (1,057,923)
Largest Towns Bruxelles/Brussels (1,057,923); Antwerpen/Anvers (661,656); Lüttich/Liège (452,417); Ghent/Gand (229,178)
Government Parliamentary monarchy
Religion Half the population are practising Roman Catholics; there are also smaller groups of Protestants and Jews
National languages Dutch and French (German is the language of minority groups in eastern cantons)
Leading foreign languages English and German
Weights, Measures Metric System
Currency unit Belgian franc (b. fr.)
Education Compulsory. Higher and university education: 72,000 students at 4 universities, higher, technical, and academic institutions
Illiteracy 3%
Paper consumption a) Newspaper: 13 kg. per inhabitant
b) Printing paper: 17 kg. per inhabitant
Membership UNESCO, IPA, ICBA, ILAB

2 Past and Present

Printing and publishing have been carried on in Belgium since the 16th century. Let it suffice to quote here the names of Christopher Plantin, Antwerp (1,600 titles), Dirk Martens (200 titles) and Jan van Westfalen, Louvain (120 titles) to illustrate the important part that Belgium has played in the development of printing and publishing in Europe. The 17th century saw the massive production of small editions of popular books, legends, and medieval verse chronicles of heroic exploits. After 1815 the freedom of the press, written into the constitution of the Low Countries, led to the founding of many publishing firms, some of which still exist. This particularly concerns Belgian publications in the French language. In the seventeenth century, after a period of great fame, Belgian publications in the Dutch language suffered a decline and did not recover until 1920; after 1945 they once again made great headway.

At present Belgian publishing and book printing is constituted as follows:

1. Belgian productions, half of which are in French and half in Dutch (French editions are destined for the home market and particularly for export; Dutch editions are intended mainly for the home market and for the Dutch markets). There are about 275 publishing houses recognized by professional associations.
2. Considerable imports from France and the Low Countries. These imports account for about 70% of the trade's total turnover. (This proportion was not so high in the past, which proves that Belgian reading habits are heavily supported by imports, which increase every year). Because of the distribution of imported books, some wholesalers and importers have established themselves on the Belgian market.

3. Some 1,700 bookshops recognized by the professional associations ensure distribution and sale to the public.

3 Retail Prices

The book trade in Belgium observes regulated selling prices, fixed by the publisher. Stock is sold to wholesalers and bookshops with the obligation of maintaining fixed retail prices (there is a clause to this effect on invoices). Two professional associations to which publishers and booksellers belong observe regulations, the most important element of which is retail price maintenance. The regulations also guarantee exclusive selling rights to booksellers who have undertaken to respect the retail price fixed by publishers. As a consequence, the retail price assures a reasonable profit to the interested parties, whether it is the author, the publisher, the wholesaler or the bookseller. This rule is agreed to at official levels and commercial courts can intervene if it is being transgressed; since undertaking to observe the price constitutes a freely accepted clause in the contract, a breach of it is a dishonorable action.

The "Cercle Belge de la Librairie" ("Belgian Book Trade Association") and the "Vereniging ter bevordering van het Vlaamse Boekwezen" ("Association for the Promotion of the Flemish Book Trade") have drawn up an agreement (1966) which guarantees the mutual decision of the members of both associations to respect the retail selling price.

With regard to imported books there are two possibilities; if there is a single importer he fixes a selling price in Belgian currency; if there is no individual importer and the import is carried out directly from the foreign publisher, the whole profession uses a "conversion table" fixed by the professional associations.

The first system (fixing of the selling price by the importer) is usual for books from the Netherlands, while the "conversion table" is used in the case of French books. This is due to the fact that there are more individual importers for Dutch books, while the import of French books is done either directly through the bookshops or by way of wholesalers who are not working individually. In any case, the price obtained on the basis of conversion-table or that fixed by the importer must be respected by the retail bookseller.

4 Organization

The book trade as organized in Belgium reflects the historical development of the profession as well as its orientation towards different markets. These two factors also define the character of the activity of publishers and booksellers belonging respectively to the French and Dutch consumer markets. As has been emphasized elsewhere: though the market is not entirely confined to them, it is largely concerned with the sale of books in French or Dutch.

The oldest organization is:

Cercle Belge de la Librairie
(The Belgian Book Trade Association)
111, avenue du Parc
B 1060 Bruxelles

Founded in 1883, it was the only association at that time, and grouped together publishers and booksellers from all over the country (including the few publishing houses and bookshops existing in the Flemish part of the country at that time). In 1921 it became necessary to form an organization for publishers only. So the

Syndicat des Editeurs Belges—Syndicaat der Belgische Uitgevers
(Association of Belgian Publishers)
111, avenue du Parc
B 1060 Bruxelles

was established. This association accepts as members publishers only and is composed of two distinct sections: one for publishers of the French language and one for publishers of the Dutch language.

The third phase in the evolution of this profession was the development of the publication and sale of books in the Dutch language after the First World War. In 1929 a decision was taken to create a third organization, grouping together publishers of Flemish works, booksellers specializing in the sale of Flemish publications, and importers of Dutch books.

This organization:

Vereniging ter bevordering van het Vlaamse Boekwezen
(Association for the Promotion of the Flemish Book Trade)
Frankrijklei 93
B 2000 Antwerpen

is composed of three sections (publishers, importers and booksellers). For a long time there was little contact between these three organizations, which can only be explained by the different interests of the professional people in the organizations: at present the "Cercle Belge de la Librairie" groups together those booksellers who essentially specialize in the sale of French books in the French language; the "Syndicat" tends particularly towards the exports of its members' publications, while the "Vereniging" deals mainly with books in the Dutch language for the home market and for export to the Netherlands. Since 1966 an agreement exists between the "Cercle" and the "Vereniging". Also in 1966 the *Conseil National du Livre—Nationale Raad van het Boek* ("National Book Council") was instituted, where the representatives of the three organizations meet regularly to discuss common problems and to represent the whole trade in contacts with other official bodies.

The aims pursued by the three organizations are identical in whatever concerns the big fields of activity: professional organization, promotion of business relations in the national and international field, publicity for books and reading matter, and the creation of information centres which will come to the help of the profession.

With regard to antiquarian bookselling, there is the

Syndicat Belge de la Librairie Ancienne et Moderne
(Belgian Syndicate of the Antiquarian and Modern Book Trade)
112, Rue de Trèves
B Bruxelles

There is also:

L'Association pour la diffusion à l'étranger des éditions belges
(Association for the Diffusion Abroad of Belgian Publications)
20, Rue Belliard
B Bruxelles

established in 1962 to further the export of Belgian books.

5 Trade Press

The "Cercle Belge de la Librairie" (→ 4) publishes

Journal de la Librairie
(Journal for the Book Trade)
111, avenue du Parc
B 1060 Bruxelles

ten times a year.

This professional bulletin contains articles of general interest for the trade, publishes technical information about selling prices, changes in the list of members, and has a bibliographical section for Belgian publications in French.

The "Syndicat des Editeurs Belges" (→ 4) regularly publishes bulletins for its members. They contain practical and technical information about the profession. The bulletins are stencilled and sent exclusively to the members.

The "Vereniging ter bevordering van het Vlaamse Boekwezen" (→ 4) publishes a fortnightly

Tijdingen (Information for the Book Trade)
Frankrijklei 93,
B 2000 Antwerpen

containing a section with general and technical information about the trade (changes of prices, publicity material available from the publishers) and a bibliographical section mentioning the Belgian publications in Dutch, and Dutch books imported through special agencies.

6 Book-Trade Literature

Literature in book form about the trade is practically non-existent. Articles which appear in the professional bulletins of the respective associations must be considered as a source of information for publishers and booksellers.

7 Sources of Information, Address Services

General information about the trade may be obtained from the three existing associations (→ 4):

Cercle Belge de la Librairie
(Belgian Book Trade Association)
111, avenue du Parc
B 1060 Bruxelles

(for information about Belgian books written in French);

Syndicat des Editeurs Belges
(Association of Belgian Publishers)
111, avenue du Parc
B 1060 Bruxelles

(for information about Belgian publications);

Vereniging ter bevordering van het Vlaamse Boekwezen
(Association for the Promotion of the Flemish Book Trade)
Frankrijklei 93
B 2000 Antwerpen

(about bookselling and Belgian publications in Dutch).

These associations give general information about all aspects of bookselling and publish bibliographies, addresses of public libraries, and are in a position to give information to foreign colleagues about any problem relating to the Belgian trade.

Naturally the three associations keep up to date and publish lists of their members.

Belgium

The "Cercle Belge" publishes an *Annuaire* (year-book) every two years (last edition 1970) containing a list of its members, Belgian publishers, a list of representatives of foreign firms, and some interesting social and financial information.
The "Syndicat des Editeurs" also publishes a *list of its members*, with details about each of the affiliated firms (year of establishment names of directors and a list of the specialities of each firm).
The *list of the members* of the "Vereniging ter bevordering van het Vlaamse Boekwezen" appears every two years (plus a supplement in alternative years) and contains lists of representatives of foreign firms and lists of collections published in Flanders etc. in addition to the lists of members who are publishers, booksellers and importers. All three associations furnish bibliographical information about works which have appeared in Belgium.
The "Vereniging ter bevordering van het Vlaamse Boekwezen" also publishes about twenty lists a year of works which have appeared in Flanders or have been imported by its members; these lists are assembled in an annual publication, *Repertorium*, under authors and titles.
Bibliographical information is also provided by the

Bibliothèque Royale de Belgique
(Royal Library of Belgium)
4, Boulevard de l'Empereur,
B 1000 Bruxelles

(→ 15).

8 International Membership

Because of its geographical situation and the influence of the importation of foreign editions, the Belgian book trade naturally seeks international collaboration. So Belgian colleagues have always answered the call of international trade associations.
The "Syndicat des Editeurs Belges" is a member of the "International Publishers' Association". One of the congresses of this association took place in Brussels. Members of the "Syndicat des Editeurs Belges" are leading members af the "IPA". The "Cercle Belge de la Librairie" and the "Vereniging ter bevordering van het Vlaamse Boekwezen" are members of the "International Community of Booksellers' Associations" (ICBA) since its foundation and regularly follow its work through the intermediary of their delegates, who are on either the executive committee or the boards of the "ICBA". The "Syndicat de la Librairie Ancienne et Moderne" is a member of the "International League of Antiquarian Booksellers" ("ILAB").
Between the "Vereniging ter bevordering van het Vlaamse Boekwezen" and the Dutch Association an agreement exists since 1949 (aiming at mutual observation of retail prices).
Belgium is a member of Unesco.

9 Market Research

At present the Belgian book trade lacks the means of starting research in this field. Six years ago, nonetheless, a first step was taken in this direction, when, in cooperation with the University of Ghent, a project was started to assemble data on the structure of bookselling in general, with regard to general costs.
It has been established that many students at sociological institutes, schools for librarians, interpreters' institutes, etc. choose for their thesis subjects relating to publishing and bookselling. Thus they are interested in the problems of the trade, the role of the paperback, and the reading and leisure activities of youth. These were interesting efforts which, however, lack unity and coordination. They would have been of greater interest to the trade if the students had worked in closer collaboration with the book trade.

The trade remains aware of the urgent need for market research, encouraged by the results obtained and published in neighbouring countries.

10 Books and Young People

In Belgium, like everywhere else, the profession is conscious of the fact that its future will very largely depend on the interest that young people have in reading and in books generally. So it is a question of putting adequate books within reach of these young people.

Several examples show the interest in this field. The "Ministère de la Culture" ("Services de l'éducation populaire et des loisirs") regularly organizes travelling exhibitions of books for young people, and equips libraries. There are many different writers' organizations for young people who also arrange exhibitions and encourage their members to produce adequate reading material for youth.

It is also the custom in Belgium to give books to pupils at the end of the school year. This custom has been criticized recently—a tendency which writers for young people as well as the trade have firmly opposed, regarding it as the wrong way to create closer contacts between schools and books. It is hoped to achieve this by means other than "book prizes"; e.g. better-equipped school libraries, etc.

There are periodicals which exclusively review books for youth and in this way help librarians to choose from a multitude of books published for youth. The trade annually organizes a referendum showing the best books for youth, with the aim of attracting attention to book production and to reading matter for the young in general.

At the book fairs an important place is always reserved for books for young people; authors are invited to give young readers the chance of meeting them.

Radio and television services, too, broadcast programmes that create an interest in books. Several competitions organized in the interests of youth are endowed with prizes, among which books often have the place of honour.

11 Training

With few exceptions, bookselling in Belgium deals in small and medium-sized enterprises; very often they are family concerns, in which knowledge is passed from generation to generation. These enterprises, the most important sources of professional training, particularly on a practical basis, are however not always founded on a scientific basis.

So there is no professional training in the book trade through schools, institutes or special courses. A limited number of proprietors or employees have taken correspondence courses given either in the Netherlands or in France. Besides, there are schools for librarians, where certain courses (bibliography, book production, etc.) would no doubt be useful for the professional training of booksellers. Libraries as well as the professional associations have encouraged booksellers or apprentice booksellers to follow these courses.

From there, the gifted and the more studious have to read the professional literature to learn more, or else to attend courses abroad.

This situation could be improved if the financial and economical standing of the profession could be raised, but this is certainly not the case at present. Because of this few people are attracted to the trade; and here we have a vicious circle: relatively few new bookshops, slow economic evolution, unattractive salaries, little interest among young people in the book business, not enough professional aptitude, a great need for organized courses and insufficient interest in the prospective courses.

As for conditions, there are no special requirements for those who want to set up a bookshop. Anyone can open one; he has the right and the chance to do so. Thus there is no incentive to train first.
What is true for the bookseller with regard to professional training applies equally to the publisher. But here there often exists a link between publishing and printing as careers. There are special schools and institutions for training printers, and several of these courses are equally suitable for editors.

12 Taxes

Belgium being a member of the Common Market, the system of "tax on the additional value" has taken effect since January 1971. In this system books are taxed at 6%.

13 Clearing Houses

Such institutions do not exist in Belgium for the book trade.

14 Copyright

Copyright in Belgium is regulated by the laws of 22 and 27 March 1886 (as well as those of 25 June and 23 September 1921).
These laws assume rights for 50 years after the author's death, in the interests of his heirs or rightful claimants (while the law of 25 June 1921 provides for the extension of copyright for a time equal to that between 4 August 1914 and 4 August 1924 for all works published before the expiry of this term and which have not fallen into public domain on 25 June 1921).
Copyright does not exclude the right to quote when this is done for purposes of criticism, polemics or teaching. There is a move at present to limit the right of quotation in the interests of teaching; one has in mind especially anthologies, where certain quotations seem to go beyond the sphere of "quotation" in the eyes of the law.
Belgium adhered to the Berne Convention (9 Sept. 1886) and to the Universal Copyright Convention (20 Apr. 1960).
The "Société Belge des Auteurs, Compositeurs et Editeurs", Brussels, which numbers 5,000 affiliated members, has as its aim the consideration and distribution of copyright for its members as well as for foreign societies with whom it has reciprocal contracts. It awards literary and artistic prizes every year. A centre for mutual help and solidarity operates in the interests of cooperative members; it can also grant subsidies to cultural works.

15 National Bibliography, National Library

On 1 January 1966 the "dépôt légal" was inaugurated in Belgium (by the law of 8 April 1965). This law provides for the obligatory deposit in the

Bibliothèque Royale de Belgique
(Royal Library of Belgium)
4, Boulevard de l'Empereur
B 1000 Bruxelles

of a copy of each of their publications by the publishers on one hand, on the other by Belgian authors living in Belgium whose works are published abroad. The term "publication" also comprises all lithographic art productions including photographical works. Phonographic and cinematographic works are excluded from the law, but the government intends to propose similar legislation with regard to these works.
The legal deposit must allow the "Royal Library" to make a representative collection of national productions and to preserve this cultural heritage for future generations. The deposit also meets the need for establishing a complete list of everything published in the Kingdom (or

published abroad by Belgian authors living in Belgium) and of putting this list at the disposal of the public. Before the establishment of copyright deposit, the "Belgian Bibliography" section of the Royal Library tried to index all publications which appeared in Belgium, or were connected with Belgium, but did not always succeed. Indeed, many publications which are nowhere mentioned escaped research and others were sometimes acquired considerably later. Often these publications were presented to the Royal Library by publishers or authors, or else the Royal Library had to do the necessary research and buy the books.
Titles acquired in this way since 1874 were filed in the

Bibliographie de Belgique
(Belgian Bibliography)
4, Boulevard de l'Empereur
B 1000 Bruxelles

This organ continues to appear under this name, but is now based on the works of the legal deposit. The bibliography is published under the auspices of the Ministry of National Education and Culture, on which in turn the Royal Library depends. It is a systematic bibliography (12 issues per year) completed by an alphabetical index of authors' names, as well as titles of anonymous works and collections, and an alphabetical list of subjects.
With regard to the Royal Library itself: history mentions an institution of this name, created by Philip II in 1559. In 1594 a copyright deposit is mentioned, established in favour of this library. Under French reign the Royal Library was integrated into the "Library of the City of Brussels". In 1837 the new Belgian state decided to create a "National Library" based on Van Hulthem's collection of encyclopedias. Since then, the Royal Library has established itself as scientific library of great value.

16 Book Production

The book market in Belgium has always been influenced in great measure by French and Dutch publications. The importance of these publications can be evaluated at 65% to 70% of the complete market, and these proportions have been even less favourable to the country in the past. In spite of these imports, or rather, within the margin of these imports, Belgian publishing firms have been established and have been able to obtain an independent place which permits the tracing of the country's scientific and cultural evolution by means of the book.
The country's French publications specialize particularly in the field of the scientific, school and general books, books for the young, and books on art.
Dutch publications are concerned with literature and literary studies, schoolbooks and books for the young, general, and philosophical works.
Many publishing houses have a mixed output (in both French and Dutch). The Belgian book written in French has a vast market abroad; books written in Dutch are more particularly intended for the home market, as well as for export to the Netherlands.
Statistics of book publication in 1969 (provided by the Royal Library in Brussels) mention the following figures:

Subject group	Titles
General	196
Philosophy	239
Religion	282
Social science	824
Philology, linguistics	389
Pure science	415
Applied science	605
Fine arts	424
Literature	1,444
History and auxiliary sciences	429
Total	5,247

Belgium

Statistics given by the Royal Library to UNESCO for 1969 (here we are only concerned with non-periodical publications) mention a total of 5,089 titles. A classification according to the language of publication is added, which shows: Dutch—2,656; French—2,026; English—159; German—34; Latin—39; Spanish—8; Italian—2; bilingual or multilingual—163.

17 Translations

With the direct import of French books (original or translated into French) the question of the translation does not arise: the majority of Belgians read French.

With regard to translation of works in other languages: French and Dutch publishing firms are in a position to offer wider openings and markets than their Belgian colleagues. The result is that several translations of German, English or American books are published in France or the Netherlands, and these translations are exported to Belgium.

As to the translation of Belgian books abroad, considerable efforts are made by Belgian publishers in order to have their most important works translated. French-speaking Belgian publishers are succesful in the field of scientific publications and children's books, whereas Flemish publishers succeed in having novels and children's books translated, as well as philosophical and religious books.

This does not apply to literary classics, which also appear in Belgium, either in French or in Dutch.

18 Book Clubs

This phenomenon is not yet known in Belgium as it is in Germany, for example. What is practised in Belgium is the system of subscription on a series of works whose number and titles are known in advance and which are provided at a fixed rate for the series. There are 5, 10, or 12 titles at a fixed price, which is cheaper than buying each separately. The subscriber undertakes to buy the complete series.

There are also some associations or clubs which publish one book per month; this is offered to the members of these organizations, but here too there is a limited choice of works.

19 Paperbacks

Belgium has had its forerunners of the present form of paperbacks: going back in history, one could say that Christopher Plantin was one of the first (16th century) to publish classics annotated by scholars in pocket-size format. Later, a uniform presentation of popular books was produced during the Second World War. These editions had a fairly wide circulation.

Like everywhere else in Europe, the real avalanche of paperbacks began around 1950. In Belgium this particularly took the form of French and Dutch imports. The first series of French paperbacks to be published was of Belgian origin. After that, several collections of Belgian paperbacks appeared, books on literature as well as popular and poetic works.

20 Book Design

We can quote three drives in this field:

a) The "Graphica Belgica" prize.

b) The "Association of Belgian Publishers" competition for the 20 best-designed books.

c) The competition run by the "Association for the Promotion of the Flemish Book Trade" for the 20 best-designed books.

The "Graphica Belgica" prize is a foundation made by an important Belgian paper-mill. It runs for a seven-year cycle, during which, each year, the most beautiful books of a certain literary type are awarded prizes. The "Graphica Belgica" prize is worth 100,00 francs.

In 1962 the best art book was chosen; 1963: the best scientific book; 1964: the best literary book (not awarded); 1965: the religious book; 1966: the schoolbook; 1967: the children's book. In 1968 the jury judged paperback and popular editions. The requirements of the jury for the "Graphica Belgica" prize are—quite rightly—very exacting. They look for the composition of a representative collection of high value of Belgian graphic art.
The competition of the "Association of Belgian Publishers" (→ 4) takes place every two years and awards 20 books, chosen from the production of the two preceding years, without making any distinction between the types of work. The prize-winning books are exhibited abroad and in Belgium. The 20 books awarded every two years take and permit a good and fair choice.
For the same reason the "Association for the Promotion of the Flemish Book Trade" (→ 4) organizes its competition every two years and also chooses 20 books. They try to award books of different kinds as often as possible, as books are not always comparable (a paperback can have the same merits in its own field as a richly illustrated art book).

21 Publishing

In the French-speaking part of the country the master-printer is well-known, established for a century or more (certain firms are even two hundred years old) and running important publishing houses at the same time. During the period between the World Wars and after 1945 several new firms were established, particularly in the capital and in university towns like Liège and Louvain.
In the Dutch-speaking part of the country the situation is different. With few exceptions, publishing is rather young. There was a decline after the 17th century and a positive change did not appear until between 1920 and 1940 and after 1945. Several firms have a mixed output in French and Dutch; nevertheless there is always a clear tendency for one or the other national language to predominate. This is the result of a historical evolution determined by the orientation of respective markets (whether towards France or towards the Netherlands, though at the same time not neglecting the home market).
The existence of a printing firm has often been the basis for the foundation of a publishing house. This is not, however, the general rule, and several firms established since 1945 have no printing works of their own.
Important publishing centres are Brussels, Antwerp, Louvain and Liège, while towns like Tournai, Namur, Bruges and Tielt have important publisher-printers.
These thus tend to concentrate in the University towns (Brussels, Liège, Louvain). This is a slighter concentration, nevertheless, than in countries with larger geographic boundaries: the distances between larger towns are shorter in Belgium; because of this, transport and delivery problems practically never arise and the place of establishment is relatively unimportant.
Almost 300 publishing firms are recognized by the existing professional associations.
With regard to business statistics, Belgian output amounted (1965) to 500 million Belgian francs. (The value of imports reaches almost twice this amount.)

Subject group	Percentage of total production
General literature	32.0
Schoolbooks	22.0
Science, technology	17.0
Encyclopedias	14.0
Children's books	11.0
Religion	4.0
Total	100.0

No figures for distribution by each publisher or group of publishers exist.

22 Literary Agents

The influence of literary agents is rather small. There are few of them, and their main endeavour is to sell translations of Belgian works abroad.
The situation in this field is that publishers generally try to establish personal contact with foreign publishers.

23 Wholesale Trade

Like everywhere else, small orders are quite a heavy burden for the publishers as well as the bookseller. The wholesaler is therefore a normal phenomenon in the book trade and a blessing at the same time. To the problem of small orders is added the important one of the import of foreign books.
These two problems are solved by the existence of wholesalers and exclusive agents of foreign firms. With regard to the import of Dutch books, there are usually agents representing one or several Dutch firms exclusively. As for French books: there are fewer exclusive agents and the firms which import French editions are mostly wholesalers, who are in a position to provide books belonging to the most important firms.
The wholesaler cannot provide schoolbooks because of a very limited discount. Besides, since he runs his business on a purely commercial basis, he cannot stock the less popular works.
The creation by the trade itself of a central warehouse could resolve all the problems which exist in this field.

24 Retail Trade

Broadly speaking, we can distinguish three groups of booksellers or shopkeepers who sell books: the normal bookshop, storing a wide variety in big towns or important centres; newspaper shops which have a more or less wide variety of popular books and paperbacks; and newsdealers in small localities, who also sell paperbacks and very often provide schoolbooks for schools or local authorities. We can add to these big department stores which almost all run successful book sections, and mail-order firms.
The professional associations have about 1,700 affiliated bookshops to which must be added the same number of other outlets (newsdealers).
Important bookshops are concentrated in centres like Brussels, Antwerp and the university towns: Liège, Ghent and Louvain, and at Charleroi, Bruges, Mons and Malines.
In general, the number of important bookshops is not noticeably increasing. Existing firms nevertheless find the trade increasing. Besides, the popular books and paperbacks are sold quite readily at subsidiary outlets. This is a general phenomenon and has obliged the professional associations to strech the rules somewhat to ensure that only members of the associations get discount. The opportunities for affiliation have been widened for this purpose.

25 Mail-Order Bookselling

The fact that many less important localities do not possess a bookshop worthy of the name opens a vast field for mail-order sales. Some firms have specialized in this while several existing bookshops have a special service which takes care of mail orders.
Besides, encyclopedias, medical works, art books and series lend themselves to sales through book-hawkers. There are several specialists of this type who obtain, indeed, surprising results, proving at the same time

that in the public there exists a latent interest in books that needs only to be stimulated.

26 Antiquarian Book Trade, Auctions

The second-hand book trade for book-lovers and scientists is managed in Belgium by about forty firms, the majority of whom are found in Brussels and Liège, and some in Flanders (Antwerp, Ghent, Courtrai). These firms are grouped together under the

Syndicat Belge de la librairie ancienne et moderne
(Belgian Syndicate of Antiquarian and Modern Booksellers)
112, Rue de Trèves
B Bruxelles

This association was founded in 1946 and is joined to the "International League of Antiquarian Booksellers", of which it is one of the foundation members.

From time to time the association organizes book exhibitions. Belgian sellers of antiquarian books direct part of their activity towards the foreign market, particularly scientific works.

The death of important collectors, the dispersal of collections and the two World Wars greatly influenced the home market. After 1918 it became a market which is orientated towards topography, folklore, local history, etc.

The number of public auctions is very restricted. Brussels and Liège remain relatively important centres.

27 Book Imports

Belgium is pre-eminently an importer of books. The value of imports is about double that of the value of Belgian book production.

Official statistics give the following figures for the years 1967 and 1969:

1967	1969
912 m. b.fr.	1,145 m. b.fr.

which is an increase of more than 25% in two years. One must of course take into account price rises during this period.

For 1969 the most important sources were the following countries:

Country	Amount b.fr. 1,000
France	541,000
Netherlands	400,883
Germany (Federal Republic)	45,245
USA	36,331
Switzerland	38,684
United Kingdom	25,600
Italy	50,973

There is a clear predominance of French and Dutch imports: from 1967 to 1969 there is an increase of value on French imports of about 13% (from 479 to 541 m. b.fr.); during the same period the value of Dutch imports increased by about 34% (from 298 to 400 m. b.fr.). About 85% of the total of Belgian imports come from France and the Netherlands.

28 Book Exports

For the years 1967 and 1969 official statistics give the following figures:

1967	1969
890 m. b.fr.	1,181 m. b.fr.

which shows an increase of about 9.2% in the total value. With regard to the year 1969 we can give the following subdivision:

Country	Amount b. fr. 1,000
France	649,000
Netherlands	199,000
Canada	55,000
United Kingdom	55,000
USA	58,000
Congo (Kinshasa)	21,000
Switzerland	47,000
Germany (Federal Republic)	40,000

Belgium

Most foreign countries count as a more or less important market for Belgian books written in French. This is not the case for Belgian books written in Dutch, whose only market is the Netherlands and to a very small extent the South African Republic. About 80% of total exports are therefore books written in French.
If France and the Low Countries are Belgium's most important book-providers (→ 27), these two countries are also the best markets for Belgian books. As the table shows, France imports more than one half of Belgiums exports. From 1967 to 1969 the value of exports to France increased by more than 37% (from 470 to 649 m. b.fr.). During the same period exports to the Netherlands rose from 148 to 199 m. b.fr., that is about 34%.
The publicity work of the "Syndicat des Editeurs Belges" (→ 4) abroad has considerably influenced Belgian exports. The Syndicat takes part in several fairs and exhibitions, distributes publicity material, and tries to establish selling sources for Belgian books. This is particularly so in Canada, "L'Association pour la diffusion à l'étranger des éditions belges" (→ 4) tries on its part to promote the export of Belgian editions, particularly to the Congo (Kinshasa). This was the special aim of founding the Association in 1962.

29 Book Fairs

Fairs and exhibitions organized in Belgium aim to draw the public's attention towards books elsewhere than in the bookshop. With this aim in mind well-known localities situated in the town centres are chosen.
Since 1932 the "Vereniging ter bevordering van het Vlaamse Boekwezen" (→ 4) organizes a yearly fair of books in the Dutch language in Antwerp. The "Syndicat des Editeurs Belges" (→ 4) has since 1964 been organizing a similar fair in Brussels, exclusively for Belgian publications. From 1969 onwards this fair has been organized as an international event (→ International Section, 29).
These central events have served as an example for local or regional fairs, organized with the help of cultural or literary associations in the region, youth movements, etc.
Official authorities help by organizing travelling exhibitions of books for young people, beautiful books, etc. The „Syndicat des Editeurs" does interesting work by organizing exhibitions of Belgian books abroad.

30 Public Relations

Organs existing under the auspices of the professional associations (→ 4) deal exclusively with collective publicity about books and reading. This publicity takes the form of posters, displays of books as presents for different occasions (Christmas, parents' birthdays, end of school year, Easter, etc.).
In spring and autumn great numbers of publicity pamphlets are distributed; on the occasion of the book fair, a publicity year-book is distributed. During the year special pamphlets are issued, dealing with specific subjects: tourism, dictionaries, books for young people, etc.
Some of this material is sent free of charge to the members, who can order additional copies at cost price.
Discussions and other activities, organized during book fairs, as well as general publicity, attract the attention of the press, radio and television throughout the country. In this way the masses are reached. The professional associations sponsor good relations with the press, radio and television. Here there are several opportunities to speak about books, authors and the book trade.

31 Bibliophily

Before 1914 there were quite a large number of important universal libraries, owned by well-known individual collectors. The death of many collectors and the war have been responsible for the disappearance of most of these great private libraries. There remains a limited number of important collectors and genuine booklovers.
This fact does not apply to modern bibliophily, which is still much practised, as well as that relating to topography, folklore, local history, etc.
The following are among the best-known bibliophile societies:

Société des bibliophiles et iconophiles de Belgique
(Belgian Bibliophile and Iconophile Society)
4, Boulevard de l'Empereur
B Bruxelles

The Society publishes 4 or 5 numbers annually of a periodical entitled *Le livre et l'estampe* ("Book and Engraving").

Vereniging der Antwerpsche Bibliophielen
(Antwerp Bibliophile Society)
Museum Plantin-Moretus,
Vrijdagmarkt 22
B 2000 Antwerpen

This Society, founded in 1877 by Max Rooses (curator of the Plantin-Moretus Museum), aims at encouraging knowledge of old books, principally in the area of the former Low Countries (Belgium and the present Netherlands). It publishes a review: *De Gulden Passer* ("The Golden Compass"), which is devoted to the study of the history of books. Since 1877 the Society has published an imposing series of works; its aim is to continue the publication of these studies.

32 Literary Prizes

There is a multitude of literature prizes, awarded either after the appearance of the works, or in the form of a competition before the appearance, in which the jury decides at manuscript stage. In the latter case they are generally voluntary efforts—not very frequent—undertaken by certain publishers or competitions organized under their auspices.
The prizes awarded after the appearance of works are more numerous, and these consist of prizes donated by official representations and academies, and prizes awarded by voluntary efforts and by cultural associations.
The state awards two *Prix quinquennal de l'Etat—Vijfjaarlijkse Staatsprijs* ("Quinquennial state award"); one for the French-speaking and one for the Dutch-speaking part of the country. They are awarded for an author's complete works. Then there are the *Prix trisannuel de l'Etat—Driejaarlijkse staatsprijs* ("Triennial state award"), awarded by the state to the French-speaking and the Dutch-speaking parts of the country respectively. These are awarded for poetry, drama and novels. Each of the nine provinces has its own literature prize.
Further, there is the *Prix des provinces flamandes—Prijs van de Vlaamse provincies* ("Literary award of the Flemish provinces") for poetry, prose, drama and books for young people. *Prix de l'académie de langue et littérature française* ("Award of the Royal Academy of French Language and Literature") has its own literature prizes for several types of book. They all have different names, e. g. the *Prijzen van de Koninklijke Vlaamse Academie voor taal- en letterkunde* ("Awards of the Royal Flemish Academy of Language and Literature"). The *Prijs der Nederlandse Letteren* ("Award of Dutch literature") is awarded alternately to a Dutch author and a Belgian author

writing in Dutch, at the annual conference of Dutch Arts.
The following are prizes awarded by private initiative and cultural associations: *Scriptores Catholici, Sabam, Bernheim, Reinert, Rossel, L. J. Krijn.*

33 The Reviewing of Books

The important newspapers carry an art and cultural page at least once a week, where the most important books are listed. When we consider the many books published, both Belgian and foreign—and considering the need to devote sufficient attention to books appearing in Belgium—not enough space is made available.
Radio (two national programmes and eight regional stations) has regular literary news, or news concerning books or authors. Television (two stations) includes regular programmes devoted to books.
In the Dutch-speaking part of the country there are a number of specialist magazines that deal exclusively with book lists for public libraries *(Boekengids* and *Lektuurgids)*. They provide a service which permits librarians to make a choice from among the multitude of books on the market.
One of these periodicals *(Boekengids)* has published a catalogue in three volumes; *(Lektuurrepertorium)*, comprising all indexed works. Authors' names are given in alphabetical order, with notes on each work for the use of librarians; this is a work of documentation which is unique in conception.
As to the French-speaking part of Belgium, we mention the *Répertoire alphabétique de 16,700 auteurs. 70,000 romans et pièces de théâtre, cotés au point de vue moral* ("Alphabetical repertory of 17,600 authors. 70,000 novels and plays, judged from a moral point of view"), Ed. Casterman, Tournai.
Here is a list of the most important journals and periodicals, having a literary page or dealing with book-review in a general way: (F = French; D = Dutch)

Journals

Het Volk, Forelstraat 22, Ghent—D
Het Belang van Limburg, Stationsplein 11, Hasselt—D
Het Laatste Nieuws, Em. Jacqmainlaan 105, Brussels—D
De Standaard, Em. Jacqmainlaan 127, Brussels—D
Gazet van Antwerpen, Nationalestraat, Antwerp—D
Journal de Charleroi, 20 rue du Collège, Charleroi – F
La Cité, rue St. Laurent 14, Brussels—F
La Dernière Heure, 52 rue du Pont-Neuf, Brussels—F
La Lanterne, 50 place de Brouckère, Brussels—F
La Libre Belgique, Montagne-aux-Herbes-Potagères 12, Brussels—F
Le Soir, Place de Louvain 21, Brussels—F
Volksgazet, Somersstraat 22, Antwerp—D

Periodicals (cultural and literary)

De Periscoop, Nationalestraat 46, Antwerp—D
Dietsche Warande en Belfort, Belgiëlei 147, Antwerp—D
La Revue Nationale, 35 avenue Van Goolen, Brussels—F
Le Thyrse, 22 rue Albertine, Rixensart—F
Marginale, 12 rue Marie-Henriette, Brussels—F
Nieuw Vlaams Tijdschrift, Somersstraat 22, Antwerp—D
Revue Générale Belge, 22 rue de la Limite, Brussels 3—F
Spectator, Forelstraat 22, Gent—D
Streven, Frankrijklei 91, Antwerp—D
Synthèses, 63 rue Gachard, Brussels 5—F
Vlaamse Gids, Em. Jacqmainlaan 105, Brussels—D

34 Graphic Arts

The Belgian graphic industry is grouped under the auspices of an association:

Union des industries graphiques et du livre
Unie der grafische bedrijven en het boek
(U.N.I.G.R.A.)
(Union of the Graphic and Book Industries)
76 Rue Renkin
B Bruxelles

which comprises printers, compositors, bookbinders and other branches of the country's graphic industries. There are also several regional and provincial groups of printers.

Bulgaria

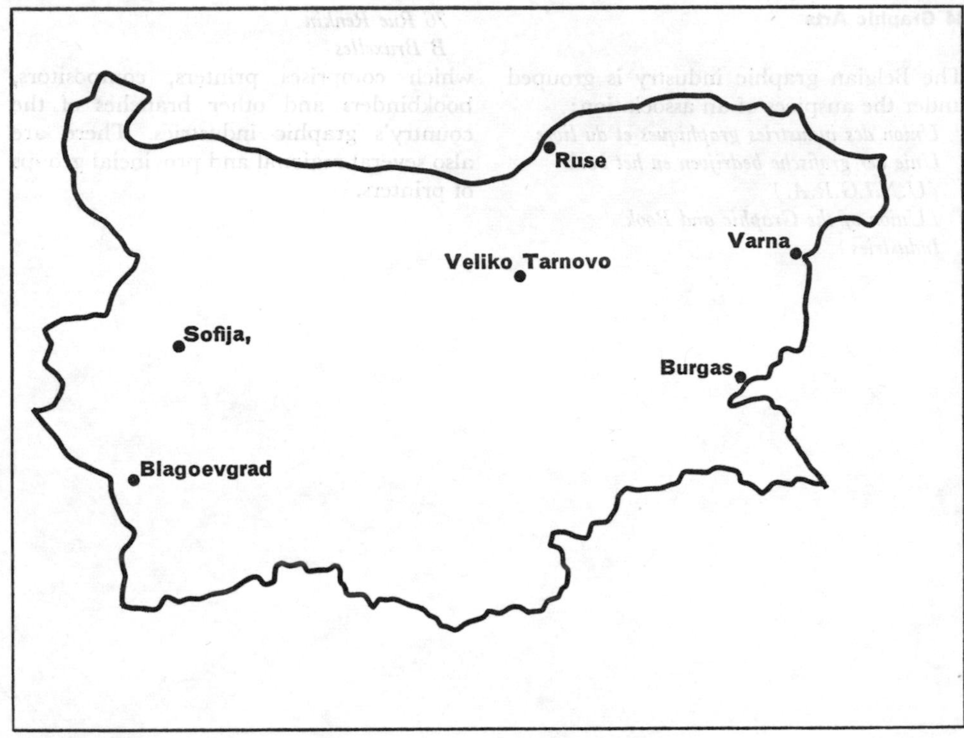

Important Book Centres

1 General Information

Area 111,000 km²
Population 8,500,000 (ca. 75 per km²)
Capital Sofia (1,000,000)
Largest towns Sofia (1,000,000); Plovdiv (223,000); Varna (180,000); Rousse (130,000); Bourgas (106,000); Pernik (76,000); Shoumen (60,000)
Government A People's Republic. Supreme legislative body: the National Assembly. Head of State: the President of the Presidium of the National Assembly. Administrative division: 30 districts
Religion Eastern Orthodox (Church separated from the State). Mohammedan and Jewish religious communities
National language Bulgarian
Leading foreign languages Russian, German, English, French
Weights and measures Metric system
Currency unit Lev
Education Compulsory; University students 82,000, of which 35,000 women
Illiteracy Nil
Paper consumption a) Newsprint 3.5 kg per inhabitant (1967)
b) Printing paper (other than newsprint) 4.8 kg per inhabitant (1967)
Membership UNESCO

2 Past and Present

The oldest written documents of the First Bulgarian Kingdom, founded by the Old Bulgar tribal chieftain Khan Asparouh in A. D. 680, show the two basic components of the Bulgarian people—Slavs and Old Bulgars (a Turkic-Tatar tribe)—to have reached a definite cultural level in the 7th and 8th centuries.

The earliest Bulgarian sovereigns felt the need of creating their own alphabet and literature for greater unity, and to ward off the strong Byzantine influence. King Boris I, who for both internal and external reasons decided to convert the Bulgarian people to Christianity, used the services of the two Christian missionaries Cyril and Methodius, who composed the first Slavonic (Cyrillic) alphabet in 855. The Gospel and other books of church ritual were thus translated into the native tongue of the South-Bulgarian Slavs. After preaching the Christian teachings in South and South-West Bulgaria, Cyril and Methodius were sent by the Patriarchy in Constantinople to the Kingdom of Moravia. After the adoption of Christianity, King Boris I invited five pupils of Cyril and Methodius to return to Bulgaria and engage in missionary and educational work. One of them, Clement, created at Ochrida (South-West Bulgaria) a large religious and lay school. Sofia State University has been named after Clement of Ochrida.

The creation of Slav-Bulgarian religious and worldly literature in the common language of the people did much to promote the rapid cultural development of the Bulgarian and other Slav peoples. The cultural and historic heritage of the nation was made accessible to every section of society (unlike many countries in Western Europe, in which the use of Latin kept people estranged from written culture).

Two cultural centres gradually emerged—at Preslav and Ochrida—which flourished during the reign of the son of Boris I, Simeon the Great (893–927), when his military power englobed almost the whole of the Balkan Peninsula, the Belgrade region, Albania, and the Carpathians including the territories between the Tissa and Dniester rivers.

Towards the end of the 9th and early in the 10th century the Bulgarian writers Joan Exarch, Chernorizets Hrabr, Presbyter Cosma and others wrote original works like the Six-Day Book, the Written Characters, Lifework of Cyril and Methodius, The Lives of Clement and Naoum, and others. The significance attached to literature is illustrated by the fact that Tsar Simcon I and his household, Tsar Peter I and many courtiers won distinction as authors and translators.

This period also witnessed the appearance of original Bulgarian schools of art, architecture and church music. The writings and translations of Bulgarian educators were copied and circulated in all other Slav countries, which readily adopted the Cyrillic alphabet, as phonetically more perfect.

Slav literature helped preserve and develop the national feelings and culture of the Bulgarian people from medieval times to our day. Books which even the common people could read and understand did more than spread the Christian teachings. The Bogomil movement (then called a dualistic heresy) appeared towards the middle of the 10th century in opposition to an oppressive feudal order. As a religious teaching with a marked social and revolutionary background, Bogomilism gained rapid popularity because it taught social equality, peace and insubordination to the king and his boyars. It influenced literature, as many apocrypha spread inside and beyond the confines of the land. Together with the Bogomil missionaries, these books spread the heresy to Serbia, Croatia, Northern Italy,

France and Kievite Russia, where its adherents were known as Bugri or Bulgari. The Bogomils undoubtedly influenced the teachings of the Patarines, Albigenses and Cathari, for whom the Bogomil "Secret Book" (also known as the Book of St. John), served as ideological guidance. The Bogomil legends about Baruch's Revelation, Enoch, Adam and Eve, and others gained broad popularity.

After the death of Simeon and his son Peter I, the feudal division of the country, the devastation of incessant warfare and the cruel exploitation of the people undermined the military power of the kingdom. After long struggles and the fall of Ochrida, capital of the Western Bulgarian Kingdom, Bulgaria fell under Byzantine rule. Several insurrections failed and it was only in 1185 that the boyars Assen and Peter rallied the people and freed the country from Byzantium. Veliko Tarnovo was the centre of the uprising, and became the capital of the Second Bulgarian Kingdom. Under Kaloyan and Assen II, who together with the former territories resumed the title of "King of all Bulgarians and Greeks", Bulgaria reached an unprecedented peak of prosperity. The head of the Bulgarian Church was given the title of Patriarch, and the church gained complete autonomy.

Official writings and Bogomil apocrypha flourished as Veliko Tarnovo grew into a new Bulgarian cultural centre. Although literature, art and music tolerated the influence of Byzantine church canon, there were original Bulgarian developments. Until the Ottoman Conquest of the Balkans, Bulgarian literature was under the strong influence of mysticism.

The Patriarchal and Royal Libraries at Veliko Tarnovo, and those at the Ochrida and Mount Athos monasteries, had vast literary collections. Works, the significance of which far transcended the borders of the country, were created by writers and thinkers like Theodossi of Tarnovo, Patriarch Evtimi, Cyprian, Gregori Tsamblak, Joasaph of Bdin, and others. Cyprian (later Metropolitan bishop of Moscow), Gregori Tsamblak and Konstantin Kostenechki emigrated to Russia or Serbia and there continued their literary activities.

Valuable written works of the period include the Teter Gospel of 1322, Ivan-Alexander's Gospel of 1356, the Vidin Collection of 1360, the so-called Vatican Chronicle of 1345, the Ochrida Psalter, the Skoplie Minei and Sofia Octoechos liturgical books, the indexed Rila Gospel, and others, many of them tastefully illuminated.

Art and wood-carving made similar progress during the 13th and 14th centuries, principally in the decoration of churches and palaces. Many architectural and artistic monuments of this period have been damaged or destroyed, but even those which have been preserved show evidence of a true Bulgarian Renaissance, preceding by half a century the Renaissance in Italy.

But the Bulgarian state—which during the reign of Ivan Assen II spread south to the Peloponnesus, east to the Adriatic Sea, north-west to Hungary and north-east to the river Dniester—was not fated to live in peace for long. Tatars, Byzantines and Magyars menaced its borders. High taxes and feudal bondage soon led the people to revolt. The swineherd Ivailo united the people, defeated the boyars one after another and showed outstanding military talent in dispersing foreign invaders. He finally ascended to the throne at Veliko Tarnovo, where he was crowned. This is one of the very few, and perhaps only, people's movement in Europe crowned with success, though of short duration. Several centuries before Thomas Müntzer and Joan of Arc, the common swineherd Ivailo, backed by the Bogomils and the people, showed that the people are able to cope with all local and foreign oppressors.

After the popular leader Ivailo fell prey to the intrigues of his foes, the political situation of the country quickly deteriorated. The Ottoman Conquest of the Balkans found Bulgaria weakened by internal struggles and constant warfare. In spite of the stubborn resistance of the last Bulgarian king, Ivan Shishman, and of certain boyars, the country was subjugated. Quarreling among themselves, the Balkan peoples realized when it was too late that they should have joined forces against the Asiatic invasion.

This was a long and hard period for the Bulgarian people, but they never lost heart. The Turks settled in the plains and gradually drove the Bulgarians towards the mountains. The attempt to convert the people to Islam was stubbornly resisted and many preferred death rather than change their faith. Many national rebellions and guerrilla detachments weakened the rear of the Ottoman forces, which after the conquest of the Balkans planned to conquer the whole of Europe. Such rebellions broke out at the decisive moments when the Ottoman armies advanced into Hungary and reached the walls of Vienna.

The monasteries, as cultural centres in out-of-the-way places, did much to preserve the patriotic feeling of the Bulgarian people during the five centuries of Ottoman rule. The monks copied old books, painted icons, made wonderful woodcarved iconostases.

Some of the old books were saved: in Russia, Serbia and the Ottoman vassal principalities of Walachia and Moldavia. Bulgarian medieval literature found its second home. During the 15th and 16th centuries these close relations between Walachians, Moldavians and Bulgarians created a number of famous literary works, such as the Rumano-Bulgarian Alexandria in 1563, the works of the monk Asynchritus in 1486, the Kotel Writings, and many others. In 1508 the monk Makari printed at Turgovishte (then capital city of the Walachian Principality) a church service book, and the Gospel in 1512. They are among the first Bulgarian printed books, representative of the Tarnovo literary school.

As the Ottoman government would not allow the opening of Bulgarian educational institutions and printing houses on the territories of subjugated Bulgaria, books for a long time were copied by hand and circulated among the people. The monasteries did useful work in this field until the middle of the 19th century. In the meantime Bulgarian writers living in exile published their works in a number of European countries, which in one way or another eventually reached Bulgaria.

Jacob Traikov of Sofia is thought to be the first Bulgarian printer, editor and publisher. He learned the printer's trade in Venice, where in 1566 he published the church service book "Chasoslovets" in the West Bulgarian dialect. Another Bulgarian, Peter Stanislavov, Catholic bishop for the whole of Bulgaria, in 1691 compiled and printed a collection under the title of "Agabar". The Bulgarian catholic priest Krustiu Peykich published, in Venice in 1717, a polemic work in Latin against Mohammedanism, which was highly valued by European philosophers and theologians.

The middle of the 18th century witnessed a sharp economic and cultural upsurge of the Bulgarian people, and a noticeable disintegration of the once mighty Ottoman Empire.

This whole period of oppressive Ottoman rule, rebellions, guerrilla warfare and outstanding heroism left deep traces in the development of folk art—songs, tales and legends of the rebel guerrillas, many of which have been preserved and enjoy popularity down to our day.

Literature also made progress, especially in the form of accounts of the lifework of

national saints—militants defending the Orthodox faith.
The Slav-Bulgarian History written in 1762 by the monk Paissy of Hilendar Monastery is considered to have marked the beginning of the Bulgarian National Revival Period, and a new stage in the struggle for freedom. This remarkable book has many elements of the new Bulgarian language. It was copied and circulated in hundreds of copies, appearing in print several decades later.
Many writers gained popularity by works describing the suffering of the Bulgarian people, calling upon the nation to rise against the oppressors. As printing on the territory of Bulgaria was persecuted, many of these works were published in Vienna, Leipzig, Brashova, Belgrade, Odessa, Moscow, Constantinople, and elsewhere. Some 360 Bulgarian books were published between 1825 and 1850, and about 2,000 between 1850 and 1878, when Bulgaria won freedom from Ottoman rule. Only few were set in Bulgarian printing houses, which were almost clandestine. The first printing office on Bulgarian territory was opened in 1823 at Samokov, soon followed by one at the village of Vatosha in the district of Tikvesh (1838) and another at Salonica, where a large part of the population in those days was Bulgarian. Their limited capacity could not meet the requirements of Bulgarian schools, and most of the books, papers and periodicals published abroad were smuggled into Bulgaria and circulated in secret.
The middle of the 19th century produced the first great names in Bulgarian literature, which will always be associated with the country's struggle for freedom. Hristo Botev, Lyuben Karavelov, Georgi Rakovski and P. R. Slaveikov were not only talented writers; they were also the leaders of the national revolutionary movement. The struggle for political and spiritual freedom formed the basic contents of Bulgarian literature between the fifties and seventies of the 19th century, regardless of views and orientations, which finally crystallized in two parties—the Educators and the Revolutionaries. The first Bulgarian publishing houses were organized, creating a periodical press. Hristo G. Danov opened his publishing house in 1856 with the calendar book "Staroplaninche".
Until Bulgaria's liberation from Ottoman rule in 1878, book publishing had a strongly non-commercial character. Books were written, printed and circulated not to bring profit to their authors, printers or publishers, but for the cultural and patriotic enlightenment of the people. Most editions were financed by preliminary subscriptions.
After several national rebellions, suppressed with much bloodshed, the last of which was the April Uprising of 1876, Bulgaria finally won national freedom as a result of the Russo-Turkish War of 1877–78, in which many Bulgarians fought as volunteers. This war of liberation did away with the Ottoman feudal system and marked the beginning of the capitalist development of the country, the rise of a Bulgarian bourgeoisie and its antithesis—the Bulgarian proletariat. There was an intensive cultural life and literary trends generally reflected West European and Russian opinion. Compulsory elementary school education quickly raised the cultural level of the people in town and country, and the number of readers steadily increased.
Soon almost all works of the world's classic writers appeared in Bulgarian translation. A small nation, for five centuries under alien rule, made bold strides to catch up with the other countries of Europe. New machinery, type and equipment created a modern printing trade. The Hristo G. Danov publishing house in Plovdiv was followed by the publishers Chipev, Hemus, the Ignatov Bros., New World, and others in the capital.

Bulgaria had internal and external problems similar to those of other West European states. In addition to the two World Wars, Bulgaria was involved in three others: the Serbo-Bulgarian war of 1888, the Balkan war of 1912, and the Inter-Allied Balkan war of 1913. One started feeling the influence of the socialist and workers' movement, which organized their own publishing houses and circulated socialist literature. Even during the years when the Bulgarian Communist Party was persecuted and led a clandestine existence it never stopped its publications, often using underground printing shops, stencilled editions, and even materials copied and circulated by hand.

There was a strong interest in foreign literature. Some 2,169 books were published in 1939 in a total of 6,484,000 copies (averaging about 3,000 copies per title). During this period the publishing trade was not properly organized and its equipment was not up to European standards. The prices of books were high, compared with the income of the people, and especially the poor rural population could not buy them. The public reading rooms were widely used in both town and country, and such rooms were opened at almost all inhabited localities. The book trade was in the hands of private enterprise. Specialized book stores did not exist. Usually school book stores sold literary publications.

The publishing trade really developed after the overthrow of fascist rule and the establishment of the People's Government on 9 September 1944. A referendum in 1946 abolished the monarchy and set up a socialist form of government. A radical change took place in every sphere of economic, cultural and social life. The publishing trade was organized on a socialist basis, in the form of a system of state publishers, which took over the assets of the private publishing enterprises. The prices of books fell sharply and circulation increased. Printing equipment was modernized. Specialized bookstores were opened, and today seven books are published per capita a year, including foreign books and translations.

3 Retail Prices

Book prices of both fiction and technical literature in Bulgaria are among the very lowest in the world, fixed by a "Unified State Price List," approved by decision No. 158 dated 5 May 1964 of the Council of Ministers. Under special circumstances a maximum of 20% price fluctuation is permissible. Prices are estimated per folio. The lowest price is that of textbooks—2.2 to 5 stotinki per folio; social and political literature—between 3 and 11 stotinki; fiction—4 to 6 stotinki; dictionaries and encyclopedias—5 to 8 stotinki; technical manuals—4 to 11 stotinki, and so on.

There is also a price list for the various types of binding, depending upon the materials, the size of the books and the number of printed copies:

- bindings of fiction and scientific editions—2 to 55 stotinki
- textbooks—to 28 stotinki
- books for children— 3 to 25 stotinki
- jackets—3 to 28 stotinki. Paperbacks are not charged extra for the binding.

The standard price can be increased by 2 stotinki whenever there is a coloured frontispiece. All prices are price maintained.

4 Organization

The printing and sale of books in Bulgaria is a monopoly of the state and social organizations. The work of the publishing sector is coordinated, planned and supplied by the

Državno Obedinenie "Bulgarska Kniga"
(State Association "Bulgarian Book")
Pl. Slavejkov 11
BG Sofia

which forms part of the system of the
Komitet za Izkoustvo i Koultoura
(Committee for Art and Culture)
Boul. Stamboliisky No. 18
BU Sofia

Bulgaria has 22 publishing houses: 20 in Sofia, 1 in Plovdiv and 1 in Varna. "Bulgarska Kniga" coordinates their plans and supervises the constant improvement of the quality of print and sale prices.

The work is divided among the various publishing houses on a thematic basis. For instance, "Narodna Prosveta", as organ of the Ministry of Education, supplies the educational institutions with textbooks, manuals, maps, visual aids, etc. The "Technica Publishing House" deals with original or translated technical manuals; "Medizina i Fizkultura" occupies itself with the problems of medicine, public health and sports, working in coordination with the Ministry of Public Health. "Narodna Mladezh" ("People's Youth") is an organ of the "Dimitrov Communist Youth Union", publishing literature for people up to the age of twenty-five. The "Union of Bulgarian Writers" also has its own publishers for the works of Bulgarian writers and poets, regardless of whether they happen to be members or not.

"Bulgarska Kniga" has set up a special "Book Circulation Service", which has offices at all district centres (30). Each district office directs the sale of books by the local stores at all inhabited localities.

6 Book-Trade Literature

Various forms are used to publicize books. "Bulgarska Kniga" (→ 4) publishes the central monthly
Informacionen bjuletin "Bulgarski Knigi"
(Information Bulletin "Bulgarian Books")
Pl. Slavejkov 11
BG Sofia

with brief annotations regarding the books which the respective publishing houses are planning to print. The "Bulletin" also surveys books which have appeared, gives the opinions of specialists, advises people as to what books they might add to their private libraries or to the local public reading rooms, etc. Some of the district services also publish "Bulletins" advising readers and bibliophiles where they might find certain books. Each publishing house prints its annual catalogues, folders, leaflets and posters. The book trade is also given publicity in the literary press, special radio and television programmes public readings, etc.

The "Bulgarian Bibliographical Institute", now united with the "National Library" in Sofia (→ 15) publishes year-books, monthly information sheets, and various bibliographical studies. Bibliographical studies were started in 1858 with the publication of the magazine "Bulgarian Bibliophile."

10 Books and Young People

Bulgarian youth is the best reader and buyer of books, and the most regular library visitor. Students, industrial and farm workers have bought or drawn from libraries thousands of different books, showing their versatile interests. Modern and classic Bulgarian and foreign authors enjoy equal popularity. Together with the works of writers and poets, young people in Bulgaria buy popular science publications, adventure stories, and purely scientific works and manuals.

The "Narodna Mladezh" ("People's Youth") Publishing House is one of the largest in Bulgaria, with 10 specialized editorial boards. Books for children and young people are published in 5,000 to 80,000 copies. These include stories, poetry, long and short novels by Bulgarian authors, as well as the works of foreign authors like the Brothers Grimm, Andersen, L. Caroll, J. Radari, Alexei Tolstoy, and others.

Books for children and young people include the series "The Golden Library", "Stories from All Over the World", "Favourite Books and Heroes", "The Small Historic Library", "Meridians", "Names from Centuries Past". The publishing house "Bulgarian Writer" has a popular Library of the Student, helping young people at school to learn about the works of Bulgarian and world classics. Adventure stories, travelogues and the like are published mainly by the "Publishing House of the Ministry of National Defence".
The "Narodna Prosveta" publishing house occupies itself mainly with textbooks, manuals, visual aids and other accessories used by our educational institutions at all levels.
The low prices of books make it possible even for very young people to start a library of various editions in Bulgarian, Russian, German, English and French.
Publishing houses and the specialized papers and periodicals for young people always have book reviews to help orientate young readers. Teachers of literature also play their part in this respect. The public libraries and reading-rooms have consulting services to direct young people's reading.
Bulgaria's Constitution and its laws do not allow publications directed against the spirit of peace, or preaching racial discrimination, hatred and ideas conducive to criminal tendencies.

11 Training

The training of editorial staff, proofreaders, typesetters and other specialists in the printing industry takes place within the general framework of the national educational plan. "Bulgarska Kniga" (→ 4) trains commercial workers for the book trade. Bookstore attendants must have at least a secondary education. Knowledge of foreign languages is required at all bookstores selling foreign books, papers and periodicals. "Bulgarska Kniga" organizes regular language courses for this category of employees.
Higher executives in the book trade must have a university degree in Bulgarian literature, bibliography, library work, or economics.

14 Copyright

All literary, artistic, architectural, decorative works and films are protected by the Copyright Law of 1951, with addenda of 1956. It also covers photographs, choreographic productions and pantomime.
Protection is given to authors personally, or to scientific institutions or public bodies, for collected works or studies which they may compile.
Radio (a state institution) has the right to broadcast works which have been published or performed.
Copyright is granted for the life time of the author, but rights are limited to 10 years for film productions, scenarios, and to five years for photographs. The copyright of juridical persons or corporate bodies is protected for a period of 15 years. Terms always run from 1 January of the year during which the work has been published or produced.
Copyright is inherited, as follows:
Until the author's descendants reach majority. If continuing their studies—until their 24th year.
If those claiming under the author are incapacitated they draw benefits under the copyright until their condition improves (possibly until the end of their days).
The author's parents or surviving spouse can draw copyright benefits to the end of their days. If the surviving spouse remarries, the right lapses.
Copyright does not pass from one heir to another. With the death of those claiming directly under the author, rights lapse.

Copyright acquired by testament is limited to a period of 10 years.
The law gives protection against plagiarism.
Bulgaria is a signatory to the Berne Convention (revised in Rome in 1928), but has not yet ratified the Stockholm version of 1967. Legal protection is given to authors of other countries, not affiliated with the Berne Union, on condition that the work has been first published in Bulgaria.

Bibliography

L. AVRAMOV AND V. TADJER, *Avtorsko i Izdatelsko Pravo Varhu Nauchni i Literatourni Proizvedenia.* (Authors' and publishers' rights over scientific and literary works.) Sofia 1956. 290 pp.

L. AVRAMOV, *Copyright and legal contracts.* In: Archiv für Urheber-, Film-, Funk- und Theaterrecht, vol. 50, pp. 98–128. Baden-Baden 1957. – In English.

L. AVRAMOV AND V. TADJER, *Avtorsko Pravo v Narodna Republika Bulgaria.* (Copyright in the People's Republic of Bulgaria.) Sofia 1965. 321 pp.

15 National Bibliography, National Library

Two types of bibliographical surveys have been organized: current and retrospective. The task has been assigned to the National Library, "Cyril and Methodios," in Sofia. The most important publications in this field are

1) Bulgarski Knizhitsi
("Bulgarian Books")
a monthly publication with quarterly suplements.

2) Bulgarski Knigopis
("Bulgarian Bibliography")
monthly.

3) Letopis na Periodicnia Pechat
("Chronicle of the Periodical Press")
every other month, with annotations. A retrospective survey of all books which have been published so far is planned to appear in the near future in 12 volumes. For the moment quite a full description of Bulgarian literary works has been given in Ivan Bogdanov's *Bulgarskata Literatoura v Dati i Karakteristiki 817–1965* ("Bulgarian literature, dated and characterized"), Sofia 1965. A complete bibliographical survey of the Bulgarian periodical press is contained in a two-volume edition under the title *Bulgarski Periodichen Pechat, 1844–1944* ("The Bulgarian periodical press 1844–1944"). A third volume will cover the period 1944–68.

The Bulgarian National Library "Cyril and Metodius"
Bulgarska Narodna Biblioteka
"Kiril i Metodi"
Boul. Tolboukhin 11
BG Sofia
was founded in 1878, right after Bulgaria's liberation from Ottoman rule.

The library is now housed in one of the most monumental and stylish buildings in the capital within a small park in the central part of the city, facing "Sofia State University". The Library has over one million old and new books, manuscripts, archive documents, ancient graphic inscriptions, and other works. In 1966 the books alone numbered 688,000. Together with Bulgarian books published in this country and abroad, the National Library has all translated editions of Bulgarian authors, which have appeared in some 80 foreign languages. There are also many foreign books, including rarities. Valuable copies are found in its "Oriental Department".

The library is open to all people with a scientific interest, regardless of nationality or citizenship. Applicants are issued cards entitling them to access to the specialized reading rooms. The public reading rooms are open to all.

Alphabetical, systematic and thematic catalogues orientate visitors. They list the books available in ordinary and specialized

reading rooms. Rare books and manuscripts and documents are listed separately by each section and department of the library. Readers also have access to index cards for periodicals and magazines, a special catalogue for UN publications, for articles in the press, for bibliographical references, for reviews, for new Bulgarian novels, art, medicine, etc.
The books in the systematic catalogue are classified under 20 basic heads, each with several subdivisions. The basic heads are: Marxism-Leninism, social sciences, history and historical sciences, economics and economic sciences, political und social life, state and legal systems, military sciences, culture, science and education, philosophical sciences and psychology, philological sciences and literature, art, religion and atheism, natural sciences, physics, mathematics and chemistry, geology and geography, the biological sciences, medicine, agricultural sciences, industry and technology, general reference books, and general publications.
The alphabetical catalogue lists works by authors' names, or after the institutes or groups by which they have been published. The thematic catalogue arranges cards according to subject discussed: poetry, belles lettres, literary criticism, fine arts, sculpture, the theatre, and so on.
The "National Library" in Sofia is not only a treasure house of Bulgarian and foreign literature: it acts as an advisory body to individuals and groups engaged in scientific research. The "Bibliographical and Information Departments" give free advice to all applicants. The library has on its staff representatives of all scientific branches: medics, engineers, historians, geographers, philosophical advisers, and others—all able to supply the required data at short notice. In 1967 the National Library in Sofia provided 480 detailed written reports and more than 20,000 oral consultations.
The "Information Department" and other services of the Library publish periodical reference books in Bulgarian and in foreign languages, specialized references for specific branches of literature, Bulgarian magazines and periodicals, Bulgarian books in foreign translations, and others.

16 Book Production

The printing industry is fairly young, because until Bulgaria's liberation from Ottoman rule in 1878 books in the Bulgarian language were usually printed abroad. Only a few clandestine printing offices existed in the country: the trade was persecuted by the Ottoman authorities. Until the Second World War there were about 400 printing and bookbinding concerns, mostly very small, with primitive and worn-out equipment. Only Sofia had several larger and more modern printing establishments.
In 1947 all printing works and publishing houses were nationalized (together with industry, mining and the banks). The printing trade expanded and was completely overhauled and modernized. 31 large enterprises with 77 branches were formed by merging smaller printing establishments. Outdated machinery was discarded.
The growth of print production is illustrated by the following figures:

	1939	1956	1965
Number of books issued	2,169	2,900	3,634
Annual number of copies	6,484,000	21,141,000	39,282,000
Books per capita	1.0	2.8	4.8

The above number does not include supplements of the periodical press, advertising prospectuses, folders, visual aids for schools. In 1965 23,384,000 copies of magazines were produced and 602,178,000 copies of newspapers.

The largest printing establishments are the "Dimiter Blagoev Polygraphic Combine" and the "Georgi Dimitrov State Printing House", both in Sofia. There has been a general change to offset and gravure printing. Annual book production at the "Dimiter Blagoev Combine" in 1966 reached 196 million folios and is planned to rise to 245 million by 1970.
While the books published in 1939 averaged 3,000 copies, in 1966 the average jumped to 10,800.
Since 1878 (when Bulgaria won freedom from Ottoman rule) Bulgaria has published a total of 179,000 different books. Between 1945 and 1966 their number was 59,000, totalling 505 million copies.

17 Translations

Translations of foreign literary and other works account for a considerable part of Bulgaria's book production, and there are many specialized translators. The "Union of Bulgarian Writers" has a section for "Translators of Foreign Literature". It discusses important aspects of the translator's art, organizes seminars for improving translator qualifications. The "Committee of Art and Culture" and the "Faculty of Philology" at Sofia State University also train qualified translators. Cultural agreements with foreign countries give Bulgarian translators an opportunity to attend courses and lectures in other countries. For instance, German translators are sent to the "Herder Institut" in Leipzig (German Democratic Republic) and to the "Goethe Institut" in the Federal Republic of Germany. Every year translators are sent for a certain period to Britain, France, the Soviet Union, and other countries.
Many writers and poets also translate prose and poetry. Bulgaria now has expert translators in all of the world's leading languages. Special attention has lately been paid to literature of the developing countries. Most of the translations are from Russian, German, English, French and Spanish.
In 1967 694 translations were published with a total of 7,510,124 copies. Most of the translations were done from Russian (224 titles and 2.6 million copies) followed by translations from German, English and French.

18 Book Clubs

The popularity of book clubs in Bulgaria is illustrated by the existence of 5,000 book clubs in towns and country, forming the *Bulgarski Chitalishten Suyuz* ("Bulgarian Reading Room Union").
They have their own buildings, stock of books, subscriptions to magazines and periodicals, with a total fund of some 23 million books.
The "reading rooms" came into being during the days of Ottoman rule, enlightening the people and preserving their patriotic spirit. Their influence was particularly great in the rural districts.
At present the "reading rooms" organize general and specialized book exhibitions, keep show cases with the latest books, organize reading circles, lectures, discussions of new books, etc.

19 Paperbacks

No special paperback editions are published. Books published in Bulgaria are sold at very low prices, and it has not been found necessary to print cheap editions, as all books are accessible to people in every walk of life.

20 Book Design

The quality of print is controlled by "Bulgarska Kniga" (→ 4) and a special research institute. They are concerned with problems of technical progress and the purchase of modern printing equipment.
A popular contest is jointly organized

every year by the "Committee of Art und Culture" (→ 4), the "Union of Bulgarian Artists" and "Bulgarska Kniga" (→ 4), with prizes for the best-designed, laid-out and printed editions. The entries are divided into six groups: novels, works for children and young people, social and political publications, popular science, technology, and albums. Prizes are also awarded for the excellent design of several schoolbooks.
The special prize in 1966 was awarded for an edition which stood out from all others: "Type through the centuries" by Vassil Yonchev, published by "Bulgarski Houdozhnik".
Bulgarian books have won several international awards: at the 1965 "International Book Design Exhibition" (Leipzig) Bulgaria was 8th among 42 participating countries, winning a total of 14 gold, silver and bronze medals and 12 diplomas. Here, too, V. Yonchev's "Type through the centuries" won high distinction.

21 Publishing

Bulgaria's publishing houses are principally in the capital (Sofia), namely: "Narodna Kultura"—for classics, general international and Slav literature, with an international information service; "Narodna Prosveta"—for all types of textbooks and manuals for the educational institutions; "Nauka i Izkustvo"—with departments for graphic art, literature on music, scores, dictionaries, and other works; "Bulgarski Houdozhnik"—for art books, monographs, children's illustrated editions, reproductions of famous paintings and other works of art; the "Military Publishing House"—papers, periodicals and books for the army and the militia; "Zemizdat"—specialized editions for the needs of agriculture; "Medizina i Fizkultura"—publications in the field of medicine, physical culture and sport; "INRA"—news about technological problems, inventions and rationalizations; "Technica"—for scientific technical literature; "Publishing House of the Bulgarian Academy of Sciences"; "Bulgarian Writer"—for works of its members and other poets and writers; "Fotoizdat"—photo albums, illustrated postcards, etc.; "Sofia-Press"—for publications in foreign languages; the "Fatherland Front Publishers"; "Publishing House of the Bulgarian Communist Party"; the "Publishers of the Dimitrov Union of Communist Youth"; the "Publishing House of the Bulgarian Eastern Orthodox Church". There is also a publishing house in Varna and another in Plovdiv for Bulgarian literature and translated works by foreign authors.
Number of publishing houses → 4
Calculation → 3
Distribution → 23

23 Wholesale Trade

Bulgarian publishing houses are not engaged in the sale of their production. This is channelled through the commercial network of the state economic enterprise

Knigorazprostranenie
(Distribution of Books)
BU Sofia

which has monopoly rights for the whole of the country. It buys the output of the publishing houses under prior contracts stating the choice of book, editing of the text, and its graphic and artistic aspects. Every edition should bear the year of publication, number of copies printed, name of the editor, layout artist, proofreader, technical editor, price, and the name of the printing house. If the book is illustrated: the name of the artist, and of the designer of the front cover.

24 Retail Trade

The term book distribution is used in Bulgaria rather than trade, because the publishing houses are not after profit. In fact, many of them exist only because of state subsidies, or with funds from the public organizations which they represent. The products of the publishing houses are sent to the state economic association, "Distribution of Books" (→ 23), belonging to Bulgarska Kniga (→ 4). The association has 30 district enterprises and 1,304 bookstores. "Distribution of Books" also supplies these bookstores with stationery, office materials and accessories—everything except newspapers. These last are circulated by the state enterprise, "Distribution of Press", with its head office in Sofia.

Many publications, particularly special series, encyclopedias, selected works of a certain author, and others, are available on a subscription basis. In the larger inhabited localities there are mobile book vendors using kiosks and little shops near busy thoroughfares, shopping centres, etc. Each mobile salesman has a certain section of the city, where he calls in on industrial enterprises, administrative and other services, and shows the workers and employees the latest publications. Workers can pay cash, or larger purchases on an instalment basis. Salesmen receive 10% commission.

The larger cities have specialized bookstores for technical literature, textbooks and manuals, for agricultural publications, and for books in Russian, German, French, Italian, English, Spanish and other languages. As they cannot keep a complete stock of all the foreign editions which readers might require, they have catalogues of publishing houses in many countries, and have a service for ordering books for readers from abroad.

The cultural centres which foreign countries have set up in Sofia sell books and periodicals as well as objects of art, publicity material, souvenirs, etc.

Bookstores have shop-window displays of the latest Bulgarian and foreign books. The shelves inside are arranged by subject matter and language for easier inspection. The larger bookstores keep author-index cards and can tell readers about new books expected in foreign countries. Readers can use these files to make their choice.

Booksellers can always give qualified advice to customers. They keep statistics about best-sellers, so as to be able to inform the central orgnization about the taste of the reading public and specialists.

For closer contact with readers, bookstores set up show windows at plants and factories, administrative services and public organizations, on the cooperative farms in the rural districts, at popular resorts, in market places, etc. to give direct information about the latest publications.

26 Antiquarian Book Trade, Auctions

In the larger cities there are antiquarian bookshops with a fairly large selection of old Bulgarian and foreign books. Every citizen can sell an unlimited part of his library to these antiquarian shops and is paid a price determined by the original price and quality of the book, its rarity, condition, year of publication, etc. Often these antiquarian bookshops buy certain editions for the state or public libraries from private individuals. The shops pay cash, less 30% commission, or less 25%, if the books are left to be paid for after sale. Foreign visitors often find interesting old books and editions in Bulgarian antiquarian bookshops.

27 Book Imports
28 Book Exports

Foreign books and publications are imported mainly by the state foreign-trade enterprise

Hemus
Russkij Bulwar 6
BG Sofia

with head offi e in Sofia (under the "Committee of Art and Culture", → 4).

The "Sofia Press Agency" markets its own editions abroad. In 1967 books valued at 2,500,000 lewa were sold to more than 30 different countries—principally to the Soviet Union, the German Democratic Republic, Yugoslavia, the Federal Republic of Germany, France, the United Kingdom, and Italy.
Book imports were valued at 2.5 million leva in 1967.

29 Book Fairs

There have been interesting book exhibitions of individual countries: the Soviet Union, the United Kingdom, France, Germany, Italy, and others. For the exchange of experience, many Bulgarian publishing houses are taking part in international book fairs, exhibitions and contests, and have staged individual exhibitions of the Bulgarian book abroad. In 1966 Bulgaria took part at international book fairs in Warsaw, Leipzig and Frankfurt a. M., and staged individual exhibitions of the Bulgarian book in Skoplje in Yugoslavia, in East Berlin, and elsewhere. In 1967—in addition to participation at several traditional international book fairs—Bulgaria staged individual book exhibitions in Prague, Warsaw, Stockholm, Bombay and Havana. Many Bulgarian editions received awards for their fine style and attractive presentation (→ 20).
In 1968 an international book fair was started in Sofia (→ International Section, 29).

30 Public Relations

The publicity which "Bulgarska Kniga" (→ 4) gives to the book trade in socialist Bulgaria resembles the role of the "Börsenverein" in the Federal Republic of Germany. There is never a danger of favouring one publishing house or book at the expense of another. Readers are able to inform themselves quickly about the quality of new books, and best-sellers disappear from the bookstores in a matter of hours. Readers keep track of new editions so as to be sure to secure a copy before it is too late.
How do they do it?
In addition to the catalogues of the various publishing houses, posters and "new books" columns in the papers and periodicals, readers are kept informed by weekly book reviews on Bulgarian Television. Bulgarian Radio also makes regular literary surveys. The district services of the "Distribution of Books" (→ 23, 24) department often organize local "Friend of the Book Councils", including representatives of the teaching body, scientific workers, pensioned executives of scientific, artistic and cultural departments, and others. These Councils are non-salaried bodies. Their members organize reading circles and literary discussion groups, stage exhibitions, arrange meetings with Bulgarian writers or foreign writers visiting the country, etc.
New editions are also given publicity by way of annual "Book Weeks": "Week of Bulgarian Literature", "Week of Bulgarian Poetry", "Week of Books for Children", and others. Attractive book exhibitions are staged on the occasion of national holidays, festivals, and rallies, at which all exhibits can be bought. Meetings and discussions with popular writers and poets and reading circles are another form in which people learn about new editions, new authors and literary trends. Thus information about books is quickly given to all sections of society.

31 Bibliophily

Although quite numerous, book collectors in Bulgaria do not at present have a printed bulletin. They collect old and rare Bulgarian and foreign books, editions specializing in some particular subject, rare books in a certain language, etc. Some of them correspond and exchange books and information with colleagues in other countries.

32 Literary Prizes

Various awards are made to writers, poets and playwrights. The highest distinction is the title of *Dimitrov Prize Laureate,* with a gold medal and a monetary award of 5,000 to 8,000 leva. The title is awarded every year to not more than two or three writers for outstanding achievements. While conferred by the Government, the title and prize are given on the advice of the "Union of Bulgarian Writers", or another of the art unions. The works nominated are publicly discussed at meetings all over the country and in the press. The proposal is then submitted to the Dimitrov Prize Commission, which approves or rejects it by a majority vote.

Poets and writers are also awarded the title of *People's Cultural Worker* or *Emeritus Cultural Worker.* These titles are conferred by a majority vote of a commission including representatives of the competent writers' union, the "Committee for Art and Culture", and the "Council of Ministers". These titles include a monthly monetary grant for life.

Prizes are also awarded for prose, poetry and drama, and literary criticism by the Union of Bulgarian Writers, the Committee for Art and Culture (four annual awards for the best translation of foreign works into Bulgarian), the Central Council of the Bulgarian Trade Unions (for best theme covering the life of the working class), the Sofia City Council, and by the municipal councils of the larger cities, like Plovdiv, Sliven, Stara Zagora, Smolian, Turgovishte, certain ministries and state departments (such as the Ministry of National Defence "the Ministry of Forestry"), and others.

33 The Reviewing of Books

Literary critics, experts and linguists show a keen interest in new books. Although there are no regular magazines dealing exclusively with the subject, the literary papers and magazines always review a new publication. The monthly magazine of the Union of Bulgarian Writers, *Septemvri,* always reviews one or several literary works of Bulgarian or foreign authors. Book-review columns are a common feature of the magazines *Plamak* ("Flame"), *Chitalishte* ("Book Club"), *Bulgarski Voin* ("Bulgarian Warrier"), *Nasha Rodina* ("Our Fatherland"), and others.

Almost all the daily papers have regular literary critics and specialists in every branch of the sciences, economics, culture and art.

The Union of Bulgarian Writers publishes the weekly paper *Literaturen Front* and the Committee for Art and Culture, another weekly—the *Narodna Kultura.* Both papers review new literary works, and publish readers' views.

The Bulgarian National Library Cyril and Metodius (→ 15) publishes a periodical, *Bulletin,* with annotations, listing new books.

Cyprus

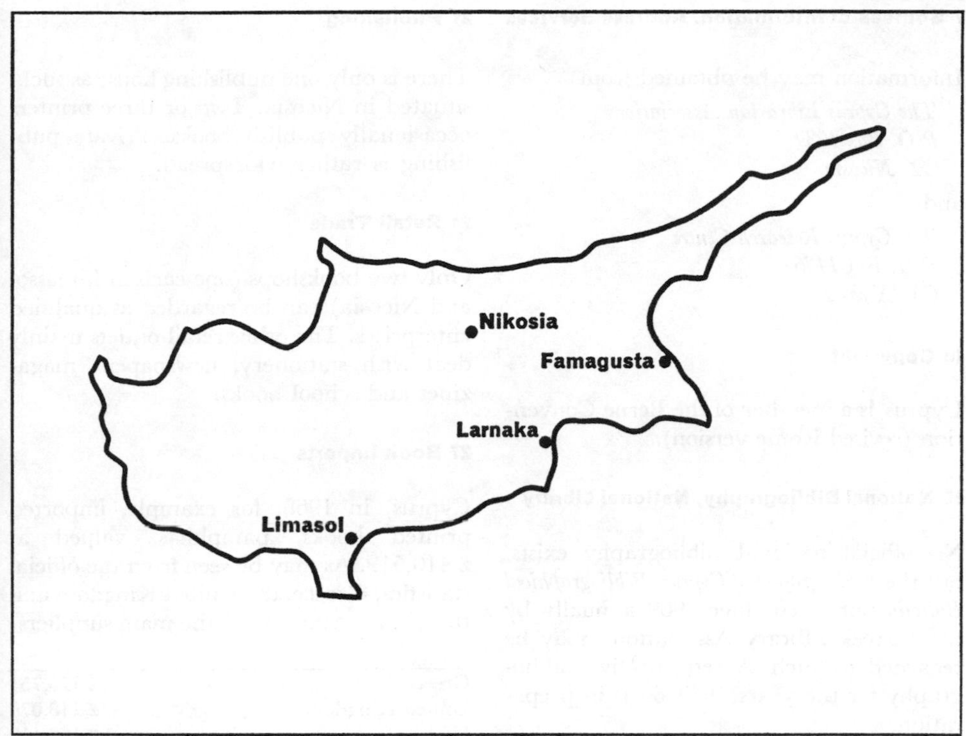

Important Book Centres

1 General Information

Area 9,251 km²

Population 614.000 (66 per km²; 80% Greeks, 18% Turks)

Capital Nicosia (112,000)

Largest Towns Nicosia (112,000); Limassol (50,000); Famagusta (40,000); Larnaka (20,000)

Government Republic with a house of representatives from the Greek and the Turkish community

Religion Greek speaking community (80%): Greek orthodox

Turkish speaking community (18%): Muslims. Other groups: Anglican, Roman Catholic, and others

Languages Greek and Turkish

Leading foreign languages English, French

Weights, measures Imperial system and metric system

Currency unit Cyprus Pound (= 1,000 mils)

Education Compulsory.
Students (3rd level) approx. 5,500

Illiteracy 30%

Paper consumption a) Newsprint 2,4 kg per inhabitant (1967)

b) Printing paper (other than newsprint) 2.0 kg per inhabitant (1966)

7 Sources of Information, Address Services

Information may be obtained from
The Cyprus Librarian Association
P.O. Box 1039
CY Nicosia
and
The Cyprus Research Centre
P.O. Box 1436
CY Nicosia

14 Copyright

Cyprus is a member of the Berne Convention (revised Rome version).

15 National Bibliography, National Library

No official national bibliography exists, but the *Bibliography of Cyprus, Bibliographical Bulletin* published since 1969 annually by the "Greek Library Association" may be regarded as such. A retrospective bibliography for the years 1930–60 is in preparation.
The Paedagogical Academy, Nicosia, issued, between 1960 and 1966, seven editions of a national bibliographical list.

16 Book Production

212 titles have been published in 1967 within the following subject groups:

Subject group	Titles
Generalities	9
Philosophy	6
Religion	7
Social sciences	57
Philology	5
Pure sciences	6
Applied sciences	38
Arts	15
Literature	48
Geography, history	21

21 Publishing

There is only one publishing house as such, situated in Nicosia. Two or three printers occasionally publish books. Private publishing is rather widespread.

24 Retail Trade

Only two bookshops (one each in Limassol and Nicosia) can be regarded as qualified enterprises. The other retail outlets mainly deal with stationery, newspapers, magazines and school books.

27 Book Imports

Cyprus, in 1968, for example, imported printed books, pamphlets, valued at £ 410,519. As may be seen from the official statistics, Greece, the United Kingdom and the United States were the main suppliers:

Greece	£ 175,751
United Kingdom	£ 118,076
USA	£ 100,418
France	£ 4,337

The imports of periodicals amounted to £ 244,966

Greece	£ 134,920
United Kingdom	£ 81,550
Turkey	£ 10,652
USA	£ 7,870
France	£ 6,499

28 Book Exports

With a total of £ 5,382 in 1968, the book exports were rather small. In approximately equal parts, the countries of destination were the United States and the United Kingdom.
The United Kingdom imported nearly 100% of the periodical exports of Cyprus (£ 1,707 in 1968).

Czechoslovakia

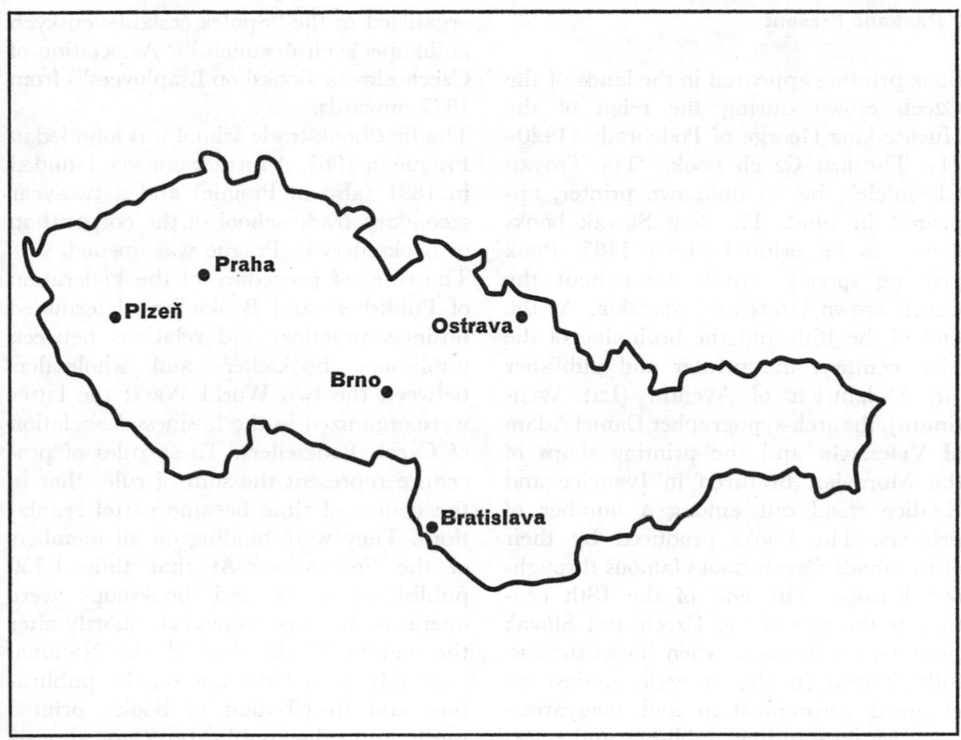

Important Book Centres

1 General Information

Area 127,870 km²
Population 14,158,000 (111 per km²)
Capital Praha (1,025,240)
Largest towns Praha (1,025,240); Brno (329,634); Bratislava (271,650); Ostrava (264,635); Plzeň (141,299); Košice (105,987)
Government Federal socialist republic composed of the Czech and Slovak Socialist Republics
Religion Roman Catholic, Protestant
National languages Czech and Slovak
Leading foreign languages Russian, German, English
Weights and measures Metric system
Currency unit Crown (Kčs)
Education Compulsory. 144,990 university students (in 1965), including 37,355 women and 3,303 foreigners. 38 universities and colleges
Illiteracy Negligible
Paper consumption a) Newsprint 3.5 kg per inhabitant (1967)
b) Printing paper (other than newsprint) 6.2 kg per inhabitant (1966)
Membership UNESCO

Czechoslovakia

2 Past and Present

Book printing appeared in the lands of the Czech crown during the reign of the Hussite king George of Poděbrady (1420–71). The first Czech book, "The Troyan Chronicle", by an unknown printer, appeared in 1468. The first Slovak books began to be printed about 1485. Book printing spread rapidly throughout the Czech crown lands and Slovakia. At the end of the 16th and the beginning of the 17th century, the printer and publisher Jiří Melantrich of Aventin (Lat. Aventinum), the arch-typographer Daniel Adam of Veleslavín and the printing shops of the Moravian Brethren in Ivančice and Kralice stood out among a number of printers. The books produced by their offices made Czech books famous throughout Europe. The end of the 18th century is the age of the Czech and Slovak national renaissance, when books successfully helped in the struggle against an enforced germanization and magyarization. An outstanding publisher and bookseller of that time was Václav Matěj Kramerius who published popular literature in Czech. Beside instructive tracts and translations he published, in 1789, the periodical "Pražské poštovní noviny" ("Prague Post"). The revolutionary movement of 1848 had a great influence on awakening mass interest in culture and above all in literature and books. Large publishing houses appeared in the second half of the 19th century. In 1897 the Czech organization of publishers and booksellers, "Spolek českých knihkupců a nakladatelů" ("Czech Publishers' and Booksellers' Association") was founded, and from it sprang the "Svaz knihkupců a nakladatelů" ("Federation of Publishers and Booksellers") in 1924.

This organization played an important role after the First World War. Employees of publishing houses and bookshops were organized in the "Spolek československých knihkupeckých účetních" ("Association of Czechoslovak Bookshop Employees") from 1877 onwards.

The first book-trade school was founded in Prague in 1867. A further one was founded in 1891 (also in Prague) and a two-year secondary trade school of the corporation of booksellers in Prague was opened.

The rules of procedure of the Federation of Publishers and Booksellers determined business practices and relations between publishers, booksellers and wholesalers between the two World Wars; the latter were organized in the Business Association of Czech Booksellers. These rules of procedure represent the sum of rules that in the course of time became cartel regulations. They were binding on all members of the Federation. At that time 1,750 publishing firms and bookshops were operating in Czechoslovakia. Shortly after the end of World War II the National Assembly passed the law on the publication and distribution of books, printed music and other publications not appearing at regular intervals. This was in consequence of the profound change in the structure of society, and provided for the nationalization of all publishing houses and bookselling enterprises.

The realization of this policy led to the establishment of State publishing houses whose operation on a national scale has been complemented by the activities of the publishing departments of various organizations (trade unions, youth organizations, sports organizations, artists' associations, etc.) and regional publishing houses.

The national enterprise "Kniha" ("The Book"), founded in 1951, has become the principal distributing agency.

3 Retail Prices

The retail price of publications not appearing at regular intervals is in principle fixed in the following manner: the size of the publication expressed by the number of printer's sheets is multiplied by the fixed rate for the particular group of reading matter. The rates for individual groups of literature are scaled to correspond above all with the intensity of public interest in the distribution of the individual groups of literature. The rate per printer's sheet ranges from Kčs 0.25 to Kčs 0.87. The number of published copies is not taken into consideration in determining the retail price.

The price for a book block increases with the number of illustrations and colours used in the printer's sheet given. On the other hand, the rate per printer's sheet is lower in a publication of large volume. A charge for bookbinding is added to the price of the book.

The building principles in fixing and controlling the prices of periodical and non-periodical publications permit individual publishing houses to deviate from retail prices (+10% in the case of textbooks, ±30% for political, specialist, literary and children's books and printed music, and ±50% for art publications), should the calculated price not correspond with the real value of the work, its design, or its saleability.

The price level of non-periodical publications can perhaps be best illustrated by the fact that in 1966 the average realization of 1 kg of paper, expressed in the net price of a publisher's production, amounted to Kčs 50 in miscellaneous stock and Kčs 32 in the case of textbooks. In 1966 the average price per copy was Kčs 15. This price level makes it possible to run a publishing firm at a profit without considering the loss due to the low number of copies of specialist and scientific books.

In Czechoslovakia the prices of non-periodical publications are printed on the binding or on the dust cover, for the information of the public and workers in the book trade.

Prices are fixed. It is not allowed to grant any discounts to individuals, organizations or libraries. For certain chosen titles the price is lowered every year; this is done centrally and applies to the whole country.

Price-fixing of non-periodical publications, based on a fixed uniform price per printed sheet in the particular group and without regard to the number of published copies, represents one of the instruments of cultural policy in Czechoslovakia by means of which the country strives to make political, specialist and scientific literature available to the mass of the people at the cheapest possible price.

The system of fixed prices for non-periodical publications represents one of the fundamental features of the organized book market in Czechoslovakia.

4 Organization

The state organization for publishing and the book trade in the Czech Socialist Republic is:

Ministerstvo kultury ČSR, Odbor knižní kultury
(Ministry of Culture of the ČSR, Section for Book Culture)
Staré město,
Na Perštýně 1,
CS Praha 1

In the Slovak Socialist Republic the same duties are performed by the

Slovenské ústredí knižní kultury
(Slovak Center for Publishing and the Book Trade)
Námestí SNP No 1
CS Bratislava

5 Trade Press

The most important trade paper for the book trade is

Nové knihy
(New Books)
Vězeňská 5
CS Praha 1

Czechoslovakia

This weekly, published by *Knižní velkoobchod* ("Wholesale Books", → 23), has a circulation of over 100,000. It offers its readers a weekly summary of all new titles in Czech, Slovak and Hungarian. The contents are divided into two parts: Bibliography with short annotations and further bibliographical matters; extensive reviews of the most interesting titles.

The second part also includes commentaries, interviews with authors, short biographies, features and extracts from selected works. In view of its completeness and the exhaustive quantity of information, this publication is widely read in the Czechoslovak periodical market.

In addition, specialized trade periodicals on books are issued. Of these particular mention must be made of

Věda a knihy (Science and Books)
Vodičkova 40
CS Praha 1

published by "Academia", the publishers of the Czechoslovak Academy of Sciences. This is a monthly bulletin of the most important Czechoslovak scientific publishing house. It provides foreigners with information in the form of extensive reviews of scientific publications, published not only in Czech but also in French, English, German, Russian and other languages.

6 Book-Trade Literature

F. Lukáš, *Propagace knih.* (Book advertising). Praha 1963.

R. Málek and M. Petrtýl, *Knihy a Pražané.* (Books and the Praguers). Praha 1964.

T. Nitranský, *Ekonomika knižného obchodu a technika predaja.* (Economics of the book trade and sales techniques). Bratislava 1966.

K. Nosovský, *Nauka knihopisná a nástin vývoje knihkupectví českého.* (Bibliography and outline of the development of the Czech book trade). Praha 1927.

J. Živný and Collective, *Vykladní skříně a knižní výstavky.* (Shopwindows and book exhibitions). Praha 1956.

J. Živný and Collective, *Knižní obchod a technika prodeje.* (Book trade and sales techniques). Praha 1964.

L. K. Žižka, *Průprava k praxi knihkupecké.* (Basic training in book trade practice). 2 vols. Praha 1938.

7 Sources of Information, Address Services

General information on publishing and the book trade is obtainable through the following institutions:

Ministerstvo kultury ČSR, Odbor knižní kultury
(Ministry of Culture of the ČSR, Section for Book Culture)
Staré město,
Na Perštýně 1,
CS Praha 1

for the Czech Socialist Republic and through the

Slovenské ústredí knižní kultury
(Slovak Center for Publishing and the Book Trade)
Námestí SNP No 1
CS Bratislava

for the Slovak Socialist Republic.

8 International Membership

The Czechoslovak Socialist Republic is a founder-member of Unesco.

It is developing initiative in all directions to further international cooperation in the field of publishing within the programme of this organization.

9 Market Research

Problems of market research are a subject of scientific interest at various universities and technical colleges, especially at the School of Economics in Prague.

The Research Institute of Trade in Prague is concerned in particular with applied market research.

Ministerstvo kultury ČSR,
Odbor knižní kultury
(Ministry of Culture of the ČSR,
Section for Book Culture)
Staré město,
Na Perštýně 1
CS Praha 1

for the Czech Socialist Republic and through the

Slovenské ústredí knižní kultury
(Slovak Center for Publishing and the Book Trade)
Námestí SNP No. 1,
CS Bratislava

for the Slovak Socialist Republic.

10 Books and Young People

Společnost přátel knihy pro mládež
(The Society of Friends of Books for Young People)
1-Staré město
Na Perštýně 1
CS Praha

deals with various problems of literature for children.

It was founded in 1959 as an institution financially supported by the "Státní nakladatelství dětské knihy" ("Children's Book Publishers") which later changed its name to Albatros. Slovakia has a publishing firm corresponding to Albatros, namely "Mladé letá, ("Young Years"), Bratislava. The Society of Friends of Books for Young People has more than 700 members. The majority are educationists, writers, librarians and those practising the fine arts; other members include scientists, literary critics, translators, representatives of radio, the theatre and the film. Students can also be found among the members. The activities of the Society include publicity and the spread of information, talks with authors, lectures and seminars, conferences, and exhibitions of books and illustrations.

In 1961 the Society became a member of IBBY—the International Board on Books for Young People (→ International Section, 10)—as its Czechoslovak section. Since 1966 it has had a representative in the executive committee of IBBY.

The Society together with Albatros and Mladé letá is the publisher of the periodical

Zlatý máj
(Golden May)
Na Perštýně 1
CS Praha 1

It appears 10 times per year (1967 being its eleventh year) and it deals with children's literature, publishes theoretical works, studies on writers and the plastic arts, reviews, news, information and bibliographical notices.

The Society has the task of laying before the Ministry of Culture proposals for awarding the *Prizes of Marie Majerová.* These have been awarded annually since 1962 to the most important works in the field of books for children and youth. Since 1966 they have been awarded every two years for a life's work in two categories: to writers and illustrators. Parallel with these prizes the *Prize Fraňo Král's* is awarded in Slovakia; this is given by the Slovak section of the Society. The Society works closely with Albatros in Prague, particularly in the field of literary enlightenment, information, publicity for children's literature, it also fosters relations with publishers abroad. Albatros awards prizes annually for successful work in the field of children's literature.

The Society co-operates further with the

Klub mladých čtenářů
(Young Reader's Club)
Staré město
Na Perštýně 1
CS Praha 1

This club is a mass organization of about 400,000 schoolchildren. It issues books for them which form obligatory reading in the nine-year elementary schools.
Theoretical problems of children's literature are systematically dealt with by members of Albatros largely through a department specifically appointed for this purpose, and also by literary critics, specialists in Czech language and literature in the faculties of philosophy and education, in the Educational Research Institute in Prague, and in certain of the larger libraries. The series of books issued by Albatros and devoted to theoretical problems concerning children's literature look back on an old tradition.
BIB — Biennale of Illustrations, Bratislava (→ International Section, 20), is a regular international exhibition of illustrations for children's books. In supporting the regulations and aims of UNESCO and its allied international organizations, the BIB makes possible an international comparison of children's book illustrations, and thus promotes this form of art. The address of the BIB is

BIB
Námestí SNP 11
CS Bratislava

Bibliography

J. ŠNOBR, *Bibliografický soupis knih vydavých SNDK v letech 1949–1963.* (Bibliographical index of the publications of the children's book publishers, 1949–63). Praha 1966.

The regular *Bibliografie české a slovenské dětské literatury* (Bibliography of Czech and Slovak youth literature) in single volumes for the years 1957–62, compiled by P. Hykeš and Z. Marčanová. Praha 1961–66.

11 Training

Training for specialists in the book trade is based on the training of apprentices. Apprenticeship lasts three years for those who have had nine years' schooling at an elementary school, and one year for owners of the school-leaving certificate from a secondary school. A contract is made with the apprentice. Theoretical instruction is given in special classes at apprentices' school. There are five months of instruction without a break each year. In 1967 such courses were being conducted in Prague, Kladno, Turnov, Gottwaldov and Bratislava. In 1967 there were 427 apprentices, 80% of them girls. Of the 13 subjects taught in the three-year course 10 are specialist subjects: Czech language and literature, Russian language and literature, German language and literature, scientific and specialist literature, commercial arithmetic, the economics of trade and sales technique, world literature, book production, book advertising, social training and psychology.
In the one-year course only the following subjects are taught: literature, scientific and specialist literature, commercial arithmetic, the economics of trade and sales technique, book production, book advertising and psychology.
During the first 18 months for those with the school-leaving certificate the first 6 months) apprentices receive a monthly 40–80 Kčs pocket money. After that they are paid 400–800 Kčs per month. At the end of their time at the apprentices' school they take the final examination, which consists of three parts: written, practical and oral. Successful candidates receive their apprentice's certificate in the book trade.
These young booksellers then start work at a bookshop.
Those who work in places where there is no apprentices' school and where no trained personnel are available, can obtain qualifications as external students at a book-trade school. This course of study, which generally lasts four years but two for former

secondary-school pupils concludes with an examination which confers a qualification sought after by all those engaged in the book trade. Those who have finished their apprenticeship can also acquire this qualification. In 1967 there were students for this course in Prague, Hradec Králové, Ostrava, Brno and Bratislava.
Booksellers and publishers' representatives attend three-day seminars at least twice a year in order to discuss plans prepared by individual publishers and to define readers' demands. Depending on the nature of the publishers' programmes, important workers in specialized bookshops attend too. Specialized schooling spread over a number of days is organized for individual groups of workers in the trade (e.g. antiquarian books, printed music).
The training of workers for the book trade has a great tradition in Czechoslovakia. As early as 1867 there were specialist schools in Prague, and later on in other towns. Their system of training has stood the test of time and has in essence been incorporated into present-day teaching methods.

12 Taxes

Since 1967 all book deliveries, including pamphlets, are no longer subject to purchase tax.

14 Copyright

Copyright is regulated by Bill No. 35/1965 concerning literary and scientific works and works of art. It came into force on 1 July 1965. This law regulates the situations that arise in connection with the creation of literary and scientific works and works of art, and the assertion of the author's rights in society. It protects the interests of the author and ensures favourable conditions for the development of works of culture and the active participation of the workers in such creation, in harmony with the development and needs of a socialist society. This law also deals in detail with the rights of performing artists, producers of sound recordings and radio and television organizations. It also contains fundamental regulations concerning the organization of authors and performing artists.
Fundamentally copyright lasts during an author's life-time and 50 years after his death, and in the case of co-authors until 50 years after the death of the one who lives longest.
In the case of works published for the first time in the last 10 years of this period, the validity of copyright is increased by 10 years from the date of such a publication. In the case of anonymous and pseudonymous works, where the identity of the author is not known, copyright continues for 50 years after the publication of the work.
In the case of film works copyright persists for 25 years after publication of the work, in the case of photographic works for the life of the author and 10 years after his death, and in the case of anthologies and periodicals published by organizations it persists for 10 years after the publication of the work.
Czechoslovakia is a party to the following international agreements: the Berne Convention (in its Berlin and Rome version), the Universal Copyright Convention and the international Convention for the Protection of Performers, Producers of Phonograms and Broadcasting Organizations.

Bibliography

Books:

K. Knap, *Autorské právo.* (Copyright). Praha 1960.

K. Knap, *Vztahy v autorském právu.* (Copyright relations). Praha 1967.

S. Luby, *Autorské právo.* (Copyright). Bratislava 1962.

Periodicals:
Právník. (The Jurist).
Právní obzor. (Jurists' Review).
Socialistická zákonnost. (Socialist legality).

15 National Bibliography, National Library

In Czechoslovakia the national bibliography is made up of two organizations: 1. the *State Library of the Czechoslovak Socialist Republic*—the *National Library* in Prague, for the historical lands Bohemia and Moravia; 2. *Matica slovenská* in Martin, for Slovakia.
1. *Czech* books and printed music together with articles in Czech periodicals are dealt with bibliographically by the State Library of the Czechoslovak Republic—the National Library in Prague. The most important bibliographical material published:
Bibliografický katalog ČSSR—české knihy (The bibliographical catalogue of the Czechoslovak Republic—Czech books).
Bibliografický katalog ČSSR—české hudebniny a gramofonové desky (The bibliographical catalogue of the Czechoslovak Republic—Czech printed music and records).
Bibliografický katalog ČSSR—články v českých časopisech. (The bibliographical catalogue of the Czechoslovak Republic—Articles published in Czech periodicals).
Once a year appears the supplement *Bibliografický katalog ČSSR—české mapy a grafiky* (The bibliographical catalogue of the Czechoslovak Republic—Czech maps and prints).
The basic series of the bibliographical catalogue of Czech books, which appears weekly, registers books, pamphlets, literature in foreign languages produced in Czechoslovakia, textbooks, and literature issued by firms.
2. *Slovak* books and printed music are dealt with bibliographically by the "Matica slovenská". The bibliography is published monthly under the title *Bibliografický katalog ČSSR—slovenské knihy* (The bibliographical catalogue of the Czechoslovak Republic—Slovak books). The *Bibliografický katalog ČSSR—články v slovenských časopisech* (The bibliographical catalogue of the Czechoslovak Republic—Articles in Slovak periodicals) appears monthly. The *Slovenské hudebniny* (Slovak printed music) is published twice a year.
All publishers have to send copies of all books and periodicals to the State Library in Prague and the "Matica slovenská" in Martin. The Bibliographical catalogue of the Czechoslovak Republic is then drawn up from these copies.
For the use by bookshops and those engaged in the book trade the national firm Wholesale Books (→ 23) issues catalogues of literature in stock. These catalogues contain indexes of books arranged according to subject.

16 Book Production

In 1965 9,043 books and similar works were published. Of these 7,366 were books and 1,677 booklets (up to 48 pages). Of the total of published titles 5,898 appeared within the framework of planned publication. In accordance with the directions of UNESCO, printed music, maps and printed material up to four pages are not included. Of the 9,043 titles 82.1% (in the case of books 79.2%) are first editions.
Book production is classified according to the enlarged international decimal classification used by UNESCO.
The most important subjects in 1965 (books only):

Subject group	Titles
Literature (Belles lettres)	1,732
Technology	1,011
Science	613
Politics	515
Medicine	386
Linguistics	369
Agriculture and forestry	355
Architecture and art	355
Education	346

17 Translations

In 1964 there appeared 7,002 titles, of which 1,733 were translations, i.e. 24.8% of all titles. This relatively high percentage of published translation shows the efforts of the publishing firms to bring to the market valuable works from other countries as well as new and classical literature written at home.
895 of the 1,733 quoted translations were literary works.

18 Book Clubs

A number of readers' clubs enables the reader to find his way more easily through the relatively high number of books appearing annually. These clubs work with individual publishing firms. Some of them have a long tradition—in some cases prewar; others were recently founded as a result of a justifiable demand for worthwhile reading material. An important feature of the clubs is that their readers are assured of obtaining books in advance on favourable terms, even before some of these books are available on the open market. The number of members is continually growing. At present the following clubs are in operation:
1. Klub čtenářů nakladatelství ODEON, Praha (Readers' Club of the publishing house ODEON), for literature and art, about 200,000 members.
2. Klub přátel poezie nakladatelství Čs. spisovatel, Praha (Poetry Lovers' Club of the publishing house Czechoslovak Writer), about 26,000 members.
3. Máj—čtenářský klub mládeže (May—Young Reader's Club) is a book club working simultaneously with the publishing houses Mladá fronta (Youth Front), Naše vojsko (Military Publishers) and Lidové nakladatelství (Popular Publishers), Praha, about 250,000 members.
4. Klub mladých čtenářů, Praha (Young Reader's Club), about 400,000 members.
5. Klub čtenářů technické literatury (Club for readers of technical literature), a club working with the following firms: SNTL-Publishers of technical literature, ACADEMIA—the publishing house of the Czechoslovak Academy of Sciences, ALFA—the Slovak publishing house of technical literature, the trade union's publishing house Práce, NADAS—the publishing house for transport and communications. About 55,000 members.
6. Členská knižnice nakladatelství SVOBODA, Praha (Reader's Library of the publishing house SVOBODA), for political and economic literature and fiction, about 90,000 members.
In Slovakia the following clubs exist in addition to those mentioned above:
8. Hviezdoslavova knižnica nakladatelství Tatran, Bratislava (Hviezdoslav's book club of the Slovak TATRAN publishing house for literary works), about 60,000 members.
9. Společnost přátel krásných knih nakladatelství Slovenský spisovatel, Bratislava (The society of lovers of Slovak books, of the publishing house Slovak Writer), about 65,000 members.
10. Kruh milovníků poezie nakladatelství Slovenský spisovatel, Bratislava (Circle of poetry lovers of the publishing house Slovak Writer), about 10,000 members.
The publishing houses maintain regular contact with their members by means of inquiries and discussions and by publishing special periodicals and informatory material.

20 Book Design

There is an annually promoted competition, The Best-Designed Book of the Year. Its aim is to raise the standard of books both artistically and technically. Best books are selected according to the basic criteria of artistic conception, technical quality, and the harmony between the artistic design and the contents of the book.

Every publication of the current year can be entered. All publishers, graphic firms, institutions and individuals can take part. The publications entered for the competition are divided into groups: scientific and technical literature, works on art and pictorial publications, works for children and youth, belles-lettres, occasional printing and books for bibliophiles, and printed music.
Points are awarded by two commissions (one technical, the other artistic) and a jury in which specialists and leading representatives in the fields of science and culture are equally represented. Books voted by the jury as the best-designed book of the year are awarded a diploma; outstanding works receive a financial award.
The judgements on the best designed books and the distribution of diplomas and awards are made in public, and during the Book Month these books are exhibited in the Museum of Czech Literature. A book is published annually about the competition and the books that received the awards.

21 Publishing

Publishing at the present time (1967) is undertaken by 59 institutions. Their activities can be seen from the following information:

	1963	1964	1965	1966
No. of published titles	7,168	7,002	6,503	6,435
No. of copies in 1000s	58,433	53,335	52,822	54,381
Retail sale of books in 1,000 Kcs.	501,227	563,156	635,138	651,237

Book publishing in Czechoslovakia has been influenced above all by a thorough coordination of the activities of individual firms. This prevents duplication in dealing with the same subject by different publishing firms and also makes possible the reduction of the number of published titles.

22 Literary Agents

In Czechoslovakia there are now two agencies for theatrical plays and literature:

DILIA
Vyšehradská 28
CS Praha

and

LITA
Obráncov mieru 38
CS Bratislava

DILIA is responsible for the Czech socialist republic and the Czech authors, and LITA which is in full operation only since 1 January, 1971, is responsible for the Slovak socialist republic and the Slovak authors.
Both represent all important writers of literary, scientific and other specialist works, and dramatists and authors of works for the film, radio and television.
DILIA and LITA arrange contracts with various publishers, for theatre and film productions and radio and television programmes.
They reprint, distribute and lend play texts, printed music, tape recordings of operas, ballets, operettas, plays and other theatrical works. Publishers, theatre directors, agencies, film producers and radio stations interested in the copyright of literary or theatrical works by Czechoslovak authors, apply to DILIA or to LITA, which supply all the information and, if necessary, arrange the appropriate contracts. The range of DILIA's activity has extended from year to year. With foreign countries alone DILIA arranged more than 1,800 contracts in 1966, of which more than 1,300 were for the transfer of the rights of foreign authors to Czechoslovakia and more than 500 for the transfer of rights of Czechoslovak authors to countries abroad.

DILIA and LITA regularly publish bulletins in English, German and French, containing short summaries of the contents of outstanding works by Czechoslovak authors.

23 Wholesale Trade

The wholesale book trade is concentrated in three state-owned wholesale enterprises. They are:

Knižní velkoobchod
(Wholesale Books)
Staré město
Vězeuská 5
CS Praha

for Czech literature

Slovenský knižní velkoobchod
(Slovakian Wholesale Books)
Dunajská 47 a
CS Bratislava

for Slovak literature and

Zahraniční literatura
(Foreign Literature)
Karlin
Sokolovská 13
CS Praha

which handles the supply of foreign language literature.

The products of the publishing houses are delivered to the wholesale book firms in Prague and Bratislava straight from the printing presses. By organized delivery methods they are then fed into the network of bookshops.

The wholesale trade is fundamentally based on the commission principle, i.e. by charging to the account of the consignor. Relations between deliverer and buyer (i.e. between publisher and wholesale organization) are governed by this system. Deliveries of new publications, which are safeguarded as regards sale, are not paid for by the wholesale organizations until they have been transferred to their depots.

The main responsibility of the wholesale institutions is to see that publication dates of new works are kept, that the fulfilment of additional orders is guaranteed, to create a reserve in order to allow for possible variations in delivery, for various advertising and sales campaigns, and generally to ensure the correct flow of supply to the network of retail shops.

In addition, these firms ensure market research (→ 9) and checking of demands in the retail trade, and the publication of periodicals for the information of readers within the framework of book advertisement.

Apart from these main responsibilities the wholesale book firm guarantees its customers the most varied services, such dealing with single inquiries or sales campaigns, the storage of books to allow for a delivery in stages, the realization of depreciation and the pulping of remainders, and the delivery of publications intended as presents.

Mechanization has advanced considerably in wholesale book firms during recent years. This has been achieved by the introduction of computers.

24 Retail Trade

Czechoslovakia has a centuries-old book tradition, with hundreds of thousands of readers transmitting their love for books from generation to generation.

The retail book trade is presented above all by eleven regional firms, corresponding to the territorial division of the country. There is a firm in each of the ten regions and an independent firm in Prague.

Apart from these main firms engaged in the retail trade there are other bodies dealing with the sale of books, in particular salesrooms of individual publishers, mainly dealing with the sale of their own productions. There is also the *Poštovní novinová služba* ("Post and Newspaper Service"), which displays literary works as well as periodicals at its stands, and *Drobné zboží*

("Stationery"), which mainly sells pictures and children's books. The *Dílo* cooperative ("Work") sells books on art as well as its main line: works of art. Books are also available in the *Dětský dům* ("The Child's House") and in the *Československá katolická charita* ("Czechoslovak Catholic Charity").
In villages which have no bookshops, books are sold in the *Jednota* ("Unity") cooperative shops. So-called book corners are to be found in these shops. Hundreds of voluntary helpers (called Literary Stewards) help the book trade in the distribution of books. They sell books of all sorts in firms, offices, schools and elsewhere. Altogether there are 844 specialized bookshops with a wide range of subjects—27 of them also sell books in foreign languages; 1,800 stalls belonging to the Post and Newspaper Service, where books are sold; 1,870 book corners in the "Jednota" cooperative shops; and about 7,000 Literary Stewards.
Antiquarian bookshops also have a great tradition. There are 44 of these, selling both old and new works.
The wide net of bookshops, etc. which is being augmented and modernized as demand increases, guarantees favourable and swift purchase of any required work.
The Czechoslovak book trade sold works and publications to a total value of 675,000,000 Kčs. in 1966.
→ 23

25 Mail-Order Bookselling

Particularly in recent times, mail-order sections have been included in individual firms, offering newly published works to individuals and organizations and dispatching them through the post. One part of the mail-order business are the book clubs already mentioned (→ 18). These book clubs have a membership of 1,518,000 readers, who purchase 6,800,000 copies annually, representing some 118,000,000 Kčs. Advertising material is published to encourage the sale of books, including book lists, prospectuses, lists of new publications, pamphlets and transparencies. The wholesale firms and publishing houses regularly publish bulletins informing readers of new publications, books in print, and works planned for the future.

26 Antiquarian Book Trade, Auctions

The purchase and sale of antiquarian publications is taken care of by special sales departments in the regional firms of the trade: the national enterprise *Kniha* ("The Book") for Bohemia and Moravia, and *Slovenská Kniha* ("The Slovak Book") for Slovakia.
All sales departments dealing with the antiquarian book trade arrange their own purchases. When second-hand books are bought the sales department concludes an agreement with the seller in the form of purchase notes, on which, among other things, the purchased work is quoted and the agreed price fixed, which the seller receives in cash. In accordance with the regulations the signature and the calculated selling price is noted in every book purchased.
The second-hand book trade is bound to the principle of offering favourable terms to scientific institutions and other libraries and organizations. Only books not purchased by the above-mentioned come onto the normal second-hand market. Every antiquarian sales department receives lists of requirements from such organizations. The majority of these second-hand sales departments regularly publish catalogues drawn up under subject headings and made available to chosen circles of recipients.
The trained bookseller can acquire the necessary qualifications for working in the antiquarian business by practical participation in the business, where outstanding specialists are at work.

Every sales department has the necessary specialist manuals and reference works in order to ensure expert service.
The second-hand trade also takes over remainders bought by the national enterprise *Knižní velkoobchod* (→ 23).

30 Public Relations

Book advertising can be divided into three categories according to the nature and responsibilities of firms:
1. Central book advertising
2. Advertising by publishers
3. Advertising by the retail trade.
1. Central book advertising is undertaken by the national enterprise *Knižní velkoobchod* (→ 23), and in Slovakia by *Slovenský knižní velkoobchod* (→ 23). It is directed both at the reader and those working in the trade.
It organizes book publicity for the whole country, such as Book Month, International Women's Day, Month of Czechoslovak-Russian Friendship, and such activities as A Book for Your Certificate, A Book for the Holidays. The most important publicity campaign covering the whole country is the already traditional Book Month, which has taken place every March since 1954. During that time press, radio and television lay particular stress on the work and contents of books. Shop-window advertising is regularly organized, and during this time the best-designed book of the year contest is also concluded. In addition educational organizations and the book trade make preparations for readers' requests; book bazaars and auctions are organized.
In order to support these activities, Wholesale Books issues posters, shopwindow material, transparent screens, etc. It also makes use of mass media, such as the press, radio, television and films. A further example of its advertising efforts is the issue of *Výherní knižní poukázky* ("Book-winning Tickets"), by means of which the reader can win valuable prizes and exchange his ticket as a book token.
Central book advertising is assisted by the periodical *Nové knihy* (→ 5), which is printed in large numbers and informs the reader of works appearing in the current and following weeks.
The effectiveness of these mass advertising schemes is strengthened in that all new works of the current week appear in the shops on Thursday. Readers' attention is drawn to new works appearing the following week by reviews in radio, television, the daily press and cultural magazines.
A further element in central book advertising is the offer of advertising material for shops and shop-windows.
For many years there have been regular sales at reduced prices. These extend over the whole country. In 1966 such sales at reduced prices totalled a sum of 7,000,000 Kčs.
Apart from advertising activities covering the whole country, various activities are organized by individual firms or shops to cater to local conditions or the particular firm. For instance, books are advertised in conjunction with International Women's Day, and at the end of the school year books are sold under the heading A Book for Your Certificate. Poetry anthologies are sold during dancing lessons and youth balls under the heading A Book of Poetry for the Dancing Lesson.
Depot catalogues, giving titles and bibliographical information, offers under subject headings, and similar material, help to make known what is available in depots.
2. Publishers' publicity consists of publishers informing their readers before and after the publication of a new work of the firm's plan and the contents, standard, illustrations and design of individual titles. They use the press, radio, television and a number of publishers' periodicals.
Under publishers' advertising come readers'

discussions, and meetings with authors, at which authors sign copies of their books.
3. Retail-trade advertising is chiefly concentrated on actual sales. In this respect it forms the last link in the campaign, and is directly connected with central and publishers' advertising. This is done chiefly through sales letters, copies sent on approval, exhibitions, special window displays, notices on local radio networks, reviews, advertisements in the local press, and placards and transparent screens.

31 Bibliophily

At present there are two societies dealing with bibliophily.

Spolek českých bibliofilů
(Association of Czech Bibliophiles)
Nové Město, Václavské náměstí 39
CS Praha

The Association was founded in Prague in 1908. It encourages the cultivation of books in the spirit of William Morris.
The Association brought together collectors, typographers and artists, and decisively influenced the development of the well-designed book in Czechoslovakia, from the first quarter of the 20th century onwards. In 1928 it initiated the Czechoslovak competition for the best-designed book. Its earliest publications are of lasting importance for the knowledge of book cultivation in Czechoslovakia, especially the collection *Český bibliofil* ("The Czech Bibliophile", 13 annual series), which ceased publication in 1942. Today this institution unites lovers of the artistically designed book.
For them the

Památník národního písemnictví
(Museum of Czech Literature)
Strahovské nádvoří 132
CS Praha 1

regularly publishes prints for bibliophiles as awards and at irregular intervals the collection *Marginálie* ("Marginal Notes"). Lectures and gatherings devoted to the art of the book are held in the Museum (→ International Section, B 1).

Sekce krásné knihy a grafiky
(Section for the well-designed book and prints)
Nové Město, Třída politických vězňů 7
CS Praha 1

This Section was founded in 1960 as part of the "Klub přátel výtvarného umění" ("Club of Lovers of the Creative Arts"), an organization associated with the "Svaz československých výtvarných umělců" ("Association of Czechoslovak Creative Artists").
It unites book lovers and devotees of fine printing in general, and publishes individual prints and a series of small studies in book form called *Obolos.* The contents of this book series consists of articles, bibliographies and short reviews of books produced at home and abroad. Three to four volumes appear regularly each year. In this series more weight is given to the wider concepts of culture than to mere bibliophily.
The Section has a number of very active local groups. In this respect the group in Brno shows great initiative.

32 Literary Prizes

There are a great many literary awards. On the one hand there are state prizes, on the other honorary titles—"Národní umělec" ("National Artists") and "Zasloužilý umělec" ("Artist of Merit"). Prizes are also awarded by some leading publishers.
State prizes are awarded annually by the President of the Republic on the recommendation of the Government to individuals and to groups for literary works.
The title "National Artists": on the recommendation of the Government the President can bestow this title on a Czechoslovak citizen whose work has enriched the natio-

nal culture by its high standard and unusual significance.
The title "Artist of Merit": this is awarded by the Government to those in the cultural fields who have shown merit through long years of outstanding work in their own particular sphere.
Literature prizes awarded by individual publishing firms: the leading publishing firms annually award prizes to outstanding writers working with them. These prizes are awarded both for original works and for translations.

33 The Reviewing of Books

All the mass media undertake reviews and criticism. Radio and television have regular programmes acquainting listeners with new works in the form of reviews. All daily newspapers, particularly the Sunday papers, weeklies and monthlies, publish reviews of recently published books in the cultural pages.

34 Graphic Arts

Svaz československých výtvarných umělců
(Association of Czechoslovak Creative Artists)
Gottwaldovo nábřeží 250
Nové Město
CS Praha 1
is an independent organization uniting all those artists working in the field of book printing.

Denmark

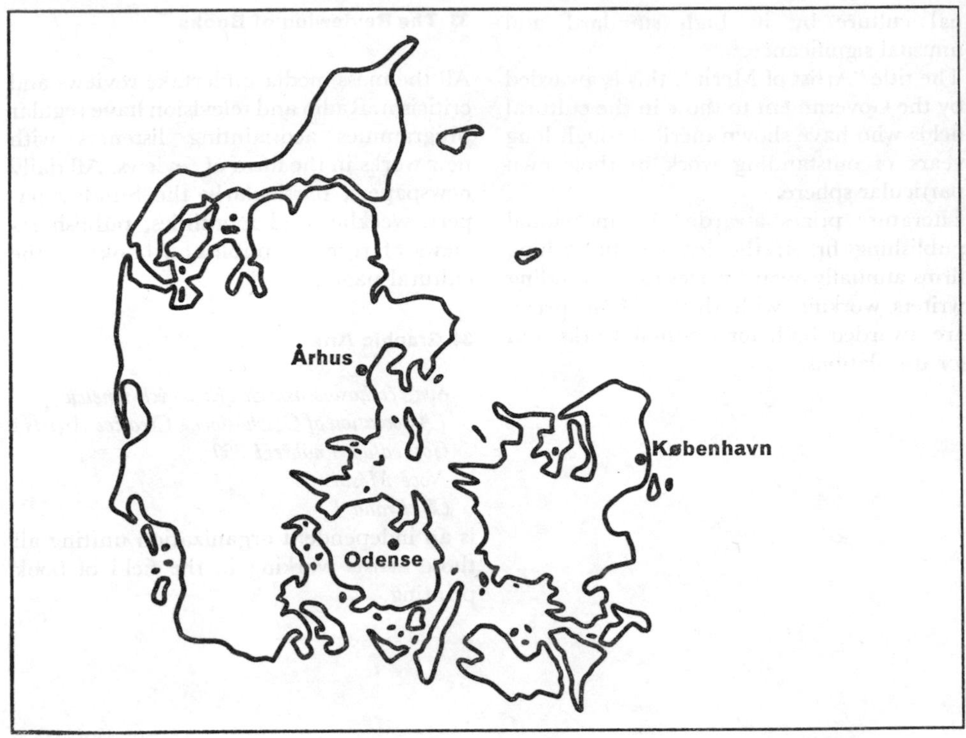

Important Book Centres

1 General Information

Area 43,000 km² excluding Faroe Islands and Greenland (→ 35)
Population 4,878,000 (113 per km²)
Capital København (Copenhagen) (1,382,000)
Largest towns København (1,382,000), Århus (233,000), Odense (164,000), Ålborg (154,000), Esbjerg (76,000)
Government Constitutional monarchy. Legislative body: Folketinget (Parliament). Local administration: 14 amter (counties). 10 stifter (dioceses)
Religion National Church (Evangelical-Lutheran) 95%. Smaller religious groups and dissidents 5%
National language Danish
Faroe Islands Faroese
Greenland Greenlandic
Leading foreign languages English, German
Weights, measures Metric system
Currency unit Danske kroner (Danish kroner, DKr.)
Education Compulsory. 43,200 (1967–1968) students at 22 universities and technical and other colleges of academic standard
Illiteracy Nil
Paper consumption a) Newsprint 28.6 kg per inhabitant (1969)
b) Printing paper (other than newsprint) 32.4 kg per inhabitant (1969)
Membership Unesco, IPA, ICBA

Past and Present

Printing in Denmark dates back to 1489, and so does the Danish book trade. As elsewhere the earliest printers acted also as publishers and booksellers, a combination which for centuries was a dominating element in Danish book distribution. Besides, books were sold retail by travelling clerks, Danes and foreigners, and by a few resident booksellers who generally had their stalls in churches. In 1638 this was forbidden by a Royal Decree but not entirely abolished.

For more than 200 years after the partial opening of the Copenhagen Bourse in 1624 importers of books tended to assemble there; here, too, such Dutch publishers as the Elzeviers and Johannes Jansson in the 17th century displayed their stocks for their Baltic trade. Book auctions are mentioned from about 1650.

In the 18th century the Danish book trade became more diversified, printers no longer necessarily being publishers or vice versa. Danish publishers took part in the Leipzig Fair. Lending libraries occur from about 1725, and publishing by subscription from approximately the same date. An act against pirating was passed in 1741, the first on the European continent.

A decisive year was 1770, when Søren Gyldendal established the firm still bearing his name. With him modern Danish bookselling began: he published books at his risk and went in for a systematic build-up of sales channels in Denmark and Norway, the two countries then forming a double monarchy. Even if publishing and retail selling were often combined under the same roof, they came more and more to be recognized as two distinct functions.

After 1837, when the forerunner of the present "Publishers' Association" (→ 4) was founded, these processes accelerated, and retail bookselling, hitherto concentrated in the capital, spread to the provinces on a growing scale. Price maintenance (→ 3) has been in force since the beginning of the 19th century. In 1894 a central cooperative "Clearing House" (→ 23) was established to supersede the many private agencies. In the 1890s retail booksellers organized themselves into an association (→ 4).

Characteristic of the Danish book trade in its present form are

(1) the dense network of bookshops (→24),
(2) the large number and variety of publishing firms,
(3) the close collaboration between publishers and booksellers (→ 4),
(4) the trade's willingness to handle books from outside publishers (→ 21),

thereby furthering the free flow of books and giving non-organized publishers a chance.

Bibliography

Sv. Dahl, *Bogens historie.* (The history of the book.) 2nd rev. edn København, Haase 1957. 311 pp.
The history of the book at all times and in many lands. The first, a somewhat shorter edition, translated into English, French, German and a number of other languages.

A. Frøland, *Bøger, bogsalg, boghandlere omkring 1875.* (Books, sale of books, booksellers about 1875). København, Forening for Boghaandværk 1969. 191 pp.

L. Nielsen, *Den danske bog.* (The Danish book.) København, Gyldendal 1941. 381 pp.
A comprehensive history of the Danish book from the earliest time to World War II.

C. Nyrop, *Bidrag til den danske boghandels historie.* (Contributions to the history of the Danish book trade.) 2 vols. København, Gyldendal 1870. 653 pp.
Still the most extensive history of the Danish book trade. With a wealth of first-hand material.

H. Koppel, *Spredte træk af boghandelens historie.* (Some traits concerning the history of the book trade.) København, Henrik Koppel 1932. 73 pp.
A short guide to the history of the book trade, particularly the Danish.

O. Andersen, *Tidsbilleder fra boghandelens verden.* (Scenes from the world of the book trade.) København, P. Haase & Søn 1965. 191 pp.
13 selected articles, rendering pictures of the times from the world of books.

3 Retail Prices

In practice Danish books have been sold at fixed prices since the beginning of the 19th century. As to foreign books, a circular issued in 1829 by the then leading book importers regulated for the first time the conversion of foreign currencies into Danish money.

In 1837, when the forerunner of the present "Publishers' Association" was founded (→ 4), these and other usages were codified.

In principle these rules, details of which have often been altered, are the same now as then. Today they are contained in the *Samhandelsregler* ("Trade Regulations" → 4). The net price is defined as the retail price (catalogue price) fixed by the publisher and can only be altered by him. With a few exceptions (see below) the publisher's price has to be maintained by publishers, booksellers and secondary outlets to the general public.

For foreign books and periodicals the net price is fixed by the principal or sole agent. If there is no such agent the net price must be calculated on the basis of the rate of exchange at any time fixed by the "Danish Booksellers' Import Association" (DANBIF). These rates are published in "Boghandleren" (→ 5).

Secondary outlets are B-booksellers (→4, 24), railway stalls (→ 4, 24) and vendors of Frisalgsartikler "open sale"-titles (→21, 23, 24).

Dispensations from these regulations are granted by the *Boghandlerrådet* ("The Council of the Book Trade," → 4). They concern bulk selling for cash, delivery of books to schools, libraries, students, etc.

Price maintenance in Denmark is abolished by law. The upholding of net prices, as practised by the book trade, rests on a dispensation from the law, granted by the "Monopoly Board" until further notice.

4 Organization

In 1837, 13 Copenhagen publishers and booksellers set up the *Boghandlerforeningen i Kjøbenhavn* ("The Copenhagen Booksellers' Association"), the aim of which was to ascertain order, firmness and solidarity within the book trade. The young association watched the interests of the whole book trade, though, as the years passed, more and more from the publishers' point of view. After various stages of transition, in 1944 it became

Den danske Forlæggerforening
(The Danish Publishers' Association)
Vesterbrogade 41 B
DK 1620 København V

In 1970 the association had 62 members, headed by a board of 7 and a representative committee of 16 members. It maintains a secretariat, and has sub-divisions for textbooks, paperbacks and publicity. A special committee watches the booksellers' accounts and settlements. Its official organ is *Det danske Bogmarked* (→ 5).

In order to become a bookseller the applicant has to be accepted by the association. The relevant rules are contained in an appendix to the "Trade Regulations" (see below).

Provincial booksellers set up an association in 1891, Copenhagen booksellers in 1893. These two associations amalgamated in 1963 and became

Den danske Boghandlerforening
(The Danish Booksellers' Association)
Siljangade 6
DK 2300 København S

With 635 members (1970) this association is divided into 9 branches, 6 in the province, 3 in Copenhagen. The chairman of the association and the chairmen of the branches constitute the board. The association's official organ is *Boghandleren* (→ 5).

These two associations adopt the *Samhandelsregler* ("Trade Regulations").

The two head organizations meet in the *Boghandlerrådet* ("The Council of the Book Trade"), a joint body consisting of 4 publishers and 4 booksellers, established for the safeguarding and discussion of common interests within the organized book trade.

Contraventions of the "Trade Regulations" are dealt with by *Boghandlernævnet* ("The Board of Arbitration"), which also has 8 members, 4 elected by the publishers, 4 by the booksellers.

Bibliography

Samhandelsregler m. v. gældende i forholdet mellem forlæggere og boghandlere ifølge aftale mellem Den danske Forlæggerforening og Den danske Boghandlerforening. (Trade regulations governing relations between publishers and booksellers as agreed between the Danish Publishers' Association and the Danish Booksellers' Association.) København 1969.

Delivery and trade regulations, etc. København 1960. – An English translation of the rules named above. Not up to date.

The book trade in Denmark. A short guide on its history, organization and functions. København 1953.
Short but useful introduction, though not up to date in all details. The English edition is out of print, but a Danish one is still available.

Bøger og forlag i Danmark i 125 år, 1837–1962. (Books and publishing in Denmark, 1837–1962.) København, Den danske Forlæggerforening 1962. 143 pp.
Covers significant chapters of the history of publishing in Denmark and the development of the "Publishers' Association".

5 Trade Press

The principal Danish book-trade paper, founded in 1854 as "Dansk Boghandlertidende," is the weekly

Det danske Bogmarked
(The Danish Bookmarket)
Vesterbrogade 41 B
DK 1620 København V

owned by the "Publishers' Association", and its official organ.

Besides topical articles and editorial matter, "Det danske Bogmarked" contains official announcements, including recognition of new booksellers, changes in ownership, etc. A main feature is the weekly *Dansk Bogfortegnelse*, the foundation of Danish bibliography (→ 15). The paper carries a great many advertisements, having almost completely superseded former individual house organs.

While "Det danske Bogmarked" can be subscribed to by anyone and has a wide circulation in libraries and other circles, the monthly paper of the "Booksellers' Association,"

Boghandleren (The Bookseller)
Siljangade 6
DK 2300 København S

is not circulated outside the book trade. Founded in 1944, it covers the activities of the association and its branches, paying special attention to trade training in its various aspects, practical bookselling, etc.

Den danske Boghandlermedhjælperforening ("The Danish Bookseller Assistants' Association") publishes

Bogormen (The Book Worm)
Siljangade 6–8
DK 2300 København S

which appears 4–6 times a year and frequently contains articles of general interest.

The "Danish Book-Craft Association" (→ 20) publishes

Bogvennen
(The Book Friend)
Furesø Parkvej 51
DK 2830 Virum

which deals with the history, technique and make-up of the book and kindred subjects in a non-technical way.

Bibliography

Det danske Bogmarked: 100 År. 1. Juli 1854–1954. Special Number. København, Den danske Forlæggerforening, 1954. 109 pp. Contains many contributions about the history of this trade paper.

6 Book-Trade Literature

Considering the size of the country, Denmark has an extensive trade literature. As a supplement to the references following the separate chapters, the titles of some general works are given below.

a) Bibliography

Dansk litteratur om bogvæsen. (Danish literature about the book.) En bibliografi udarbejdet af J. L. Laursen. Parts 1–2. København, Forening for Boghaandværk 1955–56. 384 pp.
A systematically arranged bibliography of books and articles, dealing with book matters and history in general, printing, binding, illustrations, book trade, book collecting, etc. To be completed in 3 parts.

b) Other literature

Nordisk leksikon for bogvæsen. Redigeret af P. Birkelund, E. Dansten, L. Nielsen. København, Nyt Nordisk Forlag 1951–62. 1115 pp.
An encyclopedia of book matters in Denmark, Finland, Iceland, Norway and Sweden. With national editors and collaborators.

Bogen, dens historie, fremstilling og udbredelse. (The book, its history, production and distribution.) En håndbog for boghandlere og bogvenner. Udgivet af O. Andersen og A. Frøland under medvirkning af en række fagmænd. København, BMF 1925. 352 pp.

En bog om bogen. (A book about the book.) Edited by A. Marcus. Foreword by Sv. Dahl. København, Carit Andersen 1950. 486 pp.
Two surveys for the general reader: the history of the book, its production, sale, aesthetics, etc.

A. Frøland, *Bog og handel.* (Book and commerce.) København, Gyldendal 1964. 238 pp.
29 selected articles on practical bookselling, stressing the responsibility of publishers and booksellers as caretakers of an important cultural function.

7 Sources of Information, Address Services

Information in general about the Danish book trade can be obtained from or through

Den danske Forlræggerforening
(The Danish Publishers' Association)
Vesterbrogade 41 B
DK 1620 København V

Special bibliographical inquiries about Danish books should be addressed to

Det kongelige Bibliotek
(The Royal Library)
P. R. Department
Christians Brygge 8
DK 1219 København K

and about foreign books in Danish libraries to *Bibliotekernes Oplysninpkontor*
(Library Information Service)
Niels Juelsgade 7
DK 1059 København K

A list of recognized booksellers is available on request from the "Publishers' Association". Classified addresses can be found in the yearly *Kraks Vejviser* ("Krak's Directory"), accessible at all official Danish representations abroad.

8 International Membership

Naturally the various sections of the Danish book trade are members of the relevant international associations: publishers of IPA and IBBY, import booksellers of ICBA, antiquarian booksellers of ILAB. Denmark is a member of UNESCO.

In 1935 Scandinavian publishers founded *Det nordiske Forlæggerråd* ("Northern Publishers' Council"), the object of which is to further cooperation between Scandinavian publishers, to maintain their mutual interests in dealing with authorities, authors, etc., to watch international conditions, and so forth. The council has 12 members, 3 each from Denmark, Finland, Norway and Sweden.

9 Market Research

The Danish book trade has no institute of its own for market research, but as occasions arise official and private investigations are organized. If the material is meant for publication, this generally takes place in the trade papers (→ 5) or in books. The book market is watched by a joint committee of publishers and booksellers.

Recurring features are: "Forlagsstatistik", analysed statistics of publishers' activities, turnover, etc. "Regnskabsundersøgelser", investigations instituted by the "Danish Booksellers' Association" of booksellers' costs and gain-and-loss accounts. "Dansk Bogstatistik", the yearly bibliographical statistics (→ 16).

Investigations into reading habits, use of leisure time, etc., have been undertaken by sociological and library institutions, the most recent one in 1963 and published in the book named below.

Bibliography

Læste bøger. (Books which have been read.) Voksnes læsning og biblioteksbenyttelse. 2. ændrede udgave med oplysning om de læste bøgers vurdering ved B. V. Elberling og I. Bruhns. København, Danmarks Biblioteksskole 1967.
A publication from the "Sociological Laboratory of Denmark's Library School", dealing with adult reading and the use of libraries. With numerous tables and indexes.

Bøger. Årsrapport september 1958—august 1959. København, Gallup 1959.
An investigation undertaken by the "Gallup Institute of Denmark", and commented upon in a special report by Allers Reklamebureau. Stencilled.

10 Books and Young People

In recent years the general trend of Danish books for young readers has been towards quality; parents and other buyers of juveniles are beginning to understand that high-class products cannot be had at cut prices.

Quality is also the leading principle of the many-sided informatory work done by *Bibliotekscentralen* ("Danish Library Bureau").

Of interest to librarians as well as booksellers is the running valuation of new children's books in *Bogens Verden* ("The World of Books", → 33).

During the weeks before Christmas Danish daily papers review a fairly large number of juveniles, though for the rest of the year their information as regards this branch of literature is less satisfactory.

Danish schools and libraries maintain reading rooms for young and older children and encourage home lending of books from the picture-book stage upwards.

Indbindingscentralen ("Union Binding Service"), collaborating with publishers and

booksellers, produces standard bindings for libraries. Out of the 421 juvenile titles published in 1969 350 were to be had in "Indbindingscentral" bindings.
Almost all publishers of juveniles buy advertising space in the yearly Christmas catalogue of books, *Årets Bøger* (→ 30).
Subsidized by public funds and relying upon the concerted efforts of the book trade, the schools and the libraries, "Children's Book Weeks" are held every five years, the aim being to make parents and others conscious of the importance of children's reading habits and to diffuse knowledge of good juveniles.
Each year a prize for the best "Children's Books of the Year" is distributed by the Ministry for Culture (→ 32).
Denmark is a member of the IBBY.

Bibliography

I. SIMONSEN, *Den danske børnebog i det 19. aarhundrede.* (The Danish children's book in the 19th century.) 2nd edn København, Nyt Nordisk Forlag – A. Busck 1966. 303 pp.

V. STYBE, *Fra Askepot til Anders And. Børnebogen i kulturhistorisk perspektiv.* (Children's books and cultural history.) København, Munksgaard 1962. 133 pp.
Both books contain additional bibliographies.

11 Training

Since 1889 apprenticeships in Denmark have to an increasing degree been regulated by law. No apprenticeship can be of longer duration than 4 years, the first 6 months being considered a period of mutual probation. Indentures in writing must be drawn up and legally registered. The master has to pay health insurance, trade-school fees and materials, holiday allowances, etc., for the apprentice. Remuneration is settled within the frame-work of a "General Labour Agreement". Training schemes, which of course vary from trade to trade, have to be followed, and the master can be held responsible if apprentices have not acquired the necessary trade abilities.
In the book and stationery trade, practically always combined in Denmark, the length of apprenticeships varies from 2 to 4 years, depending on the apprentice's schooling.
The number of indentures registered in 1966 was 215, approximately 40% of the apprentices being male, 60% female.
Publishing houses employ apprentices only in the office section. Their better-qualified personnel are to a large degree recruited from bookshops, and, on the editorial side, from journalistic and academic circles.
Parallel with practical apprenticeship, theoretical training is also regulated by law. Trade-school attendance is compulsory, and all commercial trade apprentices receive the same basic tuition. This, however, is augmented by supplementary schooling for each separate branch of the trade, either in special classes attached to the local school of trade or as a boarding-school course.
Courses for advanced supplementary training are progressing.

12 Taxes

The "Danish Added Value Tax" (1970 15%) includes books, thereby increasing the published price of books with this percentage. Exempted from the tax are export sales and sales to the Faroe Islands and Greenland.

13 Clearing Houses

Booksellers establish cash accounts with the "DBK" (→ 23) from which minor amounts on their behalf are paid to publishers and other suppliers against documentation in the shape of invoices and order forms.

Also, larger seasonal (monthly, quarterly) accounts between booksellers and publishers are to a certain extent settled with the assistance of the "DBK".

14 Copyright

The Danish "Copyright Act" of 31 May 1961 protects authors' rights until 50 years after their death. Transfer of copyright does not affect the author's *droit moral.* With certain limitations Radio Danmark is entitled to broadcast copyright literary works against payment, and other limitations apply as to the use of copyright texts for teaching purposes. The "Copyright Act" of 1961, covering artistic, dramatic, musical and cinematographic works too, is supplemented by a special "Act on Rights in Photographic Pictures".
Denmark belongs to the "Berne Convention" and, since 1962, is party of the "Universal Copyright Convention" of 1955.

Bibliography

a) Periodicals

NIR. Nordiskt immateriellt rättsskydd.

b) Books

T. Lund, *Ophavsret.* (Copyright.) Kommenteret udgave af lovene af 31. maj 1961 om ophavsretten til litterære og kunstneriske værker og retten til fotografiske billeder. København, G.E.C. Gad 1961.

15 National Bibliography, National Library

The Danish national bibliography is published at four stages, all of them under the collective title *Dansk Bogfortegnelse* ("Danish List of Books"):

(1) weekly in "Det danske Bogmarked" (→ 5),
(2) monthly as separate parts, called "Månedsfortegnelser" ("Monthly Lists"),
(3) annually as "Årskatalog" ("Annual Catalogue"), and
(4) every five years as "Femårskatalog" ("Five-year Catalogue").

All of these lists and catalogues are alphabetically arranged under author's name or title and cross-indexed. In and after the monthly parts classified indexes are added.
Useful also from a bookseller's point of view is the annotated catalogue *Årets Bøger* ("Books of the Year") (→ 30).
The Danish national library is

Det kongelige Bibliotek
(The Royal Library)
Christians Brygge 8
DK 1219 København K

to which printers have to send a deposit copy of every book printed by them. Special rules apply to pamphlets, graphical works, advertising matter, etc.
Deposit copies have also to be sent to the *Statsbiblioteket* ("State Library") at Århus, while the *Universitetsbiblioteket* ("University Library") in Copenhagen is endowed with the right of requisitioning a copy.
Useful practical tools are:

Fælles lagerkatalog 1970. (Common stock catalogue 1970). Containing 13,000 titles other than school textbooks in print from 68 publishers and most important contractors (→ 21) with prices, dates, etc. København, Publishers' Association and Booksellers' Association 1970. 420 pp.

Danske skolebøger 1970. (Danish school books 1970). Approximately 4,000 titles in print. København 1970. 188 pp. Published annually.

16 Book Production

According to official Danish statistics the production of books in Denmark was:

1967 4,895 titles of which
1,190 were booklets of 48 pages or less
1968 4,972 titles of which
1,201 were booklets of 48 pages or less
1969 4,978 titles of which
1,336 were booklets of 48 pages or less

Denmark

Production in 1969, books and booklets, classified according to the decimal code:

Subject	Titles	Percentage of total production
Generalities	145	2.9
Philosophy	104	2.1
Religion	165	3.3
Social sciences	693	14.0
Geography	193	3.8
Pure sciences	376	7.6
Applied sciences	861	17.2
Arts	291	5.9
Literature		
a. Critics and philology	212	4.3
b. Texts	1,503	30.2
History and biography	435	8.7
Total	4,978	100.0

17 Translations

A knowledge of foreign languages — especially English — being widespread, Denmark offers a remunerative market for foreign books. The interest taken in conditions abroad also manifests itself in many translations. Of 4,978 titles published in 1969 1,693 were translated from the following languages: English 480, American 438, Swedish 203, German 139, French 93, Norwegian 55, others 114, first-published works and reprints included. In the groups fiction and juveniles translations outnumbered works in the original, the figures being 610 against 281, and 258 against 93 respectively. The number of books printed in 2 languages or more was 171.

Not a few works by Danish scientists and technicians appear in foreign languages, preferably English, while works of this kind published in Danish often contain an English summary.

Translations of Danish books into foreign languages in 1967 amounted to 394 titles.

18 Book Clubs

When book clubs came into existence abroad, some Danish publishers attached the term (in Danish "bogklub") to book series of a fixed number of volumes to which buyers subscribed without entering into membership. Genuine book clubs, dependent on membership and the purchase of a amount and otherwise leaving the choice of titles to the members, are a recent phenomenon in Denmark. So far (1970) only a couple of clubs fully fit in with the requirements of such an enterprise.

Danish book clubs, genuine as well as nominal ones, operate in a various ways with booksellers.

19 Paperbacks

Modern pocket books were introduced 1950 on a larger scale, including quality paperbacks in 1959.

Approximately 35 organized publishers partake in the paperback trade, publishing 125 series, partly fiction, partly general literature, many of them comprising but a few titles. The total number of titles carried in stock amounts to approximately 3,500 titles. Besides the above-mentioned, a substantial number of titles, mainly detective stories, westerns and other forms of light fiction, is produced by non-organized firms, the total of paperbacks of all categories being as follows:

	Number of books of 49 pages or more	Number of paperbacks	Percentage
1967	3,705	1,025	27.7
1968	3,771	959	25.4
1969	3,642	804	22.1

As paperbacks for the greater part are "open sale" titles (→ 3, 21, 23, 24) they

can be bought in bookshops and numerous other outlets. In practice the majority of the better-class paperbacks are sold by booksellers, while non-literary titles dominate the sales in secondary outlets. Naturally no fixed borderline exists.
An annual trade list of available paperbacks is published by *Dansk Bogtjeneste* (→ 30).

20 Book Design

The best-designed books have been selected since 1934 under the auspices of the "Forening for Boghaandværk" ("The Danish Book-Craft Association") (→ 5, 31). In the beginning the jury stressed artistic features, thereby giving preference to prestige books, etc.
In 1943 the jury was split into two: one for printing, one for binding; technical workmanship, aesthetic qualities and functional suitability being laid down as guiding principles for the juries. The number of titles in each of the two groups is limited to approximately 25.
A yearly illustrated report on the findings of the juries is published under the title *Årets bedste bøger / Årets bedste bogbind* ("The best books / bindings of the year").
The chosen books and bindings are shown each year at the "Frankfurt Book Fair" as part of the international exhibit "The best-designed books of the world".

21 Publishing

In 1970 there were 62 organized publishers, i.e. members of the "Danish Publishers' Association" (→ 4). Of these only 5 are domiciled outside Copenhagen.
Some 250 persons, institutions, etc. are, however, recognized as publishers in a technical sense of the word, being entitled to have their publications sold through the organized book trade. Nearly all use the "Trade Counter" of the "Clearing House" (→ 23) as their commercial agent. In order to enjoy these facilities the publishers have to sign an agreement with the "Council of the Book Trade" (→ 4), thereby becoming contractors and binding themselves to comply with the "Trade Regulations" (→ 4) in the same way as publishers proper. A minority of these contractors, perhaps some 25, would qualify for membership in the "Publishers' Association", and out of this minority 3–5 are obvious candidates but for various reasons prefer to remain outside the organization.
From official statistics a clear picture of Danish publishing cannot be drawn, the figures not being sufficiently differentiated, but every second year statistics about organized publishers' activities are issued by the "Publishers' Association" in "Det danske Bogmarked" (→ 5). Unfortunately not all members submit material, and figures for the whole trade therefore do not exist. The participating firms, however, constitute an overwhelming part of the turnover.
Based on published price less usual bookseller's discount the total sale in 1969 from 44 members of the Publishers' Association amounted to 251.6 million DKr., to which should be added some 12 million DKr. as the estimated sale from the 18 members not submitting material for the statistical survey.
Sales channels were: Booksellers 68.2%; B-booksellers (→ 24) 0.6%; railway bookstalls (→ 24) and "open sale" outlets (→ 4) 4.4%; exports 4.6%; canvassing, mail order, book clubs 22.2%.
As to railway bookstalls and "open sale" outlets, the percentages do not indicate their total sales volume, to which must be added a considerable amount occurring from the sale of publications from non-organized publishers not included in the statistics here quoted (→ 19).
A count of titles in "Dansk Bogfortegnelse"

(→ 15) for 1969 shows the following output of titles from all organized publishers:

Groups of titles	Number publishers	Number of titles	Average of titles	Percentage of titles
0– 25	30	206	6.9	5.6
26– 50	14	516	36.8	13.9
51–100	13	1,059	81.5	28.3
101–250	2	378	189.0	10.1
251–500	2	594	297.0	16.0
501 and more	1	972	972.0	26.1
Total	62	3,725	60.0	100.0

Denmark is a member of IPA and "Det nordiske Forlæggerråd" (→ 8).

Bibliography

B. Bramsen, *Forlagskalkulation.* (Calculation in publishing.) 2nd rev. edn 182 pp. København, Den danske Forlæggerforening 1968. Also published in Swedish. A Dutch edition in preparation.

22 Literary Agents

In Denmark it is an exception for the rights in a book of Danish origin not to be negotiated directly between author and publisher.
The few literary agencies are engaged in placing Danish literary rights abroad and foreign rights in Denmark.

23 Wholesale Trade

Wholesaling only occurs within limited sectors of the Danish book trade. *Gyldendals Forhandlerekspedition* ("Gyldendal's Vendors Trade Counter") supplies B-booksellers (→ 24) with books from all publishers, *Bladhandlerforbundet* (The Union of Press Vendors) supplies railway stalls (→ 24), and *Bladkompagniet* (The Press Company) handles so-called "open-sale" books (→ 21, 24).

The sole, monopolized forwarding agent to the organized booksellers (sometimes called A-booksellers) is

Danske Boghandleres Kommissionsanstalt (DBK)
(Danish Booksellers' Clearing House)
Siljangade 6–8
DK 2300 København S.

It is a private institution, supervised by a board of booksellers and publishers, founded in 1894.
In recent years "DBK", through its *Forlagsekspeditionen* ("Trade Counter"), has become the general agent to most of the many contractors, private or others (→ 21), whose publications are sold through the organized book trade.
"DBK" also acts as a clearing house for certain payments (→ 13).
In order to keep costs down and facilitate meeting booksellers' orders a cooperative company,

Fælleseksped itionen
(Joint Trade Counter)
Njalsgade 19
DK 2300 København S

was formed by three publishers in 1955. Since then other publishers have joined the company, which in 1970 comprised 27 firms. Besides carrying out booksellers' orders its functions include warehousing, shipping (via "DBK", see above), invoicing, settlements of accounts, etc.
For bookkeeping, statistical, and related purposes three keenly competitive major publishing houses, all of which run big bookshops and have their own trade counters, have joined forces in a cooperative company, *Forlags-Data* ("Data Processing"), utilizing a combined computer system.

24 Retail Trade

Denmark is a country of many bookshops. In towns and densely populated areas there is always one close at hand, and even in the remotest parts no bookbuyer has farther than 10 km to travel in order to reach one. The average number of inhabitants per bookshop is about 7,000.

Naturally these many bookshops—about 700 in all—vary in size and activity. A few firms in the capital sell books exclusively, while the majority handles stationery and kindred goods as well, thereby broadening the point-of-sale display of books considerably.

Irrespective of the type of bookshop the vocational skill is generally high, and booksellers have played an important role in making Denmark a book-buying country. With scarcity of labour and rising costs the future of the very small shops, especially in the capital and in larger towns, does not look too bright at present.

The number of bookshops recognized by the "Publishers' Association" (→ 4) includes some 675 firms (1970). 635 are members of the "Booksellers' Association" (→ 4), which groups them as follows according to turnover:

Turnover DKr. 1,000	Number of firms	Percentage of firms
Up to 400	240	38
400–800	242	38
800–1,200	83	13
1,200 and more	70	11
	635	100

In 1969 170 firms, representing a turnover of 145.7 million DKr., took part in the annual census "Regnskabsundersøgelser" (→ 9). They were grouped in the following way:

Turnover DKr. 1,000	Number of firms	Percentage of firms	Percentage of turnover
Up to 400	20	12	4
400–800	82	48	33
800–1,200	42	25	28
1,200 and more	26	15	35
	170	100	100

Apart from the bookshops recognized by the "Publishers' Association" there are about 40 B-bookshops (→ 23), which carry all sorts of books from all publishers, but with the firm of Gyldendal as their sole supplier. Their number is diminishing, some of them are going out of business, while the successful ones are becoming recognized bookshops. Railway stalls form a third category of authorized outlets for books. They are supplied through the "Bladhandlerforbundet" (→ 23), which is entitled to booksellers' discount on all books with the exception of textbooks. There are some 150 of these bookstalls.

As mentioned above, the Danish book trade operates with so-called "open-sale" titles, i.e. with certain exceptions books priced at (1970) 17 DKr., juveniles at DKr. 10.25, or less, including added value tax. Any publisher or bookseller is entitled to deliver such items to the outlets in question. The chief supplier, however, is "Bladkompagniet" (→ 23), which serves about 1,000 outlets of this kind out of a total approximately 5,000 clients.

25 Mail-Order Bookselling

In a small market like Denmark's successful publishing of multi-volume subscription works nearly always depends on a combination of booksellers' sales over the counter and canvassing. The sales volume achieved by either booksellers or canvassers naturally varies from work to work, but ordinarily both branches have to participate in the sales efforts if all possibilities are to be exploited and a satisfying net result attained.

Practically all canvassing is done by publishers. The large houses maintain individual departments for this purpose; medium-sized and smaller firms have formed a cooperative sales organization. The majority of orders are executed by the pub-

lishers themselves, but if customers want it, orders are passed on to booksellers.
Outside the organized book trade a few publishing firms of limited importance cater for the subscription market by canvassing.
The dense network of bookshops in Denmark leaves mail-order bookselling no great possibilities. A few firms propagate specific branches of literature, domestic and foreign, and some mail-order advertising is done by publishers.
It is stipulated by the "Trade regulations" (→ 4) that publishers' order forms must contain space for a bookseller's name in case customers want to place their orders with such a firm.
Extensive circularizing is done by booksellers and/or publishers, the booksellers' material as a rule being supplied by publishers. Prospectuses etc. sent out by publishers must contain space for a bookseller's name.

26 Antiquarian Book Trade, Auctions

In general, Danish antiquarian booksellers may be said to fall into three groups: antiquarian booksellers proper, a few of them running a department for new books; appointed retail booksellers running an antiquarian department; second-hand booksellers operating in a small way.
It is stipulated by the "Trade regulations" (→ 4) that if new and antiquarian books are sold by the same firm they have to be kept apart.
The position of Copenhagen as an important factor in the North European antiquarian book trade is due to the big firms in groups 1 and 2 which do business on an international scale and issue excellent catalogues, some of them in English.
Antiquarian booksellers in Denmark are organized in

Den danske Antikvarboghandlerforening
(The Danish Antiquarian Booksellers' Association)
Kronprinsensgade 3
DK 1114 København K

founded in 1920. In 1970 it had some 40 members, the overwhelming majority domiciled in the capital. A list of members can be had on request. Requirements for becoming a member are defined in the statutes of the association.
The book-trade papers (→ 5) carry "Books Wanted" columns.
Book auctions are held by independent organizations, two of them dominating the field. Most antiquarians act as commissioners, charging a fee of 10%.
Denmark is a member of the ILAB.

Bibliography

Mennesker og bøger. (Men and books.) 46 skribenter om bogens betydning i vor tilværelse. København, Antikvarboghandlerforeningen 1945. 274 pp.

Danske Bogauktioner. Med en oversigt over bogpriserne. This list of Danish book auctions—with a survey of book prices—is published at intervals of 2 or 3 years by the "Antiquarian Booksellers' Association" and the "Book-Craft Association".

27 Book Imports

In Denmark, as probably in most other countries, a considerable but statistically invisible import and export of books takes place as postal "printed matter". In terms of money it amounts to an unknown but probably quite substantial figure.
When studying the following tables the reader should bear in mind that the two main factors in Danish book imports are: (1) the population's need for books in foreign languages; (2) the production abroad of books in Danish. The first factor accounts for imports from the United Kingdom, USA, France; the second, for imports from Czechoslovakia, Italy, the Netherlands; as for Sweden, Norway and the Federal Republic of Germany both factors operate.

The official figures for imports in 1968 were

Category	Amount DKr. 1,000
Books	39,123
Periodicals	27,814
Picture books for children	2,775
Music	1,233
Maps, etc.	2,345
Total	73,290

The most important countries of origin were:

Country	Amount DKr. 1,000	Percentage of total
United Kingdom	9,750	24.9
USA	5,430	13.9
Germany (F.R.)	5,366	13.7
Czechoslovakia	4,104	10.5
Sweden	3,694	9.4
Norway	3,098	7.9
France	1,504	3.8
Netherlands	1,491	3.8
Italy	1,284	3.3
Austria	409	1.0

The figures for the imports of periodicals are influenced in the same way as the figures for books. The most important countries of origin were (1968):

Country	Amount DKr. 1,000	Percentage of total
Sweden	8,996	32.3
Germany (F.R.)	6,993	25.1
USA	4,055	14.8
United Kingdom	2,472	8.9
Norway	1,848	6.6
France	963	3.4
Netherlands	664	2.4
Poland	588	2.1
Spain	347	1.2
Switzerland	318	1.1

28 Book Exports

The official figures for Danish export of books and kindred material in 1968 were:

Category	Amount DKr. 1,000
Books	26,692
Periodicals	16,314
Picture books for children	3,221
Music	467
Maps, etc.	516
Total	47,210

Export possibilities for books in Danish are naturally limited, the other Scandinavian countries being the only substantial purchasers. Besides exports of this kind, however, figures for Sweden and Norway include exports of books in Swedish and Norwegian, produced in Denmark. The most important consumer countries were:

Country	Amount DKr. 1,000	Percentage of total
Sweden	11,192	41.9
Norway	6,210	26.2
USA	2,100	7.8
Germany (F.R.)	1,374	5.1
United Kingdom	1,216	4.6
Iceland	956	3.6
Finland	552	2.0
Netherlands	444	1.7
China (Peoples' Republic)	325	1.2

As to periodicals, the most important consumer countries were (1968):

Country	Amount DKr. 1,000	Percentage of total
Sweden	8,061	49.4
Norway	2,965	18.2
USA	1,787	10.9
United Kingdom	1,380	8.5
Iceland	1,369	8.4
Germany (F.R.)	218	1.3
Italy	242	1.4
Austria	113	1.4

Denmark

30 Public Relations

The image of the Danish book trade may be said to be good. All the same, it has been suggested that the trade should appoint a permanent PR agent. So far proposals of this kind have only resulted in tentative attempts, leading personalities in the trade being afraid of too much stereotyped officialdom.
Besides publishers' and booksellers' individual publicity efforts very useful work is done by the publicity office

Dansk Bogtjeneste
(Danish Book Service)
Store Kannikestr. 16
DK 1169 København K

founded in 1939 for cooperative advertising purposes and now with a membership of some 650 booksellers. Publishers are not eligible, but collectively and individually they are in close contact with "Dansk Bogtjeneste".
Jointly with the trade associations "Dansk Bogtjeneste" produces the annual catalogue *Årets Bøger* ("Books of the Year"), which is distributed in $1^1/_4$ million copies. $^4/_5$ of the production costs are borne by publishers through advertisements, $^1/_5$ by booksellers, who also bear the costs of distribution. In practice it works out at 50–50.
Other important catalogues issued by "Dansk Bogtjeneste" are the lists of paperbacks (→ 19) for trade and advertising purposes, and the annual *Nedsættelseskatalog* ("Catalogue of remainders") which has superseded former individual lists of this kind.
In leaflet form: *Faglige Boglister* ("Lists of classified literature") of which in 1970 36 different ones were available. They are revised annually.
"Dansk Bogtjeneste" produces material for window displays, etc., and maintains a decoration department. It is the organizer of "Children's Book Weeks" (→ 10) and takes care of the practical work in connection with these weeks (catalogues, etc.).

Bibliography

A. G. SCHLANBUSCH, *Dansk Bogtjeneste 1939–1964*. København, Dansk Bogtjeneste 1964.

A. FRØLAND, *Kundebetjening*. (To meet the customer.) København, Boghandler Fagskolen 1953. 112 pp.
One of the few special books dealing with all practical and theoretical questions of serving the customer in the bookshops. A German version appeared in 1955 ("Kundenbedienung"). Also translated into Swedish and Serbo-Croatian.

31 Bibliophily

Measured by international standards modern Danish bibliophily may be said to rank high, counting many distinguished collectors and connoisseurs. The general trend is towards specialization, as distinct from the mere amassing of books, and while, of course, Danish bibliophiles in common with other collectors appreciate the old and the rare, quite a lot of them appreciate graphic design, printing and bindings in their modern forms, devoting much time to the study of such matters.
In 1942 the

Dansk Bibliofil-Klub
(Danish Bibliophiles' Club)
Drosselvej 31
DK 2000 København F

was founded. It has a maximum membership of 49, arranges discussions, excursions, etc.
An organization for the large public interested in beautiful books is the society

Bogvennerne
(The Book Friends)
Madvigs Alle 2
DK 1829 København V

It works on commercial lines, reprints classics, etc., in illustrated editions that would otherwise not be possible. With a membership of about 5,000 so far, it has almost a hundred titles to its credit.

Another series is "Scripta", while the

Club 13 Cicero (13 Pica)
Titangade 12
DK København N

is devoted to typographical experiments. A fairly large number of printers and publishers offer designers interesting tasks in the form of Christmas and New Year publications.

Since 1888 the

Forening for Boghaandværk
(The Danish Book-Craft Association)
Furesø Parkvej 51
DK 2830 Virum

(→ 20) has promoted the spread of knowledge of book production; it is thus paving the way to an understanding of bibliophily and book collecting. It arranges meetings, exhibitions, etc. and publishes the periodical *Bogvennen* ("The Book Friend") (→ 5), as well as monographs on typography, illustrations, bookselling, etc., and valuable reprints.

Bibliography

K. F. Plesner, *Bøger och bogsamlere. Bibliofiliens historie.* (Books and book collectors. The history of bibliophily.) København, Rosenkilde og Bagger 1962. 245 pp. Contains many remarks about bibliophily in Denmark and other Scandinavian countries.

K. F. Plesner, *Danske bogsamlere i det 19de århundrede.* (Danish book collectors in the 19th century.) København, Forening for Boghaandværk 1957. 160 pp.

32 Literary Prizes

Denmark's State Budget each year allocates a certain amount (1970; 2,200,000 DKr.), as permanent Civil List Pensions. *Statens Kunstfond* ("The State Art Fund") annually distributes some 4,200,000 DKr. among authors, artists, and compositors, to secure economic freedom to work for periods of varying length. In some ways the "Carlsberg Foundation", established in 1876, can be compared to the "Art Fund". Apart from their monetary value these grants are considered as distinctions.

Among the many private or institutional literary prizes and endowments, the best known are:

Det danske Akademis Pris ("The Danish Academy Prize"). 50,000 DKr. Since 1961; distributed each 28 November, the Academy's foundation day.

H. C. Andersen-Legatet ("The Hans Christian Andersen Endowment"). 5,000 DKr. Since 1955; distributed each 2 April, the poet's birthday.

Holberg-Medaillen ("The Ludvig Holberg Medal"). Medal and 5,000 DKr. Since 1934; distributed each 3 December, the name-giver's birthday.

Børnebogsprisen ("The Children's Book Prize"). Each year a prize for the best juvenile of the year is distributed by the Ministry for Culture.

Kritiker-Prisen ("The Critics' Prize"). 5,000 DKr. Instituted in 1957 by the "Publishers' Association". Distributed annually after a poll among literary critics.

De gyldne Laurbær. ("The Golden Laurels"). Among established Danish authors that have published books of distinction in the preceding year; since 1950. Each January/February one is chosen by booksellers' vote and handed the "Golden Laurels" at a dinner in the Booksellers' Club. From 1968 an amount of money is attached to this award.

Søren Gyldendal-Prisen ("The Søren Gyldendal Prize"). 10,000 DKr. Instituted in 1958 by the house of Gyldendal and distributed annually on 12 April, the founder's birthday.

A joint Scandinavian price, instituted 1962 by the "Nordic Council" (Denmark,

Finland, Iceland, Norway, Sweden), is *Nordisk Råds store Litteraturpris* ("The Great Literary Prize of the Nordic Council"). 50,000 DKr. Given annually to an author from one of the states named above whose book is considered the best of the year.

33 The Reviewing of Books

As a means of literary communication the daily press easily comes first. All daily Danish papers, large or small, devote a lot of space to literary matters in the form of reviews, reportage, feature articles. The bigger papers maintain permanent staffs of competent critics in many fields, while the smaller ones partly rely on syndicated contributions.
The bulk of books reviewed is naturally in Danish, but attention is also paid to outstanding works in foreign languages, especially in English.
The widest circulated Danish papers, and thus the review media of primary importance, are (in 1970):

	1,000 copies Dailies	Sundays
Berlingske Tidende		
Copenhagen, Conservative	158	299
Politiken		
Copenhagen, Liberal	134	226
Jyllands-Posten		
Århus, Conservative	81	170
B. T.		
Copenhagen, Independent	195	
Ekstra Bladet		
Copenhagen, Independent	200	

Two papers which take a special interest in literary matters are:

		Saturdays
Berlingske Aftenavis		
Copenhagen, Conservative	13	40
Information		
Copenhagen, Independent	19	

Comprehensive in its coverage of current literature, "Bogens Verden" is published by the "Danish Library Association" (→ 10); in it specialists review worthwhile books on all subjects.
Indispensable to booksellers and librarians is the weekly "Det danske Bogmarked" (→ 5).
As part of their cultural function the Danish (State) Radio and TV foster the spread of good literature.

34 Graphic Arts

Danish graphic associations meet in
De grafiske Fags Sammenslutning
(The Graphic Arts Union)
Landemærket 11
DK 1119 København K
to which all relevant inquiries should be addressed.

35 Miscellaneous

Faroe Islands/Greenland
Færøerne (The Faroe Islands) and Grønland (Greenland) are special administrative and cultural areas within the Kingdom of Denmark. These areas have languages of their own, Danish being taught and otherwise used as a secondary language.
The population (Faroe Islands approximately 37,500, Greenland approximately 44,000 in 1968) being too small to support every kind of literature, both areas are largely dependent on books in Danish.
In 1969 61 titles were published in the Faroe Islands. Booksellers accepted by "Den danske Forlæggerforening" (→ 4) numbered 8. In 1965 they bought Danish books to the value of DKr. 1,284,000.
In 1969 some 30 titles were published in Greenland, to which must be added a number of textbooks in Greenlandic, published in Copenhagen.
There are 5 private bookshops in Greenland, recognized by the "Danish Publishers'

Association", This association also recognizes *Den kongelige grønlandske Handel* ("The Royal Greenland Trade Department") as a wholesaler for Greenland. In 16 towns and villages with trade posts it maintains outlets for books, some of them organized as special sections in general stores. In 1968 Greenland bought Danish books worth DKr. 1,893,000.

Bibliography

K. Oldenow, *Bogtrykkerkunsten i Grønland.* (Book printing in Greenland.) København, privately printed 1957. 236 pp.

K. Oldendow, *The spread of printing: Greenland.* Amsterdam, Vangendt, 1969. 72 pp. Condensation of the original Danish publication (→ above).

Finland

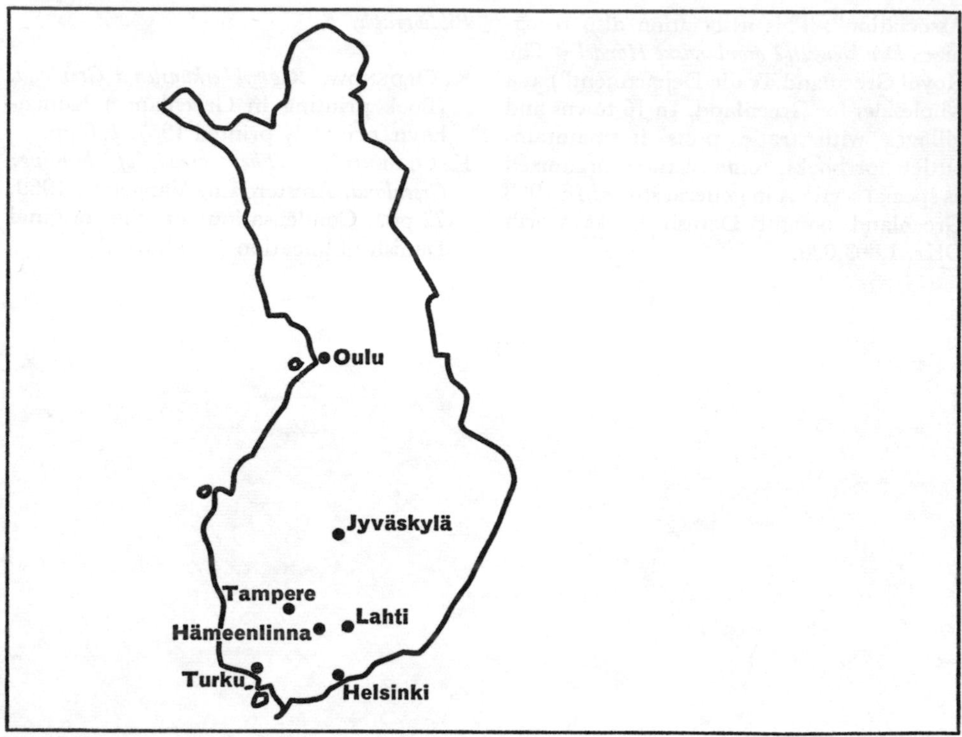

Important Book Centres

1 General Information

Area 337,032 km²
Population 4,626,000 (15.1 per km² of land area)
Capital Helsinki (506,000)
Largest towns Helsinki (506,000); Tampere (144,000); Turku (140,000); Lahti (82,000); Oulu (79,000)
Government Republic
Religion Evangelical Church 92.6%
Orthodox Church 1.3%
Other religious groups and dissidents 6.1%
National languages Finnish 92.4%, Swedish 7.4%
Leading foreign languages English, German
Weights, measures Metric system
Currency unit Finnish mark (Fmk)
Education Compulsory. 50,050 (1967) students, of whom 26,026 women and 200 foreigners at 14 universities and technical and other colleges of academic standard
Illiteracy Practically nil
Paper consumption a) Newsprint 19.6 kg per inhabitant (1967)
b) Printing paper (other than newsprint) 15.3 kg per inhabitant (1967)
Membership Unesco, IPA, ICBA, ILAB

2 Past and Present

Ever since 1488, when the "Missale Aboense", the first book to be prepared for Finland, was printed in Lübeck (Germany) on behalf of the Turku Bishop's Council, and since Finland's reformator, Mikael Agricola, had the first Finnish-language books printed in Stockholm in the 1540s and 1550s, Finnish book publishing was mainly dependent on the interest shown by Finland's leading clergy. The first public bookshop was founded in Turku in 1779 and Finland's first professional publisher started at about the same time; four decades passed with hardly one important competitor in the book trade in the whole country.

Then, slowly, the situation began to change: book printers and booksellers opened trade and new men entered the profession. In 1858 the "Publishers' Association of Finland" was founded. This was a tight organization of the book trade in Finland, for a bookshop could have no books from the publishers without the acceptance of and a guarantee given to the Association.

The next growth period in the publishing and bookselling trades was in the 1880s with the rapid increase in the amount of Finnish-language literature; this increase has continued steadily. The number of publishing companies has remained comparatively small, however, for the reason that the two oldest companies (founded in 1878 and 1890) have grown large, ranking on an international scale (together they now publish about 1,100 titles a year).

The number of bookshops in Finland is comparatively large, but many are situated in small localities and sell very small numbers of books. Unlike the small countryside bookshops, all towns and cities have very impressive bookshops; two Helsinki shops are among the largest in the world.

Bibliography

Y. A. Jäntti, *Kirjakaupan ja kustannustoiminnan historia.* (The history of bookselling and publishing.) Vol. I. The history until 1789. Helsinki, Werner Söderström 1950, XXV, 315 pp.
All important European countries and the USA are included in this general history.

A. Virtanen, *Suomen kirjakaupan ja kustannustoiminnan vaiheita.* (Events in bookselling and publishing in Finland.) Helsinki, Publishers' Association of Finland 1958. 401 pp.

O. Zweygbergk, *Om bokförlag och bokförläggare i Finland.* (Publishing in Finland.) Helsinki, Publishers' Association of Finland 1958. 199 pp.

3 Retail Prices

The net-price system was introduced to Finland with the formation of the "Publishers' Association of Finland" (1858) and was fully acknowledged in the late 1880s. The commission system still practised in Finland has helped to keep net prices intact.

The Law for the Promotion of the Economic Competition of 1964 changed this situation and the "Publishers' Association" started negotiations with the "Freedom of Commerce Board", the result being that the authorities have extended the net-price system until 31 December 1970.

From the beginning of 1971 the net-price system has been abandoned.

4 Organization

The leading publishing companies are members of the

Suomen Kustannusyhdistys ry
(Publishers' Association of Finland)
Kalevankatu 16
SF Helsinki 10

established 1858 in Helsinki.

According to its constitution, its purpose

is to take care of the general professional interests of its members, to promote the development of the production and distribution of literature, and to protect the rights of its members.

The Association has a board of directors including 6 members.

The interests of booksellers are taken care of by

Kirja- ja Paperikauppojen Liitto
(Booksellers' and Stationers' Association)
Kalevankatu 16
SF Helsinki 10

Common matters are handled by a joint committee on which publishers and booksellers are represented. The most important common undertakings are *Suomen Kirjakauppalehti* ("Finnish Bookseller" → 5), the advertising agency *Kirjapalvelu* ("Book Service" →29,30), *Kirjakauppakoulu* ("School for Booksellers" → 11) and *Suomen Kirjakaupan Säätio* ("The Foundation of the Book Branch"), which pays out old-age pensions and loans.

5 Trade Press

The trade journal is

Suomen Kirjakauppalehti
(Finnish Bookseller)
Kalevankatu 16
SF Helsinki 10

which is issued once a month.

The "Booksellers' Assistants" have their own journal,

Libristi
Box 10 242
SF Helsinki 10.

6 Book-Trade Literature

a) Bibliographies

R. Luhtanen, *Kirjakauppaa ja kustannustoimintaa käsittelevää suomalaista kirjallisuutta.* (Finnish literature dealing with bookselling and publishing.) Helsinki, Libro 1954. 40 pp.

b) General books

Jäsenet ja kirjakaupat 1970. (Members and booksellers in 1970.) Helsinki, Publishers' Association of Finland 1970. 103 pp.
Names and addresses of publishers, booksellers and organizations of the book trade. Published every other year.

Kirjakauppojen kannattavuus vuonna 1964. (The profitability of the bookstores in 1964.) Helsinki, Kirjavälitys 1966. 20 pp.
Combined sales, costs, net results, etc. of 348 bookstores.

U. Lappi, *Kirja kirjasta.* (A book about books.) Helsinki, Werner Söderström 1970. 207 pp.
The functioning and influence of the net-price system and the consequences of its abolition.

c) Textbooks

See Luhtanen (above). Most important is

A. Virtanen, *Kirjakauppaoppi.* (Textbook for bookstores.) Helsinki, Kirjavälitys 1950. 402 pp.

7 Sources of Information, Address Services

Publishing and general information:

Suomen Kustannusyhdistys ry
(Publishers' Association of Finland)
Kalevankatu 16
SF Helsinki 10

Booksellers' addresses etc:

Kirja- ja Paperikauppojen Liitto
(Booksellers' and Stationers' Association)
Kalevankatu 16
SF Helsinki 10

8 International Membership

The "Publishers' Association" is a member of the "International Publishers' Association" and of the "Scandinavian Publishers' Council". The "Booksellers' and Stationers' Association" is a member of ICBA.

9 Market Research

In Finland there is no institute specializing in book-market research. The members of the "Publishers' Association" (→ 4) send in yearly figures of production, sales, etc., and these are combined. Every few years information is collected from the bookstores and published. Occasional studies of the opinions and requirements of the public are carried out at the universities and by the trade's advertising agency "Kirjapalvelu" (→ 29, 30).

10 Books and Young People

Interest in juvenile literature has been increasing since the 1950s. In 1957
Suomen Nuortenkirjaneuvosto
(Finnish Council for Children's Books)
II linja 23 A
SF Helsinki 53
was established. It forms the Finnish section of the "International Board on Books for Young People".
The association
Suomen Nuorisokirjailijat
(Authors of Juvenile Books in Finland)
Lönnrotinkatu 19 A 25
SF Helsinki 12
was established in 1946.

11 Training

The "Publishers' Association" (→ 4) and the "Booksellers' and Stationers' Association" (→ 4) together take care of
Kirjakauppakoulu
(School for Booksellers)
Kalevankatu 16
SF Helsinki 10
The course for booksellers' assistants starts in autumn with a few days' orientation; after that students study at home. In spring an eight-week course starts with examinations.
Another course of eight weeks is arranged for managers every few years.
In addition the school arranges one-week summer and recreation courses and a few days' elementary courses for trainees.

12 Taxes

All products have an 11% sales tax, and since 1964 even books have been included.

14 Copyright

The copyright act for literary and artistic works of 1961 is almost the same as in other Scandinavian countries. According to the law the author's rights are protected for 50 years after his death.
Finland has ratified the "Berne Convention", with its amendments (Rome, 1928 and Brussels, 1948).

15 National Bibliography, National Library

The first attempt to compile a Finnish national bibliography was made by Johannes Schefferus, who included in his person- and book-catalogue *Svecia literata* (Stockholm 1680) a short section of Finnish literature. It was followed in 1719 by *Aboa literata*, compiled by a Swedish author, A. A. Stiernman, and also published in Stockholm. This bibliography contained a little over 1,400 titles belonging to the literature of Finland and published after 1640. The first general bibliography of exclusively Finnish-language literature was compiled by C. N. Keckman under the title of *Förteckning å härtills vetterligen tryckta finska skrifter* (Åbo 1821). This served as a basis for F. W. Pipping's *Förteckning öfver i tryck utgifna skrifter på finska — Luettelo suomeksi präntätyistä kirjoista*, published in Helsinki during 1856–7 and including about 6,600 printed items in Finnish, catalogued with world-renowned accuracy and completeness. The literature of Finland in all languages has been included in the bibliography of S. G. Elmgren: *Öfversigt af Finlands litteratur*, the former part of which (1861) contains Fennica literature from 1542 to 1770 and the latter part (1865) from 1771 to 1863.

Finland

The proper Finnish national bibliography, however, is a work whose title, up to volume 1936–8, was *Suomalainen kirjallisuus — La littérature finnoise*, later on *Suomen kirjallisuus — Finlands litteratur — The Finnish National Bibliography*. The first volume of this work was published in 1878, and it contains literature in Finnish from 1544 to 1877. It was followed between 1880–1934 by fourteen volumes covering Finnish literature in periods of 2–6 years up to 1932. The subsequent volumes 1933–5 and 1936–38 (published in 1937 and 1940) contain also the literature of Finland in foreign languages — except in Swedish. Fennica literature in all languages (also in Swedish) was included for the first time in the volume comprising the years 1939–43 (published in 1952), and the following volumes 1944–8 (completed quite recently). 1949–51, 1952–4, 1955–7, 1958–60 have been edited in the same way. Of the volume 1961–3 so far only the first issue has been published. Up to volume 1939–43, the publisher of this national bibliography was "Suomalaisen Kirjallisuuden Seura" ("Finnish Literature Society"), and it is included as no. 57 in the publication series of this society. The subsequent volumes have been published by the "Helsinki University Library". The editor of this bibliography was V. Vasenius for the years 1544–1900 who was succeeded by Simo Pakarinen (1901–38 — containing about 6,700 pages). The latter also collected the main part of the materials for the following volumes 1939–43 and 1944–8.

Each volume of the "Finnish National Bibliography" contains an alphabetical and a subject section. Pamphlets smaller than a printed sheet were not at first included, so that the volume 1544–1877 does not list Finnish book production as completely as the monumental work of F. W. Pipping. Newspapers were excluded before volume 1939–43.

As to Swedish literature in Finland, "Svenska Litteratursällskapet i Finland" (The Swedish Literature Society in Finland) has published a separate bibliography entitled *Katalog över den svenska litteraturen i Finland* in six volumes 1886–90, 1891–5, 1896–1900, 1901–5, 1906–15 and 1916–25. The 7th and last volume 1926–43 is in preparation.

In addition to these national bibliographies there are some general catalogues of literature published in Finland principally for the use of booksellers. So, for example, J. W. Lillja brought out a commercial catalogue *Bibliographia hodierna Fenniae* in three issues in 1846, 1848 and 1859, and in 1878–85 appeared an annual catalogue entitled *Finsk (tidskrifts) bok-katalog* (1884–85 in one volume). Thereafter an annual bookseller's catalogue was published from 1895 until 1921. After a pause of 20 years its publication was resumed and has continued uninterruptedly since 1940. It contains Fennica literature in all languages.

Mention should also be made of the general bibliography comprising the years 1850–90 in the "Helsinki University Library". It will include Fennica literature in all languages and much more completely than do the older bibliographies of that period.

All printers have to send 5 copies of each of their products to

Helsingin Yliopiston Kirjasto
(The University Library)
Unioninkatu 36
SF Helsinki 17

which is the national library and takes care of the national bibliography.

16 Book Production

In 1966 5,155 titles were published in Finland, of which 2,930 were reprints and about 43% first editions. 3,360 were books (49 pages or more), the rest pamphlets.

The most important subject groups among books (49 pages or more) were:

Subject group	Titles	Percentage of total
Literary texts	997	29.7
History, biography	223	6.6
Linguistics, philology	221	6.6
Religion, theology	205	6.1
Technology, industries, trades and crafts	187	5.6
Natural sciences	154	4.6
Medical sciences, public health	150	4.5
Geography, travel	133	4.0
Political science, political economy	129	3.9
Agriculture, forestry Stockbreeding, hunting, fishing	106	3.2

17 Translations

824 of the 3,360 published books were translations, i. e. 24.5%. The largest group was fiction (68%). Most translations were made from English (53.4%), but the Scandinavian languages were also well represented (23.3%).

18 Book Clubs

There have been several attempts by single publishing companies to start book clubs, but in 1969 *Suuri Suomalainen Kirjakerho* (The Great Finnish Book club) was established by 3 publishing companies and *Kirjakaupan Kirjakerho* (Book Club of the Bookstore) by 4 publishing companies.

19 Paperbacks

The first paperbacks in Finland were published in 1956, but development has been slow and irregular. At the moment there are about 300 titles on the market, though in the last few years the amount of quality and non-fiction paperbacks has increased considerably.

20 Book Design

Every spring a committee which includes members of several organizations selects about 25 best-designed books published during the previous year. These books, together with corresponding books from other Scandinavian countries, form a representative exhibition.

21 Publishing

Most of the leading publishing companies, or at least their head offices, are in Helsinki. There are about 400 ordinary publishers, but most of these are very small, as can be seen from the following figures (from 1966) which include the production of 28 active members in the "Publishers' Association" (→ 4):

Business volume Finnish marks	Companies	Titles (over 49 pp.)	Percentage of total
Over 9 million	3	1,206	35.9
1 – 9 million	9	892	26.5
Under 1 million	16	335	10.0
	28	2,433	72.4

If we compare the numbers of printed pages or sales, the percentage of the above-mentioned companies is even higher. Most of the publishing companies are general publishers.

22 Literary Agents

In Finland the authors have direct contact with their publishers.

23 Wholesale Trade

The largest publishing companies send their products direct to the 400 biggest bookstores, though many small orders are handled by

Kirjavälitys Oy
(Book Commissions Ltd)
Kalevankatu 16
SF Helsinki 10

"Kirjavälitys" sends commission copies to 200 small shops and is a mediator between small publishing companies and small shops. Even companies outside the "Publishers' Association" sell their books through "Kirjavälitys", which was founded in 1918.

24 Retail Trade

About 600 bookstores receive 1–3 copies from publishers on commission. When a book is sold the bookseller orders another, which is invoiced and paid for. When a publisher wants these books to be returned, the bookseller either returns them or pays. Other books ordered by the bookseller are paid within a month and are not on a sale-or-return basis.
Beside these 600 commissioners there are about 300 smaller shops and about 1,800 kiosks, stationers, etc. selling books.
Although there are bookstores in all parts of the country, bookselling is centred in the southern part, which represents about 75% of the sales.
The table below shows that most of the bookstores are very small.
Most bookstores are members of Kirja- ja Paperikauppojen Liitto (→ 4).

25 Mail-Order Bookselling

Selling by mail order is uncommon in Finland and is limited to a few specialist books.
The instalment system was started about 60 years ago, when the first Finnish encyclopedia was published. The selling and publishing of large and expensive works depend greatly on an instalment system, which represents about 20% of total book sales.

26 Antiquarian Book Trade, Auctions

The country's few antiquarian bookstores are in Helsinki, and are members of the

Suomen Antikvariaattiyhdistys
(Antiquarian Booksellers' Association of Finland)
P. Makasiininkatu 6
SF Helsinki 13

which is affiliated to ILAB.

27 Book Imports

In 1966 Finland realized the following imports:

Country	Amount Fmk 1,000	Percentage of total
Sweden	5,489	54.2
United Kingdom	1,352	13.3
Germany (Federal Republic)	1,028	10.1
USA	842	8.3
Denmark	295	2.9
Netherlands	267	2.6
Switzerland	172	1.7
Italy	159	1.6
France	154	1.5
Others	378	3.8
Total	10,136	100.0

The information for book imports and exports was given by the Customs and, therefore, many small parcels are excluded. The great percentage imported from Sweden is due to the Swedish speaking population in Finland (7.4%). When a book is printed in Sweden a special edition is often printed simultaneously for Finland. Other languages are also very well represented because most books used at the universities

10 biggest bookstores represent	19.8% of the book sales
59 medium-sized bookstores represent	30.2% of the book sales
69 bookstores represent	50% of the book sales
About 530 small bookstores represent	50% of the book sales
Total	100%

are imported, e.g. technical and medical books. Even paperbacks are imported in great amounts, in many cases to improve the knowledge of languages. The big importing bookstores can offer to their customers a selection of over 2,000 different books on art which are imported from all parts of the world, and the same situation pertains in other categories.

28 Book Exports

Because Finnish is spoken in few places, most exports of Finnish books are to Sweden, which has provided jobs for about 200,000 Finnish workers since 1945. Many of these could not speak Swedish at all at first but gradually the situation has changed. Many scientific works are written in foreign languages, which helps their export.

Country	Amount Fmk 1,000	Percentage of total
Sweden	845	56.3
USSR	159	10.6
United Kingdom	110	7.3
USA	93	6.2
Denmark	79	5.3
Germany (Federal Republic)	70	4.7
Norway	47	3.1
Others	98	6.5
Total	1,501	100.0

29 Book Fairs

Members of the book trade have assembled for a few days every autumn, but since 1968 there is a book fair for the general public. The organizer is the trade's advertising and public relations organization

Kirjapalvelu
(Book Service)
Kalevankatu 16
SF Helsinki 10

30 Public Relations

Kirjapalvelu (→ 29) takes care of joint advertising campaigns in television, newspapers, etc. and produces posters, catalogues and other material. The biggest effort is the joint book Christmas catalogue, which is distributed to every home (1.4m. copies).

31 Bibliophily

The association is

Bibliofiilinen Seura
(Society of Bibliophiles)
Lauttasaarentie 5 a C
SF Helsinki 20

32 Literary Prizes

Finland's oldest literary prizes are the "State Prizes". These were initially awarded in 1865 (a second time in 1888) and have been awarded regularly since 1898. Since 1968 "State Prizes" are also awarded for non-fiction works. The awards are made on the recommendations of a committee of government-nominated critics.

With funds obtained from publishers by the "Association of Authors of Juvenile Books" (→ 10), the best new juvenile books have been granted prizes since 1948 by an independent board of critics. The most distinguished is the "Topelius Prize".

The "Agricola Prize" also derives from publishers' donations. It has been awarded since 1958 for the best fiction prose translation into Finnish published the previous year.

The "Alfred Kordelin Literary Prize" is awarded every other year to a writer whose style is considered masterful.

The "Aleksis Kivi Prize" has been awarded annually since 1935 by the "Finnish Literature Society" to an older author who has proved his reputation.

The "Kalevi Jäntti Prize" has been awarded annually since 1942 to a promising young author in belles-lettres whose book has been published in the previous year.
The "Eino Leino Prize" differs from the above prizes in that it is not a money award. In addition to authors' prizes the larger publishers also award prizes to some of their own authors.

33 The Reviewing of Books

Publishers send between 75 and 125 copies to the daily newspapers and to a number of periodicals, which pass them to their critics for review. Some books are reviewed on television and radio. The critics are members of the

Suomen Arvostelijain Liitto
(Critics' Association of Finland)
Runeberginkatu 32 C
SF Helsinki 10

The best survey of what has been published in Finland is afforded by *Arvosteleva kirjaluettelo* ("Book-review catalogue", 10 times per year), which can be obtained from

Valtion Painatuskeskus
(Government Printing Center)
Annankatu 44
SF Helsinki 10

This publication contains a brief (10–20 lines) review of almost every book written by a Finnish author or translated into Finnish. It is published by the "Educational Board" and is chiefly designed to serve libraries. Thus it is included as a supplement in the Library Association's journal *Kirjastolehti*. A similar book catalogue concerning all literature in Swedish published in Finland is contained in the periodical

Svenskbygden
Svenska folkskolans vänner
Annegatan 12
SF Helsingfors 12

(6 times per year in Swedish, published in Helsinki).

The quarterly review

Books from Finland
Keskusk. 1
SF 00100 Helsinki 10

informs about new Finnish books and publishes articles covering all fields of the Finnish book world.

34 Graphic Arts

The printing houses are members in

Graafinen Keskusliitto
(Graphic Central League)
P. Esplanadikatu 25 a
SF Helsinki 10

France

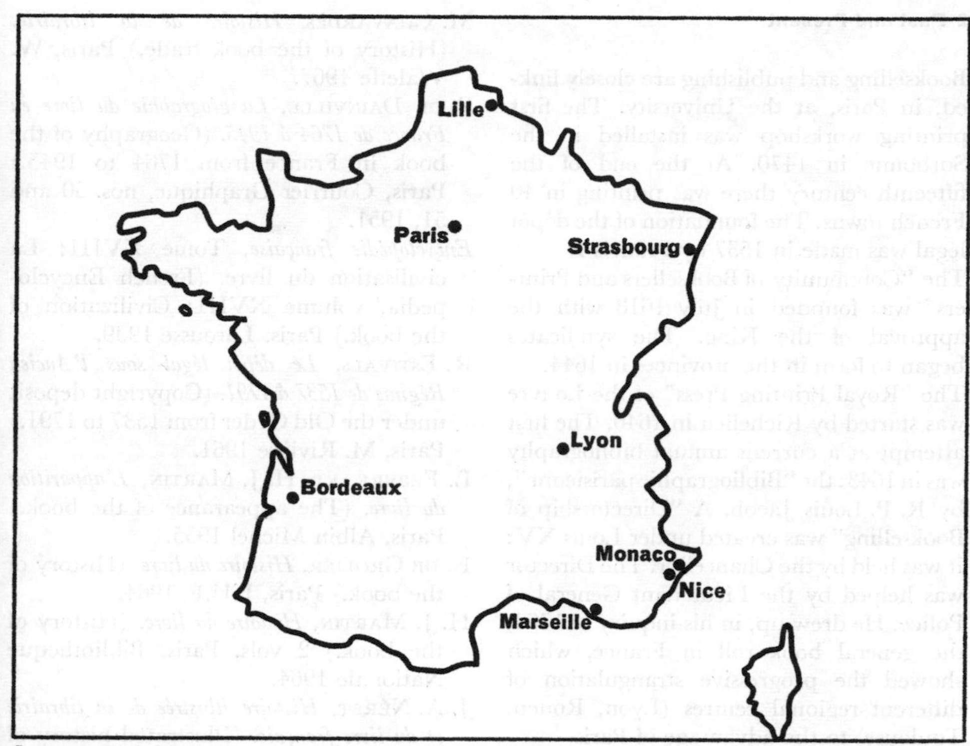

Important Book Centres

1 General Information

Area 547,026 km²
Population 50,330,000 (89 per km²)
Capital Paris (2,800,000)
Largest towns Paris (2,800,000); Marseille (813,000); Lyon (500,000); Lille-Roubaix-Tourcoing (840,000); Bordeaux (471,000)
Government Republic whose President is elected by majority vote for 7 years. Two Assemblies: Senate, National Assembly
Religion Catholic Church 80.0%
Protestant Church 1.6%
Orthodox Church 0.2%
Other groups and dissidents 18.2%
National language French
Leading foreign languages English, German
Weights and measures Metric system
Currency unit Franc (F)

Education 11,300,000 children, adolescents and college students of whom 3,200,000 are of secondary school age and 475,000 are in higher education
Illiteracy Nil
Paper consumption a) Newsprint 11.3 kg per inhabitant (1967)
b) Printing paper (other than newsprint) 31.0 kg per inhabitant (1967)

Membership UNESCO, IPA, ICBA, ILAB

2 Past and Present

Bookselling and publishing are closely linked, in Paris, at the University. The first printing workshop was installed in the Sorbonne in 1470. At the end of the fifteenth century there was printing in 40 French towns. The foundation of the dépôt légal was made in 1537 by Francis I.
The "Community of Booksellers and Printers" was founded in July 1618 with the approval of the King. The syndicates began to form in the provinces in 1644.
The "Royal Printing Press" of the Louvre was started by Richelieu in 1640. The first attempt at a current annual bibliography was in 1643: the "Bibliographie parisienne", by R. P. Louis Jacob. A "Directorship of Bookselling" was created under Louis XV: it was held by the Chancellor. The Director was helped by the Lieutenant General of Police. He drew up, in his inquiry of 1764, the general book roll in France, which showed the progressive strangulation of different regional centres (Lyon, Rouen, Toulouse) to the advantage of Paris.
With the Revolution all professions became free, but Napoleon again created a "Book Directorship" in 1810, and the following year instituted, by the Amsterdam decree, the "Bibliography of the French Empire", today called "Bibliography of France" (→ 15), the first national bibliography drawn up for the registration and control of book production.
The "Cercle de la Librairie" (→ 4) was founded in 1847; it resolved itself into a professional syndicate in 1886, and the "Syndicat des Éditeurs" (→ 4) was founded in 1892.

Bibliography

R. Castelain, *Histoire de l'édition musicale ou du droit d'éditer au droit d'auteur 1501–1793.* (History of musical publishing or editors' rights to authors' rights 1501–1793.) Paris, Lemoine 1960.

M. Chavardès, *Histoire de la librairie.* (History of the book trade.) Paris, W. Waleffe 1967.

F. de Dainville, *La géographie du livre en France de 1764 á 1945.* (Geography of the book in France from 1764 to 1945.) Paris, Courrier Graphique, nos. 50 and 51, 1951.

Encyclopédie française, Tome XVIII: La civilisation du livre. (French Encyclopedia, volume XVIII: Civilization of the book.) Paris, Larousse 1939.

R. Estivals, *Le dépôt légal sous l'Ancien Régime de 1537 á 1791.* (Copyright deposit under the Old Order from 1537 to 1791.) Paris, M. Rivière 1961.

L. Febvre et H. J. Martin, *L'apparition du livre.* (The appearance of the book.) Paris, Albin Michel 1955.

E. de Grolier, *Histoire du livre.* (History of the book.) Paris, P.U.F. 1964.

H. J. Martin, *Histoire du livre.* (History of the book.) 2 vols. Paris, Bibliothèque Nationale 1964.

J. A. Néret, *Histoire illustrée de la librairie et du livre français.* (Illustrated history of the book trade and the book in France.) Paris, Lamarre 1953.

3 Retail Prices

Two decrees of 1953 and 1958 considered it illegal to impose a minimum price on a product by means of a price list, a printed table, or a catalogue.
This means that in principle the selling price of a book to the public must be free and that the practice of discounts, rebates, bargains, etc. would be not only tolerated, but even encouraged by public authorities. One can see the profound upsets which could result from this for the profession, in particular the bookshop network. Steps therefore were taken by the professional associations, especially when work was being done on the 4th Plan, to obtain permission from the public authorities to implement this law.

Then again, refusal to sell was punishable by law, which was equally serious in that anyone could legally buy books directly from the publisher for resale.

The negotiations which were undertaken resulted in the following situation: Publishers are authorized to sell to booksellers at a fixed price which is called "catalogue price" or "public price": it is on this that copyright is calculated.

It is not forbidden for booksellers to give discount to customers (students, teachers, etc.) or to offer genuine bargains.

Refusal to sell is forbidden, but publishers are authorized to give discount with discrimination, the lowest being 18% for literature in general. Professional establishments which are authorized to buy directly from the publisher but get only the minimum discount find it difficult, in consequence, to hold a discount policy.

Monopoly contracts are permitted, with a fixed price all along the line.

This situation is in fact more or less stable, though on many occasions it has been threatened. Conditions of sale are abused by certain booksellers, by stores or by outside circuits, as much through school purchases as in discount to libraries or private buyers.

The stabilization of prices by the government in 1963, then the policy of stability and control into which it entered in 1967, help to cut the losses at consumption level in spite of the inevitable rise in prices at production level.

In giving free rein to the more or less individual practice of rebates and discount, this policy threatens to throw retailers into cut-price competition, which by limiting their margin of profit will greatly reduce the network of booksellers.

4 Organization

Three professional bodies dominate the life of the book in France.

The

Syndicat National des Éditeurs
(National Syndicate of Publishers)
117, Boulevard Saint-Germain
F 75 Paris VI

was founded in 1892.

Membership in the "Syndicat" is voluntary, but all the big publishing firms with a few exceptions belong to it and the 309 publishers at present in this Syndicate represent 88% of the total number.

Grouping is carried out according to subjects; there are 9 distinct groups (Literature, Science and Technology, Law and the Humanities, Religion, Medicine, Art, etc.). Each group elects its representatives on 6 boards (social affairs, commercial, technical, exportation, promotion, literary and artistic fields). The presidents of the groups and boards are elected for 3 years. Also, every 3 years the General Assembly of Publishers elects a Committee of 6 members who are responsible for the administration of the Syndicate. The meeting of the Committee and the presidents of groups and boards constitutes the Committee which is the directing organ of the profession: it is they who pass the Syndicate's budget and decide the big economic options of the profession.

The

Fédération Française des Syndicats de libraires
(French Federation of Booksellers' Associations)
117, Boulevard Saint-Germain
F 75 Paris VI

was drawn up in 1959 by the amalgamation of the "Syndicate of the Booksellers of France" and the "National Syndicate of Booksellers". This Federation groups together:

a) 18 regional syndicates (North, Alsace, South-East, Brittany, etc.),

b) 3 specialist syndicates (classical, religious and technical booksellers),

c) 3 professional groups.

The Directing Committee is made up of

representatives of each one of these syndicates. At the head of the Federation there is a board, elected for 3 years, a third of which is renewable every year.
The Federation also has its place in the "Cercle de la Librairie".

Cercle de la Librairie
(Book Trade Club)
117, Boulevard Saint-Germain
F 75 Paris VI

founded in 1847, is a society of individuals which goes back to the time when professional syndicates were forbidden in France. The heads of big firms in books and the graphic arts founded an association which later became a professional syndicate.
Today the "Cercle", in the heart of the publishing district, shelters the social and administrative seats of most of the professional organs; it runs public services: professional teaching, placing, information, technical library; it edits the "Bibliographie de la France" (→ 5) and different catalogues or yearbooks.
The "Cercle" is managed by an Administrative Council in which representatives of all the professional associations sit.

Bibliography

Monographie de l'édition. (Monograph on publishing.) Paris, Cercle de la Librairie 1970.
Syndicat National des Éditeurs. (National Syndicate of Publishers.) Paris, Cercle de la Librairie 1966.
Cercle de la Librairie. (Book Trade Club.) Paris, Cercle de la Librairie 1966.

5 Trade Press

First, we must mention

La Bibliographie de la France
(Bibliography of France)
117, Boulevard Saint-Germain
F 75 Paris VI

which is probably the oldest bibliographical organ still in existence since it was founded by the famous "Decret d'Amsterdam" ("Amsterdam Decree") made by the Emperor Napoleon I on 14 October 1811. Today the "Bibliographie de la France" is published weekly by the "Cercle de la Librairie". This organ is made up of three parts:
a) the official section, of which the "Bibliothèque Nationale" is in charge, and which regroups the copyright deposit entries into categories; it gives details about almost every title.
There are special publications for theses, engravings, music, periodicals, etc. They are republished annually in catalogues.
b) the report, which gives the professional news, and all economic, juridical, legislative or statutory information about the book in its different stages.
c) the publicity section, which takes in not only all publishers' announcements about their next publications, but also all the information about dates of returns of the publishers, changes in price, sales of old stock, offers and requests for old and rare books, and offers of and requests for employment. A certain number of supplements appear with the "Bibliographie":
— some repeat notices about works which have been the subject of publicity posters: Books of the Week, Books of the Month, Books of the Term, Books of the Semester, Books of the Year; it is a big recapitulatory volume which can be obtained with the yearly subscription;
— the others are purely publicity papers, but they are useful in that they group together the principal works on any subject: books about plays, religion, etc. The two best known are:
— the catalogue of school books and teaching material which, appearing every June, helps bookshops to prepare orders for the following school year;
— the catalogue of gift books which, about the month of October, groups together all

the works which will be the object of Christmas and New Year campaigns.
We must also note:

L'Officiel de la Librairie
(Official Organ of Booksellers)
117, Boulevard Saint-Germain
F 75 Paris VI

founded in 1892, which every month presents all the official or professional information about the book trade.
Finally there is

Le Bulletin du Livre
(Book News)
166, Boulevard Saint-Germain
F 75 Paris VI

a monthly which, in a very vivacious style, gives information about the trade and its different developments, as well as surveys and bibliographies about subjects chosen by number.
Les cahiers du livre et du disque ("Catalogue of books and records"); *Les cahiers du livre chrétien* ("Catalogue of the Christian book") represent a selection for booksellers, as well as different magazines, one of the best of which is

Bulletin critique du livre français
(Critical Bulletin of the French Book)
23, rue la Pérouse
F 75 Paris XVI

This gives monthly, complete, objective reviews in every field.

6 Book-Trade Literature

Unfortunately professional literature is not more highly developed in France.
Most information will be found in the *Monographie de l'édition* (→ 4, Bibliography). It contains all the necessary information about the profession, and a full bibliography.
Besides the works mentioned already, we add, published by the "Syndicat National des Éditeurs" (→ 4):
La clientèle du livre. (The clients of the book trade.) Paris 1967.
The

Centre de la Productivité du Livre
(Book Research Centre)
117, Boulevard Saint-Germain
F 75 Paris VI

has also published *La librairie française en 1966* (The French bookshop in 1966), Paris 1967, which is an annual statistical inquiry, and *L'enquête 25/25* (The 25/25 inquiry), Paris 1967, which studies the distribution of bookshops for general literature.
Finally, the official service of the

Documentation Française
(French Documentation)
31 Quai Voltaire
F 75 Paris VII

has published *Le livre en France* (The book in France), Paris 1961, as a general study.

7 Sources of Information, Address Services

All information on editing, bookselling and the graphic arts can be obtained at the

Cercle de la Librairie
(Club of the Book Trade)
117, Boulevard Saint-Germain
F 75 Paris VI

whose "Service de renseignements" ("Information Service") provides all bibliographical information to subscribers, and does all required research. The "Bibliothèque technique du Cercle" (the "Technical Library of the Club") is also at the disposal of all investigators (→ International Section, p. 68.) At the same address the "Fédération Française des Syndicats de Libraires" (→ 4) will give detailed information concerning distribution and trade.

8 International Membership

The "Syndicat National des Éditeurs" (→ 4) belongs to the following organizations; "International Publishers' Association," "Union des Éditeurs de Langue Française" ("Union of Publishers of the French Language"), "Groupe des Éditeurs de livres de la Communauté européenne" ("Publishers' Group for Books in the European Community"). The "Syndicat" is the founder of the two latter organizations. The "Fédération Française des Syndicats de Libraires" (→ 4) is a member of the "International Community of Booksellers' Associations" (→ 26).

9 Market Research

If much research has been done on books and the market, it is always with the "Cercle de la Librairie" (→ 4) at the centre, whether the "Syndicat des Éditeurs" (→ 4) entrusts the carrying out of this to outside organizations (for example, the "Institut Français de l'Opinion publique") or carries out studies of the market for schoolbooks, or of cost price by itself. The "Fédération Française des Syndicats de libraires" (→ 4) works in the same way, or co-operates with the

Centre de la Productivité du livre
(Book Research Centre)
117, Boulevard Saint-Germain
F 75 Paris VI

for the study of problems such as the standardization of order forms, etc.
Finally, the "Centre" participates with similar foreign organizations in common research on the book market.
(→ 6).

10 Books and Young People

Several efforts have been made in recent years to give young people a taste for books and to develop the practice of reading. These efforts have unfortunately been too scattered, and if their number is an indication of the interest shown, it is certainly the cause of a regrettable lack of efficiency.
Below are the names and adresses of associations and movements which have particularly interested themselves in this special field:

Fédération des Francs et Franches Camarades
(The Comrade's Federation)
66, rue de la Chaussée d'Antin
F 75 Paris IX

La Joie par les livres
(Delight through Books)
Cité de la Plaine
Rue de Champagne
92-Clamart
and 59, Avenue du Maine
F 75 Paris XIV

Loisirs-Jeunes
(Young Leisure)
36, rue de Pontieu
F 75 Paris VIII

Finally, for teen-agers, there is

Les Jeunesses Littéraires de France
(The Literary Youth of France)
117, Boulevard Saint-Germain
F 75 Paris VI

which, in France and in French-speaking countries, initiate young people's interest in reading and in the problems of literary composition.

11 Training

Professional training in France is organized on two levels:
1. For booksellers, the *Syndicat des Libraires de Paris et de l'Île-de-France* ("Syndicate of the Booksellers of Paris and the Île-de-France") organizes, in the "Cercle de la Librairie" (→ 4), a course of studies extending over two years which prepares employees of the trade for the examination for the certificate of professional aptitude for commercial booksellers. Provincial candidates are invited to follow a two-week course immediately preceding the examination;
2. For booksellers and publishers, courses created by the "Cercle de la Librairie" (→ 4) in 1908 prepare candidates who have passed the Baccalaureat for a professional

diploma in editing and bookselling, for a commercial diploma of the CAP or a diploma of the *École Estienne*.
The course lasts for two years and the bookselling and publishing branches have a certain number of lessons in common. The latter is also sub-divided into two options in the second year: economic and commercial, technical and manufacturing.
One hundred and fifty pupils are enrolled for this diploma, as many in Paris as in the provinces.
It is interesting to note that meetings for the reorganization of chiefs and employees in bookselling and publishing firms are henceforward organized by the "Cercle de la Librairie", under the direction of the "Association des Cadres de l'Édition et de la Librairie Françaises" ("Association of the Ranks of French Publishing and Bookselling").
Finally, former pupils of the "Cercle's" courses are grouped together in an association which organizes conferences and professional trips regularly.
All information about these different activities and the course and examination programmes can be obtained at the "Cercle de la Librairie", department "Service des Cours" ("Course Information Service").

12 Taxes

Besides the taxes which affect societies, and which, in the case of publishing or bookselling, present no peculiarity or exception, the production and sale of books are subject to a tax on the given value (Law of 6 January 1933).
So the book is taxed at 7.5% at each stage until it is sold to the private customer, but it is possible for each buyer to deduct from the cost the value of the tax already paid at previous stages.

13 Clearing Houses

There is no institution of compensation in France, only a general claims organization to facilitate the recovery of debts for the profession:

Union Nationale intersyndicale des industries graphiques
(UNIDIG)
(National Union of Syndicates of Graphic Industries)
117, Boulevard Saint-Germain
F 75 Paris VI

14 Copyright

Relations between publishers and authors are controlled by a law of 11 March 1957. Proportional remuneration of the author is the rule.
The duration of literary rights covers the life of the author and benefits his heirs during the present year and the 50 years following the author's death, to which must be added the duration of hostilities for the works which appeared before the war of 1914–18 or 1939–45.
On the expiry of the protection time allowed, the *Caisse Nationale des Lettres* ("National Literary Pay Office", created by the law of 26 February 1956) takes the place of the beneficiaries and collects for 15 years the principal and secondary royalties agreed on in the contracts.
France is a member of the "Berne Convention" and has approved the different amendments. In 1967 she signed but did not approve the "Stockholm Protocol" concerning the developing countries. She also signed the "Universal Copyright Convention", concluded at Geneva in 1952.

Bibliography

G. Bonnefoy, *La nouvelle législation sur la propriété littéraire et artistique*. (The new legislation on literary and artistic copyright). Paris, Montchrestien 1959.

M. CL. DOCK, *Étude sur le droit d'auteur.* (Study of copyright.) Paris, L.G.D.J. 1963.
P. MONNET, *Dictionnaire pratique de propriété littéraire.* (Practical copyright dictionary.) Paris, Cercle de la Librairie 1961.
A. LE TARNEC, *Manuel de la propriété littéraire et artistique.* (Manual of literary and artistic copyright.) Paris, Dalloz 1966.

15 National Bibliography, National Library

The
Bibliothèque Nationale
(National Library)
58, rue de Richelieu
F 75 Paris 2
the former "Bibliothèque Royale", is one of the most illustrious and the richest in the world in treasures of all sorts. It is directed by an "Administrateur général" who is at the same time "Directeur des Bibliothèques et de la Lecture publique" ("Director of Libraries and Public Reading") at the "Ministère de l'Education Nationale" ("Ministry of National Éducation"). The "Bibliothèque Nationale" looks after the copyright deposit of all books, or rather "all publications printed or reproduced by any graphic procedure (with the exception of locally printed works), sold, distributed, hired or called in for reprinting".
It is a law of 21 June 1943, that fixed the main rules of copyright deposit: the publisher provides four copies for the "Bibliothèque Nationale" and one copy for the "Ministère de l'Intérieur" ("Ministry of Home Affairs"). In his turn, the printer must send two copies to the "Bibliothèque Nationale" or to specially designated provincial libraries if his business is not in the Paris region.
The works, after they have passed into the hands of the copyright deposit, are listed and included in the national bibliographical weekly *Bibliographie de la France* (→ 5) which is arranged by subjects and compiled in annual volumes.
There exist two other distinct bibliographical publications: *Les Livres de l'année* ("Books of the Year"), published by the "Cercle de la Librairie", mentions again all the works which have been announced in the "Bibliographie de la France".
The *Tables décennales* ("Decennial Tables") give, again by title and by author, all the works which have appeared in France over a period of ten years. At the moment two editions are available (1945–55, 3 vols.; 1955–65, 4 vols. Paris, Cercle de la Librairie).

Bibliography

P. MONNET, *Dictionnaire pratique de propriété littéraire.* (Practical copyright dictionary.) Paris, Cercle de la Librairie 1962.

16 Book Production

Statistics and book production naturally come from copyright deposit, but a certain number of material conditions inherited from the past have not facilitated the establishment of classification according to the norms of UNESCO.
On the other hand, it happens that a certain number of publishers and authors —publishers particularly—publish in the "Bibliographie de la France" announcements of works which never appear in reviews at the copyright deposit.
We must thus put together the two sources, and we obtain the following picture for 1967 (books and pamphlets).

Subject group	Titles First editions	Titles New editions	Theses and official publications
General works	249	61	
Philosophy	656	170	
Religion, theology	1,028	101	4
Social sciences	2,176	259	1,497
Linguistics, Philology	378	594	
Pure science	995	309	645

Subject group	Titles First editions	Titles New editions	Theses and official publications
Medical science	552	16	1,585
Technical	1,164	372	
Fine arts	906	50	
Games and sports	234	32	
History and literary criticism	460	7	128
Literary texts	348	1,837	
History, geography	2,016	181	
Total	15,162	3,989	3,859

This gives a total of 23,010 titles, of which 19,809 are books and 3,201 are pamphlets of less than 49 pages.

Finally, but based this time on the 1966 results, the number of copies printed was as follows:

Subject group	New books	Reprints	Total
General literature	60,039,250	46,837,880	106,877,130
Teaching	16,070,824	51,162,454	67,233,278
Encyclopedias etc.	1,876,458	3,270,843	5,147,301
Books for the young	23,182,782	20,363,980	43,546,762
Science and technology	3,095,902	3,675,142	6,771,044
Piety, prayers	492,100	2,631,307	3,123,407
Catechisms	397,895	1,938,872	2,336,767
Religious literature	3,062,257	1,544,270	4,606,527
Art and architecture	1,849,443	1,196,210	3,045,653
Medicine	495,853	660,826	1,156,679
Law, political economy	1,792,014	572,757	2,364,771
Bibliophily	130,830	0	130,830
Erudition	599,686	552,190	1,151,876
Total	113,085,294	134,406,731	247,492,025

The following analysis of paperbacks and bound books gives 93.68% of titles and 93.42% of copies printed, certain publishers not being in a position to give this information.

Category	Titles	Copies printed
Paperbacks	65.7%	60.8%
Bound books	34.3%	39.2%

17 Translations

In 1967, 23,010 titles were published in France, among which were 1,815 translations.

Although about fifty languages were represented, English (including American) and German represent almost $^3/_4$ of the translations and eight principal languages make up 90% of the total figure. Here is the distribution of the main translations:

English	527
American	462
German	361
Russian	84
Italian	73
Spanish	37

In a table of the most important categories in which these translations are done, one obtains the following list:

Literature	807
History and biographies	259
Religion	189
Social science	160
Philosophy	99
Pure science	96
Applied science	81

With regard to translations from French, they represented 4,494 titles in 1965 out of 36,196 translations taken from 70 countries (according to "Index Translationum") and the biggest translating countries were:

	Titles
Spain	566
Italy	545
Germany	514
USA	495
Netherlands	298

France

The most translated groups from French into foreign languages were:

	Titles
Literature	2,042
Religion	661
History	440
Social science	340

Bibliography

Index Translationum. Paris, UNESCO.

18 Book Clubs

Book clubs were born in France after the Second World War. The clubs took it upon themselves to present works of proven quality, as much for the texts as for presentation.

French publishing had often been criticized abroad and, formerly, in France, for the bad quality of paper and paper binding.

So the clubs set about finding original and impeccable editions. There resulted from this a "Club" style which after a certain time set a fashion, and finally was adopted by general publishing.

The clubs work by correspondence or through agents. They rarely deal through the bookseller. But the methods of distribution and sale were not always up to the standard of bookmanship. Thus a great number of clubs disappeared and there remain only a few which can truly be called clubs; that is, publishing bodies of which one can become a member, and which annually put forward for individual choice a variable number of works.

Certain organizations for production and mail sales have since called themselves clubs, but in their case this name no longer means anything.

It is difficult to determine the exact number of real clubs in France. Their production counted in the general statistics could be evaluated in 1966 at 80 million francs.

19 Paperbacks

If one keeps strictly to the present characteristics of paperbacks—that is, if one does not confuse them with the concept of the popular books—France saw the first series of paperbacks in 1953.

Since that date a large number of series in paperback format have appeared. The "Cercle de la Librairie" (→ 4) publishes a catalogue of these books, which in its last edition numbered 5,600 titles for 80 series.

The last annual statistical inquiry of the "Syndicat National des Éditeurs" (→ 4) numbered 45,048,556 copies, of which 16,667,876 were new and 28,380,680 reprints.

The study of the market undertaken by the "Institut Français de l'opinion publique" ("French Institute of Public Opinion") in 1967 showed that 56% of the production of works in pocket format were bought by young people of 15 to 19 years old. This study also showed that those categories of the public called "big buyers and big readers" buy 29% of books in pocket format. Thus it would seem that the book in pocket format widens book clientèle only by very little.

Bibliography

Catalogue des livres au format de poche. (Catalogue of books in pocket format.) Paris, Cercle de la Librairie 1966.

The subject of paperbacks has been discussed in a special number of *Temps Modernes* (No. 267; Paris, Julliard 1965).

20 Book Design

As in many other countries, a selection of the best-designed books is made every year under the auspices of the

Comité permanent des Expositions du Livre et des Arts Graphiques Français
(Permanent Committee for the Exhibition of French Books and Graphic Arts)

117, Boulevard Saint-Germain
F Paris VI

Every year about 400 books are presented for selection to a jury presided over by an eminent personality, and composed of representatives of different sections of the arts and graphic industries.

The basic principles of the jury are the following: the selection takes in all the categories of books, from paperbacks to works for bibliophiles, according to the eleven established categories. The selection ("The Fifty Books of the Year") considers the following qualities: books which are a credit to French publishing as much by the creative spirit which they show in their particular domain as by the care and the artistry applied to their material production. Only those books are chosen which have been printed between 1 January and 31 December of the past year or whose copyright has been established in the same period. Priority is given to works of French conception and production. With regard to works co-edited by several authors belonging to different countries, only those whose original conception is French can be considered. The problem of works in several volumes whose production is scaled over several years is resolved according to each individual case. Among the works belonging to collections, only those which present a new and considerable effort in the collection to which they belong can be selected. Reprints are only considered if they present a really new element. Translations can be selected if they contain particularly original elements. Special presentations in France and abroad of the best-designed books are made. (115 in 1967).

21 Publishing

The analysis of the frequency of deposits gives an idea of the production of the 2,677 individual or corporate bodies, of a very varied nature, which gave works to the legal deposit in 1966.

Number of titles deposited	Number of depositors	Percentage of the total of titles deposited
more than 200 titles	5	12.5
from 151 to 200	4	4.8
from 101 to 150	9	8.2
from 51 to 100	24	12.4
from 21 to 50	75	17.8
from 11 to 20	89	9.9
from 6 to 10	125	7.2
from 1 to 5	2,346	27.2
	2,677	100.0

But nearly half of these publishers gave no titles at all in 1965. So it is usual to consider as publishers only those who have an annual turnover of over 100,000 F, and who respond to research—i. e. 319 firms.

Amount of turnover in 1966 (Francs)	No. of firms	Percentage of total turnover
more than 30 m.	9	37.6
from 20 to 30 m.	6	10.8
from 10 to 20 m.	15	17.5
from 5 to 10 m.	18	9.7
from 2 to 5 m.	54	13.6
from 1 to 2 m.	48	5.4
from 500,000 to 1 m.	55	3.1
from 200,000 to 500,000	76	1.9
from 100,000 to 200,000	38	0.4
Total	319	100.0

The figures appearing on the above table show that almost half of the publishing business is carried on by 15 firms.

More than half (52.3%) of publishing personnel belong to enterprises which employ more than 100 salaried workers, more than two thirds in firms whose total strenghth is over 50 people, and 192 firms which employ less than 10% represent only 9% of the profession's manpower.

France

Personnel occupied	Publishing firms	No. of employees	Percentage of all employees
more than 100 people	20	5,065	52.3
from 51 to 100 people	28	1,869	19.3
from 26 to 50 people	28	980	10.1
from 11 to 25 people	51	895	9.3
from 5 to 10 people	88	641	6.6
less than 5 people	104	232	2.4
Total	319	9,682	100.0

Distribution of firms according to the tonnage of paper used:

Paper tonnage	Publishing firms	Tonnage	Percentage of total tonnage
more than 1,000 tons	21	56,494	65.7
from 500 to 1,000	8	6,050	7.0
from 200 to 500 tons	35	11,242	13.1
from 100 to 200 tons	47	6,843	8.0
from 50 to 100 tons	35	2,471	2.9
from 20 to 50 tons	57	1,848	2.1
less than 20 tons	116	1,009	1.2
Total	319	85,857	100.0

The following table indicates the position of the head offices of publishing houses in Paris and the provinces.

Paris districts:

1st —	8	8th —	13	15th —	6
2nd —	9	9th —	11	16th —	7
3rd —	1	10th —	5	17th —	11
4th —	1	11th —	2	18th —	1
5th —	30	12th —	3	19th —	0
6th —	117	13th —	3	20th —	2
7th —	27	14th —	9		
		All Paris districts			266
		Provinces			53
		Total			319

from which we must deduct 11 firms in Monaco whose business figure is included in the above figures.

22 Literary Agents

Literary agents are playing an increasingly important part in France, but one which is quite different from that in, for instance, the United States.

In fact, without exception their part is limited to the buying and selling of foreign copyrights, and to the negotation of original copyright. It is very rare for an author to grant direct management of his rights and works to a literary agent.

There exists a

Syndicat des Représentants littéraires français
(Syndicate of French Literary Representatives)
117, Boulevard Saint-Germain
F 75 Paris VI

which groups together most of the members of this profession.

23 Wholesale Trade

In the book trade there are many intermediaries; they vary widely in competence, role and size.

One can distinguish several kinds of intermediary:

1. commission agents, who keep in stock all or part of French production, carry, put and group together booksellers' purchases, from whom the latter's travellers can easily stock up;
2. exclusive distributors, who ensure representation and distribution of their stock to booksellers and French and foreign selling points, for a certain number of publishers;
3. export commission-agents who range from the very big firm to the one-room bookshop and who each in their own way have their own representatives and explore foreign markets, or simply receive orders from universities, libraries and foreign booksellers and ensure they are carried out.

There exists a

Syndicat National des Importateurs et Exportateurs
(National Syndicate of Importers and Exporters)
117, Boulevard Saint-Germain
F 75 Paris VI

24 Retail Trade

The main sale of books is carried out in France by retail bookshops: 54% according to a census in 1967. This shows the importance of this profession to publishers. Research carried out in 1966 by the "Centre de Productivité du Livre" (→ 6) gave the following results for 1,877 usable replies from 4,142 booksellers questioned, which represent a business figure of 850 million F, of which 396 million F come from sales of books.
Of this figure, two thirds is realized by 460 enterprises, that is less than 20% of the total number. This analysis also gives the distribution of the business figure of "exclusive bookselling" between Paris (32%) and the provinces (67.8%).
The average turnover of stock, that is, the connection between the business figure and the value of the stock (maximum buying price increased by 30%) is 2.6 times for the whole country with 2.5 times for the provinces and 3.2 times for Paris.
Enterprises whose "all activities" annual turnover figure exceeds 500,000 F represent 68% of the business figure and their proportion in the world business figure tends to increase regularly. If one apportions the business figure of the sale of books by category, one obtains the following results, which noticeably agree with those for publishing output:

Subject	Percentage of total turnover
General literature	32.2
School books	23.6
Scientific and technical books	11.8
Religious books	4.6
Books for the young	12.1
Encyclopedias, fine arts	8.9
Foreign languages	2.5
Varied	4.3
Total	100.0

Out of these figures bulk sales (schools, libraries) represent 17.2%.
Many firms (10.8%) carry out bulk-selling; 16.5% mail-order sales; 5% sales through travellers and door-to-door agents.
Still within the framework of this research, the examination of 1,639 questionnaires shows a total of 8,284 people working in bookshops, with an average of 5 per enterprise with an average monthly salary (in 1965) of 638 F. These salaries together would represent 12.5% of the business figure.
The averages quoted here obviously have only a secondary value, the employment or salary figures varying considerably according to the importance and position of the firms.

25 Mail-Order Bookselling

Mail-order sales have developed a lot over the last ten years, to the point at which research on book clientele carried out in 1967 showed the following percentages for mail-order purchases of the last new books (altogether 11%):

Subject	Percentage
Novels	16
Detective	4
Travel	23
History	26
Philosophy	15
Art	12
Sciences	13
School	3
Children's	4

These large percentages, in particular for history and travel books, show the direction in which enterprises for mail-order sales are going.
Mail-order firms in fact buy back from classic firms books which are already successfully established, presenting them luxuriously, and flooding the market with brilliantly produced catalogues. Often publishing houses have branches which exploit,

under another name, mail-order sales of books or series from their stocks.
The publishers of specialized clubs have not formed any association to cope with mail-order business, but the "Syndicat National des Éditeurs" (→ 4) regroups them and deals with their problems.

26 Antiquarian Book Trade, Auctions

The business in old books has been practised successfully in France for a long time. But this market was so rich, and people have been coming from so far away and for such a long time, that really rare books and bargains have become more difficult to find. However, the antiquarian trade is very well organized and comprises about 500 members in Paris and the provinces. We must mention here the "bouquinistes" of the banks of the Seine, well known to tourists, and with whom, alas, finds are becoming much rarer.

Le Syndicat de la Librairie Ancienne et Moderne
(Syndicate of Antiquarian and Modern Booksellers)
117, Boulevard Saint-Germain
F 75 Paris VI

helps to sort out some of the problems peculiar to this field of bookselling. It is in charge of meetings of bibliophiles, antiquarians, etc., and represents French antiquarian booksellers at the "International League of Antiquarian Booksellers".

Bibliography

Bulletin de la Librairie Ancienne et Moderne
(Bulletin of Antiquarian Bookselling)
117, Boulevard Saint-Germain
F 75 Paris VI

Bibliographie de la France (→ 4) publishes a list of books offered and wanted in each number.

Répertoire du Syndicat de la Librairie Ancienne et Moderne (Index of the "Syndicate"). Paris, Cercle de la Librairie 1964.

27 Book Imports

Imports of books in 1966 rose in France to 180,560,000 F.
But one must distinguish in these figures given by the customs what is for books and what is not, extracting from this total at least 100 m. F for books printed abroad for French publishers or in co-production.
The main imports of new books into France originated from:

Country	Amount (million F)
Switzerland	52,767
Belgium-Luxemburg	41,842
United Kingdom	7,634
USA	5,637
Germany (Federal Republic)	4,572

French imports increase from year, but the balance between imports and exports continues to be favourable, since exports still largely outweigh imports.

28 Book Exports

Exports of French books in 1966 represent a total of 273 m. F and are divided as follows:

1) According to destination

Area	Percentage
Europe	50.8
Africa	19.5
North America	19.2
Latin America	5.3
Asia	2.2
Middle East	2.2
Oceania	0.8
Total	100.0

2) According to subject groups

Subject group	Percentage
General literature	32.3
Teaching	23.6
Encyclopedias and big publications	13.3

Subject group	Percentage
Books for the young	5.5
Science and technology	6.9
Piety, prayers	1.0
Catechisms	0.4
Religious literature	3.1
Art and architecture	5.0
Medicine	3.0
Law, political economy	2.6
Bibliophily	0.7
Erudition	1.8
Geographical, maps	0.8
Total	100.0

3) According to the importance of firms (and after research on firms which make a business total of more than 100,000 F)

Value in F	Number of firms	Percentage of total exports
more than 4 m.	13	53.9
from 2 to 4 m.	14	16.3
from 1 to 2 m.	19	10.6
from 500,000 to 1 m.	24	7.2
less than 500,000	249	12.0
Total	319	100.0

Below is a list of the twenty countries which are the best foreign customers for French books.

Country	Value F 1,000
Belgium-Luxemburg	57,431
Canada	35,033
Switzerland	29,777
USA	19,019
Italy	8,802
Algeria	8,623
Ivory Coast	7,232
Spain	7,224
United Kingdom	6,670
Germany (Federal Republic)	6,280
Marocco	5,469
Lebanon	4,835
Madagascan Republic	4,611
Senegal	3,993
Cameroons	3,642
Netherlands	3,475
Tunisia	3,282
Argentine	3,173
South Vietnam	2,838
Japan	2,543

Book exports represent in value 5.1% of general exports in France and 20% of the business figure for French publishing.

29 Book Fairs

France has never felt the need to have a book fair, for the publishing profession has gradually established itself in Paris, and is concentrated in only three parts of that city.

Thus provincial or foreign booksellers who come to Paris can, within a few days, see the whole of French book production.

On the other hand, it has seemed to be important to regroup specialized works for the French public. Two distinct Salons have thus been established in France:

1. Salon international du Livre et de la Presse Scientifique et Technique which, every two years, presents to French specialists the works of all the world and at the same time holds discussions on scientific publishing;

2. Salon du Livre sur l'Art et de Bibliophilie ("Salon of Art Books and Bibliophily"), also international.

These two meetings are organized under the auspices of the "Syndicat National des Éditeurs" (→ 4) by the

Comité Permanent des Expositions du Livre et des Arts Graphiques Français
(Permanent Committee for Exhibitions of French Books and the Graphic Arts)
117, Boulevard Saint-Germain
F 75 Paris VI

30 Public Relations

At a time when reading and books have to compete with so many rivals, it is under-

standable that members of the profession organize a public-relations system.
At the "Syndicat National des Éditeurs" (→ 4) a promotion service created in 1965 produced:
— A Reading Week in 1966.
— Book-present exhibitions in the whole of France in 1967.
— Publicity exhibitions for books and reading.
With its cooperation, the "Office de Radio-Télévision Française" ("French Radio-Television Service") produced a remarkable "Quinzaine de la lecture et des lecteurs" ("Fortnight for Reading and Readers") in 1967.
The 'Comité Permanent des Expositions du Livre et des Arts Graphiques Français" (→ 20, 29), which at first specialized in exhibitions abroad, now also covers all France and gives technical help to all enterprises requested by the "Syndicat National des Éditeurs" or the "Cercle de la Librairie". The only association for abroad contacts, the

Association Nationale du Livre français à l'étranger
(National Association for French Books Abroad)
117, Boulevard Saint-Germain
F 75 Paris VI

edits bibliographical bulletins, receives students, etc.
Finally, publishers and booksellers usually organize exhibitions, discussions, conferences for congresses, meetings, and specialist meetings such as scientific, religious, technical, medical, etc.

31 Bibliophily

French editing has always made it a point of honour to present books of a high standard. To traditional and rare original editions were added works printed on excellent paper and illustrated by the best artists and engravers; these have been followed now for about thirty years by books of painters. Thus the greatest names of the Paris School—Braque, Dunoyer de Segonzac, Léger, Matisse, Picasso, Villon—collaborated to create works of great beauty, as regards both art and typography. These volumes have made original bindings one of their objects.
These works are produced either by the publishers themselves, or by bibliophile societies whose members have a meeting at regular intervals to order a book from some illustrator or painter.
Big exhibitions take place periodically at the "Bibliothèque Nationale" (→ 15), at the "Cercle de la Librairie" (→ 4) or even abroad.
The

Comité National du Livre Illustré
(National Committee of the Illustrated Book)
Bibliothèque de l'Arsenal
1, rue de Sully
F 75 Paris IV

comprises publishers and illustrators, while

La Chambre Syndicale du Livre d'Amateur
(National Chamber of the Amateur's Book)
117, Boulevard Saint-Germain
F 75 Paris VI

consists of publishers irrespective of societies.
The "Syndicat de la Librairie Ancienne et Moderne" (→ 26) ensures the buying and selling of these works second-hand and can follow them through public sales.

32 Literary Prizes

Numerous literary prizes are awarded in France every year. Though some are known throughout the world and contribute greatly to the fame of the work thus distinguished, others are extremely specialized or else do not pass beyond the limits of a chosen circle or province. Literary prizes are awarded either by constituent bodies (the "Académie Française", etc.) or by juries drawn up for this aim. The prizes themselves are very varied, some of them honouring one book, others the complete work of an author (e.g. the "Grand Prix

National des Lettres" – "The Great National Arts Prize"). Their value is sometimes purely symbolic, at others a very substantial remuneration. We can quote in this respect the "Prix Goncourt", whose value is only 50 F, but which, by the fame which it brings to the work through translations and copyright, brings the author more than 100,000 F.
The main literary prizes are those awarded at the end of the year: the *Goncourt,* the *Renaudot,* the *Femina,* the *Interallié,* the *Medicis.*
Prizes like the *Grand Prix du roman de l'Académie Française,* the *Prix des critiques,* etc., deserve special attention.

Bibliography

Guide des prix littéraires. (Guide to literary prizes.) Paris, Cercle de la Librairie 1967.

33 The Reviewing of Books

The French press (and broadcasting) takes note of books and certain television productions are more effective than the proper literary chronicles.
The leading literary weeklies are:
Nouvelles littéraires
Figaro littéraire
Lettres Françaises
Monde des Lettres
Further literary columns of the daily or periodical press are: Pierre-Henri Simon's article in *Le Monde;* Claude Mauriac's in *Figaro;* Etienne Lalou's in the *Express,* etc.
The monthly reviews all have a very important literary column: new *NRF, Temps Modernes, Lettres nouvelles, Esprit, Critique,* etc., etc. Finally, there are publications which specialize exclusively in reviewing, about which some information has already been given (→ 5). It is useful to note that according to research done on book-buying habits in 1967, information about the last books bought showed:
9% reviewed in the press,
11% had publicity in the press,
3% were presented on television,
1% were presented on the radio.

34 Graphic Arts

The professions comprising industry and the graphic arts are grouped according to their multiple subdivisions into local, regional and national syndicates. These, whether on a national scale or in the Paris region, mostly have their head offices in the "Cercle de la Librairie" (→ 4).
The
Fédération Française des Syndicats patronaux de l'Imprimerie et des Industries Graphiques (French Federation of Patron Syndicates of Printing and the Graphic Industries)
115, Boulevard Saint-Germain
F 75 Paris VI
regroups, on a national scale, all the national, regional and local syndicates of printers, photo-engravers and binders.

35 Miscellaneous

Public Libraries
A complete view of the book situation in France should also mention the relatively poor state of France's public libraries. Though many private concerns have sprung up to cope with this deficiency, much still remains to be done, and the government has at last decided to propose a plan for improving the stock and facilities in public libraries.
The "Direction des Bibliothèques de France et de la Lecture Publique" ("Directorate of French Libraries and Public Reading") at the
Ministère de l'Éducation Nationale
(Ministry of National Education)
55, rue Saint-Dominique,
F Paris VII
is looking after this problem.

Germany — Federal Republic of Germany and West Berlin

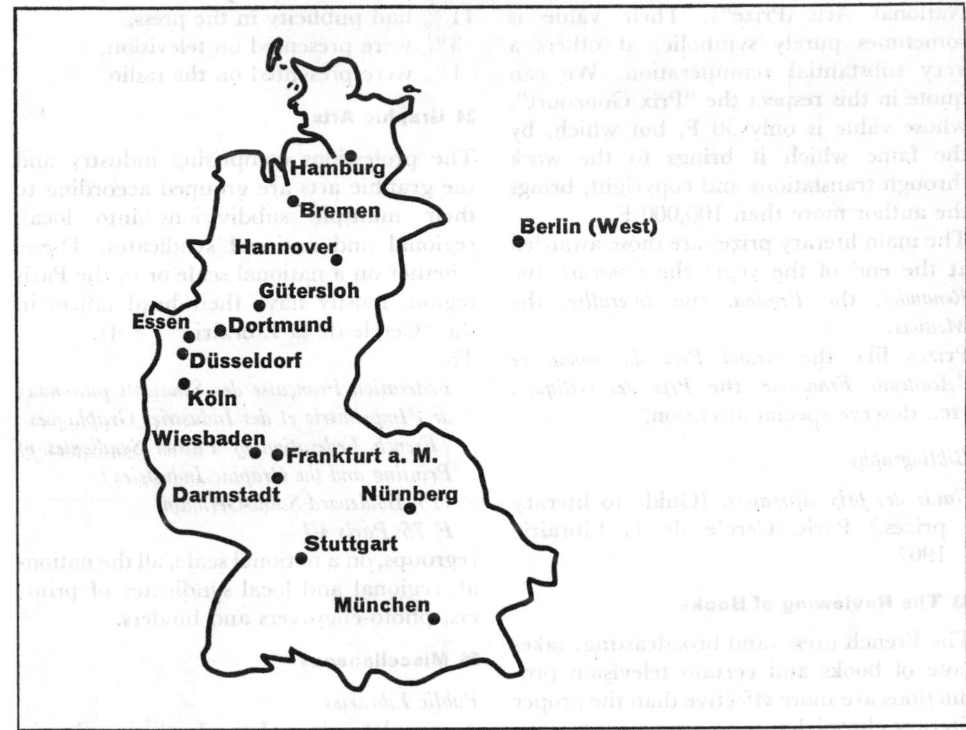

Important Book Centres

1 General Information

Area 248,553 km²
Population 60,184,000 (242 per km²)
Capital Bonn (138,000)
Largest towns Hamburg (1,826,400); München (1,260,600); Köln (853,900); Essen (702,300); Düsseldorf (686,100); Frankfurt a. M. (660,600); Dortmund (646,400); Stuttgart (615,000); Bremen (605,000); Hannover (524,500)
Government Federal Republic (F.R.G.) comprised by 10 states ("Länder"). Education and police under the control of the "Länder". The independent political unite West Berlin (2,149,700 inhabitants) is additionally represented in the Federal Parliament ("Bundestag")
Religion Protestant 50.5 %
Roman Catholic 44.1 %
Smaller religious groups and dissidents 5.4 %

National language German
Leading foreign languages English, French
Weights, measures Metric system
Currency unit Deutsche Mark (DM) = 100 Pfennige (Pf)
Education Compulsory. 406,831 (1966) students (3rd level) at 46 universities, technical and other colleges of academic standard
Illiteracy Nil
Paper consumption a) Newsprint 12.0 kg per inhabitant (1968)
b) Printing paper (other than newsprint) 26.9 kg per inhabitant (1968)
Membership UNESCO, IPA, ICBA, ILAB

2 Past and Present

The discovery by Johannes Gutenberg, citizen of Mainz (*c.* 1400–1468), of letters moulded from matrices and printing with movable types did not long remain confined within the boundaries of the old German episcopal town on the Rhine. At the end of the 15th century printing offices existed in 250 European places. It is estimated that during the first 50 years of printing about 30,000 titles were published. Johannes Gutenberg's 42-line *Biblia latina*, printed not later than 1456, ranks as the most beautiful book of this period.

The early printers of incunabula were both publishers and booksellers. Soon, however, divisions appeared between the printing trade and the book trade, which separated more and more. In the book trade, however, publishing and bookselling tended to remain the same business for some time to come. Variations began to appear, but it was not until the 18th or early 19th century that the publishing trade and the retail trade became quite distinct from each other; finally the mixed business practically disappeared. Today this means that as a rule the publisher only publishes and the bookseller only sells books. In such a system the wholesale book trade must clearly occupy a particularly important position. For this reason a first-class wholesale system has always been an influential part in the development of the modern German book trade.

This interaction between the three major pillars of the book trade—publishing, wholesaling and retailing—has led to an organization which is typical for Germany: in 1825 the German book trade joined together in the *Börsenverein der Deutschen Buchhändler* ("German Publishers' and Booksellers' Association"), the special characteristic of which was and is that it combines all branches of the trade. From the beginning this "Börsenverein" tackled not only tasks in the book trade but also those of a more general nature. It thus became part of the German cultural scene, and this in turn explains the special regard with which the public looks upon this organization. Achievements particularly noteworthy in the history of the "Börsenverein" and therefore of the book trade are the creation of a generally binding copyright and the foundation and advancement of a German national bibliographical centre.

Bibliography

a) Periodicals

Archiv für Geschichte des Buchwesens. (Archives for the history of the book world.) So far (January 1970) 9 vols. Frankfurt a. M., Buchhändler-Vereinigung, since 1956.
This continues the *Archiv für Geschichte des Deutschen Buchhandels* (Archives for the history of the German book trade) which appeared from 1878 to 1898 in Leipzig.

b) Books

FR. KAPP and J. GOLDFRIEDRICH, *Geschichte des Deutschen Buchhandels.* (History of the German book trade.) 4 vols. & index. Leipzig, Börsenverein 1886–1923.

G. SCHULZ, *Zeugnisse und Programme zur Geschichte des deutschen Buchhandels, 1794–1951.* (Documents and programmes about the history of the German book trade, 1794–1951.) München, Verlag Dokumentation 1964. 112 pp.

S. TAUBERT, *Bibliopola. Pictures and texts about the book trade.* 2 vols. Hamburg, Hauswedell (London: Allen Lane The Penguin Press; New York: R. R. Bowker) 1966. XXVI, 124; X, 524 pp.—Trilingual: English, French, German. International iconography of the book trade.

S. TAUBERT, *The German book trade today and tomorrow.* In: The Indian Publisher and Bookseller. Indo-German special number. Bombay, Popular Book Depot 1966.

FR. UHLIG, *Geschichte des Buches und des Buchhandels.* (History of the book and the book trade.) 2nd ed. München, Verlag Dokumentation 1962. 115 pp.

H. WIDMANN, *Geschichte des Buchhandels vom Altertum bis zur Gegenwart.* (History of the book trade from antiquity to the present time.) Wiesbaden, Harrassowitz 1952. 189 pp.

H. WIDMANN, H. KLIEMANN and B. WENDT (eds.), *Der deutsche Buchhandel in Urkunden und Quellen.* (The German book trade in documents and sources.) 2 vols. Hamburg, Hauswedell 1965. 448, 460 pp.

→ 6, Bibliography.

3 Retail Prices

In 1887 all branches of the German book trade came to an agreement, set down in the *Verkaufs- und Verkehrsordnung* ("Regulations for the sale of books to the public and terms and conditions between publisher and bookseller"), fixing the retail price for books. This retail price maintenance continued after 1945, though under completely changed conditions, in the form of individual pronouncements and reversions. On 1 January 1958 a new situation was created through the *Gesetz gegen Wettbewerbsbeschränkungen* (GWB, i.e. "Restrictive Practices Act"). However, the book trade has had its price-maintenance agreement confirmed. This exception to the rule allowed for individual agreements to be made between the retail trade and the publishing trade. After some further developments, a collective system of agreements was established in 1965 with the approval of the "Bundeskartellamt" ("State Monopoly Commission") which most publishers have now joined. Some publishers fix their prices themselves and about 90% of all book production can be regarded as price-fixed. Generally allowed reductions in price are: 5% for scientific libraries (yearly budget for expenditure at least DM 30,000); 10% for public libraries; 20% on a lecturer's books for his students; 15% for needy students.

The future of retail price maintenance for books depends on whether or not the present system proves to be without loopholes. Future pricing policy therefore lies in the hands of the book trade itself.

The function of the

Verein für Verkehrsordnung im Buchhandel
(Association for Book Trade Regulations)
Postfach 3914
D 6 Frankfurt a. M.

is to look after the interests of its members by taking care of the customs and usage which have developed in the relationship that the publishing trade has with its customers. The book-trade regulations which are included in the rules of the "Verein" deal with the following subjects: terms of delivery, legal validity of the orders, firm orders, conditions of consignments, transportation, agencies, arrangements for invoicing, terms of trade, and other matters.

Bibliography

H. FALTER, *Buch und Buchhandel im Rahmen der Wirtschaftspolitik verschiedener Länder unter besonderer Berücksichtigung der vertikalen Preisbindung.* (Books and the book trade in the economic framework of various countries with special reference to vertical price maintenance.) Aachen, J. A. Mayer 1965. 135 pp.

H. FRANZEN, *Tagesfragen zur Preisbindung.* (Actual problems of price maintenance.) Frankfurt a. M., Buchhändler-Vereinigung 1967. 68 pp.

H. FRANZEN and G. SCHWARTZ, *Preisbindungsfibel für den Buchhandel.* (Handbook for price maintenance in the book trade.) München, C. H. Beck 1966. XIII, 99 pp. Complete survey of the problems of price maintenance in the book trade of the Federal Republic. With bibliographical references.

H. GRUNDMANN, *Literatur ohne Preisbindung.* (Literature without price maintenance.) Bonn, H. Bouvier 1965, 33 pp.—Forschungsstelle für Buchwissenschaft an der Universitätsbibliothek Bonn, Kleine Schriften, 3.
Short survey written by a well-known bookseller.

W. NUMRICH, *Die soziologische Funktion des festen Ladenpreises im Buchhandel.* (The sociological function of the fixed price in the book trade.) Frankfurt a. M., Buchhändler-Vereinigung 1968. 44 pp. —Archiv für Soziologie und Wirtschaftsfragen des Buchhandels, III.
With a bibliography.

W. STRAUSS, *Der feste Ladenpreis im Buchhandel.* (The fixed price in the book trade.) And: P. MEYER-DOHM and CHR. UHLIG, *Zur Problematik der vertikalen Preisbindung bei Verlagserzeugnissen.* (The problems of vertical price maintenance for the printed word.) Hamburg, Verlag für Buchmarkt-Forschung 1963. 52 pp. —Berichte des Instituts für Buchmarkt-Forschung, 4.

4 Organization

The main association for all branches of the book trade is the

Börsenverein des Deutschen Buchhandels e.V.
(German Publishers' and Booksellers' Association)
Postfach 3914
D 6 Frankfurt a.M.

It continues in the tradition of the "Börsenverein" founded in Leipzig in 1825 (→ 2). Membership is on an individual basis, but a membership of firms is planned (1971).

Its most important tasks are: representing the interests of the book trade, the easing of business relations, the care of traditions and customs, developments of new forms of business, balancing the interests of the various branches, book promotion, training of young booksellers, social welfare, and contact with institutions in Germany and other countries which are related in one way or another to the book trade.

Three representatives of the publishing trade and three representatives of the retail trade as well as the chairmen of the publishers', the wholesalers' and the retailers' committees make up the board *(Vorstand)*, which is elected every three years. Apart from the board various bodies exist: the main assembly *(Hauptversammlung* = assembly of members), the representative assembly (*Abgeordnetenversammlung* = parliament of the book trade) with the assistance of the regional book trade organizations, and committees (publishers, booksellers, wholesalers). In addition there are specialists' committees (*Fachkommissionen:* for antiquarian booksellers, railway station booksellers, mail-order booksellers, book clubs) and working committees (*Arbeitsausschüsse:* copyright, taxes, book promotion, training, book-trade history, foreign trade, rationalization).

The seat of the central office is in the *Haus des Deutschen Buchhandels* (address under "Börsenverein") and consists of the following departments: secretariats for the publishers', for the booksellers' and for the wholesalers' committees, department of economics and statistics, law department, department for information and public relations, membership registry, library.

The body with responsibility for the publishing ventures of the head organization is the

Buchhändler-Vereinigung GmbH
Postfach 3914
D 6 Frankfurt a.M.

Shareholders of the "Buchhändler-Vereinigung" are the regional book-trade federations of each Land *(Landesverbände)*. Its most important publications are: "Börsenblatt für den Deutschen Buchhandel, Frankfurt edition" (→ 5), "Deutsche Bibliographie" ("German bibliography", →

15), "Archiv für Geschichte des Buchwesens" ("Archives for the history of the book world", → 2), "Adressbuch des deutschsprachigen Buchhandels" ("Directory of the German-speaking book trade", → 7), "Buch und Buchhandel in Zahlen" ("Book and book trade in figures", → 6). Apart from the "Börsenverein" there are a great number of related associations. Their addresses are to be found in the section on organizations in the "Adressbuch des deutschsprachigen Buchhandels" (→ 7).

Bibliography

A. U. Martens (ed.), *Der Börsenverein des Deutschen Buchhandels. Organisation—Aufgaben—Tätigkeit.* (The Börsenverein des Deutschen Buchhandels. Organization—tasks—activities.) Frankfurt a. M., Börsenverein 1968. 60 pp.—Schriftenreihe des Börsenvereins, 1.

W. Michael, *The organization of the German book trade.* In: The Indian Publisher and Bookseller. Indo-German special number. Bombay, The Popular Book Depot 1966.—In English.

Organisationsteil zum Adressbuch des deutschsprachigen Buchhandels. (Section on organizations in the directory of the German-speaking book trade.) Frankfurt a. M., Buchhändler-Vereinigung. Bi-annually.

Satzung des Börsenvereins des Deutschen Buchhandels e.V. (Rules of the Börsenverein.) Frankfurt a. M., Börsenverein 1967. 66 pp.

A. Werner, *Der Börsenverein des Deutschen Buchhandels nach 1945.* (The Börsenverein des Deutschen Buchhandels after 1945.) München, Verlag Dokumentation 1971. 182 pp.

5 Trade Press

The most important trade journal for all matters concerning the book trade is the

Börsenblatt für den Deutschen Buchhandel
Frankfurt edition
Postfach 3914
D 6 Frankfurt a. M.

which is published twice a week.

The "Börsenblatt", published since 1834 and one of the oldest book trade journals in the world, is the official voice of the "Börsenverein" (→ 4). Each number contains editorial matter dealing with problems of the German and foreign book trade; it makes indispensable reading for anyone interested in the development of the book trade in the Federal Republic and in West Berlin. This also applies to the section of advertisements which is regularly used by German-speaking publishers to announce new titles, new editions, changes in business, etc. The section on appointments ought to be mentioned here as well. It is not possible for publishers and booksellers to be completely efficient without reading the "Börsenblatt". There are regular supplements: "Aus dem Antiquariat" ("Antiquarian bookselling"), which deals with all matters appertaining to the national and international antiquarian and auction book trade, and "Der Junge Buchhandel" ("The young book trade"), dealing with matters of interest to the younger generation in the book trade. Another regular supplement is "Das Archiv für Geschichte des Buchwesens" ("Archives for the history of the book world" → 2) which, however, can be obtained separately from the "Börsenblatt" and the "Archive for sociology and commercial questions of the book trade" (→ 6). Each year several special editions of the "Börsenblatt" are published which appear in the following order and under the following general subjects: spring number, technical publishing, travel and hiking, calendars, Frankfurt Book Fair (about 5 weeks before the Fair), reprints, Christmas. Alle these numbers have a detailed author and subject index. The most comprehensive publication is the special number for the "Frankfurt Book Fair" in several volumes. In addition, numerous periodicals are published which deal specially with the book trade. The following list gives a selection:

Bertelsmann Briefe
(Bertelsmann Letters)
C. Bertelsmann Verlag
Postfach 555
D 4830 Gütersloh

This is an irregularly published series in which 74 numbers have appeared so far (Oct. 1971). It has long contributions dealing mainly with up-to-date problems of the book trade in various aspects.

Buchhändler Heute
(The Book Trade of Today)
Jahnstrasse 36
D 4 Düsseldorf 1

deals with questions of particular interest to the younger generation in the book trade.

Buchmarkt
(Book Market)
Magazin für den Buchhandel
Postfach 10165
D 4 Düsseldorf 10

The aim of this magazine, which appears ten times annually, is to deal—as an independent, critical voice—with important questions of the modern national and international publishing trade and its relationship with other branches of the book trade.

Much information about trends and topics of the book trade is published by

Buchreport
Postfach 1305
D 46 Dortmund

6 Book-Trade Literature

There is a very extensive range of literature on the book trade in the Federal Republic. As far as they deal with specific subjects, the most important books will be mentioned in the relevant chapters. The titles below are of particular interest either with regard to the overall picture or as bibliographies and selective lists for the whole field of the book trade.

a) Bibliographies

Die Fachliteratur zum Buch- und Bibliothekswesen. (Special literature about the book- and library-world.) 8th ed. München, Verlag Dokumentation 1967.
About this important bibliography → International Section, 6.

H. Kliemann and P. Meyer-Dohm, *Buchhandel. Eine Bibliographie.* (The book trade. A bibliography.) Hamburg, Verlag für Buchmarkt-Forschung 1963. 160 pp.—Schriften zur Buchmarkt-Forschung, 1.
A selective summary of publications about the German book trade which are relevant from an economical and sociological point of view. The work aims at completeness for titles published since 1945, and includes books as well as periodicals. It is divided into subjects and includes an index.

G. K. Schauer (ed.), *Eine Fachbibliothek für Buchhändler.* (A special library for booksellers.) 4th ed. Frankfurt a. M., Buchhändler-Vereinigung 1970. 63 pp.
Published for the first time in 1955 under the title "Grundstock einer Fachbibliothek für den Buchhändler" ("Basis for a special library for the bookseller").
—With the collaboration of well-known experts, this selective and descriptive bibliography gives the basis for a special library of the book trade. It appeals to all circles of the trade and is also an excellent source of information for the interested foreigner. The contents are grouped into subjects and include among others: reference works, the book world, production, legal aspects, bibliography, history of the book and the book trade, literary history, publicity, trade jounals.
The emphasis is on modern trade literature.

b) General Surveys

Organisationsteil zum Adressbuch des deutschsprachigen Buchhandels. (Section on organizations in the directory of the German language book trade.) Frankfurt a. M., Buchhändler-Vereinigung, bi-annually.
This work lists addresses and functions of all organizations relevant to the book trade of the Federal Republic of Germany, Austria and Switzerland.

Archiv für Soziologie und Wirtschaftsfragen des Buchhandels. (Archives for sociology and commercial questions of the book trade.) Frankfurt a. M., Buchhändler-Vereinigung, since 1967.
A supplement to the "Börsenblatt" (→ 5) with interpretations of important topical sociological and commercial problems of the book trade.

Buch und Buchhandel in Zahlen. (Book and book trade in figures.) Frankfurt a. M., Buchhändler-Vereinigung, annually.
Issued since 1952 by the "Börsenverein" (→ 4). It gives comprehensive information about all branches of the German book trade in tables, statistics and diagrams, illustrated by comments and pictures. Includes also some international material.

S. Taubert (ed.), *Indo-German special number of "The Indian Publisher and Bookseller".* Bombay, The Popular Book Depot 1966. 115 pp.—In English.
Contains numerous contributions about the situation of the modern book trade in the Federal Republic.

c) Handbooks

H. Gonski, H. G. Göpfert and others, *Der deutsche Buchhandel in unserer Zeit.* (The German book trade in our time.) Göttingen, Vandenhoeck & Ruprecht 1961. 109 pp.
Compiled from a series of lectures given in Göttingen this book offers much informative material about problems in the German book trade.

H. Hiller and W. Strauss (eds.), *Der deutsche Buchhandel.* (The German book trade.) 4th ed. Hamburg, Verlag für Buchmarkt-Forschung 1968. 462, 36 pp.
Numerous authors—all of them well-known experts in their field—have contributed to this book, which touches on all the main subjects of the book trade in the Federal Republic and its internal organization and external relationships. A comprehensive bibliographic index has been added. This book is also very suitable for the foreigner as a general introduction to the situation of the book trade in the Federal Republic.

A. U. Martens (ed.), *Buchhandel und Gesellschaft—heute und morgen.* (Book trade and society—today and tomorrow.) Frankfurt a. M., Börsenverein 1969. 94 pp.—Schriftenreihe des Börsenvereins, 3.

P. Meyer-Dohm, *Buchhandel als kulturwirtschaftliche Aufgabe.* (The book trade as cultural-economic venture.) Hamburg, Verlag für Buchmarkt-Forschung 1967. 224 pp.—Schriften zur Buchmarkt-Forschung, 11.

P. Meyer-Dohm and W. Strauss (eds.), *Handbuch des Buchhandels.* (Handbook of the book trade.) 4 vols. Hamburg, Verlag für Buchmarkt-Forschung, since 1971.
Standard work covering all aspects of modern book publishing, book wholesailing and book retailing including book clubs, etc.

H. F. Schulz, *Das Schicksal der Bücher und der Buchhandel.* (The future of books and the book trade.) 2nd ed. Berlin, de Gruyter 1960. 243 pp.
A cultural and statistical study of central problems in the functioning of the book trade.

7 Sources of Information, Address Services

General information about the book trade is to be obtained through the

Börsenverein des Deutschen Buchhandels e.V.
(German Publishers' and Booksellers' Association)
Postfach 3914
D 6 Frankfurt a.M.
(→ 4) or through its agency.
The addresses of all branches of the book trade are given in the "Adressbuch des deutschsprachigen Buchhandels" ("Directory of the German language book trade") published by the Buchhändler-Vereinigung (→ 4) bi-annually.
Special inquiries about matters of bibliography should be directed to the
Deutsche Bibliothek (German Library)
Auskunftsabteilung
Zeppelinallee 8
D 6 Frankfurt a.M. 1
Inquiries of this kind can also be directed to the firm of
O. Gracklauer
Postfach 21
D 6434 Niederaula über Bad Hersfeld 1
Trade addresses of libraries and the book trade can be obtained from the
Buchhändler-Vereinigung GmbH
Postfach 3914
D 6 Frankfurt a.M.
(→ 4). The material this association offers has been grouped under various aspects. It is a good basis for general and specific publicity in the Federal Republic and in German-speaking neighbouring countries, and as such, is of value also to the foreign user.

Bibliography

G. Schulz, *Information material about the German book market.* In: The Indian Publisher and Bookseller. Indo-German special number. Bombay, The Popular Book Depot 1966.—In English.

8 International Membership

The "Börsenverein" (→ 4) has a long tradition in supporting efforts to encourage the international book trade. It is a member of the "International Publishers' Association" (→ International Section, 4) and the "International Community of Booksellers' Associations" (→ International Section, 4). As is evident from chapter 26, the "Verband deutscher Antiquare" ("Union of German Antiquarian Booksellers") is attached to the "International League of Antiquarian Booksellers" (→ International Section, 26). The "Frankfurt Book Fair" is a member of the "Union des Foires Internationales" (UFI) with its headquarters in Paris.
Apart from this there are numerous associations which, either officially or privately, bring German publishers and booksellers together with their foreign colleagues in order to discuss problems of common interest. This applies to German-speaking as well as foreign countries. In the German-speaking book trade special mention ought to be made of the "meeting of three nations" (*Dreiländertreffen:* Federal Republic, Austria, Switzerland) at the highest level of their respective book-trade organizations.
The Federal Republic is a member of Unesco.

9 Market Research

Scientific research into the book and its market is done in two ways.
On the one hand there are, at various universities and colleges, chairs or lectureships and visiting readerships which study the book trade in historical, sociological, legal, economic, literary or cultural context. (Universities: Bonn, Frankfurt a.M., Göttingen, Köln, Mainz, München; Technical University: West Berlin; Teacher Training College, Münster; "Institut für Jugendbuchforschung an der Universität Frankfurt a. M." ("Institute for Research into Children's Books at the University of Frankfurt a.M.").

On the other hand, special institutions are working in a rather more practical way—researching, collecting and publishing.
For example, there is a section for market analysis within the economic department of the "Börsenverein" (→ 4). It publishes such works as the yearly account, "Buch und Buchhandel in Zahlen" ("Book and book trade in figures" → 6), and is responsible for researches into the book market. The "Archiv für Soziologie und Wirtschaftsfragen des Buchhandels" ("Archives for sociology and commercial questions of the book trade" → 6), issued by the "Börsenverein", partially touches market-research problems.
Independent work is being done by the

Institut für Buchmarkt-Forschung
(Institute for Book Market Research)
Eickhoffstr. 14–16
D 483 Gütersloh

which has existed since 1961. With the aid of the sciences—in particular the economic and social sciences—this institute aims to contribute to research into the book trade and its market conditions. By giving advice and procuring literature from other sources it promotes and supports scientific studies and itself commissions research projects. In its methodological work the institute retains close contact with the practical working of the book trade. The "Berichte des Instituts für Buchmarkt-Forschung" ("Reports of the Institute for Book Market Research") and the "Schriften zur Buchmarkt-Forschung" ("Publications about Book Market Research") are among the most interesting contributions of today's book-trade literature.
A "scientific working circle" for all problems of the book was founded in 1965 following a suggestion of the "Institut für Buchmarkt-Forschung". This group discusses important problems on specialized and general conferences.
The Federal Republic participates in international book market research.

The

Deutsches Bucharchiv
(German Book Archive)
Erhardtstr. 8
D 8 München 5

aims at providing complete documentation of the book trade and thus gaining a scientific insight into it. It is thus offering a multi-faceted basis for theoretical and practical work. This institute has also done valuable work over the years by making comparative studies of the trade.
Internationales Schulbuchinstitut ("International Text Book Institute," → International Section, 4).

Bibliography

L. Delp, *Das Deutsche Bucharchiv 1947–1967.* (The German Book Archives 1947–1967). München, Verlag Dokumentation 1967. 48 pp.

K.-Fr. Flockenhaus and G. Schmidtchen, *Marktforschung in der Diskussion.* (Market research in discussion.) In: Archiv für Soziologie und Wirtschaftsfragen des Buchhandels, VIII, pp. 1871–90. Frankfurt a. M., Buchhändler-Vereinigung 1969.

R. Fröhner, *Das Buch in der Gegenwart.* (The book at the present time.) Gütersloh, Bertelsmann 1961. 198 pp.
An empiric sociological study of the role of the book as conceived by the adult population of the Federal Republic.

M.-R. Girardi, L. K. Neffe and H. Steiner, *Buch und Leser in Deutschland.* (Book and reader in Germany). Hamburg, Verlag für Buchmarkt-Forschung 1965. 356 pp.—Schriften zur Buchmarkt-Forschung, 4.
Based upon an inquiry of one of the leading Western German demoscopic institutes (DIVO, Frankfurt a.M.).

H. Grundmann, *Von der Notwendigkeit und Möglichkeit einer allgemeinen Buchwissenschaft.* (About the necessity and possibili-

ty of a general book science.) In: O. Wenig (ed.), Wege zur Buchwissenschaft. Bonn, H. Bouvier 1966. pp. 399–416.
With bibliographical references.

E. Heinold, *Neue Wege zum Leser. Marketing für das religiöse Buch.* (New ways to reading. Marketing for the religious book.) In: Börsenblatt für den Deutschen Buchhandel, Frankfurter Ausgabe, 1969, pp. 1010–16.

H. Machill, *Buchmarkt-Untersuchung des Börsenvereins.* (Investigation of the book market by the Börsenverein.) In: Börsenblatt für den Deutschen Buchhandel, Frankfurter Ausgabe, 1967, pp. 113–121.

L. Muth, *Der befragte Leser.* (The questioned reader). Freiburg i. Br., Herder 1968. 48 pp.
General remarks about market research and book trade.—pp. 47–8: annotated bibliography.

L. Muth, *Perspektiven und Konsequenzen.* (Perspectives and consequences.) In: Archiv für Soziologie und Wirtschaftsfragen des Buchhandels, VI, pp. 3257–3264, Frankfurt a. M., Buchhändler-Vereinigung 1968.
Deals with the "Allensbach report" (cf. G. Schmidtchen "Lesekultur in Deutschland").

E. Noelle-Neumann and G. Schmidtchen, *Religiöses Buch und christlicher Buchhandel.* (Religious book and Christian book trade.) Hamburg, Verlag für Buchmarkt-Forschung 1969. 191 pp.—Schriften zur Buchmarkt-Forschung, 18.
An inquiry done by the "Institut für Demoskopie", Allensbach, on behalf of the two existing religious book trade organizations in the Federal Republic of Germany. Covers a wide field of reading and book buying habits.

W. Salber, *Zusammenhänge auf dem Buchmarkt—psychologisch gesehen.* (Coherences on the book market—seen psychologically.) In: Archiv für Soziologie und Wirtschaftsfragen des Buchhandels, VIII, pp. 1855–70, Frankfurt a. M., Buchhändler-Vereinigung 1969.

J. Scharioth, *Das Lesen alter Menschen.* (The reading of old people.) Hamburg, Verlag für Buchmarkt-Forschung 1969. 156 pp.—Berichte des Instituts für Buchmarkt-Forschung, special number.
The first inquiry in a special field of growing importance.

G. Schmidtchen, *Lesekultur in Deutschland.* (Reading culture in Germany F. R.). Frankfurt a. M., Buchhändler-Vereinigung 1968. 176 pp.—Archiv für Soziologie und Wirtschaftsfragen des Buchhandels, V.
The result of a representative reading study done by the "Institut für Demoskopie", Allensbach, upon request of the "Börsenverein". The findings will be used for practical approaches towards many fields of book-trade and reading activities.

G. Schmidtchen, *Eine Politik für das Buch.* (Politics for the book.) In: Archiv für Soziologie und Wirtschaftsfragen des Buchhandels, VI, pp. 3239–56. Frankfurt a. M., Buchhändler-Vereinigung 1968.

Fr. Uhlig, *Erforschung des Buchwissens.* (Book market research.) In: Gegenwart und Überlieferung. Special number: Börsenblatt für den Deutschen Buchhandel, Frankfurter Ausgabe, 1966, pp. 23–27.
With bibliographical references.

Fr. Uhlig and others, *Buchhandel und Wissenschaft.* (Book trade and science.) Hamburg, Verlag für Buchmarkt-Forschung 1965. VI, 192 pp.—Schriften zur Buchmarkt-Forschung, 5.
Contributions by several authors on all aspects of modern German book science. Numerous bibliographical references.

Die Zukunft des Lesers. (The future of the reader.) Freiburg i. Br., Herder 1969. 80 pp.

Articles about the (German) reader in past and present times and some outlooks in possible future conditions.

10 Books and Young People

As in other countries there is great interest shown in the young reader of the Federal Republic, and this is demonstrated in a number of ways. Among the organizations of interest the

Arbeitskreis für Jugendliteratur e.V.
(Working Committee on Literature for the Young)
Kaulbachstrasse 40
D 8 München 22

is the most important.

This committee is an association of friends and promoters of good books for young readers in the Federal Republic. Among its members are: federations and organizations of teachers of all types of school, of librarians, of the book trade and of people connected with youth work, as well as particular individuals whose concern is good literature for the young. The committee is also the German section of the "International Board of Books for Young People" (IBBY, → International Section, 10). It advises parents, teachers, students, librarians and booksellers, and provides them with reliable booklists, such as *Das Buch der Jugend* ("The book for young people"). The committee is responsible to the "Bundesministerium für Jugend, Familie und Gesundheit" ("Ministry for Young People, Family and Health") for organizing and selecting the annual award of the *Deutscher Jugendbuchpreis* (prize for the best book for the young → 32).

The monthly

Jugend und Literatur
(Youth and Literature)
An der Alster 22
D 2 Hamburg 1

publishes information and reviews about literature for young people.

The association

Deutsches Jugendschriftenwerk
(German Publications for the Young)
Kurt-Schumacher-Strasse 1
D 6 Frankfurt a.M. 1

annually publishes, in a so-called "White List", a selection of books for the young which have been read and recommended. This includes paperbacks, pamphlets and magazines.

There is a special

Institut für Jugendbuchforschung
(Institute for Research into Books for the Young)
Georg-Voigt-Strasse 10
D 6 Frankfurt a.M. 1

at the Johann-Wolfgang-Goethe University in Frankfurt a.M. The institute maintains a research library with approx. 30,000 volumes.

The

Arbeitsgemeinschaft von Jugendbuchverlegern in der Bundesrepublik Deutschland
(Workshop of Publishers of Children's Books in the Federal Republic of Germany)
Postfach 1124
D 87 Würzburg

deals with the special problems of this field. Close cooperation with spezialized institutions is maintained. The group sponsors an annual window-display competition for children's books.

Books likely to have a damaging influence on young readers are examined by the "Federal Examination Board"

Bundesprüfstelle
für jugendgefährdende Schriften
Postfach 190
D 532 Bad Godesberg

The basis for its work is the "Law about the circulation of literature damaging to young people" of 1953.

Internationale Bilderbuch-Ausstellung ("International Picture Book Exhibition"), Klingspor Museum, Offenbach, → Book Museums, p. 59.

Christian-Felix-Weisse Prize → 32.
Vorlesewettbewerb ("Reading competition") → 30.

Bibliography

H. ADLER, *Rund um die Jugendliteratur.* (About literature for young people.) Berlin, E. Klopp 1968. 344 pp.
A directory of all institutions, official, semi-official and private, dealing with children's books. The book covers the German-speaking countries of Europe.

H. ADLER and A. KÖHLERT, *Zehn Jahre Jugendschrifttumsarbeit in der Bundesrepublik.* (Ten years of work for literature for the young in the Federal Republic.) Frankfurt a. M., Deutsches Jugendschriftenwerk 1966. 69 pp.

M. DAHRENDORF, *Das Mädchenbuch und seine Leserin.* (The book for girls and its reader.) Hamburg, Verlag für Buchmarkt-Forschung 1970. 296 pp.—Schriften zur Buchmarkt-Forschung, 21.

I. DYHRENFURTH, *Geschichte des deutschen Jugendbuches.* (History of German children's literature.) 3rd ed. Zürich and Freiburg i. Br., Atlantis 1967. 324 pp.
With bibliography.

B. HÜRLIMANN, *Europäische Kinderbücher in drei Jahrhunderten.* (European children's books in three centuries.) 2nd ed. Zürich and Freiburg i. Br., Atlantis 1963. 288 pp.

K. CHR. LINGELBACH and CH. OBERFELD, *Jugendbuchforschung im Studium künftiger Lehrer.* (Research about books for young people within the curriculum of future teachers.) In: Archiv für Soziologie und Wirtschaftsfragen des Buchhandels, VIII, pp. 1891–1899. Frankfurt a. M., Buchhändler-Vereinigung 1969.

L. MUTH, *Der Buchhandel und die jungen Leser.* (The book trade and the young readers.) In: Archiv für Soziologie und Wirtschaftsfragen des Buchhandels, I, pp. 853–863. Frankfurt a. M., Buchhändler-Vereinigung 1967.

A. PELLOWSKI, *The world of children's literature.* New York, R. R. Bowker 1968. X, 538 pp.
pp. 140–47: text, pp. 147–73: bibliography: Germany.

11 Training

Traditional ideas and modern theories are combined in the training of future booksellers and publishers. It is felt that because of the great responsibility the publisher and bookseller have towards society, their training has to be conscientious and thorough.

Whoever wants to enter the book trade, no matter which branch, is apprenticed to a firm which is qualified to instruct trainees. Depending on the formal education of the trainee the time of training is 2 or 3 years. The Chambers of Commerce, in collaboration with the book trade, keep a watching brief on the methods and time of training as laid down in general regulations. The trainee is instructed in the theory of commerce and is given practical training. He has to keep a journal of his work and studies. This journal contains a list of all the topics to be covered during the training, and this list is regarded as equally binding on his employer. During training the trainee is payed a fee by way of an educational allowance.

The legal concept for all areas of professional training in the Federal Republic of Germany is expressed in three laws (*Arbeitsförderungsgesetz*, *Berufsbildungsgesetz* and *Erstes Gesetz zur individuellen Förderung der Ausbildung)* accepted in 1969. These laws regard professional training as important as school and university studies. Therefore they support on a collective and individual level the existing and the future means of training. Education and profession are accepted as a unity which has a decisive influence on a modern and dynamic society.

The trainee receives his theoretical instructions in special courses on commerce and the book trade which are held at vocational training centres in every large town. In addition there are correspondence courses and an extensive range of trade literature. The "Börsenverein" (→ 4) has its own school, the

Deutsche Buchhändlerschule
(School of the German Book Trade)
Wilhelmshöher Strasse 283
D 6 Frankfurt a. M NO 14

in which residential courses, lasting 6 weeks, are held. Trainees can take these courses at the end of their training. The lectures and seminars are designed to give the young bookseller or publisher an overall picture of the trade.

There are also other possibilities of further training for the keen publisher or bookseller of any age, such as regional and national courses, working groups, special courses on production, taxes and the problems of bookselling.

Young and talented booksellers or publishers who lack the means for training are assisted by the

Herbert-Hoffmann-Gedächtnis-Stiftung
Leuschnerstrasse 44
D 7 Stuttgart 1

whose programme also includes a working week in Paris once a year to which 20 young and promising booksellers or publishers are invited.

In 1965 the "Börsenverein" (→ 4) created, in Frankfurt a. M., the *Deutsches Buchhändler-Seminar* ("German Book Trade Seminar") in which young qualified booksellers and publishers are trained for leading positions in all branches of the book trade. Applicants have to have a thorough practical and theoretical knowledge of the book trade and experience in handling major problems.

Address of the "Seminar" see above, "Deutsche Buchhändlerschule".

The future training system will additionally comprise the *Fachschule des Deutschen Buchhandels* as a means of instructing promising members of the trade on a higher level. This new school will be balanced between the "Deutsche Buchhändlerschule" and the "Deutsches Buchhändler-Seminar". It cares for the training of higher paid assistants in the book trade.

In 1965 the

Stiftung Bertelsmann
zur Förderung und
Weiterbildung des
buchhändlerischen Nachwuchses
Postfach 555
D 4380 Gütersloh

was founded. Its purpose is the further training of young publishers and booksellers to become capable and responsible members of the book trade, suitable for promotion to the highest level. This foundation held its first seminar in 1967.

Trainees in the book trade, 1969

Category	Trainees Male	Female	Total	Percentage of total
Publishing	102	148	250	7.9
Bookselling	534	2,198	2,732	86.0
Antiquarian book trade	14	17	31	1.5
Wholesaling	15	40	55	1.7
Mail-order bookselling	8	11	19	0.6
Other categories	39	34	73	2.3
Total	712	2,448	3,160	100.0

Courses and trainees of the "Deutsche Buchhändlerschule"

Year	Courses	Trainees Total	Females alone
1946	1	40	29
1950	5	264	135
1955	6	332	234
1960	7	493	396
1968	6	587	486
1969	6	573	468

Bibliography

a) Periodicals

Buchhändler Heute. (Book publisher and bookseller today.) Monthly. (→ 5.) Formerly called "Der Jungbuchhandel" ("The young book trade"); finds its readers primarily amoung young members of the trade.

Der Junge Buchhandel. (The young book trade.) Monthly supplement to the "Börsenblatt für den Deutschen Buchhandel", Frankfurt edition (→ 5). Deals with all topics of interest to the young publisher and bookseller, including literary matters.

b) Books

W. ADRIAN, *Berufsbildung als gesellschaftspolitischer Auftrag.* (Professional education as a socio-political factor.) In: Börsenblatt für den Deutschen Buchhandel, Frankfurt edition 1969, pp. 2179–84.

Berufsbildung im Buchhandel. (Professional training in the book trade.) In: Börsenblatt für den Deutschen Buchhandel, Frankfurt edition, 1971, pp. 759—822.

Buchhändler werden. (Becoming a bookseller.) Frankfurt a. M., Börsenverein 1966.

R. MOHN, *Ausbildung und Fortbildung im Buchhandel.* (Training and further education in the book trade.) Gütersloh, Bertelsmann 1965. 7 pp. Gives information about the reasons for the "Stiftung Bertelsmann".

P. ZERNITZ, *Ausbildungssituation und Berufsvorstellungen angehender Buchhändler.* (Training system and professional conceptions of booksellers to be.) Hamburg, Verlag für Buchmarkt-Forschung 1967. 184 pp.—Berichte des Instituts für Buchmarkt-Forschung, special number. pp. 180–83: detailed bibliography.

Zur Einweihung des Neubaus der Deutschen Buchhändlerschule. (On the occasion of the opening of the new premises of the Deutsche Buchhändlerschule.) Special number of the Börsenblatt für den Deutschen Buchhandel, Frankfurt edition. Frankfurt a. M., Buchhändler-Vereinigung 1962. 239 pp. Contains a large number of contributions from various authors on the following three main subjects: history and work of the school; the new building; training and promotion of the young generation in the book trade, past and present.

12 Taxes*

Like all industrial undertakings, book-trade firms of whatever branch are subject to current taxation, and in particular the following four taxes:

Income Tax or *Corporation Tax.* The highest rate of the progressively graded income tax table is 53% of income; the highest rate of the essentially linear corporation tax table is 51% of income.

Trade Tax. This is divided tinto a) Trade Profits Tax, b) Trade Capital Tax and c) Total Salaries Tax, which is only levied in a few communities. There is considerable variation in the rates of taxation, which, within certain limits, can be autonomously fixed by the communities. In general the trade profits tax amounts to about 12–14% and the trade capital tax to 5–6%.

* The Editor wishes to record his thanks to Dr Herbert Haag, Frankfurt a. M., for contributing this chapter.

Property Tax. This amounts to 1% of the value of the property, after deducting certain concessions.

In the kinds of taxation mentioned above, the burdens are differentiated according to the legal form, size and strength of output of the individual undertakings; for the individual branches of the economy they are, however, equal.

Sales Tax. The general rate of taxation is 11% of the payment for the assessed deliveries or other services; the rate of taxation for most products of the publishing trade is 5.5%.

Books, periodicals and some other products of the publishing trade therefore receive considerably favoured treatment with regard to this form of taxation—as do also the most important articles of food. The charges levied in the other forms of taxation may be differentiated according to size and output of the various undertakings, but they are equal for the individual branches of the economy.

The value-added tax, which came into operation on 1 January 1968, is levied, like the earlier all-phase gross sales tax, on all stages of the production and sale of goods and also on all other remunerated services (e.g. the granting, transfer and assertion of rights arising from the Copyright Law). As compared with the old all-phase gross sales tax, which affected the cost of each transaction, the value-added tax becomes part of the cost only to the final consumer, since the salesmen can set off against their taxes any sales tax levied on the goods or services, and charge to the purchasers the tax arising from their sales.

Export deliveries are free from sales tax, and a refund is made of those taxes that have to be paid for the acquisition of goods and for the services claimed in order to effect such export deliveries. Exports enjoy no other forms of tax relief.

The following goods from the book trade and productions of the printing trade are subject to the reduced rate of tax of 5.5%:

a) books, brochures and similar products, loose sheets or leaves, also antiquarian material (from No. 4901 and 9906 of the customs tariff)
b) newspapers and other periodical publications, also with illustrations (from No. 4902 of the customs tariff)
c) picture albums, picture books, and drawing or painting books for children, whether paperback, paper-boards, or bound (No. 4903 of the customs tariff)
d) sheet music, manuscripted or printed, with or without pictures, also bound (from No. 4904 of the customs tariff)
e) cartographic productions of all kinds, including wall maps and photographic plans, printed terrestrial and celestial globes (from No. 4905 of the customs tariff)
f) objects of art and items for collections (from No. 9901–9903 and 9905 of the customs tariff)

The following are subject to the regular rate of taxation of 11%:

a) postcards, congratulatory cards, Christmas and similar cards, with pictures (No. 4909 of the customs tariff)
b) calendars of all kinds (No. 4910 of the customs tariff)
c) pictures, picture prints and other prints (No. 4911 of the customs tariff).

On imported goods the so-called *import sales tax* must be paid at the customs house. Its purpose is to charge the final consumer for imported goods in exactly the same way as for the same home goods. The rates of taxation are the same as with the sales tax for inland deliveries. Salesmen can set off such levied import-sales taxes against their sales-tax liabilities. In this way the import-sales tax, like the sales tax in general, does not affect their costs.

Printed works obtained in the form of printed-matter deliveries through the post are not subject to the import-sales tax, and so the final consumers (e.g. libraries,

private customers) do not pay it either. The weight limit for printed matter in case of book deliveries is 5 kg.
Book-trade goods and products of the printing trade are, in principle, free from *customs duty*. Exceptions are:
a) picture books b) globes c) postcards d) calendars e) pictures and prints of pictures.
The so-called external customs duties (on import from non-members of the EEC) vary between 9 and 15 % of the value of the imported goods. Internal customs duties, i.e. those within the EEC, are no longer levied.

Bibliography

H. HAAG, *Die Mehrwertsteuer im Buchhandel. Sonderfragen in Verlag und Sortiment.* (The value—added tax in the book trade. Special points concerning publishing and the retail book trade). Köln, O. Schmidt 1967. 172 pp.
This publication points out the effects of the sales-tax reform throughout the book trade, deals with special questions and, from time to time, with the importance of certain problems in practice.
K. MATHEJA, *Mehrwertsteuer der Verlage, Buchhandlungen und Druckereien.* Ein Leitfaden für die Praxis. (Value-added tax for publishers, booksellers and printers. A practical guide). Darmstadt, Stoytscheff 1967. 235 pp.
A first short book dealing in sequence with all the paragraphs and investigating the situation of enterprises engaged in the production and sale of published goods.

13 Clearing Houses

In order to help rationalize the settlement of accounts in the book trade a former Leipzig tradition was reintroduced, and in 1953 the

Buchhändler-Abrechnungs-Gesellschaft mbH (BAG)
(Booksellers' Clearing House)
Postfach 3942
D 6 Frankfurt a. M.

was formed, at first as a cooperative society. In 1956 it was turned into a limited company. Partners are the *Verein für buchhändlerischen Abrechnungsverkehr e.V.* and the "Buchhändler-Vereinigung GmbH" (→4). Through the BAG booksellers and publishers can settle their smaller accounts themselves and support by other means the rationalization of the book trade. The BAG reached a turnover of DM 107.1 m. in 1969. 3,952 firms were members at the end of 1969.
Supplementary to the BAG the

Buchhändlerische Kredit-Garantiegemeinschaft
(Credit-guarantee Community of the Book Trade)
Postfach 3942
D 6 Frankfurt a. M.

was established in 1970. This institution offers bank credits in cases where individual obligations of the members of the BAG are concerned.
The

Verleger-Inkasso-Stelle
Spaldingstr. 64
D 2 Hamburg 1

cares for the settlement of publishers' claims.

14 Copyright*

The law of copyright in force today in the Federal Republic of Germany is governed by the Act dealing with Copyright and Related Rights (Gesetz über Urheberrecht und verwandte Schutzrechte) dated 9 September 1965. This Act became effective on 1 January 1966, and covers the whole field of copyright and related matters. It is a

*The Editor wishes to record his thanks to RA Dr Heinz Kleine, Frankfurt a. M., for contributing this chapter.

very modern copyright act of the Western world and its systematic arrangement as well as its dealing with new questions, that have been arising from technical developments, are the results of many years of preparative work.

The focal point of this act is the author. As the creator of the work he is protected in his intellectual and personal relationship to the work (droit moral) and in the right of exploitation. There is no definitive enumeration of the protected works; the act merely quotes by way of examples the familiar categories of works, such as literary works, works of music, artistic works, works of artistic craftsmanship, photographic and cinematographic works, and designs of scientifical or technical nature: so that new types of works, too, arising as the result of new technical developments, can be protected. The decisive factor for the protectability of a work is that it shall be a personal intellectual creation: The work must bear the imprint of the author's personality. The artistic value or the quality of the intellectual effort is not decisive. The so-called "small change" of copyright, like forms, model contracts, advertisements, also enjoy copyright protection. As a result of his moral rights, the author has the right to determine whether and how his work is to be published and whether it has to bear an author's designation. He further has the right of recognition of his authorship and he can prohibit even a licensee (e.g. publisher, theatre or broadcasting company) from any deterioration of his work that might endanger his intellectual or personal interest in the work. Finally, he has the right to revoke a given licence, if it is not exercised or if he subsequently realizes that the work no longer reflects his views.

The rights of exploitation give the author the most comprehensive views of his work. Apart from the right to exploit the work in any material form (reproduction and distribution), the author is also granted the right to communicate the work in a non-material form. This comprises the right of recitation, performance, and broadcasting, and also the so-called secondary rights as the right of communication to the public (in restaurants, hotels, education or entertainment centres) through visual or sound recorders and through broadcasting. If new methods of reproduction are discovered through new technical development, these rights are also reserved for the author. Additional rights are granted to the creators of works of fine art; they receive a share of the price if their works are later on sold in the art trade *(droit de suite)* and the authors of literary works and works of music receive a participation if their works are professionally loaned.

In the interest of the public the rights of the author are subject to certain limitations. The reproduction of whole literary works without paying remuneration is only possible in some limited cases, for instance for collections for church, school, and otherwise educational purposes. A new law that has already been submitted to Parliament proposes that in these cases a remuneration shall be paid. The right to make free quotations is still the same as under the old act which took into account the needs of cultural life. Musical performances are only exempt from fees if they do not serve business purposes and if the audience is admitted free and the performing artists do not receive any special remuneration. The "reproduction for personal use" is dealt with in greater detail. The law differentiates between personal use and other internal use. With exception of tape-recordings, reproductions for personal use are permitted without limitation, and those for other internal use are generally permitted, if they serve a scientific purpose or if it is a matter of small sections of already published works or of single articles which have been published in newspapers or periodicals. But if the reproduction serves the internal use of some commercial enterprise, remuneration has to be paid in any case. The provision that permits the reproduction of whole books for personal and scientific use is already outdated by technical development, for a copy of a book can be produced in the same quality as the original, and sometimes it is even cheaper. Apart from that, storage and reproduction through television and computers are not yet dealt with. There are no proposals to change the law in these points.

The term of copyright of 50 years, which is practised by most other countries and which is laid down as minimum in the Berne Convention (International Section 14) has been extended to 70 years by the new act for all works that enjoy copyright protection on 31 December 1965. With regard to this extension of the term of copyright one has renounced the introduction of a levy in favour of a cultural fund on the sale of works whose copyright has expired (the so-called "*domaine publique payant*").

Apart from these provisions concerning the law of copyright the act also contains a number of important provisions concerning the law of copyright contract, especially the law of contract between author and publisher that was laid down in an Act of the year 1901. Only two rules of construction shall be mentioned here. If a licence (right of exploitation) is granted, it does not relate to kinds of exploitation that were not known at the time when the contract was made. If the kinds of exploitation that shall be transferred are not expressively mentioned, the scope of the rights transferred is determined by the purpose of the contract. If the so-called secondary rights shall be transferred to a publisher, it is not possible to determine that beside the right of publishing and distributing all other rights shall be transferred to the publisher; all the secondary rights that the parties want to transfer have to be named expressly.—If the parties of a publishing contract have agreed to a lump sum and it turns out that this sum stands in a grossly unfair relationship to the profit made by the publisher, the author can demand such an alteration of the contract as shall guarantee him a fair share under the given circumstances.

Apart from these provisions the copyright act also coordinates as related rights the rights of performing artists with regard to their performances. These may not be recorded or broadcast in visual or sound records without their consent. The performing artists and the producers of records receive a share of the revenue that comes out of the secondary exploitation of their works. The broadcasting societies and the producers of records are also protected against their works being broadcast and record producers against their records being reproduced and distributed. Apart from these rights, that have a term of 25 years beginning with the publication of the picture or the record, the law gives a 10-years' protection, similar in effect to copyright protection to publishers of scientific editions of unprotected works and texts and to publishers of posthumous literary works whose copyright has expired or never existed.

There are special provisions for copyright in films. The film producer does not enjoy copyright protection, but he has a lesser right classified among the neighbouring rights (Leistungsschutzrecht) in the film strip on which the film work or the sounds are recorded.

The law of copyright applies to German nationals irrespective of where their works appear. Foreign nationals enjoy the protection of the law for those of their works that first appeared in the Federal Republic, and for works appearing elsewhere if they are citizens of a country belonging to the Berne Convention and the work first appeared in a country associated with the Berne Convention, or if their country of origin has signed the Universal Copyright Convention, or if bilateral agreements exist between their country of origin and the Federal Republic (→ International Section, 14).

The Federal Republic is a signatory to the Revised Berne Convention in its Brussels version of 1948 and the Universal Copyright Convention of 1952. (→ International Section, 14). The Federal Republic has signed the Paris versions of the Copyright Convention (24 July 1971, → International Section, 14).

The application of copyright and other related rights when not applied individually, especially in the collection of fees, is undertaken by the following companies which are subject to the Law of 9 September 1965 for the appraisal of copyright and related rights:

GEMA
(Gesellschaft für musikalische Aufführungs- und mechanische Vervielfältigungsrechte)
(Performing and Reproduction Rights Society)
Bayreuther Str. 37–38
D 1 Berlin 30

VGW (Verwertungsgesellschaft Wort)
(Copyright Society for the Spoken Word)
Damenstiftstr. 7
D 8 München 2

Gesellschaft zur Verwertung von Leistungsschutzrechten mbH
(Society for the Application of Protective Rights on Performance)
Charlotte-Niese-Str. 8
D 2 Hamburg 52

Inkassostelle für urheberrechtliche Vervielfältigungsgebühren
(Encashment Office for Copyright Fees for Reproduction)
Großer Hirschgraben 17–21
D 6 Frankfurt a. M.

Verwertungsgesellschaft Bild – Kunst
(Copyright Society for the Arts)
Seckbächer Gasse 4
D 6 Frankfurt a. M.

and

Interessengemeinschaft Musikwissenschaftlicher Herausgeber und Verleger – IMHV
(Community of Interests of Musicological Editors and Publishers – IMHV)
Heinrich-Schütz-Allee 29
D 35 Kassel-Wilhelmshöhe

Bibliography

a) Text editions

L. Delp, *Das gesamte Recht der Presse, des Buchhandels, des Rundfunks und des Fernsehens.* (The whole law relating to the press, book trade, radio and television). Neuwied, Luchterhand. Loose-leaf.

K. Haertel and K. Schiefler, *Urheberrechtsgesetz und Gesetz über die Wahrnehmung von Urheberrechten und verwandten Schutzrechten.* (The law of copyright and of the protection of copyright and associated rights of protection). Köln, Heyman 1967. IX, 557 pp.

Urheber- und Verlagsrecht mit den internationalen Verträgen und dem Recht Österreichs und der Schweiz. (Copyright and right of publication, together with international treaties and the law of Austria and Switzerland). 4th ed. München, C. H. Beck.

b) Manuals

Bussmann, Pietzcker and H. Kleine, *Gewerblicher Rechtsschutz und Urheberrecht.* (Industrial legal protection and copyright). 3rd ed. Berlin, de Gruyter 1962. 791 pp.

H. Hubmann, *Urheber- und Verlagsrecht.* (Copyright and right of publication). 2nd ed. München, C. H. Beck, 1966. 296 pp.

E. Ulmer, *Urheber- und Verlagsrecht.* (Copyright and right of publication). 2nd ed. Berlin, J. Springer 1960. 471 pp.

c) Commentaries

Fr. K. Fromm and W. Nordemann, *Urheberrecht. Kommentar.* (Copyright. A commentary). 2nd ed. Stuttgart, Kohlhammer 1970. 538pp.

O.-Fr. Freiherr v. Gamm, *Urheberrechtsgesetz. Kommentar.* (The law of copyright. A commentary). München, C. H. Beck 1968. 902 pp.

E. Gerstenberg, *Die Urheberrechte an Werken der Kunst, der Architektur und der Photographie.* (Copyright as applied to works of art, architecture and photography). München, C. H. Beck 1968. 323 pp.

Ph. Möhring and K. Nicolini, *Urheberrechtsgesetz.* (The law of copyright). Berlin, Vahlen 1970. 904 pp.

H. Riedel, *Urheberrechtsgesetz und Verlagsgesetz mit Nebengesetzen. Hand-Kommentar.* (The law of copyright and of publication with associated laws. A handbook commentary). Düsseldorf, Deutscher Fachschriften Verlag 1968. Loose-leaf edition.

E. Schulze, *Kommentar zum deutschen Urheberrecht unter Berücksichtigung des internationalen Rechts.* (Commentary on German copyright as related to international law). Frankfurt a. M., A. Metzner 1969. Loose-leaf edition.

d) Collections of Verdicts

E. Schulze, *Rechtssprechung zum Urheberrecht. Entscheidungssammlung mit Anmerkungen.* (Verdicts in copyright cases. A collection with annotations). München, C. H. Beck. Loose-leaf edition.

e) Periodicals

Archiv für Urheber-Film-Funk und Theaterrecht. (Archive for authors' film, radio and theatre copyright). Ed. by G. Roeber. München, Verlag Dokumentation.

Gewerblicher Rechtsschutz und Urheberrecht. Zeitschrift der Deutschen Vereinigung für gewerblichen Rechtsschutz und Urheberrecht. (Industrial legal protection and copyright. Periodical of the German Association for Industrial Legal Protection and Copyright). Ed. by K. Bussmann and L. Heydt. Weinheim, Verlag Chemie.

ibid, *International Section.* Ed. by Ulmer and Fr.-K. Beier. Weinheim, Verlag Chemie.

The text of the Urheberrechtsgesetz (Law of Copyright) is printed in English in the English edition of "Droit d'Auteur". (cf. "Internationaler Urheberrechtsschutz", 1965, p. 251 ff.).

15 National Bibliography, National Library

After 1945, differing developments in the Eastern Zone of Germany (later German Democratic Republic) and the Western Zones (later Federal Republic of Germany) have led to the existence of two German archives for works written in the German language. In addition to the *Deutsche Bücherei* ("German Library"), founded in Leipzig in 1913 (→ Germany: GDR, 15), the

Deutsche Bibliothek
(German Library)
Zeppelinallee 8
D 6 Frankfurt a. M.

was created in Frankfurt a. M. in 1947. Since 1969 this library has been incorporated in the public statutes of the Federal Republic. According to these statutes it has the following aims: to collect, keep and make available, as complete as possible, all literature written in German or a foreign language and published since May 1945 in Germany, and all literature written in German and published in another country, as well as compile and publish the *Deutsche Bibliographie* ("German bibliography") based on scientific principles. In this way it fulfils the task of a complete archives of German literature and the German book trade, as well as that of a national bibliographical centre. In addition the "Deut-

sche Bibliothek" shall collect works about Germany published in foreign languages in other countries, translations of German books into other languages, as well as the literature of German emigrants; apart from this all other publications in German meant for trade distribution, visual materials with or without text, and printed music.
The general public has direct access to the collected literature.
The publishers are obliged to send their books to the "Deutsche Bibliothek" (*dépot légal*).
The "Deutsche Bibliothek" assists with the compiling of several bibliographic publications which are all published by the "Buchhändler-Vereinigung" (→ 4). They bear the collective title

Deutsche Bibliographie
(German bibliography)
Postfach 3914
D 6 Frankfurt a.M.

and are published as "Wöchentliche Verzeichnisse" (weekly lists). These weekly lists are collected in half-year lists. Next are the five-year lists which are published with the cooperation of the "Austrian National Library", Vienna, and the "Swiss National Library", Berne. This also applies to the lists of periodicals of the "Deutsche Bibliothek". A bibliography of official publications appears every two years.
The bulletin *Deutsche Bibliographie. Das deutsche Buch* ("German bibliography. The German book"), in the form of a *bibliographie raisonnée*, serves mainly to provide information for other countries.
The bibliographic work of the book trade is much helped by the catalogues issued by the wholesalers and by the lists of trade literature published by various other institutions.
A catalogue of books in print ("Verzeichnis lieferbarer Bücher") has been published in 1971 by the Verlag Dokumentation, München.

Bibliography

Bibliographie und Buchhandel. Festschrift Deutsche Bibliothek. (Bibliography and book trade. Festschrift German Library.) Börsenblatt für den Deutschen Buchhandel, Frankfurt edition. Frankfurt a. M., Buchhändler-Vereinigung 1959. 242 pp.

K. Köster, *The Deutsche Bibliothek (German Library) in Frankfurt a. M.* In: The Indian Publisher and Bookseller. Indo-German special number. Bombay, The Popular Book Depot 1966.—In English.

R. Weitzel, *Die deutschen nationalen Bibliographien.* (The German national bibliographies). 3rd ed. Frankfurt a. M., Buchhändler-Vereinigung 1963. 92 pp.

16 Book Production

Books have for hundreds of years held a special place in the lives of the Germans, whose reading of books has been comparatively extensive. This has influenced book production, which in its extent, variety and quality has placed Germany high among the book nations of the world.
It is, as yet, not possible to establish the exact order of precedence of book production, as the basis for a definition is still not generally agreed upon (→ International Section, 16). But it is certain that the Federal Republic with its yearly more than 30,000 publications takes a prominent place with the USSR, the United Kingdom, Japan and the USA.
In 1969 35,577 titles were published, among them 29,929 first editions. Of these publications 28,257 were books (49 pages and more). The rest were leaflets, brochures and maps.
From 1951 to 1969 the publishers of the Federal Republic and West Berlin produced more than 400,000 titles.
In the book production field the leading subjects were (1969):

Subject group	Titles	Percentage of total production
Fiction	6,555	23.2
Economics, sociology	2,066	7.3
Law, government	1,957	6.9
History, cultural history, folklore	1,919	6.8
Religion, theology	1,597	5.7
Linguistics, literary history	1,523	5.4
Natural sciences	1,389	4.9
Technical	1,308	4.6
School books	1,223	4.3
Education	1,201	4.3

Bibliography

H. Machill, *Book production in the Federal Republic of Germany.* In: The Indian Publisher and Bookseller. Indo-German special number. Bombay, The Popular Book Depot 1966.—In English.

The latest figures are regularly given in "Buch und Buchhandel in Zahlen" (→ 6) and, even more detailed, in "Archiv für Soziologie und Wirtschaftsfragen des Buchhandels" (→ 6).

17 Translations

Among the 35,577 titles published in 1969 there were 3,512 translations from other languages: 9.9% of the total book production. This figure is traditionally high in the German book market, and it indicates a varied readership. Interest in foreign literature is great and apart from translations many foreign books are read in the original languages.

Most of the translations are literary works (48.6%) and books for young people (9.8%). The whole field of translations is very varied, and in 1969 it included altogether 43 foreign languages.

59.2% of the translations were based upon originals published in the USA and the United Kingdom. Next in order were translations from the French (16.9%).

→ 35 a.

Bibliography

J. Levy, *Die literarische Übersetzung.* (Literary translation.) Frankfurt a. M., Athenäum 1969. 308 pp.

→ 16.

18 Book Clubs

It was in Germany that the idea of the modern book club was first introduced and put into practice. The first club was started in 1891, followed by others in subsequent decades. Two major book clubs emerged in the mid twenties and are still functioning today.

At the present time there are 15 book clubs in the Federal Republic, with a total membership of about 5 million. The range of choice of the various clubs lies between 25 and 700 titles. Between 6 and 182 new titles per year are introduced into their lists. Charges for membership range between DM 16 and DM 50.

The German book clubs originally arose from the desire for learning by workers and employees. This educational stress, linked with price considerations, is still relevant in some book clubs today, but the availability of a greater range of books at lower prices and generally improved financial standards have made this aspect to some extent less important. Apart from the choice of suitable reading material of good quality, the standard of production and design plays an important part in competition between book clubs.

At first the book trade viewed the spread of book clubs with some distrust, as unwanted competitors. Recent developments have, however, modified this impression. Closer cooperation between book clubs and the book trade has led to the widening of the distribution of books and stimulated reading habits among potential book buyers. The majority of the 5 million members of book clubs are now being catered for by the book trade.

Germany: FRG

The

Arbeitskreis der Buchgemeinschaften
(Book Club Circle)
Postfach 16220
D 6 Frankfurt a.M.

deals with special problems of this area.

Bibliography

H. HILLER, *The German book clubs.* In: The Indian Publisher and Bookseller. Indo-German special number. Bombay, The Popular Book Depot 1966.—In English.

G. EHNI and FR. WEISSBACH, *Buchgemeinschaften in Deutschland.* (Book clubs in Germany.) Hamburg, Verlag für Buchmarkt-Forschung 1967. 124 pp.—Berichte des Instituts für Buchmarkt-Forschung, 37–39.
Covers many interesting aspects of German book clubs including information about book clubs in the German Democratic Republic.—pp. 103–21, the best bibliography of this special field.

W. STRAUSS, *Die deutschen Buchgemeinschaften.* (The German book clubs.) In: H. HILLER and W. STRAUSS (eds.), *Der Deutsche Buchhandel.* 4th ed. Hamburg, Verlag für Buchmarkt-Forschung 1968.

19 Paperbacks

As we know them today, paperbacks in their design, method of pricing and distribution are based on American and English principles, and as such were introduced to Germany in about 1950. This modern concept of the paperback was, however, somewhat influenced by the low-priced paper-covered books that were earlier published in Germany (*Tauchnitz-Edition* since 1841, *Reclam-Universalbibliothek* since 1867, the *Albatross-Library* since 1932, etc.).

The methods of mass distribution, publication for impulse purchase and promotional methods by extensive point-of-sale merchandising soon emerged in West Germany despite some initial reluctance on the part of the traditional bookseller. The channels of distribution differ from the North American methods in so far as most paperbacks are sold in bookshops rather than in any other kind of outlet. The number of paperback series is growing yearly and therefore the number of titles and editions has become an increasing proportion of total book production. The average quality is high. Some 100 paperback series provide a high number of original titles every year. In 1969 2,060 paperback titles represented 5.8% of total book production. Many paperback series have established a high standard of book design and typography. There were 12,000 titles available in early 1970.

Bibliography

a) Catalogue

KOEHLER & VOLCKMAR, *Katalog der Taschenbücher.* (Catalogue of paperbacks.) Köln, Koehler & Volckmar. Twice annually.
Index according to authors, titles, subjects and series with publishers and prices.

b) Other literature

H. FRIEDRICH, *The pocket book in Germany.* In: The Indian Publisher and Bookseller. Indo-German special number. Bombay, The Popular Book Depot 1966. —In English.

H. FRIEDRICH, *Paperbacks in Deutschland.* (Paperbacks in Germany.) In: Paperbacks. A catalogue, pp. VIII–XVI. Frankfurt a.M., Ausstellungs- und Messe-GmbH des Börsenvereins 1969.

FR. HINZE, *Organisation des Taschenbuchverkaufs im Sortimentsbuchhandel.* (Organization of paperback distribution in the retail book trade.) Hamburg, Verlag für Buchmarkt-Forschung 1966. 115 pp.—Berichte des Instituts für Buchmarkt-Forschung, 24–26.

H. PLATTE, *Soziologie des Taschenbuchs. Bemerkungen zur Taschenbuchproduktion in der Bundesrepublik Deutschland von 1948 bis*

1962. (Sociology of the paperback.) Gütersloh, Bertelsmann 1962. 28 pp.—Bertelsmann Briefe, 15.
With numerous other references, covering the German development from 1948 to 1962.

20 Book Design

The idea of choosing every year the "best-designed German books" originated between 1930 and 1933 and was re-introduced by the "Börsenverein" (→ 4) in the Federal Republic in 1952. Since 1965 it is organized by the
Stiftung Buchkunst
Sophienstrasse 8
D 6 Frankfurt a. M.
Sponsors of this foundation are the "Börsenverein" (→ 4), the "Bundesverband Druck" (→ 34) and the "Deutsche Bibliothek" (→ 15).
The choice of the "Best-designed books" (mostly 50 titles a year) is governed by the quality of layout, print, illustration and binding. They are mainly chosen from books in general circulation. The aim of this competition is to give book buyers a greater awareness of the aesthetic pleasure to be had from books and thus to influence book production. Traditional as well as modern technical, typographical and artistic aspects are controlling factors.
For a period of 3 years the "Stiftung Buchkunst" selects a jury of 12 people to award the prize. The jurors are chosen from the book trade, the library world and the graphic industries.
The special competition *Der werbende Umschlag* ("The promoting book jacket") is held by the
Bund Deutscher Buchkünstler
(Union of German Book Artists)
Herrnstr. 80
D 6050 Offenbach a. M.
in collaboration with the
Bund Deutscher Grafik-Designer (BDG)
(Union of German Graphic Designers)
Postfach 6405
D 4 Düsseldorf 1
and with ICTA (→ International Section, 34).

Bibliography

Yearly catalogue of the "Schönste deutsche Bücher". Frankfurt a. M., Buchhändler-Vereinigung.
Text and pictures inform about the chosen books. A detailed report about the work of the jury is published yearly in the "Börsenblatt für den Deutschen Buchhandel" (→ 5).

B. Hack, *Modern art of the book in Germany and its traditional background.* In: The Indian Publisher and Bookseller. Indo-German special number. Bombay, The Popular Book Depot 1966.—In English.

21 Publishing

The division in 1945 of Germany into East and West brought about a great change in German publishing. Before 1945 first Leipzig und then, increasingly, Berlin were the publishing centres. Not only were many publishing houses concentrated there, but most German publishers were represented in Leipzig by agents or had their trade counters there. Today the publishing trade is dispersed among a number of cities in the Federal Republic, although important publishers can be found outside these centres. There are today about 400 locations with publishing houses, but some contain only one or two. The table below shows which towns have most publishing houses. Frankfurt a. M. is today regarded as the organizational centre of the book trade, being the seat of the "Börsenverein" (→ 4), the "Frankfurt Book Fair" (→ 29), the "Deutsche Buchhändler-Schule" (→ 11), and other institutions of the book trade, but in terms of the number of publishing houses it takes only fifth place behind Munich, Stuttgart, Berlin (West), and Hamburg.

Because of this dispersion of the publishing trade over the whole country a foreign observer needs much more time for his studies than in France, the United Kingdom, the USA or the USSR, where one can expect to find most information in the capitals. In Bonn, the capital of the Federal Republic, however, there are only 25 publishing houses.

According to the number of firms entered into the "Adressbuch des deutschsprachigen Buchhandels" (→ 7) the ten leading publishing cities (in 1968) are:

	Publishers
Munich	238
Stuttgart	180
Berlin (West)	178
Hamburg	136
Frankfurt a. M.	102
Darmstadt	62
Düsseldorf	54
Cologne	48
Hannover	46
Wiesbaden	42

Seen from the annual title output the leading publishing centres were in 1968: Munich (4,253 titles), Stuttgart (2,900 titles), Frankfurt a. M. (2,357 titles), Berlin West (2,241 titles), Hamburg (2,011 titles).

The turnover tax statistics give a good idea of the extent of the publishing trade. On the basis of 1966 the following number of firms were quoted:

Publishers of books, scientific and trade journals	1,670
Publishers of newspapers, magazines, etc.	523
Other publishers	696

The turnover of publishers of books, scientific, and trade journals, according to the official turnover tax statistics, in 1968 amounted to DM 2,788 million; that of publishers of newspapers, magazines, etc. to DM 3,240 million; that of other publishers to DM 404 million.

From the same source the following table shows firms (publishers of books, scientific and trade journals) arranged by size of turnover (1968):

Turnover DM	Firms	Turnover (1,000 DM)
12,000–100,000	584	28,550
100,000–500,000	523	140,447
500,000–1 mill.	189	144,177
1 mill. and more	415	2,475,289
Total	1,711	2,788,463

According to the book-production statistics of 1968 the number of publishers existing (regardless of official publications, institutional publishing) is given below.

Up to 1960 a comparative study of the publishing trade was carried out in Munich, and, in 1966, was restarted at the *Institut für Handelsforschung an der Universität zu Köln* ("Institute for Trade Research of the University of Cologne"), parallel to the comparative study of the retail book trade. The findings of this institute are published annually in the "Archiv für Soziologie und Wirtschaftsfragen des Buchhandels" (→ 6) and in "Buch und Buchhandel in Zahlen" (→ 6).

Published titles	Publishers	Percentage of publishers	Titles	Percentage of titles
Up to 5	1,166	63.6	2,333	9.4
6–20	430	23.4	4,676	18.8
21 and more	239	13.0	17,852	71.8
Total	1,835	100.0	24,861	100.0

Bibliography

a) Periodicals (→ 5)

School-book publishing problems are discussed in

Blickpunkt Schulbuch
(Focus on Schoolbooks)
Neue Mainzer Strasse 40–42
D 6 Frankfurt a.M. 1

This trade journal is published by the *Verband der Schulbuchverlage* ("Association of Schoolbook Publishers").

b) Books

CL. MARX, *Werbung im Buchverlag*. (Promotion in publishing.) Düsseldorf, Buchhändler Heute 1962. 137 pp.

W. OLBRICH, *Einführung in die Verlagskunde*. (Introduction to the technique of publishing.) 3rd ed. Stuttgart, Hiersemann 1955. VIII, 247 pp.

PH. REEG, *Scientific publishing in Germany*. In: The Indian Publisher and Bookseller. Indo-German special number. Bombay, The Popular Book Depot 1966. —In English.

C. A. SCHROEDER, *The modern textbook in Germany*. In: The Indian Publisher and Bookseller. Indo-German special number. Bombay, The Popular Book Depot 1966.—In English.

B. SPATZ, *Marketing im Verlagsbuchhandel*. (Marketing in the publishing trade.) Hamburg, Verlag für Buchmarkt-Forschung 1964. 92 pp.—Berichte des Instituts für Buchmarkt-Forschung, 10–11.

FR. UHLIG, *Der Verlags-Lehrling*. (The publishing apprentice.) 8th ed. Hamburg, Hauswedell 1969. 266 pp.

S. UNSELD, *Literary publishing firms in Germany*. In: The Indian Publisher and Bookseller. Indo-German special number. Bombay, The Popular Book Depot 1966.—In English.

→ 6 Bibliography: *Eine Fachbibliothek für Buchhändler*.

22 Literary Agents

In sharp contrast to the great importance literary agencies have in the USA and in the United Kingdom, their role is a minor one in the Federal Republic. Following an old tradition most authors as well as publishers prefer to make their arrangements in direct talks without a mediator. Negotiations are seldom made in any other way, thus giving the few existing literary agencies only a limited scope for activity.

International transactions are a different matter. Here the literary agent in the Federal Republic has a greater chance. But even here the German publisher generally prefers direct contact with his foreign counterpart.

23 Wholesale Trade

In the development of the modern German book trade, since the middle of the last century, the wholesale trade has had an influential and mediating role. Up to World War II it had, especially in Leipzig, taken a unique form, which, with its reliability and speed, made it exemplary far beyond the boundaries of Germany. It made possible a retail trade able to obtain any book not in stock within the shortest space of time.

As with other branches of the book trade, the wholesale trade was affected by the change after 1945. This change meant not only the absence of Leipzig as a centre for the Western German book trade, but also—apart from heavy war damage and resulting restrictions—a completely different set of circumstances following the development of a federal system in West Germany. Because of the growth in the number of bookselling and publishing centres a new method of distribution had to be adopted by the wholesale trade. It was possible to overcome the difficulties that arose within a few years not least because of an adaptable and far-seeing wholesale trade. Today the Federal Republic has a dense supply network, situated in various cities and linked with the names of several large firms. The centres are: in the south—Munich, Stuttgart and Frankfurt a. M.; in the west—Cologne; in the north—Bielefeld, Bremen, and Hamburg; and in the east—Berlin (West). It remains to be added that, as an importer and exporter, the wholesale trade also plays a part in the foreign trade in books and periodicals.

According to the official turnover statistics (1968) 564 wholesale firms handled books and scientific and trade journals at a value of DM 1,380 million. 6 firms had a turnover in excess of DM 25 m. with a combined turnover of DM 707.2 m.

24 Retail Trade

The classical form of book distribution is symbolized by the retail trade, which in tradition and achievement is indispensable for the marketing of books and is therefore the publisher's most important partner. Its structure and its distribution over the country guarantee that, through the bookshop, readers have easy and quick access to the book of their choice. The efficiency of the retail trade gives it a responsible role as entrepreneur, while the German reader, unlike readers in some other countries, likes to rely upon the bookseller for service. To maintain and improve the high standard of the retail trade is considered one of the great tasks of the book trade in the Federal Republic.

In 1968, according to turnover tax statistics, there were 3,368 firms in the economic group "retail trade with books, scientific and trade journals".

The 3,378 retail bookshops represented in the "Börsenverein" (→ 4) in 1968 were situated in the following leading cities:

Berlin (West)	286
Hamburg	257
Munich	205
Stuttgart	176
Frankfurt a.M.	107
Hannover	79
Cologne	78
Düsseldorf	62
Nuremberg	46
Essen	41

Apart from these 10 leading places there are 984 others where bookshops exist with approx. 600 additional places with book outlets.

Under the influence of a comparatively favourable economic development in the book trade after 1950, the retail trade underwent a remarkable revival, so that today there are many very modern and efficient bookshops in the Federal Republic. This applies equally to special paperback shops, to the incorporation of mail-order departments, and to the service provided for members of book clubs.

According to turnover tax statistics the "retail trade with books, and scientific and trade journals" and the "retail trade with other magazines and newspapers" (i.e. mainly shops where, apart from books, other reading matter and stationery are sold) in 1968, together reached 1,742 million DM, the "retail trade with books, scientific and trade journals" alone 1,146 million DM.

For this group the following turnover groups were established:

Turnover groups in DM	Firms	Turnover (1,000 DM)
Up to 100,000	1,242	66,729
100,000–500,000	1,367	398,895
500,000 and more	489	680,959
Total	3,368	1,146,583

The development of costs, turnover and other important and decisive facts of the retail book trade are expressed in the findings of a regular analysis done by the "Institut für Handelsforschung an der Universität zu Köln" ("Institute for Trade

Research of the University of Cologne", → 21) and regularly published in "Buch und Buchhandel in Zahlen" (→ 6) and in the "Archiv für Soziologie und Wirtschaftsfragen des Buchhandels" (→ 6).

To improve the efficiency of the retail book trade, to support its image and public relations, and to rationalize its activities the

Arbeitsgemeinschaft der Buchhandlungen
(Community of the Bookshops)
Bleichstr. 38a
D 6 Frankfurt a.M. 1

has been founded in 1969. This community has 500 bookshops as members.

Bibliography

a) Periodicals (→ 5)

b) Books

B. v. Arnim and Fr. Knilli, *Gewerbliche Leihbüchereien.* (Commercial lending libraries.) Hamburg, Verlag für Buchmarkt-Forschung 1966. 315 pp.—Schriften zur Buchmarkt-Forschung, 7.

G. Fesenfeld, *Buchverkaufskunde.* (Book retailing.) Düsseldorf, Buchhändler Heute 1968. 104 pp.

R. B. Förster, *Das Buch vom Buchfenster.* (The book of the display window for books.) Düsseldorf, Buchhändler Heute 1963. 54 pp.

W. Götze and W. Bormann, *Die Landkarte im Buchhandel.* (The geographical map in the book trade.) Hamburg, Verlag für Buchmarkt-Forschung 1963. 96 pp.

Fr. Hinze, *Erfahrungsaustauschgruppen im Sortimentsbuchhandel.* (Joint discussion groups in the retail book trade.) 2nd ed. Hamburg, Verlag für Buchmarkt-Forschung 1966. 62 pp.—Berichte des Instituts für Buchmarkt-Forschung, 15–16.

Fr. Hinze, *Registrierkassen als Buchungsmaschinen im Sortimentsbuchhandel.* (Cash registers as accounting machines in the retail book trade.) 3rd ed. Hamburg, Verlag für Buchmarkt-Forschung 1964. 34 pp.—Berichte des Instituts für Buchmarkt-Forschung, 2.

Fr. Hinze and V. Lohr, *Organisation des Schulbuchverkaufs.* (Organization of textbook distribution.) 2nd ed. Hamburg, Verlag für Buchmarkt-Forschung 1963. 34 pp.—Berichte des Instituts für Buchmarkt-Forschung, 5.

Fr. Hinze and U. Nitschke, *Kundenkarteien und Adressieranlagen im verbreitenden Buchhandel.* (Customers' card index and mailing lists in the distributive book trade). 3rd ed. Hamburg, Verlag für Buchmarkt-Forschung 1968. 96 pp.—Berichte des Instituts für Buchmarkt-Forschung, 20.

E. D. Hüttermann, *Verkauf und Erwerb von Buchhandlungen.* (To sell and buy a bookshop.) Hamburg, Verlag für Buchmarkt-Forschung 1964. 56 pp.—Berichte des Instituts für Buchmarkt-Forschung, 12.

E. D. Hüttermann, *Gründung einer Buchhandlung.* (Establishing a bookshop.) Hamburg, Verlag für Buchmarkt-Forschung 1966. 115 pp.—Berichte des Instituts für Buchmarkt-Forschung, 27–29.

G. Fr. Karcher, *Warenkunde des Buches.* (Product knowledge in the book trade.) 2nd ed. Stuttgart, Poeschel 1964. 119 pp.

P. Meuer, *Die kulturelle Bedeutung der Buchhandlung in der kleineren deutschen Stadt.* (The cultural significance of the bookshop in the small German town.) 2nd ed. Hamburg, Verlag für Buchmarkt-Forschung 1966. 44 pp.—Berichte des Instituts für Buchmarkt-Forschung, special number.

P. Meyer-Dohm (ed.), *Das wissenschaftliche Buch.* (The scientific book.) Hamburg, Verlag für Buchmarkt-Forschung 1969. 240 pp.—Schriften zur Buchmarkt-Forschung, 16.

P. Otto, *Kleinstadibuchhandel.* (The book trade in small towns.) Hamburg, Verlag für Buchmarkt-Forschung 1970. 172 pp.—Schriften zur Buchmarkt-Forschung, 17.

B. SPATZ and FR. WIENINGER, *Schallplattenverkaufslehre für den Buchhandel.* (Selling records in the book trade.) Hamburg, Verlag für Buchmarkt-Forschung 1961. 88 pp.

R. G. STECHER, *Praktische Werbekunde für das Sortiment.* (Practical promotion guide for the retail book trade.) Düsseldorf, Buchhändler Heute 1967. 189 pp.

W. STÖCKLE, *Der Buchabsatz im Warenhaus.* (The sale of books in department stores.) 2nd ed. Hamburg, Verlag für Buchmarkt-Forschung 1967. 78 pp.—Berichte des Instituts für Buchmarkt-Forschung, special number.

W. STRAUSS, *Der Buchhandel und seine potentiellen Kunden.* (The book trade and its potential customers.) Hamburg, Verlag für Buchmarkt-Forschung 1963. 34 pp. —Berichte des Instituts für Buchmarkt-Forschung, 6.

W. SUSSMANN, *Der Wettbewerb im westdeutschen Bucheinzelhandel.* (Competition in the West German retail book trade.) Hamburg, Verlag für Buchmarkt-Forschung 1967. 82 pp.—Berichte des Instituts für Buchmarkt-Forschung, 35–36.

K.-G. THIELE, *The retail book trade.* In: The Indian Publisher and Bookseller. Indo-German special number. Bombay, The Popular Book Depot 1966.—In English.

H.G. TÖLKEN, *Die Bedeutung des Standorts für das Ladengeschäft im Buchhandel.* (The importance of the location of the retail book trade.) In: Archiv für Soziologie und Wirtschaftsfragen des Buchhandels, IX, pp. 2687–2751.

Detailed bibliography on pp. 2747–2751.

FR. UHLIG, *Der Sortiments-Lehrling.* (The retail book-trade apprentice.) 16th ed. Hamburg, Hauswedell 1967. 324 pp.

A. VATTER, *Schreibwaren als Verkaufsartikel.* (Stationery as an article of sale.) 3rd ed. Stuttgart, Poeschel 1964. VIII, 76 pp.

25 Mail-Order Bookselling

This branch of the distributive book trade has also developed strongly in the Federal Republic, but it does not have quite the same importance as for instance in the USA. The turnover of the mail-order book trade is considerable; there are, however, no valid statistics as yet. This applies equally to the marketing of certain publishing projects (subscription works, encyclopedias, etc.) and in particular to the sales of the modern second-hand book trade (remainders) which result almost exclusively from mail-order promotion.
The number of bookshops that have a mail-order department has greatly increased in recent times. The formation of international economic organizations, such as the EEC, favours the further spread of the mail-order business.
Special mail-order firms are represented in the

Bundesverband der
Deutschen Versandbuchhändler e.V.
(Federal Association of the
German Mail-Order Book Trade)
Burchardstr. 14
D 2 Hamburg 1

Bibliography

E. GREINER jr., *Mail-order im Buchhandel.* (Mail-order in the book trade.) Hamburg, Verlag für Buchmarkt-Forschung, 1969. 52 pp.—Berichte des Instituts für Buchmarkt-Forschung, 42.

Mail-order in publishing and retail bookselling.—Bibliography on p. 45.

P. OTTO, *Das moderne Antiquariat. Der Restverkauf im Buchhandel.* (The modern remainder business.) Hamburg, Verlag für Buchmarkt-Forschung 1966. XI, 274 pp.—Schriften zur Buchmarkt-Forschung, 8.

26 Antiquarian Book Trade, Auctions

During the Nazi period and World War II and its aftermath the German antiquarian book trade suffered very heavy and sometimes irreparable damage. It had reached its peak in the second half of the 19th century and in the first three decades of this century. During that time it fulfilled a world-wide function, and in the history of the development of the modern book trade several names of important German antiquarian booksellers take a special place. After the unfortunate repercussions of World War I on the German antiquarian book trade there followed a promising interlude in the twenties, but in 1933 the trade began to decline. The expulsion and persecution of the German Jews had a grave and tragic effect on the antiquarian book trade, and on its leading representatives. Many large firms disappeared at that time, and, if they could, re-established themselves in another country. Numerous connections between the German antiquarian book trade and the rest of the world were broken off, and World War II and the destruction it caused amongst book stocks left the antiquarian book trade in an almost hopeless situation. Despite this, however, it picked up again after 1945. Today, under completely different circumstances, it has reached an important position within the country as well as in the international book world.
At the moment there are in the Federal Republic more than 200 bibliophile and scientific antiquarian bookshops. They are incorporated in the

Verband Deutscher Antiquare e.V.
(Union of German Antiquarian Booksellers)
Zum Talblick 2
D 6241 Glashütten Ts.

This association, being a member of the "International League of Antiquarian Booksellers" (→ International Section, 26), holds an annual selling exhibition in Stuttgart. The catalogue of this exhibition ("Gemeinschaftskatalog Deutscher Antiquare") offers a good introduction to the regional distribution of the antiquarian book trade and its subjects. The membership list contains, apart from other information, the special subjects of the antiquarian bookseller. This specialization is increasing, above all in the scientific and technical field.
Everything that has been said in this section about the antiquarian book trade also applies on the whole to the auction trade. Especially in Hamburg and Munich, but also in West Berlin, Frankfurt a. M., Cologne, Braunschweig, Heidelberg and Marburg, it has revived in importance far beyond thc boundaries of the Federal Republic, thus re-establishing connections with the book world of all continents.
The leading book and print auctioneers are members of the

Bundesverband Deutscher Kunstversteigerer
(Federal Association of
German Art Auctioneers)
Neumarkt 3
D 5 Köln 1

Bibliography

a) Periodicals

Antiquariat
Finkenweg 6
D 7261 Stammheim

This journal was founded in 1945 by the late Walter Krieg, Vienna. It incorporates the supplement "Der Bibliophile" ("The bibliophile") and a special section "Books offered and wanted."

Aus dem Antiquariat. (From the antiquarian book trade.) Monthly in the Börsenblatt für den Deutschen Buchhandel, Frankfurt edition. Frankfurt a. M., Buchhändler-Vereinigung (→ 5).

b) Search lists

Angebote und gesuchte Bücher. (Books offered and wanted.) In: Börsenblatt für den Deutschen Buchhandel, Frankfurt edition. Frankfurt a. M., Buchhändler-Vereinigung (→ 5).

c) Books

E. Carlsohn, *Der Antiquariatsbuchhandel.* (The antiquarian book trade.) In: H. Hiller and W. Strauss (eds.), Der Deutsche Buchhandel. 4th ed. Hamburg, Verlag für Buchmarkt-Forschung 1968. 22 pp.

Der deutsche Antiquariatsbuchhandel 1971. (The German antiquarian book trade.) In: Aus dem Antiquariat, vol. 27, no. 1, pp. 1–74. Frankfurt a. M. 1971.

B. Wendt, *Der Antiquariatsbuchhandel.* (The antiquarian book trade.) 2nd ed. Hamburg, Hauswedell 1952. 178 pp.
→ 25.

d) Auction Prices

Jahrbuch der Auktionspreise für Bücher, Handschriften und Autographen. (Yearbook of auction prices for books, manuscripts and autographs.) Hamburg, Hauswedell, annually.
Reports results in Germany (F.R.G.), the Netherlands, Austria and Switzerland. With a supplement: special subjects of the firms of the antiquarian book trade.

27 Book Imports

The Federal Republic of Germany signed and ratified the Unesco "Agreement on the importation of educational, scientific and cultural materials" (→ International Section, 27) and supports the "free flow of books".

As one of the leading European book importing countries between 1950 and 1969 her book imports grew from DM 10.4 million to DM 141.7 million. Including periodicals, picture books for children, musical publications and geographical maps and atlases the respective figures are DM 17.3 million and DM 187.4 million.

The main countries of origin for book imports in 1969 were:

Country	Amount DM 1,000	Percentage of total
Austria	35,690	25.2
Switzerland	26,942	19.2
Netherlands	16,672	11.8
USA	15,136	10.7
United Kingdom	11,539	8.1
Italy	11,384	8.0
France	5,711	4.0

This table shows the dominant position of the two German-speaking countries. Not less than 44.4% of the book imports came from Austria and Switzerland. The importance of the Netherlands is due to the influential position as middleman which this country has in today's international book trade.

Some information about the import of periodicals of the Federal Republic, also for 1969 (all countries: 35.9 m.):

Country	Amount DM 1,000	Percentage of total
Italy	10,911	30.4
Switzerland	6,711	18.7
Netherlands	4,832	13.4
USA	3,937	11.4
France	3,148	8.8
United Kingdom	2,977	8.3
Austria	1,537	4.3

The import of goods connected with the book trade is fully liberalized and free of duty (→ 12).

Bibliography

The annual results of the book and periodical imports are published in "Buch und Buchhandel in Zahlen" (→ 6) and in the "Archiv für Soziologie und Wirtschaftsfragen des Buchhandels" (→ 6).

H. Machill, *The export/import of books and periodicals in th Federal Republic of Germany.* In: The Indian Publisher and Bookseller. Indo-German special number. Bombay, The Popular Book Depot 1966.—In English.

28 Book Exports

After a very modest fresh start—in 1950 the book exports of the Federal Republic surpassed for the first time the DM 10 million—book exports have increased to a considerable amount. The yearly total for 1969 amounted to DM 297.4 m. In addition there are other goods exported within the book trade. The following survey quotes the official export statistics of 1969:

Category	Million DM
Books	297.4
Periodicals	228.3
Picture books for children	2.5
Music publications	6.5
Cartographical products	9.9
Total	544.6

The method of gathering these statistics offers almost complete accuracy.
Divided up by continents the book exports in 1969 offer the following panorama:

Area	Million DM
Europe	225.6
America	54.3
Asia	12.7
Africa	3.1
Australia	1.7
Total	297.4

It is estimated that in 1969 book exports amounted to about 15% of the total turnover of publishing.
In 1969 the Federal Republic exported books to 130 countries. The most important of these were:

Country	Amount DM 1,000	Percentage of total
Switzerland	75,448	25.4
Austria	50,575	17.0
USA	46,315	15.6
Netherlands	18,538	6.2
France	18,477	6.2
United Kingdom	12,818	4.3
Italy	11,633	3.9
Belgium/Luxembuurg	10,231	3.4
Japan	9,133	3.1
Denmark	4,319	1.5
Sweden	3,995	1.3
Canada	3,644	1.2

These figures show that 42.4% of the book exports went to the other two German-speaking countries, Switzerland and Austria. It is assumed that in these exports the general book played a much more important part than to non-German-speaking countries, where, although varying from country to country, the scientific and technical book predominates.
This also applies to periodicals exports (1969):

Country	Amount DM 1,000	Percentage of total
Austria	52,752	23.1
Switzerland	44,506	19.5
Netherlands	15,931	7.0
France	14,782	6.5
Belgium/Luxembourg	14,452	6.3
USA	14,137	6.2
Italy	13,777	6.0
United Kingdom	5,199	2.3
Spain	4,519	2.0
Denmark	4,397	1.9
Japan	4,315	1.9
Yugoslavia	4,298	1.9
Sweden	3,493	1.5

The quota for German-speaking countries is little less than in book exports. 57.4% of periodicals are exported to non-German-speaking countries. Here, too, scientific and technical periodicals play a major part, although the export of entertainment journals, fashion magazines, etc. must not be underestimated.
There are no reliable statistics as to how large a share wholesalers and booksellers

have in the export of books and periodicals. The influence of some larger wholesale firms on the export trade is certainly quite considerable.
Taxes → 12.
The export figures mentioned are an indication of the success which individual book exporters, whether they are publishers or wholesalers, have achieved. The efforts made by the German book trade as a whole to promote book and periodical exports, however, has to be mentioned too, and here book exhibitions in foreign countries are of primary importance.
The

Ausstellungs- und Messe-GmbH des Börsenvereins des Deutschen Buchhandels (Exhibition and Fair Society of the German Publishers' and Booksellers' Association) Postfach 3914 D 6 Frankfurt a. M.

has held exhibitions in foreign countries since 1950. This company is concerned with various programmes: representative German book exhibitions, which are held in close cooperation with the Bonn Foreign Office: medium-sized exhibitions of collections of paperbacks, the "Best-designed Books" etc.; exhibitions of German books at foreign industrial and trade fairs and at similar occasions when German products are on show.
Representative book exhibitions have so far been held in all five continents. From 1950 to 1969 they took place in 222 towns of 43 countries, and on each occasion some 2,000 to 3,000 titles are displayed to give a cross-section of the contents and design of modern book production.
The "Ausstellungs- und Messe-GmbH des Börsenvereins" supports the export drive of publishers also insofar as it analyses the foreign export market and passes on information, for which it publishes the special journal *Auslandsinformationen für den Deutschen Verlagsbuchhandel* ("Foreign Information for the German publishing world"), giving new leads to stimulate individual efforts.
(→ 29)
Bibliography
(→ 27)

29 Book Fairs

In 1949, to make book trading easier within Germany, the

Frankfurter Buchmesse (The Frankfurt Book Fair) Postfach 3914 D 6 Frankfurt a. M.

was re-established, in keeping with an old tradition. Originally it was only intended to support and promote the work of the book trade within the country. Soon, however, it became evident that there was a need for a fair like this on an international basis. Already in 1950 seven foreign countries took part, and since 1953 the number of countries actively taking part in the *Frankfurt Book Fair* (→ International Section, 29) has increased steadily from year to year. Thus the "Frankfurt Book Fair" has become the most important international event of this kind. Every year, either in September or October, it brings the book trade of the whole world together. In 1971 59 countries took part, with over 3,500 exhibiting publishing houses. For some time now foreign publishers have constituted about 70% of the representation.
The "Frankfurt Book Fair" derives its importance not only from this large-scale international showing, but also from the fact that despite all political, religious, racial and other dividing lines everyone is invited to take part. It thus brings together publishers, booksellers, librarians, authors, bibliophiles and designers from all five continents; and, apart from promoting the international book trade, it has become an important place for discussions on translation rights, co-productions, etc.

The organizer of this Fair is the "Ausstellungs- und Messe-GmbH des Börsenvereins" (→ 28).
The Frankfurt Book Fair is a member of the "Union des Foires Internationales" (UFI).
Apart from the "Frankfurt Book Fair" there are other events, though not comparable in kind, as they are of a more regional character. One of these is the *West Berlin International Book Exhibition*, held each year after the "Frankfurt Book Fair" (→ International Section, 29). Others take place in *Hamburg*, *Munich*, and *Stuttgart*, and are primarily intended to promote the Christmas trade.

Bibliography

H. Presser, *Der Markt der Märkte.* (The market of markets.) Mainz, Eggebrecht-Presse n.d. 7 pp.
S. Taubert, *The Frankfurt Book Fair.* In: The Indian Publisher and Bookseller. Indo-German special number. Bombay, The Popular Book Depot 1966.—In English.
S. Taubert, *The old Frankfurt Book Fair. The new Frankfurt Book Fair.* In: Henricus Stephanus, Francofordiense emporium. Frankfurt a. M., Frankfurter Buchmesse 1968.—In English.

30 Public Relations

The existence of a "Head department for information and public relations" within the "Börsenverein" (→ 4) indicates the importance the book trade attaches to the contact with the public and with public institutions. This department originated from the former "Department for press and publicity" of the "Börsenverein". It is responsible for a variety of programmes. Basic decisions are made by a special committee, and these are then approved by the board of the "Börsenverein". This means that the interests of the entire book trade are guaranteed.

The work of this department can be classified under six groups:

1. The creation of posters and similar publicity material for important occasions like Easter, Christmas, the *Jugendbuchwoche* ("Book week for the young"), etc.
2. The promotion of the idea of reading, which of course primarily means the reading of books. In this connection a yearly *Vorlesewettbewerb des deutschen Buchhandels* ("Reading competition of the German book trade") has taken place since 1959, and it now has a considerable response. More than 100,000 competitors take part in this event. This competition is aimed at 12- to 13-year-old pupils. It starts in the schools, going on from there to the towns, the districts and finally to the "Länder". The successful candidates from the "Länder" meet every year in Frankfurt for the final competition.
3. The organization of lectures which relate to travelling exhibitions in Germany during the yearly "Jugendbuchwoche" (e.g. "Books on Europe", "Hobbies in books", "Prizewinning books for children and young people", etc.).
In addition special mention should be made of the colour slides which are made on the subject of books and the book trade and are at the disposal of lecturers.
4. Following the example of Sweden and especially the United Kingdom, a system of book tokens was developed which has, however, not yet proved very successful.
5. Contact and cooperation with press, radio and television are of great importance, too. Because of the distribution of the West German press throughout the country and the federal structure of radio and television there are many possibilities for coverage, especially as these institutions have, beyond mere publicity, extensive cultural programmes. For these there is a special press service, *Buch + Leser* ("Book and Reader").
6. The publication of the series "Schrif-

tenreihe des Börsenvereins" ("Pamphlets of the Börsenverein"), dealing with many aspects of the book trade of the Federal Republic of Germany.

Bibliography

W. Ensslin, *Werbung im Sortiment.* (Publicity in the retail book trade.) München, Verlag Dokumentation 1958. 76 pp.

R. B. Forster, *Das Buch vom Buchfenster.* (The book of the bookshop window.) Düsseldorf, Buchhändler Heute 1963. 54 pp.

B. Hack, *Der Bücherkatalog. Wesen, Anlage und Herstellung buchhändlerischer Kataloge.* (The booklist.) München, Verlag Dokumentation 1955. 160 pp.

H. Kliemann (ed.), *Die Werbung fürs Buch.* (Publicity for the book.) 4th ed. Stuttgart, Poeschel 1950. IX, 384 pp.
The basic handbook in the German language about almost all questions relating to publicity in the book trade.

A. U. Martens, *General book publicity.* In: The Indian Publisher and Bookseller. Indo-German special number. Bombay, The Popular Book Depot 1966.—In English.

Cl. Marx, *Werbung im Buchverlag.* (Publicity in publishing.) Düsseldorf, Buchhändler Heute 1962, 137 pp.

P. Meuer, *Öffentlichkeitsarbeit im Buchhandel—Allensbach und Aktion '69.* (Public relations in the book trade—Allensbach and Action '69.) In: Börsenblatt für den Deutschen Buchhandel, Frankfurt edition 1969, pp. 1947–54.
Discusses the findings of the demoscopic researches of Allensbach (→ 9) and the establishment of an action by the "Arbeitsgemeinschaft der Buchhandlungen" (→ 24).

H. Riediger, *Organisation von Buchausstellungen.* (The organization of book exhibitions.) Hamburg, Verlag für Buchmarkt-Forschung 1964. 56 pp.—Berichte des Instituts für Buchmarkt-Forschung, 13.

W. Strauss, *Öffentlichkeitsarbeit im Buchhandel.* (Public relations in the book trade.) 2nd ed. Hamburg, Verlag für Buchmarkt-Forschung 1967. 42 pp.—Berichte des Instituts für Buchmarkt-Forschung, 14.

31 Bibliophily

In the Federal Republic there are nine associations of book-lovers. Of these the three most important ones are:

Gesellschaft der Bibliophilen
(Association of Bibliophiles)
Sambergerstrasse 31
D 8 München 71

This association was founded in 1899 in Weimar. Its aim is to preserve the culture of the book in a time of changing values. Four times a year members receive a magazine, *Wandelhalle der Bücherfreunde* ("Lobby of Bibliophiles"), and about every second year the yearbook *Imprimatur*, of which so far (at the beginning of 1970) 18 volumes have been published and which is certainly one of the most influential publications for book-lovers in the German-speaking countries.

Gutenberg-Gesellschaft
(Gutenberg Society)
Liebfrauenplatz 5
D 65 Mainz

The international Gutenberg Society was founded in 1901 with the aim of circulating the findings of the "Gutenberg Museum" (→ Book Museums, p. 59). The main purpose of the society is to encourage research into the invention of printing and its technical and artistic development up to the present time and to pass on the results of these researches in quality publications. An important secondary purpose is to offer financial support to the "Gutenberg Museum". The society is internationally recognized for its publishing activity, notably the "Gutenberg Jahrbuch" ("Gutenberg Yearbook"), pub-

lished yearly since 1926 as the leading voice for the past and present development of printing. Since 1968 the "Gutenberg-Gesellschaft" distributes the *Gutenberg Preis* ("Gutenberg Prize") for outstanding achievements in the field of printing.
The
Maximilian-Gesellschaft
(Maximilian Society)
Pöseldorfer Weg 1
D 2 Hamburg 13
was founded in 1911. The name of its patron, the German Emperor Maximilian I (1459–1519), who was devoted to literature and the arts, is symbolic of its programme. As his interest for beautiful manuscripts, calligraphy and printing stimulated new forms, this socicty wants to perform the same function in our time. Originally founded as an exclusive society, since 1945 it has turned into a wider circle of book-lovers. Its publications, apart from those on bibliophile and literary subjects, also deal with bibliography and bibliology. Since 1957 it has published the quarterly journal
Philobiblon
Pöseldorfer Weg 1
D 2 Hamburg 13
to which non-members can also subscribe. This journal, which is also interesting for its typography and illustrations, publishes bibliophile and bibliographic contributions in a synthesis of the traditional and the modern. At the same time it expresses the aim of the "Maximilian Society".
Regional societies exist in Hamburg, Cologne, Lichtenfels, and Munich.
For the *Vereinigung Freunde des Klingspor-Museums* (Association "Friends of the Klingspor Museum") → Book Museums, p. 59.
The friends of the ex-libris meet in the
Deutsche Exlibris Gesellschaft
(German Exlibris Society)
Bebelallee 146
D 2 Hamburg 39

Dedicated to the art of the book are
Blätter für Buch und Kunst
(Leaves for Book and Art)
Blumenau 86
D 2 Hamburg 76
which appear irregularly since 1969 and
Illustration 63
Seyfriedstr. 15
D 894 Memmingen
with special impetus on book illustration (since 1964).
→ 26.

32 Literary Prizes

There are a great number of literary prizes, about a hundred, if one includes all the medium and small awards. However, no literary prize exists that would have a fundamental influence on the literary scene and on the sales of award-winning books, as, for instance, is the case with the top literary prizes in France. The German prizes tend more to highlight an existing literary work and to give its author his well-deserved place on the literary scene. Very often they confirm the acclaim of many years.
As in other western countries, the literary prizes are sponsored by various official or semi-official institutions, by municipal corporations, literary societies, academies, but also by private enterprises. Some of these prizes have gained an international reputation as well as inside the country.
The prize best known internationally is probably the *Friedenspreis des Börsenvereins des Deutschen Buchhandels* ("Peace prize of the Börsenverein of the German book trade"), awarded every year during the "Frankfurt Book Fair". This prize has existed since 1950 and has been awarded to great personalities at home and in foreign countries who, through their written works and their personal example, have

contributed to peace in the world. The prize is sponsored by the whole book trade of the Federal Republic and is one of the few international awards given by the book trade itself. Because of its purpose, it is not an exclusively literary prize, as are most of the others.

Some influential and noteworthy literary prizes are listed below:

Hansischer Goethe-Preis (Freiherr-vom-Stein-Stiftung), Hamburg;
Georg-Büchner-Preis (Deutsche Akademie für Sprache und Dichtung), Darmstadt;
Droste-Preis, Münster/Westfalen;
Theodor-Fontane-Preis, West Berlin;
Goethe-Preis, Frankfurt a. M.;
Johann-Peter-Hebel-Gedenkpreis (Kultusministerium), Baden-Württemberg;
Heinrich-Heine-Preis, Hamburg;
Wilhelm-Raabe-Preis, Braunschweig;
Hörspiel-Preis der Kriegsblinden (Bund der Kriegsblinden), Bonn;
Preis der Gruppe 47, West Berlin;
Friedrich-Schiller-Gedächtnis-Preis des Landes Baden-Württemberg;
Übersetzer-Preis der Deutschen Akademie für Sprache und Dichtung, Darmstadt (This academy in addition regularly chooses a "book of the month").

Some political and literary weekly papers, as e.g. "Die Zeit", Hamburg, or "Der Spiegel", Hamburg, regularly publish bestseller lists which are compiled on a private basis and according to sales figures.

To support good reading for children and teen-agers the *Bundesminister für Familie und Jugend* ("Federal Ministry for Family and Young People") offers the *Deutscher Jugendbuchpreis* (1953 and since 1956 annually), adjusted to various book categories (picture books, books for younger children, books for teen-agers). The annual list "Die besten Jugendbücher" ("The best books for children and teen-agers") is based upon these awards. The "Arbeitskreis für Jugendliteratur" (→ 10) is responsible for the procedures.

Supported by the "Federal Ministry for Family and Young People" and some publishing houses the "Deutsches Jugendschriftenwerk" (→ 10) sponsors the *Christian-Felix-Weisse Preis*. This prize is given for excellency in research work dealing with periodicals for young people.

Gutenberg-Prize → 31.

Bibliography

20 Jahre Friedenspreis des Deutschen Buchhandels. (20 years "Peace Prize of the German book trade.") Frankfurt a. M., Börsenverein 1969. 110 pp.—Schriftenreihe des Börsenvereins, 4.

Fischer Welt-Almanach, 1961. Paragraph on "Literary Prizes". Frankfurt a. M., Fischer-Bücherei 1960.

Mentions the German and most important foreign literary prizes. The list in each year's new edition of this almanac is brought up to date.

→ International Section, 32.

33 The Reviewing of Books

Because of the widely distributed communications network in the Federal Republic the reviewing of books in newspapers, magazines, radio and television varies considerably.

Every newspaper and magazine of any standing publishes a literary section as a matter of course; therefore book reviews play an important and often influential part in the history of a publication.

Radio and television, in a slightly different form, are in the same position. Because of competition between stations of the different "Länder", and because non-commercial programmes are markedly cultural in tone, books are given a considerable coverage.

The list of newspapers and journals with extensive book reviewing is large. There are, among others: *Das Sonntagsblatt*, Hamburg (weekly paper with religious—protestant—tendency); *Die Welt*, Hamburg (with the weekly literary supplement *Die Welt der Literatur* "The world of literature"), *Die Zeit*, Hamburg; *Rheinischer Merkur*, Koblenz (weekly paper with religious—catholic tendency); *Frankfurter Allgemeine Zeitung*, Frankfurt a. M.; *Frankfurter Rundschau*, Frankfurt a. M.; *Christ und Welt*, Stuttgart (weekly paper with religious—protestant tendency); *Stuttgarter Nachrichten*, Stuttgart; *Süddeutsche Zeitung*, München.

The "Börsenverein" (→ 4) issued a list comprising the addresses of most of the literary and cultural periodicals of the Federal Republic.

Lesen
(Read)
An der Alster 22
D 2 Hamburg 1

reviews and promotes books and is almost entirely distributed through the retail book trade.

Die Bücherkommentare
(The Book Commentaries)
Rosastr. 9
D 78 Freiburg Br.

is published six times a year.

The "Börsenblatt für den Deutschen Buchhandel" (→ 5) includes a column, "Books about books", which deals with publications of this kind not only in German but in other languages as well. This column has a reputation extending beyond the bounds of Germany.

Bibliography

A. Carlsson, *Die deutsche Buchkritik von der Reformation bis zur Gegenwart.* (The German book critique from the Reformation to the present time.) Bern, Francke 1969. 420 pp.

P. Glotz, *Buchkritik in deutschen Zeitungen.* (Book reviews in German newspapers.) Hamburg, Verlag für Buchmarkt-Forschung 1968. 228 pp.—Schriften zur Buchmarkt-Forschung, 14. With a bibliography.

Der Leitfaden für Presse und Werbung. (The manual for press and publicity.) Essen, Stammler. Published annually in revised editions.

34 Graphic Arts

The graphic societies of the Federal Republic are represented in the

Bundesverband Druck
(Federal Association of Printing)
Postfach 503
D 62 Wiesbaden

This institution gives information on the graphic arts industry, on production problems and on other special questions of this kind. In 1970 it organized the first issue of *Imprints*, an exhibition and congress touching all means and methods from the original to the printed result.

The monthly journal

Gebrauchsgraphik
(Advertising Art)
Nymphenburger Str. 86
D 8 München 2

includes many topics of national and international book and graphic design. The texts are given in English, French and German.

→ 20.—*Drupa* → International Section, 34.

35 Miscellaneous

a) Authors

To support the cultural, legal, professional and social interests of authors the

Verband deutscher Schriftsteller e.V.
(Association of German Authors)
Clemensstr. 58/I
D 8 München 23

was founded in 1969. It comprises ten regional and two subject groups (translators, critics). Since 1970 this association issues the periodical *VS-Informationen*.

Special questions regarding translation are dealt with by the

Verband deutschsprachiger Übersetzer literarischer und wissenschaftlicher Werke (Association of German-speaking translators of literary and scientific texts)
Schloss Remseck
D 7141 Neckarrems

The association publishes the journal *Der Übersetzer* ("The Translator").

The
Verband der deutschen Kritiker e.V.
(Association of German critics)
Dernburgstr. 57/IV
D 1 Berlin 19
handles general questions of literary criticism.

The address of the Western German P.E.N. Centre is
P.E.N. Zentrum der Bundesrepublik Deutschland
Sandstr. 10
D 61 Darmstadt

b) German Interzonal Trade

The special relationship between the Federal Republic of Germany and the German Democratic Republic has led to a form of mutual trading which is unique in the national and international book trade. This *Interzonenhandel* ("inter-zonal trade") is, when defined as "inter-zonal trade in products of the book trade", part of the "trade with printed matter". It is mainly in scientific, technical and specialized books and sheet music. The following table shows the volume of trade in 1968.

Category	Deliveries to the FRG 1,000 currency units	Deliveries from the FRG 1,000 currency units
Books	5,119	9,872
Newspapers and journals	5,587	3,206
Art reproductions and post cards	—	175
Other printed matter	686	489
Total	11,392	13,742

This inter-zonal trade is undertaken either by clearing houses or with barter-trading agreements. In the first case the buyer purchases in his own currency, whilst the seller is recompensed in his own currency. There are two methods of barter trading: one by the direct exchange of books and journals, the other by sales of books being offset by purchase of print. The latter method is more common in barter trading.

Bibliography

The development of this trade between the two Germanies is regularly reported in "Buch und Buchhandel in Zahlen" (→ 6).

Germany — German Democratic Republic

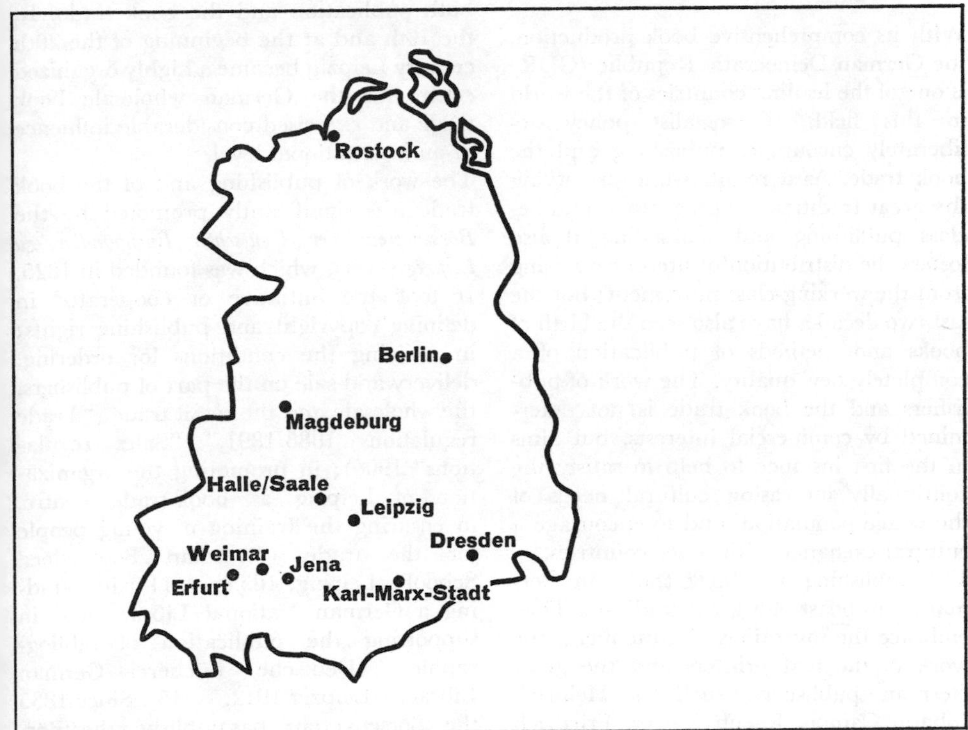

Important Book Centres

1 General Information

Area 108,174 km²
Population 17,066,000 (158 per km²)
Capital Berlin, the capital of the GDR (1,083,000)
Largest towns Leipzig (585,000); Dresden (501,000); Karl-Marx-Stadt (298,000); Magdeburg (269,000); Halle/Saale (259,000); Erfurt (194,000); Rostock (194,000); Zwickau (127,000); Potsdam (110,000); Gera (110,000)
Government The German Democratic Republic (GDR) is divided into 14 districts and the capital, Berlin.
National language German
Leading foreign languages Russian, English, French
Weights and measures Metric system
Currency unit Mark (M) = 100 Pfennige (Pf)
Education Compulsory; basic education—10 years' attendance at a polytechnic. 189 technical training colleges with 151,000 students (including 67,800 women). 54 universities and other colleges of university standard with 122,790 students (including 41,661 women). Figures for 1969.
Illiteracy Nil
Paper production: 40.3 kg per inhabitant (1968)

2 Past and Present

With its comprehensive book production, the German Democratic Republic (GDR) is one of the leading countries of the world in this field. Its socialist policy deliberately encourages publishing and the book trade. As a result, while preserving the great traditions of progressive middle-class publishing and bookselling, it also fosters the distribution of literature arising from the working-class movement; but the last two decades have also seen the birth of books and methods of publication of a completely new quality. The work of publishers and the book trade is not determined by commercial interests, but aims in the first instance to help to satisfy the continually increasing cultural needs of the whole population, and to encourage a cultural exchange with other countries.

The publishing and book trades in Germany can boast of a great tradition. They embrace the inventions of Gutenberg, the work of the first printers and the great German publishers, such as Heinrich Johann Campe, Joseph Meyer, Friedrich Perthes and Philipp Reclam. To these must also be added the outstanding work of publishers such as Wilhelm Bracke, J. H. W. Dietz and Paul Singer for their part in the struggle of the working-class movement, and such outstanding organizers in the retail trade as Julius Motteler.

The "Leipziger Platz" plays a special part in the history of the German book trade. Within forty years of Gutenberg's inventions Leipzig had developed into one of the most important centres of printing, publishing and the book trade. The first book catalogue at the Leipzig Fair appeared in 1594. The importance of Leipzig increased, particularly in the 18th and at the beginning of the 19th century, since the division of work led to the ever greater separation of publishing and the retail trade, while the wholesale trade, which was concentrated in Leipzig, influenced both publication and the book trade. In the 19th and at the beginning of the 20th century Leipzig became a highly organized centre for the German wholesale book trade and exercised considerable influence at an international level.

The work of publishing and of the book trade was significantly promoted by the *Börsenverein der Deutschen Buchhändler zu Leipzig* (→ 4), which was founded in 1825. It took the initiative or cooperated in defining copyright and publishing rights; in unifying the conditions for ordering, delivery and sale on the part of publishers, the wholesale and the retail trade ("Trade regulations 1888/1891," "Sales regulations" 1906); in promoting the organization of Leipzig as book-trade centre, in ensuring the training of young people for the trade ("German Booksellers' School", Leipzig, 1853, → 11); in founding a German National Library and in supporting the publication of bibliographies (Deutsche Bücherei—German Library—Leipzig 1912, → 15). Since 1835 the "Börsenverein" has published the "Börsenblatt für den Deutschen Buchhandel", founded in 1834, an important source of information for publishers and booksellers (→ 5).

The division of work between publishing and the retail trade has been taken to its logical conclusion in the German Democratic Republic. About 80 state-owned and private publishing firms are in the main responsible for the production of booklets, books and periodicals, and their publishing plans are specified and carefully balanced with one another. Their task is to develop a systematic supply of reading material corresponding with the needs of society. Important centres of publication are Berlin, the capital of the GDR, and Leipzig. After 1945 and above all after the birth of the GDR the concentration in favour of Leipzig was consistently continued. In spite of the concentration in Leipzig, the wholesale trade was still scattered. This was overcome by the founding of the "LKG Leipziger Kommissions- und Grossbuchhandel", a socialist wholesale undertaking which delivers the products of all publishing firms in the GDR and all imported literature from a central point (→ 23). In this way it has been possible to introduce the most modern techniques in the trade and to offer the most economical method of ordering for the retail trade. Import and export are also carried on centrally through the "Deutscher Buch-Export und -Import GmbH" (→ 27, 28).

In the GDR more than 2,000 bookshops and book stalls are engaged in the sale of reading-matter. Of these more than 775 are state-owned. The state-owned book trade has become an important factor in the sale of reading-matter. It is particularly characterized by the fact that it reaches large areas of the population without bookshops and has thus created completely new circles of readers. Publishing and the wholesale and retail book trade are governed by the

Ministerrat der Deutschen
Demokratischen Republik
Ministerium für Kultur,
Hauptverwaltung Verlage und Buchhandel
(Council of Ministers of the GDR,
Ministry of Culture,
Main Department—Publishing and
Bookselling)
Clara-Zetkin-Str. 90
DDR 108 Berlin 8

Bibliography

a) Periodicals

Beiträge zur Geschichte des Buchwesens. (Contributions on the history of books and the book trade. Edited by K.-H. Kalhöfer and H. Rötzsch on behalf of the Historical Commission of the Börsenverein Leipzig.) Since 1965. Leipzig, VEB Bibliographisches Institut. 4 vols. had appeared by the end of 1969.

b) Books

Bibliographie zur Geschichte der Stadt Leipzig. (Bibliography to the history of Leipzig.) Special volume IV: The book. Weimar, H. Böhlau 1967. XVI, 383 pp.

Die DDR—ein Land des Buches (The GDR—a country of books). Leipzig, Börsenverein 1969.

FR. KAPP and J. GOLDFRIEDRICH, *Geschichte des Deutschen Buchhandels.* (History of the German book trade.) 4 vols. plus index. Leipzig, Börsenverein 1886–1923.

Ordnung für den Literaturvertrieb (Conditions for ordering, delivery and sale on the part of publishers, the wholesale and the retail trade). Leipzig, VEB Fachbuchverlag 1969.

Ökonomik des Buchhandels. (The economics of the book trade.) Leipzig, VEB Verlag für Buch- und Bibliothekswesen 1962.

Verlage der Deutschen Demokratischen Republik. (Publishing firms in the German Democratic Republic.) Leipzig, Börsenverein 1969.

3 Retail Prices

In the GDR there is a fixed retail price for all articles in the book trade, fixed by the publisher and binding on all concerned on the distributive side.

Before the GDR was created, fixed retail prices for books, booklets and periodicals were determined in accordance with the principles laid down in the Trade Regulations and Sales Regulations of the "Börsenverein". They had been valid since the turn of the century. In the GDR this method of price fixing was not only maintained but was placed on a higher footing by state price regulations. In 1967 price regulation No. 4586 came into force; it lays down the retail price of all forms of property for publishers and bookshops. The publishing firm is responsible for

determining prices, bearing in mind that the retail price must be both stable and in accordance with cultural policy.
Uniform contracts determine the economic relations between the publishing firms, the Leipzig Book Trade Wholesale Organization (→ 23), the German Export and Import Book Co. (→ 27, 28) and the state-owned and privately owned retail bookshops.

4 Organization

The professional and trade organization for publishers and booksellers in the GDR is the

Börsenverein der
Deutschen Buchhändler zu Leipzig
(German Publishers' and
Booksellers' Association in Leipzig)
Gerichtsweg 26
DDR 701 Leipzig

The Association was founded in Leipzig in 1825. It significantly influenced the development of publishing and the book trade in Germany (→ 2). In the GDR the character of the Association has changed; from being above all a union representing an employers' association, it has become the professional and trade organization for all publishers and booksellers in the GDR. Membership is therefore open not only to owners and directors of publishing firms and bookselling enterprises, but also to their colleagues and those enganged in publishing and the book trade in general.
Its most important tasks are: to bring together all those engaged in publishing and the book trade in the GDR, and so promote their common interests; to advise the departments of state, cultural organizations and institutions on matters concerning publishing, the book trade and the distribution of reading matter; to awaken public interest in books, publishing, the book trade, the general distribution of reading matter and book publicity, especially in relation to books abroad that have been produced in the GDR; to cooperate with similar organizations outside the GDR and those on an international level; to promote the theory and practice of publishing and the book trade; to foster and promote the art of book production; to advise members on matters connected with their profession; to promote the training and further training of publishers and booksellers; to distribute publications dealing with publishing and the book trade.
The General Meeting is the ruling body in the Association. Every three years it chooses the chairman and other members of the governing body, which in turn nominate members of specialist committees. The Association contains the following committees and boards:
publishing committee, retail-trade committee, antiquarian book-trade committee, committee for the publication and sale of printed music; commission on bibliography, commission for public relations and the historical commission; the advisory board for the "Börsenblatt" (→ 5). Publishing and bookselling firms in Berlin are at the same time members of the

Berliner Verleger- und Buchhändlervereinigung
(Berlin Publishers' and Booksellers' Association)
Rungestrasse 20
DDR 102 Berlin

Bibliography

Börsenverein der Deutschen Buchhändler zu Leipzig. Leipzig, Börsenverein 1968.

5 Trade Press

The "Börsenverein" publishes the

Börsenblatt für den Deutschen Buchhandel
Gerichtsweg 26
DDR 701 Leipzig

It has appeared regularly since 1834 in Leipzig and is one of the oldest book-trade publications in the world. The "Börsenblatt" is indispensable to publishers and booksellers in the GDR, provides foreign countries with information on the book trade in the GDR, and promotes international cooperation among publishers and booksellers. It appears weekly. The editorial section publishes articles, contributions, reports and information on the work of the "Börsenverein" and on problems connected with publishing and bookselling in the GDR and abroad, especially in connection with the development of reading material, proof-reading, the art of book production, book-market research, the promoting of literary publicity, book publicity and distribution. The advertisement section gives detailed information on book production in the GDR. Every March and September, at the time of the Leipzig Trade Fair, two special editions appear with detailed indexes. In addition, several thematic editions of advertisements appear in the course of the year, e.g. "Books of Export" or "Calendars and Annuals".

The home edition includes the "Vorankündigungsdienst des LKG" ("Advance-notice service of the LKG," → 23); with the foreign edition, the "NOVA forth-coming books" of the German Export and Import Book Co. (→ 27, 28), and the "Bibliographie der Kunstblätter" ("Bibliography of art prints") are included.

6 Book-Trade Literature

Book-trade literature is substantially published by three firms, corresponding with the specialized branches of the publishing business:

VEB Fachbuchverlag
Karl-Heine-Strasse 16
DDR 7031 Leipzig

This firm deals among other things with publishing and the book trade.

The

VEB Verlag für Buch- und Bibliothekswesen
Gerichtsweg 26
DDR 701 Leipzig

publishes the most important bibliographies, in particular those of the "German Library" (→ 15).

VEB Bibliographisches Institut
Gerichtsweg 26
DDR 701 Leipzig

This firm deals among other things with book questions, library matters and documentation.

Among the most important publications in past years are:

Beiträge zur Geschichte des Buchwesens. (Contributions on the history of books and the book trade.) Edited by K.-H. Kalhöfer and H. Rötzsch on behalf of the Historical Commission of the Börsenverein, Leipzig. Since 1965. Leipzig, VEB Bibliographisches Institut.—4 vols. had appeared by the end of 1969.

Continuing the great tradition of Kapp-Goldfriedrich and the "Archives for the History of the German Book Trade", this annual publication has as its aim the collection of monographs to serve as the preliminary work for a comprehensive Marxist presentation of the history of the German book trade. Each volume contains several essays and a complete index.

Leben und Werk deutscher Buchhändler. (The life and work of German booksellers.) Edited by K.-H. Kalhöfer. Leipzig, VEB Bibliographisches Institut 1965. 160 pp.

This little work contains 20 essays in chronological order on the life and work of important booksellers from the 18th century to the present day, beginning with Philipp Erasmus Reich and including Breitkopf, Göschen, Cotta, S. Fischer and Anton Kippenberg. With an index of names.

Ökonomik des Buchhandels. (The economics

of the book trade.) Leipzig, VEB Verlag für Buch- und Bibliothekswesen 1962. 221 pp.
This publication provides a survey of the development of the book trade to the present day and deals with problems of planning and directing the wholesale and retail book trade. It is particularly intended for those holding leading positions in the socialist book trade.

H. Fauth and W. Lehmann, *Taschenbuch des Buchhändlers*. (The bookseller's pocketbook). Leipzig, VEB Verlag für Buch- und Bibliothekswesen 1958. 180 pp.
A short work of reference, intended as a guide to the bookseller in his daily work.

W. Richter and H. Baier, *Literaturpropaganda im Schaufenster*. (Publicity in the shopwindow). Leipzig, VEB Verlag für Buch- und Bibliothekswesen 1962. 172 pp.
A guide to the decoration of the bookseller's shopwindow. The text and copious illustrations offer suggestions for making the shopwindow an effective part of the movement for promoting reading to further the socialist cultural revolution.

L. Fröhlich, *Grundlagen der Verkaufskultur im Buchhandel*. (Fundamentals of the art of selling books.) Leipzig, VEB Fachbuchverlag 1970. 108 pp.

The book is arranged in the form of a guide for practical purpose and deals with subjects such as sales talk, display and representation of goods, sales promotion, advertising of publications and book information, the bookseller's activities outside the bookshop.

7 Sources of Information, Address Services

Information on the book trade and publishing in the GDR is obtainable from the (→ 4)

Börsenverein
der Deutschen Buchhändler zu Leipzig
(German Publishers' and Booksellers' Association in Leipzig)
Gerichtsweg 26
DDR 701 Leipzig

Spezialized questions are answered by

Deutsche Bücherei
Abteilung Auskunft und Beratung
(German Library, Information Service)
Deutscher Platz 1
DDR 701 Leipzig

The comprehensive nature of the "Deutsche Bücherei" enables it to answer specialized questions; one of its special departments consists of international literature on book and library matters. Unique among works on German library matters is the "Catalogue of Publishers and Institutions" ("Verleger- und Institutionenkatalog", 1913–), which presents the literature under the headings of publishers and other editing bodies. Also of importance is the "Deutsche Buch- und Schriftmuseum" (German Book and Writing Museum), which is attached to the German Library and includes the former library of the "Börsenverein". It also contains circulars, trade catalogues and records of great importance for information on the history of the book trade (→ Book Museums, p. 61).

Fees for information are laid down in the "List of fees for the German Library". M 0.10 is charged for each query and proof of a title. The location of books can be obtained from the

Deutsche Staatsbibliothek
Auskunftsbüro der deutschen Bibliotheken
(German State Library,
Information Office on German Libraries)
Unter den Linden 8
DDR 108 Berlin

Bibliography

M. Debes and L. Reuschel, *Die ehemalige Bibliothek des Börsenvereins der Deutschen*

Buchhändler zu Leipzig. (The former library of the Börsenverein, Leipzig). In: Deutsche Bücherei 1912–1962, pp. 243–257. Leipzig 1962.

Der Verleger- und Institutionenkatalog der Deutschen Bücherei. (The catalogue of publishers and institutions of the German Library.) 2 vols. Revised reprint. Leipzig 1965.—Neue Mitteilungen aus der Deutschen Bücherei, 20.

Das Sachgebiet Allgemeine Auskunft. (General information.) 2 vols. Leipzig 1962.—Neue Mitteilungen aus der Deutschen Bücherei 39.

8 International Membership

Publishers and the book trade in the GDR support international understanding and peace both through printed matter, which is humanistic and free from nationalism, and through the promotion of international cooperation. The latter is encouraged in many ways in the fields of publishing and the book trade. For instance, the First Conference on Publishing in Socialist Countries was held in the GDR in 1957. The GDR is also the home of the "International Book Art Exhibition in Leipzig" (1959, 1965 and 1971, → 20) and the annual exhibition, "The Best-designed Books in the World" (→ 20).
As part of the Leipzig Trade Fairs, the International Leipzig Book Fair is a member of the "Union des Foires Internationales" (UFI), ("Union of International Fairs"), which has its headquarters in Paris.

9 Market Research

A number of universities, colleges and institutes in the GDR are engaged in book research. Among them are: Karl Marx University, Leipzig; Humboldt University, Berlin; Martin Luther University, Halle-Wittenberg, Halle/Saale; College of Education, Potsdam; College of Education "Dr Theo Neubauer," Erfurt; Institute of Sociology of the Central Committee of the Socialist Unity Party, Berlin; Institute for Youth Research of the Council of Ministers of the GDR, Berlin.
Book research is also undertaken by the publishing firms, the wholesale trade and the state-owned book trade. The Department for Publishing and the Book Trade in the Ministry of Culture of the GDR (→ 2) is responsible for coordinating all research plans on the book market. It is assisted by an advisory body for book-market research, consisting of representatives of publishing houses, the wholesale and retail trades, the "Börsenverein", Leipzig, and the Central Institute for Library Matters.
The Wholesale Book Trade Organization in Leipzig (→ 2, 23) has a department for book-market research which works under the instructions of the government department for Publishing and the Book Trade. In addition, the government gives assignments to Institutes and the Faculties of the universities and colleges which are intended to supplement its own economically orientated research plans by sociological research. The department for book-market research in the Wholesale Book Trade Organization has above all two main tasks:
1. Continuous research with a defined aim: this is intended to produce results that can be utilized when taking into account the cultural and economic angles in the publication and distribution of books.
2. Basic research: its aim is to test methods experimentally, so that they can be put to general use on the book market.
In accordance with the usual twofold division of market research into investigations related to subjects and those related to objects, the department for book-market research is mainly occupied with

research related to subjects, i.e. readers, buyers and non-readers.

In the GDR the advantages of a socialist order of society can be used in the field of book-market research. In book-market research related to objects new methods have been developed and have been successfully applied for some time. Among these are:

Study groups, convened by the Ministry of Culture, whose members include scientists, authors, representatives of publishing houses, the book trade, the Ministry of Culture, and other social institutions. At the present time there are about 20 study groups, e.g. for philosophy, medicine, mathematics, eletrical engineering, cultural heritage, present-day literature and literary history. They analyse the position reached to date in the development of reading material, and plan its development in the future. They take as their basis the future plans which have been scientifically worked out in each subject and the resulting requirements with regard to content and range from the literature which will appear up to 1980. These study groups make recommendations for the coordination of the annual and prospective thematic plans of the publishers, and thus prevent duplication of work which could be economically wasteful.

Subject discussions. These are done in the majority of publishing firms. Plans for the forthcoming year are minutely discussed with specialists in the wholesale and the retail trade, in export and library matters. The publishers thus receive valuable recommendations which are particularly important for determining the size of an edition, and the policy with regard to reprints, but also for the price and layout of a book.

Experimental bookshops. The state-owned book trade has become highly specialized in certain sectors. From its circle of specialized bookshops experimental bookshops are chosen for literature on particular subjects, and they work closely with the publisher responsible for that particular specialized literature.

Overall statistics. The creation of a central socialist wholesale undertaking (→ 2, 23) has made it possible to include production, market, distribution of the market and development of stock in a uniform system and evaluate them for book-market research.

Bibliography

J. Harz and P. Leopold, *Bedarfs- und Buchmarktforschung.* (Research into requirements and book-market research.) In: Börsenblatt für den Deutschen Buchhandel, Leipzig, no. 22, 1965.

J. Harz, R. Brendel, P. Meier, *Einführung in die sozialistische Buchmarktforschung* (Introduction into socialist book-market research). Leipzig, VEB Fachbuchverlag 1970.

10 Books and Young People

The literature intended for children and youth in the GDR differs in content and artistic quality from that in non-socialist countries: the child's environment and the world of the adult are treated as an organic whole. They are presented artistically in such a manner that important social discernment is transmitted to young readers and humanistic feelings are awakened in them. Good literature for children and youth in the GDR is widely supported and promoted by the government, the schools and a democratically minded public.

The Decree for the Protection of Youth (15 Sept. 1953) and the Law for the Advancement of Youth (4 May 1964) are the most important legal foundations on which the development of a socialist literature for youth and children is based.

For the promotion and coordination of all

schemes and plans for the development of a socialist literature for juveniles conforming to highest art standards, a controlling board for socialist juvenile literature of the German Democratic Republic was established whose members are appointed by the Ministry for Culture. The board contributes towards the production of effective and exciting works which inspire readers of the young generation, developing their class-consciousness, to fulfil their duty as young socialists. The secretary-general is responsible for the direct control of the GDR juvenile literature centre which was established in conjunction with

Der Kinderbuchverlag
(Juvenile Books Publishers)
Behrenstrasse 40/41
DDR 108 Berlin

Its particular tasks are: Coordination and planning of research and of scientific publications in the field of juvenile literature, coordination and planning of sociologic research in readership, development of a scientific documentation on theory and practice of juvenile literature, advertising and sales promotion, e.g. organization of the Day of Juvenile Books held every year. Further, there is the

Arbeitsgemeinschaft
für das Kinder- und Jugendbuch
(Study group on books for youth and children)
Deutsche Demokratische Republik
Unter den Linden 8
DDR 108 Berlin

The study group is a meeting of friends and promoters of the socialist children's book and youth literature in the GDR. The organizations, authors, teachers, publishers, librarians and booksellers who belong to it have undertaken the following tasks in particular:

1. to work for the ideas of a humanistic education and upbringing, for international understanding, against moral and mental brutalization and against trashy and obscene publications;
2. to cooperate internationally in the field of books for children and youth, and to organize exhibitions;

Since 1963 the study group has published *Beiträge zur Kinder- und Jugendliteratur* ("Contributions on literature for children and youths") which appears at irregular intervals two or three times a year.

Since 1951 the Ministry of Culture has organized open competitions for the promotion and development of socialist literature for children and youths. In addition various authors of children's books have been awarded the highest state decorations for their work. A special section of the Ministry for Popular Education is the

Zentralstelle für Kinder- und Jugendbücher
(Central Office for Literature
for Children and Youths)
Nöthnitzer Strasse 2/III
DDR 8027 Dresden

It publishes lists of recommendations for school libraries and for the "Pupils' Book Club" (→ 18) and issues material and analyses relevant to literature for children and youth and particularly intended for teachers and educationists.

Critical discussion on literature for children and youths is undertaken by the

Aktiv für Kinder- und Jugendliteratur
beim Deutschen Schriftstellerverband
(Department of Literature for Children and
Youth within the
German Authors' Association)
Friedrichstrasse 169
DDR 108 Berlin

This department, together with the Ministry of Culture and the Kinderbuchverlag, Berlin, annually organizes "Conferences on Literature for Children and Youth" and "Colloquiums" with authors, experts, teacher, librarians, etc.

Bibliography

Beiträge zur Kinder- und Jugendliteratur. (Articles on literature for children and youth.) Berlin, Kinderbuchverlag 1963ff.

11 Training

Every child and citizen of the GDR is entitled to be trained comprehensively and completely according to his ability. The foundation for this is laid in the "Law concerning the uniform socialist educational system," (25 May 1965).
In publishing and book trading the GDR possesses a well-developed, varied system of training and advanced training; its particular characteristic is that transition from one stage of training to the next above it is always guaranteed. All forms of training and advanced training are arranged not only to fit the trainee for a limited trade with books, but, above all, to enable him to fulfil the cultural tasks presented by publishing and the book trade. Trained personnel thus become more versatile and are equal to the constantly growing tasks brought about by the spread of books. Pupils leaving after 10 years at a general polytechnic or pupils who have passed their Abitur (final school-leaving certificate, 13th grade) can train to become booksellers. The apprenticeship is 2 years in the former case and 1 ½ years in the latter. About 200 pupils annually begin their apprenticeship. Training is mandatory in the book trade, both state-owned and private. Contracts are drawn up by individual bookshops and publishing firms (insofar as they train assistants for the sales departments of publishing houses). Practical and theoretical training includes instruction in all branches of the book trade—in problems arising in the cultural and financial fields and in trading methods as they affect literature for children and youth, fiction, scientific and specialized literature, art literature and reproductions, printed music and records, and second-hand sales. Plans for theoretical training at school and practical training in the firm are based on training schemes which are binding and carefully synchronized. The theoretical training is done centrally through the

Deutsche Buchhändler-Lehranstalt
(German Book Trade Educational Institution)
Goldschmidtstrasse 26
DDR 701 Leipzig

In the majority of cases, theoretical instruction is in the form of courses at a boarding school. Trainees are further encouraged by competitions; those with the best results are awarded medals and prizes. Older colleagues who are already working in the trade and have had no opportunity to undergo training can also take the trade examination. The body responsible for this is the

Schulungszentrum der Zentralen Leitung des Volksbuchhandels der DDR
(Training Centre of the Central Board of the State-Owned Book Trade in the GDR)
Friedrich-Ebert-Strasse 25
DDR 701 Leipzig

To ensure uniformity in training, booklets for teaching and training are published. This form of training gives women considerable assistance, e.g. free qualifying facilities during working time.
The Training Centre also provides special courses regularly for booksellers who wish to acquire special knowledge and for those in responsible positions. These courses are free and are financed from the profits of the bookshops.
The training of those in responsible positions at middle level is done through the

Fachschule für Buchhändler
(Trade School for Booksellers)
Walther-Rathenau-Strasse 40
DDR 7033 Leipzig

In order to be accepted for three years' study at the Trade School or for four years' study as an external student, the applicant must have passed the "Facharbeiterprüfung" (specialist's examination) as a bookseller. Internal students receive a scholarship of M 300 per month, older and married students up to 80% of their

monthly salary; all teaching apparatus is free.
A college for the continuous training and further training of persons in responsible positions in publishing and bookselling is being founded. Those who have passed their examinations at the Trade School as well as students coming from universities and similar institutions will be admitted to this college.
In 1968 a university institute for training and postgraduate education of leading staffs of publishing houses and the book trade was established:

Karl-Marx-Universität Leipzig
Institut für Verlagswesen und Buchhandel
(Leipzig Karl-Marx University
Institute for Publishing and Book Trade)
Querstrasse 28
DDR 701 Leipzig

The institute started teaching in 1969, conducting training courses for postgraduates—especially for readers and editors of publishing-houses—and courses for enrolled students. Fourth-year undergraduates (e.g. students of German philology, economics or a branch of natural science) receive special training to prepare them for a post in a publishing-house or the book trade. The institute also conducts research work necessary for teaching in the field of the publishing, graphic and book trades.
A special form of further training is given in the "Betriebsakademien," in Leipzig and Berlin:

Betriebsakademie
Verlage und Buchhandel Leipzig
(Publishing and
Book Trade Academy of Leipzig)
Querstrasse 28
DDR 701 Leipzig

Betriebsakademie
Verlage und Buchhandel Berlin
(Publishing and
Book Trade Academy in Berlin)
Glinkastrasse 13/15
DDR 108 Berlin.

They provide 50–60 courses per year, given by specially invited lecturers. Each course includes lectures on the natural sciences, economics, literary history, the history and organization of publishing and the book trade, data processing, and foreign languages. About 1,000 students take advantage of this opportunity every term, free of charge.

Bibliography

Buchhändler-Rahmenausbildungsunterlage für die sozialistische Berufsausbildung (Bookseller. Foundation for the socialist vocational training). Leipzig, VEB Fachbuchverlag 1969.
W. Kahlenberg, *10 Jahre Fachschule für Buchhändler*. (Ten years' Trade School for Booksellers.) In: Börsenblatt für den Deutschen Buchhandel, Leipzig, no. 30, 1967.

12 Taxes

The system of taxation varies according to ownership. Owners of private publishing and bookselling firms pay income or corporation tax. This is also the case with publishing and bookselling firms in which the state is part-owner. Socialist publishing and bookselling firms hand over their profits to the state after the creation of works funds.
In accordance with the development of society, publishing and bookselling firms in all classes of ownership paid trade and turnover taxes until 1956. In the case of socialist publishing firms, both forms of tax were unified into a production levy in 1957. With the introduction of industrial price reform the production levy and the trade and turnover tax need no longer to be paid by publishing firms since 1967. Bookselling firms in all classes of ownership now only pay the turnover tax.

13 Clearing Houses

A special clearing institution is not necessary in the GDR since the Leipzig Wholesale Book Trade Organization (→ 23), as the central body, is linked with all publishing and bookselling firms and undertakes any necessary settlement of accounts between firms.

14 Copyright

All copyright, contractual rights and rights protecting output are covered in the Copyright Law of 13 Sept. 1965, which came into force on 1 Jan. 1966. It guarantees without formality comprehensive protection to all authors and to all those permitted by the author to exercise powers covered by copyright.

Copyright covers works in literature, art and science presented in an objective manner and offering an individual creative effort. The work can also be produced by a group. The means or method by which a work is produced is of no importance.

Copyright is understood as a socialist right related to the person, and this right gives the author powers both of a monetary and non-monetary nature. Because copyright has the character of a right related to the person it is not transferable in its entirety. The author can merely transfer to others authority to use his work. In accordance with the socialist "principle of output" an author has a right to reimbursement for transferring his rights; transfer without charge requires a special agreement. The principles of transfer are laid down in the section "Urhebervertragsrecht" (contractual rights) and in the specimen contracts based on them; these contracts are agreed between authors' organizations and institutions responsible for determining the cultural use of a work. Copyright expires fifty years after the death of the author. The fifty-year period begins after the expiry of the calendar year in which the author died. After his death the powers of an author are transmitted to his heirs in accordance with the general law of inheritance. The terms of the law of copyright also apply to authors who are not citizens of the GDR, insofar as their works and productions are published for the first time in the GDR, or in accordance with international agreements to which the GDR is a partner. Where such agreements are lacking, copyright is guaranteed by reciprocal agreement. The GDR is a member of the Berne Convention in the Rome version (1928) and the Montevideo Agreement of 11 Jan. 1889 plus the additional minutes of 13 Dec. 1889.

Bibliography

A. Haufe, *Zum neuen Gesetz über das Urheberrecht.* (Concerning the new law on copyright.) In: Börsenblatt für den Deutschen Buchhandel, Leipzig, no. 13, 1965.

W. Knittel, *Zum Verlagsrecht im neuen Urheberrechtsgesetz.* (Concerning the right of publishing in the new law on copyright.) In: Börsenblatt für den Deutschen Buchhandel, Leipzig, no. 50, 1965.

Neue Justiz, no. 21/1966.

Urheberrecht der Deutschen Demokratischen Republik — Lehrbuch. (Copyright law of the German Democratic Republic—manual). Berlin, Staatsverlag der DDR 1970. 626 pp.

15 National Bibliography, National Library

On the initiative of the "Börsenverein" (→ 2, 4) the

Deutsche Bücherei
(German Library)
Deutscher Platz 1
DDR 701 Leipzig

was founded in 1912, in order to establish a complete record of literature written in the German language. By continually widening its area of activity and its bibliographical tasks it has developed into the German National Library and the Centre for German General Bibliography. At the present time the following have to be collected:

All literature that has appeared in Germany since 1913, such as books, booklets, magazines and other periodicals, dissertations and theses, cartographical productions and literature in German.

Translations of German works that have appeared abroad since 1941 and works in foreign languages about Germany and personalities in the German-speaking world.

Printed music that has appeared in Germany since 1943 and music printed abroad with German titles and texts.

Art prints that have appeared in Germany since 1943 and art prints published abroad with German titles.

German literary records that have appeared since 1959.

Letters patent that have appeared in Germany.

A selection of the international literature on books and library matters.

This collected literature is kept in a reference library accessible to the general public. Copies of the above material for the archives of the "Deutsche Bücherei" are guaranteed by law insofar as the territory of the GDR is concerned; in the case of the Federal Republic of Germany, West Berlin and foreign countries, it is done on a voluntary basis.

The extent of the bibliographical material corresponds with the field under review: *Deutsche Nationalbibliographie und Bibliographie des im Ausland erschienenen deutschsprachigen Schrifttums* (Reihe A: Neuerscheinungen des Buchhandels; Reihe B: Neuerscheinungen ausserhalb des Buchhandels; Reihe C: Dissertationen und Hochschulschriften; "Jahresverzeichnis des deutschen Schrifttums"; "Deutsches Bücherverzeichnis"; "Jahresverzeichnis der deutschen Hochschulschriften"; "Deutsche Musikbibliographie"; "Jahresverzeichnis der deutschen Musikalien und Musikschriften"; "Bibliographie der Übersetzungen deutschsprachiger Werke"; "Bibliographie fremdsprachiger Werke über Deutschland und Persönlichkeiten des deutschen Sprachgebiets"; "Bibliographie der deutschen Bibliographen").

The series "Sonderbibliographien der Deutschen Bücherei" (Special bibliographies of the German Library) and "Bibliographischer Informationsdienst der Deutschen Bücherei" (Bibliographical information service of the German Library) are compiled on selected themes, with special reference to present-day problems in social developments in the GDR. The material contained in the basic bibliographies can also be obtained from the German Library in the form of title prints in international library format.

Bibliography

Die Deutsche Bücherei—die deutsche Nationalbibliothek. (The German Library—the German national library.) In: Deutsche Bücherei 1912–1962, Leipzig 1962.

G. Rost, *Tradition und Fortschritt in der bibliographischen Arbeit der Deutschen Bücherei.* (Tradition and progress in the bibliographical work of the German Library.) In: Börsenblatt für den Deutschen Buchhandel, Leipzig, no. 30, 1966.

H. Rötzsch, *Die Deutsche Bücherei und die deutsche Allgemeinbibliographie.* (The German Library and German general bibliography.) In: Börsenblatt für den Deutschen Buchhandel, Leipzig, no. 30, 1961.

H. Rötzsch, *Der Börsenverein der Deutschen Buchhändler zu Leipzig und die Deutsche Bücherei.* (The Association of German Publishers and Booksellers in Leipzig and the German Library.) Leipzig, Deutsche Bücherei 1962.

Germany: GDR

16 Book Production

Book production in the GDR aims at providing the people with the wealth of German literature past and present, with the best literature of other countries that is committed to humanism and progress, with an extensive range devoted to training and advanced training, to study, instruction and research. One significant expression of the cultural and educational revolution in progress in the GDR is a continually growing demand for reading material, reflected in the quantitative and qualitative development in book production. In 1969 there appeared 5,169 titles in 113.980 million copies. The average edition in the case of books has risen from 14,500 copies in 1962 to 22,050 copies in 1969. The GDR can claim a leading position in the world with a book production totalling nearly 7 copies per head of the population. The greater part of production of books for 1969 falls under the following headings:

Subject group	Titles	Percentage of total production
Literature (belles lettres)	999	19.3
Applied science, technology, industry	545	10.5
Books for children and youths	438	8.4
Religion, theology	282	5.4
Natural sciences	270	5.2
School textbooks	257	4.9
Linguistics, literary sciences	252	4.8
Educational theory, youths movement	252	4.8
Maps, atlases	232	4.4
Economics, social sciences, statistics	187	3.6

Bibliography

Also 1969: nearly 7 books per head of the population. In: Börsenblatt für den Deutschen Buchhandel, Leipzig, no. 35, 1970.

17 Translations

Translations of foreign works, particularly of literature, have always assumed an important place in the book production of the GDR. Her international inheritance and contemporary humanistic literature of other countries are represented in large quantities on her book market. Of the 5,169 titles in 1969 there were 660 translations, 12.7% of all titles. The number of copies was 12.950 million, i.e. 11.3% of all books produced. Predominant among such translations are those from Russian, English, American and French. In addition it should be noted that the import of foreign literature, in the original, especially from socialist countries, is continually increasing (→ 27).

18 Book Clubs

Several book clubs exist in the GDR. By offering good reading material exclusively, they are continuing the tradition of the great book clubs of the German working-class movement. Since the price of books in the GDR is low, even compared with international standards, the task of book clubs today is not so much, as in former times, to offer books at reduced prices, as to gain new circles of readers and to make permanent readers of them through subscription schemes. For this reason book clubs take specific themes in order to attract particular classes of readers, and so the "Buchklub der Jugend" ("Book Club for Youth"), the "Buchklub der Schüler" ("Pupils' Book Club") and the campaign for subscribers in country districts are particularly encouraged. A further characteristic, arising out of the close cooperation generally existing in the socialist publishing business, is that the book clubs are supported by many publishers; the "Buchclub 65" ("Book Club 65") is a joint undertaking of several publishers, the "Kleine Hausbibliothek" ("Small Home Library") is directed by the "Buchhaus Leipzig" (→ 25), the central mail-order organization in the GDR. Books issued by book clubs reach their readers exclusively through the local book trade or by mail-order.

19 Paperbacks

For some years paperback production has been part of the programme of many publishers. With an ever-increasing demand for reading material in the GDR there has been a rise in the number of paperback editions. The oldest and at the same time the most famous pocket-book series is the "Reclams Universal-Bibliothek", founded in 1867. With its high standard both of content and presentation it stands at the head of pocket-book series and also proves that the best publishing traditions are preserved in the GDR. During 1945–1966 this library produced over 900 titles, 120 of which, with a total of more than two million copies, appeared in 1966.
Paperback production in the GDR is also characteristic of socialist division of work and cooperation. In each particular field of literature 2–3 series are published. Every paperback series has a special task; there is no trade rivalry among the series.

20 Book Design

The art of making books is greatly encouraged in the GDR not merely out of love of books, but, above all, to foster interest in well-produced books suitable for the general public.
Since 1952 an annual choice has been made of the Best-Designed Books in the GDR, to enable the general public to see a high standard of performance in the art of making books, and to set new standards and provide suggestions for the future. The jury, on which well-known book artists, typographers, and bookmen of the general book world are represented, is appointed jointly by the Department for Publishing and the Book Trade of the Ministry of Culture (→ 2) and the German Publishers' and Booksellers' Association in Leipzig (→ 4). In 1958 the jury formulated the following principles of assessment:
"Book design must correspond with its contents and be of service to a socialist culture; the design must harmonize with its purpose, the type of reader, the value and the maximum quality attainable; a book worthy of special notice can only be produced when all its elements are in harmony. In making it a principle to observe the laws and to appreciate the experience in classical book production, the jury encourages experiments that aim not at transitory effects but search for new methods of expression; the central aim must be the creation of a book for the general public that is good value for money and lively in presentation".
About every six years the International Book-Art Exhibition takes place in Leipzig, the last occasions being 1959 and 1965; the next will be 1971. Its aim is to encourage the exchange of experience at an international level and to further cooperation and thus foster the art of book-making which can unite the peoples of the world. In 1965 the work of 44 countries in this field was represented in Leipzig. Apart from exhibitions from various countries, there are numerous special stands devoted to book production in particular fields of literature or special problems of typography and the graphic arts. The International Book-Art Exhibition is preceded in many countries by national competitions; the organizers also arrange international competitions. Outstanding performances at the Exhibition are awarded gold, silver and bronze medals and diplomas.

In order to keep these developments in the public eye during the intervening years, the City Council of Leipzig and the "Börsenverein" in Leipzig (→ 4) annually organize an exhibition called "Best-Designed Books in the World", during the International Book Fair in Leipzig in the autumn; about 25 countries regularly take part. Here too medals and diplomas are awarded.

Bibliography

The *Börsenblatt* (→ 5) regularly provides detailed reports on the Best-Designed Books in the GDR, the International Book-Art Exhibition and the exhibitions Best-Designed Books in the World.

The detailed report of the jury on their choice of the Best-Designed Books in the GDR is published every year in book form by the "Börsenverein" in Leipzig.

At the *International Book-Art Exhibitions* in 1959 and 1965 catalogues appeared in book form, published by the international exhibition management.

21 Publishing

In the GDR publishing once again developed under anti-fascist and democratic conditions and later, after the destruction of Hitlerite fascism, in a socialist environment. In addition to many traditional and internationally famous publishers, like the Bibliographic Institute or F. A. Brockhaus in Leipzig, which have continued their activity, new publishers have appeared, such as the Dietz Verlag, Berlin, the Akademie Verlag, Berlin, the Aufbau-Verlag, Berlin and Weimar, the VEB Fachbuchverlag Leipzig, or the Kinderbuchverlag, Berlin, all of which have grown to become important publishing houses well known beyond the frontiers of the GDR. Leipzig and Berlin remain the centres of publishing, the publishers of literary works being particularly in Berlin. However, there are several publishing firms in other towns, such as Dresden, Halle/Saale, Jena, Gotha and Rostock.

At present there are 78 firms publishing books and specialist periodicals in the GDR of various types of ownership—publishing firms of social organizations, nationalized, half-nationalized and private firms. They are as follows:

22 scientific publishers
4 medical publishers
15 specialist publishers
5 theological publishers
16 literary publishers
6 childrens' and youth book publishers
3 art publishers
7 music publishers

There are a further 100 or so publishing firms, most of them small-scale, dealing with calendars, picture and painting books, post cards, games, etc.; this does not, however, include firms publishing daily and weekly papers or monthly magazines.

The volume of production by book firms, excluding music, averages about 77 titles and 1.4 million copies per firm annually, i.e. almost all firms have a considerable capacity for production, even by international standards.

After a period of satisfying the desire for such literature as was withheld from the public during the Third Reich and the Second World War, the publishing firms regarded as their pressing task the need to streamline their activities, harmonizing with the progressive political, economical and cultural development in the GDR, and assisting in building up a socialist order of society. And so in the years 1960–1963 whole sectors of the publishing world were overhauled, corresponding to the rising socialist structure in the economy and culture, and in agreement with the wishes and suggestions of the publishing firms themselves. This was particularly the case in technology and science, where

the firms were made to fit the structure of the economy:
VEB Deutscher Verlag für Grundstoffindustrie
Literature of mining, metallurgy, power, chemistry
VEB Verlag für Bauwesen
Literature for all branches of building
VEB Verlag Technik
Literature for mechanical engineering, electrical engineering and electronics
TRANSPRESS
VEB Verlag für Verkehrswesen
Literature for transport and communications
VEB Deutscher Landwirtschaftsverlag
Literature for agriculture, forestry and gardening.

In the literary field a certain amount of concentration was also undertaken; the following firms in particular produced the works indicated below:

Aufbau-Verlag Berlin–Weimar
Humanistic, progressive literary works of the 20th century in German, contemporary socialistic literary works in the GDR, literary works of former ages both home and foreign
Verlag Volk und Welt/Kultur und Fortschritt
Foreign contemporary literary works
Mitteldeutscher Verlag
Contemporary German socialist literature

Similar demarcations were drawn in other fields. These changes, which have without exception proved to be justified, did not lead to monopolization, but to a sensible and rational use of the means and potentialities of the publishing firms; several firms continue to be active in many fields, but they now supplement each other. In order to harmonize the thematic plans of the publishers, study groups (→ 9) have been functioning for the last ten years or so; they also act as bodies for the interchange of experience gained in individual firms.

Today the GDR's leading publishers have an important place in its cultural and scientific life as centres of intellectual and cultural activity.

Bibliography

Verlage der Deutschen Demokratischen Republik. (Publishers in the GDR.) Leipzig, Börsenverein 1969.

Konferenz des Verlagswesens der sozialistischen Länder. (Conference of the publishing world of the socialist countries.) Leipzig 1957. 304 pp.

A. Kapr, *Buchgestaltung.* (Book design.) Dresden, VEB Verlag der Kunst 1963.

L. Pflug, *Verlagsarbeit zwischen VI. und VII. Parteitag der SED.* (Publishing activity between the 6th and 7th Party conference of the Socialist Unity Party.) In: Börsenblatt für den Deutschen Buchhandel, Leipzig, no. 10, 1966.

Periodicals: → 5.

22 Literary Agents

In the usual sense literary agents do not exist in the GDR. Publishers and authors usually contact each other without an intermediary. However, agreements about copyright and reproduction with partners outside the GDR always require the authority of the

Büro für Urheberrechte
(Copyright Office)
Clara-Zetkin-Strasse 105
DDR 108 Berlin

This office has the exclusive right to collect fees and reproduction charges and to pass them on to those entitled to them. It guarantees legal information to all interested parties and legal aid by special request.

23 Wholesale Trade

With the development of the book trade in Germany the wholesale trade took shape; it included both wholesale bookselling and distribution. Its most prominent centre was Leipzig (→ 2). The need for this arose from the need to supply the bookseller with any required title quickly and at a low cost.

The development of a socialist publishing and bookselling trade after 1945 did not imply any necessity to depart from proven methods in the wholesale trade and its concentration in Leipzig. Thus a state-owned wholesale business was created to work side by side with new publishing firms.

In 1946 the

LKG Leipziger Kommissions- und Grossbuchhandel
(Leipzig Book Trade Wholesale Organization)
Leninstrasse 16
DDR 701 Leipzig

was founded, at the traditional Leipzig centre, to act as wholesaler to newly formed publishing firms. Later it became necessary to create a state-owned wholesaler for the music trade, the "Zentralvertrieb für Musikalien und Volkskunstmaterial" ("Central Distributors for Musical Goods and Material for Popular Art", 1954). In a socialist society the development of these two wholesale enterprises was bound to lead to greater centralization than in a non-socialist society. After the fusion of these two state-owned businesses in 1965 the LKG distributed the whole production of state-owned publishing firms and the greater part of the production of other firms to the book trade as a whole and to other trade organizations.

As a wholesaler, the LKG completely takes over production of all publishers' distribution in accordance with orders from booksellers. The retail trade is informed of the appearance of every book title through advance notices by the LKG and the "Börsenblatt" (→ 5). Orders are sent to the LKG on individual order forms. The whole retail book trade has therefore only one partner representing its interests at publishing level. This organization is of great advantage economically and educationally; educationally because each order for works from all publishers is so carried out by the LKG that the consignment leaves the house on the day after the order has arrived—economically because orders from booksellers can be delivered from a single place, resulting in savings on transport costs.

The further development of the wholesale book trade in a socialist society has led to a significant simplification of work. The use of order-slips and parcels becomes superfluous because nearly all publishers are principals of the LKG, and their goods are stored there. Payment to the LKG for complete delivery to a bookshop is made only at the end of the month. The bookseller usually places his order against a firm invoice, but deliveries on sale-or-return are also possible with the publishers' consent.

Although the LKG relieves the publishers of a large part of the work of distribution, informs them about sales and the situation of the market, and advises them on editions, the publishers still remain fully responsible for their production. They are responsible particularly for stock on hand and the consequent measures taken for advertising, in which the LKG plays only a supporting role. As wholesaler, the LKG is completely responsible to publishers for the correct maintenance and care of stocks.

The LKG is at the same time a wholesale dealer. It buys up a small part of the production, chiefly of private publishers, just as it buys imported books. Here the LKG has taken over a function similar to the earlier "Barsortiment" which sold both to retailers and to the public. On the basis of contracts with publishers in the GDR and the German Export and Import Book Co. (→ 27, 28) as to what material shall be imported, the LKG decides on titles and editions. Through the purchase of these works the LKG becomes the owner and carries full responsibility for sales to the retail trade. A consequence of this is that the publicist activities of the LKG are confined almost entirely to this literature.

As the central organization for the delivery of publications in the GDR and for export, the LKG was given tasks which concern the whole field of publishing and the book trade: research into requirements and the book market (→ 9), and information and documentation. The maintenance of such arrangements by a wholesaler has only become possible since the abolition of a dispersed wholesale trade and the creation of a socialist wholesale business as a third party between publisher and the retail trade.

Bibliography

Die Geschichte des LKG Leipziger Kommissions- und Grossbuchhandel 1946–1967. (History of the Leipzig Book Trade Wholesale Organization). Leipzig 1968. 96 pp.

Die Aufgaben und die Organisation des LKG Leipziger Kommissions- und Grossbuchhandel. (Tasks and organization of Leipzig's Wholesale Book Trade). Leipzig 1969. 100 pp.

24 Retail Trade

The retail book trade in the GDR possesses an efficient network, thus making it possible to acquire quickly any book required. Altogether there are more than 2,000 bookshops engaged in the sale of books, state-owned bookshops, bookshops that have concluded an agreement with the state-owned book trade, bookshops that are partly state-owned, and privately owned bookshops.

Most book sales take place through the organizations of the state-owned book trade, which, with its 800 or more bookshops, covers about 80% of all book sales in the GDR. All state-owned bookshops in the GDR are united into a uniform undertaking whose work is planned, directed and settled by the

Zentrale Leitung des Volksbuchhandels der DDR
(Central Board of the State-owned Book Trade in the GDR)
Friedrich-Ebert-Strasse 25
DDR 701 Leipzig

Branch managements in the 14 districts of the GDR and in the capital are under the direction of this Central Board; they are responsible for the work of all state-owned bookshops within their districts. Two special institutions are part of the state-owned book trade, the "Buchhaus Leipzig" (→ 25), and the "Zentralantiquariat" (→ 26). A special feature of the work of the state-owned book trade is the fact that it successfully carries out intensive publicity outside bookshops as well. In this work it is supported by its 5,000 agencies: book departments in other socialist trading organizations that are not bookshops, particularly in villages and small towns—and about 12,000 private persons, who in an honorary capacity sell books in factories, schools and other establishments. In addition, the state-owned book trade organizes some 15,000 book exhibitions annually, chiefly in factories, agricultural production cooperatives, or on social occasions. This comprehensive outside activity makes an essential contribution to the creation of new classes of book buyers. It is supported by a many-sided propaganda to foster reading. Not only are the mass media, such as radio, press and television, used:

the state-owned book trade also cooperates with publishers and authors in arranging book events, in which the population shows growing interest. This book publicity places emphasis on awakening the urge to read, on information about reading matter

and on the development of the reader's critical faculties. In this way book publicity supports the general desire for education in all sections of the population.
The 1,200 or more private bookshops and book departments which distribute books in the traditional manner also play an important role in providing the population with reading matter. Notable in this branch of the book trade is an increasing trend in its activities towards matters that concern society as a whole, and in increasing cooperation with the state-owned book trade. Concrete examples of this are a growing participation in organized events in the book world and agreements on the basis of sale-or-return which embrace a continually widening circle of readers.

Bibliography

Ökonomik des Buchhandels. (The economics of the book trade.) Leipzig, VEB Verlag für Buch- und Bibliothekswesen 1962. 221 pp.

25 Jahre Volksbuchhandel der Deutschen Demokratischen Republik 1945–1970. (25 years of the state-owned book trade in the GDR). Leipzig, VEB Fachbuchverlag 1970.

25 Mail-Order Business

The most important organization for these activities is the

Buchhaus Leipzig,
Zentraler Versandbuchhandel der DDR
(Leipzig Book House,
Central Mail-Order Office for Books of the GDR)
Täubchenweg 83
DDR 705 Leipzig

This institution is an establishment of the state-owned book trade which in agreement with the local state-owned book trade throughout the GDR attends to customers, especially in country districts. Comprehensive catalogues and prospectuses, booksellers' representatives, and advertisements in the press publicize book offers. The "Buchhaus Leipzig" does not solicit merely for a comprehensive and general range of reading matter, but also uses special methods of publicity and distribution for the sale of particular works or limited fields of scientific or specialized literature. The "Buchhaus Leipzig" also has large special departments for the distribution of works published in parts and for book subscriptions (→ 18). It is thus an important establishment for supplementing the work of the local book trade in satisfying the needs of readers without competing with it. It achieves an annual turnover of over M 30 million.
In addition to the "Buchhaus Leipzig" there are a number of private mail-order firms. Books are also offered for sale in the mail-order firms for industrial goods in Leipzig and Karl-Marx-Stadt.

26 Antiquarian Book Trade, Auctions

The great traditions of the antiquarian book trade in Germany are preserved and encouraged in the GDR. Since many well-known firms were shut or driven abroad during the Nazi regime, the state-owned book trade built up a network of second-hand bookshops after 1945, and they, together with a series of efficient private firms, perform a great service; the need for older literature is on the increase with the development of educational facilities.
In the district capitals and in Berlin there are state-owned antiquarian bookshops offering their goods both in sales-rooms and through catalogues. In the publication of catalogues for different specialized fields cooperation has developed between the various state-owned second-hand bookshops.
The

Zentralantiquariat der DDR
(Antiquarian Book Centre of the GDR)

Talstrasse 29
DDR 701 Leipzig
has assumed a special position in the GDR. It is the largest antiquarian bookshop and at the same time it deals with the export side on behalf of all other second-hand bookshops and in cooperation with the German Export and Import Book Co. (→ 27, 28). It has a publishing department for scientific reprints. The Committee of the "Börsenverein" (→ 4) is the democratic forum of all antiquarian booksellers, where questions concerning this branch of the trade can be discussed in common.
The distribution of nazi, militaristic and anti-humanistic literature by second-hand bookshops in the GDR is forbidden under the Directions concerning the Antiquarian Book Trade, from 20 June 1960.
The international importance of the antiquarian book trade of the GDR continues to grow; export amounts to about 25% of the total turnover.

27 Book Imports

In the GDR the state has the monopoly of the export trade. This monopoly, which is part of the socialist economic system, is delegated to the appropriate enterprise for export trade. In the case of publishing and the book trade it is the
Deutscher Buch-Export und -Import GmbH
(German Export and Import Book Co.)
Leninstrasse 16
DDR 701 Leipzig
Its function is to coordinate commercial and trade interests, to conclude export contracts on the basis of trade agreements and to safeguard their realization. In this it works closely with publishers in the GDR and with the organizations responsible for the purchase and distribution of imported published material. The import and export of books is not subject to customs duty in the GDR.
The import of published material serves in the first place to supplement home production and information on the latest developments in the arts andsciences throughout the world. As a result the non-fiction book is naturally in the forefront. In view of the demand for up-to-date information technical journals and trade papers assume a high proportion of the total import. With the thematic streaming of publishing in the GDR it is possible to recognize thematic requirements without great expense, and to adjust imports accordingly. Of the total imports of published material, 52% comes from non-socialist and 48% from socialist countries. Import from the socialist countries are based on long-standing trade agreements which allow the coordination of requirements over a long period.
Direct ordering is done through the LKG (→ 23), which collects and coordinates all orders from the retail trade. It also has the duty of synchronizing thematically retail-trade imports with what the publishers in the GDR can offer.
Imports from the Federal Republic of Germany and West Berlin are covered by a trade agreement.

28 Book Exports

The publishing firms of the GDR export to over 100 countries throughout the world. The main concern in exporting published material is to provide comprehensive information on developments in the GDR in the fields of science, technology and culture; this book export to an ever-increasing number of countries on a trade basis is of advantage to both sides. It can best be achieved where long-standing reciprocal trade agreements can be concluded through the German Export and Import Book Co. (→ 27) on the basis of trade treaties between states. The work of the central and coordinating section of the department for export trade is supplemented by individual responsibility on

the part of publishers for opening up and concluding export deals according to the line of business of the individual publisher. This presupposes that publishers undertake market and price research of their own in particular types of book they publish and take the results into consideration in producing their editions. Characteristic of the export activities of publishers and the German Export and Import Book Co. is a varied activity abroad, reflected in zealous participation in trade fairs, at exhibitions, and in the continual provision of information to potentially interested parties.
Cooperation between the department for export and the publisher is on the basis of agreements. Acquisition and delivery are undertaken by the LKG (→ 23), where all available literature from the publishers is stored.
The continually growing demand of foreign business partners for publications from the GDR is expressed in the rising export figures:

Year	Proportional increase in %
1960	100
1962	132
1964	153
1966	166
1967	172

Increased interest is shown in all fields of production, in particular for scientific and specialized works, for children's books and art-book production.
A definite increase in trade with the Federal Republic of Germany and West Berlin could also be noted, but it does not correspond with any objectively calculated requirement for publications from the GDR.

29 Book Fairs

Within the framework of the traditional Leipzig Trade Fair, organized by the
Leipziger Messeamt
(Leipzig Trade Fair Office)
Markt 11–15
DDR 701 Leipzig
the International Leipzig Book Fair takes place twice a year (Spring Fair, in March for 10 days; Autumn Fair, in September for 8 days). In Leipzig, being one of the most important centres of world trade, the book fair enjoys great interest from foreign countries. As part of the Leipzig Trade Fair, the book fair is not only of importance for those directly interested in the publishing and book trades, but exhibitors in all branches of industry take the opportunity of informing themselves of the latest international publications. An essential factor in the increasing importance of the Leipzig Book Fair is the complete equality of all exhibitors. The book fair serves in the first place to spread information, to bring about contacts and to make business deals. This is true for trade in books, booklets and periodicals, and in co-production and the granting of licenses. In addition, the retail book trade in the GDR, the institutes, universities, academies, research centres and libraries of large industrial undertakings etc. acquire information on the latest international works and plan their foreign publications accordingly. During the Spring Fair the distinction "Best-Designed Books in the GDR" is awarded, and during the Autumn Fair the City Council of Leipzig and the Leipzig "Börsenverein" (→ 4) organize the exhibition known as "Best-Designed Books in the World" (→ 20).
In previous years an average of 750 publishers exhibited their works to buyers and interested parties.
A further advantage of the book fair is that in the city of Leipzig a comprehen-

sive and many-sided trade-fair service is at the disposal of exhibitors and buyers.
As part of the Leipzig Trade Fair, the International Leipzig Book Fair is a member of the "Union des Foires Internationales" (UFI).

30 Public Relations

With the transformation of society in the GDR there no longer exists any separation of the people from culture and education, and a new relationship is developing between the printed word and society as a whole. An obvious expression of this is the growing desire to read and to learn, evident at all levels. In such conditions book advertising assumes a character touching the whole of society and increasingly becoming a part of the work of general education. It requires and achieves the mutual working of all publishers, the book trade and the "Börsenverein" (→ 4), together with all libraries and many social and cultural organizations and institutions.
The annual climax of this advertising work is the Book Week, organized since 1953/4 in all districts and communities. During that time thousands of meetings take place, discussions, readings by authors, conversations with writers, book exhibitions, visits to libraries, etc.; these are devoted to literary, scientific and specialized works. Children's books receive special attention on a particular Children's Books Day.
Reading needs for the younger generation are also served by annual Exhibitions of Children's Literature, organized by the German Writers' Association in cooperation with publishers, children's libraries and schools (→ 10).
In addition, social events such as commemoration days, holidays and festivals are used for intensive book advertising. One expression of the interest of the whole population in reading are the literary and art-prize discussions (→ 32). Reading circles, book committees of local councils, working committees on books in houses of culture, libraries, bookshops and other cultural institutions promote direct discussions on subjects. Traditional forms of advertising used by wholesale and retail traders—such as posters, slides, films, catalogues and prospectuses—are at the disposal of all social organizations and individuals. A number of publishers produce readers' newspapers which contain comprehensive information on their publications. During recent years the library catalogues have achieved increasing importance.
Part of book advertising consists of numerous radio and television programmes. A permanent association between publishers and cultural and technical editors of the press assures the public of expert information on the book market (→ 33).

31 Bibliophily

The only organization of bibliophiles is the

Pirckheimer-Gesellschaft
(Pirckheimer Society)
Otto-Nuschke-Strasse 1
DDR 108 Berlin

a special association founded in 1956 within the German Cultural Association. There are local groups in several cities. The Society organizes meetings, exhibitions and lectures to inform members and nonmembers about books, particularly the art of making books; it also promotes personal contacts. The Society publishes the periodical *Marginalien* and booklovers' prints for its members.

Bibliography

Marginalien. Zeitschrift für Buchkunst und Bibliophilie. (Journal for book-art and bibliophily.) Berlin, Aufbau-Verlag (Französische Strasse 32).—Quarterly.

32 Literary Prizes

In the GDR literary prizes are donated by the government, local councils, organizations and institutions. They honour outstanding authors, artists and individual works of art, while simultaneously promoting significant tendencies in art and literature. The most important prize is the "National Prize for Art and Literature", awarded every year on 7 October, the day of the foundation of the GDR. Further literature prizes awarded by the state are:

the Johannes R. Becher Prize (for lyric poetry)
the Heinrich Heine Prize (for lyric poetry and literary journalism)
the Lessing Prize (for dramatic works, art theory and criticism)
the Cisinski Prize (for Sorbian works of art)

The Heinrich Mann Prize and the F. C. Weiskopf Prize are awarded by the German Academy of Arts, Berlin.

Among the most important literary prizes awarded by social organizations are the Art Prize of the Free German Trade Union Federation, the Erich Weinert Medal, the Art Prize of the Free German Youth Organization and the Literature Prize of Domowina (the Union of Lausitz Wends).

Town and district councils also award art and literary prizes. Among the most noteworthy are: the Goethe Prize of the City of Berlin, the Carl Blechen Prize for Art and Literature (Cottbus district), the Händel Prize of Halle District, the Art Prize of Karl-Marx-Stadt district, the Theodor Fontane Prize for Art and Literature (Potsdam district), the John Brinckman Prize of the Council of Rostock district, the Fritz Reuter Art Prize of the Council of Schwerin district, the Martin Andersen Nexö Prize of the City of Dresden, the Art Prize of the City of Halle, the Art Prize of the City of Leipzig, the Erich Weinert Prize of the City of Magdeburg, the Literature and Art Prize of the City of Weimar.

The nature of these literature prizes in the GDR is best seen in the Art Prize of the Free German Trade Union Federation. The award of the prize is preceded by several months' discussions, in which thousands of people in the factories and in country districts talk about works of art and put forward names for the award. In this way the bestowal of the prize sets in motion discussions that are both a form of propaganda on behalf of books and a means of creating understanding of art.

Outstanding work in the field of book art and production can be awarded the Gutenberg Prize of the Council of the City of Leipzig.

Bibliography

L. Fröhlich, *Literaturpreise der DDR.* (Literary Prizes in the GDR.) In: Börsenblatt für den Deutschen Buchhandel, Leipzig, no. 44–7, 1962.
A supplement appears annually in April, containing the awards of the previous year.

33 The Reviewing of Books

The systematic reviews and critical articles in the daily and weekly papers as well as in specialist journals play an important role. They inform readers on home and foreign works, and thus arouse public interest in reading. The same is true of radio and television.

The leading daily papers provide a continuous series of reviews and critiques. Among these are *Neues Deutschland* ("New Germany"), the official paper of the Socialist Unity Party, and *Junge Welt* ("World of Youth"), published by the Central Council of the Free German Youth Organizations, with monthly literary supplements. The district newspapers of the democratic parties, especially that of the

Socialist Unity Party, also reach a large circle of readers with comprehensive reviews and regularly published literary supplements. To these should be added papers whose readership extends beyond local areas, like the *Berliner Zeitung* (a daily from the capital), *Tribüne* (official paper of the Free German Trade Union Federation), *Nationalzeitung* (official paper of the National Democratic Party), *Neue Zeit* (official paper of the Christian Democratic Union), and *Der Morgen* (official paper of the Liberal Democratic Party).

Of particular importance among the weekly papers are *Sonntag* ("Sunday") published by the German Cultural Federation, and *Weltbühne*, which has a proud tradition. In addition there are *Forum*, a paper appearing twice a month and dealing with the intellectual problems of youth, and the *Neue Deutsche Literatur*, published by the German Writers' Association and devoted to reviews of the most important editions of contemporary literature in the German language.

Mention must also be made of the specialized publications like the *Börsenblatt für den Deutschen Buchhandel* (→ 5) and *Der Bibliothekar*, published by the "Zentralinstitut für Bibliothekswesen", ("Central Institute for Library Matters"), Berlin, and appearing monthly. These publish both specialist information in their own field and also regular and up-to-date contributions and reports on the world of books and literature.

34 Graphic Arts

The direction of the printing industry is in the hands of the

Zentrag
Rosenstrasse 18
DDR 102 Berlin

From this address information can be obtained on the industry, production and other specialist matters.

Greece

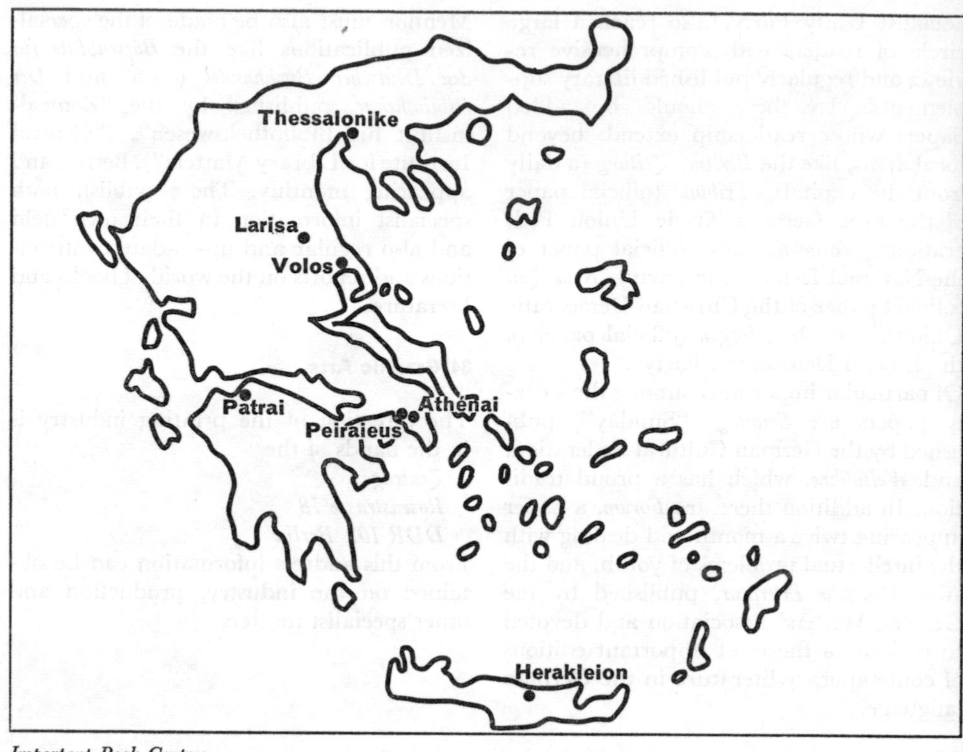

Important Book Centres

1 General Information

Area 131,944 km²

Population 8,716,000 (= 66 per km²)—estimated population in mid-1967

Capital Athenai (1,853,000)

Largest towns Athenai (1,853,000); Thessaloniki (378,000); Patras (102,000); Heraklion (70,000); Volos (67,000); Larissa (55,000)

Government Crowned democracy (literal translation of "Vassilevomeni Dimokratia"—meaning a parliamentary democracy with the King as head of State)

Religion Eastern Orthodox

National language Greek

Leading foreign languages English, French, German

Weights, measures Metric system

Currency unit Drachma (in Greek: Drachmi, plural Drachmai)

Education Free at all levels, including free text-books. Primary education (compulsory): 6 years, secondary-school education: 6 years. Number of students in universities and other higher educational institutions (academic year 1966–7): 60,624, of whom 19,358 female. (Athens University: 18,794—University of Thessaloniki: 19,681—National Technical University, Athens: 3,384—Graduate School of Economic and Commercial Sciences, Athens: 5,465—Pantios Graduate School of Political Sciences, Athens: 6,206)

Illiteracy (1961 census) 17.8% (males: 7.6%; females 27.3%)

2 Past and Present

The first mention of a bookseller in Greece is made by the comic poet Nicophon, a contemporary of Aristophanes, from whom we learn that bookselling existed as a trade in Athens in the fifth century B.C. Manuscripts were displayed and sold in a certain part of the Agora. With the expansion of Greek culture, after Alexander's conquests, the demand for manuscripts from learned men, but especially from the great libraries of Alexandria, Pergamon and others, led to a flourishing of the trade in Athens, Rhodes and Alexandria. After the destruction of the Western Roman State, bookselling declined, and existed only in the Eastern Roman Empire, mainly in Constantinople, and in Alexandria (later in the Islamic cultural centres).

When the rest of Europe discovered typography, Greece was under Frankish domination and Byzantium was soon to fall to the Turks. With the fall of Constantinople the Greek people entered a long period of cultural darkness, from which it emerged four centuries later. So Greece did not benefit immediately from Gutenberg's discovery.

During the Turkish domination few books were printed. These were didactic texts or ecclesiastic books and were bought by wealthy Greeks to be presented to schools and communities. The first printing centres of Greek books were in Italy, where the first printed book wholly in Greek was produced (1476); later also in Constantinople and Moschopolis.

In the modern Greek State, printing activity began during the War of Independence, but the structure of the book trade, as we know it today, took shape as late as the second decade of the present century. Until then the demand was small and books were sold directly to the public by the publisher or the author, or by subscription. Very often the same person was publisher, printer and bookseller at the same time. Gradually, important bookshops were created in Athens and Thessaloniki, some of them belonging to publishers. A few of the bookshops belonged to foreigners (like the German Wilhelm Bart), and sold only imported books.

After the Second World War the sale of voluminous works (encyclopedias, multivolume histories and science works) in weekly parts made it possible for a great number of low-income readers to possess books.

Today books are sold in three ways: through bookshops, by door-to-door salesmen, and in weekly parts by newsagents. A great number of titles are still being published by the authors, but sold mainly in the bookshops.

3 Retail Prices

The retail price of books is fixed by the publisher, who allows a trade discount (varying from 20% to 50%) to the bookseller. There is no formal trade agreement for the enforcement of retail-price maintenance, though the publisher can make a private contract with the bookseller to that end. The bookseller can offer a discount not only to libraries and educational institutions, but also to individual customers.

The law governing the retail trade in general, however, does not permit the advertisement of a reduction of prices except twice a year (twenty days in February and twenty in August). All retailers, then (including booksellers), are free to offer their goods to the public at any discount, advertising the discount offered. In general the law protecting retailers from unfair competition is also applicable to booksellers.

4 Organization

Until recently the Greek book trade was organized in independent local associations. Only the Athens-Piraeus association and the Thessaloniki association were united into a federation before the Second World War. In 1966 the provincial associations joined too, and a body named

Panellinios Omospondia Ekdoton—
Vivliopolon—Chartopolon
(Panhellenic Federation of Publishers,
Booksellers and Stationers)
Stadiou 51
GR Athenai (121)

was formed. It includes as members the "Athens Association" and 17 provincial ones (about 140 publishers and 800 booksellers).

The aims of the Federation are the promotion of books in general, the improvement of their quality, and the safeguard of the interests of the book trade.

5 Trade Press

The only trade journal is:

O Kosmos Tou Vivliou
(The World of Books)
Veranzerou 5
GR Athenai (141)

It is published twice a month and contains news of the trade, articles and advertisements, but no bibliography.

7 Sources of Information, Address Services

Inquires concerning book-trade matters should be addressed to the "Panhellenic Federation of Publishers, Booksellers and Stationers" (→ 4)

Panellinios Omospondia Ekdoton—
Vivliopolon—Chartopolon
Stadiou 51
GR Athenai (121)

Bibliographical inquiries to the National Library:

Ethniki Vivliothiki
GR Athenai

Some bookshops with international connections will readily answer inquiries concerning either the trade, or bibliographic matters. The addresses of the Greek book trade are contained in

Odigos Ekdotikon Oikon Kai
Vivliopoleion Ellados
(Guide of Publishing Houses
and Bookshops of Greece)
O Kosmos Tou Vivliou
Veranzerou 5
GR Athenai (141)

8 International Membership

Greece is a member of UNESCO and a signatory to the agreement for the "Free Flow of Books" (→ International Section, 27/28).

10 Books and Young People

The

Kyklos Tou Ellinikou Paidikou Vivliou
(Circle of the Greek Children's Book)
c/o George Zombanakis, President
Akadimias 57
GR Athenai (143)

is a private organization for the promotion of good children's literature in Greece and abroad. It awards prizes for the best children's books. It also selects and translates the best children's book to participate in the honour list for the international "Andersen Prize" (→ International Section, 10).

The

Gynaikia Logotechniki Syntrofia
(Women Writers' Group)
c/o Mrs Tatiana Stavrou
President of the Selection Committee
Evrou 4
GR Athenai (611)

another private organization, was the first to institute, twelve years ago, an award of prizes for the best children's books and continues to do so. The prizes are for the best unpublished novel, collections of short stories, poetry, fairy tales and travel books, all for children.

The funds for the prizes come from dona-

tions by publishers, booksellers and private individuals.
An exhibition of children's books takes place in Athens every year.

12 Taxes

Books published in Greece are not subject to any taxes. Foreign books and periodicals are free of import duty, but liable to a 2% stamp duty. Books published abroad in the Greek language are subject to import duty.

14 Copyright

The first Greek copyright law dates from 1920. Greece joined the "Berne Convention" with the decree of 18 August 1931, which, due to administrative difficulties, became valid on 25 February 1932. The Brussels version was ratified in 1956. The "Universal Copyright Convention" of 1952 was signed by Greece in 1962, due to certain reservations on her part.
Copyright expires 50 years after the death of the author.

15 National Bibliography, National Library

The National Library was founded in 1827 on the island of Aegina and was later moved to Athens, where it was housed for a period in the Byzantine church of Saint Eleftherios, and, later still, in the University building. In 1902 it was finally moved to its present building,

Ethniki Vivliothiki
(National Library)
GR Athenai

donated to the State by the Vallianos brothers and built by the German architect, Ziller.
Depositing of 2 copies of every book published is obligatory. Also, one copy is deposited at the municipal library of the town where the book was published.
In 1934 the National Library began issuing a bibliography, which was discontinued in 1938. As from 1970, however, publishing was resumed and under the title *Helliniki Vivliographia* ("Greek Bibliography") the National Library will issue annually a catalogue of books and periodicals deposited during the year. Volume 1 will cover the year 1968 and the contents will be classified by author and by subject.

16 Book Production

The constantly rising standard of living in Greece resulted in an increased demand for books. This fact, as well as the postwar development of communications and cultural exchanges, had a beneficial effect both on the choice of books published and on their standard of production. In 1968 1,800 titles were published and deposited in the "National Library". Some of the leading subjects were:

Subject group	Titles
Fiction	106
Poetry	147
Theology	210
Law	130
Medicine	156
Technical	157
Social sciences	184
Translations	114
Education	194

It is worth noting the number of poetry books published, but it should be remembered that a big percentage of them were privately published by their authors.

21 Publishing

Athens is the undisputed publishing centre of Greece. Of the existing 141 publishers (1967) only 4 are in Thessaloniki, 1 in Patras, 2 in Piraeus and 1 in Volos; 133 are in Athens.

Greece

23 Wholesale Trade

The existing few wholesalers deal only in imported books, mainly paperbacks and books of interest to tourists as well as magazines.

24 Retail Trade

The increasing demand over the last twenty years for books in general, and for imported books in particular, has been an invigorating factor for the retail trade. It led to the creation of new bookshops and the modernization of many existing ones. Today, Athens and Thessaloniki have some very modern bookshops, both in design and in methods. It is these cities which have the leading bookshops.
Bookshops in Greece can be divided roughly into three categories:

1. Bookshops selling only Greek books.
2. Bookshops selling only foreign books.
3. Bookshops selling both Greek and foreign books.

27 Book Imports

There has been a very important increase in book imports during the last decade. This is due to many factors, mainly the constant rise in the standard of living, the increasing number of people learning foreign languages and the industrialization of the country. The comparative figures for 1965 and 1968 show the extent of the increase:

Book imports in 1965—Drachmas 9,465,000
Book imports in 1968—Drachmas 38,424,000

There has also been a qualitative change: a growing demand for scientific and technical books.
The great majority of imported books are in English, with the United Kingdom as the largest supplier. The figures for 1968 are as follows:

1968
United Kingdom—Drachmas 28,264,000
USA —Drachmas 8,061,000

28 Book Exports

Exports of Greek books in 1968 amounted to Drachmas 11,243,000.
The largest importer of Greek books was Cyprus (Drachmas 7,565,000). The other comparatively large importers were:

Country	Amount (1,000 Drachmas)
USA	1,238
Australia	638
Canada	411
Federal Republic of Germany	390
United Kingdom	256
Republic of South Africa	217

It is worth noting that the above-listed countries have strong Greek colonies.
To the export figure for 1968 should be added an additional amount of Drachmas 405,000 representing books published in Greece in languages other than Greek.

Hungary

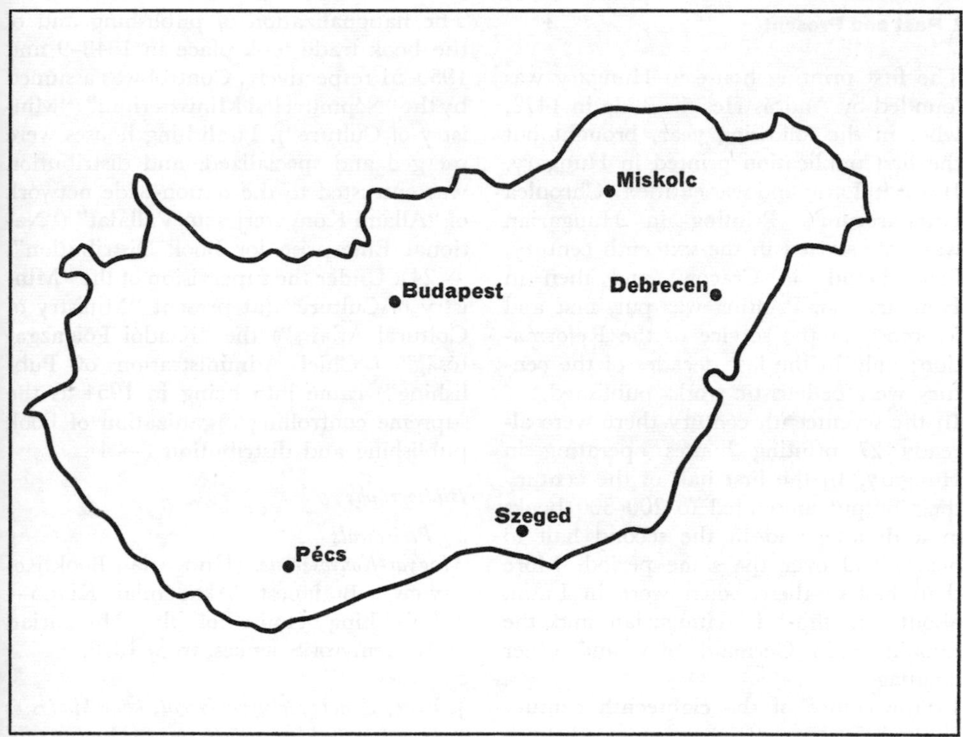

Important Book Centres

1 General Information

Area 93,030 km²
Population 10,160,00 (109.2 per km²)
Capital Budapest (1,969,000)
Largest towns Budapest (1,969,000); Miskolc (175,000); Debrecen (151,000); Pécs (137,000); Szeged (118,000)
Government People's democracy, with 19 counties ("megye") as administrative units. Parliament with one chamber. The head of the state is the President of the Presidential Council
National language Hungarian
Leading foreign languages German, English, Russian, French
Weights, measures Metric system
Currency unit Hungarian forint (FT)
Education Compulsory. 1,756,000 elementary and secondary school pupils. 65,621 students (3rd level), of whom 44.8% are women, at 31 universities and other colleges of academic level.
Illiteracy 2.5% (1963)
Paper consumption a) Newsprint 3.9 kg per inhabitant
b) Printing paper (other than newsprint) 1.8 kg per inhabitant
Membership UNESCO

2 Past and Present

The first printing house in Hungary was founded by András Hess in Buda in 1472, who, in the following year, brought out the first publication printed in Hungary. It was in Latin and was entitled "Chronica Hungarorum". Printing in Hungarian was only started in the sixteenth century, first abroad (in Cracow) and then in Hungary too. Printing was put, first and foremost, in the service of the Reformation; only in the last decades of the century were belletristic works published.

In the seventeenth century there were already 27 printing houses operating in Hungary. In the first half of the century their output amounted to 200–300 books in a decade, and in the second half to nearly 600 over the same period. More than half of these books were in Latin, about one third in Hungarian and the remainder in German, Slav and other languages.

In the course of the eighteenth century booksellers came to be separated from printer-publishers. The first decree regulating the book trade was issued in 1772. The publishing and selling of books was mostly carried on by people of Austrian or German origin. The social and independence movements that commenced after 1825 (the Era of Reforms) and the 1848–9 war of independence gave a tremendous impetus to the development of Hungarian literature and publishing. In the last third of the nineteenth century the great publishing houses, which up to 1948, when they were nationalized, had played a decisive role in Hungarian book publishing, were established. The "Magyar Könyvkereskedők Egyesülete" ("Association of Hungarian Booksellers") was founded in 1878 and later pursued its activity under the name of "Kiadói és Könyvkereskedelmi Egyesület" ("Association of Publishing and the Book Trade").

The nationalization of publishing and of the book trade took place in 1948–9 and 1950–51 respectively. Control was assumed by the "Népmüvelési Minisztérium" ("Ministry of Culture"). Publishing houses were merged and specialized, and distribution was entrusted to the nation-wide network of "Allami Könyvterjesztő Vállalat" ("National Enterprise for Book Distribution", → 24). Under the supervision of the "Ministry of Culture" (at present "Ministry of Cultural Affairs") the "Kiadói Főigazgatóság" ("Chief Administration of Publishing") came into being in 1954 as the supreme controlling organization of book publishing and distribution (→ 4).

Bibliography

a) Periodicals

Magyar Könyvszemle. (Hungarian Book Review). Budapest, Akadémiai Kiadó—Publishing House of the Hungarian Academy of Sciences, from 1876.

b) Books

J. Fitz, *A magyar nyomdászat, könyvkiadás és könyvkereskedelem története.* (History of Hungarian printing, publishing and the book trade.) 1. rész. A mohácsi vészig. (First Part. Up to the defeat at Mohács.) 2. rész. A reformáció korában. (Second Part. At the time of the Reformation.) Budapest, Akadémiai Kiadó Publishing House of the Hungarian Academy of Sciences 1959–67.

A könyv és könyvtár a magyar társadalom életében. Összeállitotta Kovács Máté. (Books and libraries in Hungarian society.) Compiled by Máté Kovács. Budapest, Gondolat Publishing House 1963.

A. Tevan, *A könyv évezredes utja.* (The millenary course of books.) Budapest, Müvelt Nép Publishing House 1959.

3 Retail Prices

The calculation of the retail prices of books is regulated in Hungary by the prescriptions of the "Minister of Cultural Affairs" (→ 21). The retail price is printed indelibly into every publication that is placed on the market, and the book trade has to adhere to these prices.

4 Organization

In Hungary both branches of the book trade, publishing and distribution alike, are under social ownership. The highest controlling organ of the book trade is the

Kiadó Föigazgatóság
(Chief Administration of Publishing)
Szalay utca 10–14
H Budapest V

which operates within the framework of the "Ministry of Cultural Affairs", as one of its departments. The "Chief Administration of Publishing" lays down the guiding principles, in accordance with national cultural policy, to be followed in the different branches of the book trade, it elaborates long-term plans, coordinates the activity of publishing and distribution enterprises and allocates, according to plans, the stocks of paper and the printing houses' capacity. Nevertheless, the enterprises under its control maintain their independence; this refers, first and foremost, to the publishing houses (→ 21), which choose the works they wish to bring out.

Nationwide publicity promoting the interests of the whole book trade (→ 30) is carried out by

Magyar Könyvkiadók
és Könyvterjesztök Egyesülése
(Hungarian Publishers'
and Booksellers' Association)
Vörösmarty tér 1
H Budapest V

Its work is connected with the activity of the editorial section of publications both in Hungarian and in foreign languages of the "KTTK" (→ 9), which is in charge of the periodicals of the book trade. Other tasks within the scope of the "KTTK" are carried out by the "Economic and Market Research Group" (→ 9) as well as by the "Section for Bibliography and Book Statistics" (→ 15).

5 Trade Press

The monthly

Könyvtájékoztató
(Information on Books)
Deák Ferenc utca 15
H Budapest V

provides information for the public and trade alike. Printed in a large edition, this information journal contains a list of the books published every month, grouped according to special lines and provided with annotations. It publishes reports on the plans of publishing houses, statements made by writers, reviews of books and a bibliography of the publications that appeared in the preceding month (→ 1).

Books from Hungary—Livres de Hongrie—
Bücher aus Ungarn
Petöfi Sándor utca 17
H Budapest V

are the quarterlies of the Hungarian book trade, published with identical contents in three foreign languages. They report on significant events in Hungarian publishing and in the cultural life of the country—events that may be of interest for foreign readers; they introduce writers to the public and present a list with annotations of the most important new publications as well as a bibliography with the translations of the titles of the books published in Hungary in the three months preceding by half a year the appearance of each number (→ 15).

The six annual numbers of

A Könyv—Dokumentációs
(The Book—Review of Documentation)
Deák Ferenc utca 15
H Budapest V

deal with trade questions in the narrower sense. In addition to articles referring to the Hungarian book trade it contains the translation of articles published in foreign trade journals, which may be of interest for the members of the Hungarian book trade.

All three papers are published by "Könyvkiadók és Terjesztők Tájékoztató Központja" ("Information Centre of Publishers and Distributors of Books", → 4).

7 Sources of Information, Address Services

General information concerning the Hungarian book trade can be obtained from

Kiadói Föigazgatóság
(Chief Administration of Publishing)
Szalay utca 10–14
H Budapest V

as well as from

Magyar Könyvkiadók
és Könyvterjesztök Egyesülése
(Hungarian Publishers'
and Booksellers' Association)
Vörösmarty tér 1
H Budapest V

The

Bureau Hongrois pour la Protection des
Droits d'Auteur—ARTISJUS
(Hungarian Bureau for the Protection of
Copyright)
Deák Ferenc utca 15
H Budapest V

provides information on copyright questions.

9 Market Research

The central market-research organization of the Hungarian book trade is the

Könyvkiadók és Terjesztök Tájékoztató
Központja Közgazdasági és Piackutató
Csoport
(Information Centre of Publishers and
Distributors of Books—Economic and
Market Research Group)
Báthory utca 10
H Budapest V

which, since its foundation in 1964, has conducted systematic investigations into the structure of the Hungarian book market. In 1964 it carried out a comprehensive and representative investigation into the reading and book-purchasing habits of the adult population of the country and published the results in a volume entitled "Könyvolvasás és könyvvásárlás Magyarországon. Egy reprezentativ közvélemény-kutatás eredményei" ("The reading and purchasing of books in Hungary. Results of a representative public opinion poll"). The Research Group investigates the relationship between books and different sections of society. In 1966 it conducted a public-opinion test among working class readers, whereas its schedule for 1967 comprised an exploration entitled "Youth and books". A continual analysis of the purchases in bookshops and the composition of buyers also falls within its scope of activities. Year after year the turnover achieved during special drives by the book trade ("Poetry Day", "Week of Books", winter season of presents, → 30) as well as the efficiency of publicity media are investigated. Among management questions of publishing and distribution the group explored the development of book prices, the nature of the demand for different types of book, questions of where to place bookshops, etc.

Investigations about certain aspects of the Hungarian book market are conducted by two more organizations. In the course of public-opinion research pursued in 4,000 families about household statistics in 1962, the

Központi Statisztikai Hivatal
(Central Office of Statistics)
Keleti Károly utca 5–7
H Budapest II

assessed what was read in Hungary and by how many people. It also tried to discover from what layers of society the reading public was recruited. The results of the investigation were brought out as a separate publication entitled "Mit olvasunk? 4,000 háztartás könyvolvasási adatai" ("What do we read? Data on the reading of books in 4,000 households"). The "Office of Statistics" also carried out a comprehensive survey on the prices of books; in its sociological researches it discusses the role which reading plays in the life of the population.

Within the framework of library work an analysis of reading is conducted by the

Országos Széchényi Könyvtár—
Könyvtudományi és Módszertani Központ
(National Széchenyi-Centre of
Librarianship and Methodology)
Múzeum utca 3
H Budapest VIII

chiefly among the rural population. The most significant publication on this theme is "Ezer falusi lakos és a könyv" ("One thousand village-dwellers and the book").

Bibliography

Könyvolvasás és könyvvásárlás Magyarországon. Egy reprezentativ közvéleménykutatás eredményei. (The reading and buying of books in Hungary. Results of a representative public-opinion poll.) Budapest, KTTK (Information Centre of Publishers and Distributors of Books) 1965.

Mit olvasunk? 4,000 háztartás könyvolvasási adatai. (What do we read? Data on the reading of books in 4,000 households.) Budapest, Központi Statisztikai Hivatal 1965.

J. Ughy, *Ezer falusi lakos és a könyv.* (One thousand village-dwellers and the book.) Budapest, OSzK Könyvtártudományi és Módszertani Központ 1965.

10 Books and Young People

The *Móra Ferenc Ifjúsági Könyvkiadó (Móra Ferenc Publishing House for Youth Literature)*
Lenin körút 9–11
H Budapest VII

is responsible for the publication of children's and young people's books in Hungary. It publishes about 150–160 titles annually.

A "Department for Children's and Youth Literature" operates under the auspices of the *Magyar Irók Szövetsége*
(Hungarian Writers' Union)
Bajza utca 18
H Budapest VI

One of the Union's secretaries is the Chairman of the Department. The Department has several sections: for children's literature, youth literature, science fiction and popular science, as well as for criticism. The Department stages public debates every month in the course of which problems concerning children's and youth literature are discussed.

The central depot of works for children and young people is the

Országos Padagógiai Könyvtár
(National Library of Pedagogy)
Honvéd utca 20
H Budapest V

which also collects theoretical works, both Hungarian and foreign, dealing with youth literature. Every second month it publishes a journal, *Könyv és Nevelés* ("Books and Education") containing articles on aspects of literature for young people, on the psychology of reading, on the work of school libraries, etc. Within the framework of its work on bibliography and methodology the Library compiles and publishes the so-called "Bibliographies of subjects of instruction", richly annotated lists of reading matter for young people. These bibliographies are published in separate series for general and for secondary schools.

Bibliographies, grouped according to special subjects, are also published by

Fővárosi Szabó Ervin Könyvtár
(Municipal Szabó Ervin Library)
Szabó Ervin tér 1
H Budapest VIII

of which the network of children's libraries in the capital is a part.
For several semesters youth literature is a subject at independent and compulsory courses of teachers' training academies (at Eger, Pécs and Szeged) where teachers of Hungarian at general school level are trained. In teachers' training colleges for kindergarten teachers, youth literature is a compulsory subject as well.

11 Training

In Hungary the training of newcomers to the book trade differs for those who are to work in publishing and those to be engaged in distribution.
The latter are trained by the department for special training of the "Allami Könyvterjesztő Vállalat" ("National Enterprise for Book Distribution", → 24) as well as by the "Földmüvesszövetkezeti Könyvterjesztő Vállalat" ("Enterprises for Book Distribution of Cooperative Farms", → 24) with the same curriculum and equal tuition time.
The distribution trade only engages people over 18 who have completed their secondary schooling and matriculated. For a year they work as junior clerks in shops. For 30 weeks during that year they must attend a basic course twice a week (comprising 360–400 lessons). Having finished the course they sit for an examination, and having passed it they obtain a skilled worker's certificate, recognized by the state. The curriculum comprises special subjects (rudiments of book distribution, a general knowledge of books, booksellers' bibliography, publicity, branches of science and of industry and administration) as well as general subjects (Hungarian and world literature, contemporary literature, Russian or German language, the history of books and the book trade). In Budapest the pupils can attend day classes or take correspondence courses, whereas in the bigger provincial towns junior clerks in the book trade are trained in correspondence courses only. Having finished their one-year basic course, they can attend two-year continuation courses (for sheet music, for antiquarian bookselling, for technical books, etc.) at which experts give lectures on their special lines.
Publishers recruit young clerks from among university graduates. These attend a special one-year minimum course arranged by the "Kiadói Főigazagatóság" ("Chief Administration of Publishing", → 4) and pass an examination on the editor's work from the point of view of content and technique, knowledge of printing and legal questions, etc. This examination, however, does not qualify them. Up to 1967 the "Chief Administration of Publishing" provided training for publishers' technical staff (technical editors, art editors); since then, however, these specialists have been trained at a newly established department of the "Magyar Iparmüvészeti Főiskola" ("Hungarian Academy of Applied Arts").

14 Copyright

In Hungary Act No. LIV of 1921 protects copyright. The protection of copyright extends over 50 years following the author's death (in which the calendar year of death is not included). A new Hungarian Copyright Act is being prepared.
Hungary enacted the Rome version of the revised "Berne Convention" (1928). The agreement about the protection of works of art and literature concluded in Montevideo (1889) as well as the supplementary protocol (1889) were made law in Hungary in 1931. Argentina, Bolivia and Paraguay recognized Hungary's having joined the agreement.
A bilateral agreement about the mutual

protection of copyright has been in force between the United States of America and Hungary since 1912. This agreement has been confirmed after the Second World War by both contracting parties.
On 17 November 1967 government representatives of the Hungarian People's Republic and of the Soviet Union signed a bilateral agreement on the mutual protection of copyright. In force since 1 January 1968, the agreement extends provisionally over three years.

15 National Bibliography, National Library

In Hungary the
Országos Széchényi Könyvtár
(National Széchényi Library)
Múzeum körút 14–16
H Budapest VIII
founded in 1802, fulfils the tasks of a national library. The basic principles of its operation are determined by a decree issued in 1956 by the Government of the Hungarian People's Republic, which states: "The Országos Széchényi Könyvtár (henceforth abbreviated OSzK) in its capacity of a national library collects, keeps in display and discloses publications produced in Hungary; furthermore Hungarian authors' works published abroad, as well as publications with Hungarian references that are published abroad.
"Within the framework of its work in library science, methodology and bibliography, the OSzK prepares current and retrospective national bibliographies and a current repertory of articles in scientific journals.
"As an authority of libraries the OSzK is to fulfil the tasks entrusted to it with regard to copyright deposits."
The delivery of copyright deposits is regulated by a decree issued by the Government in 1951: "For scientific purposes copyright deposits are to be delivered, free of charge, of publications produced in Hungary by printing or multiplication processes in at least 25 copies. 16 copies of the publications are to be delivered as copyright deposits to the OSzK within 48 hours after their appearance."
Published by the OSzK the *Magyar Nemzeti Bibliográfia—Bibliographia Hungarica* ("Hungarian National Bibliography") is a bi-monthly list of books, sheet music, records and maps that have appeared in Hungary. The OSzK endeavours completely to catalogue, within the limits of possibility, the copyright deposits delivered to it. This material is published annually in a cumulative volume entitled *Magyr Könyvészet* ("Hungarian Bibliography"). The monthly supplement of "Magyr Nemzeti Bibliografia" entitled "Magyar Folyóiratok Repertóriuma—Repertorium Bibliographicum Hungaricum" ("Repertory of Hungarian Periodicals") is the bibliography of the articles published in general periodicals, scientific and special journals, and the three greatest Budapest dailies "Népszabadság", "Népszava", "Magyr Nemzet", → (27).
The supplement *A Hónap Könyvei* ("Books of the Month") in "Könyvtájékoztató" (→ 5) contains a bibliography of books on the market. The material of "A Hónap Könyvei" is published by the "KTTK" (→ 4) every year under the title *Altalános Könyvjegyzék* ("General List of Books"). "KTTK" also publishes *A Hónap Zeneművei* every other month. ("Sheet Music Publications of the Month".)
The quarterly periodicals published in three foreign languages and entitled "Books from Hungary"—"Bücher aus Ungarn"—"Livres de Hongrie" (→ 5) contain the three-monthly crop of Hungarian books.

16 Book Production

Book production in Hungary is constantly increasing, both as regards number of

titles and volumes published. This proves that the demand for reading matter is growing. In 1966 5,969 publications appeared in Hungary with a total of 54,979,544 copies, of which 4,660 (45,262,225 copies) were books (that is to say, publications of 49 or more pages), whereas the rest were brochures, sheet music, pictures and maps.
Broken down according to their subjects the books show the following distribution:

Subject group	Number of titles	copies
General works, library science, bibliography	142	2,424,653
Social sciences, economics	486	3,628,517
History, geography, ethnography	347	5,137,126
Pedagogy	164	784,534
Natural sciences, mathematics	495	4,660,924
Applied sciences	1,263	3,036,768
Commerce, transport	222	1,608,033
Fiction, youth literature	992	16,449,250
Arts	231	2,057,134
Linguistics	175	4,027,253
Religion, criticism of religion	38	338,664
Other subjects	105	1,070,370
Total	4,660	45,263,225

Bibliography

A magyar könyvkiadás. 1945–1959. (Hungarian book publishing. 1945–1959.) Compiled by J. Bak. Budapest, Kiadói Főigazgatóság (Chief Administration of Publishing) 1960.

J. Bak, *Husz év magyar könyvkiadása. 1945–1964.* (Twenty years of Hungarian book publishing. 1945–1964.) Budapest, Könyvkiadók és Terjesztők Tájekoztató Központja (Information Centre of Publishers and Distributors of Books) 1965.

17 Translations

From among 4,660 titles published in 1966 708 were translated from foreign languages and amounted to 8,516,162 copies.
Of the languages from which more than 10 titles had been translated into Hungarian, the following were the most important ones:

Language	No. of titles
Russian or other languages of the USSR	140
German	112
French	72
Czech and Slovak	66
American English	47
English	41
Romanian	39
Polish	29
Italian	12

In 1966 translations of 315 works of fiction and belles-lettres were published in Hungary (5,122,700 copies).

18 Book Clubs

At present there are no book clubs in Hungary, in the narrower sense of the word, which publish for their members publications that would not be available in the bookshops. However, there are some ventures run by publishers and distributing enterprises, with the characteristics of book clubs. They ensure for their members an allowance and permanent information on books they are particularly interested in or on works that deal with their special lines—if the members undertake to buy books for a fixed amount every year.
Ventures of this kind are the "Club for Technical Books", which operates within the framework of "Müszaki Kiadó" ("Publishers for Technical Literature"), and the "Circle of Friends of Agricultural Literature" run by the "Mezőgazdasági Kiadó" ("Publishers for Agricultural Literature"), as well as the "Friends of Gondolat Kiadó" ("Gondolat Publishing House"), which is

mainly engaged in publishing popular scientific works. The "Müvelt Nép Könyvterjesztő Vállalat" ("Cultured People") Book Distributing Company (→ 24) has "Women's Bookshelf", which provides for its members, at reduced prices, publications of interest chiefly for women. This organization is closest to book clubs in the real meaning of the word, for some of its books are supplied to members in bindings different from those available in the trade.

19 Paperbacks

The publication of contemporary Hungarian paperbacks was launched in the mid-1950s, although this type of book has had a considerable tradition in Hungary too. The paperbacks brought out in the last third of the 19th century, the "Olcsó könyvtár" ("Inexpensive Library") and later the "Magyar könyvtár" ("Hungarian Library") imitated the German "Reclam-Universal-Bibliothek". However, after the 1920s these series were no longer published.
The growing size of the reading public after the liberation of Hungary in 1945 made it necessary to publish inexpensive books in large numbers. The first series of modern paperbacks, the "Olcsó Könyvtár" ("Inexpensive Library"), was launched in 1954 and has, since then, remained the most popular. At first a new volume was brought out every week, later once fortnightly. The average number of copies for every title published is about 40–50,000. In 22 current series of paperbacks, 175 titles were published in 1966; they are mostly works of fiction, but there were also quite a number of popular scientific and specialist books ("Európa Paperbacks", "Minerva Paperbacks", etc.). At present the most important task for the publishers of Hungarian paperbacks is to raise standards; with a view to this several series have been started in recent years. In 1967 the covers and typography of the "Inexpensive Library" were modernized.

20 Book Design

Ever since 1957 a competition for the title "Most beautiful book of the year" has been staged annually in Hungary. All Hungarian publishers take part in the competition, which is sponsored by the "Kiadói Főigazgatóság" ("Chief Administration of Publishing", → 4). The jury, composed of leading figures in the publishing and printing trade, eminent typographers, illustrators and book designers, also acts as an advisory council.
Books entered for the final competition are chosen by separate committees consisting of two or three members. Once every three months, in consultation with the manager and technical staff, they discuss with each publishing house all of its books from the point of view of design.
A presidium of five and a working committee of twenty take part in the jury sessions, held at the end of the year. In the course of debates lasting a week the chosen books are discussed; out of the year's output about 40 books are awarded money prizes and about 50 receive honourable mention.
At the final session the committee summarizes the results achieved in the course of the year and points to possible shortcomings as well.
The list of prize-winning books is published in the press and the books themselves are displayed at an exhibition. Every year the "Chief Administration of Publication" publishes a richly illustrated brochure entitled *A szép magyar könyv* ("Beautiful Hungarian books"), which contains appraisals and reviews by members of the jury about the prize-winning books and about the work of publishers with regard to good book design and lay-out.

Hungary

Bibliography

A szép magyar könyv. (Beautiful Hungarian books.) Published annually since 1957.

Reports of the adjudicating committee of the competition of beautiful books have been published in the following numbers of the periodical *Magyar Grafika* ("Hungarian Graphic Arts"): 1959–2, 1960–2, 1961–2, 1962–2, 1964–2, 1965–2, 1966–2.

21 Publishing

The present pattern of Hungarian book publishing emerged in 1948 when, after the nationalization of the largest publishing houses, five great nationalized publishing houses came into being. In subsequent years all firms previously engaged in publishing were nationalized and the "Népmüvelési Minisztérium" (Ministry of Culture"), which was founded in 1949, took over the control of nationalized publishing houses.

Under the supervision of the "Ministry of Culture" the "Kiadói Főigazgatóság" ("Chief Administration of Publishing", → 4), which at present operates within the framework of the "Ministry of Cultural Affairs" and controls, according to the principles of the prevailing cultural policy, the publishing of books on a nationwide scale, was founded in 1954.

In 1955 the "Chief Administration of Publishing" merged some of the publishing houses into greater units with a view to achieving the necessary specialization. In 1966 there were 16 publishing houses operating in Hungary, 12 under the direct control of the "Chief Administration of Publishing" and the rest under various other scientific or social organizations. However, as far as the determination of general principles, the coordination of plans, the allocation of paper and printing capacity are concerned, these latter publishers are also under the aegis of the "Chief Administration of Publishing".

As regards their internal structure, publishing houses, as a rule, comprise three departments: editorial, technical and administrative. Some publishers, who deal with the distribution of books too, also have a smaller distributive staff. Editorial councils operate in affiliation with the publishing houses; acknowledged specialists in the lines in question are members of these councils.

The general guiding principles for the different branches of publishing are determined by the "Chief Administration of Publishing". According to these principles the publishers prepare annual as well as long-term plans for several years, indicating the works they wish to publish in different fields. When coordinating these plans the "Chief Administration of Publishing" decides to what extent they correspond with the guiding principles of cultural policy and readers' demands, and ascertains whether there is no overlapping in the plans. The initiative, however, lies with the publishers when drawing up their plans; they choose the books they want to bring out and they bear the responsibility for their contents.

After discussions with the distributing enterprises the publishers decide on the number of copies of each publication. If the two parties agree, the distributing enterprise takes over the book at its own risk. If no such agreement can be reached, the publisher delivers the book on a commission basis and—after a fixed period—the distributing enterprise returns the unsold stock to the publisher.

Prices of books are determined according to genre and size according to the following uniform principles and not their actual production costs. Thus different prices prevail for fiction and belles lettres, for youth and children's literature, for popular scientific, scientific and special

works. To arrive at a retail price for the different categories prices are set for one sheet and this price is multiplied by the number of sheets the volume contains. The retail prices of popular series are set even lower than the price per sheet. This means that some books are sold below their actual production price. And yet, globally, the publishing of books, does not show a deficit, because losses are covered by the profits of other books and the centralized structure of nationalized book publishing makes clearing between different publishing houses possible.
In addition to publishing houses, which publish books professionally, churches also bring out publications. Moreover, scientific institutes, universities, libraries and organizations of municipal councils may publish their own publications. Private persons, too, can publish their own works if they have them licensed by the "Chief Administration of Publishing".

22 Literary Agents

In Hungary any contracts concerning the international exploitation of copyright are concluded through the foreign department of the "Bureau Hongrois pour la Protection des Droits d'Auteur"

ARTISTJUS
Deák Ferenc utca 15
H Budapest V

which operates as an international agency of literature, drama and music (→ 7).
"ARTISTJUS" not only represents all Hungarian authors and their legal successors, but also acts as an intermediary between the holders of foreign copyright and Hungarian users of copyright. The "Bureau Hongrois pour la Protection des Droits d'Auteur" is a member of several international organizations.

23 Wholesale Trade

Due to the peculiarities of the Hungarian book trade the wholesale trade of books has a restricted role. The three great distributing enterprises (→ 24) buy the books from the publishers direct; only business enterprises that deal with books as merely a sideline (department stores, stationers' shops, toy shops and newsagents) avail themselves of the intermediate trade.
The wholesale department of the "Allami Könyvterjesztő Vállalat" ("National Enterprise for Book Distribution", → 24) supplies them.

24 Retail Trade

In 1957 the distributing enterprises sold books of a total value of 310 million forints, in 1966 this amount rose to 787.5 million forints. This means that in 1966 the *per capita* purchase of books in the country was 78 forints. The increase is the more significant as in the past decade books prices have remained essentially unchanged.
In 1966 there were altogether 357 bookshops in Hungary; 104 in the capital and 253 in the country. The bookshops sell only books, which means that great care can be taken to give readers a high standard of service and to give employees training in the trade.
A new and special feature of Hungarian book distribution is the widespread network of agents who sell the books on a commission basis in factories, industrial works, villages, at bookstalls in the streets, in schools and other public places. There are 15,000 people engaged in this work, either as a main occupation or as a sideline.
The distribution of books in Hungary is in the charge of three companies. The largest of them is the

Allami Könyvterjesztö Vállalat
(National Enterprise for Book Distribution)
Deák Ferenc utca 15
H Budapest V

In 1966 it had 1,506 employees. It has 70 bookshops in the capital and 75 in the country, of these 25 are second-hand bookshops (→ 26). Its most important task is the book trade in the capital, in industrial centres in the country and in busy resorts. It also tasks after the distribution of books in factories and deals with resale (→ 23). The supply of public libraries and the marketing of important books in foreign languages also fall in its domain. In 1966 the retail turnover of the "Enterprise" amounted to 419.7 million forints.

The

Müvelt Nép Könyvterjesztö Vállalat
("Cultured People"—
Book Distributing Company)
Népköztársaság útja 21
H Budapest VI

is chiefly engaged in distributing books through commission agents in factories, offices, etc., through circular letters and mail-orders (→ 25). It has 496 employees and gives work to about 5,000 people on a commission basis. It has 31 bookshops in Budapest and 33 in the provinces. In 1966 its turnover amounted to 99.8 million forints.

The

Földmüvesszövetkezeti Könyvterjesztö Vállalat (SZÖVKÖNYV)
(Enterprise for Book Distribution of Cooperative Farms)
Petöfi Sándor utca 3
H Budapest V

provides for the distribution of books in villages through 20 shops run by itself and 125 run by the cooperatives, as well as through the mail order service. The number of those who work for it on a commission basis (teachers, shopkeepers, employees in villages) is 9,900. The Enterprise has 680 employees of its own. The turnover it achieved in 1966 was 141.8 million forints.

The "Allami Könyvterjesztő Vállalat" ("National Enterprises for Book Distribution") and the Művelt Nép Könyvterjesztő Vállalat" ("Cultured People-Book Distributing Company") are under the direct control of the "Kiadói Főigazgatóság" ("Chief Administration of Publishing", → 4), whereas the supervising authority of "SZÖVKÖNYV" (Enterprise for Book Distribution on Co-Operative Farms") is the "Szövetkezetek Országos Központja" ("National Centre of Co-Operatives").

In addition to the three great distributing enterprises there are some privately owned bookshops.

25 Mail-Order Bookselling

Mail-orders are gaining ground too. All the three distributing enterprises (→ 24) have a "Books by mail" service.

26 Antiquarian Book Trade, Auctions

In Hungary the second-hand book trade has a dual task. On the one hand, with a view to completing the stock of the bookshops, it sells books second-hand, or books taken over in big lots and remaindered at about two thirds of the original price (the modern second-hand trade). Its other task is the sale of old publications, etchings and maps.

There are 15 antiquarian bookshops in Budapest and 10 in the provincial towns. They are all run by the (→ 24)

Allami Könyvterjesztö Vállalat
Országos Antikvár Osztály
(National Enterprise for Book Distribution National Department for Antiquarian Books)
Múzeum körút 21
H Budapest V

These shops only sell second-hand books.

In 1966 the antiquarian bookshops of the "National Enterprise for Book Distribution" achieved a turnover of 21.8 million forints; the total number of employees was 134.

27 Book Imports
28 Book Exports

KULTURA
Hungarian Trading Company for Books and Newspapers
Fö utca 32
H Budapest I

is in charge of the export and import of books in Hungary. The basic data of the 1966 turnover of the Company are:

Import of books:
1.8 million volumes valued at 61.118 million forints;

Import of periodicals:
6.6 million items for 43.390 million forints.

Export of books:
2.6 million volumes valued at 81.150 million forints;

Export of periodicals:
12.6 million items for 24.180 million forints.

As regards books, the main suppliers have been:

Country	Amount FT 1,000
Czechoslovakia	11,400
Yugoslavia	11,000
USSR	7,960
Germany (Democratic Republic)	6,940
Germany (Federal Republic)	5,720
United Kingdom	4,870
Bulgaria	4,600
Romania	2,060
USA	1,590
France	1,430

The most important buyers of Hungarian books have been:

Country	Amount FT 1,000
USSR	16,560
Germany (Democratic Republic)	14,050
Czechoslovakia	11,590
Yugoslavia	9,940
Romania	6,990
Germany (Federal Republic)	5,750
France	2,580
USA	2,430
Poland	2,420
United Kingdom	1,870

Hungarian authors' books brought out in joint editions with foreign publishers by

Akadémiai Kiadó
(Publishing House of the Hungarian Academy of Sciences)
Alkotmány utca 21
H Budapest V

as well as by

Corvina Kiadó
(Corvina Press)
Váci utca 12
H Budapest V

represent a particular form of the Hungary's book export. Readers of the foreign partner revise the translations of the works in question, but the printing is done in Hungary. The publication bears the emblem of the foreign publisher, who is entitled to distribute exclusively the work in the countries indicated in the agreement.

29 Book Fairs

The International Exhibition of Technical Books, staged annually by

Müszaki Könyvkiadó
(Publishers of Technical Literature)
Bajcsy-Zsilinszky út 22
H Budapest V

within the framework of the "Budapesti Nemzetközi Vásár" ("International Fair of Budapest") is a noteworthy event in the publishing and distribution of Hungarian technical literature. In 1967 90 publishers of technical books from 15 countries took part, displaying nearly 4,000 works. The interest of foreign publishing houses in the exhibition is increasing year by year.

30 Public Relations

The central publicity organization of the Hungarian book trade is the (→ 4)
Magyar Könyvkiadók
és Könyvterjesztök Egyesülése
(Hungarian Publishers'
and Booksellers' Association)
Vörösmarty tér 1
H Budapest V
Its publicity department is in charge of promoting the interests of the whole trade as well as running the three drives staged every year for selling books and popularizing literature.
Chronologically the first of these occasions is the "Költészet napja" ("Day of Poetry") held on 11 April, the birthday of Attila József, the greatest figure in twentieth-century Hungarian poetry, who had so tragic a life. The "Day of Poetry" is aimed at popularizing poetry; lyrical poetry has long been the most eminent genre in Hungarian literature.
The "Ünnepi Könyvhét" ("Book Week"), arranged late in May and early in June, has been going for several decades. It is the largest annual event for popularizing books and reading. Every year over 50 publications are published in connection with it; the solemn inauguration of "Book Week" is a cultural and social event; parallel with the central inauguration festival, celebrations are staged in the provincial towns too. The distributing enterprises (→ 24) set up several hundred bookstalls in the streets both in the capital and in provincial towns. Since one of the chief aims of "Book Week" is the popularization of living Hungarian literature, writers appear at bookstalls and write dedications into their books; several hundred meetings between writers and their readers are organized all over the country.
The latest publicity drive for books is connected with the Christmas season, which starts in the last week of November and lasts for five weeks, during which the "MKKE", the publishing houses and the distributors stimulate public interest in books through radio, the press and advertisements in the cinemas.
In addition to organizing the three annual book drives the "MKKE" maintains a close connection with radio, the press and television. The central publicity campaigns are completed by the publicity work of the publishers and the distributing enterprises. Apart from the drives mentioned above, there are additional publicity campaigns for the book trade, of a more specialized nature.

31 Bibliophily

In 1966 the
Magyar Bibliofil Társaság
(Hungarian Society of Bibliophiles)
Bródy Sándor utca 16
H Budapest VIII
was reorganized within the framework of the "Tudományos Ismeretterjesztő Társulat" ("Society for the Propagation of Popular Science"). The Society fosters an interest in the cultural treasures of world and Hungarian literature, in beautiful volumes worthy of their contents. In return for their membership dues, members of the Society (about 350 in 1967) receive numbered, autographed volumes.

32 Literary Prizes

Hungarian literary prizes are aimed, first and foremost, at expressing society's appreciation of a writer's *œuvre* or of his work over a considerable period of time. That is why they do not exert so direct an influence on the success of a book with the reading public or on its sales in bookshops as, for example, prizes do in France.

The most important literary prizes are:

The "Kossuth Prize", bestowed by the Government; it has three grades and is generally awarded every three years.

The "József Attila Prize", awarded yearly by the Minister of Cultural Affairs; it has three grades.

The "SZOT Prize", awarded annually by the "Trades Unions Council".

33 The Reviewing of Books

Hungarian dailies and literary weeklies consider it an important task to review new books. Once a week the three national dailies (*Népszabadság, Magyar Nemzet, Népszava*) have book reviews several columns in extent; they also reserve space for more extensive criticism on different works. The literary journals *(Kortárs, Uj Irás, Elet és Irodalom, Nagyvilág, Valoság, Jelenkor, Alföld, Tiszatáj)* always have book reviews and publish criticisms of new books; these help to formulate public opinion.

Of particular importance for the book trade is the (→ 5)

Könyvtájékoztató
(Information on Books)
Deák Ferenc utca 15
H Budapest V

published by the "Information Centre of Publishers and Distributors of Books" (→ 4).

34 Graphic Arts

The central organization for the sale, both on the domestic and on foreign markets, of the work of Hungarian artists and illustrators is the

Magyar Népköztársaság
Képzömüészeti Alapja
(Fine Arts Fund of the Hungarian People's Republic)
Báthory utca 10
H Budapest V

This organization gives information on all questions bearing on works of the graphic arts.

Iceland

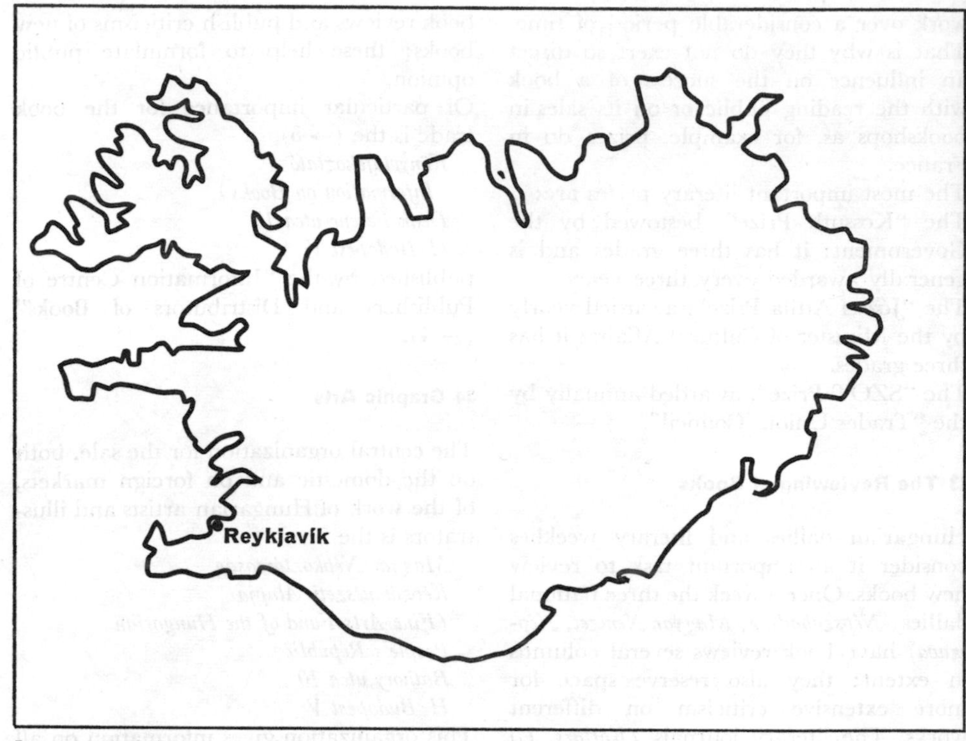

Important Book Centres

1 General Information

Area 102,846 km²
Population 200,000 (1968) (2 per km²)
Capital Reykjavík (78,309)
Largest towns Reykjavík (78,309); Akureyri (9,642); Kópavogur (9,204); Hafnarfjördur (8,135); Keflavik (5,128); Vestmannaeyjar (5,012)
Government Republic (since 17 June 1944)
Religion Evangelical Lutheran Church: over 90% Roman Catholic and smaller religious groups: 7%
National language Icelandic
Leading foreign languages English, Danish
Weights, measures Metric system
Currency unit Icelandic krona (I.kr.)
Education Compulsory and free for all children between the ages of 7 and 15 years. 1,158 undergraduates (1965–6) at the University of Iceland, Reykjavík, of whom 283 are women and 40 foreigners
Illiteracy Nil
Paper consumption a) Newsprint 11.5 kg per inhabitant (1968)
b) Printing paper (othe than newsprint) 6.4 kg per inhabitant (1967)
Membership UNESCO, IPA

2 Past and Present

Long before the advent of the art of printing in Europe, Icelanders wrote books which were in later centuries fated to bring them renown the world over. The thousand-year history of the Icelanders testifies to their relentless passion for writing; they have been more energetic in their copying of books than most other nations, no less so when they were most harassed in the economic field and the population was less than a third of what it is today. The first written book on record in Iceland was the law code "Vígslódi" (A.D. 1118), and the writing of history in Icelandic commenced in the years immediately following with "Islendingabók" ("The Book of the Icelanders") by Ari Thorgilsson the Learned. After the early years of the 13th century the making of books may be said to have increased to a considerable extent. Then the Icelandic family Sagas began to appear: the famous historical work "Heimskringla" by Snorri Sturluson and the ancient poetic "Edda" (or "Elder Edda") were committed to parchment. The period ranging from about 1300 until the early 15th century is the era when vellum books flourished in Iceland.

Printing and paper came to Iceland in the 16th century. The last Catholic Bishop of Hólar, Jón Arason, bought a printing office abroad in about 1525, whereupon the printing of books commenced. About 1600 there existed numerous printed books in Iceland, including a complete translation of the Bible (1584), and in the 17th century a total of 196 books and booklets were printed at Hólar and Skálholt.

Printing was monopolized by the Church and publishing was in the care of the bishops until the close of the 18th century. The publishing activities of the episcopal sees were almost entirely restricted to religious literature, so that secular literature desired by the public, such as tales and narrative works (rímur), remained unprinted. The Icelanders therefore continued to copy books with singular industry and application long after this had become an obsolete method in other countries, and the output was more extensive than before, as paper was now used for this purpose. Thus copying continued in Iceland during the 17th and 18th centuries and far into the 19th, even after printed stories became available.

Throughout these centuries the printing and sale of books was in the hands of the same people. Travelling salesmen frequently took books around on horseback or on foot. Publishers generally dispatched these men on sales excursions without laying down any general rules to regulate their activity. It was not until the "Icelandic Booksellers' Association" was founded in 1889 that publishers formed a union and appointed agents in various parts of the country. In the year the Association was founded there were 32 of them, and on its 75th anniversary there were 93 retailers, 18 of them in Reykjavík. But to the present day publishers deal directly with booksellers and other retail outlets, as there is no central distribution of Icelandic books. Booksellers do, on the other hand, have an import union for foreign books, periodicals and papers.

Bibliography

B. S. Benedikz, *The spread of printing: Iceland.* Amsterdam, Vangendt 1969. 64 pp.—p. 64: short bibliography.

J. Helgason, *Handritaspjall.* (Causerie on manuscripts). Reykjavík, Mál og menning 1958. 118 pp.

H. Hermannsson, *Icelandic books of the sixteenth and of the seventeenth centuries.* In: Islandica 1916–1917.

Islandica. An annual relating to Iceland and the "Fiske Icelandic Collection" in Cornell University Library. Ithaca.

3 Retail Prices

In Iceland the retail prices of books are fixed. An association of publishers authorizes booksellers to operate in various places and concludes contracts with them. At the same time the bookseller will pledge a personal guarantee of one or more individuals or security in the form of real estate in respect of debts arising out of commission sales. In each individual case the bookseller may decide whether he buys a book on cash terms at a sales discount of 30% or conducts the business on the basis of a 20% commission, in which case he must render settlement once a year. There have been discussions on an amendment to the effect that more of the business should be done on a cash basis or that settlement should be effected more frequently, e.g. twice a year.

4 Organization

Under an amended law of 1952 the

Bóksalafélag Islands
(Icelandic Booksellers' Association)
c/o Valdimar Jóhannsson
Skeggjagötu 1
IS Reykjavík

is clearly defined as an association of publishers to negotiate arrangements with the

Félag íslenzkra bókaverzlana
(Association of Icelandic Bookshops)
c/o Lárus Blöndal
Skólavördustíg 2
IS Reykjavík

which had recently been established at the time. The association of publishers therefore decides as before who may become bookseller, and only those bookstores which have been approved may become members of the "Association of Icelandic Bookshops". The object of the "Association of Icelandic Bookshops" is to strengthen the cooperation of members and to protect their trade.

The

Innkaupasamband bóksala n.f.
(The Booksellers' Import Union, Ltd.)
Brautarholt 16
IS Reykjavík

was established in 1956. The Union undertakes the importation of foreign books and periodicals and their distribution to the booksellers who make up the Union. The "Icelandic Booksellers' (Publishers') Association" has an executive board of 7; the "Association of Icelandic Bookshops" a board of 3. The boards are elected for one year at a time.

5 Trade Press
6 Book-Trade Literature

7 Sources of Information, Address Services

The "Landsbókasafn Islands" ("Icelandic National Library", → 15) issues an annual report on the publication of books and periodicals in Iceland. This is the chief source of information, but the "Booksellers' Association" (→ 4) has also issued an annual book list since 1930.
In Iceland there is no specialized publication on book news or the production or sale of books. There are, on the other hand, several literary periodicals with regular book news and reviews of Icelandic books. These include *Skírnir* (established 1827), the annual publication of the

Hid íslenzka bókmenntafélag
(The Icelandic Literary Society)
c/o Sigurdur Líndal
Bergstadastraeti 76
IS Reykjavík

and the quarterlies *Eimreidin* (1905), *Tímarit Máls og Menningar* (1940) and *Birtingur* (1953).
The addresses of publishers and booksellers are contained in *Bóksalafélag Islands sjötíu og fimm ára*, obtainable from "Bóksalafélag Islands" (→ 4). The "State Broadcasting Service" frequently broad-

casts news of recently published Icelandic books, inviting authors or others to give readings from their works.

Bibliography

Bóksalafélag Islands sjötíu og fimm ára. 1889—12. janúar—1964. (Icelandic Booksellers' Association, 75th anniversary.) Reykjavík, Bóksalafélag Islands 1964. 60 pp.

8 International Membership

In 1956 the "Icelandic Booksellers' (Publishers') Association" (→ 4) enrolled as a member of the "International Publishers' Association". After Iceland became a signatory to the "Berne Convention" on 7 September 1947 it undertook to abide by the rules and regulations contained in the Convention. When the Universal Copyright Convention entered into force on 16 September 1955 a bill to the effect that Iceland should become a party thereto was presented, and this was enacted in that year. Previously, in the course of the debate on the "Berne Convention", it was maintained that despite the fact that the "Icelandic Booksellers' (Publishers ers') Association" did not dispute copyright and Icelandic publishers generally endeavoured to reach agreement with foreign authors on the translation of their works, Icelandic publishers were evidently incapable of effecting such high payments for the translation rights of books by foreign authors as are customary among larger nations, owing to the small population of Iceland.

Icelandic publishers and bookshops have now and again participated in international book exhibitions, among them the "Frankfurt Book Fair", and held exhibitions of foreign books at Reykjavík. They have also been in contact and have cooperated with foreign publishers.

→ 14.

10 Books and Young People

A special state institute supplies children with textbooks free of charge. It was established in 1937 by an Act revised in 1956

Ríkisútgáfa námsbóka
(The State Educational Publishing Department)
Tjarnagötu 10
IS Reykjavík

according to an "Act of Parliament", revised in 1956. Since then all children aged 7–15 have equal rights to get free textbooks, regardless of where they live in the country.

The activities of the "State Educational Publishing Department" can be divided into three chief parts:

(1) The publishing of the proper textbooks which are delivered free of charge to the pupils or the schools.

The expenses of the publishing of these books are paid in the following way:

$^1/_3$ is payable by the State, $^2/_3$ is paid by means of a special textbook tax levied on all those who support one or more children in compulsory school.

(2) The publishing of various handbooks or manuals and teaching material for use in the schools to give study more variety. These articles are usually sold at approximate cost price as their publication is not financed by the State or by the textbook tax.

(3) A store for school supplies. The "State Educational Publishing Department" runs a special store for school supplies.

In other respects the publishing of books for children and youth has not been organized, but several publishing houses engage in this field. Only one publishing house, "Youth" (Aeskan) has specialized in books for children and teenagers. One children's magazine of the same name, established in 1899, has long been popular and publishes 9 issues annually, with a circulation of 15,000.

Iceland

11 Training

There are no special requirements for the training of those engaging in bookselling and there is no special school in that field.

12 Taxes

Iceland has a free flow of books. Consequently there are no import dues on books or periodicals, but there is a general sales tax of 11 %.

14 Copyright

An Act relating to copyright came into force in Iceland in 1905; since then this Act has been revised several times. The provisions of this Act covered literary and musical compositions only. Under an Act of 1912 it was decreed that the protection should extend also to illustrations and drawings of artistic value. The most important amendment was made by an Act of 1943, under which the sphere of copyright was greatly widened and extended to all works of art.

It may be said that under the present copyright laws of Iceland the protection of authors is comparable to that of most other nations, and the legislation was deemed sufficient to satisfy the demands imposed by the "Berne Convention" upon member countries. The Scandinavian countries, Denmark, Finland, Norway and Sweden, have recently cooperated in compiling a copyright law. Icelandic legislation is also undergoing revision and a new bill has been drafted, but not yet enacted.

Iceland became a signatory to the "Berne Convention" in 1947 and ratified the "Universal Copyright Convention" in 1956. Iceland was also one of the states represented at the "Rome Congress" of 1961 and voted for the "International Convention for the Protection of Performers, Producers of Phonograms and Broadcasting Organizations" (→ 8).

Copyright ceases to be valid 50 years after the death of an author.

STEF Samband tónskálda og eigenda flutningsréttar
(Federation of Composers and Copyright Owners)
Bókhlödustíg 2
IS Reykjavík

was founded in 1948 and given legal performance rights over musical compositions. Authors have not established an organization to operate in the same fashion as STEF, but the

Rithöfundasamband Islands
(Authors Association)
Vesturgötu 25
IS Reykjavík

has formed a special federation which has concluded a contract with the "State Broadcasting Service", relating to payment to authors.

Bibliography

Pordur Eyjolfsson, *Lagastafir.* (Letters of law.) Reykjavík, Hladbúd 1967, 331 pp.

15 National Bibliography, National Library

The

Landsbókasafn Islands
(National Library of Iceland)
Safnahúsinu vio Hverfisgötu
IS Reykjavík

was established in 1818 under the name of "Stiftsbókasafnid".

In law the object of the library is:

"to undertake the collection and preservation of Icelandic writings and writings relating to Iceland or Icelandic subjects of ancient and current origin, printed and unprinted;

to maintain a collection of foreign literature in all branches of science, art, technology and current affairs;

to undertake research into Icelandic bibliography;

to disseminate information about Icelandic literature and culture abroad . . ."
All printers in Iceland have to furnish the "National Library" with 12 free copies of each book, 4 copies of all leaflets and 8 copies of periodicals. All Icelandic books and other printed matter should therefore be available in the "National Library", which also preserves an extensive collection of manuscripts.
Of the obligatory copies the "National Library" has to preserve two, one must be supplied to the "University Library" and one to the "North Country Library" at Akureyri. The "National Library" sends other obligatory copies to libraries and scientific institutions.
Until the last few decades the "National Library" was the nation's only educational library, but by now there have come into being, or are about to do so, several other educational libraries. The largest of these is the "University Library", which is also located in Reykjavík.
Since 1944 the "National Library of Iceland" has been publishing *Arbók Landsbókasafnsins*, a year book with a list of all books, papers and periodicals received during the preceding year, as well as articles on bibliographic subjects.

Bibliography

Landsbókasafn Islands. Arbók. National Library of Iceland. Year Book.

16 Book Production
17 Translations

Icelanders have gained renown for books, and it will be difficult to find a nation that has a better record for book reading. This has been true throughout the country's history. During the present century publishing has been greatly augmented, particularly in recent decades, although the increase has been only slight in the last few years.

When the 75th anniversary of the "Icelandic Booksellers' Association" was about to take place a detailed register of books published in Iceland from 1888 until 1962 was compiled and published in the Association's anniversary report (1964). A mention must be made of the fact that tracts and booklets exceeding 16 pages are included in the list. "Iceland 1966" (a handbook published by the "Central Bank of Iceland") draws conclusions from this report and comments:
"The decade 1941–1950 saw by far the largest expansion in Icelandic publishing history. The total output during that ten-year span was 4,781 books, ranging from 302 titles in 1942 to 603 titles in 1946 (an all-time record). In those ten years there appeared 262 Icelandic works of fiction, 821 translated works of fiction, 256 collections of Icelandic poetry, and 13 anthologies of translated poems".
The last decade, 1951–1960, was similar in output to the preceding one: 4,927 books, ranging from 427 in 1953 to 546 in 1958. During that decade there were 272 Icelandic works of fiction, 506 translated works of fiction, 301 collections of Icelandic poetry, and 22 anthologies of translated poems.
During the 75 years from 1888 to 1962 the total number of books published in Iceland was 17,642. Out of these there were 1,006 Icelandic works of fiction, 2,155 translated works of fiction, 1,156 collections of Icelandic poetry, and 74 anthologies of translated poems. Of other categories the most prolific were: educational books, 1,026; religious books, 869; translated children's books, 848; and biographies, 810.
It may be added that during the same period some 870 Icelandic books were published in Canada and about 950 in Copenhagen. Translations of Icelandic books abroad during the same period were: Germany, 330 titles, Norway, 160,

Sweden, 130, England, 120, USA, nearly 100, and other countries, about 260.
After deducting tracts and booklets and including only books of 48 pages and over, it will be found that in recent years an average of about 350 book titles have been published annually. Despite the growth of the population the publishing of books remains static, but the number of copies printed is considerably smaller than before. The average number of copies printed is 1,500 and only a few books each year are printed in runs of over 3,000.
During 1967 631 titles (including pamphlets) were published. These included:

Subject group	Titles
Belles lettres	209
Social sciences	188
Geography, History	81
Applied sciences	66

The Icelandic title production (including pamphlets) of 1967 contained 160 translations from foreign languages, mostly English.

18 Book Clubs

The oldest existing literary association in Iceland, "Hid islenzka bókmenntafelag" ("The Icelandic Literary Society"), was established in 1816; it is thus 155 years old. The Society has published an annual, "Skírnir", since 1827. The Society was organized for the restoration of the Icelandic language and literature while Iceland was under Danish rule. During this extended period the Society has discharged much work of national importance and published good books, but rarely more than 2–3 a year, due to the low membership subscription. In recent years the Society has increased its publications. During the present century three more literary associations have appeared on the scene.

The first one

Bókmenntafélagid Mál og menning
(The Book Society Language and Culture)
Laugavegi 18
IS Reykjavík

was formed in 1937 at a time of financial depression, when it was difficult to procure books. Young radical authors applied themselves to the poverty-stricken public, inviting cooperation to reduce the price of books and offering a solution by means of organizing an association to publish six books annually at very reasonable prices. The response was enthusiastic beyond all hopes. A membership of over 5,000 was enrolled. The population at the time was less than 150,000 and, estimating 4–5 readers per copy, it may be concluded that nearly every sixth Icelander read the society's books.
Two years later the Legislative Assembly formed

Bókaútgáfa Menningarsjóds og þjódvinafélagsins
(The Publishing Department of the Cultural Fund)
Hverfisgötu 21
IS Reykjavík

on the same basis as "Mál og menning". This literary society, being supported by the State, could offer still better terms, and their membership was even greater for a time, without reducing the growth of "Mál og menning". But this abnormal membership was not retained for long. Both societies have the disadvantage that members do not have a choice of books, and the low annual fee of I.kr. 600–650 left little room for diversified publishing activities. However, the societies engage in general publishing operations as well, granting discounts to their members.
In 1955 a public literary association

Almenna Bókafélagid
(The General Book Society)
Austurstræti 18
IS Reykjavík

was organized on a new basis. It does not charge an annual fee, but membership rights are subject to the purchase of any 4 books published by the association each year. In return members are granted a 20% discount off the publication price.
This association has a membership of 5–6,000.
Together these literary societies publish 50–60 books annually and their aggregate membership is about 15,000.

19 Paperbacks

Inexpensive editions of this type have been attempted but have not been a success. The market is too limited. Besides, the people of Iceland seem to be more inclined than those of other countries to collect books for keeps, and so they desire elaborate editions, well bound, and printed on quality paper. In the neighbouring countries, e.g. Scandinavia, paperbacks are gaining ground, and foreign paperbacks are widely bought by Icelanders. There must therefore be a demand for inexpensive and simple editions, and further attempts in this field must evidently be made by Icelandic publishers.

20 Book Design

There are frequent complaints to the effect that books are not being sufficiently well finished in Iceland, although considerable advances have been made in that respect during past decades. Bookbinding is often criticized, but bookbinders' equipment in Iceland is of poorer quality than in many other countries. It must, however, be admitted that there is an increased interest in elaborate finish and the beautiful appearance of books, and several publishers have endeavoured to produce quality books. It was not until 1965 than an exhibition was held to show "the best-produced books of the year" along with the best books selected in Sweden, Norway, Denmark and Switzerland. The

Félag íslenzkra teiknara
(Association of Icelandic Draftsmen)
c/o Gísli B. Björnsson
Lindargötu 9
IS Reykjavík

sponsored the exhibition, and various professional associations displayed an interest in this matter, nominating their representative to a panel of judges to discuss the material quality of the books and pass judgement on them. Another exhibition was held during 1968.

21 Publishing

There are at present 50 publishing firms in Iceland, most of them in Reykjavík. Numerous individuals also publish books now and again, and they include writers—poets in particular. Of the 50 firms of publishers 34 publish fewer than 6 books annually, 13 publish 6–20 books annually and three firms 20–40 books. Sales figures can thus be analysed as follows: 34 publishing firms, or 68%, effect annual sales of less than I.kr. 1 million; 13 publishers or 26% annually sell books worth for I.kr. 1–5 million and 3 firms, or 6%, a total value of I.kr. 5–10 million a year.
Several of the largest publishing houses have their own printing works and bookbinding facilities, or operate their own bookshops. Publishers employ about 360 people apart from those engaged in the publishing of newspapers and periodicals, but in 1962 a total of 265 newspapers and periodicals was published in Iceland.
About 1,150 people are engaged in the production of books, periodicals and papers.

24 Retail Trade

There are no wholesale booksellers in Iceland. Publishers are in direct contact with bookshops or salesmen. They send 2, 5, 10 or 20 copies of each new book to booksellers, who have an option of accepting these on a commission basis or against cash payment (→ 3). Many of the larger bookshops also sell foreign books, periodicals and weeklies, as well as stationery, and most of them sell Icelandic weeklies.

The annual turnover of 10 of the 16 bookshops in Reykjavik is between I.kr. 1 and 5 million; 4 stores have an annual turnover of I.kr. 5–10 million and two between I.kr. 10 and 20 million. (These are 1967 figures.)

Travelling salesmen occasionally collect subscriptions to specific editions—larger works in particular; for instance, a large number of subscriptions to foreign encyclopedias has been collected in this way. Icelandic publishers do also now and then dispatch salesmen to offer their books for sale.

26 Antiquarian Book Trade, Auctions

There are 5 second-hand bookshops in Reykjavík. Book auctions, particularly of old and rare books, are also held 3–4 times a year or so.

27 Book Imports

The importation of books, papers and periodicals has greatly increased since the end of World War II.

In 1969 the book imports amounted to I.kr. 21.162 million and the largest suppliers were:

Country	Amount I.kr.1,000
Denmark	6,592
United Kingdom	3,941
USA	3,019
Netherlands	2,424
Germany (F.R.)	2,005
Switzerland	1,646

The importation of books has, on the other hand, fluctuated a great deal in recent years. In 1964, for example, the total imports amounted to I.kr. 14.7 m.; of these books from the United States were worth I.kr. 6 m.; but in 1966 the total figure was I.kr. 53.5 m.; books from the United States were worth I.kr. 41.1 m. Imports of books from Denmark, Great Britain and other countries have, on the other hand, remained steady during all these years. The explanation is to be found in the importation of encyclopedias from the United States, the "Encyclopaedia Britannica" in particular, to which there were thousands of subscriptions during these years.

Imports of newspapers and periodicals have been much more even from one year to another. In 1969 these amounted to I.kr. 19.7 m., the three largest supplier countries being:

Country	Amount I.kr. 1,000
Denmark	13,887
Germany (F. R.)	3,028
United Kingdom	1,674

As mentioned above, foreign books, newspapers and periodicals are not subject to import duty.

28 Book Exports

It goes without saying that exports of Icelandic books are practically nil, for only a very small number of people abroad read Icelandic, though a considerable number of Icelanders live in Canada and Denmark. Only a few libraries, universities and scientists abroad are buyers of Icelandic books. Very few books are printed in Iceland in foreign languages. A mention may, however, be made of two editions on the volcanic eruption at Surtsey:

"Surtsey" by Sigurdur Thorarinsson, and "The Surtsey Eruption" by Thorleifur Einarsson. Surtsey is the island which was suddenly formed off the south coast of Iceland and has attracted world-wide attention. These books were printed in Icelandic and also in English, Danish and German; the number of copies was unusually high (35–40,000). The same is true of a book about Reykjavík. Books like these are mainly intended for tourists, but also for sale abroad. A few books on Iceland are also printed in foreign languages, e.g. "Facts about Iceland" has been printed in large numbers. All the same, it is hardly possible to speak of any exports of books. Two periodicals in English are being published

Iceland Review
tímarit og útgáfustarfsemi
Laugavegi 18a
IS Reykjavík

a quarterly, and

65°
Laugavegi 59
IS Reykjavík

32 Literary Prizes

Literary prizes have been rare, and there are no literary funds. Individual publishers have now and again given prizes for specific books, and two years ago newspaper critics initiated a prize, a silver horse, for what in their opinion was the best book of the year. Iceland also participates in the annual award of the "Nordic Council's" literary prize.

Ireland

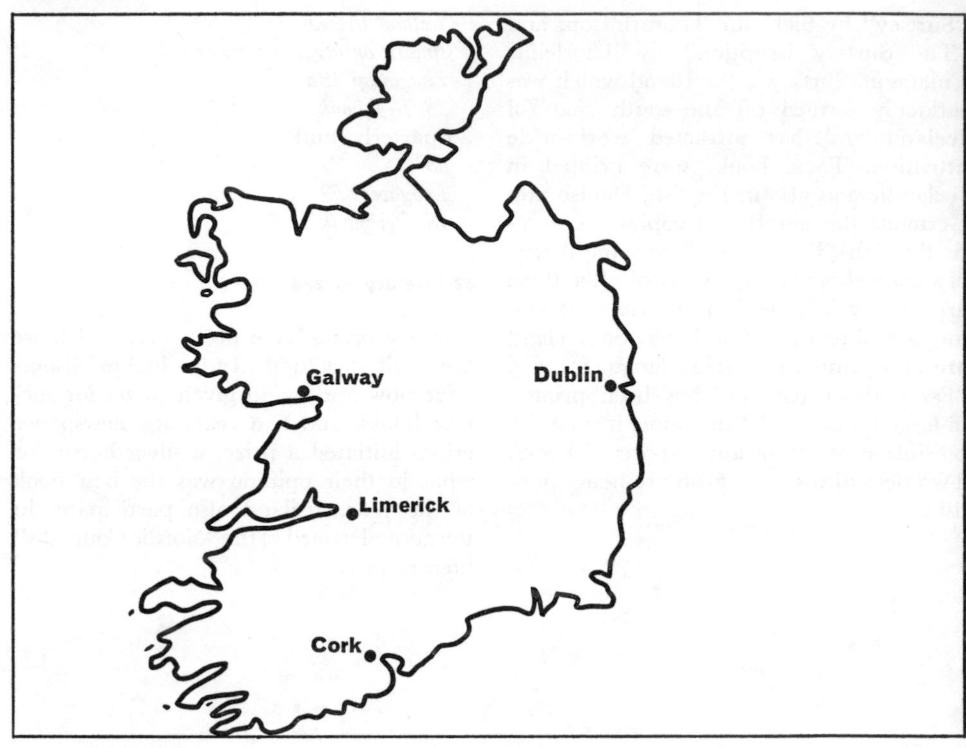

Important Book Centres

1 General Information

Area 84,000 km²
Population 2,884,002 (1966) (33 per km²)
Capital Dublin (718,332)
Largest towns Dublin (718,332); Cork (218,126); Galway (149,887); Limerick (82,553)
Government Republic (since 1949)
Religions Roman Catholic 94.3 %
Anglican, Presbyterian, and other smaller religious groups 5.0 %
Dissidents 0.7 %
National languages English; Irish (or Gaelic) is spoken in some small parts of the West, Southwest and Northwest mainly
Leading foreign languages French, Spanish and German
Weights, measures metric
Currency unit Ir. £ (= 100 p)
Education Compulsory and free for all children between the ages of 7 and 14 years. Free for all children to the age of 18 years. There are four universities in the country, viz.: University College Dublin, University College Cork, University College Galway, and Trinity College Dublin.
Illiteracy Nil
Paper consumption a) Newsprint 17.0 kg per inhabitant (1964)
b) Printing paper (other than newsprint) 4.5 kg per inhabitant (1964)
Membership UNESCO (→ 8)

2 Past and Present

The earliest Irish books are in manuscript form, and date from the 8th century. They include the famous "Book of Kells" and the "Book of Durrow". The first book printed in Ireland was "Aibidal Gaoidheilige et Caillicosma", dated 1571. From then on, printing and publishing was largely concentrated in Dublin, then under British domination, which accounts for the fact that most books were printed in the English language. Ireland has had a reasonably flourishing publishing industry ever since then. During the 17th and 18th centuries there was quite a lot of "illegal" publishing, as the British authorities rigorously suppressed all pro-Irish and pro-Catholic publishing. Nevertheless the output of this kind of publishing continued to grow, even though many of the books had to be printed on the continent, and it reached its zenith during the 19th century, when the British "Penal Laws" were relaxed. During the 19th century, and well into the present century, Ireland became the centre of Catholic publishing in the English-speaking world. This kind of publishing still flourishes in Ireland today, although the leadership has gone to the USA. As in Britain, the printer became a publisher, and then had to open a shop to sell his books. For quite some time this position was maintained, and printer-publisher-bookselling establishments flourished in Dublin, Cork, Galway and Limerick. During this century, specialization set in, and, with a very few exceptions the roles of printer, publisher and bookseller are now separated.

Bibliography

→ United Kingdom, 2, 5, 6.

3 Retail Prices

The retail prices of books are fixed by the publishers. Most books are sold by their publishers on a firm basis at a discount of $33^1/_3\%$. In a few cases publishers offer, in the hope of stimulating sales, books "on sale or return" at the same discount rate. Publishers generally will not accept the return of unsold copies unless they have agreed in advance to the "on sale" terms. Credit terms are 30 days for settlement of accounts.

4 Organization

When the "Booksellers' Association of Great Britain and Ireland" was founded (→ United Kingdom, 4) in Great Britain during the nineteenth century, a branch was established in Dublin very shortly afterwards, and this continues to operate in Ireland because most of the books sold in Irish bookshops are published in Great Britain:

The Booksellers' Association of
Great Britain and Ireland
28/29 Nassau Street
IRL Dublin C 2

Through this large organization the Irish booksellers are enabled to negotiate terms of discount and work in contact with the (British) "Publishers' Association" (→ United Kingdom, 4), a group which technically controls the licensing of bookselling premises even in Ireland. In fact, the supply of books to retail outlets is largely in the hands of Irish wholesale firms, and some of the Irish publishers decide for themselves (mainly on a credit-status basis) where their books will be sold. Paperback editions are sold, for instance, in hotel foyers, supermarkets and at airport terminals.

The

Irish Publishers' Association
179, Pearse St.,
IRL Dublin, 2

was formed in 1969. The government's "Department of Education" supplies the "Association" with advance educational

syllabuses, so that textbooks may be prepared in advance for school purposes.
In 1964 the government's "Department of Education" organized a library scheme for the primary schools, circulating a list of what was considered to be basic titles for children between the ages of 7–14 years. Each school was allowed to requisition the titles it thought most suitable for its children. After a trial period, however, the direct purchase of books ceased, and the administration of the school libraries passed over to the County Libraries. Free school textbooks are provided for children whose parents are needy. The distribution of these free texts is left entirely to the discretion of each headmaster, and no details are available of the extent to which it is made use of.

5 Trade Press

The English-language book-trade papers of Great Britain and the United States are in general use (→ United Kingdom, 5; vol. II: USA, 5).

6 Book Trade Literature

As in the case of the trade press, the special literature of Great Britain (→ United Kingdom, 6) may be consulted.

7 Sources of Information, Address Services

Inquiries about book-trade questions are handled by the "Irish Publishers' Association" (→ 4) or by the "Publishers' Association" or the "Booksellers' Association of Great Britain and Ireland" (→ United Kingdom, 4).

8 International Membership

Through individual memberships of Irish publishers, booksellers and antiquarian booksellers to the respective British associations (→ United Kingdom, 4, 26) the Irish book trade is affiliated to IPA, ICBA, and ILAB.

11 Training

There is no special Irish training course for young people entering the book trade. This is usually met by a period of apprenticeship of no fixed duration.

12 Taxes

There is no tax on books entering Ireland, but the bookseller must provide for "Turnover Tax", a sales tax of 5%. Imports of foreign-made paper (except newsprint) are liable to a duty of 30%. In view of the size of the publishing industry, the Irish-made paper mills cannot provide a wide enough range of qualified paper to satisfy the requirements of the publisher of specialized books. If a publisher is able to show that 75% of a book printed on an imported paper has been exported, he can claim a rebate of the duty paid. This, however, is a lengthy process, requiring great patience and careful records.

14 Copyright

Copyright is automatic on publication. Ireland became a signatory to the "Berne Convention" in 1947 and signed the "Universal Copyright Convention" in 1956. Copyright ceases 50 years after the death of an author. There is no "Society of Irish Authors", but many Irish writers are members of The Irish Academy of Letters, c/o The Abbey Theatre, Dublin.

15 National Bibliography, National Library

A national bibliography is not, as yet, being published. Information on books on Ireland or books by Irish authors in English or Irish may be obtained free of charge from

The Director
The National Library of Ireland
Kildare Street
IRL Dublin 2

In the "National Library" every effort is made to ensure that a copy of every book on Ireland or by Irish writers is readily available to students from its shelves. The catalogue cards of the National Library form a basic national bibliography, but so far they have not been issued in volume form.

16 Book Production

Ireland's annual book production varies between 150 and 200 titles. The leading categories are religion and the social sciences.
In 1967 Irish publishers produced 233 titles with 55 titles on literature, 50 on religion, 40 on social sciences, and 36 on geography and history.

17 Translations

Between 5 to 10% of the country's annual book production consist of translations taken from various languages.
The number of translated titles was 16 in 1967, all of them in the field of religion.

18 Book Clubs

At present there is only one book club in Ireland, "An Club Leabhar", with a membership of some 2,000 readers of modern Gaelic literature. The club publishes between 6 and 12 books each year of poetry, fiction and biography. It is subsidized by a yearly grant from government funds.

19 Paperbacks

As British publishers have free entry to the Irish market, the full range of British paperbacks is available in stores throughout the country. Irish publishers on the whole did not enter into competition in this field until one firm published a series of Irish folklore and novel reprints in 1960. Since then several publishers have added paperback editions to their lists. The firm which began this trend has now almost 300 paperback titles on its list, and these are almost all of Irish interest.
More and more paperback editions are now being published each year, and it seems as though an expanding market has been discovered for such editions of Irish books.
The major Irish paperback publishers are: The Mercier Press Ltd, Cork; M. H. Gill & Son Ltd, Dublin; and Anvil Books Ltd, Tralee; Allan Figgis Ltd; Sáirséal agus Dill.
Each of these firms has salesmen calling on the book- and allied shops and ensuring that their titles get the largest possible public display.

21 Publishing

As the vast majority of books published in Ireland are written in English, the Irish publishers offer their titles in all parts of the English-speaking world. They sell directly to what used to be called the British Empire Market Area, which now covers Australia, New Zealand, the Africas, Malta, Gibraltar, Trinidad, etc.
Where possible, the Irish publisher endeavours to find a publisher in the United States to reprint and market titles in that larger area and in Canada. Where this is not possible, they try to sell directly to bookstores, but in practice this can be a most expensive mode of marketing.
There are 11 principal Irish trade pub-

lishers, 8 of them located in Dublin, 2 in Cork and 1 in Tralee.
The productions of these firms are mostly divided between books of Irish interest and religious books. About 80% of the books of Irish interest are sold in Ireland, and 20% exported. In the matter of religious books, 80% are exported, and 20% sold on the home market.

Bibliography

J. M. Feehan, *An Irish publisher and his world.* Cork, Mercier Press 1969. 137 pp.

24 Retail Trade

There are approximately 30 regular booksellers in the country whose main business is selling books. But hundreds of other smaller outlets exist to whom bookselling is a sideline. The Irish booksellers are members of the "Booksellers Association of Great Britain and Ireland", with headquarters in London, and a branch office in Dublin (→ 4).
About one third of all regular bookshops are located in Dublin. Other important places are Cork, Waterford, Tralee, Limerick, Galway, Sligo, Kilkenny, and Clonmel.
The book-buying public in Ireland have the full benefit of the productions of the British publishers. Practically 85% of the books available in Irish bookshops come from England, and virtually the same conditions apply in Ireland as in England. The Irish public tend, however, to give preference to books published in Ireland, about Ireland.

26 Antiquarian Book Trade, Auctions

Ireland boasts of some first-class and internationally renowned antiquarian bookshops, mainly situated in Dublin. All in all 9 firms may be mentioned (Dublin 6, Cork 2, Galway 1).

27 Book Imports
28 Book Exports

Ireland imports approximately £1,000,000 worth of books each year, mainly from England and the USA, and exports approximately £ 300,000 worth of books, mainly to England, the USA, Australia, New Zealand and Africa.
The government-sponsored "Irish Export Board" is particularly keen on the development of a larger export trade in Irish publications, and it provides generous travel and promotion incentives to publishers. The Irish diplomatic missions abroad generally display books on Ireland or by Irish authors in embassies and legations.
A proportion of the profits on books published and printed in Ireland and exported is free of income tax.

33 The Reviewing of Books

The main book-review media in Ireland consist of four daily newspapers, each of whom publishes a weekly page:
Irish Press (Burgh Quay, Dublin); *Irish Times* (Westmoreland Street, Dublin); *Irish Independent* (Middle Abbey Street, Dublin); *Cork Examiner* (Patrick Street, Cork).
Special book reviews are also broadcast over Radio Eireann, G.P.O., Dublin.

Italy

Important Book Centres

1 General Information

Area 301,125 km²
Population 53,650,000 (178 per km²)
Capital Roma (2,160,773)
Largest towns Roma (2,160,773); Milano (1,580,978); Napoli (1,178,608); Torino (1,019,230); Genova (775,106); Palermo (587,063); Bologna (441,143); Firenze (483,138); Catania (351,466); Venezia (336,184); Bari (311,268); Trieste (273,390).
Government Unitarian Republic
Religion Catholic
National language Italian
Leading foreign languages French, English, German
Weights and measures Metric system
Currency Lira (L.)
Education Obligatory up to 14 years of age. University students: 474,727 (academic year 1969–70) at 39 universities or institutes of an academic type.
Illiteracy 3%
Paper consumption a) Newspaper: 8.1 kg per inhabitant
b) Writing and printing paper: 5.3 kg per inhabitant
Membership UNESCO, IPA, ICBA, ILAB.

2 Past and Present

Booksellers, in the modern sense of the word, i.e. exclusively booksellers and not copyists as well, began to appear in Italy at the beginning of the fourteenth century. During that time prices were still high, especially for manuscripts, because good copyists were well paid. Conditions in the book trade underwent a remarkable change after the invention of printing. Books were put on the market which, because of their low price, were accessible to persons of modest means. In the early stages, it was the printers themselves who sold their own books; towards the end of the fifteenth century publishers started selling books too. Venice soon became one of the most important cities in the world in the book trade. At the end of the fifteenth century the art of printing had developed considerably. Printing, publishing and bookselling were still carried out by the same person.

In 1500 the book-trade associations assumed considerable importance and the statutes of these associations permitted the sale of books only to persons of sufficient culture who had undergone a difficult examination.

In the seventeenth century, according to the statutes of the "University of Booksellers in Rome", those wishing to become booksellers had to undergo an apprenticeship of eight years.

Prices varied according to conditions in the trade. In the eighteenth century the book trade in Italy was governed exclusively by the book-trade associations, but went through a phase of decadence, especially in Venice, due to religious censure, the piratical printing of books, and competition between booksellers. This situation improved with the beginning of the "Risorgimento" movement, with the passing of the first laws on copyright, and the widening of public education.

With the arrival of national unity in the second half of the nineteenth century, both production and trade in books expanded considerably. The first national organizations appeared and important bibliographic works were printed; in 1869 the "Italian Publishers' and Booksellers' Association" was founded; in 1870 the publication of "Bibliografia Italiana" started; in 1891 the "Catalogo Collettivo della Libreria Italiana" was published and ten years later the "Catalogo Generale della Libreria Italiana" (Paglianini). The largest bookshops were run by publishers. Milan was the most important publishing and bookselling centre. The first specialized bookshops were opened, especially those for antiquarian books.

During the First World War and immediately afterwards, powerful commercial organizations appeared which monopolized the sale of books.

After the crisis during the Second World War the book trade improved considerably. Free associations between publishers and booksellers (which had been disbanded during the fascist period) were recreated (→ 4). The new atmosphere of freedom, the improvement in the standard of living which gradually reached all social strata, school reform which aimed at a higher level of education for young people, the spiritual enrichment of the public are all factors which have increased cultural interests throughout Italian society and have given a strong fillip to the book trade, which itself has assumed a more modern structure to cope with new requirements in the distribution of books.

Bibliography

A. Adversi, *Storia del libro.* (History of the book). Firenze, Sansoni 1963. 362 pp.

M. Bonetti (ed.), *Storia dell'editoria italiana.* (History of publishing in Italy.) 2 vols. Roma, Gazzetta del Libro 1960. 876 pp.

U. Dorini, *Breve storia del commercio librario.* (Short history of the book trade.) Milano 1938.

3 Retail Prices

In Italy books are sold to the public at a price determined by the publishers. The principle by which the fixed price is to be respected was sanctioned in 1935 in a collective economic agreement on the running of the book trade laid down by the "Federazioni Industriali Editori e Commercianti del Libro". This principle was re-confirmed in the new collective economic agreement on the sale of books laid down by "AIE" and "ALI" (→ 4) in 1965. This agreement was re-examined in 1968 because of new developments in the book market which called for the modification and integration of some of the rules. Based on this agreement, the discount on cover price is exclusively granted to booksellers, to publishers who are members of "AIE" (limited to copies for work purposes only) and to the "National Institute for Public and School Libraries", in consideration of the special task of this body. The discount is 30% on non-educational books and 25% on educational books. Shipping and packing costs have to be paid by the booksellers, with the exception of packing expenses on supplies of books worth more than L. 5,000. The agreement signed by "AIE" (→ 4) and "ALI" (→ 4) is of a private nature and from a strictly legal point of view is therefore only binding on those companies which are members of the two associations. As a matter of practice, however, publishers and booksellers who are not members of these two associations generally abide by these rules too.

4 Organization

During the first "Italian Book Congress" in 1869 an association was founded in Milan with the aim of improving, both morally and materially, the conditions of the book trade and of developing business relations between its members. This association—the "Associazione Libraria Italiana"—initially consisted of publishers and booksellers, and later on of printers too. In the course of time it has undergone several transformations and has had several names ("Associazione Tipografico-Libraria Italiana", "Associazione Editoriale Libraria Italiana"). Nowadays publishing and bookselling are represented by two separate associations:
the

Associazione Italiana Editori
(Italian Publishers' Association)
Foro Buonaparte 24
I Milano

and

Associazione Librai Italiani
(Italian Booksellers' Association)
Piazza G. G. Belli 2
I Roma

"AIE" was founded in 1946 and "ALI" in 1945.

"AIE's" aims are: to represent all those who are engaged in publishing, to take care of the moral and material interests, to encourage initiative in promoting the further spread of culture and the Italian book abroad. Even though it is a single unit, "AIE" consists of two groups called the "Group for Educational Publishers" and the "Group for Publishers of Literary, Scientific, Technical, Art Books", etc. Only publishers of books and cultural periodicals are represented by "AIE". Newspaper publishers are represented by the

Federazione Italiana Editori Giornali
(Italian Newspaper Publishers' Federation)
Via Petrarca 6
I Milano

The official organ of the "AIE" is the "Giornale della Libreria" (→ 5). Further "AIE" covers the publication of *Editori,*

librai, cartolibrai e biblioteche d'Italia (addresses of publishers, booksellers, stationers and libraries), of *Elenco dei quotidiani e periodici italiani* (addresses of periodical publications) and of *Catalogo dei libri italiani in commercio* (Italian books in print, arranged according to authors and titles).
The aims of "ALI" are to represent and look after the economic, cultural and moral interests of Italian booksellers, and in particular to give help to its members within the structure of Italian law.

Bibliography

80 anni di vita associativa degli editori italiani. (80 years of associative activities of the Italian publishers.) Milano, AIE-SABE 1950. 111 pp.

A. VALLARDI, *L'editoria italiana e la sua associazione dal 1869 al 1949.* (The Italian publishing world and its organization from 1869 to 1949.) Milano, SABE 1950. 16 pp.

5 Trade Press

The most important source of information and documentation for booksellers and all those interested in the problems of publishing and bookselling is the

Giornale della Libreria
(Journal of the Book Trade)
Foro Buonaparte 24
I Milano

which is the official organ of "AIE" (→ 4) and comes out monthly. This magazine was founded in 1881 and is one of Italy's oldest periodicals. It is in two parts: the first part (editorial) contains articles on subjects regarding books, news from Italy and abroad, reviews of the specialized press, studies and surveys, etc.; the second part (bibliographic) contains publishers' advertisements, and data on new Italian works or reprints, divided up by subject (according to the Universal Decimal Classification) under publishers and authors. Each year there are five special issues devoted to special events (the Milano Sample Fair—April; the Frankfurt Book Fair—September/October) or to special sectors of the industry (Educational Books —May; University Books—October; Christmas Gifts—November).
Another important publication for booksellers is

La Libreria
(The Book Trade)
Piazza G. G. Belli 2
I Roma

which is the official organ of "ALI" (→ 4) and was founded in 1946.
Other monthly publications on subjects of interest to booksellers and stationers are:

Selecart
Via Madonna dei Prati 5
I Ponte Ronca (Bologna)

and

La Cartoleria
(Stationery)
Via Teodosio 69
I Milano

6 Book-Trade Literature

In Italy there are many publications, both specialized and general, dealing with publishing, printing and bookselling in their various aspects (historical, economic, technical and sociological). Below are some of the most important works of a general nature:

A. ADVERSI, *Storia del libro.* (History of the book.) Firenze, Sansoni 1963. 362 pp.
The author describes in a lively manner the history of the book over a period of 7,000 years. The six chapters are devoted to manuscripts, printed books, the illustration of books, publishing and bookselling, preservation of books, bibliography etc.

A. BIGNAMI, *L'economia dell'impresa editoriale nel suo divenire storico.* (History of the economies of book production.) Milano, Bignami 1968. 1,800 pp.

An excellent monograph on the evolution of book-producing companies. The author goes back to the very beginnings of publishing; she looks for the causes which were at its origin; she analyses the different structures which she covers during the different periods, and studies the reasons for its continuous transformation.

M. Bonetti (ed.), *Storia dell'editoria italiana.* (History of publishing in Italy.) 2 vols. Roma, Gazzetta del Libro 1960. 876 pp.
Various authors have collaborated on this volume, which contains a comprehensive, well-documented historical survey of publishing in the various regions of Italy. A good part of vol. 2 is dedicated to information on Italian publishers and major Italian newspapers and magazines.

A. Ciampi, *Il tempo libero in Italia.* (Leisure time in Italy.) Milano, Bompiani 1965. 223 pp.
The author is concerned with problems related to the spending of leisure-time.

Ottanta anni di vita associativa degli editori italiani (→ 4). Milano, AIE-SABE 1950. 111 pp.
This booklet gives a lively picture of Italian publishing in the second half of the nineteenth and the first half of the twentieth century.

G. M. Pugno, *Trattato di cultura generale nel campo della stampa.* (Treatise on the general culture of printing.) Torino, SEI 1964. 408 pp.
This vast work on the history of the art of printing has been written by a famous professor at the Turin Polytechnic.

F. Riva, *Il libro italiano.* (The Italian book.) Milano, Scheiwiller 1966.
A history of the Italian book from the beginning of the last century to the present day.

S. H. Steinberg, *500 years of printing.* London, Penguin Books 1955.
The history of graphic design in its various artistic movements, the beginning of new types of education influenced by the intellectual climate of the moment, the development of printing techniques due to a growing demand for printed matter, the appearance of low-prized editions, together with a description of the works of great printers, are some of the subjects which the author describes. A small glossary of technical terms, specially written for the *Italian edition* (Torino, Einaudi 1964) explains techniques, machines and systems now used in the printing industry.

P. Trevisani, *Storia della stampa.* (History o printing.) Roma 1953.
The author, a well-known expert in the field of books, has produced a comprehensive history of printing covering the whole world.

7 Sources of Information, Address Services

Information on production and the book trade may be obtained from

Associazione Italiana Editori
Foro Buonaparte 24
I Milano

and

Associazione Librai Italiana
Via G. G. Belli 2
I Roma

Bibliographic information can be requested from

Biblioteca Centrale Nazionale
Piazza Cavalleggeri 1
I Firenze

→ 4.

8 International Membership

Both "AIE" (→ 4) and "ALI" (→ 4) take an active part in international life. "AIE" is a part of the "International Publishers' Association" and "ALI" is a member of

the "International Community of Booksellers' Associations".
The "Circolo dei librai antiquari italiani" (→ 26) is a member of the "International League of Antiquarian Booksellers".

9 Market Research

The most recent and complete survey on reading in Italy was made in 1965 by the "Central Institute of Statistics" on behalf of the "Information and Copyright Service of the Office of the Prime Minister". The data of the survey give a comprehensive view of how, how much, where and what Italians read: of how they react to reading, with respect to their age, standard of education, sex and social status; of the costs involved in the purchase of books and magazines; of the size of family libraries, etc. A similar study was made by the same Institute in 1957.
Surveys on books and the book market have also been made by the market research institute "DOXA". Some of these surveys have been made on an exclusive basis for private companies; the results thus obtained have not therefore been published. The data collected in some other surveys were published in the "Doxa Bulletin" (see below).

Bibliography

Bollettino Doxa. Milano 1957, 1961, 1964, 1965.

Indagine speciale sulla lettura in Italia al 15 aprile 1965. (Special research about Italian reading habits.) Roma, Istituto Centrale di Statistica 1965. 52 pp.

Italy. Documents and Notes, Roma, Presidenza del Consiglio dei Ministri, 1970, no. 3.

10 Books and Young People

Each year more than one thousand books are published for young people; this represents about 7% of the total production. This figure is in itself indicative of the attention Italian publishers pay to young people and of the contribution which they offer to their formation, both moral and intellectual.
Since 1964 Italy has organized an *International Children's Book Fair* held in Bologna and exclusively devoted to books for children and young people. This fair, in which publishers from all over the world take part, is rapidly becoming an important centre for international exchanges in the field of literature for young people. During this fair two prizes are awarded: one for the best illustrated book and the other for the most beautiful book from a graphic point of view (→ International Section, 29).
In several Italian cities there are specialized libraries for young people. Rome has an international library dedicated to children and adolescents. It contains the best foreign literature for youngsters.
A special section of the "Centro Didattico nazionale di studi e documentazione" in Florence looks after juvenile literature and publishes a bi-monthly bulletin called

Schedario
Via Buonarroti 10
I Firenze

A literary prize named after *Giana Anguissola*, a well-known Italian woman author of children's books, is awarded every year to a new novel for youngsters. Another important prize (bi-annual) takes its name from the novelist *Olga Visentini*.

11 Training

At the moment there are no real training schools. In the past, courses for assistants in bookshops have been held in some Italian towns. These have, however, been the fruit of special initiative on the part of private and public bodies and are not part of an integrated programme of compulsory studies.

Bibliography

Operatori del libro. Padua, Consorzio Provinciale per l'Istruzione Tecnica 1963. 138 pp.

12 Taxes

Based on current laws, the sale of books is subject to a turnover tax "una tantum" of 2.4% on cover price.
This tax must be paid when the book is sold or delivered to the purchaser or retailer.
The same taxes apply to the sale of those newspapers which are not dailies, magazines, maps and printed sheet music. The sale of daily newspapers of all kinds and magazines of a largely political nature are exempt from this tax.
Imported books are also subject to a turnover tax of 2.4% on cover price converted into Italian currency (→ 27).
During manufacture, books are subjected to a 4% turnover tax on paper, composition, printing and binding. Magazines of a political, trade-union or cultural nature are exempt from the turnover tax on composition and printing.
Copyright is also subjected to 4% turnover tax.
In accordance with the general instructions of the Council of the "EEC" for the unification of taxation on turnover, the turnover tax will be discontinued as of 1 January 1972 in favour of the one on added value.

Bibliography

P. Molino, *Imposta Generale sull'Entrata*. Grosseto, Il Corriere Tributario 1964. 680 pp.

14 Copyright

In Italy copyright is regulated by Law no. 633 of 22 April 1941, which became effective on 18 December 1942. All works of a creative nature, in literature, music, the arts, architecture, the theatre or the cinema are thus protected, whatever their manner or form of expression may be.
Copyright protection is not subjected to any kind of formality.
Rights last for the entire duration of the life of the author and up to the end of the fiftieth year after his death.
Translation rights are tied to the rights on the original work.
For posthumous works the duration of rights is 50 years from the date of initial publication, provided that this take place within 20 years from the death of the author.
Italy has been a member of the "International Union for the Protection of Literary and Artistic Works" since 1887, i.e. since the "Berne Convention" of 9 September 1886.
Italy adheres to the Rome Act (1928), the Brussels Act (1948) and the Stockholm Act (1967).
Italy subscribed to the "Universal Copyright Convention" of 6 September 1952. This convention has been effective in Italy since 24 January 1967.
Italy adheres to the "Montevideo Convention" of 11 January 1889, but only in respect of certain countries.

Bibliography

E. P. Caselli, *Codice del diritto d'autore*. (Copyright law.) Torino, UTET 1943. 760 pp.

G. Jarach, *Manuale del diritto d'autore*. (Handbook of copyright.) Milano, Mursia 1968. 461 pp.

E. Valerio and Z. Algardi, *Il diritto d'autore*. (Copyright law.) Milano, Giuffré 1943. 513 pp.

15 National Bibliography, National Library

In Italy a copy of each publication must be sent, according to the laws of the country, to the

Biblioteca Nazionale Centrale
(National Central Library)
Piazza Cavalleggeri 1
I Firenze
and the
Biblioteca Nazionale Centrale
Vittorio Emanuele II
(National Central Library
Vittorio Emanuele II)
Via Collegio Romano 27
I Roma
which are the greatest authorities on national bibliography. Since 1958 the National Central Library of Florence publishes monthly the *Bibliografia Nazionale Italiana*, in which works are cla s fied according to the Universal Decimal Classification.
The "Centro Nazionale per il Catalogo Unico delle Biblioteche Italiane" (Roma, Viale Collegio Romano 27) has edited the "Comprehensive Catalogue of Italian Publications from 1886 to 1957" (41 volumes). Other book trade bibliographies → 4.

16 Book Production

Italian book production is approximately 14,000 titles a year. This figure may seem high in relation to the actual absorption possibilities of the Italian market. However, it should be remembered that approximately 35% of the annual production is usually made up of reprints and re-editions. The data on book production in 1968 has been obtained from a statistical survey made by the "Information and Copyright Service of the Office of the Prime Minister". As a source and field of analysis the "Bibliografia Nazionale Italiana" (→ 15) was used.
The processing of data has been carried out according to criteria given in the well-known "recommendation" by UNESCO and according to specific evaluations. Only book-like works of at least 49 pages have been taken into consideration and these must be fully completed and capable of being objectively considered as new works.
This survey shows that in 1968 11,612 new titles were published. In the classification, by subject, first place is given to literature, with 3,060 titles, followed by social science, history, geography and biography, applied science, art, games and sport, religion, pure science, philosophy and psychology, languages, and general works.
The following table gives data on book production in 1968 (new titles) classified according to the "Universal Decimal Classification":

Subject group	Titles	Percentage of total production
General works	142	1.2
Philosophy, psychology	455	3.9
Religion	918	8.0
Social science	2,494	21.5
Languages	282	2.4
Pure science	526	4.5
Applied science	1,187	10.2
Art, games, sport	1,034	8.9
Literature	3,060	26.4
History, geography, biography	1,514	13.0

Bibliography

Annuario delle Statistiche Culturali, Roma, Istituto Centrale di Statistica 1968.
Bibliografia Nazionale Italiana. Firenze, Biblioteca Nazionale Centrale 1967.
Vita italiana. Roma, Presidenza del Consiglio dei Ministri, pamphlet no. 6.

17 Translations

Books by foreign authors, translated into Italian, represent about 13–14% of the total annual book production. According to data from the "Index Translationum", the number of foreign works translated into Italian in 1964 amounted to 2,122. A similar figure was registered in 1965 (2,099). Most of the translations are from English (953 in 1964), French (581) and German (259). Most of the foreign works translated are of a literary nature (in 1964

46.8% of total), history and geography texts, books on religion, law and sociology. There are about 800–900 translations a year from Italian (752 in 1964, 907 in 1965). Approximately 40 countries normally translate Italian works: among the most important are France, Germany, the USA, Spain and the UK. The Italian books most frequently translated abroad are literary works (in 1964, 52.6% of total), religion, art, law and sociology.

Bibliography

Bibliografia Nazionale Italiana. Firenze, Biblioteca Nazionale Centrale 1964–1965.
Index translationum. Paris, UNESCO.

19 Paperbacks

In Italy there are several series of low-priced books. Up to a few years ago only classical works or particularly well-known works were obtainable in economically priced editions. Furthermore, this production was not as extensive as it was in the USA. Paperbacks became particularly important in Italy in 1965 because a number of leading publishers started printing some economical series of books which were available to the public not only through bookshops but also from newspaper stalls.
These series were characterized by the high numbers of copies they printed (150,000–250,000 copies) and the low price (350–600 Lire). After an initial boom this phenomenon stabilized itself.
The graphic standard of Italian paperbacks is excellent.

21 Publishing

According to the results of a census made in 1967 by "AIE" (→ 4) there are 1,050 publishers operating in Italy. This number refers exclusively to publishers of books and, therefore, excludes publishers of music, newspapers and magazines. Actually almost 90% of production comes from no more than 320–350 firms. These are nearly all firms on an industrial scale and are managed accordingly. The remainder are mainly family businesses. The lack of homogeneity in the Italian publishing field, which is caused by the existence of publishers of different structure and management, creates a series of delicate problems which concern not only the production of books but also their distribution (→ 24).
The most important publishing centre is Milan (347). Other important centres are:

Roma	260
Torino	82
Firenze	52
Napoli	41
Bologna	28
Palermo	19
Genova	17
Venezia	17
Padova	16
Bari	12

Classification of publishers in the various Italian regions is as follows:

Lombardia	387
Lazio	262
Piemonte/Val d'Aosta	98
Toscana	70
Emilia/Romagna	50
Campania	45
Veneto	33
Sicilia	25
Liguria	20
Puglia	18
Friuli/Venezia Giulia	12
Marche	10
Umbria	6
Abruzzi/Molise	5
Calabria	5
Trentino/Alto Adige	2
Sardegna	2
Basilicata	–

In Italy no official figures are published on the turnover in publishing. A survey on reading in Italy made in 1965 by the "Istituto Centrale di Statistica" (→ 9) revealed that between April 1964 and April 1965 Italians spent more than 344 billion L. on books, both educational and non-educational, magazines and newspapers. More than one third of the amount was spent in north-western Italy, 21.7% in central Italy, 18.8% in north-east Italy and 23.9% in the Islands. On average each Italian family spends L. 24,537 on books. Approximately three million families purchase books for reading, 800,000 in order to make presents.
The above-mentioned survey gave an annual expenditure of about L. 140 billion on books. The estimate for 1969 is about L. 160 billion.

Bibliography

A. Bignami, *L'economia dell'impresa editoriale nel suo divenire storico.* (→ 6.)
Editori, librai, cartolibrai e biblioteche d'Italia. Milano, AIE. (→ 4.)
Indagine speciale sulla lettura in Italia al 15 aprile 1965. (→ 9.)

22 Literary Agents

In Italy there are excellent literary agents who act as mediators, especially in international relations. The role of these agents is, however, limited with regard to the sale and purchase of rights in Italy, which are normally arranged directly between author and publisher.

23 Wholesale Trade

Most Italian publishers have a commercial organization which permits them to supply retailers directly through their own branches in the main cities. Other publishers use agents or representatives who promote contracts for the publishers.
Quite a few publishers make use of specialized organizations for book distribution. Some of these agencies are of considerable size and operate on an international scale.

24 Retail Trade

The process of economic and social transformation which has been taking place in Italy for some years now embraces all sectors of production and distribution.
Both publishers and booksellers have felt this transformation. Many publishers nowadays work on an industrial scale. The constant increase in production has obliged publishers to increase their market and, therefore, to look for new outlets, though the bookshop is still the main channel through which books reach the public.
There are approximately 2,000 real bookshops. There are also about 5,000 stationers who sell books. A further 7,000 sales outlets are to be found in newspaper stalls.
The most important bookshops are to be found in:

Milano	418
Roma	370
Torino	230
Napoli	96
Firenze	95
Genova	71
Bologna	65
Venezia	40
Palermo	36
Brescia	33
Padova	32
Cagliari	26
Catania	26
Bari	25

Bookshops in big towns devote ample space to the presentation of foreign books. In order to operate a retail bookshop it is necessary to obtain a licence from the municipal office, as for any other kind of shop.

Among the new channels for the sale of Italian publications an important role has been played by the newspaper stands, especially in the sale of low-priced books, which are published periodically (weekly, fortnightly, monthly). Part publications (mostly encyclopedias) are also sold from news-stands. This formula was first introduced on the Italian book market some fifteen years ago and makes the promotion of books possible among larger strata of the population.
Another important channel through which retail sales are made is by instalments. This particularly applies to voluminous, expensive works (encyclopedias, dictionaries, scientific treatises, etc.).
Shops devoted exclusively or partially to the selling of books are spread over the regions as follows:

Lombardia	3,673
Piemonte/Val d'Aosta	2,173
Lazio	2,037
Toscana	1,976
Veneto	1,653
Emilia/Romagna	1,620
Campania	1,342
Sicilia	1,293
Puglia	1,168
Liguria	806
Calabria	794
Abruzzi/Molise	782
Sardegna	729
Marche	670
Friuli/Venezia Giulia	467
Trentino/Alto Adige	333
Basilicata	304
Umbria	294

25 Mail-Order Bookselling

The system of book sales by mail-order is not very widespread in Italy at the moment. Some publishers use this system especially for the sale of handbooks. It is not difficult to foresee great future developments of this channel.

26 Antiquarian Book Trade, Auctions

Antiquarian books have always been an object of study and collection in Italy, but their commercial value in past centuries has been irrelevant; very few auctions and few people dedicated themselves exclusively to the sale of old books. The evaluation of the antiquarian book as an object of commercial exchange was undertaken not long ago by a number of cultured, intelligent booksellers who, with cleverly illustrated catalogues and other forms of advertising, created an interest and a curiosity which had previously only existed in the restricted world of the learned, but now started a major demand.
There are few antiquarian books of great value and importance kept by or circulating among private individuals, compared to the number to be found in some of the greatest libraries and public institutions in Italy (Biblioteca Marciana, Venezia; Laurenziana, Firenze; Estense, Modena; Nazionale, Roma) which own texts of enormous value. There are more than 200 Italian antiquarian book dealers.
In 1947 the

Circolo dei Librai Antiquari
(Circle of Antiquarian Booksellers)
Via Manzoni 39
I Milano

was founded for the purpose of regulating the sale of antiquarian books, promoting love for these books, by means of displays, fairs, art, etc., and the publication of a periodical bulletin with articles on bibliophily, news, information on books "wanted" and "for sale", etc. The "Circolo" is a member of the "International League of Antiquarian Booksellers".
The special journal for books wanted and offered is

Gazzettino Librario
Piazza Lotario 6
I 00162 Roma

Italy

Bibliography

G. AVANZI, *Bibliografia storica dell'arte della stampa in Italia.* (Historical bibliography of the art of printing in Italy.) Milano 1939–30.

La Bibliofilia. Rivista di storia del libro e delle arti grafiche. Firenze, Olschki, since 1899.

U. COSTA, *Codice delle biblioteche italiane.* (Codex of Italian libraries.) Milano 1937.

D. FAVA, *Di alcuni importanti libri a stampa.* (About some important books and prints.) Modena 1931.

L. FERRARI, *Onomasticon.* Milano, Hoepli 1947.

G. FRATI, *Dizionario dei bibliotecari e bibliofili italiani dal secolo XIV al XIX.* (Dictionary of librarians and bibliophiles in Italy from the 14th to the 19th century.) Firenze 1934.

G. FUMAGALLI, *Lexicon typographicum Italiae.* Firenze, Olschki 1905.

G. FUMAGALLI, *Vocabolario bibliografico.* Firenze, Olschki 1940.

G. MIRA, *Manuale teorico pratico di bibliografia.* (Theoretical-practical manual of bibliography.) Palermo 1861–2.

27 Book Imports

Italian book imports have increased seventeenfold from 1954 to 1969 from L. 472,094,000 to L. 8,415,899,000. It should be noted that these figures, which have been obtained from statistics on foreign trade drawn up by the "Istituto Centrale di Statistica" (as were those indicated above) do not have any absolute value but refer exclusively to imports documented by bills from customs and not to those sent by mail in small quantities. Considering the importance of mail shipping in international exchanges of works of graphic art and publishing, it is estimated that the actual value of imports of such products is more than 50% higher than the official figures.

Below are the the values of publishing/graphic imports in 1969, classified under the principal groups of products:

Category	Amount (L. 1,000)
Books	8,415,899
Newspapers and magazines	3,266,969
Books, albums of pictures and drawings for children	53,209
Maps	310,968
Printed music	14,703
Total	12,061,748

It is interesting to note that books occupy the first place among imported products. The official statistics from the countries of origin include all publishing and graphic products.
From these statistics it can be seen that in 1969 the major exporters to Italy were:

Country	Amount (L. 1,000)
USA	6,185,000
Germany (Federal Republic)	5,399,500
France	2,098,400
United Kingdom	1,290,000
Switzerland	1,119,700
Belgium/Luxembourg	785,700
Netherlands	620,100

Italy adheres to the "Florence Agreement" on the import of objects of an educational, scientific and cultural nature (1950) and therefore assures free circulation of books. Book imports were liberalized and are exempt from customs duty.
Imported books are subject to a turnover tax at 2.4%, as are Italian books (→ 12) and to an equalization tax of 4% on the paper used. The latter tax is levied so as to equalize fiscally all products from home and abroad, since the former are exempted from taxes which directly or indirectly derive from the taxation of turnover in the countries for which they are destined.

Bibliography

Statistica mensile del commercio con l'estero. December 1969. Roma, Istituto Centrale di Statistica.

28 Book Exports

In 1969 Italian book exports amounted to L. 19,592,369,000.
Since 1954 (the year taken into consideration in the previous chapter regarding imports) exports have increased twenty-fourfold.
The remarks on the reliability of the import data also apply to exports.
The classification of publishing and graphic exports by principal sectors of products is as follows:

Category	Amount L. 1,000
Books	19,592,369
Magazines	32,027,664
Books and children's albums of pictures or drawings	562,702
Maps	916,763
Printed music	25,599
Total	53,125,097

The main purchasers of Italian graphic/publishing products in 1969 were:

Country	Amount L. 1,000
France	28,193,200
United Kingdom	7,930,500
Germany (Federal Republic)	7,004,800
USA	4,815,300
Switzerland	4,355,100
Yugoslavia	1,861,100
Belgium	1,627,700
Netherlands	1,566,900
Canada	963,000
Spain	625,200

The export of books is completely liberalized and is not subject to the turnover tax.
Moreover, provision is also made for the reimbursement of turnover tax on the paper used in accordance with the rules regulating relations in international exchange, by which the turnover tax is paid in the country of destination (→ 27).
In order to improve the knowledge of Italian culture abroad, a law of 1955, modified in 1961 and 1969, provides for the assignment of annual contributions to exporters of books and other publishing and graphic products.
Many publishers send books directly abroad through their own commercial organizations. There are also some excellent firms specializing in both export and import trade.
In order to increase the distribution of Italian books abroad, "AIE" (→ 4) usually organizes a collective stand for Italian publishers at the Frankfurt Book Fair—and at all other fairs of international importance (the Warsaw Fair, the Belgrade Fair, the Brussels Fair).
"AIE" also organizes special displays of Italian books in various countries in collaboration with the Italian cultural and commercial Institutes.

Bibliography

Statistica mensile del commercio con l'estero. December 1969. Roma, Istituto Centrale di Statistica.

29 Book Fairs

In 1958, "AIE" (→ 4) sponsored and organized the first National Book Exhibition in Milan. It had no direct commercial aims but attempted to attract the public to books and to create a dialogue between publishers and readers. In 1968 the Exhibition took place in Rome, and will probably be repeated in other major Italian centres in future years.
A specialized exhibition which, although fairly recent, has already attracted the

attention of both Italian and foreign publishers, writers and illustrators, as well as the general public, is the *International Children's Book Fair*, which takes place each spring in Bologna (→ 10).
There is also the "Fair of Economic Books" in Modena (spring) and the "Viareggio Book Fair" (summer).

30 Public Relations

Advertising investments are made by the Italian publishing houses in the following descending order: press, radio and television. The table below gives the figures for expenditure in 1966, compared with those for 1965:

	1965 L. 1,000	1966 L. 1,000	Percentage of difference
Press	7,831,509	8,603,199	+ 9.85
Radio	618,007	736,972	+19.24
TV	108,353	151,600	+39.91
Total	8,557,869	9,491,771	+10.91

In just one year advertising investment increased by nearly 11%. In these figures expenditure for direct advertising by publishers either in their own press, or by posters, etc., is not included. Publishing houses rate eighth on the list of trades using space for advertising. During the "Reading Week", which took place in Italy for the first time in 1967 and which will be repeated in future years, the "Office of the Prime Minister" cooperated with "RAI-TV", "AIE" and "ALI" in starting a vast advertising campaign for the promotion of books.

Bibliography

La pubblicità in Italia. (Advertising in Italy). Milano, l'Ufficio Moderno.

Publirama italiano. Milano, l'Ufficio Moderno.

32 Literary Prizes

Though they do not lead to a great increase in the sale of works, literary prizes play an important role in Italy in the book trade. The influence of prizes on sales relates to the importance of the prize, as well as to the kind of book which gets the prize.
There are quite a number of literary prizes in Italy, some of which are of international repute. They cover fiction, essay writing, poetry, literature and science. Prizes are given by town councils, private individuals, academies, foundations, companies, trade and scientific associations, etc.
The oldest is the *Bagutta* prize (for fiction) which was given in Milan for the first time in 1927. Other important prizes are: *Viareggio* (Viareggio—fiction and essay writing), *Strega* (Rome—fiction), *Bancarella* (Pontremoli—fiction), *Marzotto* (Valdagno—fiction, essay-writing and science), *Campiello* (Venice—fiction), *Cortina—Ulisse* (Cortina—essay writing, science), *Chianciano* (Chianciano—poetry), *Anguissola* (Milan—children's literature), *Accademia dei Lincei* (Rome—science), *Visentini* (Milan—children's literature).
In 1958 the Italian government set up the prizes *Penna d'Oro* ("Golden Pen") and the *Libro d'Oro* ("Golden Book").
The "Penna d'Oro" is granted every year to a writer who has significantly enriched Italian culture in philosophy, history, literature, science, or economics.
The "Libro d'Oro" is given annually to a publisher who has contributed in an original manner to the diffusion of culture among the people.

33 The Reviewing of Books

Many Italian literary magazines regularly contain book reviews:
Libri e riviste d'Italia (monthly), Roma, Presidenza del Consiglio dei Ministri

Via Boncompagni 15. Printed in Italian, English, French, German and Spanish.
L'Italia che scrive (monthly), Roma, Via della Quattro Fontane 16.
Letture (monthly), Milano, Piazza S. Fedele 4.
Vita e Pensiero (monthly), Milano, Largo A. Gemelli 1.
La parola e il libro (monthly), Roma, Ente Nazionale Biblioteche Popolari e Scolastiche, Via S. Caterina da Siena 57.
Il ragguaglio librario (monthly), Milano, Via Mercalli 23.
Uomini e libri (monthly), Milano, Viale Emilio Caldara 8.
Schedario (bimonthly). Firenze, Sezione Giovanile del Centro Nazionale Didadattico di Studi e Documentazione di Firenze, Via Buonarroti 10.
L'Osservatore Politico e letterario (monthly). Milano, Via Solferino 32.
All the major dailies devote one or more pages a week to presenting and reviewing new books (*Corriere della Sera*, Milano; *La Stampa*, Torino; *La Nazione*, Firenze; *Il Resto del Carlino*, Bologna; *Il Piccolo*, Trieste; *Il XIX Secolo*, Genova; *Il Messaggero*, Roma; *Paese Sera*, Roma).
Book presentations are also made by "RAI-TV" (Italian Radio and Television Company) in its various cultural programmes.

34 Graphic Arts

The trade association of the printing industry in Italy is:

Associazione Nazionale Italiana
Industrie Grafiche
Cartotecniche e Trasformatrici
Piazza Conciliazione 1
I Milano

The official organ of this association is: *L'Italia Grafica.*

35 Miscellaneous

(a) Libraries

There are about 15,000 libraries in Italy, 7,000 of which are open to the public (they belong to the State, the universities, the local authorities and various public or religious institutions) and 8,000 are connected with high schools.
The total amount of books and booklets owned by libraries is about 86 million copies, of which more than 13 million are borrowed each year. Visits to libraries (the so-called inside readings) were more than 20 million in one year.
These data came from a statistical survey, the most exhaustive ever carried out so far in this field, made by the "Istituto Centrale di Statistica" in cooperation with the "Direzione Generale delle Accademie e Biblioteche" of the "Ministry of Education" and with the "Ente Nazionale per le Biblioteche Nazionali e Scolastiche". The data refer to 1965.

(b) Daily press

At present 83 dailies are published in Italy, of which 17 are evening papers, 4 sports papers and 3 published in languages other than Italian (English, German, Slovene). 48 dailies are published in Northern Italy (10 in Milan), 20 in Central Italy (16 in Rome, one in the Vatican City), 6 in Southern Italy (4 in Naples) and 10 on the Italian islands. Dailies are published in 34 towns (22 in the northern regions, 4 in central regions, 3 in southern regions and 5 on the islands).

Luxembourg

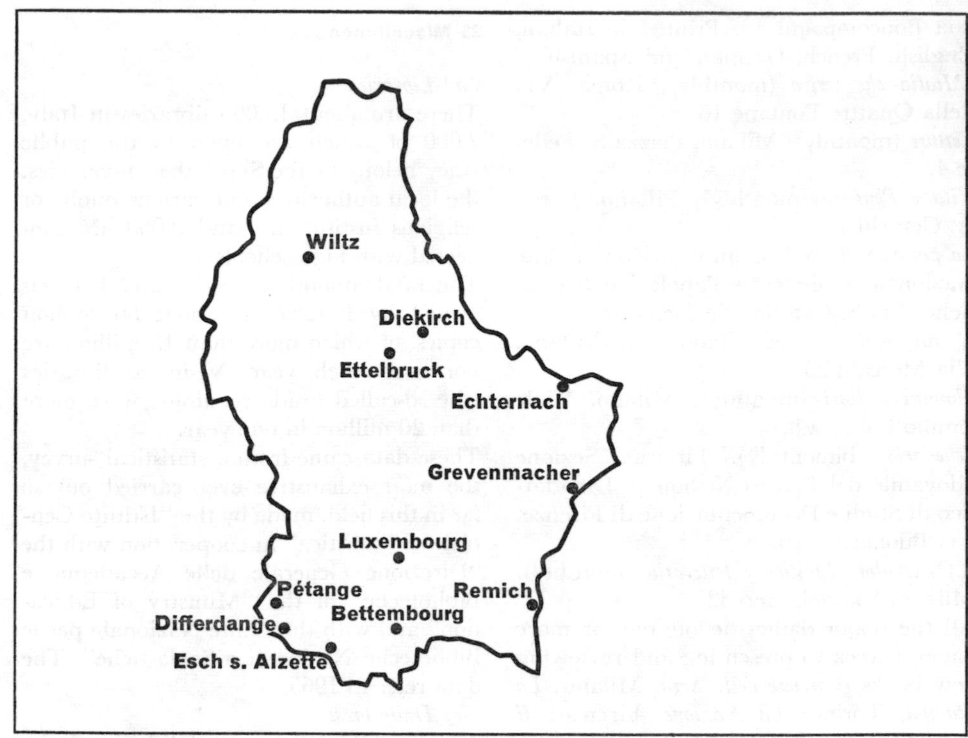

Important Book Centres

1 General Information

Area 2,587 km²

Population 333,000 (127 per km²)

Capital Luxembourg (78,000)

Largest towns Luxembourg (78,000); Esch-Alzette (28,000); Dudelange (15,000).

Government Legislature is the Chamber of Deputies, with 56 members directly elected for 5 years, in cooperation with the Grand-Duke, who names the Ministers (7 Ministers) and Councillors of State. The country is divided into 12 cantons with 126 parishes. The latter are autonomous corporations.

Religion Roman Catholics 95.5%
Protestant 1.8%
Jews 1.2%
Dissidents 1.5%

National language Letzeburgesch (Moselle-Frankish dialect)

Leading foreign languages French (the official language), German, English.

Weights and measures Metric system

Currency unit Lux. Franc = 100 Centimes = 1 Belgian Franc, which together with the Lux. Franc is legal tender.

Education 6,000 boys and 3,000 girls attend 9 central schools in Luxembourg, Esch-Alzette, Diekirch and Echternach (5 classical and 4 modern schools) and 2 girls' schools. 1,600 girls attend private central schools.
4,500 pupils attend state trade schools, technical central schools and agricultural schools.

Illiteracy Nil

Paper consumption (incl. Belgium)
a) Newsprint 14.4 kg per inhabitant (1967)
b) Printing paper (other than newsprint) 22.8 kg per inhabitant (1967)

2 Past and Present

About 140 years after Johannes Gutenberg had invented the printing of books with moveable cast letters, Mathias Birthon introduced the art of book-printing into Luxembourg. On the advice of the Provincial Council of Luxembourg, Philip II of Spain granted him a patent on 10 April 1598 which gave him the right to print and sell all printed material passed by the censor in all the provinces of the Spanish Netherlands. One of the decisive reasons for the granting of this permit was the proposed foundation of the Jesuit College in 1594, which needed various classes of books for its pupils.

The first of Birthon's printed works was a German translation of royal patents of 25 August 1598, in which Isabella and Albert of Austria, the new rulers of the Netherlands, confirmed in their functions those who had held office under Philip II, who had abdicated.

Birthon, who gave up printing on 18 July 1618, was followed by Hubert Reulandt of St Vith, who had learned his trade in Antwerp and Cologne and obtained possession of a patent through the Grand-Dukes. As a result of serious disagreements with the town authorities, Hubert Reulandt left the country in 1646 and settled in Trier.

Luxembourg was without a printer for forty years, but two booksellers, one of whom, Michael Cantzeler, was well known beyond the frontiers of the country, dealt with the provision of books, particularly for the pupils of the Jesuit College, the most important educational institution in the country, founded in 1603.

The early printers were simultaneously writers, booksellers and publishers. This is particularly true of André Chevalier, who began a printing firm in Luxembourg on 2 June 1686 and played an outstanding part in the cultural life of the time.

Chevalier signed an agreement with Louis XIV's military administrative officer concerning the printing of all schoolbooks needed in the country, and their exclusive delivery to professors and students. In addition he printed books on theology, history, mathematics, numismatics, medicine and novels. Among the most important historical publications of the Chevalier press are a biography of Governor Mansfeld and an 8-volume work on civics and church history by the Jesuit Jean Bertholet, printed from 1740 to 1743, a real masterpiece of old Luxembourg printing. Chevalier also printed and published the first Luxembourg monthly magazine: "La Clef du Cabinet des Princes de l'Europe, ou Recueil Historique et Politique sur les matières du temps", which historians of today still find invaluable. It proves, among other things, that Chevalier was in communication with numerous booksellers and publishers abroad, e.g. Briasson, Chaubert, Coignard, Mariette, Saillant and Lacombe of Paris, Brandmüller of Basle, Guillot of Verdun, Desain and Collette of Liège, Gervais and Babin of Nancy, Fontaine of Colmar, Auerbach of Leipzig and Mortier of Amsterdam. Further we learn that clergy, judges, lawyers, doctors, chemists and all the intellectuals of the country regularly frequented Chevalier's bookshop in order to discuss the books and magazines displayed there, and matters concerning literature, history, architecture, theology, science, archaeology and politics.

André Chevalier died in April 1747, aged 86. He assumes a distinguished place in the cultural life of the country. He was succeeded by his son-in-law, François Perle, legal adviser to the Provincial Council. The editing of Chevalier's magazine was taken over by the Jesuit F. X. de Feller, who changed its lengthy title to "Journal Historique et Littéraire". François Perle printed, among other things,

French translations of Cicero and Xenophon, biographies of Philip II of Spain and Louis XIV, several works of Marivaux, and a large number of travel books.

Prominent booksellers and printers of the same period were Paul Barbier and Jacques Ferry, who in 1694 and 1706 respectively were granted permission to print and sell books. The successors of Ferry and François Perle were Jean-Baptiste Kleber and Pierre Brück.

In 1821 J. P. Müllendorf opened a bookshop in the centre of Luxembourg and combined it with a literary society. As a widely educated man he was soon playing an outstanding part in the cultural life of the town. The members of his reading circle had more than 5,000 volumes at their disposal.

About this time there is an increasing number of booksellers and stationers competing with each other and yet continually striving to acquire and preserve their individuality. J. F. Schmit-Brück founded a spacious bookshop in 1825, Jacques Lamort opened several stationery shops, E. Hoffman founded a stationery shop and a lending library, J. M. Scheid stocked mainly schoolbooks, in particular educational works and grammars, while J. P. Küborn specialized in novels and travel books.

In 1845 J. P. Küborn handed over his bookshop to his former apprentice, Victor Bück, who seven years later acquired the printing works of Jacques Lamort. Intellectuals were able to procure scientific works and French and German literature from Victor Bück, and all the works of the best-known French and English writers from E. Hoffman.

Well-known booksellers around the middle of the nineteenth century were Francis Rehm, Pierre Brück (son of J. F. Schmit-Brück) the brothers Heintzé and M. Beaucolin (about 1870).

Today there are some 100 bookshops and book outlets in the Grand Duchy selling the latest works of international reputation in modern editions and carrying the scientific spirit across the frontiers.

Bibliography

E. van der Vekene, *Die Luxemburger Drucker und ihre Drucke bis zum Ende des 18. Jahrhunderts. Eine Bio-Bibliographie.* (The Luxembourg printers and their printings up to the end of the 18th century. A bio-bibliography). Wiesbaden, Harrassowitz 1968. XV, 571 pp.—Beiträge zum Buch- und Bibliothekswesen, Bd. 15.

3 Retail Prices

In Luxembourg the retail prices of books is fixed in the form of price control. Rebate is in principle not permitted. Exceptions (maximum 10%) are brought to the notice of all members as they arise by circular from the National Federation.

4 Organization

All branches of the book trade are united in the

Fédération des Commerçants du
Grand-Duché de Luxembourg
(Mercantile Federation of the Grand Duchy of Luxembourg)
5 rue Jean-Origer
L Luxembourg

This Federation includes 23 professional groups, and more than 100 bookshops and book outlets belong to the bookselling professional group.

The Federation works for the preservation of professional interests and fights for all the vital demands of booksellers. It also lays down the guiding principles to be pursued in particular professional matters. Its official publication

Le Journal du Commerce
(Trade Journal)

5 rue Jean-Origer
L Luxembourg
informs the 23 professional groups of all meetings and deals with current problems in an objective and intelligible manner.
Publishers have no federation of their own, but they belong to the "Mercantile Federation".

7 Sources of Information, Address Services

Addresses of publishers and booksellers in the Grand Duchy can be obtained from the *Chambre de Commerce*
8 Avenue de l'Arsenal
L Luxembourg
or the "Fédération des Commerçants du Grand-Duché de Luxembourg" (→ 4).

11 Training

Potential booksellers must serve a three-year commercial apprenticeship.
The best method is to attend one of the four state trade schools in Luxembourg, Esch-Alzette, Ettelbruck or Grevenmacher, where instruction is clear and realistic. Students register in the department of "Business Studies".
The training lasts two years. Entrance depends on fulfilling one of the following conditions: attendance at a secondary or central school for two years, or two years' preparatory business study; or passing an entrance examination (in German, French and arithmetic based on the eighth school-year syllabus).
Admittance to the first year of preparatory business studies depends on the completion of the sixth year at primary school and the passing of an entrance examination in German, French and arithmetic based on the sixth school-year syllabus; admittance to the second year depends on the completion of the seventh year at primary school or the first year at a secondary or central school, plus an entrance examination in German, French and arithmetic, based on the seventh school-year syllabus. Training at the state trade schools includes German, French and English (including correspondence), book-keeping, shorthand, typewriting, business arithmetic, business and fiscal law, market research, civics, business practice, geography and hygiene. The two years' studies conclude with an examination. Successful students receive a diploma. The most successful receive bursaries. In all cases travelling expenses are refunded. The prospective booksellers, both male and female, now do a year with a recognized firm, during which time they get financial assistance. At the end of the year they take an examination, and successful candidates receive the "Certificat d'Aptitude Professionelle", which entitles them to manage a bookshop. This permit is granted by the so-called "Middle Class Ministry".

12 Taxes

Book-trade firms of whatever branch are subject to the sales tax. The general rate of taxation is 10% of the payment for the assessed deliveries or other services; the rate of taxation for most products of the publishing trade is 5%.
The Value-added Tax, which came into operation on 1 January 1970, is levied on all stages of the production and sale of goods and also on all other remunerated services. It becomes part of the cost only to the final consumer.
Export deliveries are free from sales tax.
The following goods from the book trade and productions of the printing trade are subject to the reduced rate of tax of 5% (Art. 40 of the law of 5 August 1969 published in the "Memorial" A No. 40 of 16 August 1969): Books, brochures, newspapers and other periodical publications, cartographic productions of all kinds.

All other kinds of cultural productions are subject to the regular rate of taxation of 10%.

14 Copyright

Luxembourg is a signatory to the "Berne Convention" in the revised form of Rome (1928) and Brussels (1948).
Copyright on works of literature and the fine arts operates for fifty years after the death of the author. It then expires. The "Berne Convention" obliges the signatories to introduce the agreed legislation, and in particular to entitle authors of member countries to the same legal rights as the authors in the home country.
Such legislation does not yet operate in Luxembourg; however, an appropriate draft has already been worked out.

15 National Bibliography, National Library

The first public library in Luxembourg came into being during the second French period by the decrees of 15 April and 29 June 1798. It embraced the "Bibliothèque des anciens États du Pays de Luxembourg", the "Bibliothèque des Jésuites" and the library of the various religious congregations that had been suppressed by the revolutionaries and incorporated with the central school.
After the dissolution of this school, the library was placed, in 1802, at the disposal of the city authorities, who placed it under the care of a librarian.
When the secondary school was founded in 1804, the post of librarian was abolished and the administration handed over to the headmaster of the particular school. In 1837 a special library was founded for the "Athenaeum". In 1848 the reform of secondary instruction brought with it the merging of the city library and the library of the Athenaeum. The librarian in charge of the combined libraries was appointed by the general administrator of public education and was given an assistant. The regulations of 24 January 1850, 24 May 1853, 13 February 1871 and 10 June 1893 determined the powers of the librarian and his assistant. The term "National Library" is first used in the budget of 1899 and with appropriate words of appreciation, thus fittingly underlining the role played by this cultural institution in the life of the community.
In 1945 the 30,000 volumes of the "Bibliothèque Pédagogique" and the 10,000 volumes of the "Bibliothèque Professionelle" were incorporated into the "National Library", which today consists of some 400,000 volumes.
The

Bibliothèque Nationale
14 a Boulevard Royal
L Luxembourg

has the task of collecting, keeping and placing at readers' disposal all literature appearing in the country. Further, it has to acquire as many as possible of the fundamental scientific works published abroad. It also has the task of compiling and publishing annually the *Bibliographie luxembourgeoise*.
The "Bibliographie luxembourgeoise" (about 200 pages) deals with the publications of Luxembourg authors that have appeared in the course of a year and those foreign publications that concern or interest the Grand-Duchy: 1. New books; 2. maps and atlases; 3. printed music; 4. newspapers and magazines; 5. records; 6. articles appearing in newspapers and magazines dealing with science, local history or folklore.
The bibliography is compiled under the following headings: theology, philosophy, psychology, education, linguistics, literature (German, French, dialect, history and criticism), history, local history, folklore, law, administration, economics, politics, archaeology, fine arts, geography, tourism, mathematics, physics, chemistry, botany,

zoology, medicine, technology, industry, business, trade and transport, sport, leisure, agriculture, forestry, press and newspapers, authors, publishers, printers.
Publishers are obliged to deliver copies of works to the "National Library" by the law of 5 December 1958 and the regulation of 6 May 1960. Delivery of literary and musical works of all kinds must be made before these can be sold or distributed.

16 Book Production

On average about 130 new publications by Luxembourg authors appear every year.
The annual book output of 1967 was 200 titles.

18 Book Clubs

There is one book club in Luxembourg, called "Der Freundeskreis" (the "Friends' Circle"), founded in 1936. Each year it publishes from one to three works by Luxembourg authors (2 books on average); these are either novels, poetry, stories, essays, biographies or drama. Registered members undertake to acquire all the books published. As the range of the works published varies in size, the contribution varies from year to year. After the books have been delivered to members they are displayed for sale in the bookshops.

21 Publishing

In the Grand Duchy there are 17 publishing houses, situated in Luxembourg and Esch-Alzette. These firms publish on average 130 works by local authors per year, mostly literary. In addition individual firms publish specialist literature on the following subjects: law and taxation, education, local history, documentation, travel, cartography, photography, calendars. Not infrequently an author will share in the cost of printing and deal with the sale of his book. A few privileged authors receive subsidies from the "Ministry of Cultural Affairs".

24 Retail Trade

The 100 bookshops and book outlets are primarily concentrated in the capital, in Esch-Alzette, Diekirch, Ettelbruck, Echternach, Dudelange, Remich, Grevenmacher and Bettembourg.

26 Antiquarian Book Trade, Auctions

Before the Second World War there were a number of very successful antiquarian book dealers in Luxembourg. They were mostly Jews, who at the German invasion of Luxembourg in 1940 either emigrated or were carried off to concentration camps by the German civil administration.
Since 1945 the antiquarian book trade in Luxembourg has not yet succeeded in regaining its former splendour.

27 Book Imports

According to the official statistics for 1967, about 30 million L. francs' worth of books were imported into Luxembourg.
The countries from which those books were imported in that year were as follows:

Country	Amount in L. fr. 1,000	Percentage of total
Germany (Federal Republic)	20,968	69.0
France	5,593	18.3
Switzerland	1,064	3.3
Belgium	1,026	3.3
Italy	610	2.0
United Kingdom	288	1.0
Netherlands	287	1.0
Austria	246	1.0
USA	201	0.8
Denmark	56	0.3
German Democratic Republic	6	—
Total	30,345	100.0

Luxembourg

30 Public Relations

The book trade in Luxembourg maintains close and regular contact with the public, thus preserving maximum interest in all branches of bookselling.
By means of posters and other advertising material, attention is drawn to various changes in opening times, to events important in the book world, New Year's festivals, seasonal sales in the form of "Semaines du Livre Soldé" (remainder sales), combined book exhibitions, etc.

32 Literary Prizes

A ministerial decree of 8 July 1924 created a *Prix de littérature luxembourgeoise* ("Luxembourg Literature Prize"), to be awarded in rotation to a work of literature, science and art. This decree has subsequently undergone various changes, e.g. under the ministerial instructions of 15 December 1927 and 1 December 1938. Today this Luxembourg Literature Prize of 25,000 L. fr. is only occasionally awarded, the most recent being in 1966. 25,000 L. fr. were awarded to each of two works, one in the Luxembourg language and one in German. None of the submitted works in French was considered by the jury to have reached the required standard.
Only rarely has a scientific work received the award. Up to now it has never been given to a work of art.

33 The Reviewing of Books

Cooperation between press, radio and television is encouraged and is of great importance. New works are without exception discussed in local newspapers and magazines, and on the radio.
Daily newspapers and magazines publish, monthly and free of charge, a list of new publications drawn up by the "Fédération" (→ 4) under the heading *Letzeburger Bichermaart* ("Luxembourg Bookmarket").

Malta

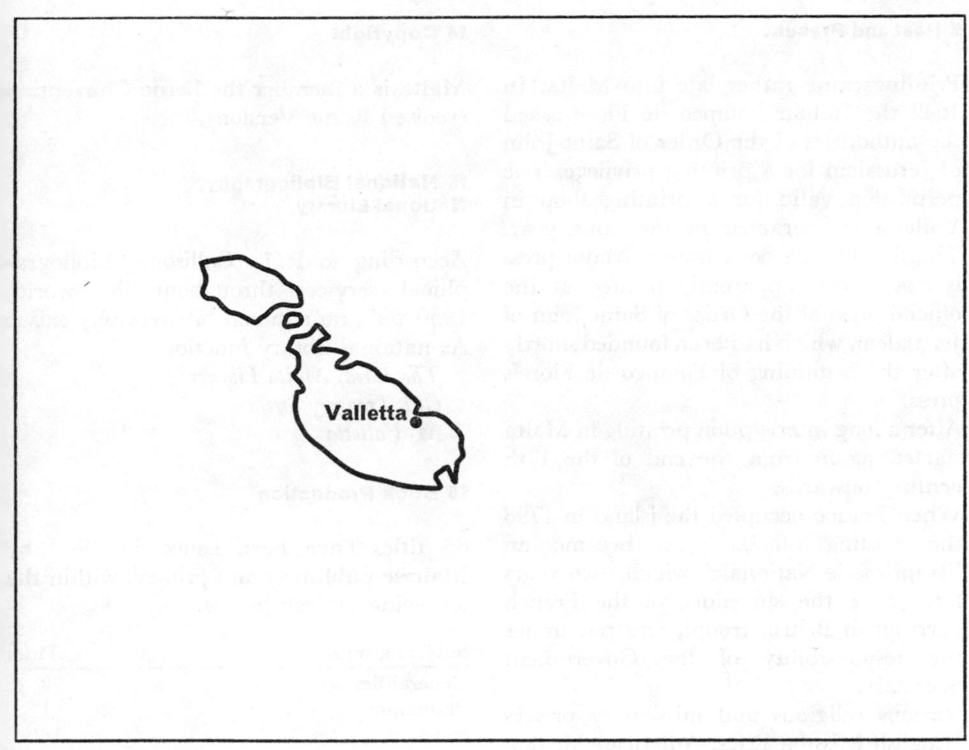

Important Book Centres

1 General Information

Area 316 km²

Population 316,000 (1,000 per km²)

Capital and largest town Valletta

Government According to the constitution of 1964 Malta is independent within the British Commonwealth. The governing cabinet is responsible to the House of Representatives.

Religion Roman catholic (state religion)

National languages English and Maltese are the official languages, Italian is widely spoken.

Weights, measures Imperial system

Currency unit Maltese Pound (at par with the Pound Sterling)

Education Compulsory between 6 and 14 years, one University with 1,010 students

Illiteracy 30 %

Paper consumption a) newsprint 2.2 kg per inhabitant (1968)
b) printing paper 3.8 kg per inhabitant (1968)

Malta

2 Past and Present

Printing came rather late into Malta. In 1642 the Italian Pompeo de Fiore asked the authorities of the Order of Saint John of Jerusalem for a printing privilege. The permission valid for a printing shop in Valletta was granted in the same year. The first known book from a Malta press is from 1644, apparently printed at the official press of the Order of Saint John of Jerusalem, which had been founded shortly after the beginning of Pompeo de Fiore's press.
After a long interruption printing in Malta started again from the end of the 17th century onwards.
When France occupied the island in 1798 the existing official press became an "Imprimerie Nationale" which, two years later after the surrender of the French garrison to British troops, was put under the responsibility of the Government Secretary.
Various religious and missionary presses (English Mission Press, American Mission Press) were established on Malta. They produced a remarkable amount of Bible texts.

Bibliography

C. Clair, *The spread of printing: Malta.* Amsterdam, Van Gendt 1969. 35 pp. With a short bibliography on p. 30.

7 Sources of Information

Information may be obtained from

The Librarian
The Royal Malta Library
Old Treasury Street
M Valletta

or

Department of Information
24 Merchants Street
M Valletta

14 Copyright

Malta is a member the Berne Convention (reoised Rome Version).

15 National Bibliography, National Library

According to R. L. Collison, "Bibliographical services throughout the world, 1950–59", no national bibliography exists. As national library functions

The Royal Malta Library
Old Treasury Street
M Valletta

16 Book Production

65 titles have been issued in 1967 by Maltese publishers and printers within the following subject groups:

Subject group	Titles
Generalities	2
Philosophy	1
Religion	16
Social sciences	8
Philology	1
Pure sciences	3
Applied sciences	4
Arts	1
Literature	22
Geography, history	7
Total	65

21 Publishing

The four active publishers have their premises in Valletta.

24 Retail Trade

Bookselling is centralized in Valletta where 5 bookshops and stationers, catering also for books, are situated.

26 Antiquarian Book Trade, Auctions

There are no antiquarian booksellers as such, but some private collectors buy and exchange early works, maps, prints, e.g., relating to Malta.

27 Book Imports

In 1968 Malta imported books, brochures and leaflets valued at £ 160,531.
The leading countries of origin were:

United Kingdom	£ 142,146
USA	£ 8,042
Italy	£ 6,197

In addition £ 4,413 worth of children's picture and printing books and £ 3,309 worth of atlases were imported.
The imports of periodicals were valued at £ 165,962, with the United Kingdom as by far the most important supplier (£ 141,128) and Italy coming next (£ 21,445).

28 Book Exports

In 1968 Malta exported books, brochures e.g. valued at £ 151,219.
The leading countries of destination were:

United Kingdom	£ 85,292
Lebanon	£ 22,739
Libya	£ 21,052
Nigeria	£ 9,892
Italy	£ 3,508

Netherlands

Important Book Centres

1 General Information

Area 36,150 km²
Population 12,370,000 (370 per km²)
Capital Amsterdam (862,000)
Seat of the government Den Haag (593,000)
Largest towns Amsterdam (862,000); Rotterdam (728,000); Den Haag (593,000); Utrecht (271,000); Eindhoven (181,000); Haarlem (172,000); Groningen (154,000); Tilburg (147,000); Nijmegen (142,000); Enschede (135,000)
Government The Netherlands are a monarchy with a Parliament consisting of two Chambers: the First and Second Chamber. The country has eleven provinces.
Religion Roman Catholic 40.4%
Dutch Reformed and Calvinist 37.5%
Smaller religious groups and dissidents 3.6%

National language Dutch
Leading foreign languages English, French, German
Weights, measures Metric system
Currency unit Gulden (guilder) (Hfl)
Education Compulsory to 15; 163,213 students (3rd level)
Illiteracy Nil
Paper consumption a) Newsprint: 18.9 kg per inhabitant
b) Printing paper: 28 kg per inhabitant
Membership UNESCO, IPA, ICBA, ILAB

2 Past and Present

The first printing in the Netherlands was done in 1473 and in 1477 the first Dutch Bible came off the presses in Delft. The seventeenth century, in Holland commonly called "the Golden Age" because of its cultural and economic expansion, is also of the utmost importance with regard to books, the Dutch book trade being the world's largest during that century. The eminent printer families of those days are world-famous: Elsevier, Van Waesberghe, Blaeu and, in the eighteenth century, Enschedé, whose printing office, established in Haarlem in 1703, is a going concern until this very day.

As in Germany, "book trade" for a very long time (well into the nineteenth century) included publishing and bookselling. Not until after *c.* 1850 do the publisher and the bookseller begin to lead a life of their own. The original situation, however, has left some recognizable traces: one of these is that the publisher still has the prerogative to sell straight to the consumer. An intermediate book trade, linking publisher and bookseller, has so far played no significant role in the Netherlands, except that for a number of years it has been serving as a link between the publisher and the booksellers.

On 11 August 1815 a trade group of nineteen reached an agreement pledging themselves to take legal action against pirate printers and sales. For in those days reprinting the works of fellow-publishers was the most natural thing in the world, in spite of existing prohibitory laws. The above-mentioned date may be regarded as the birth date of the "Vereeniging ter bevordering van de belangen des Boekhandels" ("Dutch Book Trade Association—henceforth referred to as the "Association", → 4).

This young organization soon met with success; within seven years piratical printing had almost become a thing of the past and it was not long before members could begin to devote their time to other problems.

The above serves to illustrate the fact that the members of the Association were engaged in publishing as well as bookselling. Until this day both publishers and booksellers are members of the Association. But apart from this, the publishers are organized in the "Koninklijke Nederlandsche Uitgeversbond" ("The Royal Dutch Publishers' Association", → 4) which dates back to 1880; and the booksellers in the "Nederlandse Boekverkopersbond" ("The Dutch Booksellers' Association", → 4), founded in 1907. Since then publishers and booksellers have each gone their own way, for both groups felt the need to have their separate interests served. The Association may be considered as the master - organization.

Bibliography

E. de Bock, *Beknopte geschiedenis van de boekhandel in de Nederlanden.* (A concise history of the book trade in the Netherlands.) Antwerpen, Nederlandsche Boekhandel 1943. 144 pp.

Bont-boek over bond en boek. Een gevarieerde verzameling opstellen over het uitgeven, produceren en distribueren van boeken. Bijeengebracht ter gelegenheid van het 75-jarig bestaan van de Nederlandsche Uitgeversbond, voorafgegaan door een geschiedenis van de N.U.B. van 1931 tot 1955. (A varied anthology of essays on the publishing, production and distribution of books. Compiled on the occasion of the 75th anniversary of the Dutch Publishers' Association with a prefatory history of the D.P.A. from 1931 to 1955.) Amsterdam 1955. 158 pp.

H. Furstner, *Vereeniging ter bevordering van de belangen des Boekhandels 1940–1965.* (Vereeniging 1940–65.) Amsterdam, Vereeniging 1965. 122 pp.

Netherlands

A. C. KRUSEMAN, *Bouwstoffen voor een geschiedenis van den Nederlandschen boekhandel, 1830–1880.* (Materials for a history of the Dutch book trade, 1830–80.) 2 vols. Amsterdam, P. N. van Kampen & Zoon 1886–7. 864, 873 pp.

V. LOOSJES, *Geschiedenis van de Vereeniging ter bevordering van de belangen des Boekhandels 1815–1915.* (History of the Vereeniging, 1815–1915.) Amsterdam, Vereeniging 1915. 171 pp.

A. LOOSJES, *Vereeniging ter bevordering van de belangen des Boekhandels 1915–1940.* (Vereeniging, 1915–40.) Amsterdam, Vereeniging 1940. 170 pp.

De Nederlandsche Uitgeversbond, Gedenkboek 1880–1930. (The Dutch Publishers' Association. Memorial volume 1880–1930.) Amsterdam 1930. 202 pp.

De Nederlandse Boekverkopersbond 1907–1947. (The Dutch Booksellers' Association, 1907–47.) Den Haag 1947. 135 pp.

3 Retail Prices

In the Netherlands the fixed retail price was regulated in 1907. In that year the Association's bye-laws (which may be regarded as its statutes) inserted a clause which made adherence to the fixed retail price compulsory for every member. The fixed price has been the pillar supporting the Dutch book trade ever since. In the Netherlands it is also the general concensus of opinion that price competition is undesirable when dealing in cultural commodities. The obligation to adhere to the fixed retail price has now been laid down in a series of sections of the bye-laws of the "Dutch Book Trade Regulations". If a bookseller or publisher fails to comply with this ruling, the supervisory committee may call him to account for his transgression of the regulations.

These bye-laws recognize a few exception to the fixed-price regulations. Thus in the Netherlands we recognize: prices for members (reduced prices for members of an association), quantity prices (20 copies or over), prices of series (not to be less than 50% of the retail price), prices on subscription terms and prices of books, regarded as public-relations gifts (from a certain quantity upwards, varying according to the price of the book). Lawful reductions are: 5% on supplies of textbooks to or on behalf of schools, 5% on supplies of scientific books to government institutions or scientific libraries, 10% on supplies of belles-lettres and juvenile books to public libraries and 15% in the last-mentioned category on orders of 15 copies or over.

In 1964 the Dutch government passed a law prohibiting the application of collective vertical price-control in vertical price maintenance in competition agreements. This also affected the above-mentioned bye-laws of the "Book Trade Regulations". Fortunately the government law contained a modification, providing a means to apply for exemption. Naturally the Association applied for this exemption. In 1967 the government granted the Association the right to fix net prices for its books.

Bibliography

P. NIJHOFF ASSER, *De verticale prijsbinding en het boek.* (Vertical price control and the book.) In: De Vertegenwoordiger 1965, no. 1/2. Amsterdam 1965.

4 Organization

The master-organization is the

Vereeniging ter bevordering van de belangen des Boekhandels
(Dutch Publishers' and Booksellers' Association)
Het Boekhuis
Jan Tooropstraat 109
Postbox 8014
NL Amsterdam-W. 2

founded in 1815.

Membership consists of about 1,950 booksellers, 400 publishers and ten importers. Legally everyone in Holland has the right to practise as book trader and/or a publisher. However, anyone wishing to participate in the "Book Trade Regulation" must be accredited by the Association as either a bookseller or a publisher. In order to qualify for accreditation one must meet certain requirements, which includes obtaining the certificate (→ 11). Books up to Dutch fl. 25.— may be sold in every shop. The most important obligations taken on by those accredited are: adherence to the fixed price, and the purchase of books only within the closed circuit of acknowledged dealers and publishers.

Responsibilities of the Association are: Promoting the combined interests of publishers and booksellers, furthering mutual consultation between publishers' and booksellers' groups, preservation of bye-laws ensuring smooth commercial traffic between publishers, booksellers (or library managers) and the public (including a ruling preventing the publication of two Dutch translations of a foreign work that is unprotected by the "Berne Convention"), management of the commercial institutions, "Centraal Boekhuis" ("Single Copy House"), "Bestelhuis van de Boekhandel" ("Book Trade Clearing House"), "Nieuwsblad voor de Boekhandel" ("Book Trade Review"), carrying on publicity for the Dutch book, preservation and advancement of arbitration and jurisdiction, providing professional training for assistants in the book trade, publishing firms and libraries, financial support of former colleagues if it is needed, granting premiums for covering special expenditures, and supervising the publication of books of a bibliographical or iconographical nature.

The board consists of eight members, 4 booksellers and 4 publishers. They serve a four-year term on the board. They cannot be re-elected immediately. The authority in the Association is the annual general meeting, usually held in early July. The board has delegated a number of duties to committees, such as the "Commissie voor het Handelsverkeer in de Nederlandse Uitgeverij en Boekhandel" ("Committee for Book Trade Regulations"), the "Commissie voor de Collectieve Propaganda van het Nederlandse Boek" ("Book Development Committee"), the "Commissie voor het Ondersteuningsfonds" ("Relief-fund Committee"), the "Commissie voor de Martinus Nijhoff Reisbeurs" ("Martinus Nijhoff Travel Foundation Committee"). The Association has established an independent body, doing research on buying, reading and study habits. This organization is called "Stichting Speurwerk betreffende het Boek" ("Book Research Foundation, →9)".

In addition to the Association there are:

De Koninklijke Nederlandsche Uitgeversbond
(The Royal Dutch Publishers' Association)
Herengracht 209
NL Amsterdam-C.

and

De Nederlandse Boekverkopersbond
(The Dutch Booksellers' Association)
Waalsdorperweg 119
NL Den Haag

An entirely separate organization is the

Nederlandse Organisatie van Tijdschriftuitgevers
(Dutch Organization of Periodical Publishers)
Herengracht 257
NL Amsterdam

The Association is housed in the "Boekhuis" ("Book House") as are the secretariat, the management, the administration, the editorial staff of the "Nieuwsblad voor de Boekhandel" ("Book Trade Review", → 5) and the "Centraal Boekhuis" ("Single Copy House").

The *Bestelhuis van de Boekhandel* ("The Book

Trade Clearing House"), founded in 1871, is an institution of the Association. It is a shipping agency for the forwarding of books from the publishers to the booksellers, situated now in Zwanenburg. The *Centraal Boekhuis* ("Single Copy House"), founded in 1926, is also an institution of the Association. It is a record-office which has on file virtually every important book title published by the majority of Dutch publishers. Its purpose: a prompt delivery to the book trade of smaller quantities (→ 23).

The Library. The Association owns a library with "books about books", the largest collection of its kind in Europe, perhaps in the world. The "Library" is not housed in the "Book House": the University Library of Amsterdam has it on loan. The "Library's" temporary home is a building on the Nieuwe Prinsengracht 57, Amsterdam (→ p. 70).

Bibliography

Catalogus der Bibliotheek van de Vereeniging voor de Boekhandel. (Library catalogue of the Vereeniging.) 7 vols. Den Haag, Nijhoff 1920–65.

H. Furstner, *In en om Het Boekhuis.* (In and around the Book House.) Amsterdam 1969. 48 pp.

Mr. C. Vrij, *De Vereeniging voor de Boekhandel en het Reglement voor het Handelsverkeer in de Nederlandse Uitgeverij en Boekhandel.* (The Vereeniging and Book Trade Regulations.) Amsterdam 1967. 55 pp.

5 Trade Press

The most important organ is the weekly

Nieuwsblad voor de Boekhandel
(Book Trade Review)
Postbus 8014
NL Amsterdam

The first issue appeared on 1 October 1834. It contains an editorial section with articles and news items concerning the book trade and publishing at home and abroad, an official section giving information from the board and committees and finally advertisements of publishers announcing their titles. The editorial section includes a column, "Nieuwe uitgaven verschenen in het Nederlandse taalgebied" ("New publications in the Dutch language"), including a description of virtually all the titles published in the Netherlands. Publishers are bound by law to send a copy of each of their new publications and new editions to the "Review" to have a title description written (the copy will be returned to them). A few times a year special issues appear: for instance, a "Spring Issue" on the occasion of the "Book Week", and an "Autumn Issue".

De Uitgever
(The Publisher)
Doezastraat 1
NL Leiden (Administration)
Editorial Offices
Herengracht 209
NL Amsterdam-C.

appears monthly and is the organ of the "Royal Dutch Publishers' Association" (→ 2, 4). It mainly contains thorough and reliable articles concerning the publishing trade.

De Boekverkoper
(The Bookseller)
Waalsdorperweg 119
NL Den Haag

is another monthly publication and the organ of the "Dutch Booksellers' Association" (→ 2, 4). It gives information primarily of interest to booksellers.

Het Nederlandse Tijdschriftenwezen
(Dutch Periodical Publishing)
Herengracht 257
NL Amsterdam

This monthly magazine is the organ of the "Dutch Organization of Periodical Publishers" (→ 4).

6 Book-Trade Literature

As most Dutch people are able to read English, German and French, they can consult foreign-language trade literature. Simple, yet thorough and practical, are the textbooks of the "Professional Training Courses", which the Association sets up for assistants in the book trade and publishing:

P. Hagers, *Inleiding tot het uitgeversberoep.* (Introduction to the publishing profession.) Amsterdam 1964. 95 pp.

J. W. Holsbergen, *Vandaag voor Morgen. Principiële richtlijnen voor de reclame.* (Today for tomorrow. Fundamental directives for advertising.) Amsterdam 1964. 50 pp.

G. J. van der Lek, *Bibliographie. Beknopte Handleiding.* (Bibliography. Concise guide.) Amsterdam 1969. 148 pp.

A. W. Vogelsang, *Geven + nemen = mededelen.* (Give + take = inform.) Amsterdam 1967. 192 pp.
Deals with advertising knowledge for the bookseller.

A. W. Vogelsang and Joh. van Doorn, *Praktijk voor de Boekverkoper.* (Practice for the bookseller.) Amsterdam 1966. 209 pp.

A. Witte, *De vormgeving van het Boek.* (Book design). Amsterdam 1965. 159 pp.

W. G. Hellinga, H. de la Fontaine Verwey, G. W. Ovink, *Copy and printing in the Netherlands.* Amsterdam, North-Holland Publ. Co. 1962. XXVII, 253 pp.

H. van Krimpen, *Het Boek: Over het maken van Boeken.* (The book: on making books.) Arnhem, Van Loghum Slaterus 1966. 440 pp.
A standard work of vast importance on publishing and the book trade.

Th. Wink, *Auteursrecht in Nederland.* (Copyright in the Netherlands.) Revised by Th. Limperg. Amsterdam 1970. 92 pp.

As directories for the book trade, publishing firms, etc. there are available two titles that appear annually:

Lijstenboek van de Vereeniging. (Directory of the Vereeniging.) Amsterdam, Vereeniging.
Lists the names of all accredited booksellers, publishers, wholesalers, importers foreign sole agencies in the Netherlands and Dutch publishers' representatives. Also a membership list of the Association. This directory comes out every year early February.

Sijthoffs Adresboek voor Boekhandel, Uitgeverij, Grafische industrie, Gids voor dagbladen en tijdschriften. (Sijthoff's directory for book trade, publishing firms, the printing trade, guide for dailies and periodicals.) Leiden, Sijthoff.
This directory (103rd volume 1969/1970) also appears annually.

7 Sources of Information, Address Services

For general information, apply to the

Vereeniging ter bevordering van de belangen des Boekhandels
(Dutch Publishers' and Booksellers' Association)
Postbus 8014
NL Amsterdam

The Association will, if necessary, forward those letters which it does not feel qualified to answer.

For specific questions of a bibliographical nature one may apply to the

Bibliotheek van de Vereeniging ter bevordering van de belangen des Boekhandels
(Library of the Association)
Nieuwe Prinsengracht 57
NL Amsterdam-C.

or to the

Koninklijke Bibliotheek
(Royal Library)
Lange Voorhout 34
NL Den Haag

Netherlands

8 International Membership

As the master organization the Association is not a member of any international body. The "Koninklijke Nederlandsche Uitgeversbond" (→ 4 "Royal Dutch Publishers' Association") is a member of the "International Publishers' Association" and the "Nederlandse Boekverkopersbond" ("Dutch Booksellers' Association", → 4) of the "International Community of Booksellers' Associations". → 26.
The Kingdom of the Netherlands is affiliated with UNESCO.

9 Market Research

At the "Municipal University" of Amsterdam there are three chairs in connection with the book: Prof. G. W. Ovink lectures on "History and aesthetics of the art of printing and allied graphic techniques" and Prof. H. de la Fontaine Verwey and Prof. Th. P. Loosjes on "Book and bibliography".
Of great importance is the
Stichting Speurwerk betreffende het Boek
(Book Research Foundation)
Jan Tooropstraat 109
NL Amsterdam W. 2
This foundation does market and comparative research among book traders and publishing firms. Also, in 1965, it had an econometric model built concerning the the future of the Dutch book market during the ten years to come (1965–75). Basing its projection on economic statistical and mathematical data, the "Foundation" forecasts a 220% increase within the next 10 years. The "Foundation" maintains relations with similar institutions in other countries. The foundation has published the following reports:

Rapport betreffende: standaardadministratie boekverkopers; bestelformulieren boekverkopers; facturen uitgevers. (Report on standard administration for booksellers; order forms for booksellers; invoices for publishers.) 1960.

Handleiding standaardadministratie boekverkopers. (Standard administration, bookseller's annual.) 1960.

Mensen en Boeken 1961. Onderzoek naar de koop-, lees- en studiegewoonten 18 jaar en ouder. (People and books 1961. Study of buying; reading and study habits, of readers of 18 years and over.) 1961.

Memorandum inzake de facturering van het Centraal Boekhuis. (Memorandum concerning invoicing of the Single Copy House.) 1961.

Memorandum inzake de Buchhändler Abrechnung Gesellschaft. (Memorandum about a Book-trade Clearing Company.) 1961.

Het belang van rationeel bedrijfsbeheer van boekverkopersbedrijven. (The importance of rational management in bookselling concerns.) 1962.

Samenvatting der enquêtegegevens betreffende de rechtstreekse importen in Nederland in 1961 van boeken, wetenschappelijke en semi-wetenschappelijke tijdschriften. (Summary of inquiry data concerning direct imports of the Netherlands in 1961 of books, scientific and semi-scientific periodicals.) 1962.

Rapport van de resultaten Boekenweek 1962. (Report on the results of Book Week 1962.) 1962.

Kinderen en boeken 1963. (Children and books, 1963.) 1963.

Rapport betreffende bedrijfsvergelijkend onderzoek bij boekverkopersbedrijven over 1962. (Report on a comparative study of bookselling for concerns, 1962.) 1963.

NIPO-wekelijks consumentenonderzoek, Jaarrapport 1963. (NIPO-Weekly consumer research, annual report, 1963.) 1964.

Rapport betreffende de pocketboekenquête over de jaren 1958–1963 bij uitgevers. (Report on study on paperbacks during the years 1958–1963 of publishing.) 1964.

NIPO-wekelijky consumentenonderzoek, Jaarreport 1964. (NIPO-Weekly consumer research, annual report, 1964.) 1964.

Structuuranalyse en toekomstvisie betreffende de nederlandse boekenmarkt. (Structure and future analysis of the Dutch book market.) 1965.

Rapport betreffende de pocketboekenquête bij uitgevers over het jaar 1964. (Report on study on paperbacks during the year 1964.) 1966.

NIPO-wekelijks consumentenonderzoek rapport over de jaren 1963–1964–1965. (NIPO-Weekly consumer research report for the years 1963–1964–1965.) 1966.

10 Books and Young People

In the Netherlands much is done to stimulate the reading of good books among young people. Apart from the book trade the lending libraries are also very active. In this connection the

Bureau Boek en jeugd
(Book and Youth Office)
Bezuidenhoutseweg 231
NL Den Haag

of the "Centrale Vereniging voor Openbare Bibliotheken" ("Central Association of Public Libraries") is an important informative body for, amongst others, the juvenile departments of public libraries. Every month this office sends cards bearing titles and short reviews to the juvenile departments of various institutions wishing to receive this information. The Commissie voor de Collectieve Propaganda van het Nederlandse Boek (Book Development Committee, briefly called the "CPNB", organizes a "Juvenile Book Week" every autumn. It lasts for ten days. Reading contests are held with a country-wide finale on the eve of "Juvenile Book Week"; there is a gift for everyone spending a specified amount or more on children's books. In addition to this there are window-display contests in many towns, the various schools doing the window-dressing. In many cases there is close cooperation between the book trade and the public libraries.

In 1963 a large "Juvenile Book Convention" was held, where all sorts of problems connected with juvenile literature came up for discussion. It is expected that such a convention will again take place.

The "CPNB" awards two prizes annually to the authors of juvenile books: one for a book for children under ten years and one for a book for children of ten years and over. Once every three years the government awards the "State Prize for the Juvenile Book". This took place three times: 1965, 1968 and 1970.

(→ 30, 32).

Bibliography

Boek en Jeugd. Gids voor Jeugdlectuur. (Book and youth. Juvenile literary guide.) Den Haag and Amsterdam, Leopold & Ploegsma 1965–1967. 144, 52; 48 pp.

L. M. Boerlage, *Jeugdboeken lezen en kiezen.* (Reading and selecting juvenile literature.) Groningen, Wolters 1964.

Laat ze lezen. (Let them read.) An annual juvenile book guide of a number of firms jointly publishing children's books.

W. H. J. Niemöller, *Een onderzoek naar de kwaliteit van het Nederlandse kindertijdschrift.* (An inquiry into the quality of Dutch children's magazines.) Groningen, Wolters 1964. 76 pp.

11 Training

Since 1937 the Association has been organizing a two-year correspondence course for the vocational training of booksellers and publishers. Until 1967 this course was open only to those who were employed in bookshops and/or publishing firms, but the Government no longer permits this restriction. At the end of the first year students must take an examination and at the end of the second year they must take a final examination. The certificate students receive on passing this examination is one of the requirements

necessary to become an accredited bookseller or publisher (→ 4).
Students receive instructions in the following subjects: Organization of the book trade, social history, business administration, bibliography and book techniques. In addition to these the booksellers' course includes the following subjects: Practical training for the bookseller, salesmanship for the bookseller and the antiquarian bookshop. The publishers' course includes: Practical training for publishers, salesmanship for the publisher, copyright and book design. Towards the end of the second year, about a month before final examinations, there is one day of oral instruction.
607 students followed the 1966–7 course. Of that number 262 completed the first-year booksellers' training course and 149 completed the second year. 46 students followed the first-year publishing course, 34 the second year. 79 students took both courses at once for the first year, while 37 completed the second year.
In 1969 a day school started, giving a three-year executive training course in publishing and bookselling. Twice during this course there will be a six-month break during which the students will do practical work in bookshops and publishing firms.
In 1952, on the occasion of its 100th anniversary, the firm of Martinus Nijhoff in The Hague created the *Martinus Nijhoff Travel Foundation*, to enable capable personnel in publishing firms, bookshops and antiquarian firms to gain experience abroad. Assistants in our profession wishing to get practical foreign experience may apply to this foundation. In addition to this, the foundation organizes occasional instructional tours abroad. Thus in 1963 and 1967 one-week study-tours were made to Germany; in 1964 to Paris and in 1970 to London.
Many young people have joined forces in the *Studiegroep Boekhandel en Uitgeverij Elspeet* ("Study group of the book-trade and publishing firm Elspeet"). This group was the result of a post-graduate course that has been held twice, namely 1955–7 and 1957–9. Each time these courses have concluded with a study-week held in the village of Elspeet. Every year since, people have been getting together there in order to discuss all sorts of professional problems, draft reports and promote good fellowship.
In order to get a sufficient number of people to enter our profession, the *Commissie Beroepsvoorlichting* ("Vocational Guidance Committee") has been established in 1965. This committee tries to stimulate interest in our profession by giving information relevant to the book trade and by giving lectures to students and parents.

12 Taxes

Since 1970 the Netherlands have a purchase tax on books of 4%.

13 Clearing Houses

A clearing institution such as the "BAG" in Germany (→ Germany, F.R., 13) does not exist in the Netherlands. Book-gift certificates, which are very popular in this country, are settled via a clearing system, created by the "Nederlandse Boekverkopersbond" (→ 4).

14 Copyright

The Dutch Copyright Act of 1912, although—on minor points—revised repeatedly has in general been effective for nearly sixty years.
At present up for parliamentary discussion is a new series of amendments, aimed at achieving an adjustment to the Brussels text of the "Berne Convention", as well as to the changing views that are the result of social and technical development since 1912.
The "Copyright Act" grants exclusive rights of publication and multiplication to

the maker of a literary, scientific or artistic piece of work or to his legal representative. Roughly, eligible for protection are the same works as enumerated in section 2,1° of the "Berne Convention". The right may be assigned in whole or in part. Nevertheless, in that event the consent of the maker continues to be required for possible revisions in his work.
The copyright remains in force until 50 years after the author's death. Copyright on posthumous works expires 50 years after their first publication.
The Netherlands are a member of the "Berne Convention" in the text of Rome (1928). A bill for approval of the Brussels version (1948) is presently up for parliamentary discussion.
The "Universal Copyright Convention" has been approved by both chambers of the "States General" and is shortly expected to take effect officially.

15 National Bibliography, National Library

Publications coming out in the Netherlands are included as soon as possible in the weekly *Nieuwsblad voor de Boekhandel* (→ 5). The accredited publishers have pledged themselves to sending one copy of each of their publications to this weekly review in order to have a title-description written. The copy is returned to the publisher concerned.
Brinkman's Cumulatieve Catalogus van Boeken ("Brinkman's cumulative book catalogue"), a monthly publication, enumerates the titles published in the Netherlands (and Flanders); an annual issue lists the titles published during the past year, and every five years *Brinkman's Catalogus van Boeken en Tijdschriften* ("Brinkman's catalogue of books and periodicals") publishes the titles of the past 5 years. Corresponding to this catalogue is the repertory and title catalogue on "Brinkman's Catalogue". The publishers are A. W. Sijthoff's Publishing Company in Leiden.
The *Koninklijke Bibliotheek*
(Royal Library)
Lange Voorhout 34
NL Den Haag
could be regarded as being the *National Library*. As the Netherlands know no "dépôt légal", the "Koninklijke Bibliotheek" does not have at its disposal a copy of every book published in the Netherlands. However, they do have a central catalogue listing every title in the large scientific libraries in the Netherlands.

16 Book Production

The Dutch read a great deal and the number of titles produced for this small country may be called very large indeed. In 1966, 10,582 titles were published in the Netherlands. We must add here that this figure includes books and brochures of 48 pages and less. It is not possible to extrapolate these brochures from the statistics. The above-mentioned figure does not include sheet music. Of these 10,582 titles, 5,816 are new editions and 4,766 are reprints. Schoolbooks number 3,527. The foreign-language publications number 1,592 titles (15.1 %).
The most important categories are:

Subject group	Titles	Percentage of total production
Linguistics and literature	1,775	16.8
Novels and short stories	1,541	14.6
Science	1,081	10.2
Social science and economics	1,039	9.8
Juvenile literature	994	9.4
Political and general social history and history of economics	676	6.4
Technical science	541	5.1
Religion	503	4.8
Geography and ethnology	342	3.2
Philosophy	312	2.9

Netherlands

17 Translations

As many Dutchmen, who have the reading habit, also have a command, albeit passive, of French, German and English, a fairly large number of books are read in the original language. Yet the number of translated titles amounts to 3,680 or 34.8%. Fiction tops the list: 956 foreign-language novels were translated into Dutch. Translations from the English lead with 1,274 titles (12.1%), followed by German with 383 titles (3.6%) and French with 248 titles (2.3%).

18 Book Clubs

Book clubs in the modern sense of the word are new in the Netherlands. In September 1966 "De Nederlandse Lezerskring" ("Dutch Reading Society") was launched, followed in January 1967 by the "Europaclub for Books and Records". The several-year-old "Bosch and Keuning Book Club" has joined "De Nederlandse Lezerskring". The book club "Succes", a non-accredited publishing-firm, dates back further.
As both clubs are still in their infancy, little can be said about either their offers or their results.

19 Paperbacks

As in many other countries, the paperback in the modern sense of the word has undergone a tremendous development during the fifties, so that we may speak of a true avalanche. The paperback is sold either in large, separate basements (which may or may not be part of a bookshop), in magazine or newspaper stands, or alongside the hard-cover book in the regular bookshop. In order to present the paperback adequately, many bookstores needed to be remodelled.
There exist over 30 series of paperbacks. Only a few of the 36 firms that publish paperbacks market titles in the large quantities suitable for the nature of the pocket book.
Some publishers have gradually moved from pocket books towards paperbacks.

Bibliography

Every autumn the printer's firm of Semper Avanti in the Hague puts out the *Pocketgids* (Pocket-book guide) listing the titles of pocket books and paperbacks published by Dutch and Flemish firms and adding a few notes on contents or praise for each title.

In 1966 the *Gids voor buitenlandse pockets* (Foreign-language pocket-book guide), edited by A. A. van der Hoek and Jacques den Haan, was published by Ditmar in Rotterdam.

J. P. BARTH, *Pocketproblemen. Kostprijscalculatie en prijsbepaling bij de uitgever.* (Pocket book problems. Publishers' cost and price calculations.) In: Maandblad voor Handelswetenschappen, 1959, no. 12. Leiden, Ned. Uitgevers Mij.

Rapport betreffende de pocket-enquête over de jaren 1958–63 bij de uitgevers. (Report on study on pocket books during the years 1958–1963.) Amsterdam, Stichting Speurwerk betreffende het Boek 1964 (→ 9).

20 Book Design

In the Netherlands, too, the 50 best-designed books are selected annually by a jury. Selection is made on the basis of quality of material, print and binding of the ordinary book, not necessarily the bibliophile book, although the latter is not excepted. The improved quality in book design (especially schoolbook design) is undoubtedly the result of the annual jury reports. The fifty best-designed books are, among others, exhibited at the "Frankfurt Book Fair".

21 Publishing

Amsterdam, the nation's capital, is the traditional centre of the book trade. Since 1815 it has been the seat of the "Association", the "Book House" (→ 4), as well as of the majority of publishing firms, as illustrated by the following list of Dutch towns accommodating most publishing houses (as of 1967):

Amsterdam	102
Den Haag	39
Utrecht	22
Haarlem	15
Rotterdam	14
Leiden	12
Hilversum	10
Groningen	8
Baarn	8
Tilburg	6
Alkmaar	6

In all, almost 400 publishers are accredited by the Association. They are located in 100 different towns and villages. Because of the country's small size, good communications and an excellent network of roads, it does not greatly matter where a publisher is located. The total turnover of Dutch publishing for 1965 was estimated at Dutch fl. 200 million (excluding textbooks and export).
Exact turnover figures per publisher or per group are not available. However, figures can be given on the title production of publishers putting out more than 10 titles yearly. They number 144, all told. Those publishing less than 10 titles a year number 238. The production of the abovementioned 144 firms is:

Publishing firms	Titles annually
44	10– 20
53	20– 50
16	50–100
23	100–200
2	200–300
4	300–400
1	over 500

Textbooks are included in this count.
There is evidence of the growing concentration of concerns: publishing firms merge with publishing firms but also with printers, binderies, etc. It is the only possible way to combat rising costs and to compete with the very large concerns in our profession.

Bibliography

R. Boltendal, *Boekmakers. Portretten van uitgevers.* (Makers of books. Portraits of publishers). Amsterdam, Moussault 1965.

P. Hagers, *Inleiding tot het Uitgeversberoep.* (Introduction to the publishing profession.) Amsterdam, Vereeniging 1968.

A. Witte, *De vormgeving van het Boek.* (Book design.) Amsterdam, Vereeniging 1970.

22 Literary Agents

There are in the Netherlands a few large literary agencies concerned almost exclusively with foreign books. That is to say, they try to find a Dutch publisher willing to have foreign-language books translated into Dutch. Dutch authors are in direct touch with their publishers.
In order to advance a favourable climate for Dutch-language literature abroad, there has been established the

Stichting ter bevordering van de vertaling van Nederlands letterkundig werk
(Foundation for the Promotion of the Translation of Dutch Literary Works)
Herengracht 400
NL Amsterdam

This "Foundation" publishes the quarterly bulletin *Writing in Holland and Flanders*, which contains in English selected passages of Dutch books with a brief description of the author and a summary of the book's contents. This bulletin is sent to prominent foreign publishers. The "Foundation" itself does not conclude contracts but, if necessary, assists literary agents abroad; for instance, with preparing and editing a volume of poetry that is to include Dutch and/or Flemish poems. The "Foundation" is subsidized by the Dutch and Belgian governments.

23 Wholesale Trade

As concerns the normal book trade, the publisher generally supplies the bookseller directly. However, in the last few years an increasing number of wholesale firms have been established: on a regional, but even more especially on a local level, booksellers have joined forces in order to enlarge their stock by buying in bulk, particularly schoolbooks, though gradually other current saleable books as well.
The *Centraal Boekhuis*, lodging in the "Book House" (→ 4) in Amsterdam, is not a wholesale firm but functions as an intermediary agency. The "Centraal Boekhuis" is a book depository of virtually every title published by the majority of Dutch publishers. The copies remain the property of the publishers: they deposit a certain number of each there. Repeat orders on credit are settled with the individual publisher. The bookstore orders smaller quantities of one title from the "CB". By combining a variety of titles the book trade manages to get a more sizeable discount. The "CB" is geared for prompt delivery. The administration is handled by means of a punch-card system. In 1966 the turnover was Dutch fl. 7.6 million.
The importer serves as intermediary for the foreign book. There are about ten of them in the Netherlands. In many cases they act as sole representative of a foreign publisher as well.
Apart from this, some accredited booksellers and a few non-accredited firms act as sole agents for foreign publishers. In the event of an exclusive representation the bookstore may order its books from these non-accredited firms.
The large book dealers generally order directly from the foreign country concerned.

24 Retail Trade

The backbone of the trade is the bookstore with its stock on hand, where the public can go for information and select from as varied a stock as possible.
In this day and age the rendering of such a service involves ever-increasing expenditures and the bookseller must continually ask himself to what extent the service of ordering single copies of an inexpensive book is still justified. Indeed, there are bookstores—though relatively few in number—which limit this service and there are those—and their number is increasing—which charge the customer for the expense incurred.
In the Netherlands there are 1,944 sales centres under the management of accredited booksellers, 261 of which are branch stores. 36 supply schoolbooks exclusively. The 1,944 bookstores—about half of which have a turnover of less than Dutch fl. 50,000—are spread out over 595 towns and villages. The cities and villages with the largest number of bookstores are:

Amsterdam	209
Den Haag	105
Rotterdam	101
Utrecht	50
Haarlem	32
Arnhem	30
Groningen	29
Nijmegen	24
Eindhoven	21
Leiden	20

Modern sales methods demand that the lay-out of the store be convenient and encourage easy browsing. Consequently, since the fifties, many stores have been remodelled. The rise of the paperback book, too, has sometimes made it necessary for many bookstores to undergo alterations. Some shops have introduced a special basement for paperbacks.

Bibliography

A. W. Vogelsang and J. G. van Doorn, *Praktijk voor de Boekverkoper.* (Practice for the bookseller.) Amsterdam, Vereeniging 1966.

25 Mail-Order Bookselling

A few firms, which used to sell by mail order almost exclusively, have been forced to discontinue this sales method due to the enormous increase of postal rates which makes the mailing of folders and prospectuses a prohibitively expensive affair.
In the antiquarian book trade selling by mail-order catalogue still prevails.

26 Antiquarian Book Trade, Auctions

The Netherlands have always been a booksellers' country and what could be called a kind of antiquarian book trade "avant-la-lettre" dates back until the early seventeenth century. Throughout the seventeenth and eighteenth centuries "antiquarian" books formed part of the stock in trade of the larger bookshops in Holland, which were traditionally established in the four towns of Amsterdam, Den Haag, Utrecht and Leiden. The scope of these firms, a few of which have even survived until the present day, has been international from the start: large quantities of books in languages other than Dutch—a great many in French—have been published and sold, imported and exported from Holland. This typical international pattern has also remained a feature of Dutch antiquarian bookselling. Old books and modern books were found next to each other on the shelves of booksellers throughout the seventeenth and eighteenth centuries, and up to the first half of the nineteenth century. Antiquarian bookselling as a separate and independent form of business was virtually unknown until then.
A more definite separation between the selling of modern books and that of antiquarian books took place towards the last quarter of the nineteenth century. This saw the beginnings of firms, also operating on an international scale, exclusively or mainly devoted to the selling of antiquarian books.
The Dutch antiquarian booksellers got their own trade organization (recent membership: 65) in 1935, when the

Nederlandsche Vereeniging van Antiquaren
(Association of Dutch Antiquarian Booksellers)
c.o. A. Gerits
Delilaan 5
NL Hilversum

was founded.
Its periodical

Het Nederlandsche Antiquariat
(The Dutch Antiquarian Bookshops)
c. o. A. Gerits
Delilaan 5
LN Hilversum

appears monthly.
The "Dutch Association of Antiquarian Booksellers" is one of the member associations of the "International League of Antiquarian Booksellers", which was founded in 1946 at the initiative of the Dutch antiquarian bookseller Menno Hertzberger. The Dutch have played an active part in this international body since its founding. Today Dutch antiquarian booksellers have a prominent and esteemed place among their colleagues all over the world. Many firms are widely known abroad, not in the least on account of their specialization. The majority of them issue catalogues at regular intervals.
The first auction of books ever to be organized took place in Holland: on 6 July 1599 the library of the well-known Dutch

statesman and poet Philips van Marnix van St Aldegonde was sold by auction by the Leiden bookseller Christophorus Guyot. Since that date book auctions have regularly taken place in our country. Libraries of famous men of letters such as Lipsius, Scaliger, Vossius, Heinsius and Huygens were sold in this way. The cities of Amsterdam, Den Haag, Utrecht and Leiden were also the chief centres for book auctions. Today the Netherlands can boast of five internationally reputed auction houses for books.

Bibliography

J. G. Frederiks, *Belangrijke auctiën in vroeger tijd.* (Important auctions in former times.) In: Bijdragen tot de geschiedenis van de Nederlandsche boekhandel. vol. 5. Amsterdam 1892–95.

B. de Graaf, *Het antiquariaat. Beknopte handleiding.* (The antiquarian bookshop. Concise manual.) Amsterdam, Vereeniging 1968.

R. van der Meulen, *Over de liefhebberij voor boeken.* (On books as a favourite pastime). Leiden 1896.

27 Book Imports

Thanks to their favourable location on the continent and excellent intercontinental communications, the Netherlands have always played an eminent role in transit traffic. For the book trade the import and re-export of books is a factor which is not to be underestimated. Just as the Netherlands advocate free trade on every sea, so do they heartily accept one of the basic principles of "Unesco" and "ICBA"—the free flow of books. In 1966 the Netherlands imported Dutch fl. 39.856 m. worth of books and brochures and Dutch fl. 28.203 m. worth of magazines. (These figures refer to registered imports only.) The most substantial imports come from the following countries:

Country	Books Hfl.	Periodicals Hfl.
Germany (Federal Republic)	6,360,000	8,748,000
France	2,000,800	2,640,000
United Kingdom	5,685,000	2,887,000
USA	8,276,000	5,380,100
Switzerland	1,007,900	461,000
Belgium and Luxembourg	10,767,000	7,317,000

The import of books is only subject to the so-called compensating import duty (a substitute for purchase tax) on 4% and not to other taxes.

For importers of foreign books → 23.

28 Book Exports

In 1966 the Netherlands exported Dutch fl. 84.709 million worth of books and Dutch fl. 32.874 million worth of periodicals (these figures refer to registered exports only and mainly concern printing orders).

The main body of exports goes to the following countries:

Country	Books Hfl.	Periodicals Hfl.
Belgium and Luxembourg[1])	21,200,000	19,000,000
Germany (Federal Republic)	6,000,000	7,000,000
France	10,700,000	400,000
Italy	1,300,000	188,000
United Kingdom	17,000,000	1,470,000
USA	14,000,000	1,500,000

The Netherlands have a number of scientific publishers who exclusively, or almost exclusively, publish books and periodicals in foreign languages, mainly English. They

[1]) With reference to Belgium it may be assumed that a large portion of the figures refers to the furnishing of books not produced on printing orders from abroad (→ 35).

have earned the Netherlands an excellent reputation in the world of science and the scientific book.
According to the data of 23 of these scientific publishing firms, their exports for 1966 amonted to Dutch fl. 27 million. This figure may be broken down into Dutch fl. 12.6 million worth of books and Dutch fl. 14.4 million worth of periodicals. Of this amount 86.8% has been sent through the mail and therefore has not been registered.
In Belgium the people of Flanders reading and speaking Dutch are the leading recipients of the export of Dutch books and periodicals. There also is some export to South Africa for the benefit of the Dutch-reading part of its population.
The

Graphic Export Centre
Prinsengracht 668
NL Amsterdam

promotes the export from the Netherlands of books and printed matter.

29 Book Fairs

The Netherlands have no book fairs comparable to the "Frankfurt Book Fair". This German Fair, however, is attended by many Dutch colleagues and the number of Dutch stands—either collective or individual—is relatively large.
In 1965 a fair for the buying public was organized on the occasion of the 150th anniversary of the Association, the "Nationale Boekenmarkt 1965" ("National Book Mart 1965").
Similar "Marts" have been held in 1968 and 1970.

30 Public Relations

One of the most important committees is the *Commissie voor de Propaganda van het Nederlandse Boek* ("Book Development Committee"), the "CPNB". It looks after general promotion, which the "Committee" is enabled to carry on by means of a compulsory contribution from accredited publishers. Collective promotion was started in 1930 when a "Book Day" was organized. The first "Book Week" was organized in 1932. To this day it is the most important event for drawing the nation's attention to the book. The "CPNB" is guided in its policy by reports of the "Stichting Speurwerk betreffende het Boek" (→ 9). Since 1966 an important deviation from its course of action has become noticeable: attempts are made to popularize the book in order to get through to the large body of not-yet-readers.
The "CPNB's" chief promotional methods are:
1. "Book Week". This is held in February or March and earns the book tremendous publicity. In 1967 92% of Dutch adults had heard of "Book Week", as compared with 72% in 1951. "Book Week" opens with a great gala, which was televised in 1967. Opening nights are attended by numerous officials. Often members of the Royal Family are present to watch a performance of either drama, ballet or cabaret, which precedes the so-called "Writers' Ball". Many Dutch authors are invited to attend. During "Book Week" bookstores individually or together organize local "Book-week Evenings", lectures, etc.
2. The "Book-Week Gift Book". During "Book Week" anyone buying books for or over a specified amount receives a free book, published by the "CPNB". In 1967 the size of the edition was 237,400 copies.
3. A juvenile publication. On the occasion of the "Book Week" the "CPNB" publishes a very low-priced work, intended for youthful buyers. The 1967 edition: 43,830 copies.
4. "Book Week" flags and banners are displayed throughout this week.
5. Posters. The "CPNB" has posters made not only for the "Book Week", but also for "Juvenile Book Week", "Mother's

Day", "Father's Day", examination time, and summer recess.
6. "Juvenile Book Week", held from the end of October until early November. Here, too, a gift (often a picture) is received by anyone purchasing children's books for or over a specified minimum. A newspaper or folder with classified titles lists juvenile books available. Every "Juvenile Book Week" has its leading theme (1965: the animal; 1966: fairy tales, myths and legends; 1967: children in other countries).
An important part is played by a reading contest in which children from all over the country participate. The televised country-wide finale is held during "Juvenile Book Week".
Two children's books receive prizes during every "Juvenile Book Week".
The author of a book for children's books under 10 receives the "Annual Juvenile Book Prize Up to Ten", another the "Annual Juvenile Book Prize From Ten Up".
7. *Books in the Home,* a quarterly or semi-annual newspaper distributed by the book trade, is aimed at a large public. The size of the 1966 spring edition of this publication was 810,000 copies. It contains mainly publishers' advertisements informing readers of their publications.
8. The "*Book Guide*" contains an extensive list of titles and advertisements. It is intended for the more sophisticated reader who feels at ease when entering a bookstore.
Size of the 1966 spring edition: 211,500 copies.
9. "Literary Criticism Prize". This prize is awarded every other year by the "CPNB" in cooperation with the "Maatschappij der Nederlandse Letterkunde" ("Dutch Literary Society").
The "Dutch Booksellers' Association" (→ 4) has very successfully introduced the "Book Gift Certificate": if uncertain what book to give, one can buy such a book token, which is honoured anywhere in this country, in Belgium and in England. Settlement is made via a clearing system.

31 Bibliophily

With regard to the bibliophile book, we mention the "De Roos Foundation" in Utrecht. A limited number of lovers of the "book beautiful" become members. A few times a year they receive a bibliophile edition, brought out by the Foundation.
The address:
De Roos Foundation
c/o Chr. Leeflang
Boekhandel Broese
Nachtegaalstraat 20
NL Utrecht
In Den Haag is situated:
Museum van het Boek
(The Museum of the Book)
Prinsessegracht 30
NL Den Haag
(→ p. 63).

32 Literary Prizes

Dutch authors can hardly expect to live on their purely literary labours. They must also write articles, criticism, etc. In order to allow a writer more time for creative writing, the authorities have, for a number of years now, made available sums of money in the form of literary commissions, travel exhibitions, honorary allotments, etc. Another means of providing an author with money as well as a reputation is the institution of literary prizes.
The Dutch government makes annual awards of the *Staatsprijs voor Letterkunde,* better known as the *P. C. Hooftprijs* (named after the 17th-century Dutch poet P. C. Hooft).
Furthermore, once every three years the Dutch government awards de *Staatsprijs voor het Kinderboek* (for a children's book). Apart from the prizes awarded by the

"CPNB", we list here the following important Dutch prizes:

Prijs t.g.v. de jaarlijkse Conferentie der Nederlandse Letteren[1]*)*
Martinus Nijhoffprijs voor vertalingen
Prijs Fonds voor de Letteren
Gouden Ganzeveer (awarded by the KNUB, → 4)
Anne Frankprijs
Anna Blamanprijs
Van der Hoogtprijs
Reina Prinsen Geerligsprijs
Brand-Van Gentprijs
ANWB-prijzen
Van Kuilenburgprijzen
Friese Romanprijs
Amsterdamse Romanprijs
Amsterdamse Poezieprijs
Amsterdamse Novellenprijs
Amsterdamse Essayprijs
Literaire Aanmoedigingsprijs Eindhoven
Toneelprijs Contact Nederlandse en Vlaamse Toneelauteurs.

33 The Reviewing of Books

Every newspaper of any consequence devotes some space to reviews of newly published books. These book reviews apply to both the original Dutch book and the foreign-language book translated into Dutch. Some newspapers put out special book sections in the autumn and in the spring, on the occasion of the "Book Week".

Apart from inserting articles on literature and other subjects relating to the humanities or politics, a few generally excellently edited periodicals publish reviews that are sometimes very extensive and detailed.

Thus the Dutch public can, it so wishes, be very well informed on both the domestic and the foreign book. A critical informative periodical dealing with the foreign book exclusively is:

Literair Paspoort
(Literary Passport)
Beulingstraat 2–4
NL Amsterdam

34 Graphic Arts

Anyone requiring information on matters concerning book-production techniques may apply to the

Instituut voor Graphische Technieken
(Institute for Printing Techniques)
Ter Gouwstraat 1
NL Amsterdam

35 Miscellaneous

Flanders

There is close cooperation with Flanders, i.e. Dutch-speaking Belgium. To many publishers the Flemish market is very important (particularly when they bring out books by Flemish authors) and Belgian firms publishing well-known Flemish authors may be assured of a sizeable Dutch market.

Dutch and Flemish organizations in the field of books work together in a most congenial atmosphere. They have an agreement ensuring the mutual observance of the various rules that apply to their respective book-trade regulations.

[1]) This Conference is held alternately in Belgium and the Netherlands.

Norway

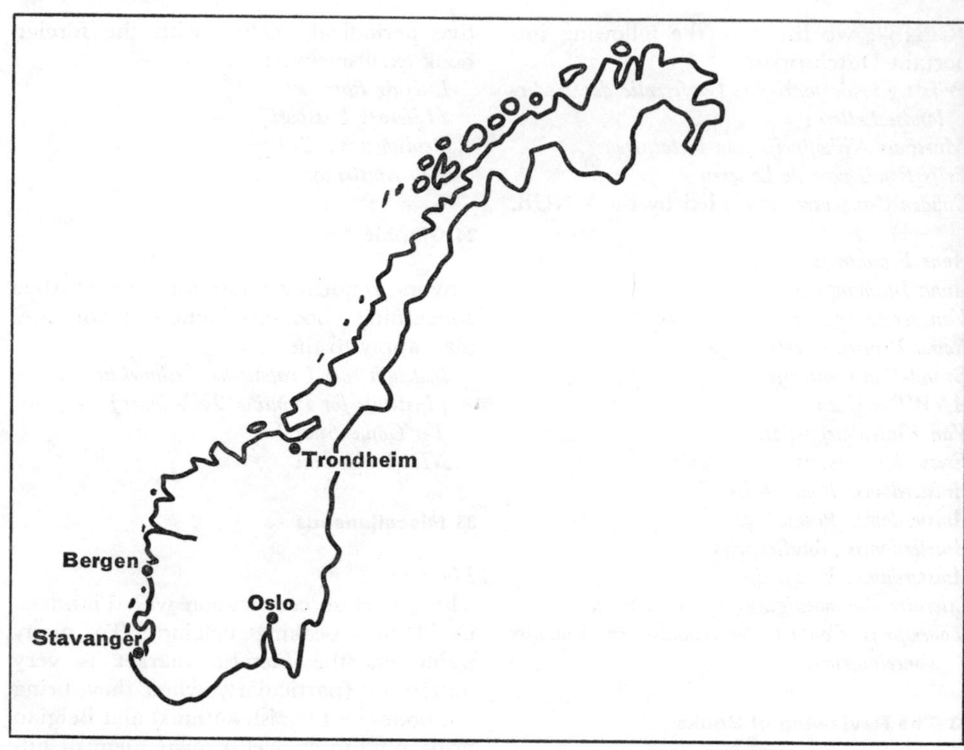

Important Book Centres

1 General Information

Area 324,000 km²
Population 3,723,000 (11.5 per km²)
Capital Oslo (485,000)
Largest towns Oslo (485,000); Bergen (117,000); Trondheim (123,700); Stavanger (79,400)
Government Monarchy with parliamentary government
Religions National church (Lutheran) 96.3 %
Smaller religious groups 3.1 %
Outside all religious communities 0.6 %
National language Norwegian
Leading foreign languages English, French, German
Weights, measures Metric system
Currency unit Norske kroner (n.kr.)
Education Compulsory. 27,414 (1969) students at 10 universities and technical and other colleges of academic standard, of whom 7,371 are women
Illiteracy Nil
Paper consumption a) Newsprint 20.0 kg per inhabitant (1969)
b) Printing paper (other than newsprint) 20.0 kg per inhabitant (1969)
Membership Unesco, IPA, ICBA, ILAB.

2 Past and Present

Due to Norway's great size, its widely dispersed settlements, and the difficulty of communication it was not until the second half of the 19th century that the Norwegian book trade became organized. In 1851 "Den norske Bokhandlerforening" ("Norwegian Booksellers' Association", → 4) was started as a union for both booksellers and publishers. The association concerned itself more and more with the task of developing an efficient bookselling network throughout the whole of Norway, following the same principles adhered to today: regulated cooperation between bookseller and publisher; technical knowledge (→ 11), i.e. practical experience in bookselling required of all who run bookshops; and emphasis on the principle of fixed net prices.

To stimulate the sale of books in rural or sparsely populated areas various tactics have been employed. Until the 1920s the "Norwegian Booksellers' Association" advertised places "open for the establishment" of bookshops; they also introduced the category "book agent" (with salesroom), without the technical requirements of "booksellers", and they encouraged existing bookshops to open branches. In 1962 "Den norske Forleggerforening" ("Norwegian Publishers' Association", → 4) introduced the concept "book sales outlets"; such outlets must not ge started nearer than 15 km to regular bookshops or their branches.

Time and experience showed that it was desirable for the two associations to have special organs through which each might promote its special interests. Thus, within the framework of the common association, subdivisions were formed: in 1888, "Norsk Provins-Bokhandler-Forening" ("Norwegian Association for Booksellers outside Oslo"); the "Norwegian Publishers' Association" in 1895; "Oslo Bokhandlerforening" ("Oslo Booksellers' Association") in 1920; and gradually also district associations in other parts of the country.

Around 1950 several publishers began to feel that it was not satisfactory to belong to a common association of both publishers and booksellers, and in 1956, after amicable agreement, all the publishers withdrew from the "Norwegian Booksellers' Association". This association thus became a purely general association, while the publishers are organized in the "Norwegian Publishers' Association". Although these two organizations are mutually independent, there is, naturally, continual close cooperation, aided by a common contact-committee. This consists of the two associations' chairmen, vice-chairmen, and directors; its task is for the parties to inform each other of their views concerning questions which are, or may be, of current importance. In this way unnecessary misunderstanding and disagreements may be avoided through mutual knowledge at an early stage.

The "Norwegian Booksellers' Association" has (in 1970) 398 member firms throughout the country, 68 of them in Oslo. 28 publishing houses—among them most of the leading ones—are members of the "Norwegian Publishers' Association". In principle these publishers distribute their total production through the organized bookshops. The relation between bookshops and publishers is regulated by "Bransjeavtalen" (the "Trade Rules"), which is recognized by the price authorities. The rules set forth in this agreement are in general also followed by the many smaller publishing houses which are not members of the Association.

Bibliography

H. L. Tveteraas, *Den norske bokhandels historie.* (History of the Norwegian book trade). To date 2 vols. Oslo, Norsk Bokhandler-Medhjelper-Forening 1936–64.

Published under the auspices of the "Norwegian Bookshop Assistants' Association" (→ 4), this history of a national book trade is one of the finest ever written. The work is supposed to be completed in two more volumes.

H. M. LANGE and P. JOHANSEN, *Seksti år for norsk bokhandel. Norsk Provins-Bokhandler-Forening, 1888–1948.* (Sixty years for the Norwegian book trade. The Norwegian Rural Booksellers' Association 1888–1948). Oslo 1948.

O.-ST. ANDERSSEN, *Bilder av bokhandelens historie.* (Pictures from the history of the book trade). Oslo, Den norske Bokhandlerforening 1951.
History of the book trade in Norway—from the Middle Ages to 1948.

3 Retail Prices

The principle of fixed prices in bookshops is rigidly upheld. Discounts can be allowed only in special circumstances formulated in the Trade Rules: 10% discount is allowed to libraries and to schools when these purchase books for the free use of the pupils. The case is different with older books, which may be sold more cheaply at price-reduction sales. Concerning this, the Rules say:

"Price-reduction sales may occur only once a year, and within a period of time to be determined by the 'Norwegian Publishers' Association' (→ 4) and the 'Norwegian Booksellers' Association' (→ 4). Booksellers may make use of this sales period to liquidate their stock of unsaleable books, provided these have not appeared in the present or the two previous calendar years. Price reduction on books in categories 4 and 5 (larger connected works, and subscription to such) is allowable only after the publisher has recalled the sample copy".

"During such a price-reduction sale publishers may, at reduced rates, deliver further copies of books which have not appeared in the present or the three previous calendar years. Publishers may not themselves start price reductions of books which have appeared within the period mentioned, i.e. the present or the two previous calendar years."

The period permissible for price reduction sales is a three-week period in the spring. Booksellers may then sell books at reduced prices until 31 July, but without posters or other forms of advertising. After 31 July prices return to normal for those books which publishers still have in stock.

For the time being (1970) there is nothing to indicate that the authorities will contest the principle of fixed prices in bookshops even though it is otherwise forbidden, in all other branches of trade, to operate with prices fixed by the supplier.

The "Norwegian Booksellers' Association" (→ 4) has an "Import Commission" which decides the rates of exchange for books imported from abroad. The prices thus arrived at are then the fixed retail prices for imported books.

4 Organization

The head organization of the Norwegian retail book trade is

Den norske Bokhandlerforening
(The Norwegian Booksellers' Association)
Övre Vollgt. 15
N Oslo 1

The "Bokhandlerforening" is under the management of an executive committee of 5 members, chosen for a 2-years period, and 2 deputies. While there is no formal stipulation of district representation, care is usually taken that the various parts of the country are represented in the executive committee. Within the framework of the "Norwegian Booksellers' Association", district associations have their local meetings. These district associations may not, however, negotiate directly with the

"Norwegian Publishers' Association" or other professional associations: this right is reserved for the "Norwegian Booksellers' Association". For recognition as a regular bookshop → 11.

Den norske Forleggerforening
(The Norwegian Publishers' Association)
Övre Vollgt. 15
N Oslo 1

is under the management of an executive committee of 7 members and 2 deputies, elected for a 1-year period.

Also situated in the professions' headquarters, "Bokhandelens Hus" ("Book Trade House") are the forwarding agents "A/S Bokcentralen" (the "Book Centre", → 13) and the centre for import of foreign books, "Norsk Bokimport A/S" ("Nor wegian Book Import", → 23).

Bookshop assistants are organized in the

Norsk Bokhandler-Medhjelper-Forening
(Norwegian Bookshop Assistants' Association)
Arbeidersamfunnets plass 1
N Oslo 1

Between this association and the "Norwegian Booksellers' Association" there is a wage agreement, the provisions of which follow, in the main, those of agreements in other branches of trade. The agreement is, however, quite independent, so that its provisions are not influenced by possible tariff conflicts elsewhere in trade.

5 Trade Press

The chief organ for the Norwegian book trade is the weekly

Norsk Bokhandlertidende
(Norwegian Book Trade News)
Övre Vollgt. 15
N Oslo 1

existing since 1879, edited by the "Norwegian Booksellers' Association" (→ 4). The magazine contains material of current interest in the trade, both domestic and foreign news, and is widely used by publishers as an advertising medium for their books, reaching booksellers, bookshop assistants, and libraries. It also contains the official weekly bibliography, prepared by the University Library in Oslo.

The "Norwegian Bookshop Assistants' Association" (→ 4) has as its organ

Krebsen
(The Crab)
Arbeidersamfunnets plass 1
Vaer. 301
N Oslo 1

which appears bi-monthly and was founded in 1906.

6 Book-Trade Literature

Most of the purely professional literature available in Norwegian on the subject is in the form of pamphlets and booklets, but the "Bokhandlerskolen" ("Booksellers' Training College", → 11) has published:

A. Andersen, *Bibliografi for Bokhandlerskolen.* (Bibliography for the Booksellers' Training College). Oslo, Bokhandlerskolen 1966.

→ 2.

7 Sources of Information, Address Services

Though some of the larger bookshops have specialities, in principle all Norwegian bookshops carry all kinds of books. Therefore no address lists of specialized bookshops exist; there is only the total list of recognized bookshops, set up according to geographical location. It is issued by "A/S Bokcentralen" (→ 4).

In addition, the "Norwegian Bookshop Assistants' Association" (→ 4) issues, irregularly, "Norsk Bokhandlermatrikkel" ("Register of Norwegian bookshops", latest edition 1966). It contains data on all bookshops and publishing houses, including owners and staff.

The best and easiest medium for reaching the book trade in general is the "Norsk Bokhandlertidende" (→ 5).

The "Norwegian Booksellers' Association" (→ 4) and the "Norwegian Publishers' Association" (→ 4) answer inquiries addressed to them.

8 International Membership

The "Norwegian Booksellers' Association" is a member of "ICBA". The "Norwegian Publishers' Association" is a member of "IPA".
→ 26.

9 Market Research

The "Norwegian Booksellers' Association" (→ 4) has to date four times, in cooperation with "Norges Handelshöyskole" ("Norwegian College of Commerce") published investigations of economic conditions within the book trade.
These investigations deal with the years 1931, 1963, 1966 and 1969. The results of the latter three investigations are available in two booklets (one giving text, the other tables).

Bibliography

A. J. PEDERSEN, *Økonomiske forhold i Norsk bokhandel 1963.* (Economical situation in the Norwegian retail book trade, 1963). Oslo, Den Norske Bokhandlerforening 1965. The same for the years 1966 and 1969.
A German version ("Norwegische Buchhandlungen im Betriebsvergleich") appeared 1966 (Hamburg, Verlag für Buchmarkt-Forschung).

10 Books and Young People

The "Norwegian Booksellers' Association" (→ 4) is a member of

Norsk kuratorium for barne- og ungdomsbøker
(Norwegian Curatory for Children's Books)
C. Carlsen
Högaasvn. 38
N 1346 Gjettum

and is thus connected to the international Curatory (→ International Section, 10). For literary prizes for children's books → 32.

11 Training

In cooperation with the booksellers' and the publishers' associations the "Norwegian Bookshop Assistants' Association" (→ 4) startet the

Bokhandlerskolen
(Booksellers' Training College)
Övre Vollgt. 15
N Oslo 1

in 1915. Each year, from January to May, if offers evening courses for pupils who during the day work in Oslo's bookshops. The College has an average of 20 applicants a year. Its programme is both theoretical and practical; excursions are arranged so that pupils may get a glimpse of fields related to the book trade; in addition visits to theatres, concerts, etc. are planned.
There is also the *Bokhandelens Sommerskole* ("Book Trade Summer School"), with courses lasting up to a week, held alternately in various parts of the country. Further, in connection with the yearly general meeting of the "Norwegian Booksellers' Association" (→ 4), courses are often offered for booksellers, publishers, and bookshop assistants.
In addition, "Bokhandlerskolen" arranges meetings in the larger towns to inform bookshop assistants and librarians about new children's books. These meetings take place before Christmas.
In order that a firm be recognized as a regular bookshop, the "Norwegian Publishers' Association" requires, among other things: In a firm with full liability the owner must possess a business license. If there is more than one owner, the requirement applies to the one who actually manages the shop.

If the firm is a stock company or other form of limited liability corporation, the shop manager under whose business licence the shop is to be run must be a member of the board, and he must further be the actual head of the corporation.
The possessor of this business licence must furthermore have 5 years' practical experience in an authorized bookshop, or 7 years' practical experience in his own book-sales outlet. Half of this practical experience must have been acquired within the past 10 years. The examination certificate from the "Booksellers' Training College" corresponds to 1 year's practical experience.
Exemption from these requirements may be granted under certain conditions which guarantee that the applicant possesses corresponding qualifications—for example, higher education or practical experience gained in a publishing firm or a bookshop abroad.
Exemption may also be granted when an existing bookshop changes ownership through inheritance, and the conditions make immediate fulfilment of these requirements impossible. Further, in certain cases of change of ownership, exemptions may be granted to allow for shorter periods of time, when local conditions make it desirable that the existing bookshop continues its activity.

12 Taxes

The general sales tax, introduced in Norway in 1933, had from the beginning applied to books, but not to newspapers and periodicals. As of 1 April 1967, however, the Storting (Norwegian Parliament) has exempted books from this 12% tax (later: 20%), a decision arrived at after many years' perseverance from the book trade. It is hoped that this exemption will be an important stimulus to increased reading.

13 Clearing Houses

One of the services offered to booksellers by *A/S Bokcentralen* (→ 4) is to arrange payments from booksellers to publishers, and from bookseller to bookseller.

14 Copyright

Questions of copyright are governed by the "Copyright Act" of 12 May 1961. The Act covers all kinds of writings, lectures, stage performances, music, painting and architectural works, maps, films, etc., and translations and adaptations thereof. (For photographs, see below.)
The copyright runs during the author's life and for 50 years from the end of the year of his death. If two or more authors have contributed to a work in such manner that their respective contributions cannot be separated, they will acquire joint copyright thereto, which right will run for 50 years from the end of the year of the last surviving author's death.
Photographs come under the "Photography Act" of 17 June 1960. The copyright under this Act lapses when 15 years have passed since the death of the first owner.
Norway has ratified the "Universal Copyright Convention", and the "Berne Convention" and its amendments of 1948.

15 National Bibliography, National Library

Norsk Bokfortegnelse ("The Norwegian National Bibliography") is prepared at the

Universitetsbiblioteket
(University Library)
Drammensveien 42
N Oslo 2

and distributed for the book trade by the "Norwegian Booksellers' Association", (→ 4). Titles are classified according to the Dewey Decimal System. The bibliography is published weekly in "Norsk Bokhand-

lertidende", (→ 5); yearly (together with a subject index), and every five years (also with a subject index).
The first independent national bibliography for Norway was published privately by Chr. C. A. Lange in 1832, and covered the years 1813–31. This bibliography was later included in the bibliography for 1814–47 published—also privately—by M. Nissen. After this the "Norwegian Booksellers' Association" issued larger bibliographies for the years 1848–1920, and, from 1920, five-year catalogues are available, issued by the "University Library" in Oslo.
The Law of 1882 requires that one copy of all documents printed or issued in Norway be sent to the University Library in Oslo. According to the same law, the University Library must also publish each year a bibliography of documents which have been sent in. Starting with the year 1883, there has thus been a yearly catalogue of Norwegian literature. In addition to the required and indeed automatic delivery of one copy to the University Library in Oslo—which also functions as the "National Library"—every Norwegian publisher is required to send free of charge one copy to the University Library in Bergen and one to the Library of the "Royal Norwegian Society of Arts and Sciences" in Trondheim, if these institutions so desire.
Since 1893 the "Norwegian Booksellers' Association" has been issuing quarterly bibliographies of various types, rotaprinted, with a view to practical use in bookshops. It consists of an alphabetical list, with references to which issue of "Norsk Bokhandlertidende" the title originally appeared in, plus a subject index.
Every year the "Norwegian Booksellers' Association" produces a stock catalogue listing all books available from most Norwegian publishers.
In time for the new school year, the "Norwegian Booksellers' Association" also annually publishes a bibliography: *Alt for alle skoler* ("Everything for every school"), a list of all school- and textbooks on the market.
For *Felles julekatalog* (the "Christmas Catalogue", → 30).

16 Book Production

In proportion to its population, Norway's book production is both large and versatile. 2,473 books were published 1968 (non-periodical publications of not less than 49 pages).

Subject group	Titles	Percentage of total production
General	47	1.6
Philosophy	62	2.0
Religion	171	5.7
Social sciences	437	14.6
Philology	187	6.2
Natural sciences	261	8.7
Applied sciences	389	12.9
Fine arts, recreation	110	3.7
Literature	1,022	34.1
History, geography	302	10.1
Total	2,988	99.6

17 Translations

1.133 translations appeared in 1968. The most important languages of origin were:

English	467
American	333
Swedish	100
Danish	50
German	50
French	39

These translations were devided up in the following subject groups:

Subject group	Titles
General	9
Philosophy	27
Religion, theology	45
Law, social sciences, education	76
Philology	49
Natural sciences	96
Applied sciences	101
Fine arts, recreation	16
Literature	625
History, geography, biography	89
Total	1,133

18 Book Clubs

Book clubs have only quite recently become important in Norway. The year 1961 saw the formation of "Den norske Bokklubben" ("The Norwegian Book Club"), started when several leading publishers combined to form a book club. While the "Norwegian Book Club" attempts to reach the broadest possible public and thus makes ample use of advertising in newspapers, magazines, and direct mail, it also cooperates with the authorized bookshops. This cooperation is a natural result of the book club's background, as it was formed by publishers who otherwise use the authorized bookshops as main distributors for the rest of their total production. The number of members of the "Norwegian Book Club"—whether these have joined directly, or in part through bookshops—was 142,000, in 1970.

19 Paperbacks

Series of cheaply produced quality books have been available in Norway since 1887. It was not until 1960, however, that series of quality paperbacks, produced and distributed similarly to those long known in England and the USA, were offered by Norwegian publishers. Many of the regular publishers now have fiction and specialized paperbacks. Unlike the rest of a publisher's production, paperbacks may also be sold through such retail outlets as general stores, tobacconists, and newspaper kiosks.

20 Book Design

The year's best-designed books are chosen in close cooperation between the Scandinavian countries (Denmark, Finland, Norway, Sweden), according to rules drawn up at a meeting in Oslo in 1946. In each country there is a working committee for good book design and the "Nordisk Boktrykkerråd" ("Nordic Bookprinter's Council"). These committees arrange exhibitions of the books chosen, and take care of all publicity. The national juries who select the year's best-designed books in each country consist of experts on various aspects of graphic design and technical aspects. The working committees themselves have nothing to do with the jury's evaluations: they only publicize the results in connection with the exhibitions. Every other year it is the country's own books, and every alternate year books chosen from all the Scandinavian countries, which form the display.

The announcement of the jury's nominations is usually preceded by general remarks on recent development in book-design techniques and quality; the nominations are accompanied by detailed commentaries on the books—in general, 25 of them—chosen from each country within the various fields: literature, pictorial works, textbooks, handbooks, artistically illustrated works, children's books, catalogues, etc.

Working expenses are covered by donations from organizations in the graphic trades, the book trade, and the publishing world.

Each year the "Norwegian Booksellers'

Association" awards a prize for good book design, on recommendation of the Norwegian working committee. The prize is an engraved crystal cup.
"Kirke- og undervisningsdepartementet" ("Ministry of Church and Education") presents annual awards for good children's books; among these awards are cash grants to children's book-illustrators.

21 Publishing

Practically all important Norwegian publishing houses belong to the "Norwegian Publishers' Association" (→ 4). The great majority of these are in Oslo. In addition there are many smaller publishing houses, and other firms which sometimes publish books. While there are no reliable statistics available, it is safe to say that the nonmembers' share in the total amount of books published is relatively small. Neither are there statistics concerning the individual publishing houses' sales turnover, number of titles published, etc.

22 Literary Agents

Literary agents have no part in publishers' dealings with Norwegian authors. Also, as far as translations are concerned, publishers prefer to be in personal contact with authors.

23 Wholesale Trade

Wholesalers, in the sense of the word as used in larger countries, are lacking in Norway. Booksellers have direct contact with each individual publisher; however, this is generally done through *Bokcentralen* (→ 4). Recently publishers have begun to set up cooperative delivery and business offices; but this is only for increased efficiency, and has nothing to do with independent wholesalers.
To some extent the largest bookshops import foreign books directly, and in a few cases function as wholesalers for such books. But most book imports are arranged through the wholesale firm *Norsk Bokimport A/S* (→ 4), which was started by, and is still under the control of, the Norwegian booksellers as a whole.

24 Retail Trade

Despite its small and somewhat scattered population, and the great distances within the country, Norway has a highly developed network of qualified booksellers. In Norway there are altogether 398 authorized booksellers, 68 of them in Oslo. Even in small villages there are bookshops which carry out their important function extremely well, regarding premises, professional level, and efficiency. The authorized bookshop is in principle the sole distributor for books produced by members of the "Norwegian Publishers' Association" (→ 4). To be allowed to receive books from these publishers, the owner of the bookshop must be officially recognized by the "Norwegian Publishers' Association" as a distributor, fulfilling the requirements of professional training (→ 11) in a bookshop; he must have sufficient economic resources for running a bookshop efficiently, and must be housed in satisfactory premises. All ordinary schoolbooks are distributed via such bookshops. Until recently, all sales to public libraries took place through bookshops, but now there is an official centre for library purchases which buys directly from publishers and distributes to all smaller public libraries. A certain amount of the public-library fund must be used on purchases arranged by the library centre, but in many places there is still lively contact between bookshops and libraries.
There are two types of book for which the authorized bookshop does not have the status of sole distributor. The first concerns

larger works bought on the instalment plan; more and more of these have in recent years been sold directly to the public through publishers' representatives. Previously the practice had been that publishers' representatives drew up contracts with the public, and then left these contracts with the local bookseller, who took charge of distribution and payments.
The second group covers paperbacks, i.e. books whose price does not exceed a certain limit (1970: n. kr. 18.00). These books may be distributed by the publishers directly to newspaper kiosks, tobacconists, and other outlets.
To the firm

Narvesens Kioskkompani A/S
Bertrand Narvesens vei 2
N Oslo 6

which runs all railway bookstalls, publishers may distribute all kinds of books except school- and textbooks, and subscription books.
While many bookshops have chosen specific fields which they cover especially well, there is no Norwegian bookshop which is truly a specialist one. On the contrary, not only can all bookshops supply all books: they are required by the publishers to carry a representative selection.
Previously all sales to bookshops were on a commission basis; in 1962, however, a new arrangement was started, whereby all books ordered from publishers must be paid for, whether or not they are sold. When a new book is published, the bookseller may receive a free sample copy, which he may keep for three years without charge. If he sells the sample copy, he is required to re-order from the publishers; but he may return the book free of charge after three years. Any bookshop whose yearly purchase from members of the "Norwegian Publishers' Association" exceed 0.2% of the total amount purchased by all the country's bookshops must receive a sample copy, and keep a complete stock. Booksellers with smaller yearly purchase amounts can order sample copies, but are not required to do so.
Both booksellers and book-sales outlets must in the course of each year have purchased a certain amount from members of the "Norwegian Publishers' Association" if the "Association" is to allow them to continue as distributors.
At every payment deadline, publishers who are members of the "Norwegian Publishers' Association" report to the "Association" which booksellers have not paid up their balance of debt in time. The "Association" then warns the bookseller concerned that he must have paid up the total balance of debt recorded within a certain period of time; if he fails to do so the "Association" will instruct its members to stop all deliveries to the bookseller, whether or not he may have settled his debts to some of the member publishers.

25 Mail-Order Bookselling

In Norway's authorized book trade there are no special mail-order firms. However, many booksellers choose special fields in which they feel they have good chances of making special contributions. Every bookseller must follow the rule that in sales to customers living outside the geographical limits normally covered by that particular bookshop, the bookseller must add the cost of postage for delivery. This rule ensures that the numerous smaller bookshops in sparsely populated areas throughout the country will have a sufficient basis for their function in the community, and that they will at all times have a varied stock of current literature. If these smaller bookshops were exposed to intense competition from the larger, more powerful bookshops in the cities, they would lose many of the local sales that are the prerequisite for their very existence as bookshops.

26 Antiquarian Book Trade, Auctions

While there are relatively few second-hand bookshops in Norway—most of them in Oslo—they maintain an extremely high standard. They are organized in

Norsk Antikvarbokhandlerforening
(Norwegian Antiquarian Booksellers' Association)
Tollbugt. 25
N Oslo 1

which is a member of the "International League of Antiquarian Booksellers".

27 Book Imports

Figures from the "Central Bureau of Statistics" for 1969:

Category	m. n.kr.
Books	21.1
Periodicals	13.9
Picture books for children	0.8
Notes	0.5
Maps	1.8
Total	38.1

The most important sources for book imports were:

a) in Norwegian language total n.kr. 6,630,000

Country	n.kr. 1,000	Percentage of total
Denmark	1,716	26
Italy	1,350	20
Sweden	1,483	22
Netherlands	773	12

b) in other languages total n.kr. 14,519,000

Country	n.kr. 1,000	Percentage of total
United Kingdom	3,969	27
USA	1,377	10
Denmark	4,542	31
Sweden	2,425	17
Germany (Federal Republic)	812	6

The most important sources for imports of periodicals (total n.kr. 13,975,000):

Country	n.kr. 1,000	Percentage of total
Sweden	5,036	36
Denmark	2,783	19
USA	1,396	10
Germany (Federal Republic)	2,115	15
United Kingdom	1,465	10

Norsk Bookimport → 4, 23. → 3.

28 Book Exports

Figures for 1969 from the "Central Bureau of Statistics" are:

Category	m. n.kr.
Books	4.2
Periodicals	3.4
Picture books for children	0.01
Notes	0.05
Maps	0.5
Total	8.16

The most important countries for book exports:

a) in Norwegian language total n.kr. 1,063,000

Country	n.kr. 1,000	Percentage of total
Denmark	644	61
Sweden	196	19

b) in other languages total n.kr. 3,101,000

Country	n.kr.1,000	Percentage of total
Sweden	2,125	70
Denmark	552	18
USA	135	4
United Kingdom	38	1

The most important countries for exports of periodicals (total n.kr. 3,435,000):

Country	n.kr. 1,000	Percentage of total
Sweden	1,866	54
Denmark	1,459	42

29 Book Fairs

The only book fairs in Norway are those held annually at Christmas, arranged in many places throughout the country, often in cooperation with booksellers, libraries, newspapers, councils for popular education, etc. These Christmas fairs exhibit a selection of the year's production especially intended for Christmas sales; frequently authors attend these functions.

30 Public Relations

The "Norwegian Booksellers' Association" attends in various ways to the interests of the profession and to its public image. It inserts answers to any unjust criticism of the profession in the papers; collectively prepares promotional material such as posters and catalogues, which are then distributed to booksellers; and, not less important, together with the "Norwegian Publishers' Association", prepares and issues the *Felles julekatalog* ("Christmas catalogue"), which represents an enormous advertising contribution. More than one million copies are printed of this annual catalogue; it is mailed to the majority of households throughout the country.
The Christmas catalogue contains 96 pages, and has a soft cover printed in several colours. Its yearly budget is n.kr. 700,000. Two fifth of the costs are borne by the booksellers, and three fifth by the publishers. The share to be paid by the booksellers is allotted in proportion to their annual purchases from the publishers, while the publishers' share is covered by the advertising space they buy in the catalogue. The catalogue starts with a complete bibliography of all the year's books which are suitable for Christmas presents—whether fiction or popular non-fiction.
In connection with the abolition of the purchase tax on books in April 1967, the "Norwegian Booksellers' Association" and the "Norwegian Publishers' Association" cooperated in a massive advertising campaign in the newspapers. This cooperation will continue, with publishers and booksellers sharing expenses equally.

31 Bibliophily

The
Bibliofilklubben
(Bibliophiles' Club)
c/o Riksbibliotektjenesten
Drammensvn. 42
N Oslo 2
is an active society. It is of great importance for the development of antiquarian bookshops, but does not aim at the public en masse: its membership is limited to 33.

32 Literary Prizes

Several publishers, newspapers, councils for public education, and other institutions give more or less regular awards for individual books. The "Ministry of Church and Education" provides several prizes annually for good children's books. One literary prize which receives much publicity is that organized by "Norsk Kulturråd" ("Norwegian Cultural Council").

33 The Reviewing of Books

Most of the daily papers provide generous space for comprehensive book reviews. There is also a special literary periodical, *Vinduet* ("The Window"). At present, however, there is no publication containing book reviews only.

34 Graphic Arts

→ 20.

Poland

Important Book Centres

1 General Information

Area 312,700 km²
Population 32,426,000 (104 per km²)
Capital Warszawa (1,279,000)
Largest towns Warszawa (1,279,000); Łódź (750,000); Kraków (565,000); Wrocław (512,000); Poznań (457,000); Gdańsk (364,000); Szczecin (332,000); Katowice (292,000); Bydgoszcz (275,000)
Government System of people's democracy established by Constitution of July 22, 1952
Religion No statistics available
National language Polish
Leading foreign languages Russian, English, French, German
Weights, measures Metric system
Currency unit Złoty (zł.)
Education Compulsory primary education. All schools free of charge. 304,600 students (3 levels) of which 118,700 are women, in 77 schools of higher learning (1968/69)
Illiteracy About 2.7%
Paper consumption a) Newsprint 2.7 kg per inhabitant (1969)
b) Printing paper (other than newsprint) 6.5 kg per inhabitant (1969)
Membership UNESCO

2 Past and Present

The bookseller first appeared in Polish documents in the late Middle Ages, when he was mentioned in a privilege by King Casimir III the Great in 1364 as one of the members of the Congregation of Cracow University. As throughout the whole of Europe at the time, he was called 'stationarius' and performed such functions that he could be regarded as the forerunner of the present-day publishers and booksellers, as well as university librarians. The book trade of Poland commemorated its 600th anniversary in 1964. The first printed book, a calendar of 1474, came out in Cracow. This city was the main centre for the production and distribution of books until the end of the seventeenth century, although a network of print shops and bookshops covered the entire country. In the eighteenth century the centre of intellectual life shifted entirely to Warsaw. The number of titles published in the 1780s and 1790s exceeded 1,000 a year.

During the partitions of 1794–1918, Polish books played a great role in the ceaseless struggle for the very existence of national culture, in maintaining and promoting national conciousness, in integrating Poles from the three sectors of partitioned Poland, and in making up in learning and the arts those irreversible losses which the Polish nation had suffered in political and economic life. Publishers and booksellers played a noble part in that period. An average of some 1,300 titles a year appeared on Polish lands in the second half of the nineteenth century, and before the First World War this number grew to about 3,000 a year, more than half of them published in Warsaw. The political conditions did not allow the creation of a central organization.

Under the Second Republic (1918–45) the publishing industry in Poland developed considerably, to reach an output of about 7,000 titles a year in editions totalling 20–25 million copies. The Second World War was a catastrophic period for the Polish book as well. A ban on the publication of books was in force throughout the five years of the occupation. About 85% of all public libraries were destroyed.

In the People's Republic of Poland, the cultural policy of the state at first aimed at rapidly rebuilding and then greatly expanding institutions involved in the production and distribution of books. A completely new organization of publishing houses and bookshops was created. The 1968 output in Poland was 10,306 titles with a total of 119 million copies. The planned economy of the state has made it possible to rationalize the production and distribution of books. This rationalization has resulted in the establishment of large, specialized publishing houses, in a well-planned organization of networks of bookshops covering the entire country, in the creation of a unified publishing plan coordinated by central bodies, and in a unified system of cooperation between publishers and bookshops, and publishers and print shops. The particularly privileged position enjoyed by books in present-day Poland stems from the principle of decommercializing culture; consequently books are produced and distributed primarily in order to promote culture and not for gain. This principle is implemented by setting low prices on books and exempting publishing houses and bookshops from turnover tax.

Bibliography

K. Budzyk, *Wiadomości o książce.* (About books). Warszawa 1961. 200 pp.

R. Cybulski, *Popyt na rynku księgarskim na tle przemian społeczno-gospodarczych w Polsce Ludowej.* (The demand on the book market against the background of the socio-economic transformations in People's Poland). Warszawa 1966. 256 pp.

M. Czarnowska, *Ilościowy rozwój polskiego ruchu wydawniczego 1501–1965.* (The quantitative development of the Polish publishing trade, 1501–1965). Warszawa 1967. 202 pp.

S. Dahl, *Dzieje książki.* (The history of books). 1st Polish ed., supplemented with extensive information about the history of Polish books. Warszawa 1965. 455 pp.

K. Górski, *Sztuka edytorska, zarys teorii.* (The art of publishing. An outline of theory). Warszawa 1956. 230 pp.

A. Klimowicz, *Sześćset lat w służbie książki, 1364–1964.* (600 years in the service of books, 1364–1964). Warszawa 1964. 35 pp.

L. Marszałek, *Kulturotwórcza rola książki.* (The culture-generating role of books). Report to "Congress of Polish Culture". Warszawa 1966. 27 pp.

J. Muszkowski *Życie książki.* (The life of books). Kraków 1951. 468 pp.

3 Retail Prices

Publishing houses set the prices of books in keeping with detailed guidelines established by the state. In force at present is a "list of uniform prices for non-periodic publications" which was introduced in 1954 by decision of the "Council of Ministers" and partially revised by the "Ministry of Culture and Art" in 1957, when the prices of paper and printing services were adjusted.

Book prices constitute an important instrument of the cultural policy of the state, a policy which is aimed at disseminating books as broadly as possible. Hence the low prices of books, coupled with the free loan of books from libraries, have contributed to a substantial increase in reading. Prices in Poland today are several times lower than before the war.

The retail price, also called the catalogue price, of a book only partly reflects the production costs, the profit of the publisher, and the commercial profit margin (wholesale and retail). Prices are differentiated according to type of publication. Not every book brings the publisher a profit; indeed, he sells many books to the bookselling enterprises below cost, that is, at a loss. The losses on some books can be covered in the publishing house by profits from others, so that the overall financial result will be in the black. Most publishing houses in Poland today yield a profit and only a few incur losses because of unprofitable books (e.g. scientific) in their publishing programme. Overall, the financial performance of all publishing enterprises in Poland is favourable, notwithstanding the low prices of books.

The principles underlying the price setting are:

1) the state has established prices per "publisher's sheet" (a unit of measure containing 40,000 typographical marks) for various kinds of publication;

2) the lowest prices are set for schoolbooks, mass political and popular science publications, and professional publications for teachers, while the highest are applicable to scientific publications for narrow specialities;

3) a publisher can make a 25% reduction in the price of books deserving of a large edition for political or economic considerations, and conversely, may raise the price by 25% for titles with small editions;

4) the prices of special publications, such as multicolour, decorative, and commemorative, are determined on the basis of the production cost.

The commercial profit margins are also fixed by the state in Poland. The size of this aggregate margin in the bookselling trade was set in 1951 at 32% for domestic publications and 25% for imported publications. The wholesale organization "Składnica Księgarska" (→ 4) always receives 7% while the retail organization

"Dom Książki "(→ 4) gets 25% on domestic publications and 18% on imports. A system of wages introduced in bookshops in 1959 made a large fraction of the overall earnings of the employees dependent on the bookshops attaining the given margin. Concurrently with this, the retail discounts (profit margins) were differentiated so that the figure for, say, scientific publications is 35%, belles-lettres 25%, children's books, encyclopedias and dictionaries 20%, and textbooks, guidebooks, and maps 18%. A balancing account set up in "Składnica Księgarska" shows that the aggregate rebates given the bookshops runs at less than 25% of the total sales in catalogue prices.

4 Organization

The organization of the publishing and book trades in Poland is distinguished by two basic features: firstly, the publishing and bookselling enterprises are almost entirely owned by the state, with a slight fraction owned by cooperatives or public organizations; secondly, the organizational and economy activity is based on the system of a planned economy.

Organization of publishing houses: The number of publishing enterprises in Poland in 1969 was 32 (29 state-owned and 3 cooperative) while other publishing enterprises or bureaux were operated by public organizations (e.g. the "Central Council of Trade Unions", the "Polish Scouts' Association", the "Association of Lay Catholics Pax"), state offices (e.g. the "Main Statistical Office"), scientific institutes, higher schools of learning, and religious organizations. A characteristic feature of the publishing enterprises is a high degree of concentration and specialization. Only a few publishers have their own printing works, while all others avail themselves of the services of state-owned printing works. These have their own organization:

Zjednoczenie Przemysłu Poligraficznego
(The Printing Industry Association)
ul. Jasna 26
PL Warszawa

For supervising and coordination of the ensemble of publishing activities in Poland

Zjednoczenie Przedsiębiorstw Wydawniczych
Naczelny Zarząd Wydawnictw
(The Union of Polish Publishing Houses
Central Board of Publishing Houses)
Krakowskie Przedmieście 15/17
PL Warszawa

was created on 1 October 1970.

This organization encompasses 22 publishing houses directly controlled by the Ministry of Culture and Art; a further 22 publishing houses, controlled by other ministries or public organizations, are linked to the union by special understandings.

The Central Board of Publishing Houses has the following collegiate bodies: the Board of Directors comprising the directors of the Union and of all publishing houses, the Programme Council, and the Technical and Economic Council. Among the main objectives of the Central Board of Publishing Houses are: the elaboration of development lines and coordination of publishing programmes, initiation of actions with the aim to improve book layout, establishing general principles of collaboration with the printing and paper-manufacturing industries, and with book distributors, as well as allocation of paper and funds, organization of research work, professional training of editorial personnel, and organization and coordination of international relations.

All publishing houses and bureaux are completely independent in their publishing activities, within the framework of the indices which are assigned centrally each year as binding directives. These indices are: the amount of paper, the number of full-time employees, the size of the wages fund, the size of the emolument fund (for authors, reviewers, editorial committees, etc.), and the financial performance. A characteristic feature of publishing houses in Poland is that their editorial side has been built up. Thus 30% of all the employees in these enterprises in 1969 were editors.

Polskie Towarzystwo Wydawców Książek
(Polish Society of Book Publishers)
ul. Mazowiecka 1
PL Warszawa

which has been in existence since 1926 (with interruptions), is an organization which associates individuals (editors, typographers, book designers, employees of sales departments in publishing houses). It is the aim of the "Society" first and foremost to improve the qualifications of its members, and for this purpose it is engaged in training and lecturing, organizes an annual competition for the most beautiful published book, and initiates studies on publishing operations. The "Society" also represents the opinion of publishers to state agencies on matters of book production and distribution. It also promotes international cooperation and is a co-organizer of the "International Book Fair" in Warsaw (→ 29). In 1969 the "Society" had about 1,300 members.

The organization of bookselling: A unified bookselling organization was set up in 1950, covering both wholesale and retail. This has now been broken down into seperate organizations.

Since 1958 there has been a state wholesale enterprise

Składnica Księgarska
(Book Repository)
ul. Mazowiecka 9
PL Warszawa

It sells books on a commission basis, that is, on behalf of the publishing enterprises. Stocks of books in the warehouses of the "Składnica Księgarska" belong to the publishers. Apart from selling the output of the domestic publishing trade, this enterprise buys and sells publications imported by the Foreign Trade Enterprise, "Ars Polona Ruch". "Składnica Księgarska" has 9 branches with their own warehouses.

At the retail level, the principal organization is

Centrala Księgarstwa "Dom Książki"
("Book House" Central Bookselling Agency)
ul. Jasna 26
PL Warszawa

in existence since 1950. This central agency comprises 17 voivodship enterprises, an enterprise in Warsaw, a general mail-order bookshop, and a sales department for artistic and graphic publications. Eeach voivodship enterprise manages the bookshops in its area. "Dom Książki" handles about 95% of the bookselling trade in Poland.

The retail sale of books is also carried on by the "International Book and Press Clubs" in the principal towns, "Ruch" kiosks, and purchase and supply cooperatives in the countryside.

The "Związek Księgarzy Polskich" ("Union of Polish Booksellers") existed in Poland from 1908 to 1950, and since 1956 there has been the

Stowarzyszenie Księgarzy Polskich
(Association of Polish Booksellers)
ul. Mokotowska 4/6
PL Warszawa

The "Association" is an organization of booksellers employed in state bookshops. According to its statute, its aim is to organize bookshop employees for active vocational and civic work in the promotion of books and reading, to raise the qualifications of the employees, and to represent and defend their vocational, material, and moral interests. The "Association" (membership in 1969: c. 4,500) organizes regular meetings of readers and booksellers with writers and scientific workers, and initiates the establishment of booklovers' clubs at bookshops.

The organization of book and periodical imports and exports:
The separate state enterprise
Ars Polona Ruch
Krakowskie Przedmieście 7
PL Warszawa
handles all book and periodical imports and exports. It has the sole right to export and import books, sheet music, records, and periodicals, and also concludes contracts on co-editions and printing services.

5 Trade Press

Przegląd Księgarski i Wydawniczy
(Publishing and Bookselling Review)
ul. Jasna 26
PL Warszawa
a fortnightly published in Warsaw, is the joint organ of publishers and booksellers. The publication carries articles and provides an extensive informative bibliographical section on new books and titles in press. The articles deal with the principal aspects of the work of publishing houses and the book trade, various types of literature, and cooperation with the printing industry, and also give information about publishing activities abroad.
The "Składnica Księgarska" (→ 4) puts out a weekly,
Zapowiedzi Wydawnicze
(Publishing Announcements)
ul. Mazowiecka 9
PL Warszawa
which presents information about titles to be published in forthcoming months. Each title has a detailed bibliographical description and an informative note. It is printed in a form making it easy for booksellers and other subscribers to place an order and make a card index for their own purposes. Bookshops place their orders for a given title on the basis of the "Zapowiedzi Wydawnicze" and the total orders enable the publishers to determine the size of the edition more accurately.
The "Association of Polish Booksellers" (→ 4) has been publishing a quarterly,
Księgarz
(The Bookseller)
ul. Mokotowska 4/6
PL Warszawa
as its organ since 1956. Apart from articles treating on the key aspects of Polish bookselling today, this publication runs a regular department devoted to the history of Polish bookselling and information about bookselling in other countries.
Articles about the publishing industry are also carried in the monthly
Poligrafika
(Typographical Art)
ul. Wiezska 12a
PL Warszawa
published by the typography section of the "Association of Mechanical Engineers".
New Polish Publications → 7.

6 Book-Trade Literature

T. Hussak, *Poradnik kolportera.* (The book salesman's guidebook). Warszawa 1960. 131 pp.

T. Hussak, *Reklama i propaganda książki.* (Book advertising and promotion). Part I. Warszawa 1969. 280 pp.; part II. Warszawa 1970. 288 pp.

A. Klimowicz, *Księgarstwo.* (Bookselling). Warszawa 1953. 380 pp.

St. Malawski, *Obrót księgarski, organizacja i technika.* (The book trade, organization and technique). Warszawa 1960. 395 pp.

St. Malawski, *Ekonomika księgarstwa.* Cz. I. (The economics of bookselling, part I). 2nd ed. Warszawa 1969. 271 pp.

St. Pożeć, *Organizacja i ekonomika księgarstwa.* (The organization and economics of bookselling). Warszawa 1962. 391 pp.

St. Pożeć, *Ekonomika księgarstwa.* Cz. II. (The economics of bookselling, part II). 2nd ed. Warszawa 1969. 303 pp.

B. Rudecka, *Bibliografia*, Cz. I: Metodyka. (Bibliography, part I: Methods). Warszawa 1969. 330 pp.

K. Rzewuski, *Księgarstwo i towaroznawstwo.* (Bookselling and the science of commodities). Warszawa 1968. 332 pp.

St. Tarkowski, *Antykwariat księgarski.* (The antiquarian bookshop). Warszawa 1960. 58 pp.

T. Zadrożna-Gołaszewska, *Publisher's glossary.* Warszawa 1967. 27 pp.—In English.

7 Sources of Information, Address Services

Information concerning the publishing trade in Poland can be obtained by writing to

Zjednoczenie Przedsiębiorstw Wydawniczych
Naczelny Zarząd Wydawnictw
(The Union of Polish Publishing Houses
Central Board of Publishing Houses)
Krakowskie Przedmieście 15
PL Warszawa

General information about bookselling in Poland is available from

Centrala Księgarstwa "Dom Książki"
("Book House" Central Bookselling Agency)
ul. Jasna 26
PL Warszawa

Queries concerning export and import of printed matter are answered by

Centrala Handlu Zagranicznego
"Ars Polona Ruch"
Krakowskie Przedmieście 7
PL Warszawa

The monthly, *New Polish Publications*, which appears in English, French, German, and Russian, is an important source of information for foreign buyers. This monthly bulletin prints articles about Polish publishers and writers, and about interesting series, and also gives reviews, a chronicle, and a bibliography. Fortnightly supplements to this monthly periodical of announcements of publication with information about books to come off the press within a few months. The editorial address is:

New Polish Publications
ul. Marszałkowska 124
PL Warszawa

8 International Membership

The "Polish Society of Book Publishers" (→ 4) and the "Association of Polish Booksellers" (→ 4) are not members of international organizations. They do, however, cultivate lively international contacts of a bilateral nature and have concluded agreements on regular cooperation with their opposite numbers in other countries.
The "International Book Fair" in Warsaw (→ 29) is a member of the "Union des Foires Internationales" (UFI) whose headquarters are in Paris.

9 Market Research

It is primarily the universities which are engaged in book research in Poland. The "Institute of Library Science and Scientific Information" at "Warsaw University" has the task of organizing courses in library science and pursuing studies in the realm of book science. "Wrocław University" also offers courses in library science, and book research is conducted chiefly by the team in the department of library science. Such research is also pursued at "Łódź University" by the "Department of Library Science".
The main centre of book research is the

Biblioteka Narodna
(National Library)
ul. Hankiewicza 1
PL Warszawa

The "Institute of Books and Readership", which is part of the Library, comprises departments of library science, organization and promotion of reading, and library personnel training. Moreover, the "Bibliographic Institute" at the library has a "Bookselling Documentation Laboratory" and a "Laboratory of Publication Statistics" (annual figures on publishing activities).

Each year the "Institute of Books and Readership" publishes works devoted chiefly to research on reading habits in Poland, while the "Bibliographical Institute" puts out the yearbook *Ruch wydawniczy w liczbach* ("Publishing operations in figures"), the yearbook *Bibliografia bibliografii* ("Bibliography of bibliographies"), and *Przegląd pismiennictwa o książce* ("Review of literature about books"), a quarterly supplement to "Przegląd biblioteczny" ("Library Review"). In addition, dissertations on the science of books are contained in the *Rocznik Biblioteki Narodowej* ("National Library yearbook"; since 1965) and *Roczniki Biblioteczne* ("Library annals") scientific organ of the libraries of institutes of higher learning (since 1956).

Bibliography

J. Ankudowicz, *Czytelnictwo na tle życia kulturalnego i struktury społecznej mieszkańców małych miast.* (Readership on the background of cultural life and social structure of communities of small towns). Warszawa 1967. 228 pp.

K. Ziembicka and J. Ankudowicz, *Biblioteki i czytelnicy wybranych małych miast.* (Libraries and readership in selected small towns). Warszawa 1968. 215 pp.

St. Siekierski, *Recepcja literatury pięknej na wsi.* (Reception of belles-lettreslitterature in the countryside). Warszawa 1968. 228 pp. → 10.

10 Books and Young People

A keen interest in books for children and young people goes far back in time in Poland. Thus, immediately after the Second World War, these traditions were taken up again and even in the early postwar years much attention was paid to this area of literature.

A big conference organized in October 1946 by the "Czytelnik" "(Reader) Publishing House" was attended by writers, scholars of many specialities, and critics. Then, in 1947, a national congress on literature for children and young people took place. Papers read at the congress dealt with children's literature in other countries as well as in Poland. An exhibition of children's books was held along with the congress.

The main centre of studies and discussion on books for children and young people in Poland is

Instytut Wydawniczy "Nasza Księgarnia"
("Our Bookshop" Publishing Institute)
ul. Spasowskiego 4
PL Warszawa

In 1960 it organized an international meeting of publishers and scholars on the key aspects of present-day literature for children and young people; at this meeting much attention was devoted to the question of cooperation among children's periodicals. A seminar held in Zakopane in 1964 with the participation of Czechoslovak publishers heard a report on the results of a study into children's reading in Poland by the "Reading Commission of the Central Board of the Polish Teachers' Union". Another 1964 seminar, this time in Opole, dealt with the reception of children's books. A conference on popular literature for children took place in 1966 and a second one in 1970. A special conference discussed translations from other languages for children in 1967.

Various aspects of books for children and young people are also studied by a number of centres of learning, chiefly departments of pedagogy and psychology in the universities.

Annual seminars have been held since 1959 for children's reading instructors in public libraries and for the heads of children's libraries.

Bibliography

St. Aleksandrzak, (ed.), *Kim jesteś Kopciuszku, czyli o problemach współczesnej literatury dla dzieci i młodzieży*. (On the problems of present-day literature for children and young people). Warszawa 1968. 348 pp.

Wł. Goriszowski, *Czytelnictwo i jego wpływ na wyniki nauczania*. (The reading habit and its influence on the results of learning). Katowice 1968. 255 pp.

"*Nasza Księgarnia*", *40 lat działalności dla dziecka i szkoły*. ("Our Bookshop" Publishing House, 40 years of work for child and school). Warszawa 1961. 182 pp.

T. Parnowski (ed.), *Dziecko i młodzież w świetle zainteresowań czytelniczych*. (Children and young People in the light of reading interests). Warszawa 1960. 201 pp.

Problemy literatury popularno-naukowej dla dzieci i młodzieży. (Problems of popular science publications for children and young people). Warszawa 1966. 135 pp.

A. Przecławska, *Książka w życiu młodzieży współczesnej*. (The book in the life of modern young people). Warszawa 1962. 182 pp.

A. Przecławska, *Młody czytelnik i współczesność*. (The young reader and the present day and age). Warszawa 1966. 143 pp.

11 Training

The training of publishers and booksellers takes place in two different organizational systems.

There are no special secondary or higher schools for publishers. Publishers' training is looked after by the "Polskie Towarzystwo Wydawców" (→ 4), which organizes courses and seminars for various specialities in the publishing industry. The courses for editors are of fundamental importance, and editors from various publishing houses take part. Some of the courses are the same for all, while others are for specialized groups (e.g. belles-lettres group, scientific publications group).

The programme encompasses general knowledge about the publishing industry in Poland and the world and about copyright, extensive information about editorial work, and an insight into the printing trade. Specialized seminars (say, on encyclopedias, translations) are held for more experienced editors. Another type of course is that given for typographers. The accent in this programme is on the technology of printing processes, the technique of the typographer, and practice sessions in printing works and paper mills. In addition, special courses are given on copyright.

Postgraduate studies in publishing are to begin at "Warsaw University" in 1971 for university graduates employed in publishing institutions. The studies, which are evening courses, will run for three semesters.

Booksellers are trained in a system of state-run schools and in a system of courses organized by the "Dom Książki" (→ 4). At the secondary-school level there is an economic and bookselling high school in Warsaw, together with a school boarding house, and 8 schools in voivodship towns (17 such towns all told) have special departments of bookselling. These schools had 1,820 pupils in the year 1968/9. "Warsaw University" has a two-year antiquarian bookselling course for employees of "Dom Książki" (→ 4). The curriculum consists of 280 hours of lectures on such subjects as the history of books, bibliography, the organization of learning, the sociology of culture, libraries, and periodicals, manuscripts, the graphic arts, and cartography in antiquarian bookshops. Some 50 students took this course in 1969.

Apart from the training in schools, "Dom Książki" organizes additional extra-mural training coupled with lectures. Courses in various specialities last from 3 to 12 month, and are taken by about 500 persons each year. So far courses have been arranged on such subjects as organization of bookselling work, bibliography in bookshops, bibliographical information, sale of agricultural publications, advertising and promotion of books in bookshops, and the activities of bookshops in rural districts.

12 Taxes

Publishing and bookselling enterprises in Poland are exempt from taxes, especially turnover tax, which is the mainstay of the Polish tax system. This is due to the cultural policy which implements the principle of de-commercializing culture, as manifested in the low prices set on books, frequently below cost.
The foreign-trade enterprise "Ars Polona Ruch" (→ 4) is also exempted from taxes. The principle of the free flow of books is fully respected in Poland.

13 Clearing Houses

There are no clearing institutions in the book trade in Poland.

14 Copyright

The basic legal act in the realm of protecting the author's rights is the "Copyright Act of 10 July 1952". The copyright covers works expressed in print, word, or writing, musical works, works of the plastic arts, and choreographical or cinematographical works recorded in scenarios, drawings or photographs. The elaboration of other people's work (translation, adaptation, making into a film, etc.) also comes under the Copyright Act.
The "Copyright Act" encompasses the right to 1) protection of an author's personal assets, 2) exclusive control of a work, 3) payment for use of a work. The copyright expires twenty years after the death of the author.
Provisions were made in the "Copyright Act" for the "Council of Ministers" to lay down detailed principles for drawing up publishing contracts, to present model contracts, and establish the principles for payment. The "Council of Ministers" laid down these principles in ordinances on 11 June 1955 and 2 June 1964. These ordinances are thus important supplements to the "Copyright Act". The schedule of authors' emoluments given in these ordinances fixes the rates of payment for various kinds and species of publication; the basis for calculating the payment is the amount of text, expressed in "author's sheets" (40,000 typographical marks, 700 lines of verse, or 3,000 sq. cm. of art-work).
Poland ratified the "Berne Convention" according to the text signed in Rome on 2 June 1928. Thus far, however, she has not ratified the "Universal Copyright Convention" adopted in Geneva in 1952.

Bibliography

E. Drabienko (ed.), *Prawo autorskie, przepisy i orzecznictwo.* (Copyright, regulations and court rulings). 4th ed. Warszawa 1965. 503 pp.

15 National Bibliography, National Library

Publication of periodicals recording the output of the Polish publishing trade began back in 1856 ("Bibliografia Krajowa" —"National Bibliography", Warsaw). The "Przewodnik Bibliograficzny" ("Bibliographical Guide"), which came out in Cracow from 1878 to 1914, was succeeded by Bibliografia Polska" ("Polish Bibliography"), which appeared from 1914 to 1933.
A national bibliography, giving an alpha-

betical listing of all Polish publications on the basis of compulsory copies, was first printed in 1928 as the weekly, "Urzędowy Wykaz Druków" ("Official index of printed matter"). It was published until 1930 by the "Ministry of Religious Denominations and Public Education", and from 1930 to 1939 by the "National Library". This bibliography was revived in 1946 as a weekly called

Przewodnik Bibliograficzny
(Bibliographical Guide)
ul. Hankiewicza 1
PL Warszawa

arranged in sections with each entry denoted by a symbol of the decimal classification. Monthly and annual alphabetical indexes as well as annual subject indexes are provided for the Guide.

A Polish bibliography encompassing all Polish publications, a work of vast importance for Polish culture, was published by Karol Estreicher (1827–1908). He personally put out 22 volumes, taking it to the letter M, and the work was carried on to the letter Z (vols. 23–33) by his son, Stanisław Estreicher (1869–1939), who died in Sachsenhausen concentration camp. The publication, from vol. 34 onwards, has been continued by a grandson, Karol Estreicher (b. 1906).

The fundamental bibliography concerning Polish literature is "Literatura Polska od początków do wojny światowej" ("Polish literature from its beginnings to the World War"). 4 vols. 1929–31. 2nd ed. by G. Korbut.

This is being continued by the "Institute of Literary Research, Polish Academy of Sciences", which has published "Bibliografia literatury polskiej Nowy Korbut" ("Bibliography of Polish literature. A new Korbut"), Vol 1.

The central state library is

Biblioteka Narodowa (National Library)
ul. Hankiewicza 1
PL Warszawa

which was founded in 1928. Its main purpose is to collect Polish and foreign publications which are connected with Poland in any way whatever. Unfortunately, the "National Library" suffered grievous losses during the Second World War; thus collections of manuscripts and old prints were burned.

The "National Library" is now the central library, and since 1954 it has also been an institute engaged in research on book science. It acquires all books published in Poland and foreign Polonica (Polish literary documents) since 1801, and is the main centre for bibliographical documentation and standardization, as well as for expert counselling. It engages in research on books, libraries, bibliography, and reading habits. Apart from the library proper, it consists of a "Bibliographical Institute", an "Institute of Books and Reading", and an "Office for the International Exchange of Publications"; moreover, it has its own publishing department and printing works. The principal publications of the National Library are "Rocznik BN" ("National Library annals"), Catalogue of Manuscripts, Catalogue of Microfilms (annual), "Przewodnik Bibliograficzny" ("Bibliographical guide")—an official index of printed matter published in the People's Republic of Poland (weekly), "Bibliografia Zawartości Czasopism" ("Bibliography of contents of periodicals", a monthly); "Ruch Wydawniczy w Liczbach" ("The publishing trade in figures"; annual), and a subject index of the principal bibliographical compilations published by libraries and scientific institutes.

Attention should also be drawn to

Ośrodek Dokumentacji i Informacji Naukowej Polskiej Akademii Nauk
(Documentation and Scientific Information Centre of the Polish Academy of Sciences)
ul. Nowy Świat 72, Pałac Staszica
PL Warszawa

The "Centre" publishes a bulletin "Przegląd informacji o naukoznawstwie" ("Review of information about the study of human knowledge"; a quarterly), and "Polish scientific periodicals: contents" (about 10 issues a year).

16 Book Production

Production of books has grown substantially in Poland since World War II. The 6,367 books and brochures (excluding offprints) published in Poland in 1938 came out in editions totalling some 29 million copies. By contrast the 1968 figures for the production of books and brochures were 10,306 titles in a total of 119 million copies, with a steady upward trend. In regard to kinds of publication, the 1968 production can be broken down as follows:

Subject groups	Titles	Mill. copies
Scientific	3,681	6.3
University textbooks	1,060	2.5
Vocational publications	2,362	17.1
Popular science publications	1,147	21.7
School books	459	27.4
Belles-lettres	1,006	16.6
Books for children and young people	321	17.4
Total	10,306	119.0

Inasmuch as there is a planned economy in Poland, the proportions between the particular kinds of publication can be set more rationally, taking due account of the hierarchy of needs in the given period and the means available to the publishing industry (paper, printing facilities, financial means). By the same token the structure of the subject matter covered in book production can be affected indirectly through the allocation of appropriate means to various specialized publishing houses.
The pattern of subjects in the production of books and brochures (in titles), according to data for 1967, is characterized by the figures given below. These figures are tabulated in the system recommended by Unesco, but in order of volume of production, and only for the basic groups.

Subject group	Titles	Percentage of total production
Engineering and technology	1,778	18.3
Belles-lettres	1,355	13.9
Natural sciences	833	8.5
Politics, economic sciences	757	7.8
Agriculture	672	6.9
Organization and technique of commerce and industry	443	4.5
Medicine	437	4.5
History, biographies	396	4.0
Education and teaching	331	3.3
Fine arts	313	3.3
Linguistics	299	3.0
Law, administration	253	2.5
Science about literature	241	2.4
Sociology, statistics	204	2.1
Mathematics	198	2.0
Total	9,694	87.0

Of these 9,694 titles first editions accounted for 7,848, or 80%.
The breakdown of the production of books and brochures (in percentage) in 1968 in regard to size of edition was:

up to 500 copies	20.8
501– 1,500	23.6
1,501– 3,500	14.8
3,501– 6,500	11.3
6,501– 10,500	10.5
10,501– 20,500	6.9
20,501– 40,500	5.6
40,501– 75,500	3.1
75,501–150,500	2.1
above 150,500	1.3

17 Translations

The 10,306 titles published in Poland in 1968 included 894 translations from other

languages, that is 8.7% of the total. Most translations appeared in belles-lettres (360 titles), and scientific (252), popular science (128), and vocational (95) publications.
Translations from the English had first place (248) followed by Russian (210), French (134), and German (103).

18 Book Clubs

Immediately after the war the initiative was taken to organize book clubs as a means of promoting reading more rapidly. The "Spółdzielnia Wydawnicza Czytelnik" ("Reader Publishing Cooperative") set up three clubs in 1946–49: "Klub Odrodzenia" ("Club of Odrodzenie", a literary weekly at the time), "Klub Dobrej Książki" ("Good Books Club"), and "Towarzystwo Biblioteki Obiegowej" ("Circulating Library Society"). The Society organized groups of ten persons each, who received books at very low prices. After each member of the group had read a given book, that book became the property of one of them.
At present book clubs are not widespread in Poland, chiefly because the attraction of such clubs lies above all in lower prices—and books in Poland are already cheap. Several clubs do exist, however, and in the main they are attached to mass-circulation periodicals. The "Union of Rural Youth" and the editors of the weekly "Nowa Wieś" ("New Countryside") have organized three clubs: the "New Countryside Book Club" (with more than 25,000 members) in 1964, the "Club of 20th Century Poetry" (membership approx. 6,000) in 1967, and the "Club of Lovers of Songs" (membership of over 20,000) in 1968. In 1969 the editors of the popular monthly "Horyzonty Techniki" ("Horizons of Technology") founded the "Horizons of Technology Club of Popular Science Books" which works together with four specialized publishing houses. The club's list of books for 1969 includes 43 titles. The organizational side of distributing the books for these clubs is looked after by the "Powszechna Księgarnia Wysyłkowa Dom Książki" (General Mail-order Book Shop "Book House") in Warsaw.
In addition to the above, the "Śląsk" ("Silesia" Publishing House), in conjunction with the "Naczelna Organizacja Techniczna" ("Central Technical Organization"), has organized a "Club of Mining and Metallurgical Books" for engineers and technicians employed in these branches of industry.
The first club of socio-political books, "Człowiek-Swiat-Polityka" ("Man-World-Politics"), came into being in 1968. It was organized by "Dom Książki", party newspapers and some publishing houses. This club has proposed 42 titles to its members for 1971.

19 Paperbacks

In the years 1946–51 the "Czytelnik" ("Reader") Publishing Cooperative issued a series of popular science publications, "Wiedza Powszechna" ("General Knowledge"), in the form of brochures of several dozen pages each. This initiative, undertaken with much vigour, resulted in 23 series of booklets written by eminent Polish scholars. All told, 619 titles appeared. Paperbacks are beginning to spread at an increasing rate, although the large low-price editions of many books in Poland makes this form of publication less attractive than elsewhere. Several series that do come out are worthy of mention. The popular science series, "Omega" (a title every two weeks); two series put out by "Książka i Wiedza" ("Books and Knowledge Publishers") – the "Koliber" ("Hummingbird") series of stories from belles-lettres, in which editions exceed 100,000 copies, and the "Światowid" history series (named after a mythical Slav god); two series put out by the "Ministry of National Defence Publishers" —the"Żółty Tygrys" ("Yellow Tiger") series about the events of the Second World War, and the series "Sensacje XX Wieku" ("Sensations of the 20th Century"). The books in the last two series reach editions of 240,000 copies. Several series of thrillers and mysteries are carried by Czytelnik, Iskry, and other publishers.

20 Book Design

The "Polish Society of Book Publishers" (→ 4) is the organizer of an annual contest for the best book published. The first such contest took place in 1958, when books published in 1957 were adjudicated.

Publishers enter 170–200 books each year. The contest jury awards about 10 prizes and some 30 honorable mentions. The prizes have been established by the "Polish Society of Book Publishers", the "Union of Book, Press and Radio Employees", the "Union of Printing Trade Workers", and the "Foreign Trade Enterprise Ars Polona".

The monetary awards are shared by the artists, and employees of the publisher, printing works, and, in special cases, of the paper mill as well.

Books entered in the contest are judged in the following categories: 1) socio-political and popular science publications, 2) scientific publications, 3) vocational technical publications, 4) schoolbooks, 5) belles-lettres for adults, 6) belles-lettres for children and young people, 7) art albums, 8) music publications, 9) export publications. Bibliophile editions are appraised outside these categories.

In the 12 years of the contest so far, the jury has worked out objective criteria for its appraisal. When a book is being classified, four elements of publishing work are taken into account: (1) the publishing conception, (2) the expediency of the form and other features chosen as compared to the contents and value of the book, (3) the book design, (4) the choice of type, make-up of columns, and technical preparation of illustrations. Next, consideration is given to four elements of print-shop work: (5) composition and paging, (6) blocks and reproductions, (7) printing, (8) book-binding. Moreover, the jury takes account of two elements which are common to the work of both printer and publisher: (9) choice of paper, (10) choice of other materials. Professors of universities and academies of fine arts serve on the committee and jury along with publishers, graphic artists, and printers. Furthermore, representatives of other countries—from the Soviet Union, Czechoslovakia, the German Democratic Republic, Hungary, Romania, and Bulgaria—also participate as observers.

The contest plays a major role in raising the level of the get-up of books.

→ 34.

Bibliography

R. Tomaszewski (ed.), *Cztery konkursy na najlepiej wydaną książkę w latach 1957–61.* (Four contests for best-designed books published 1957–1961). Warszawa 1963. 126 pp.

21 Publishing

When organization was dicussed in section 4, it was mentioned that specialization and, in great measure, concentration were characteristic features of the publishing trade in Poland. A consequence is that the great majority of the publishing houses are in Warsaw, although since 1956 regional publishing houses of a more universal nature have come into being in all major centres, and in addition some of the big publishers have branches in other towns.

In the category of scientific publishers, mention should be made of two: the "Zakład Narodowy im Ossolińskich" ("Ossolineum Foundation") in Wrocław, which has been in existence since 1817 and is now the "Polish Academy of Sciences Press" (307 titles in 1968), and "Państwowe Wydawnictwo Naukowe" ("Polish Scientific Publishers") in Warsaw (1,300 titles). A major role in putting out books on the social and political sciences is played by "Książka i Wiedza", which also publishes mass-edition political publications and belles-letters (246 titles).
Scientific and vocational publications on technical subjects are concentrated mainly in three Warsaw publishing houses: "Wydawnictwa Naukowo-Techniczne" ("Scientific and Technical Publishers"; 182 titles), "Arkady" ("Arcades"; 109 titles), and "Wydawnictwo Komunikacji i Łączności" ("Transport and Communications Publishers; 143 titles). Agricultural publications are the domain of "Państwowe Wydawnictwo Rolnicze i Leśne" ("State Agricultural and Forestry Publishers; 485 titles), economic texts—Państwowe Wydawnictwo Ekonomiczne" ("State Economic Publishers; 105 titles), and medical books—"Państwowe Zakłady Wydawnictw Lekarskich" ("State Medical Publishers"; 214 titles).
The principal role in the belles-lettres category is played by three publishing houses in Warsaw: "Państwowy Instytut Wydawniczy" ("State Publishing Institute"; 223 titles), "Czytelnik" ("Reader" Publishing Cooperative; 225 titles), and "Iskry" ("State Publishers "Sparks"; 145 titles), and the "Wydawnictwo Literackie" ("Literary Press"; 96 titles) in Cracow. The main publisher of children's books is the Instytut Wydawniczy Naszy Księgarnia ("Our Book Shop" Publishing Institute; 249 titles) in Warsaw.
Other publishing houses are: "Państwowe Zakłady Wydawnictw Szkolnych" ("State School Publications Press") which puts out school books (385 titles), "Ludowa Spółdzielnia Wydawnica" ("Peasant Publishing Cooperative"; 133 titles), "Wydawnictwo Ministerstwa Obrony Narodowej" ("Ministry of National Defence Publishers"; 159 titles), "Wiedza Powszechna" ("General Knowledge" State Publishers), the main publishers of popular science books and dictionaries (107 titles), "Instytut Wydawniczy PAX" (Publishing Institut PAX, Lay catholic publishers), and "Polskie Wydawnictwo Muzyczne" ("Polish Music Publishers"; 320 titles) in Cracow.
A network of regional publishing houses which came into being throughout the country in 1955–9 put out publications concerning their region but also publish scientific and popular science books as well as belles-lettres. Katowice has the "Sląsk (Silesia) Publishing House", Gdynia its "Wydawnictwo Morskie" ("Maritime Publishers"), while Poznań, Łódz, and Lublin have their own regional publishing houses as well.
The structure of the 38 publishing enterprises and various publishing bureaux breaks down as follows in regard to size: 13 publishing houses issue fewer than 100 titles a year (1968 figures), 14 publish 100–200 titles, 6 put out 200–300 titles, while 5 publishers produce more than 300 and, of these, one turns out more than 1,300 titles.
Apart from books, publishing houses in Poland also publish periodicals in the "Robotnicza Spółdzielnia Wydawnicza Prasa" ("Press Workers' Publishing Cooperative"; 169 titles in 1968, incl. 44 newspapers), and of the publishing houses 17 issue periodicals as well.
For calculating and price-fixing in publishing → 3.

22 Literary Agents

Operating since 1965 is the agency

Agencja Autorska Sp. z.o.o.
(Authors' Agency Ltd)
ul. Hipoteczna 2
PL Warszawa

The "Agency" is owned jointly by four associations: "Stowarzyszenie Autorów ZAIKS" ("ZAIKS Authors' Association"), "Związek Kompozytorów Polskich" ("Union of Polish Composers"), "Związek Polskich Artystów Plastyków" ("Union of Polish Artists") and "Związek Polskich Artystów Fotografików ("Union of Polish Artistic Photographers").

The purpose of the "Agency" is to represent Polish authors and artists abroad and to sell copyright for books, plays, music compositions, and artistic and photographic works. To perform its tasks, the "Agency" provides extensive information services. It issues the quarterlies *Literatura Polska* ("Polish Literature") in English and French, and *Muzyka Polska* ("Polish Music" in English and German). It has published the handbook *Polskie Sztuki Współczesne* ("Contemporary Polish Plays") in four languages, covering 100 plays written by contemporary Polish authors in the period 1960–67. The "Agency" also collaborates with foreign periodicals in preparing special issues about Poland. In 1968–9 the "Agency" organized an exhibition called *Literatura polska w świecie* ("Polish Literature in the World"), encompassing some 1,300 titles, most of them works by contemporary writers, translated into about 70 languages. The exhibition was on show in London, Milan, Padua, Rome and Paris. The Agency also supplies encyclopedic publications with information such as biographical details concerning Polish authors.

The Authors' Agency cooperates with several hundred publishing houses and agencies and several hundred translators of Polish literature, providing them with literary periodicals, books and dictionaries. The cooperation with translators was inaugurated by the "First International Congress of Belles-Lettres Writers", which met in Warsaw in 1965. The second conference was held in 1970.

23 Wholesale Trade

There is one central book wholesale organization in Poland, *Składnica Księgarska* (→ 4). Its first task is to poll the demand of bookshops for every title announced by publishers. Several months before printing begins, publishers send the "Repository" a memo about the given title. The weekly "Zapowiedzi Wydawnicze" (→ 5) appears on the basis of these notes. Within 14 days, bookshops and voivodship "Dom Książki" enterprises place their orders, which give the publisher a basis on which to fix the size of the edition. All titles printed are delivered to the warehouses of the "Składnica Księgarska", which stores them and sends them out to bookshops in keeping with orders placed. Similarly, the "Repository" handles sales of books imported by the foreign trade enterprise "Ars Polona Ruch" (→ 4).

The various branches of the "Repository" have display rooms which show all titles in stock in its warehouses, in a bibliographical arrangement.

The "Składnica Księgarska" puts out informative and promotional material. Each quarter a balance sheet is published of all deliveries, sales, and stocks of all titles received by the "Repository" in the given and earlier quarters of the current year. Moreover, a catalogue of all titles in stock in the warehouses of the "Składnica Księgarska" is issued each year.

24 Retail Trade

A unified retail organization, concentrated in the "Dom Książki" (→ 4), exists in Poland. In 1968 "Dom Książki" operated a total of 1,720 bookshops. The territorial location of these shops in 1968 broke down as follows: 439 in voivodship towns, 680 in district towns, and 601 in localities below district towns. The index for the density of the network is improving steadily and in 1968 there was an average of one bookshop for every 12,625 inhabitants in voivodship towns, and one for every 20,701 in other localities.

Bookshop sales have been growing at 8 to 9% a year. Sales reached 1,708 million złotys in 1968, and of these 67.8% was to individuals and 32.2% to institutions (libraries, organizations, etc.).

The structure of bookshop sales of publications apart from textbooks in 1968 was:

Subject group	Amount million zł.	Percentage of total sales
Belles-lettres	336.0	28.1
Scientific and popular science publications	283.9	23.7
Technical and scientific-technical publications	155.4	13.0
Books for children and young people	103.9	8.7
Socio-political and economic publications	80.5	6.7
Agricultural publications	40.4	3.4
Art publications	26.6	2.2
Others	169.1	14.2

It should be added that apart from books, some bookshops also sell gramophone records, stationery, etc. Total sales of these items ran to 1,455 m złotys in 1968.

25 Mail-Order Bookselling

The "Dom Książki" (→ 4) has organized mobile bookselling service in several voivodships and in 1969 had a fleet of 20 mobile bookshops (in minibuses). The main purpose of these bookshops on wheels is to reach remote localities. The mobile bookshops sell books and take orders, especially on the basis of the books they display.

There is a *Powszechna Księgarnia Wysyłkowa* ("General Mail-Order Bookshop") in Warsaw and bookshops in Poznań, Wrocław, and Katowice have mail-order departments. The Mail-Order Book Shop in Warsaw works together with mass-circulation periodicals in organizing reader clubs.

26 Antiquarian Book Trade, Auctions

There is a network of state-owned and private antiquarian bookshops in Poland. The state-owned antiquarian bookshops are run by the "Dom Książki". Most of the 24 state-owned shops specialize in old publications of lasting scientific and historical value; next in number are general antiquarian bookshops (of a mixed nature) while there are a few shops for contemporary books; but these are to increase in number substantially over the next few years. There are 50 private antiquarian bookshops.

Priority in the option to buy old publications is enjoyed by the "National Library", the "Jagiellonian University Library" in Cracow, the "Ossolineum Foundation Library" in Wrocław, and the "Warsaw University Library". Antiquarian bookshops are obliged to offer newly acquired old books to the aforementioned libraries, and old documents to the Head Office of the "State Archives".

"Dom Książki" publishes specialized catalogues in order to standardize and regulate purchase prices for old books. The prices of publications listed in them are fixed by a commission of experts.

Four auctions are held each year by the four largest "Dom Książki" antiquarian

bookshops in Warsaw, Cracow, Poznań, and Bydgoszcz.
Training of antiquarian booksellers → 11.
Bibliography
→ 6.

27 Book Imports

All imports (and exports) of printed matter are handled by
Ars Polona Ruch
Krakowskie Przedmieście 7
PL Warszawa
(→ 4), a state enterprise established by uniting the former institutions "Ars Polona" and "Ruch".
The value of books imported into Poland in 1968 ran to US $ 4.618 m. The principal exporters of books to Poland were:

Country	Amount US $ 1,000
USSR	2,321
Germany (Democratic Republic)	764
Germany (Federal Republic)	389
United Kingdom	293
Czechoslovakia	179
France	172
Hungary	120
Netherlands	103

Periodicals were imported into Poland in 1968 to the tune of US $ 3.753 m. The biggest suppliers of periodicals imported into Poland were the following countries:

Country	Amount US $ 1,000
USSR	1,914
Germany (Federal Republic)	511
Germany (Democratic Republic)	310
USA	292
United Kingdom	201
France	177

28 Book Exports

Poland exported 2.534 m dollars worth of books in 1968. The group of countries which were the biggest importers of books from Poland consisted of:

Country	Amount US $ 1,000
USSR	1,726
Germany (Democratic Republic)	342
Czechoslovakia	139
USA	118
Germany (Federal Republic)	69

Exports of periodicals from Poland in 1968 amounted to US $ 2.871 m. The biggest exports went to:

Country	Amount US $ 1,000
USSR	2,010
Czechoslovakia	200
Germany (Democratic Republic)	155
Germany (Federal Republic)	148
USA	108

The foreign-trade enterprise *Ars Polona Ruch* (→ 4) and the various publishing houses organize exhibitions of books in other countries, frequently in connection with fairs. Some 40 such exhibitions are held each year.
Ruch → 27 (Ars Polona Ruch).

Bibliography

New Polish Publications → 14.

29 Book Fairs

The "International Book Fair" held in Poland was at first, i.e. in 1956 and 1957, part of the International Trade Fair in Poznań. Since 1958 it has been held each

May in the "Palace of Culture and Science" in the centre of Warsaw.
The "International Book Fair" Warsaw is organized by the Foreign Trade Enterprise "Ars Polona" (→ 4) and the "Polish Society of Book Publishers" (→ 4). The 1969 Fair was participated in by exhibitors from 26 countries of Europe, America, and Africa, representing the books of 2,200 publishers. The "Book Fair" in Warszwa has gained the reputation of being the most important such event in Europe, after the "Frankfurt Book Fair", and constitutes a meeting place for publishers and booksellers from East and West, for discussing translations, joint editions, and printing services, as well as negotiating import and export transactions.
Although all kinds of publications are presented at the "International Book Fair" in Warsaw, it is mainly a scientific book fair.
→ International Section, 29.

30 Public Relations

Advertising of books is carried out by the publishers, the wholesale organization "Składnica Księgarska" (→ 4), and the retailing organization "Dom Książki" (→ 4). Inasmuch as the organization is unified, this activity is coordinated to a substantial degree. The publishers engage in the promotion chiefly of new titles and work together with wholesale in advertising books in stock. The "Składnica Księgarska" (→ 4) provides bookshops with information and also in part reaches readers directly. The main advertising for customers is organized by "Dom Książki" (→ 4).
The bookshops play a noteworthy role in promoting reading. This is furthered by their cooperation with youth organizations and schools. The "Union of Rural Youth" has appointed reading-promotion organizers who are book salesmen at the same time. Collaborating closely with the "Union of Polish Writers", the bookshops also arrange meetings with writers. "Dom Książki" holds contests for readers, mainly through the papers.
A major book-promoting event is the annual "Book and Press Day", held each May, when some 3,000 book fairs are organized on the squares and streets of cities and towns throughout the country over a period of three weeks.

31 Bibliophily

In Poland bibliophily is the domain of
Towarzystwo Przyjaciół Książki
(Society of Friends of Books)
ul. Hipoteczna 2
PL Warszawa
The "Society" also has branches in Cracow, Katowice, and Wrocław.

32 Literary Prizes

An extensive system of prizes for writers exists in Poland, the awards being made by state agencies, periodicals, towns, publishers, and civic societies.
The committee appointed by the "Council of Ministers" for State Prizes in Science, Technology, and Culture and the Arts awards "First Class" and "Second Class" prizes every two years for outstanding works in the realm of science and belles-lettres. The "Minister of Culture and Art" also makes biannual awards in three classes for a particular work or for the whole of a writer's literary output. The "Minister of Education and Higher Schools" gives annual prizes for the best university textbooks. And the "Minister of National Defence" assigns awards for literary work on a military subject.
Regular prizes have been set up by towns such as Warsaw, Cracow, Poznań, Łódź, Wroclaw, Katowice, Lublin, Bydgoszcz, and Opole. Similarly, the voivodships of

Olsztyn, Rzeszów, Kielce, Zielona Góra, and others have done the same.

Annual awards are made by literary and social periodicals such as *Polityka* ("Politics"), *Kultura* ("Culture"), and *Życie Literackie* ("Literary Life").

Since 1929 the "Polish Pen Club" has been giving two annual prizes for translators: 1) for outstanding accomplishments in translating world literature into Polish, and 2) for outstanding achievements in translating works of Polish literature into other languages.

Prizes are also awarded by such civic organizations as the "Union of Rural Youth", the "Marine Writers' Club", and the "Association of Lay Catholics PAX".

33 The Reviewing of Books

The principal book-review publication is the fortnightly

Nowe Książki
Przegląd literacki i naukowy
(New Books, Literary and Scientific Reviews)
ul. Mazowiecka 11
PL Warszawa

The main part of this publication is an extensive section carrying reviews of books of all kinds and a survey of new titles with informative notes. The reviewers are eminent scholars and critics. Furthermore, the publication contains articles on literary criticism and the publishing trade as well as vignettes of authors.

Reviews, chiefly of belles-lettres, are carried in the literary weeklies such as *Kultura* ("Culture"—published in Warsaw), *Życie Literackie* ("Literary Life"—Cracow), *Współczesność* ("The Present Day"—Warsaw), and *Kierunki* ("Trends"—Warsaw), in the monthly *Twórczość* ("Creativeness"—Warsaw—organ of the Union of Polish Writers), *Miesięcznik Literacki* ("Literary Monthly"—Warsaw), and the monthly *Litery* ("Letters"—Gdańsk). Reviews of social and factual publications also appear in the weekly *Polityka* ("Politics"—Warsaw). Of the daily newspapers, regular review sections are conducted by *Trybuna Ludu* ("People's Tribune"—Warsaw), *Życie Warszawy* ("Warszawa Life"—Warsaw), *Trybuna Robotnicza* ("Workers' Tribune"—Katowice), and *Dziennik Polski* ("Polish Daily"—Cracow).

34 Graphic Arts

Book designers belong to the graphic artists section of the

Związek Polskich Artystów Plastyków
Zarząd Główny Sekcji Grafików
(Union of Polish Artists
Head Office of Graphic Artists Section)
ul. Foksal 2
PL Warszawa

This section organizes displays of book design in Poland and participates in international exhibitions. It has been co-organizer since 1965 of the "International Biennale of Bookplates" in Malbork, which is an extremely popular event with book-lovers.

In addition, a book-design section exists in the "Polish Society of Book Publishers" (→ 4).

Portugal

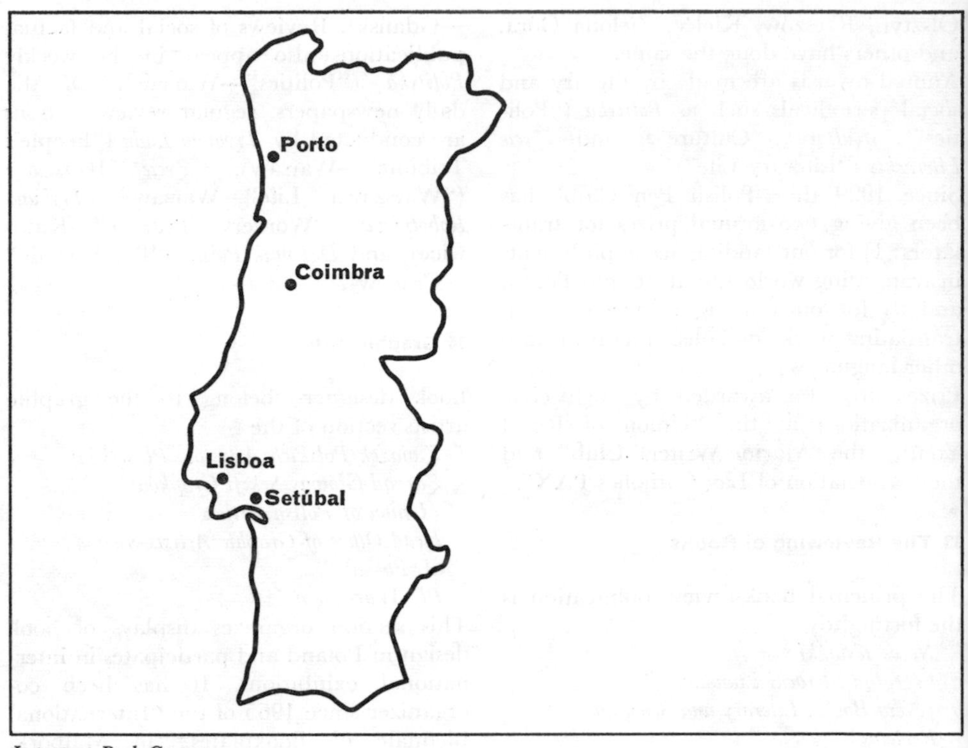

Important Book Centres

1 General Information

Area 91,971 km²

Population 9,400,000 (103 per km²); (metropolitan Portugal, Azores and Madeira)

Capital Lisboa (1,000,000)

Largest towns Lisboa (1,000,000); Porto (400,000); Setúbal (51,000); Coimbra (40,000)

Government The Republic of Portugal is a unified and corporate State governed by the following notices: the National Constitution approved by a national plebiscite on 19 March 1933 and amended in 1935, 1936, 1937, 1938, 1945 and 1958, and decrees announcing a separate foreign policy from 1930 and amended to the present date

Religions In Portugal the church and the state are separate. All religions and their branches are recognized and may be practised freely. The great majority of the population are Roman Catholic

National language Portuguese

Leading foreign languages French, English, Spanish, and German

Weights, measures Metric system

Currency unit Escudo

Education The "Ministry of National Education" supervises primary education (five years), secondary education (seven years), and secondary technical education. Classical and technical universities provide diversified and specialized courses. University instruction is the responsibility of the state. Primary and secondary school administration is largely private

Illiteracy Exists on a large scale, although primary education is compulsory

Membership Unesco, IPA

2 Past and Present

The first Portuguese printing press was assembled in Leiria about 1465, preceding by about 22 years the establishment of the Hebrew press in Faro in 1487. In 1495 Valentim Fernandes and Nicolau de Saxónia introduced the first Portuguese illustrated books. The Portuguese printing and publishing industry suffered a setback as a result of the great earthquake in Lisbon in 1755, at which date there were in existance about ten printing presses and printers. In 1768 the politician Marquis de Pombal created an "Impressão Régia" ("Royal Press"), which gave a great fillip to the production of books. In 1837 there was a lithographic office. The first newspaper to be printed on a steam press was "O Nacional", an organ of liberation. In 1955 there were 700 printing presses in Portugal and today their number exceeds one thousand. The publishing industry made great progress until shortly after the first two decades of the twentieth century. After 1920 Portuguese publications were primarily works of national classical authors, translations and local publications. Shortly before the beginning of the Second World War a movement of self-appraisal emerged with the founding of the editions "Cosmos" and "Inquérito", being the last and dynamic efforts of their founder, Eduardo Salgueiro. This vast movement not only covered the translations of foreign authors but also the works of modern Portuguese writers. An important date in the history of the Portuguese printing movement was 1945. At that time a number of new publishers emerged, despite a period of inflation which hindered the development and acquisition of new techniques.

Bibliography

a) Periodicals

A Tipografia. (Typography). Lisboa 1909–15.

Livros de Portugal. (Books of Portugal). Bulletin of the National Association of Publishers and Booksellers (→ 4).

b) Books

M. Amzalac, *A tipografia hebraica em Portugal no séc. XV.* (Hebrew printing in Portugal in the 15th century). Lisboa 1922.

A. I. Anselmo, *Bibliografia das obras impressas em Portugal no séc. XVI.* (Bibliography of the printed works of Portugal in the 16th century). Lisboa 1926.

Br. Aranha, *A imprensa em Portugal nos séc. XVI e XVII.* (The press in Portugal in the 16th and 17th centuries). Lisboa 1898.

E. Cerdeira, *A imprensa.* (The press). História de Portugal, vol. 4. Barcelos 1932.

V. Deslandes, *Documentos para a história da typografia portuguesa nos séc. XVI e XVII.* (Documents on the history of Portuguese printing in the 16th and 17th centuries). 2 vols. Lisboa 1881–2.

K. Haebler, *The early printers of Spain and Portugal.* London, Bibliographical Society 1897.

K. Haebler, *Bibliografia Ibérica del siglo XV.* (Iberian bibliography of the 15th century). 2 vols. Den Haag 1903–17.

G. do Monte, *Subsídios para a história da tipografia em Évora nos séc. XVI e XVII.* (Contributions to the history of printing in Evora in the 16th and 17th centuries). Evora 1968.

O Mundo da edição Luso-Brasileira. (The world of Luso-Brazilian publishing). Lisboa, Publicações Europa-América 1969.

A. C. Pinto, *Da famosa arte da imprimissão.* (The famous art of printing). Lisboa, Ed. Ulisseia 1948.

J. Tengarrinha, *História da imprensa periódica portuguesa.* (History of Portuguese periodical publications). Lisboa, Portugália Editora 1965.

Qu. Veloso, *Bibliografia geral Portuguesa.* (General Portuguese bibliography). vol. 1 and 2. Lisboa 1941–2.

Portugal

3 Retail Prices

There is no national convention referring to the determination of prices beyond a tacit agreement between publishers and booksellers, who receive a margin of 30% discount on the recommended retail price. This decision taken by the "Grémio Nacional dos Editores e Livreiros" (→ 4) prohibits a concessionary to allow any discount to the customer.

4 Organization

The principal association for all branches of the industry and commerce of books in Portugal is the

Grémio Nacional dos Editores e Livreiros
(National Association of Publishers and Booksellers)
Largo de Andaluz, 16, 1.°, E.
P Lisboa 1.

Its most important functions and responsibilities are representing the interests of publishers and booksellers, establishing advantageous and good commercial relations, developing new forms of negotiation and simultaneously informing institutions of other countries and being alert to the legal notices and orders relating to the commercial world of books. This independent association publishes the periodical *Livros de Portugal* ("Books from Portugal", → 5). It organizes an annual national book fair in Lisbon and Porto, and in other cities.

5 Trade Press

The official paper is

Livros de Portugal (Books of Portugal)
Largo de Andaluz, 16, 1.°, E.
P Lisboa 1

which appears monthly, published by the "Grémio" (→ 4). *Livros* contains official information, articles about all aspects of the book trade, announcements of forthcoming publications arranged by publishers, and a selection from the national bibliography (→ 15).

6 Book-Trade Literature

Very little literature exists beyond the publications already quoted (→ 2,5). However, it is possible to find further information in the monthly bulletin of the *Instituto Nacional de Estatística* ("National Institute of Statistics") and the reports of the *Direcção-Geral do Comércio* ("General Direction of Trade"). No special books or pamphlets concerning the activities and the system of the modern Portuguese book trade exist.

For addresses of the Portuguese book trade → 7.

7 Sources of Information, Address Services

Information about the book trade may be obtained from the "Grémio" (→ 4) and in certain cases from the

Secretariado Nacional de Informação
(National Information Secretariat)
Praça dos Restauradores
P Lisboa

or, for Portuguese overseas questions, from the

Agência-Geral do Ultramar
(Overseas General Agency)
Ministério do Ultramar
Restelo
P Lisboa.

The addresses of the Portuguese book trade and that of the overseas provinces (and the Brazilian book trade) are to be found in *O mundo da edição* (Lisboa, Publ. Europa-América), which appeared for the first time in 1969 (→ 2).

8 International Membership

Portugal is a member of the International Publishers' Association (IPA).

10 Books and Young People

Though, as in other countries, young people and university students are interested in reading and literary problems, nothing exists of an elementary analytical nature from which it is possible to obtain statistical information. This interest is expressed in the few academic magazines and journals in Portugal.
Talks and forums to discuss literary problems at the level of the "Associações de Estudantes" ("Associations of Students") have always been successful.
As to the selection of books for Portuguese youth, nothing has been done to promote any guidance, and to reward the initiative of publishers striving to offer better recreational books.
In 1969 the

Comissão de Literatura e de Espectáculos para Menores
(Commission Concerning Literature and Films for Minors)
Secretaria de Estado de Informação e Turismo
Palácio Foz, Praça dos Restauradores
P Lisboa

was officially founded, to which were submitted all works suitable for young people.

11 Training

In Portugal no institution of instruction suitable for the advanced education and technical advancement of future publishers and booksellers exists. Training and advancement can only be obtained by professional experience and the matter has not yet been dealt with by the "Instituto de Investigação Industrial" ("Institute of Industrial Investigation"), which maintains numerous courses of professional training in other professional branches.

12 Taxes

All imports exceeding in value 2,500 Escudos require special authorization. All foreign printed works in the Portuguese language, including dictionaries, children's books, plans and geographical maps, are subject to a special tariff regulation, from which are excluded books in Portuguese originating in Brazil.

14 Copyright

Copyright is strictly controlled by the "Código dos Direitos de Autor" ("Code of authors' rights" promulgated by legal decree no. 46980 on 27 April 1966. This code was based on the project of the commission established in 1946 at the "Berne Convention". The "Regulamento do Registo da Propriedade Literária" ("Regulation for registering literary works"; decree 4 114) is the basic judiciary document for the protection of intellectual and literary works. Portugal is a member of the Berne Convention and of the World Copyright Convention.

Bibliography

Código dos direitos de autor e dos direitos vizinhos. (Code of authors and similar rights). Ed. M. da Silva. Coimbra 1965.
Código dos direitos de autor. (Code of authors' rights). Ed. M. da Silva. Coimbra 1966.
O mundo da edição Luso-Brasileira. (The world of Luso-Brazilian publishing). Lisboa 1969.

15 National Bibliography, National Library

The national bibliography

Boletim de Bibliografia Portuguesa
(Bulletin of Portuguese Bibliography)
Biblioteca Nacional
P Lisboa

was founded in 1935, but suspended from 1940 to 1945. Up to 1954 it appeared as an annual publication, from 1955 as a monthly.

The "Academy of Sciences", Lisbon, continues the preparation of the famous "Bibliografia geral Portuguesa", covering Portuguese books printed in the 15th century. The first two volumes written by Queirós Veloso were published in 1941 and 1942 (→ 2).

Thirteen legal-deposit copies of each forthcoming book have to be sent to the "Biblioteca Nacional" for distribution to various libraries.

16 Book Production

Portugal produced 5,522 titles in 1967, divided into the following categories:

Subject group	Titles
General	244
Philosophy	79
Religion	348
Social sciences	1,183
Philology	143
Pure sciences	401
Applied sciences	1,012
Arts	208
Literature	1,397
Geography	507
Total	5,522

17 Translations

There is a lively interest in translations from foreign languages. In 1967 982 titles were translated into Portuguese, primarily from Spanish (364), English (266) and French (251).

In 767 cases the translations were in the field of literature.

18 Book Clubs

There are no book clubs in Portugal which correspond to clubs existing in some other countries. Some private associations have recently shown interest in this special problem. A reunion of the "Feira Internacional das Artes Gráficas" ("International Fair of Graphic Art") in Lisbon during 1969 may have had a beneficial effect in promoting a desirable impulse for the growth of permanent book clubs.

19 Paperbacks

As elsewhere pocket books and paperbacks are becoming a growing proportion of national book production. There are six paperback series with widespread distribution throughout the country.

21 Publishing

Nearly all of the existing publishing houses are centralized in Lisbon. Other important publishing towns are Porto and Coimbra. Some publishers are active in Portuguese overseas provinces.

22 Literary Agents

The few literary agencies of Portugal are not prosperous. Contacts between foreign authors and publishers have always been maintained directly by the Portuguese publishers or through foreign literary agencies.

23 Wholesale Trade

A special wholesale book trade does not exist.

24 Retail Trade

The main centres of the retail book trade are Lisbon, Porto, Setúbal, Coimbra, Viana do Castelo, Braga, and Faro. Lisbon is the most important place for leading import and export booksellers.

The 813 retail enterprises existing in

modern Portugal include stationers' shops and other outlets where books are sold as a sideline.

25 Mail-Order Bookselling

This method of selling has been introduced recently into Portugal but it is still not fully developed. Publishers are rarely involved and the successful adoption of this system requires appreciable outlay in modern filing equipment and convenient assembly services.

26 Antiquarian Book Trade, Auctions

The trade in second-hand books has a long tradition in Portugal. In the cities of Lisbon and Porto there are special shops for the sale of rare books, which also do business in modern second-hand books (remainders). There are frequent auctions where rare books, mostly from aristocratic or the old urban and provincial families, are offered to a general book-minded public. No special organization uniting the antiquarian book trade of Portugal exists, but some of the leading firms are members of the "Antiquarian Booksellers' Association" (A.B.A., → United Kingdom, 26). In this way they also became members of the I.L.A.B. (→ International Section, 26).

27 Book Imports

In 1968 Portugal imported books and brochures valued at Esc. 46.6 million. The leading countries of origin were

Country	Amount (Million Esc.)
United Kingdom	19.3
France	10.8
USA	5.3
Spain	3.9
Germany (Federal Republic)	2.0
Italy	1.1

The imports of periodicals reached Esc. 13.3 m in 1968.

28 Book Exports

In 1968 Portugal exported books valued at Esc. 19.6 m and periodicals valued at Esc. 1.3 m.
Books were primarily exported to Brazil and to the Portuguese Overseas Provinces.

Country, Province	Amount (Million Esc.)
Brazil	12.4
Angola	3.0
Moçambique	1.1
Other Overseas Provinces	0.6

Periodical exports were nearly exclusively to the Overseas Provinces of Portugal (Cape Verde, Guinea, S. Tomé e Príncipe, Angola and Moçambique).

32 Literary Prizes

The following selective list gives an idea of the numerous literary prizes: the prize *Diário de Notícias* (two prizes every two years); the *Prémios do Secretariado Nacional da Informação* ("Prizes of the National Information Secretariat" – history, plays, dramas, novels and children's books). The most important prizes of all are the prize *Antero de Quental* (poetry) and *Eça de Queirós* (fiction), the *Prémio Nacional de Poesia* and the *Prémio Camões* (Portuguese topics). Further prizes are: *Prémios da Agência Geral do Ultramar* ("Overseas General Agency"); *Camilo Pessanha* (poetry) and *Fernão Mendes Pinto* (short stories); and the annual prize of the *Câmara Municipal de Lourenço Marques* ("Municipal Chamber of Lourenço Marques"). Some organizations (publishers, regional associations, etc.) occasionally award cultural and literary prizes.

Portugal

33 The Reviewing of Books

Book reviewing in Portugal was started by the generation of the so-called "Presença" (1927), which was very popular. The reviewers' basic functions in the large daily newspapers of Lisbon and Porto and their weekly literary supplements has been to reveal sources of information and create violent controversies. On a more moderate level the critics actively write reviews in almost all magazines published in Portugal. There are book reviews on radio programmes, but their absence is noted in television, the more popular medium of information. Influential media of reviews are e.g. *Livros de Portugal* (→ 5), the Lisbon dailies, *Diário de Lisboa, Diário Popular, Diário de Notícias, A Capital, Século, República, Diário da Manhã, Novidades* and *A Voz*, and the Porto dailies, *Comércio do Porto, Primeiro de Janeiro, Jornal de Notícias;* further there are the magazines *Brotéria, Seara Nova, O Tempo e o Modo, Vértice, Jornal de Letras e Artes.*

Romania

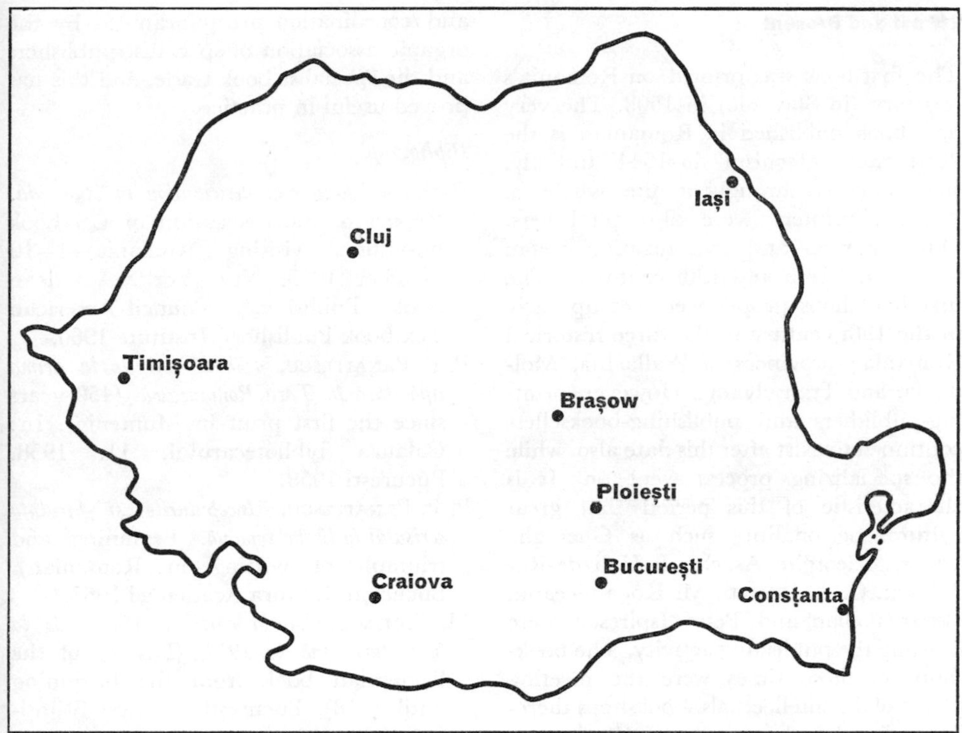

Important Book Centres

1 General Information

Area 237,500 km²
Population 20,140,000 (1970) (177 per km²)
Capital București (1,457,802)
Largest towns București (1,457,802); Cluj (197,902); Timișoara (189,264); Iași (179,405); Brașov (179,316); Galați (172,687); Craiova (171,676); Constanța (170,026); Ploiești (160,011); Brăila (149,686); Oradea (135,361); Arad (135,181); Sibiu (118,893)
Government Romania is a socialist republic, a unitary, independent, and sovereign state of the working people in towns and villages; its territory is inalienable and indivisible.
Religion Anybody is free to embrace a religious creed or not (The Constitution of the Socialist Republic of Romania).
National language Romanian; the main languages of the coinhabiting minorities: Hungarian, German, Serbian.
Leading foreign languages French, English, Russian
Weights and measures Metric system
Currency unit The Leu
Education Compulsory general education with a duration of ten years, free of charge; 147,637 students (1968/69) in 187 universities and higher educational departments.
Illiteracy Nil
Membership UNESCO

2 Past and Present

The first book was printed on Romania's territory (in Slavonic) in 1508. The very first book published in Romanian is the "Lutheran Catechism" in 1544. Initially, the same as throughout the whole of Europe, printers were also publishers. Differentiation and specialization began only in the 18th and 19th centuries. The first bookshops proper were set up early in the 19th century in the three historical Romanian provinces of Wallachia, Moldavia, and Transylvania. However, printing-publishers and publishing-booksellers continued to exist after this date also, while the specializing process went on. It is characteristic of this period that great cultural personalities such as Gheorghe Lazar, Gheorghe Asachi, I. Heliade-Radulescu, C. A. Rosetti, M. Kogalniceanu, Cezar Bolliac and Petre Ispirescu were heading the publishing activity. The bookshops of those times were the meeting places of the intellectuals. Bookshops therefore played an important role in our country, and some have earned a place in history.

Today the book trade is the concern of the whole state and is directed by the "State Committee for Culture and Art", which ensures the application of cultural principles in the book trade through the "Centrala Cărţii" ("Book Centre", → 4). Within the framework of a socialist planned economy the continual correlation between the publication of books and their distribution is more advantageous from the economic and cultural point of view, since the size of an edition plays an important role in culture; it must therefore not be determined on statistics alone, by the mere addition of various demands for it. Bookshops, book-kiosks in shops in the country, bookstalls in institutions and firms are successful intermediaries between publisher and purchaser. Both specialization and coordination are guaranteed by the organic association of specialist publishers and the specialist book trade, and this has proved useful in practice.

Bibliography

Book publishing and distribution in Rumania. Report of the delegation of US book publishers visiting Rumania—1–10 October 1965. New York, American Book Publishers' Council–American Textbook Publishers' Institute 1966.

P. P. Panaitescu, *450 de ani de la prima tipăritură în Ţara Românească.* (450 years since the first print in Muntenia). In: Calauza bibliotecarului, 11. 1958. Bucureşti 1958.

P. P. Panaitescu. *Inceputurile şi biruinţa scrisului în limba română.* (Beginnings and triumph of writing in Romanian). Bucureşti, Editura Academiei 1965.

M. Tomescu, *Istoria cărţii româneşti de la începuturi pînă la 1918.* (History of the Romanian book from the beginning until 1918). Bucureşti, Editura Stiinţifică 1968. 216 pp.

D. Trançă *and* I. Marinescu, *A general survey of the Romanian book.* Bucureşti, Meridiane Publishing House 1968.—Also in French and German versions.

3 Retail Prices

Since the publishing houses in Romania are state firms organically integrated in the general effort of culturalization, book prices are established independently of the real costs, on the basis of certain fixed norms relating to the number of printed sheets, to the literary genre, to the standard of writing, to the conditions of artistic and graphical presentation. This system permits a reasonable price to be retained for technical and scientific works, and for publications in the languages of the various nationalities, which have a small printing that makes them unprofitable.

The profits brought in by some books counterbalance the losses recorded with others, either within the same publishing house or within the system of socialist publishing houses. A harmonious development of the various kinds of books required for the cultural, economic, and scientific development of the country is thus promoted. As it is on the whole profitable, Romanian production of books ensures low stable prices that favour the spread of culture among the masses. In Romania book prices are stable.

4 Organization

The
Centrala Cărţii
(Book Centre)
Str. Biserica Amzei nr. 7
R Bucureşti
sees to the interests of booksellers in matters of book circulation, popularization, and advertising, of professional education and specialization, of facilitating the relations with institutions at home and abroad that have the same pattern of specialization, and acts on their behalf in all professional circumstances. Since there is no association of publishers or booksellers and all these institutions are run by the state or on cooperative lines (the bookshops in the villages), the "Centrala" is devided into various spheres of activity, among which are: the determination of the size of editions, public opinion, annual sale statistics, operation and checking of the network of retail shops in the whole country including second-hand sales and stationery, the organization of national and international exhibitions, book imports and exports, trade publications, advertisements, the organization of special activities in the book world ("Book Month in the Country", "Week of the Lyric", "Decade of the Technological Book", etc.). The "Centrala" is responsible for the "Baza pentru Desfacerea Carţii" ("Book Distribution Central Agency", → 23). Bucharest deals with the distribution of books in the countryside. This department of the "Central Association of Cooperatives" is split up regionally and has at its disposal bookshops, departments in large stores, book kiosks, a mail-order department and other activities.

5 Trade Press

Cărţi noi
(New Books)
Str. Biserica Amzei nr. 7
R Bucureşti
the monthly bulletin of the "Centrala" (→ 4), has been in existence since 1957. Currently 125,000 copies are printed. It contains reviews of new publications, reports of forthcoming works, second-hand offers, foreign books, information on national and international events connected with the book trade, publishing, book prints, exhibitions, trade fairs and competitions.
Romanian Books
Russian Version: Rumynskíje Knigi
Str. Biserica Amzei nr. 7
R Bucureşti
is a quarterly publication intended for distribution abroad which calls attention to the most important works published in Romanian and foreign languages in the country. It also contains publishers' addresses and their special fields and information on export matters.

7 Sources of Information, Address Services

Information on the book trade in general is supplied by
Centrala Cărţii
Str. Biserica Amzei nr. 7
R Bucureşti
→ 4, 5.

8 International Membership

The "Centrala" (→ 4) is not a member of any international organization, but it enthusiastically encourages the exchange of information, exhibitions and persons with numerous countries, regularly takes part in the international book fairs at Frankfurt a. M., Leipzig, Warsaw, Belgrade, Tokio, Washington, Plovdiv, and in exhibitions arranged on a reciprocal basis.

9 Market Research

This is undertaken by the "Centrala" (→ 4) with the help of printed publishers' programmes which are distributed to all bookshops in the country in order to determine book demands. The "Centres" collect the suggestions and requests, and during the negotiations with the publishers the size of editions is fixed. The "Centrala" makes an annual statistical inventory of all the books existing in the bookshops. On the basis of this inventory it is possible to ascertain the rate of sale of certain books, genres and series, by social groups, geographic zones, and so on. This inventory is useful for settling the printings, and at the same time it reflects clearly the state of the stocks.

Restricted inquiries are organized for special books. About 200,000 printed questionnaires were distributed in 1966, when a vast social investigation on the subject of books was organized. The regional results of this investigation and certain general data are used at present in the activity of correlating market demand with the production of books. As a consequence of the reorganization which took place in 1969, publishing houses are entitled to issue, apart from copies destined to satisfy the demand registered by the bookshops, further copies for distribution in their own display bookshops, by subscriptions, etc.

Bibliography

M. Florea, N. Mocanu and V. Deleanu, *Ce loc ocupă cartea în viața dumneavoastră? Ancheta a 100 persoane.* (What part do books play in your life? An inquiry among 100 people), Scînteia, 36, no. 7296, May 30, 1967.

St. Haralamb, *Arta de a oferi o carte.* (The art of offering a book). Scînteia tineretului, 22, no. 5213, 20 February, 1966.

I. Marina, *Cartea tehnico-științifică. Anchetă în regiunea Ploiești.* (The technical and scientific book. An inquiry in the region of Ploeshti). Contemporanul, no. 47, 1963.

I. Marinescu, *Elemente de economie editorială neglijate.* (Neglected elements of publishing economics). Scînteia, no. 7, 343, 1967.

S. Movileanu, *Se face un studiu științific al cererii de carte?* (Is there a scientific investigation of book demand being made?). Scînteia, 36, no. 7112, September 25, 1966.

D. Trancă, *Cartea – implicații sociale.* (The book. Social implications). ("Studin în psiho-sociologia culturii de masă". A study in mass-media psycho-sociology), București, Scientific Publishing House 1968.

D. Ursuleanu, and H. Lerea, *Cartea și librarul.* (The book and the bookseller). Luceafarul, 9, no. 25, July 16, 1966.

M. Vasiliu, *Plusuri și minusuri în tirajele cărților.* (Plusses and minuses in the printing of books). Scînteia, 36, no. 7090, September 30, 1966.

10 Books and Young People

Reading for youth is guided in several ways. Inexpensive book series like the "Biblioteca școlarului" ("The Pupil's Library"), and the "Lycaeum", in accordance with the school curriculum and the optional reading recommended by specialized institutions, ensure very large editions for young readers. Other series address different ages, on a large variety of subjects, also cater for younger readers. Worth mentioning among these are "Traista cu povşeti" ("The Bag of Stories)", "Oameni de seama" ("Outstanding Personalities"), "Aventura" ("Adventures"), "Povestiri ştiinţifico-fantastice" ("Science Fiction"), "Cutezatorii" ("The Daring"), "In jurul lumii" ("Around the World"), "Stiniţa învinge" ("Science Carries the Day"). These readings are viewed as an instructive whole; they are listed among the bibliographical recommendations of various schools, in competitions, and in the lists of recommended books issued by the "Central State Library of the Socialist Republic of Romania". Public libraries with departments for children and youth, or the special libraries for children (which are endowed with significant amounts of public funds) place the means of information and selecting at the disposal of young people. All this encourages them to read. In radio and television programmes, but above all in children's and young people's papers and periodicals, there are regular suggestions for book discussions and competitions to stimulate their hunger for reading, which in turn can be satisfied by low book prices and numerically large editions of young people's books. Special events organized by bookshops and librarians are intended to stimulate young people to start their own library. By means of a recommended bibliography the "Association of Communist Youth" has arranged an annual competition, "Love Books" or "Be a Booklover". This started in 1955.

Bibliography

I. D. Balan, *O colecţie de largă popularizare "Biblioteca şcolarului"*. (A widely distributed series: "Small School Library"). In: Scînteia no. 6417. Bucureşti 1964.

B. Buzila, *Biblioteca şcolarului trebuie să fie a . . . şcolarului.* (The "Small School Library" ought to belong to the pupil). In: România Libera, 23, no. 6593. Bucureşti 1965.

H. Culer, *100 de elevi răspund la un chestionar sociologic.* (100 pupils answer a sociological questionnaire). In: Colocvii, no. 1. Bucureşti 1966.

I. Hobana, *Literatura ştiinţifico-fantastică.* (Science fiction). In: Lupta de clasă, no. 12/1963. Bucureşti 1963.

Gh. Martin, *Literatura în colecţiile pentru şcolari.* (Literature in the book series for pupils). In: Călăuza bibliotecarului, 18, no. 9. Bucureşti 1965.

Gh. Stroia, *Aspecte actuale ale literaturii pentru copii.* (Present-day aspects of children's literature). In: Scînteia, no. 6138. Bucureşti 1964.

D. Trancă, *Biblioteca copiilor noştri.* (Our children's library). Bucureşti, Didactic and Pedagogic Publishing House, 1969.—Also in German and Hungarian versions.

N. Ungureanu, *"Aventura" o noua colecţie pentru tineret.* ("Adventures", a new book series for young people). In: Scîenteia tineretului, 20, no. 4807. Bucureşti 1964.

Cărţile vîrstei de aur. (Books of the golden age). In: Luceafărul, no. 47/1966. Bucureşti 1966.

Colocviu despre romanul de aventuri. (A colloquium on the novel of adventure). In: Tribuna, no. 20, 21/1966. Bucureşti 1966.

11 Training

At the moment there are two main forms of training in Romania:

1. The
   Şcoala tehnică de librari
   (Technical School for Booksellers)
   Şoseaua Străuleşti no. 1
   R Bucureşti

with a duration of one year. Young people between 17 and 25 years of age with a secondary school education, but not necessarily having passed the leaving examination, are admitted on the basis of an entrance examination. The number of places (about 60 every year) depends upon the capacity of the "Bookselling Centres" to secure jobs in bookshops for the students after leaving.
The curriculum includes both theoretical and practical instruction in bookshops. The theoretical teaching touches upon such subjects as the fundamentals of scientific, technical and belletristic literature, the elements of the history of art, of books, and of book illustration, the organization and techniques of the book trade, the advertising of books and stationery articles, the office records and routine of the book trade; one foreign language is taught of the pupils' choice, and physical training classes are held.
For the duration of schooling, 25 to 40% of the students receive grants in the order of the average marks received for the entrance:
2.

Cursuri de ridicarea calificării profesionale
(Courses Leading to Professional Qualifications)
Calea Dorobanţi nr. 99 A
R București

for those employed in book distribution (salesmen in bookshops and stationers', bibliographers, advertising experts, window dressers, etc.). The duration of the course is 30 days. Two or three such courses are held annually with about 35–40 employees participating. Fresh employees are sent on these courses by the regional centres.
Those taking part in this course also receive board and lodging via the "Centrala" (→ 4). The cost of the courses is paid for by the regional centres.
The teaching programme for this course is determined by the "Centrala" and the lectures are given by specialists in book distribution.
Each course concludes with an oral examination in the main subjects, after which each participant receives a certificate confirming his specialist training.
Apart from these courses the "Centrala" annually organizes two or three courses of instruction with leaders of book departments, second-hand departments, window-dressers, etc. Such a course lasts from six to ten days and functions under the same conditions as the courses leading to professional qualifications.

12 Taxes

In order to promote the development of book production and the book trade, the taxation authorities have exempted the book trade from taxation.

14 Copyright

Copyright was guaranteed in Romania by the "Press Law" of 1862 and the "Law Concerning Literary and Artistic Property" of 28 June 1923, which was set aside by Decree No. 17 in 1949.
At present copyright is guaranteed by Decree No. 321 of 27 June 1956 and the "Resolution of the Ministerial Council" No. 632 of 15 July 1957. Romanian law on copyright protects all works in the literary, artistic and scientific fields, regardless of content and form, merit and aim.
Romanian law does not permit the transference of copyright to another by any acts of a living person. The exercise of copyright can be inherited, but only for a limited period.
After the death of an author the task of ensuring the inviolability and utilization of a work devolves on the association dealing with the author's particular form of art.

After the death of an author rights of inheritance are transferred to his descendants for 50 years, but for life to associations and wife (or husband).
In 1936 Romania signed the "Berne Convention".

Bibliography

Decretul No. 17 privind editarea şi difuzarea cărţii. (Decree No. 17 concerning the publishing and distribution of books). Monitorul Official No. 11 of 14 January 1949. Bucureşti 1949.

Decretul No. 321 privind dreptul de autor. (Decree No. 321 concerning copyright). Buletinul Official No. 18 of 27 June 1965. Bucureşti 1965.

I. ANGHEL, *Organizaţia modiala a proprietăţii intelectuale.* (The world organization of intellectual property). In: Justiţia Nouă, No. 6/1965. Bucureşti 1965.

O. CAPATINA, *Alcătuirea masei succesorale în cazul transmiterii prin moştenire a dreptului de autor.* (Summary of succession in the event of a transference of copyright by inheritance). In: Legalitatea populăra, No. 10/1957. Bucureşti 1957.

A. IONASCU, *Dreptul de autor în legislaţia R.P.R.* (Copyright in legislation of the Romanian People's Republic). In: Justiţia Nouă, No. 6/1961. Bucureşti 1961.

A. IONASCU, *Transmiterea prin succesiune a dreptului patrimonial de autor.* (The transference of inheritance of patrimonial copyright). In: Justiţia Nouă, No. 5/1960. Bucureşti 1960.

A. IONASCU, *Conţinutul, valorificarea şi apărarea dreptului de autor în lumina Decretului No. 321/1956.* (Content, utilization and protection of copyright in the light of decree no. 321/1956). In: Justiţia Noua, No. 7/1963. Bucureşti 1963.

C. ZIRRA, *Cîteva aspecte privind reglementarea dreptului de autor asupra operei realizate în comun.* (Some aspects of the settlement of copyright in the case of works produced in collaboration). In: Justiţia Noua, No. 8/1965. Bucureşti 1965.

15 National Bibliography, National Library

There are two national libraries in Romania:

Biblioteca Academiei Republicii Socialiste România
(Library of the Academy of the Socialist Republic of Romania)
Calea Victoriei 125
R Bucureşti

founded in 1867 and

Biblioteca Centrală de Stat a Republicii Socialiste România
(Central State Library of the Socialist Republic of Romania)
Strada Ion Ghica 4
R Bucureşti

founded in 1955.

The "Romanian Academy" has issued its own publications:
"Bibliografia românească veche 1508–1830" ("Old-Romanian bibliography" 1508–1830) by I. Bianu and N. Hodoş; "Publicaţiunile periodice româneşti: ziare, gazete, reviste, 1820–1906" (Romanian periodic publications: newspapers, gazettes, periodicals, 1820–1906) by Al. Sadi Ionescu and Nerva Hodoş.
The "Library of the Academy of the Socialist Republic of Romania" will continue the publication of the national bibliography up to 1952. From that year onwards the "Central State Library of the Socialist Republic of Romania" has continuously published national bibliographies: *Bibliografia Republici Socialiste Române* ("The bibliography of the Socialist Republic of Romania)—in the series: books, albums, maps, printed music, and in the series: articles in periodicals. Both series appear bi-monthly. The "Central State Library of the Socialist Republic of Rumania" has published the *Anuarul cărţii din R.P.R. 1952–1954* (Year book on books

in the PRR 1952–1954) and is working on further volumes.

These two libraries as well as the "Central University Libraries" are provided by law with a copy of all published works. By virtue of this law the "Central State Library" draws up the "National Bibliography" and the special bibliography for public libraries; it also prints catalogue filing slips which are distributed to all interested bodies through lists of subscribers. The "Central State Library" is planning the "Catalogul colectiv al cărţii româneşti" ("Comprehensive catalogue of Romanian books", 1508–1952). In addition it is coordinating the work on the "Index Translationum". Like the "Library of the Academy", it is continuously working on the completion of the fund of books and other printed matter produced in Romania. The two libraries also buy from abroad works on Romania and works by Romanian authors that have appeared abroad. The books of the "Library of the Academy" are at the disposal of research workers and scholars; the "Central State Library" is a free public library; it contains over five million books.

Bibliography

Anuarul cărţii din R.P. România. 1952–1954. (Yearbook on books in the PRR. 1952–1954). Published by the Central State Library of the Socialist Republic of Romania. Bucureşti, Editura Stiinţifica, 1957.

Bibliografia analitică a periodicelor româneşti 1966. (Analytical bibliography of Romanian periodical publications 1966). Vol. 1: 1790–1850. 3 parts. Bucureşti, Biblioteca Academiei 1966–1967.

T. Vianu, *Bibliografia literaturii româneşti 1948–1960.* (Bibliography of Romanian literature 1948–1960). Bucureşti, Editura Academiei R.S. România 1965.

16 Book Production

Romanian book production has made notable progress since the Second World War as a result of the organization of the socialist publishing system. Production is continually on the increase as regards both titles and impressions. In terms of the not as yet uniform international statistics, Romania was fifteenth in the list of book-producing countries in 1964.

In 1965 Romanian publishing houses issued 8,422 titles (books and pamphlets in 78,024,000 copies). Grouped in subjects the situation was as follows:

Subject group	Titles	Percentage of total production
General	219	2.6
Philosophy	38	0.5
Atheism, religion	32	0.4
Science and sociology	1,980	23.5
Philology and linguistics	84	1.0
Natural sciences, mathematics	408	4.8
Technology, industry, agriculture, medicine	3,121	37.1
Art, games, sport	1,158	13.7
Literature	1,123	13.3
History, geography, biography	259	3.1
Total	8,422	100.0

The average annual rate of growth is about 10%.

Bibliography

15 ani de activitate a Edituri Academiei Republicii Socialiste România. (15 year's work of the Academy Publishers of the Socialist Republic of Romania). In: Viaţa Româneasca, 17, XXX. Bucureşti 1964.

A. Dima, *Probleme ale editării.* (Problems of publication). In: Gazeta literara, No. 22/1967. Bucureşti 1967.

D. Raducana, *Producţia editorială, Realizari şi perspective.* (The production of publishing firms. Achievement and prospects). In: Călăuza bibliotecarului, 18, No. 8. București 1965.

M. TOMESCU, *Cartea în România—ieri și azi.* (Books in Romania—yesterday and today). In: Calauza bibliotecarului, 16, No. 8, București.

D. TRANCĂ, *Cartea românească dupa 20 de la eliberare.* (The Romanian book 20 years after the liberation). In: Călăuza bibliotecarului, 17, No. 8. București 1964.

17 Translations

Romanian publishing firms lay great stress on translations from other languages. From 1949 until 1966 translations were made of 12,792 literary, technological and scientific works from some 67 countries, which resulted in 184,385,000 copies.

From 1946 until 1966 translations were made of 1,520 Romanian literary, technological and scientific works into 61 languages representing 47 countries.

According to information contained in the "Index Translatorium" (vol. 17), Romania holds 17th place among the 63 translating countries of the world.

Works of literature hold pride of place both in translations from other languages into Romanian and in those from Romanian into other languages.

Most translations are made from French, Russian, English, German and Italian.

Bibliography

A. BALACI, *Traducerile literare în R.P.R.* (Literary translations in the PRR.). In: Strudii de literatură universală, VI. București 1965.

B. BUZILA, *Considerații privind editarea clasicilor literaturii universale.* (Opinions on the publication of the classics of world literature). In: "România Libera", No. 6610. București 1966.

I. M. SADOVEANU, *Traduceri și traducători.* (Translations and translators). In: Gazeta literară, 19/9. București 1963.

19 Paperbacks

The first Romanian publisher to produce a series of paperbacks was Carol Müller with the launching of his "Biblioteca pentru toți" ("Everyman's Library") in 1895. Number 1,000 of this series appeared in 1919, and number 1,550 in 1949. The series is still being continued today, and it is the most representative paperback series printed in Romania. From 1960 until 1965 there appeared in this series 320 titles from 26 different literatures with a total of 17,425,000 copies. In recent years interest in paperbacks has grown; more series are being published, the editions increase from year to year, and their appearance is becoming more attractive. In this connection the following can be mentioned: "Biblioteca școlarului" ("Small school library"), "Cele mai frumoase poezii" ("The finest poems"), "Enciclopedia" de buzunar" ("The pocket encyclopedia), "Orizonturi" ("Horizons"), "Meridiane".

Bibliography

Catalogul colecției "Biblioteca pentru toți". (Catalogue of the series "Everyman's Library"). 9. 1. 1960–31. 12. 1965. București, Editura pentru Literatura, 1966.

V. NICOLESCU, *Biblioteca pentru toți. Sugestii și perspective editoriale.* (Everyman's Library. Suggestions and publishing prospects). In: Scînteia, 35, No. 6971, București 1966.

V RIPEANU, *Biblioteca pentru toți.* (Everyman's Library). In: Scînteia, 34, No. 6506. București 1965.

Z. STANCU, *Cartea de buzunar. Opinii.* (The Paperback. Opinions). In: Scînteia, 35, No. 6978. București 1966.

GH. TOMOZEI, *O carte mică pentru Maria Sa Cititorul. 70 de ani de la apariția colecției "Biblioteca pentru toți".* (A small book for his majesty the reader. 70 years since the first appearance of the series "Everyman's Library"). In: Munca, 22, No. 5760. Bucureşti 1966.

20 Book Design

A competition for the best-designed books of the year was held for the first time in 1962. As a result of discussions among members of the jury the basic principles of the competition prescribed in the rules as well as the criteria for the choice of the best-designed books were made harder in the course of the next five years. The jury consists of illustrators, art historians, writers, experts from publishing and printing firms, librarians and booksellers. Particular attention was given to books with very large editions. Thus, the following series received awards in 1964: "Scriitorii români" ("Romanian writers") with 35,000 copies, "Traista cu poveşti" ("Treasury of tales"), with 100,000–150,000 copies, and in 1965 "Biblioteca pentru toţi" ("Everyman's Library"), with 100,000 copies.
Some of the titles which received awards or commendations at the international book competitions were chosen from among those that had already received awards in the national competition. Thus the principles on which the jury works have proved to be correct in many instances and the high standard of artistic and graphic appearance was confirmed.
Those 32 book producers responsible for the best-designed books received diplomas and medals and were able to take part in an informatory journey abroad.
The books sent in to be judged are appreciated by the readers, and have proved useful for comparing the jury's opinion with that of book lovers. Specialists in the art of books from the friendly countries are invited to participate in the proceedings of the jury.

Bibliography

A. Balaci, *Cele mai frumoase cărţi.* (The finest books). Gazeta Literara, 13, No. 17, April 28, 1966.
A. E. Baconsky, *Cele mai frumoase cărţi ale anului 1965.* (The finest books of 1965). Poligrafia, No. 1, p. 12–14, 1966.
G. Bratescu, *Cartea frumoasă.* (The fine book). Scînteia, 33, No. 6326, July 23, 1964.
I. Marinescu, *Cele mai frumoase cărţi ale anului.* (The finest books of the year). Poligrafia, No. 1, December, 1963.
C. Maciuca, *Stimul pentru o grafică de carte elevată.* (Stimulus for an elevated book illustration). Scînteia, No. 7352, 1967.
D. Trancă, *Funcţia estetică a cărţii.* (The aesthetic function of books). Contemporanul, No. 36, p. 9, September 3, 1965, No. 37, p. 9, September 10, 1965.

21 Publishing

Properly speaking, the first state publishing houses were founded after 1948, although some of them had already started their activity after 1945 and 1946. After the 1969 reorganization, there are at present 14 publishing houses controlled by the State Committee for Culture and Art, and seven others belonging to different Departments. The recent organization of the publishing houses has resulted in their greater specialization and has led to the founding of new publishing houses in the provinces (Iasi, Cluj) as well as in Bucharest (the publishing house, "Litera", where the authors are given the chance of publishing at their own expenses, the publishing nuclei belonging to the important daily papers, the publishing house of the coinhabiting nationalities, "Criterion". It has also led to the unification of the financial management (granted to a single publishing house "Litera") to the creation of a foreign trade office, "Libri",

under the dependence of the "Centrala cărţii" (→ 4) as well as to some organizational rationalization. These 21 publishing houses concentrate in their hands 50% of the number of titles published, and 90% of the number of copies produced in the whole country.
There are, however, 94 publishing institutions carrying on their activity in Romania at present.
Although the most important ones are in Bucharest, publishing is being carried on in every great centre.
The state publishing houses are juristic persons and act independently according to their own programme, which is integrated in the general publishing programme. Economically, after the 1969 reorganization, the publishing houses in the "State Committee for Culture and Arts" division are managed by the "Centrala", which grants subsidies to certain publishing houses when the highly specialized pattern of their production does not admit of large print runs.
All publishing houses have publishing committees and councils for drawing up annual and long-term publishing programmes. They consist of specialists, university professors and lecturers, members of the Academy, writers, artists, and leading cultural personalities. The preparation of the general publishing programme for a period of one year is considered a collective work concentrating the most varied suggestions and ensuring an equilibrium between the various fields depending on the requirements of the development of social life, and on public demand. The long-term programmes are flexible enough to leave room for any new proposals that could not be foreseen when they were drawn up.
Printing business is organized on the principle of specialization. Publishing houses have not their own printing plants, but use the services of the

Centrala Industriei Poligrafice
(Polygraphic Industry Centre)
Piaţa Scînteii nr. 1
R Bucureşti

This office is subordinated to the same State Committee for Culture and Art that coordinates the activity of the publishing houses.

Bibliography

H. CULER, *Date comparative privind dezvoltarea tipăriturilor în R.P. Română.* (Comparative data concerning the development of printed works in the Romanian People's Republic). Studii şi cercetări de bibliologie. 1961, IV.

I. DODU BALAN, *Cartea românească într-o nouă condiţie editorială.* (The Romanian book in a new publishing context). Scînteia No. 8282, December 19, 1969.

I. IORGA, *Editarea manualelor şcolare şi a cursurilor universitare.* (Printing of schoolbooks and textbooks). Lupta de clasa, No. 46, May, 1966.

G. IVASCU, *Cartea.* (Books). Contemporanul, No. 23, June 10, 1966.

D. MIHALACHE, *Tipărituri de popularizare a ştiinţei.* (Printed works for the popularization of science). Contemporanul, No. 27, July 5, 1963.

C. MACIUCA, *Literatura de informare.* (Information literature). Luceafarul, 10, No. 7, February, 1967.

C. MACIUCA, *Perfecţionarea sistemului editorial.* (The improvement of the publishing system). Contemporanul No. 51, December 1969.

V. STANESCU, *Cartea ştiinţifică şi exigenţele editoriale.* (Scientific books and publishing exactingness). Lupta de clasa, 47, No. 3, May, 1967.

D. TRANCĂ, *Enciclopediile—act de cultură naţională.* (Encyclopedias—an act of national culture). Contemporanul, No. 2, January, 1967.

Romania

22 Literary Agents

Between authors and publishing houses in Romania there is an immediate relationship through direct contracts. Royalties, however, are paid through the "Literary Fund" ("Fondul Literar"), which is controlled by the

Uniunea Scriitorilor din
Republica Socialistă România
(The Writers' Association)
Soseaua Kiseleff 10
R București

The system of direct contracts is also used in dealings with foreign authors, and payments are effected according to the author's wish in any foreign currency, free of taxes, when the book comes out, and not according to the rate of sales. If they so wish, foreign authors whose books have been published in Romania can be paid in Lei, which they are free to spend in this country, and if they do so they receive an increase of 30% calculated on the initial amount in Lei. The "Literary Fund" also negotiates foreign contracts.

23 Wholesale Trade

The wholesale trade in the case of both home production and imported books is handled at state level through the business concern

Baza pentru Desfacerea Cărţii
(Book Distribution Central Agency)
Calea Moşilor nr. 62–68
R București

It receives from the publishers and import firms the quantities and ranges laid down by agreement, and supplies the 21 district enterprises ("Centres for Bookshops") according to orders placed when the annual fixing of editions was made. These orders are determined by reference to the planned projects of the publishing firms, and they are sent in printed form to all bookshops and bookselling departments. The Central Agency also stocks the 39 district offices of the consumers' cooperative system as well as the 19 branches of the Libraries Stock Office. The "Book Distribution Central Agency" receives from the publishers a rebate of 20% of the income from the sale of books, of which it gives 17% to the districtual "Centres". These "Centres" supply both the wholesale and the retail trade.

24 Retail Trade

In Romania as in other countries the bookseller is at the very heart of the book trade. In this country the term "bookseller" must be understood in the widest sense of the word, if only on account of the frequent use of the term "book distribution". The word actually means the following: in the spread of books it is not the commercial but the cultural function that stands in the forefront; it is therefore a special trade. Therefore, apart from trained booksellers and employees, there are some thousands of people engaged continually and without payment in the sale of books in firms and institutions. In this way they are helping both booksellers and their colleagues at work, and thus contributing towards the spread of books among the masses.

The organization of the retail trade is as follows:

Each "District Centre" is a juridical person, economically and financially independent within stated instructions.

1. Administratively the 21 District Centres depend upon the Executive Committees of the Popular Councils of the Districts. Directions in special book problems are given by the Central Agency; the distribution network includes:

34 specialist bookshops (with exclusive rights of distribution)
17 units of "The book at places of work", which supplies some 5,000 bookstalls

484 bookshops and stationers
13 stationers
41 kiosks
23 second-hand and antiquarian bookshops
18 centres for the supply of libraries
43 wholesale departments (stationery and standardized printing matter)

Total: 673 units, of which 617 distribute books.

2. The distribution—net of the "consumer cooperative" comprises 39 district and 59 sub-district enterprises with depots for supplying the distribution—net with books and stationery.

Bookshops (of which 70 are town, and 660 country bookshops)	730 units
Bookselling outlets in general stores	1,070 units
Bookstands in mixed shops	3,700 units
Bookmobile services	18 units

3. The distribution system of the "Book Centre" comprises 9 display bookshops, three of which are in Bucharest and the remaining in other main towns.

Bibliography

R. Boureanu, *Cartea şi satul.* (Books and the village). Luceafarul, 6, No. 3, February, 1963.

Cartea şi librarul. (Books and the bookseller). Luceafarul, 9, No. 32, August, 1966.

R. Constantinescu, *Cartea la locul de muncă.* (Book distribution at the place of employment). Scînteia, 36, No. 7290, March, 1967.

K. Tanenbaum, *Evidenţa circulaţiei cărţii la cooperativă. Difuzarea cărţii la sate.* (Records of book circulation in cooperatives. Distribution of books in the villages). Editura Centrocoop, 1966.

V. Teodorescu, *Difuzarea cărţii—sarcina permanentă a muncii culturale la sate.* (Distribution of books as a standing task of cultural work in the villages). Scînteia, 32, No. 5859, April, 1963.

G. Tomozei, *Librarii, Filigran.* (Bookshops. Filigree). România Liberă, 22, No. 5810, July, 1966.

25 Mail-Order Bookselling

Cartea prin poştă
(Mail-Order Bookshop)
Calea Moşilor nr. 62–68
R Bucureşti

accepts orders from readers and supplies them from its own stock, from that of the "Centre for Bookshops" or, if they are still to be found there, from bookshops. If the desired book has not yet appeared, the order is noted for later.

Mail-order bookshops advertise and take orders for technical and scientific books before publication. Payment is made C.O.D.

In 1966 "Cartea prin poştă", sector "Centre for Bookshops" achieved 0.63% of the total book sale.

In 1966 "Cartea prin poştă", sector cooperatives, was responsible for large sales.

"Mail-Order Bookshop" comprises: a) 2 central units in Bucharest (at the "Book Distribution Central Agency", and "Centrocoop", the Centre for Cooperatives)
b) 32 departments within other units (one department in each regional "Centre" and with the Cooperative).

Bibliography

D. Iancu, *Pentru o mai vie circulaţie a cărţii.* (For the quicker circulation of books). In: Calauza bibliotecarului, 18, No. 1, Bucureşti 1965.

Serviciul "Cartea prin poşta" va satisface? O ancheta printre intelectuali de la sate. (Are you satisfied with the services of "Books by Mail?" A questionnaire among village intellectuals). In: Scînteia, 36, No. 7172. Bucureşti 1966.

26 Antiquarian Book Trade, Auctions

Second-hand and antiquarian bookshops, as individual shops or sections of bookshops, are to be found in all large towns in the country. In general they deal both with buying and selling. Bucharest is an exception; here there are three purchasing centres which supply the nine second-hand bookshops, which in turn deal only with sales. In the case of very valuable books—incunabula, old Romanian works up to 1700—the prices are fixed by a central commission consisting of experts. With other books the buyer fixes the price, or in the case of larger sums, a local commission.

The second-hand network comprises 23 units and 10 departments in bookshops (among which are 2 seasonal stands in Mamaia and Suceava). Four second-hand bookshops in Bucharest, Timisoara and Mamaia sell books against payment in convertible currency, for which a rebate of 20% is given.

Second-hand books are exported through "Centrala Cărţii—Oficiul de comerţ exterior" "Libri" ("Book Centre—Foreign Trade Office", "Libri" the former "CARTIMEX"). In recent years, a growing interest for Romanian second-hand books was shown by firms in the Federal Republic of Germany, France, the USA, the United Kingdom, Belgium and Israel.

27 Book Imports

28 Book Exports

The export and import of books is carried out by the

Centrala Cărţii—Oficiul de comerţ exterior "Libri"
(Book Centre—Foreign Trade Office "Libri")
P.O.B. 134–135
R Bucureşti

In 1966 42,000 titles of foreign books in French, Russian, English, German, Hungarian, Italian, and Spanish were imported into Romania.

Romanian book exports consist of printed works in Romanian, of Romanian works printed in languages of world-circulation, and of works by Romanian authors printed in various languages on customers' orders. Various reprints of foreign works are also carried out in this country as ordered by the customers, either with Romanian materials, or on the basis of other arrangements. These arrangements are carried on by the

Centrala industriei poligrafice
(Polygraphic Industry Centre)
P. O. Box 4126
Piaţa Scînteii nr. 1
R Bucureşti

The main countries which are partners to the export dealings mentioned above include the USSR, France, the United Kingdom, the Hungarian People's Republic, the German Democratic Republic, the Socialist Federal Republic of Yugoslavia, Israel. Romanian publishing houses participate in co-productions on a basis of mutually profitable import and export conditions. In 1968, the value of the printed works (books and periodicals) imported into Romania was 22,400,000 foreign-exchange Lei, whilst the value exported was of 26,200,000 foreign-exchange Lei.

Bibliography

Direcţia Centrala de Statistica. Breviarul statistic al Republicii Socialiste România. (Central Office of Statistics. Short statistical survey of the Socialist Republic of Romania). Bucureşti.

30 Public Relations

Contact with readers is made through the booksellers, publishers and the "Centrala"

(→ 4), which coordinates all activities connected with distribution and publicity as well as any special activities intended to further contact with readers.
The publishers prepare various kinds of publicity material which they hand to bookshops free of charge. The press, radio and televison provide a permanent place in their papers and programmes for publishers in provincial towns and in the capital. Public libraries and "Houses of Culture" organize activities to learn the opinions of readers and to maintain permanent contact with them.
The "Centrala" (→ 4) organizes hundreds of meetings every year with readers from all parts of the country—historical evenings, lectures, open discussions, etc., in which writers, lecturers and booksellers also take part, and at which young authors and new books are presented to the public. Numerous meetings are arranged for young people according to their age, environment and interests.

Bibliography

Consideraţii asupra reclamei publicitare. (Thoughts on the advertising of publications). In: Poligrafia, 2, No. 3–4. Bucureşti

Cum ni se ofera cartea? Propuneri şi observaţii din regiunile Galaţi, Crişana. (How are books offered to us? Suggestions and remarks from the Legions of Galati and Crisana). In: Scînteia No. 7060. Bucureşti 1966.

P. Mirescu, *Metode eficiente de difuzare a cărţii.* (Successful methods of book distribution). In: Gazeta Cooperaţiei, 17, No. 33. Bucureşti 1966.

S. Movileanu, *Se face un studiu ştiinţific al cererii de carte?* (Is book-demand research done on a scientific basis?). In: Scînteia, 36, No. 7112. Bucureşti 1966.

O anchetă utila. Sondaj efectuat de revista Ramuri. (A useful inquiry. In: Tribuna, No. 39. Bucureşti 1966.

31 Bibliophily

The present interest in bibliophily is quite recent and therefore it has not been completely surveyed. However, a few publishers have issued interesting works on the subject (books with original drawings; small editions signed by the author, etc.). There are already signs of greater developments in Romanian bibliophily.

Bibliography

T. Banuta, *Frumuseţea cărţii.* (The beauty of books). In: Poligrafia, No. 3–4, 1964. Bucureşti 1964.

D. Grigorescu, *Frumuseţea cărţii.* (The beauty of books). In: Poligrafia, No. 1, 1963. Bucureşti 1963.

D. Trancă, *Gînduri despre bibliofilie.* (Thoughts on bibliophily). In: Poligrafia, No. 3, 1966. Bucureşti 1966.

32 Literary Prizes

Among the more significant prizes for stimulating literary and scientific activities we shall mention the following:

a) The "State Prize". This is granted every second year for meritorious works in the field of prose, poetry, drama, literary and art criticism, on the basis of open proposals made by specialized institutions. In addition to the title, winners of the "State Prize" receive a diploma, a medal and a corresponding sum of money.

b) The "Academy of the Socialist Republic of Romania Prizes". These prizes are granted on the basis of carefully considered proposals of the Academy departments for valuable works in poetry, prose, drama, literary history and criticism.

c) The "State Committee for Culture and Art Prizes". These prizes are granted for stimulating present-day literature, and cover the novel, poetry, short stories, sketches, children's literature, and literary criticism.

d) The "Writers' Union of the Socialist Republic of Romania Prizes". These prizes are granted for poetry, prose, translations, literature for youth and children, reportage, journalism, dramatic works, and literary criticism.
e) The "Union of Communist Youth Prizes". These prizes are granted for prose, poetry and drama written especially for youth.
f) Various literary magazines and local writers' associations are also awarding different annual prizes, especially to young writers.

33 The Reviewing of Books

The reviewing system is highly varied. It includes practically all the newspapers and magazines, broadcasting and television. All specialized journals publish book reviews. The central and local press permanently provide space for these and the literary press has regular columns for the discussion of Romanian and foreign works. "Carţi noi" ("New Books"), the official publication of the "Centrala" (→ 4), regularly prints reviews, notices and summaries of contents. The quarterly bulletin "Romanian Book" and "Rumynskije Knigi" (→ 5) contain extracts from book discussions. The large free public libraries contain files on reviews in their information and documentation departments.
Among the more important publications printing book reviews are: *Scînteia*, *România Liberă*, *Lupta de clasă*, *Contemporanul*, *Gazeta literară*, *Luceafărul*, *Secolul 20*, *Viaţâ Românească*, *Ramuri*, *Viaţa economica*, all in Bucharest.

34 Graphic Arts

Since they are concerned with artistic criteria, illustrations for books and advertising lie within the competence of the

Uniunea Artiştilor Plastici din Republica Socialistă România (Union of Artists of the Socialist Republic of Romania)
Calea Victoriei 155
R Bucureşti

The "Centrala" (→ 4) has an advisory committee consisting of graphic artists who provide the link between publishers and graphic artists, discuss the guiding principles for book illustration and select work for competitions etc.

Bibliography

D. Grigorescu, *Grafica 1967.* (Graphic art 1967). In: Contemporanul, No. 17, 1967. Bucureşti 1967.
I. Manolescu, *Ilustraţia de carte.* (Book illustration). In: Contemporanul, No. 23, 1964. Bucureşti 1964.
I. Marino, *Architectura cărţii.* (The architecture of books). In: Contemporanul, No. 18, 1965. Bucureşti 1965.
I. Mereuta, *Afişul publicitar.* (Publishing posters). In: Scînteia, No. 7111, 1966. Bucureşti 1966.
N. Stanculescu, *Ilustrarea manualelor şcolare.* (School book illustration). In: Contemporanul, No. 38, 1965. Bucureşti 1965.

Spain

Important Book Centres

1 General Information

Area 504,750 km²
Population 33,790,000 (67 per km²)
Capital Madrid (3,030,700)
Largest towns Madrid (3,030,700); Barcelona (1,759,200); Valencia (624,200); Sevilla (622,100); Zaragoza (439,400); Bilbao (400,500).
Government Spain is officially a monarchy, but political power is vested in the Chief of State, General Francisco Franco, and in the government appointed by him. Strong centralization. For administrative purposes Spain is divided into fifty provinces and the towns of Ceuta and Melilla in North Africa.
Religion Roman Catholic, nearly 100%
Protestant 0.02%
National language Castilian *(castellano)*, universally known as Spanish *(español)*, which is spoken by practically all the inhabitants
Regional languages Catalan *(catalá)*, which includes the Balearic and Valencian dialects and is spoken by some 6,000,000 people; Galician *(galego)*, spoken by some 2,700,000 people; Basque *(euskera)*, spoken by some 550,000 people.
Leading foreign languages French, English. Most educated Spaniards can read Portuguese
Weights and measures Metric system
Currency unit Peseta
Education Education is controlled by the central government and is compulsory from 6 to 14 years. In 1967–68 there were 115,590 students (upper level) at 12 State and 3 Free (Roman Catholic) Universities; 42,700 students at Technical High Schools and other centres of university level; 1,347,796 pupils (2nd level) at State and private Centres. Three new State Universities were created in 1968

Spain

Illiteracy 2.1 % of the total population in 1970

Paper consumption a) Newsprint: 5.3 kg per inhabitant (1968)
b) Printing paper (other than newsprint) 8.2 kg per inhabitant (1968)

Membership Unesco, IPA, ICBA, IBBY

This essay on the book trade in Spain could not have been realized without the assistance of numerous friends in the publishing and bookselling professions, experts in both domaines and especially the *Instituto Nacional del Libro Español*, to all of whom I express my sincere thanks. Needless to say, they are not responsible for the evident insufficiencies of this text which would have been even greater without their help; nor are they responsible for my remarks or interpretations. For these I alone must remain accountable. *The Author*

2 Past and Present

Printing began in Spain between 1470 and 1474, but it cannot be said with absolute certainty where the first printed book appeared. It was probably in Valencia, where a short literary work was printed in 1474, in Catalan, on a religious subject entitled *Les obres e trobes en lahors de la Sacratissima Verge Maria.*

The invention quickly spread, and by the end of the 15th century numerous printing works were already operating.

The book trade was soon (1480) protected by a very liberal decree of the Catholic Kings, who ordered that books of whatever kind should be tax free. However, this did not last long, for even during this reign censorship limited book imports, domestic production and exports to the newly discovered American territories. Later favoured by the wealth of high-quality literary production in Castilian (Spanish) that characterized the 16th and 17th centuries, stimulated by intellectual ferment, and at the same time hindered by the Inquisition, the history of the Spanish book trade, with all its ups and downs, offers us a picture of expansion more or less parallel to that of the rest of Europe.

Professional specialization also ran parallel. In the course of time the printer became more and more distinguished from the bookseller. The publisher, as such, appeared later, often coming from one or the other of the aforementioned professions. The nature of the three professions was fixed in the 19th century and has remained fundamentally the same to the present day. In the second third of the 19th century (when freedom of the press was permanently established after the death of king Fernando VII in 1833) the first great printers-cum-publishers of modern Spain began to appear (Rivadeneyra, Bergnes, Cabrerizo). During the last quarter of the century, after the upheavals of the years 1868–1875 (revolution, first Republic, Civil War) and within the context of a nascent capitalist society developing under the liberal monarchy of the Alfonsos, many publishing and bookselling firms were founded, the distinctions between them becoming more clearly defined each day. Some of these firms survive until today.

Spain's geographical balance was maintained during several centuries owing to the presence of various kingdoms, each one independent of the other but, nevertheless, strongly linked since the end of the 15th century by a common dynasty. This balance became progressively weakened in the course of time. Whereas in the 15th, 16th and 17th centuries Spain had several intellectual and spiritual centres, only one existed by the late 17th century—Madrid. This centralizing process was quickened by the Bourbon dynasty at the beginning of the 18th century and completed by the liberal governments in the 19th century. As a result of the increasingly centralized spiritual, intellectual and political activity, publishing and bookselling also became concentrated in the capital.

Nevertheless, since the middle of the 19th century a rival centre has sprung up on the Mediterranean coast—Barcelona. The reason for Barcelona's cultural blossoming lies not only in local language and tradition, but also and above all in a remarkable economic prosperity and in a new social structure based on the fact that Barcelona gave birth to the first modern Spanish industry and the first modern Spanish bourgeoisie. The publishing and selling of books in Catalan, although important, is but a small part (→ 16) of Barcelona's publishing and bookselling activities. Since the end of the 19th century, Barcelona has been, and remains, one of the great centres of book production in Castilian (Spanish) and it owes its prominent position in the book markets of the world to the enormous geographical area covered by this language.

The last 100 years have therefore seen a bipolar development in intellectual, publishing and bookselling activity in Spain—in Madrid and Barcelona. This bipolar development also manifests itself in the origins and growth of the professional organizations. After the old associations and guilds became inactive and fossilized, the world of Spanish books awoke to new corporate life at the beginning of the 20th century. In 1900 the *Centro de la Propiedad Intelectual* ("Copyright Association") was founded in Barcelona, and in 1901 there followed in Madrid the *Asociación de la Libreria* ("Book Trade Association"). These two bodies united publishers, booksellers and all other branches of the professions contributing to book production and trade. The cooperation between the two bodies led to the *Asambleas Nacionales* held in Barcelona (1909), Valencia (1911) and again in Barcelona (1917). The result of this third "Asamblea", which was decisive for the structural development of these associations, was the creation, in 1918, of the *Cámara del Libro* with its main office in Barcelona and a branch in Madrid. These enterprises were the brainchild of the famous Barcelona publisher Gustavo Gili Roig. A few months later the government granted the association the title of *Cámara Oficial del Libro* ("Official Book Chamber"). At about the same time, in Madrid, the "Asociación de la Librería" changed its name to that of *Federación Española de Productores, Comerciantes y Amigos del Libro* ("Spanish Federation of publishers, booksellers and book-lovers") which became, in 1922, the *Cámara Oficial del Libro*. In 1925 the government broadened the scope and the economic base of the "Cámaras" of Madrid and Barcelona and introduced compulsory membership for all publishers and booksellers. The organization was thus formed and remained intact until 1941 when a new structure arose which continues in essence to the present day (→ 4).

Bibliography

P. Bohigas, *El libro español.* (The Spanish book). Barcelona, G. Gili 1962.

J. Madurell Marimon and J. Rubio y Balaguer (eds.), *Documentos para la historia de la imprenta y librería en Barcelona, 1474–1553.* (Documents concerning the history of printing and book trade in Barcelona, 1474–1553.) Barcelona, Gremios de Editores, de Libreros y de Maestros Impresores 1955.

S. Olives Canals, *Un centenario: Conferencia de editores españoles y amigos del libro el año 1917 en Barcelona.* (A centenary: Conference of Spanish publishers and booklovers in Barcelona, 1917.) In: *El libro español* (The Spanish book → 5), October issue, 1967.

F. Vindel, *El librero español. Su labor cultural y bibliográfica en España desde el siglo XV hasta nuestros días.* (The Spanish bookseller. His cultural and bibliographical work in Spain from the 15th century to the present day.) Madrid, Góngora 1934.

3 Retail Prices

With few exceptions, it is a generally recognized principle that a book must be sold to the public at a price determined by the publisher. It has been possible to maintain this principle in spite of the doctrine of freedom of trade that prevails in Spanish economics and is laid down in the law of 20 July 1963 "for combating practices that restrict competition". Nevertheless, many booksellers are offering their customers discounts amonting to 5% to 10% of the retail (publisher's) price. Following a favourable opinion by the *INLE* (→ 4), the *Sindicato Nacional del Papel, Prensa y Artes Gráficas* (→ 4) issued on 20 June 1956 the *Ordenación del Comercio del Libro* ("Regulations for the book trade"). These regulations are not legally binding but are, rather, a "collection of customs and usages observed by the book trade". Although the introduction to these regulations expressly states that "their provisions are to be strictly adhered to by all who are engaged in the aforementioned trade", neither the "Sindicato" nor the "INLE" is in a position to verify adherence or to punish offenders.

Article 3 of the regulations says: "All books must be sold to the customer by bookshops, kiosks, etc., at the retail prices determined by the publisher, whether listed in the book itself, publisher's catalogue or price list—without rebate, special offers or free gift of any kind." The only exceptions are the rebates on the *Día del Libro* ("Book Day") and during the *Ferias del Libro* ("Book Fairs" → 29, 30).

The regulations do not provide for any rebate to libraries, but paragraph 2 of article 8 provides for a total maximum rebate of 10% for "orders from the State or other official bodies". This was expressly drawn up to facilitate the purchase of books by libraries maintained by the State, provinces and towns, i.e., almost all of the libraries in the country. Paragraph 1 of the same article 8 provides for a rebate of 10% to professors, teachers and teaching institutions, but only "when they purchase textbooks for teaching purposes in their own teaching institute". In practice this rebate is very often much greater when the institute buys directly from the publisher. The increasing frequency of this practice has seriously diminished the participation of bookshops in the sale of textbooks, and is a source of unrest and anxiety in the book trade.

Article 9 of the regulations permits the increase of retail prices by up to 20% in the case of books sold in instalments.

On 15 May 1969, the presidents of the "INLE" and the "Sindicato" launched the *Ordenación de la Venta de Libros a Precios de Saldo* ("Regulations for establishing bargain prices of books") which possess the same legal value as the "Ordenación del Comercio del Libro". These regulations took effect on 1 June 1969; they clearly distinguish between bargain-priced books and second-hand books. Bargain-priced books may be sold only in second-hand bookshops or in ordinary bookshops that dispose of a clearly separate bargain book section. Publishers may declare "bargain prices" on those books that remain unsold two years after publication; the new price cannot be more than 50% of the retail price. Booksellers and wholesalers may declare a "bargain price" on a book two years after its appearance *and* at least 18 months after its purchase from the publisher. Finally, a book that has been declared a "bargain-price" book for two years no longer falls under the regulations and may then be considered as a second-hand book.

4 Organization

Spanish law decrees that all branches of economic activity be incorporated into the *Organización Sindical.*

The

Sindicato Nacional del Papel y Artes Gráficas
(National Syndicate for the Paper and
Graphic Trades)
Paseo del Prado, 18 y 20
E Madrid

works within this Organization.

The "Sindicato Nacional" is divided into "*Sindicatos Provinciales*". Of the three sectors that make up the "Sindicato Nacional", there is one which, under the name of "Editores" ("Publishers"), comprises five groups whose activities are pertinent to this study. These five groups are as follows: publishers, wholesalers, booksellers, kiosks and philately. The publishers' group is divided into three sub-sections: general publishers, textbook publishers and publishers of records and sheet music. The booksellers' group is divided into two sub-sections: ordinary bookshops and second-hand bookshops. The sub-section of ordinary bookshops is further sub-divided into three categories: general, textbook and religious literature. In this syndicate, as in all other branches of the "Organización Sindical", there is a department called "economico" which embraces the employers, and a department called "social", embracing the employees. Membership in the "Sindicato" is compulsory for all employers and employees. For publishers and booksellers the "Sindicato" is the framework within which labour and fiscal problems are resolved.

For matters that do not concern labour or fiscal problems, Spanish publishers and booksellers act within the framework of another professional organization, the

Instituto Nacional del Libro Español (INLE)
(Spanish National Book Institute)
Ferraz 11
E Madrid

and the

Instituto Nacional del Libro Español
Delegación en Barcelona
(Barcelona Branch)
Mallorca, 274
E Barcelona

The "INLE", for all practical purposes, is the successor to the "Cámaras Oficiales del Libro" (→ 2). It thus continues to represent the interests of the book trade.

Membership in "INLE" is compulsory for all publishers and booksellers, as is membership in the "Cámaras de Comercio" ("Chambers of Commerce"). "INLE" was founded in 1941 and legally inherited the effects and functions of the "Cámaras Oficiales del Libro", in particular the promotion of the book trade and the production of bibliographical catalogues (→ 15). "INLE" was reorganized in 1957, when it took over the functions of the "CIPLE" and the "CECEL" (→ 35), and again in 1960, when it became a more representative body. "INLE" represents the interests of its members vis-à-vis public administrative bodies, individuals and corporations at home and abroad; it promotes Spanish book production through its own publications and the staging of book fairs and exhibitions; it obtains global permission for export and import which it repartitions according to the needs of its members; it sponsors competitions, awards and prizes and acts as a clearing house for the distribution of "papel editorial protegido" (subsidized printing paper → 35); it furnishes information and acts as a watchdog over the usages and customs of the book trade; it promotes the specialized training of book-trade employers and employees by founding and supporting schools and special and supplementary courses; it analyses the problems arising from export and import, from production and trade, and proposes solutions to individuals and public bodies; it negotiates agreements (on credit, insurance, tax refunds and transport facilities), signing and applying them on behalf of its members.

The official organ of the "INLE" is the monthly journal *El Libro Español* ("The Spanish Book" → 5). "INLE" is linked to the administration through the "Ministerio de Información y Turismo" ("Ministry of Information and Tourism"). The President of the "Consejo de Administración" ("Administrative Council") and the Director of the "INLE" are nominated by the Minister of Information and Tourism. The Ministry covers part of "INLE"'s financial needs and supports some of its activities, in particular book fairs and exhibitions abroad (→ 28, 29).

5 Trade Press

The most important publication devoted to books is the monthly journal

El Libro Español (The Spanish book)
Ferraz 11
E Madrid

official organ of the "INLE" (→ 4). This publication contains much information, articles, studies and comments on book trade matters, a bibliographical index (→ 15) and numerous pages of advertising. Although "El libro español" first appeared under its present title in 1958, its history goes back all the way to 1901. In May, 1901, appeared the first issue of the journal "Bibliografía española" ("Spanish Bibliography") which was replaced in 1923 by the "Bibliografía General Española e Hispano-Americana" ("General Spanish and Hispano-American Bibliography"). From 1926 to 1936 an annex to the "Bibliografía" appeared called "Boletín de las Cámaras Oficiales del Libro de Madrid y Barcelona" ("Bulletin of the Official Book Chambers of Madrid and Barcelona"). After the Civil War, in 1942, it reappeared under the name "Bibliografía Hispánica" ("Hispanic Bibliography") and was so named until 1958.

Almost every year "El libro español" publishes special issues on such subjects as children's literature and the *Feria Nacional del Libro* ("National Book Fair" → 29). In some years there appeared a special number in three editions—English, French and German—dealing with Spanish participation in the Frankfurt Book Fair.

From the summer of 1953 to the winter of 1958 the "CECEL" (→ 35) published a quarterly journal of the same character and excellent quality: "Novedades editoriales españolas" ("Spanish Book News").

The "Gremio Sindical de Libreros de Barcelona" ("Barcelona Booksellers' Guild"), an independent local group within the "Sindicato" (located at the Barcelona branch of "INLE" and closely associated with it), publishes the journal

Librería
(The Bookshop)
Mallorca, 274
E Barcelona

This journal has appeared since 1962. It contains information and commentaries of interest to the profession. Barcelona's "Diputación Provincial" ("Provincial Council") has published annually since 1950 the "Catalogo de la Produccion Editorial Barcelonesa" ("Catalogue of Barcelona Book Production"), listing books published in the previous year by Barcelona publishers and given by them to the Provincial Library. The presentation of the books to the Library is an annual event, preceded by a lecture which forms the text of the introduction to the Catalogue. The Catalogues embrace some two thirds of Barcelona's book production over the past two decades.

A detailed bibliographical list of new books appears monthly in the journal *Insula*, published by

Insula
Benito Gutiérrez, 26
E Madrid

In addition to publishing this list, "Insula" makes an important contribution as a journal of reviews and criticism. Other publications print similar lists.

6 Book-Trade Literature

The "INLE" (→ 4) publishes the *Guía de editores y de libreros de España* ("Guide to Spanish publishers and booksellers"), the last edition appearing in 1969. It publishes annually a detailed catalogue of textbooks and teaching material. It further publishes specialized catalogues (children's literature, religion, gift books, management, fiction, Spanish language and culture, books in Catalan, etc.) and has published two other catalogues (in three versions: English, French and Spanish), each one covering 100 titles proposed for translation in other languages. Each title is accompanied by bibliographical data, a brief critical resumé and biographical-bibliographical information concerning the author.

An overall view of publishing and bookselling is to be found in *Evolución del libro español en los XXV años de paz* ("The development of the Spanish book in 25 years of peace"), published by "INLE" in 1964. An account of a similar nature, giving exact and detailed statistical data and good, short summaries of various aspects of the book trade, is to be found in the second volume of the *Estudio sobre los medios des comunicación de masas en España* ("Study of mass media in Spain"), published by the "Instituto de la Opinión Pública" ("Institute of Public Opinion"), Madrid, 1964. It was produced by a group of experts led by Sr. González Seara.

The "INLE" publishes three monographs for the *Escuelas de Librería* ("Booksellers' Schools" → 11): *Los procedimientos gráficos de la ilustración del libro* ("The graphic processes of book illustration") by F. Esteve Barba, 1960; *El papel y su fabricación* ("Paper and its production") by J. L. Asenjo Martínez, 1961; and *El librero y la publicidad del libro* ("The bookseller and book advertising") by J. A. Castro Fariñas, 1961. This last author also wrote the interesting work *El librero y su mundo* ("The bookseller and his world"), Madrid, Paraninfo, 1963. The book-marketing expert A. Puigvert, is the author of various important works: *Organización comercial de la librería* ("The commercial organization of the bookshop"), Madrid, Paraninfo, 1964; *Mercados del libro español. Argentina.* ("Markets for Spanish books. Argentina."), Madrid, 1967 (published by the author), which contains, among other things, much information on book production and export in Spain; *Organización general de la librería* ("General organization of the bookshop"), Madrid, Paraninfo, 1970. Equally worthy of mention are the works of H. Marcos, *Gestión y administración de la librería* ("Bookshop management and administration"), Madrid, Paraninfo, 1970. and J. Pol Arroyo, *El libro y su comercialización* ("Books and their commercialization"), Madrid, Paraninfo, 1970. Most of the works mentioned were prize winners in the professional monograph competition sponsored by the "INLE" in 1968.

P. Bohiga's work, *El libro español* ("The Spanish book"), Barcelona, G. Gili, 1962, which contains numerous bibliographical references, is also valuable as a sound and scholarly account of historical events. The work of the great publisher Gustavo Gili Roig, *Bosquejo de una política del libro* ("Outline of a book trade policy"), Barcelona, G. Gili, 1944, is an excellent review of the bookselling trade during the first half of the 20th century. Although many of the details cited are now out of date, its description of the broad picture remains valid and it presents sound criteria for considering many of the most important current problems of the book trade.

7 Sources of Information, Address Services

A great variety of information concerning the book trade, together with other information of use to publishers and booksellers, can be obtained from the "INLE" (→ 4) in Madrid or Barcelona. A bibliographical information service is free of charge.

The main office of the "INLE" houses a *Servicio de Mercados y Documentación* ("Marketing and Documention Service") which, for a very small fee, supplies more than 60,000 addresses of libraries, bookshops, teaching centres and university chairs in all Spanish-speaking countries, as well as addresses of other foreign individuals and institutions interested in Spanish books.

The *Servicio Nacional de Información Bibliográfica* ("National Bibliographical Information Service" → 15), with its office at the

Biblioteca Nacional
(National Library)
Avenida de Calvo Sotelo, 20
E Madrid

has, among its other duties, the task of

supplying information on available publications.

The library of the "INLE" branch in Barcelona has one of the best collections in Europe devoted to the subject of books. It is an inexhaustible source of data for the specialist, the scholar and the interested layman (→ "Books about Books", p. 71).

Bibliography

INLE. *Circular 32/65* (Supplement to No. 17/62). *Servicio de Mercados y Documentación*, Madrid, 1965.

8 International Membership

Spain has regularly participated in the International Publishers' Congresses ever since their early days. The Sixth Congress was held in Madrid in 1908. The "Cámaras Oficiales del Libro" (→ 2) and, later, the "INLE" (→ 4) both belonged to the professional bodies that arranged these Congresses and founded the "International Publishers Association" (IPA → International Section, 4) in 1952. The Sixteenth Congress was held in Barcelona in 1962 and was organized by "INLE". The "INLE" also participates in the "International Community of Booksellers Associations" (ICBA → International Section, 4) which held its 1960 Congress in Barcelona.

The first "Congreso Iberoamericano de Asociaciones y Cámaras del Libro" ("Ibero-American Congress of Book Trade Associations" → Vol. II, General Section, 4) met in Mexico City in 1964. The "INLE" took part in it and strongly supported the creation of the "Federación Iberoamericana de Instituciones Editoriales y Libreras" ("Ibero-American Federation of Publishers' and Booksellers' Associations". → vol. II, General Section, 4).

Since 1955, "INLE" has been associated with the "International Board on Books for Young People" (IBBY →International Section, 10) whose Spanish National Section is "INLE"'s "Comisión de Literatura Juvenil e Infantil" ("Commission on Books for Children and Young People"). This "Comisión" organized the Eighth Congress of the IBBY in Madrid in 1964.

Spain is a member state of UNESCO.

Bibliography

INLE: El libro español. (The Spanish book → 5), May and July/August issues, 1962, on the Congresses of the IPA and in particular those held in Spain. November issue, 1964, on the Congress of IBBY in Madrid.

9 Market Research

Book-market research in Spain is still very undeveloped. Some attempts by "INLE" (→ 4) in limited regions met with difficulties and did not produce the results expected.

The results of a scientific investigation involving ten thousand households throughout Spain are to be found in the *Anuario del Mercado Español* ("Spanish Market Yearbook") of the Banco Español de Crédito (Madrid, 1965). According to this study, between 0.04 and 0.38 books were acquired per person (over ten years old) within a fortnight. In 1968 the figures were 0.078 and 0.408, with an average of 0.181. These data show a remarkable improvement within a very short period but they are insufficient and need careful supplementation in order to give scientifically exact knowledge of the state of the market. A more complete and successful study, although limited in scope to Madrid, is the *Estudio sobre los medios de comunicación de masas en España* ("Studies of mass media in Spain"), Madrid, 1964/65, a 3-part work published by the "Instituto de la Opinión Pública" ("Institute of Public Opinion"). A significant part of this study is devoted to books and the book market.

10 Books and Young People

Production and trade of books for children and young people considerably increased in Spain towards the end of the 19th century and the beginning of the 20th. This was due to the efforts of certain publishers, among whom Saturnino Calleja of Madrid and Ramón Sopena of Barcelona deserve particular mention. Native storybook characters soon appeared who later achieved great popularity and deserve a place of honour in the history of children's literature.

Since 1950, Spanish production of children's books has improved rapidly and, accordingly, so has their share of the book market. This development has been positively influenced by the foundation of the "Lazarillo Prizes" by the "INLE" (→ 4); by Spain's participation in international competition for the "Hans-Christian Andersen Prize" (→ International Section, 10) which has been awarded since 1956; and by the creation of numerous public and private awards and prizes (→ 32) for published and unpublished works.

In 1969, 458 books of over 48 pages and 723 booklets of from 5 to 48 pages intended for children and young people were published. These publications amount to 5.9% of domestic production of books and booklets. In addition to these are numerous magazines for children and young people.

The *Comisión de Literatura Juvenil e Infantil* ("Commission on Books for Children and Young People") of the "INLE", which is the Spanish National Section of the IBBY (→ International Section, 10), promotes good literature for children and young people in various ways. Particular mention should be made of the following: *Semana Nacional del Libro Infantil* ("National Children's Book Week"), held annually before Christmas; the annual celebration of International Children's Book Day, on April 2 (the birthday of Hans-Christian Andersen); the "Lazarillo Prizes", awarded annually to an author, illustrator and publisher, 90,000 pesetas being shared between the author and illustrator; the organization of children's book fairs and exhibitions; and Spain's participation in the international competition for the Hans-Christian Andersen Prize". For some years the "Feria Nacional del Libro" ("National Book Fair" → 27) was coupled with a "Feria Nacional del Libro Infantil" ("National Children's Book Fair").

Of the private undertakings assisting in the spread and promotion of books for young people, two deserve particular mention: the

Gabinete de Lectura "Santa Teresa de Jesús"
(Reading Cabinet "Santa Teresa de Jesus")
Alfonso XI, 4
E Madrid

and

Biblioteca y Documentación
(Library and Documentation)
Doctor Cárcer, 22
E Valencia

and at

Lagasca, 79
E Madrid

The first of these, with the assistance of the "Dirección General de Archivos y Bibliotecas" ("Service of Archives and Libraries"), has published annotated bibliographies containing much useful information.

The network of school libraries is unfortunately still rather thin and insufficient, considering the needs of the readers. In order partially to fill this gap the

Biblioteca de Iniciación Cultural
Ministerio de Educación y Ciencia
Alcalá, 34/36
E Madrid

has arranged a circulating book service (excluding textbooks) which reaches more than 8,000 schools throughout Spain in areas where the necessary means are lacking to provide an individual library.

Special mention must be made of the work by Carmen Bravo-Villasante in respect to the history of books for children and young people.

Bibliography

C. Bravo-Villasante, *Historia de la literatura infantil española.* (History of children's literature in Spain). Madrid, Editorial Doncel 1963.

C. Bravo-Villasante (ed), *Antología de la literatura infantil en lengua española.* (Anthology of Spanish-language literature for children). 2 vols. Madrid, Editorial Doncel 1963.

C. Bravo-Villasante, *Historia y antología de la literatura infantil iberoamericana.* (History and anthology of Ibero-American children's literature). 2 vols. Madrid, Editorial Doncel 1966.

Dirección General de Archivos y Bibliotecas y Gabinete de Lectura "Santa Teresa de Jesús", Catálogo crítico de libros para niños. (Critical catalogue of books for children). Madrid 1954.

Gabinete de Lectura "Santa Teresa de Jesús", Selección de lecturas para niños y adolescentes. (Selection of reading material for children and adolescents). Madrid 1963.

Instituto Nacional de Estadística, Estadística de la producción editorial, año 1969. (Book production statistics, 1969). Madrid 1970.

INLE: Catálogo de libros infantiles y juveniles. (Catalogue of books for children and young people). There are several editions which appear almost annually.

INLE: El libro español. (The Spanish Book → 5). Almost every year a special number is published devoted to books for children and young people.

Servicio Nacional de Lectura y Gabinete de Lectura "Santa Teresa de Jesús", Catálogo crítico de libros para niños 1957–1960. ("Critical catalogue of books for children 1957–1960"). Madrid 1961.

11 Training

As yet, there exists no compulsory systematic training for book-trade personnel in Spain, and the number of pupils at the *Escuelas de Librería* ("Booksellers' Schools") is thus limited.

The first Booksellers' School operated in Madrid from the school year 1929–30 to 1935–36. Its activity was arrested by the Civil War. The present Booksellers' Schools in Madrid and Barcelona were opened during 1962–63. They were founded by "INLE" (→ 4) and are linked to it through the corresponding local professional groups. The School in Valencia was opened in 1964–65 and is linked to "INLE" and the Valencia "Ateneo Mercantil" which provides the premises and gives the School moral and financial support. Attendance at the three Schools is as follows (school year 1969–70):

Madrid	enrolled	1st year	44
		2nd year	19
	diplomas		18
Barcelona	enrolled	1st year	23
		2nd year	11
	diplomas		10
Valencia	enrolled	1st year	17
		2nd year	6
	diplomas		6

To gain the final diploma the student must attend for two academic years and must pass the examination given at the conclusion of each year. During the first year all students study the same subjects; in the second year, elective courses are added from which the student may select according to whether he wishes to specialize in publishing or selling.

Apart from their normal programmes, the Schools organize lectures and special courses given by experts, authors, publishers and well-known booksellers. The students visit libraries, printers, publishing houses and booksellers of particular importance; they undertake study trips and, at the end of the course, travels abroad, etc.

Three intensive one-week training courses are held for sellers of scientific and technical books. These courses, given annually since 1968, are organized within the framework of the Booksellers' Schools of Madrid, Barcelona and Valencia, and are financed by Spanish and French publishers of scientific and technical works. Students are selected from among bookshop employees throughout Spain and they may benefit from scholarships and transportation allowances.

Since 1967, a 25-day *Cursillo Intensivo de Formación Profesional* ("Intensive Professional Training Course") has been held annually in Madrid. From 20 to 25 students attend this Course; they are selected, in alternate years, from bookshop employees in those Spanish provinces where no School is available, or from bookshops in Hispano-American countries. All students receive scholarships endowed by the "INLE" and the most important publishing and bookselling firms.

Since 1962 much shorter but more technical courses have been held for managers and experienced employees.

Bibliography

F. Vindel, *Manual de conocimientos técnicos y culturales para profesionales del libro.* (Manual of technical and cultural information for members of the book trade.) Madrid, "INLE" 1943.

The "INLE" publishes annual prospectuses giving the programmes and conditions of admission to the Booksellers' Schools.

12 Taxes

Publishers and booksellers were exempt from the so-called "utilidades" ("profit") tax, now called the *industrial tax,* until 1942. Since the tax reform of that year they have been subject to this charge, as are all other branches of the economy. The "Ley de Protección al Libro" ("Law for the Protection of Books") of 18 December 1946 (→ 35) brought a partial exemption under certain conditions for publishers only. But this too disappeared with the tax reform of 1964.

The sale of books is free from the so-called "impuesto sobre el tráfico de las empresas" (turnover tax). Contrary to the norms applied to all other branches of the economy, publishers are authorized by law to deduct from the value of their stock the value of their unsold books, which are not considered for tax purposes as part of the firm's capital.

Books from Spanish, Portuguese or Ibero-American publishers enjoy a 50% reduction on postage. This reduction is also valid for periodicals published by Spanish, Portuguese or Ibero-American citizens, no matter where printed.

14 Copyright

The *Ley de Propiedad Intelectual* ("Copyright Law") in force in Spain dates from 10 January 1879 and the regulations concerning its application date from 3 September 1880. Among the subsequent directives that explain these laws and partly re-shape or complete them, the most important are Articles 428 and 429 of the *Código Civil* ("Civil Code") of 1889; the decrees of 24 January 1963, which reshaped the *Código Penal* ("Penal Code") and defined the crime of premeditated infringement of copyright law; and the Law of 31 May 1966 on film rights.

In view of the antiquated text in some of these laws, attempts have been made on various occasions to carry out a general reform, but at present no results have been forthcoming.

Spain is a party to the Berne Convention and has also ratified the subsequent agreements of Paris (1896), Berlin (1908), Rome (1928), Brussels (1948) and the annexed protocol of Berne (1914). Since 16 September 1955, Spain has been a party to the Universal Copyright Convention of Geneva (1952). Spain is a party to the Convention of Montevideo of 1889 which regulates the relation of Spain to Argentina (since 30 April 1900) and of Spain to Paraguay (since 10 September 1903). (Bolivia, Peru and Uruguay are also parties to this agreement, but it is not certain whether they have accepted the participation of Spain.) Furthermore, Spain has concluded numerous bilateral agreements with various countries.

The fixed period for the legal protection of copyright is 80 years after the death of the author. In order to ensure reciprocity, this period is often adapted by special agreement to the period laid down by international agreements and the laws of other countries.

In 1965 the "INLE" (→ 4) established a list of *Recomendaciones para tener en cuenta en la redacción de los contratos de edición* ("Recommendations to be considered in the drawing up of contracts between author and publisher"). Since 1 June 1969 these Recommendations have become compulsory norms for all Spanish publishers. They were designed to guarantee, in the most effective way possible, the rights and obligations incumbent upon both author and publisher. According to Section 39 of these norms, a system of monthly press-run verification has been in force since October, 1966. The titles selected for verification are chosen at random and checked by employees of the "INLE". The results of the verification are communicated only to the author and publisher concerned.

Bibliography

M. Danvila Collado, *La propiedad intelectual.* (Copyright). Madrid 1892.

INLE, La comprobación de tiradas en las ediciones de libros españoles. (Press-run verification of Spanish books). In: *El libro español*, February issue, 1967.

H. Lopez Quiroga, *La propiedad intelectual en España.* (Copyright in Spain). Madrid 1918.

A. Miserachs Rigalt, *El copyright norteamericano, comparado con el derecho de autor en Inglaterra y en España.* (North American copyright compared with copyright in England and Spain). Barcelona, Bosch 1946.

Unesco, *Repertorio universal del derecho de autor (RUDA).* (Copyright treaties and laws of the world). Madrid, Aguilar 1960. 1st supplement: 1961. 2nd supplement: 1969. 3rd supplement: 1971.

15 National Bibliography, National Library

A "Real Decreto" ("Royal Decree") of 1896 made it compulsory for a copy of every book printed in Spain to be deposited with the

Biblioteca Nacional
(National Library)
Avenida de Calvo Sotelo, 20
E Madrid

This duty had existed legally since 1714 when the first Bourbon king, Philip V, founded the "Biblioteca Real" ("Royal Library"), the predecessor of the "Biblioteca Nacional", but the practice had fallen into disuse. The decree of 1896 suffered the same fate until a new one on 23 December 1957 organized and regulated the "Depósito Legal" ("Copyright deposit"), which operates satisfactorily. Thanks to this system, Spain, for the first time, possesses a practically exhaustive set of statistics on domestic book production.

The first comprehensive catalogues appeared in the 19th century, the most important of which were the work of Salvá, a bookseller of Valencia (→ 26) and the Madrid bookseller, Hidalgo. Their catalogues were periodically updated. Antonio Palau y Dulcet, a Barcelona bookseller, is the author of the first among the comprehensive catalogues appearing in the

20th century: the *Manual del librero hispano-americano* ("Manual for the Hispano-American bookseller" → 26).

In 1932 the "Cámaras Oficiales del Libro" (→ 2) of Madrid and Barcelona took over the publishing of the *Catálogo General de la Librería Española e Hispanoamericana* ("General catalogue of the Spanish-language book trade"), which embraced the first thirty years of this century: 92,670 titles in 5 volumes, the last of which was published by "INLE" (→ 4) in 1951. This work was continued for 20 years (1931–50) by the *Catálogo General de la Librería Española* ("General catalogue of the Spanish book trade"): 4 volumes covering 69,575 titles, Madrid, INLE, 1954/63. Works published in Latin America are not included in the latter catalogue owing to difficulties in obtaining satisfactory data. This work was not continued after 1950, all the more regrettable since, thanks to the introduction of the "Depósito Legal", the production of recent years could very easily have been collected in an exhaustive inventory.

The *Servicio de Depósito Legal* has partially filled in this gap by publishing 3 volumes of an annual directory, the *Bibliografía Española* ("Spanish bibliography"). These volumes refer to the years 1958, 59 and 60. The "Servicio" also published, at irregular intervals, the *Boletín del Depósito Legal de Obras Impresas* ("Copyright Deposit Bulletin"). These publications have been replaced by a monthly journal called *Bibliografía española*. The "Depósito Legal" is attached to the "Dirección General de Archivos y Bibliotecas" ("Service of Archives and Libraries") in the "Ministerio de Educación y Ciencia" ("Ministry of Education and Science") and has its seat in the "Biblioteca Nacional".

The publishing firm of Bowker, New York and Buenos Aires, published in 1964 *Libros en Venta* ("Books in print"), which today is the most detailed bibliographical reference work on book production in the Spanish language. An extensive supplement on book production from 1964 to 1966 appeared in 1967.

Apart from these general catalogues there are numerous specialized catalogues.

Bibliography

P. Bohigas, *El libro español.* (The Spanish book). Barcelona, G. Gili 1962.

F. Cendan, *Historia del derecho de prensa e imprenta en España.* (The history of press law in Spain). Not published.

Diputación Provincial de Barcelona, *Catálogo de la Producción Editorial Barcelonesa* (Annual → 5).

16 Book Production

According to the statistics of the "Cámaras Oficiales del Libro" (→ 2) which, because of their incompleteness, can give us only an indication, the annual average of published titles between 1920 and 1929 was a little over 2,000. Between 1930 and 1935 this figure increased to some 4,000 titles. After the Civil War (1936–39) the number never dropped below 4,000 and in 1943 it reached 5,000 for the first time. In order to arrive more closely at the real figures it is necessary to increase all those quoted above by between 20 and 40%, according to the year. Proof of this can be found in the fact that when the "Depósito Legal" (→ 15) began to function in 1958 the number of titles jumped from 4,248 (books and booklets) in 1957 to 7,968 (books only) in 1959. Books are defined as having more than 48 pages and booklets as having between 5 and 48 pages.

Since 1958, two sets of statistics have been available: those of the "INLE" (→ 4), which are a continuation of the earlier statistics and are chiefly compiled for commercial purposes and those (practically exhaustive) of the "Depósito Legal", which have been elaborated by the "Instituto Nacional de Estadística" (National

Institute of Statistics). The figures for 1969 are as follows:

	Books	Booklets	Total
INLE	10,451	2,590	13,041
Depósito Legal	14,693	5,338	20,031

According to the statistics of the "Depósito Legal" on books registered in 1969, first editions account for more than 90% of the total. Textbooks account for 10.1% and children's books (including booklets) for 5.9%.
According to the same statistics, in 1969 production in the different fields was as follows:

Subject groups	Titles	Percentage of total production
Literature (belles-lettres)	7,463	37.3
Applied sciences	2,814	14.1
Social sciences	2,449	12.2
Religion	1,513	7.6
Geography and history	1,295	6.5
Generalities	1,239	6.2
Arts	1,035	5.1
Pure science	1,009	5.0
Philology	642	3.2
Philosophy	428	2.1

From the language point of view, books and booklets in Castilian (Spanish) claimed 95.04%, Catalan (including the Balearic and Valencian dialects) 2.06%, Basque 0.28%, Galician 0.12%, and the remainder (foreign languages or multilingual editions) 2.50%.
According to the same statistics, book production (apart from booklets) is concentrated mainly in the provinces of Barcelona (40.8%) and Madrid (40.2%), a confirmation of the bi-polarity of Spanish book publishing (→ 2,21). Among the remaining provinces the following are the most notable: Biscaye, 3.3%; Valencia, 3.3%; Zaragoza, 1.7%; Salamanca, 0.9%.

Bibliography

Instituto Nacional de Estadística, España, Anuario estadístico 1970. (Statistical yearbook 1970). Madrid 1970.
Instituto Nacional de Estadística, Estadística de la producción editorial, año 1969. (Statistics on book production 1966). Madrid 1970.
INLE, El libro español. (The Spanish book → 5), January issue of each year.
Ministerio de Información y Turismo, Boletín de información estadística. (Bulletin of statistical information). Quarterly.

17 Translations

Spain is one of the world's three leading translating countries (after the USSR and the Federal Republic of Germany) and a considerable percentage of its book production therefore comes under this heading. The statistics of the "INLE" (→ 4, almost exclusively for books) indicate the following percentages: for 1969, 27.61%; for 1970, 25.06%. The statistics of the "Depósito Legal" (→ 15,16, for books and booklets) indicate, for 1969, 15.3%.
As regards the languages from which the translations are made, both sets of statistics agree as far as the order of the first four are concerned (the figures given in brackets are those of the "Depósito Legal"). For the year 1969, English, including North America, 38.9% (44.0%), French 32.2% (25.4%), German 14.8% (14.3%) and Italian 7.0% (6.2%). This order has remained the same for years. As far as subjects are concerned, literature (belles-lettres) heads the list, accounting each year for about half the translations. In 1967, 850 titles were translated from Spanish into other languages (a considerable number of these works were by authors from Spanish-speaking American countries. To promote translation of works by Spanish authors, "INLE" publishes special catalogues in Spanish, French and English,

each of which lists 100 titles recommended for translation (→ 6).

In 1970 Spanish publishers paid 258,543,000 pesetas abroad for translation rights. The most important recipients were: the USA (63,547,000 pesetas), France (47,053,000 pesetas) and the United Kingdom (40,124,000 pesetas). Against this important export of foreign currency it should be noted that Spain exports great quantities of translated works, thus playing an intermediary role between the Spanish-speaking countries of America and other book-producing countries of the world.

Bibliography

INLE, El libro español. (The Spanish book → 5) The January issue of each year.

Instituto Nacional de Estadística, Estadística de la producción editorial, año 1969. (Statistics on book production 1969). Madrid 1970.

Ministerio de Información y Turismo, Boletín de información estadística. (Bulletin of statistical information). Quarterly.

Servicio Nacional de Información Bibliográfica, Dirección General de Archivos y Bibliotecas, Bibliografía Española. (Spanish Bibliography). Monthly.

UNESCO, *Index translationum.* Annually. (→ International Section, 17).

UNESCO, *Statistical yearbook.* Annually.

For the years before 1958, → 2, 15.

18 Book Clubs

Compared with a number of other countries, Spain's book club development is very feeble. The most important organization of this nature is the *Círculo de Lectores* ("Readers' Circle"), started in 1962 by Editorial Vergara, Barcelona, in cooperation with the German firm, Bertelsmann. It later became independent of Vergara and its current membership is more than one million in Spain alone. Branches are located in several Spanish-speaking American countries and in Portugal.

Bibliography

INLE, El libro español. (The Spanish book → 5). October issue, 1970.

19 Paperbacks

The paperback book in its present form (a product of the English-speaking world) did not appear in Spain until 1960. However, long before then Spanish publishers produced pocket books of a different sort; they were more sober, less attractive and striking and were frankly derivative of similar publishing efforts in other countries. They enjoyed great popularity with the public and some of them still do. In 1919 the firm of Calpe published the first number of its famous *Colección Universal*, inspired by the German *Reclam-Universal-Bibliothek*, and with 360 carefully selected titles in 564 small volumes it did a great service to culture in all Spanish-speaking countries.

Paperback production has increased from year to year, both in quantity and quality. Among the existing collections, one in particular stands out for its sales volume. Published by Salvat, the collection introduces a new title weekly at a price of 25 pesetas. Between 300,000 and 400,000 copies are sold weekly in Spain and about 250,000 copies in Latin America. The overwhelming success of these series is due, in a large part, to the free radio and television publicity granted Salvat after the firm won a publishing competition sponsored by the state-run "Radio y Televisión Española".

Among other paperback series, that of Alianza Editorial stands out for its prestige and quality. We must also mention *Libros Rotativa* published by Plaza y Janés; *Novelas y Cuentos* published by El Magisterio Español and the series of Editorial Bruguera. The *Austral* collection of Espasa-Calpe, one of the precursors of the pocket book in Spain, has published more than 1500 titles since its founding in 1938.

Bibliography

INLE, El libro español. (The Spanish book → 5), February issue, 1971.

20 Book Design

To promote higher standards of production quality, the "INLE" (→ 4) sponsors an annual competition among Spanish publishers. In order to encourage the domestic production of well-designed books for the general public, non-purchasable editions are excluded from the competition as are numbered and special bibliophile editions, international co-editions and those books partially or totally reproduced from foreign publishers.
The candidate titles (up to a maximum of 50) are chosen by the "Comisión de Ferias, Congresos y Exposiciones" ("Commission for Fairs, Congresses and Exhibitions") of the "INLE". These books are then submitted separately to experts in the different fields of book production. Each expert grades each book according to a point system ranging from 1 to 10. Books not receiving at least 5 points from every expert are automatically eliminated. The final decisions are proposed by the above-mentioned Commission to the General Commission of the "INLE". The following medals are awarded: The "Ibarra" medal for a book displaying the highest quality for the greatest number of readers; 3 "Arnaldo Guillén de Brocar" medals for an art book, a scientific or technical book, and a work of fiction; 2 "Antonio de Sancha" medals for the best binding (soft-cover and hard-cover); the "Apeles Mestres" medal for the best illustration.

21 Publishing

In 1936, immediately before the Civil War, there were 280 registered publishers. By 1940, after the Civil War, the number had increased to 420. Thus began a process, which might be called a "publishing inflation", whose end is not yet in sight. The number of printed works increased annually after the war (→ 16) but the number of publishing firms has been increasing at an even greater pace. Booksellers, printers and authors contributed to this phenomenon by registering as publishers in order to exploit the advantages of the "Ley de Protección al Libro" ("Law for the protection of books" → 35). Nevertheless, the current publishing picture seems to be stabilizing: while only 18 Spanish publishers issued more than 100 titles in 1965, by 1969 their number had increased to 34. By 1970 the "INLE" census (→ 4) included 1,173 publishers of whom 258 were authors publishing their own works (many publishing as few as one, two or three works in their publishing career). 76% of the publishers are located in Madrid or Barcelona, where 81% of the books are published (→ 2,16). Below are the figures of the seven leading provinces:

	Madrid	Barcelona	Valencia	Vizcaya	Zaragoza	Guipúzcoa	Navarra
Publishers	391	312	38	35	15	15	11
Author and Publisher	139	52	7	3	6	2	0
Total	530	364	45	38	21	17	11

Of the 43 other provinces, not one has a total of 10 in either of the two categories and 5 provinces have no publishers at all. An analysis of the production figures reveals that only approximately 200 firms regularly publish more than 10 titles per annum.

The following table gives the classification for 1969 (author-publishers not included):

Number of published titles	*Number of publishers*
1–10	136
11–25	94
26–50	54
51–100	46
101–200	18
201–250	6
more than 250	10
Total	364

Author-publishers apart, it is estimated that about 300 of the 915 registered publishers in Spain publish regularly and continuously.

The trend among publishers is to specialize, but there are still many firms who spread their work over a wide range of subject areas.

It is very difficult to convert the capital of publishers into figures, let alone figures which might offer a basis for comparison. Almost half the publishers (excluding author-publishers) are one-man enterprises without the character of companies and without registered capital. About a quarter of the publishing firms are joint-stock companies which, especially in Barcelona, supply the juridical framework for a family enterprise. These companies sometimes own important printing plants, wholesale outlets or bookshops, while others strictly limit themselves to publishing. Almost all prominent publishing firms have branches in the most important Latin American countries.

Spanish publishing firms are generally of recent date. Most were founded after the Civil War and only some 30 current publishing houses were in existence in the 19th century. According to an investigation based on data from 1961, only 3 publishing firms appear to be more than 100 years old; however, these data are incomplete.

Figures relating to press-run are not satisfactory at the moment and the related statistics must thus be treated with the greatest reserve. A critical analysis of the appropriate data (which do not always agree) employed in estimating the use of printing paper reveals that publishers must have used about 75,000 tons in 1969.

Lack of statistics on the volume of sales means that only estimates can be made, based on certain factors which in themselves are not exact and which, therefore, do not easily lend themselves as the basis for accurate figures. It would appear reasonable for 1969 to quote a figure of about pesetas 10,000 million as the total net invoice for all publishers.

Various publishing houses that sell books in the higher price ranges sell directly (→ 25), especially through "corredores" (door-to-door salesmen) who may be representatives of the publishing firm or the wholesaler (the latter often being a branch of the publishing house itself). Although it cannot be asserted that Spanish books are expensive (→ 19), it is fair to claim that prices could be considerably lower if demand permitted larger press-runs and if the technical equipment were better and paper cheaper.

The abolition of compulsory censorship in 1966, after its liberalization in 1962, has been of great benefit to Spanish publishers. However, the present system is still far from satisfactory.

For this reason many publishers prefer to submit works to the inspection of the "Servicio de Orientación Bibliográfica" ("Bibliographical Orientation Service") which undertakes pre-censorship on a voluntary basis.

Bibliography

P. Bohigas, *El libro español.* (The Spanish book). Barcelona, G. Gili 1962.

R. Calleja, *El editor.* (The publisher). Madrid 1922.

Evolución del libro español durante los XXV años de paz, 1939–64. (The development of the Spanish book in 25 years of peace, 1939–64). In: *El libro español* (The Spanish book → 5), July issue, 1964.

Instituto Nacional de Estadística, Estadística de la producción editorial, año 1969. (Statistics on book production, 1969). Madrid 1970.

INLE, Guía de editores y de libreros de España. (Guide to Spanish publishers and booksellers). Madrid. Latest edition: 1969.

Instituto de la Opinión Pública, Estudio sobre los medios comunicación de masas en España. (Study of mass media in Spain). Part 2. Madrid 1964.

Ley de prensa e imprenta. (Press and printing law). Boletín Oficial del Estado, special edition for the "INLE". Madrid 1966.

A. Mas Esteve, *El contrato de la venta de libros a plazos, arma decisiva.* (A decisive weapon: the instalment-purchase agreement). In: *El libro español* (The Spanish book), October issue, 1970.

Ministerio de Información y Turismo, Boletín de Información Estadística. (Bulletin of statistical information). Quarterly.

J. Pol Arroyo, *El libro y su comercialización.* (Books and their commercialization), Madrid, Paraninfo 1970.

A. Puigvert, *Mercados del libro español. Argentina.* (Markets for Spanish books. Argentina). Madrid, the author 1967.

22 Literary Agents

The number of literary agents in Spain is very small and their field of activity is not comparable to that of the influential agencies of other countries.

Spanish authors and publishers negotiate directly. This is not the case when it concerns granting rights abroad or acquiring Spanish translating and publishing rights for books published abroad, but even here agents do not play a large part, although their importance in this respect is increasing continuously.

23 Wholesale Trade

The position of the "distribuidor" ("wholesale dealer") as intermediary between publisher and bookseller is increasing in importance as production grows, although his activity in Spain is not so important as it is in some other countries. According to the census of the "INLE" (→ 4) dated 30 September 1970, there are 410 wholesalers in Spain. Madrid with 161 and Barcelona with 58 are, as in the publishing field, the two main centres; but in this case Madrid has an enormous advantage not evident in publishing matters (→ 16,21). Well behind are Biscaye (32), Las Palmas de Gran Canaria (18), Valencia (17), Salamanca (17), Seville (13) and Zaragoza (12). The overwhelming majority of wholesalers restrict their activities geographically as representatives of one or several publishing houses within a province or, at the most, within a group of provinces. Only a few extend their activities across the entire country.

About half of the wholesalers (42% in 1961) have dealings with the foreign book trade, as importers, exporters or both. Their share in export is small. On the other hand, there are wholesalers who deal extensively with the import trade as branches of foreign publishers (especially French, Argentinian or Mexican). Others have successful mechanisms for direct sale to the reader, including door-to-door salesmen and instalment purchases →(25). In 1961, 20% of the wholesalers were at the same time publishers, and 60% were retail booksellers. This situation seems to be maintaining itself with slight variations.

Spain

Bibliography

INLE, Guía de editores y de libreros de España. (Guide to Spanish publishers and booksellers). Madrid. Latest edition: 1969.

Instituto de la Opinión Pública, Estudio sobre los medios de comunicación de masas en España. (Study of mass media in Spain). Part 2. Madrid 1964.

A. MAS ESTEVE, *El contrato de la venta de libros a plazos, arma decisiva.* (A decisive weapon: the instalment-purchase agreement). In: *El libro español* (The Spanish book → 5), October issue, 1970.

Ministerio de Información y Turismo, Boletín de Información Estadística. (Bulletin of statistical information). Quarterly.

24 Retail Trade

In Spain, as in the other European countries, the traditional retail bookseller remains the chief intermediary between publisher and reader. Bookshops are spread over the entire country but their density varies, depending on the economic and cultural standard of the area; rural districts, for example, are at a disadvantage.

Of the 3,629 ordinary bookshops mentioned in the "INLE" census (→ 4) dated 30 September 1970, 490 are in the province of Madrid and 286 in the province of Barcelona; taken together, these figures represent 21% of the total. In 1968 (last year for which population data are available) the number of ordinary bookshops per 100,000 of the population amounted to 11.2 in Madrid and 7.6 in Barcelona; the national average was 9.26. The ten provinces where the proportion was the highest are as follows:

Oviedo	18.6
Navarra	16.8
Huesca	15.7
Guipúzcoa	15.7
Alava	15.5
Logroño	15.2
Vizcaya	14.4
Valencia	14.1
Santander	13.3
Segovia	12.8

As can be seen, the first nine are concentrated in the North in an area whose centre is the Basque country.

In the large cities (Madrid, Barcelona—and not so strongly in Valencia, Zaragoza, Bilbao) booksellers are becoming increasingly specialized. On the other hand, in the small and medium-sized towns where the book trade is thinly and less evenly represented, the number of general bookshops without distinct specialization has increased in recent years. This increase is a result of both population growth and a steady rise in the cultural level. These two trends, while not as pronounced as they are in the large cities, would seem to indicate that the phenomenon of specialization cited above will eventually spread through the entire country.

Today, as in the past, many bookshops are compelled to sell stationery if they are to stay in business and in most cases these articles are the most profitable sources of income—even in many bookshops in Madrid and Barcelona. The census of the "INLE" no longer differentiates between "librerías de nuevo" (ordinary bookshops) and "librerías-papelerías" (book-and-stationery shops), but in 1963, when this distinction was still being made, 40.1% of the ordinary bookshops indicated that they dealt in stationery.

The sale of records and, occasionally, works of art has recently spread to booksellers.

The Spanish bookshop is, in most cases, owned by one man and his trade comes up against many serious difficulties. Some of them can be ascribed to humdrum and routine, an endemic lack of means and a limited view of the trade. Others, which are much more difficult to surmount, come from outside although they are often aggravated by the abovementioned structural weaknesses.

The kiosk is another point of sale for Spanish books. Dealing mainly in newspapers and magazines, there are nevertheless 245 kiosks licensed to sell books. Their economic importance is not significant because they are unevenly scattered, principally in the small and medium-sized towns, and because the main bookselling kiosks in the largest cities are licensed as bookshops, their sales thus not being attributed to the category "kiosks".

Bibliography

J. A. CASTRO FARIÑAS, *El librero y la publicidad del libro.* (The bookseller and book advertising). Madrid, INLE 1961.

J. A. CASTRO FARIÑAS, *El librero y su mundo.* (The bookseller and his world). Madrid Paraninfo 1963.

INLE, Guía de editores y de libreros de España. (Guide to Spanish publishers and booksellers). Madrid. Latest edition: 1969.

Instituto de la Opinión Pública, Estudio sobre los medios de comunicación de masas en España. (Study of mass media in Spain). Part 2. Madrid 1964.

Librería. (The bookshop, → 5). Almost all its editions publish reports on professional problems in the book trade.

H. MARCOS, *Gestión y administración de la librería.* (Bookshop management and administration). Madrid, Paraninfo 1970.

Ministerio de Información y Turismo, Boletín de Información Estadística. (Bulletin of statistical information). Quarterly.

J. POL ARROYO, *El libro y su comercialización.* (Books and their commercialization). Madrid, Paraninfo 1970.

A. PUIGVERT, *Organización comercial de la librería.* (The commercial organization of the bookshop). Madrid, Paraninfo 1964.

A. PUIGVERT, *Organización general de la librería.* (General organization of the bookshop). Madrid, Paraninfo 1970.

A. PUIGVERT, *La rentabilidad de las librerías.* (The profitability of bookshops). In: *El libro español* (The Spanish book → 5). February issue, 1971.

25 Mail-Order Bookselling

Mail order bookselling is gradually developing in Spain—especially through a number of publishers and wholesalers. Specialized bookshops which distribute their catalogues to interested readers are engaging in this business to a greater extent than ever. There are, however, no statistics to give an idea of the percentage share of this kind of sale. It is in any case quite small.

A much greater development has taken place in the sale through travelling salesmen who visit potential customers in their homes. Retail booksellers make little use of this method which is exploited chiefly by the publishers (→ 21) and the wholesalers (→ 23). This is still another limit to expansion by the retail bookseller, which aggravates the structural weakness of this branch of the trade.

26 Antiquarian Book Trade, Auctions

The second-hand and antiquarian book trade gradually developed in the framework of the trade fairs (→ 29) of the 16th, 17th and 18th centuries. However, it acquired professional standing only in the second half of the 19th century, thanks to the efforts of three booksellers: Pedro Salvá in Valencia, Antonio Palau in Barcelona and Pedro Víndel in Madrid. Among his many other significant contributions, Palau was responsible for the extremely important "Manual del librero hispanoamericano" ("Manual for the Hispano-American bookseller" → 15). Pedro Salvá published the famous "Catálogo de la biblioteca Salvá" ("Catalogue of the Salvá library") in two volumes (Valencia, 1872; reprinted by the Barcelona bookseller José Porter in 1963). According to the census of the "INLE"

(→ 4) dated 30 September 1970, there are 491 antiquarian booksellers in Spain; almost one third of these are to be found in Madrid (83) and Barcelona (75). There are 32 in Zaragoza, 28 in Valencia and 27 in La Coruña; the remainder are spread over the other provinces where the turnover is less important. Many of Madrid's antiquarian booksellers are located in the picturesque "cuesta de Claudio Moyano", near the Retiro Park, and they form the well-known *Feria de libros* ("Book Fair") which lasts throughout the year and which flourished best in the first three decades of this century. This fair must not be confused with the book fairs dealt with in chapter 29. Since 1952 the *Feria del Libro de Ocasión antiguo y moderno* ("Second-hand Book Fair, old and new" → 29) has been celebrated annually in Barcelona; it has recently become a national event and a number of dealers from other cities are also participating. This fair comprises some 50 stalls which sell direct to the public.
Auctions of antiquarian books have developed little in Spain up to now. The only two of any importance were held in Madrid in 1913 and in Barcelona in 1931.

Bibliography

P. Bohigas, *El libro español.* (The Spanish book). Barcelona, G. Gili 1962.

P. Cid Noe (pseud. for F. Víndel), *Historia de una librería.* (History of a bookshop). Madrid, Imprenta Góngora 1945.

A. Palau, *Memorias de un librero catalán 1867–1935.* (Memoirs of a Catalan bookseller 1867–1935). Barcelona, Librería Catalonia 1935.

A. Palau, *Memorias de libreros.* (Booksellers' memoirs). Madrid, Librería para bibliófilos, 1949.

A. Rodriguez Moñino, *Catálogos de libreros españoles (1661–1840). Intento bibliográfico.* (Catalogues of Spanish booksellers, 1661–1840. A bibliographical essay). Madrid, Imprenta Langa y Cía 1945.

F. Vindel. *El librero español. Su labor cultural y bibliográfica en España desde el siglo XV hasta nuestros días.* (The Spanish bookseller. His cultural and bibliographical work in Spain from the 15th century to the present day). Madrid, Imprenta Góngora 1934.

F. Vindel, *Manual gráfico-descriptivo del bibliófilo hispanoamericano.* (Handbook of the Hispano-American bibliophile). 12 vols. Madrid, Imprenta Góngora 1930.

→ 24, 34.

27 Book Imports

The import of books and periodicals has been increasing constantly for a long time. This growth has been particularly marked since 1958 as a result of several factors: the liberalization of foreign trade (1959); the rise in the standard of living and of purchasing power since 1961; the relaxation of censorship since 1962; the enormous flow of foreign tourists (since the exchange rate of the peseta was standardized in 1959) who demand newspapers, magazines and books from their own countries; and the increase in the appearance of international co-editions. The last factor has stepped up the bulk import of completely or partly finished books (of which many are later exported by the Spanish co-publisher to Latin American countries).
By its control of import licences, the "INLE" (→ 4) is in a position to provide very accurate and reliable statistics. The separation of books and periodicals has only been made since 1966:

	Books million pesetas	Periodicals million pesetas	Total million pesetas
1961	—	—	203
1966	421	228	670 [1])
1967	465	287	793 [2])
1968	489	368	909 [3])
1969	541	451	1033 [4])
1970	639	435	1120 [5])

[1]) includes 21 million pesetas for illustrations, maps, sheet music, etc.
[2]) includes 41 million pesetas for illustrations, maps, sheet music, etc.
[3]) includes 52 million pesetas for illustrations, maps, sheet music, etc.
[4]) includes 41 million pesetas for illustrations, maps, sheet music, etc.
[5]) includes 46 million pesetas for illustrations, maps, sheet music, etc.

During these ten years the same seven countries have remained at the head of the list of suppliers to Spain, and since 1962 France has held first place.
The following figures are for 1970 in million pesetas:

	Books	Periodicals	Total [1])
France	112.1	134.4	250.0
Italy	161.1	29.8	206.4
United Kingdom	72.1	68.8	148.3
Germany (Fed. Rep.)	32.4	106.0	143.7
USA	55.6	36.3	96.9
Mexico	73.9	8.3	82.8
Argentina	65.1	0.8	66.0

[1]) includes also illustrations, maps, sheet music, etc.

The percentage of books (as opposed to periodicals) is much higher among imports from Argentina and Mexico than from the remaining countries. If the imports from all Spanish-speaking countries are added together, the total is 169 million pesetas (15.1% of the total sum); 158 million of this total is accounted for by books (24.7% of the total number) and of these 158 million, Argentina and Mexico account for 139 million. Imports from Spanish-speaking countries in America have slightly decreased (both in absolute figures and percentages) since 1967.
Spain ratified the "Florence Agreement" (→ International Section, 4). In addition, book imports from Portugal and Latin American countries (almost none of which are signatories to the above agreement), including Brazil, are exempted from Spanish customs duties. Also exempt are technical dictionaries and publications in foreign languages, whatever their country of origin. A tax of 9% ad valorem is imposed on all Spanish-language books and periodicals imported from countries other than Latin America and Portugal. This tax is equivalent to those taxes which would be imposed on the books had they been produced in Spain.

Bibliography

INLE, El libro español (The Spanish book → 5). This monthly periodical publishes numerous statistics and many articles on subjects dealt with in this chapter.
Ministerio de Información y Turismo, Boletín de información estadística. (Bulletin of statistical information). Quarterly.

28 Book Exports

If the growth of imports since 1959 appears spectacular, this is no less true of exports. Spain is thus continuing its tradition as a book-exporting country, a tradition that goes back to the early years of the 16th century.
In Spanish statistics, periodicals and other printed matter such as sheet music, maps and illustrations have been included with books until 1967. Until that same year books always represented about 90% of the total. The maintenance of an artificial exchange rate for Spanish currency hindered progress and led to a stagnation in exports which amounted to only 4,675 tons in 1958. The currency readjustment of 1959 eliminated this hindrance and the result that year was over 5,000 tons, or 600,000,000 pesetas, in exports. The continuous growth in the export of books and periodicals since 1959 has brought Spain to fifth place among the great book-exporting countries of the West, after the USA, the

United Kingdom, the Federal Republic of Germany and France. Below are the data for 1961–70 according to the accurate and reliable statistics provided by the "INLE" (→ 4). Books were not separated from other printed material until 1967:

Year	Books, periodicals, etc. Weight in tons	Books, periodicals, etc. Amount million pesetas	Books only Weight in tons	Books only Amout million pesetas
1961	9,393	1,079	—	—
1962	9,475	1,153	—	—
1963	10,502	1,357	—	—
1964	11,208	1,575	—	—
1965	13,073	1,760	—	—
1966	17,660	2,341	—	—
1967	18,566	2,588	16,400	2,359
1968	22,120	3,236	19,632	2,928
1969	27,504	4,011	24,555	3,638
1970	35,208	4,720	31,001	4,240

The Spanish-speaking countries absorb the overwhelming majority of these exports. The percentage for individual areas is given below:

Area	Books, periodicals, etc. 1961	1965	1969	1970
Spanish-speaking countries	88.8	84.2	78.6	76.6
Portugal and Brazil	3.6	3.0	3.9	4.1
Total Latin America/Portugal	92.4	87.2	82.5	80.7
Rest of Europe	4.2	6.6	12.5	13.9
USA	2.9	5.2	3.9	3.4
Other countries	0.5	1.0	1.1	2.0
Total	100.0	100.0	100.0	100.0

Area	Books only 1969	1970
Spanish-speaking countries	83.4	81.5
Portugal and Brazil	3.4	3.6
Total Latin America/Portugal	86.8	85.1
Rest of Europe	8.9	9.9
USA	3.5	3.3
Other countries	0.8	1.7
Total	100.0	100.0

It will be noticed that there is a very small but continuous decrease in the percentage of sales to the Spanish-speaking area; this does not mean that there is not an increase in actual sales, but that exports to other areas are more repidly increasing, especially to other European countries.

Since 1961 the same five countries have stood at the head of the book-export list. Their relative positions since 1967 are as follows:

1967	*1968*	*1969*	*1970*
Argentina	Argentina	Argentina	Argentina
Mexico	Mexico	Mexico	Mexico
Venezuela	Venezuela	Venezuela	Venezuela
Chile	Chile	Chile	Columbia
Columbia	Columbia	Columbia	Chile

The relative positions of the five leading non-Spanish speaking countries on the book export list are as follows:

1967	*1968*	*1969*	*1970*
USA	USA	USA	France
Brazil	Brazil	France	USA
Germany (Fed. Rep.)	United Kingdom	Brazil	Brazil
United Kingdom	France	United Kingdom	United Kingdom
France	Germany (Fed. Rep.)	Germany (Fed. Rep.)	Germany (Fed. Rep.)

In 1970 the main purchaser of Spanish periodicals was Argentina, followed by France, Brazil, Mexico and Venezuela.

In 1970, 26 firms exported 51% of the total (nine of them exporting 28%), publishers accounting for 85% and wholesalers and retail booksellers accounting for the remaining 15%.

Exports by Spanish publishers (not considering wholesalers and retail booksellers) amount to about 35% of their total turnover; this large proportion is explained above all by the weakness of the domestic Spanish book market and the enormous size of the Latin American market. The great importance of this market is, at the

same time, the best explanation for the situation—unique in the Western world—whereby Spain's book exports in recent years have amounted to almost 4% of her total exports and to more than 10% of her total exports to Latin America.
On completing a book-export order, an exporting firm acquires a 9% tax refund. This refund is made in a lump sum through the "INLE" which in turn repartitions the amount according to the particular firm's share of exports. On request, every exporting firm can participate, at a very small premium, in an all-round insurance policy concluded by the "INLE" for the protection of exports.
Since 1963 a special credit system has existed in order to make possible the long-term extended payments which Spanish exporters must grant to their Latin American customers. These credits may amount to as much as 55% of the previous year's export value. As of 1972 this credit limit will change to 55% of the average of the publisher's *received* payments for the preceding two years. Each credit is granted by a public or private bank and, after having been authorized by the "Instituto de Crédito a Medio y Largo Plazo" ("Institute for Medium and Long-term Credit"), it is compulsorily rediscounted through the "Banco de España" ("Bank of Spain") at an exceptionally low interest rate. In actual fact, Spanish exporters receive about 60% of the total credit they could theoretically claim under this system (1,232 million pesetas in 1969). Exports represent one of the decisive factors in determining the quota of "papel protegido" (subsidized printing paper) and the amount of priority credit granted to the publisher (→ 35).
In order to promote exports the "INLE" organizes annual exhibitions abroad, both in Europe and America. It also takes part in international book fairs (Frankfurt, Warsaw, Brussels, etc.).
By virtue of a multi-lateral agreement, postal charges for mail (not only for books) from Spain to Portugal or Latin America, and vice-versa, are the same as domestic rates. → 12; 27, 35.

Bibliography

A. Puigvert, *Mercados del libro español. Argentina.* (Markets for Spanish books. Argentina.) Madrid, the author 1967.

29 Book Fairs

Historical documents as well as literary works testify to the existence of bookstands at Spanish trade fairs as far back as the middle of the 16th century. Although this custom persisted through the centuries, Spain claims no tradition of book exhibitions comparable to the grand tradition of the German book fairs.
Thanks to the initiative of the students of the "Escuela de Librería" (→ 11), the first "book fair" was held in Madrid in the spring of 1933, founded and supported by the "Cámara Oficial del Libro" (→ 2). Its character and influence were felt beyond the immediate vicinity and called into being a whole series of open-air events that have been regularly held since then. They have been named *Ferias Nacionales del Libro* ("National Book Fairs") and form one of the typical phenomena of the Spanish book world.
Since the end of the Civil War they have been organized annually by the "INLE" (→ 4), except for the years 1950 and 1954. The "Feria Nacional del Libro" has always been held in Madrid except in 1946 and 1952 (Barcelona) and 1948 (Sevilla). The stands, erected in the city centres, are visited by hundreds of thousands. Customers receive a discount of 10%, as is the case on the *Día del Libro* ("Book Day" → 3,30). The fair takes place at the end of May and the beginning of June.
Publishers and wholesalea nd retail book-

sellers take part in this "Feria". They all sell direct to the public. The number of stalls varies between 100 and 150, and the fair lasts for 10–17 days. Sales have risen rapidly and in 1970 they surpassed 27 million pesetas. The "Feria" always offers the opportunity of presenting many new works and of engaging in a strong promotion campaign on behalf of books (→ 30).
The effect of the "Feria Nacional" in promoting sales has led many booksellers in various provinces to hold local fairs. These fairs take place with increasing frequency and often bear the title "National" because firms and publishing houses of other provinces are represented as well as local publishers, booksellers and wholesalers.
Of the specialized book fairs, mention must be made of the *Feria del Libro de Ocasión antiguo y moderno* ("Second-hand Book Fair, old and new") held annually in Barcelona (→ 26) and the *Feria del Libro Juvenil e Infantil* ("Children and Young People's Book Fair"). The latter may be attached to the *Feria Nacional del Libro* in Madrid or it may be independently held in Madrid and/or the other provinces (→ 10).
Spanish publishers also take part in book fairs abroad (→ 28).

Bibliography

J. Simon Diaz, *Las ferias de Madrid en la literatura.* (The Madrid trade fairs in literature). In: *Anales del Instituto de Estudios Madrileños.* (Annals of the Institute of Madrid Studies). Vol. 2. Madrid 1967.

During the year the monthly periodical *El libro español* (The Spanish book → 5) usually discusses book fairs, in particular the *Feria Nacional del Libro* in Madrid.

30 Public Relations

Events such as the "Ferias del Libro" (→ 29), the "Semana Nacional del Libro Infantil" (→ 10) and the awarding of literary prizes (→ 32) provide opportunities for effective book propaganda through the various mass media.
Independent of these opportunities, advertising campaigns of a general nature are launched with carefully chosen slogans that are then circulated throughout the country or special regions. The efforts of publishers and booksellers in Barcelona are particularly worthy of mention.
In addition, window-display competitions are organized among bookshops, competitions are held for advertising posters for book fairs and book weeks, as are competitions for journalistic and radio works that are published when these events take place.
But the promotional event most peculiar to Spain is the well-known *Día del Libro* ("Book Day").
Instituted by royal decree on 6th February 1926 and then fixed for 7 October (the alleged date of Cervantes' birthday), this festival was changed four years later to 23 April, the date of the death of the author of "Don Quixote". It is celebrated in all the provincial capitals and other important cities. On the "Día del Libro" many booksellers (including the most important ones) erect stalls in the streets in the town centre; the press, radio and television devote articles and commentaries to books; in many towns authors autograph their latest books, and book buyers receive lottery tickets for book prizes—often of considerable value—and in all elementary and secondary schools pupils are told about books and the importance of reading. In some schools special performances are devoted to the same theme. And, finally, on this day all books are sold at a discount of 10%.
In recent years the celebration of the "Día del Libro" has re-captured the splendour and enthusiasm of its early days. The festival has traditionally reached its most brilliant heights in Barcelona.

31 Bibliophily

Bibliophily in Spain went through a relatively brilliant period as a result of the foundation in Madrid of the *Sociedad de Bibliófilos Españoles* ("Society of Spanish Bibliophiles") whose publications appeared from 1866 until 1918. The activity was later resumed, under the name of *Librería de Bibliófilos Españoles* ("The Bookshop of Spanish Bibliophiles"), by Gabriel Molina, but this second epoch did not enjoy the importance of the first.
The *Asociación de Bibliófilos de Barcelona* ("Association of Barcelona Bibliophiles") was founded in 1944 with a limited membership of 100. It still exists but its excellent publications do not appear frequently. In other towns are other associations with some signs of life. In 1939 and 1957 the publishing house of Castalia (Jávea, 30; Valencia) produced a volume entitled *Bibliofilia.*

Bibliography

F. VINDEL, *Los bibliófilos y sus bibliotecas. Desde la introducción de la imprenta en España hasta nuestros días.* (Bibliophiles and their libraries. From the introduction of printing in Spain to the present day). Madrid, Imprenta Góngora 1934. (→ 26).

32 Literary Prizes

The increase in literary prizes (the January 1971 issue of "El libro español", → 5, cited more than 300) is one of the phenomena typical of the Spanish book world in the last two decades. The immediate success of the *Nadal* Prize, awarded for the first time in January 1945 by Ediciones Destino, Barcelona, was a decisive factor. It developed into the most prestigious literary award in Spain for unpublished works.

Some prizes are awarded for already published books. Two of the most important of these are the highly esteemed *Premio Fastenrath*, awarded by the "Real Academia Española" ("Royal Spanish Academy") and worth 6,000 pesetas; and the *Premios Nacionales de Literatura*, consisting of 8 individual prizes, each worth 50,000 pesetas and awarded by the Ministry of Information and Tourism. The *Lazarillo* Prizes for young people's books (→ 10) are almost always awarded to works already published. The coveted *Premio de la Crítica* ("Literary Critics' Prize"), carrying no financial reward, is given annually.
However, the huge majority of prizes (awarded by corporations and public institutions as well as public or private publishers) are intended to honour unpublished works. They represent one of the ways in which publishing houses can discover talented new writers. Public and private publishers, provincial councils, Ministries and local authorities vie with each other in creating and awarding these prizes, some of which are worth considerable sums of money. The most important are listed below:

For novels	
Planeta prize	1,100,000 pesetas
Aguilas prize	500,000 pesetas
Ateneo de Sevilla prize	500,000 pesetas
Alfaguara prize	300,000 pesetas
For essays	
Taurus prize	500,000 pesetas
For journalism	
Meliá prize	500,000 pesetas
Ciudad de Vigo prize	400,000 pesetas

The *Premi d'Honor de les Lletres Catalanes* ("Honour Prize of Catalan Literature") is worth 500,000 pesetas. The *Adonais* prize, although not the most financially well endowed, is the most esteemed prize for poetry.
Many literary prizes are explicitly or implicitly open to foreign authors who

write in Spanish or in one of the regional languages, in particular Latin American authors.

Although their origin and aims are international, the *Formentor* and *Internacional de Literatura* prizes have a close association with Spain where they were instituted and awarded during their early years. Both are held in high esteem throughout the world. From 1960 to 1965 they were awarded annually; since 1967, bi-annually. The name of the former has been changed to *Selección Formentor.*

Bibliography

INLE, El libro español. (The Spanish book). All issues contain detailed accounts of competitions and awards of literary prizes.

33 The Reviewing of Books

Book reviews appear very frequently in daily and weekly newspapers and in periodicals of a general, specialized, private or official nature and published at varying intervals. The most important daily newspapers devote a large weekly space to them. The *Bibliotheca Hispana,* with the sub-title "Revista de información y orientación bibliográficas" ("Review of bibliographical information and orientation"), published by the "Instituto Nicolás Antonio", a branch of the "Consejo Superior de Investigaciones Científicas" ("Council for Scientific Research"), Madrid, regularly reviews a large number of titles divided into two categories: arts and sciences. The *Enciclopedia de Orientación Bibliográfica* (4 vols., Barcelona, Juan Flors, 1964/65) contains reviews of 4,730 titles covering natural and human sciences, mathematics, religion and some fiction. It includes both Spanish and foreign books and periodical articles.

Of special importance are the comprehensive book reviews by the authoritative periodicals *Insula* and *Indice* of Madrid, and *Destino* of Barcelona.

There are also various critical catalogues of books for children and young people (→ 10, Bibliography).

34 Graphic Arts

The *Sindicato Nacional del Papel y Artes Gráficas* (→ 4) embraces the whole field of the graphic arts in Spain under the section *Artes gráficas y manipulados* ("Graphic arts and trades"), sub-section *Artes gráficas,* which in turn is sub-divided into machine composition, typography, all types of photogravure and bookbinding. Another sub-section is *Industrias auxiliares de las artes gráficas* ("Auxiliary industries of the graphic arts").

The excellent work of the "Instituto Catalán de las Artes del Libro" (1898–1936) was resumed in 1960 by the *Conservatorio de las Artes del Libro* ("Academy of Book Arts") which falls under the "Escuela de Artes y Oficios" in Barcelona. It is one of the most outstanding training centres for the graphic trades. Madrid and Bilbao each have a school for graphic arts.

35 Miscellaneous

Under this heading we will take a brief look at special regulations for the protection of publishing.

In order to improve the equipment of the graphic arts industry, the *Comisión Ejecutiva del Comercio Exterior del Libro* ("Executive Commission for Foreign Book Trade")—known as "CECEL"—was founded in 1951. To purchase equipment and machinery, the "CECEL" was given a portion of the convertible currency received by Spain for book exports. In 1958 "CECEL"'s functions were transferred to the "INLE" (→ 4). As a consequence of the liberalization of foreign trade, this role has lost much of its former importance.

The *Ley de Protección al Libro* ("Book Protection Law") of 18 December 1946 provides, among other measures, a system to reduce the prices of domestic paper which, despite bad quality, and owing to a protective tariff, were very high. Through a clearing-house fund administered by the *Comisión Interministerial para la Protección del Libro Español* ("Interministerial Commission for the Protection of Spanish Books") —known as "CIPLE"—the price of printing paper is partly subsidized by the sale of non-printing paper. This subsidy amounts to 2 pesetas per kg. The quantity of this "papel editorial protegido" ("subsidized printing paper") increases from year to year and amounted to 44,000 tons in 1970. The subsidy of 2 pesetas, which in 1946 was a considerable percentage of the price for 1 kg of printing paper, is today only 3 to 8% of the price. Although the quality of domestic paper has considerably improved, the high protective tariff still exists and with it the difficulty of importing cheaper foreign paper. The clearing-house fund has been administered by the "INLE" since 1958.

Since 1964 publishing activities have been regarded as a priority sector for obtaining credit within the "Planes de Desarrollo" (Development Plans). The interest payable amounts to 5.625 or 5.87%, according to the length of time.

Bibliography

F. Cendan, *La industria editorial, sector prioritario.* (The book industry: priority sector). In: *El libro español* (The Spanish book → 5), March issue, 1964.

F. Cendan, *El crédito editorial.* (Publisher's credit). In: *El libro español*, May issue, 1964.

INLE, El libro español. (The Spanish book → 5). January issue, 1971, p. 3, 46/47.

Sweden

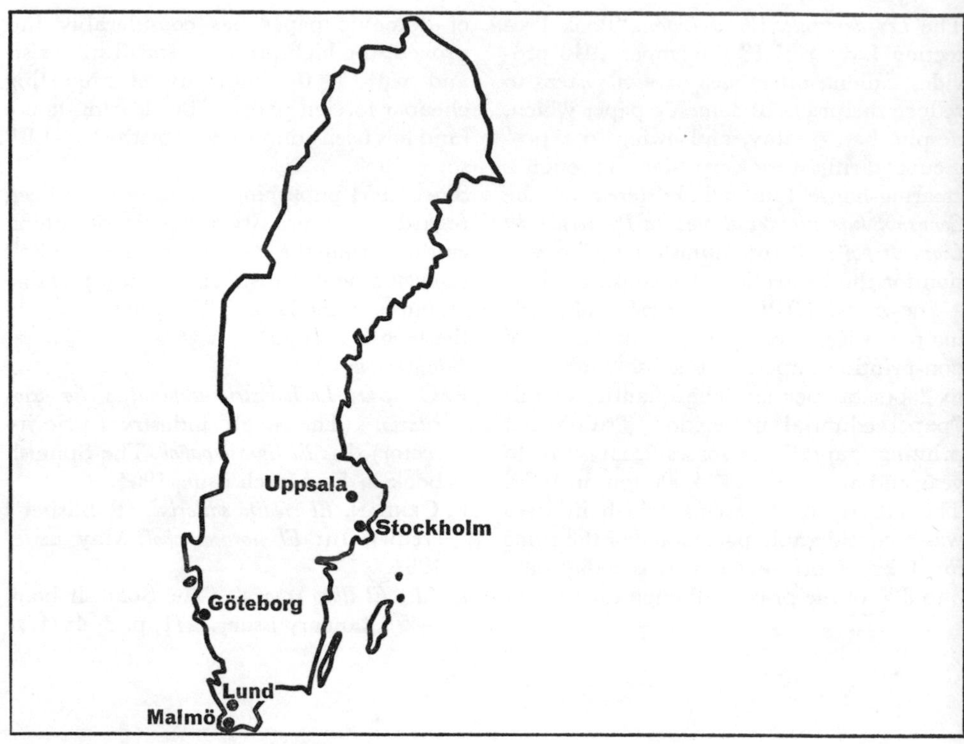

Important Book Centres

1 General Information

Area 449,750 km²

Population 7,951,000 (17 per km²)

Capital Stockholm (747,490; Greater Stockholm 1,274,731)

Largest towns Stockholm (747,490); Göteborg (446,875; Greater Göteborg 636,718); Malmö (258,311; Greater Malmö 421,070); Västerås (113,389; Uppsala 101,696); Norrköping (95,851)

Government Constitutional monarchy. The legislative power is shared between the Government and Parliament
Administrative units: 24 countries, 13 dioceses, 25 provinces

Religion The Lutheran State Church of Sweden 95.5%
Other groups and dissidents 4.5%

National Language Swedish

Leading foreign languages English, French, German

Weights, measures Metric system

Currency unit Swedish crown skr. = 100 Öre

Education Comprehensive school, 9 years
90,250 students at 9 universities, 28,800 students at 9 colleges

Illiteracy Nil

Paper consumption a) Newsprint 32.2 kg per inhabitant (1966)
b) Printing paper (other than newsprint) 24.1 kg per inhabitant

Membership UNESCO, IPA, ICBA, ILAB

2 Past and Present

In the sixteenth century books were distributed in Sweden by travelling salesmen, usually German bookbinders. There were hardly any booksellers' shops in the seventeenth and eighteenth centuries in Sweden outside Stockholm, Uppsala and to some extent Lund. Other parts of the country got their books from these cities. Since the bookbinders had the sole and exclusive right to sell bound books in those days, expansion was restrained. Lars Salvius became the reformer of the Swedish book market. He was a printer, a publisher and a bookseller. In 1752 regulations were issued on his initiative, stipulating that the printers, for the sales of their publications, might keep agents in the big cities and sell bound books.

The foundation of organized Swedish bookselling and publishing was laid in 1843, when the "Swedish Publishers' Association" was established and 79 booksellers were engaged as agents on a sales-or-return basis. The "Swedish Bookshops' Association" was also established, and in 1918 adopted the name of "The Swedish Booksellers' Association". Within a few years of the foundation of the "Swedish Publishers' Association" an independent forwarding agency was founded in Stockholm on the initiative of the publishers. It operated as a privately owned enterprise till 1917, when it was taken over by a group of booksellers under the name of Seelig & Co. and became the forwarding and distribution centre which is employed by all Swedish booksellers. In 1968 its turnover amounted to skr. 55 million. In 1966 the total sales of books in Sweden ran to skr. 430 million gross, skr. 50 million of which passed through the booksellers.

On 1 January 1970 the "Swedish Publishers' Association" numbered 78 members. The 9 largest of these are responsible for 75% of the books sold by the booksellers to private customers. Also on 1 January 1970 the "Swedish Booksellers' Association" had 312 members. These booksellers are all accepted by the "Swedish Publishers' Association" as agents on a sales-or-return basis and are called "A-booksellers" ("primary booksellers"). Without ordering they are sent on commission one copy of each title published by the members of the Publishers' Association.

1 April 1970 marks a turning point in the Swedish book trade, since fixed published prices were then abolished (→ 3). As from that date all books may also be distributed through the 190 "B-booksellers" ("secondary booksellers"), who carry a limited stock and order their books from Seelig & Co., the distribution centre, which stocks all books currently in print. Total sales of the secondary booksellers equal those of 2 or 3 large primary booksellers. Since 1 April 1970 all books are also "free" and may, in principle, be sold by all kinds of dealers, department stores among them.

Under the system of 1 April 1970, 293 primary booksellers are accepted by the "Swedish Publishers' Association" as fully stocked bookshops and receive, much as before, one copy of each new title published by the publishers subscribing to the new system. The main part of the secondary booksellers continue as before.

Up till now (August 1970) no new outlets have been established under the new system, with the exception of some small activities in the department stores. On the other hand the free pricing has made competition keener, and demands for discounts have increased, especially on books for official institutions, schools and libraries. Booksellers today allow a discount of 25% to schools and 20% to libraries.

State-owned publishing houses are a new feature of the Swedish book trade. So far there are two: "Utbildningsförlaget" which, in competition with private pub-

lishers, produce textbooks for all stages and also university literature, and "Allmänna Förlaget", which is supposed to publish all publications issued by governmental departments and institutions.
The history of Swedish libraries originates from the cathedral libraries of the fifteenth century. Such libraries were to be found in Skara, Lidköping, Uppsala, Strängnäs, and at the convent of Vadstena.
The first book auctions took place in Stockholm and Uppsala in the seventeenth century. Today there are regular auctions in the Stockholm and Lund auction rooms. There are also second-hand bookshops in the big cities. 34 of these are members of the "Swedish Antiquarian Booksellers' Association" (→ 26) associated with ILAB. → 6, Bibliography.

3 Retail Prices

As long as organized publishing and bookselling have existed in Sweden, fixed book prices have been strictly maintained. Prices were set by the publishers and upheld by the booksellers. This was done under an exemption from the law against restrictive trade practices. As from 1 April 1970, however, this exemption is repealed, and the publisher may no longer stipulate a minimum price nor indicate a price without explicitly stating that it may be quoted lower. The price set thus is an approximate one, and includes added-value tax. In the official "Swedish Book List", however, the price given does not include added-value tax. Authors' royalties are also based on these new conditions. → 2.

4 Organization

Svenska Bokförläggareföreningen
(The Swedish Publishers' Association)
Kungsholmstorg 13 A
S 112 21 Stockholm

founded in 1843, has at present 78 members in all (→ 21).

Svenska Bokhandlareföreningen
(The Swedish Booksellers' Association)
Skeppargatan 27
S 114 52 Stockholm

founded in 1893, consists of the following groups: The Skåne group, The Småland group (Småland, Blekinge, Öland), The Western group (Västergötland, Halland, Bohuslän, Dalsland), The East group (Östergötland, Södermanland), The Stockholm group (Stockholm, Uppland, Gotland), The Bergslags group (Närke, Västmanland, Värmland, Dalarna), The Lower Norrland group (Hälsingland, Medelpad, Ångermanland, Jämtland, Härjedalen, Gästrikland), The Upper Norrland group (Västerbotten, the Norrbotten county).
Number of members: about 330.

Sveriges B-Bokhandlareförbund
(The Swedish Association of Secondary Booksellers)
S 280 10 Sösdala

founded in 1946, has about 180 members

Svenska Bokhandelsmedhjälpareföreningen
(The Swedish Union of Bookshop Assistants)
Luntmakargatan 15
S 111 37 Stockholm

founded in 1888, membership about 1,450, dedicates itself mainly to the professional training of its members. It is a part of the "Swedish Commercial Employees' Union".

5 Trade Press

In succession to "Svensk Bokhandelstidning" (Swedish Booksellers' Review) founded in 1853, and "Bokhandlaren" (The Bookseller) founded in 1908 the official organ of the "Swedish Publishers' Association" (→ 4) and the "Swedish Booksellers' Association" (→ 4) is

Svensk Bokhandel (Swedish Book Trade)
Karlsrogatan 2,
S 171 90 Solna

The Organ of the "Swedish Union of Bookshop Assistants" (→ 4) is
BMF
Luntmakargatan 15
S 111 37 Stockholm

6 Book-Trade Literature

There are few Swedish books about bookselling and publishing, and there is no special bibliography of this subject. The most important summary works are:

a) History of the book trade and publishing

I. A. Bonnier and A. Haanell, *Anteckningar om svenska bokhandlare.* (Notes on Swedish booksellers). 2 vols. Stockholm 1912–35.

K. O. Bonnier, *Bonniers. En bokhandlarefamilj.* (The Bonniers. A family of booksellers). 5 vols. Stockholm 1930–56.

Liber Librariorum. Bokhandlarnas bok. (The book of the booksellers). 2 vols. Stockholm 1919–20.
Memorial publication published for the 25th anniversary of the "Swedish Booksellers' Association" (→ 4).

Pro Novitate. Festskrift utgifven av Svenska Bokhandelsmedhjälpareföreningen till minne af dess 10-årige tillvaro. (Memorial volume published in connection with the 10th anniversary of the Swedish Union of Bookshop Assistants). Stockholm 1898.

Pro Novitate. Pars secunda. Utgifven af Svenska Bokhandelsmedhjälpareföreningen till minne af dess 25-åriga tillvaro 1888–1913. (Published by the Swedish Union of Bookshop Assistants in memory of its 25th anniversary 1888–1913). Stockholm 1914.

S. Rinman, *Svenska Bokförläggareföreningen 1843–1887.* (The Swedish Publishers' Association 1843–1887). Stockholm 1951.

H. Schück, *Den svenska förlagsbokhandelns historia.* (History of the Swedish publishing world). 2 vols. Stockholm 1923.

Vi valde boken. (We chose the book). Pro Novitate III, published in connection with the 75th anniversary of the Swedish Union of Bookshop Assistants on 29 September 1963. Stockholm 1963.

b) Practical knowledge

P. I. Gedin, *Den nya boken.* (The new book). Stockholm 1966.
Paperbacks: Introduction and analysis.

M. Härlin (ed.); *Bokhandels ABC.* (ABC of bookselling). Compendium for booksellers' apprentices. Solna, Seelig 1970.

7 Sources of Information, Address Services

"Svenska Bokförläggareföreningens matrikel", the annual directory of the "Swedish Publishers' Association" (→ 4) lists the members of the "Publishers' Association", the "Booksellers' Association", the "Association of Antiquarian Booksellers", and other organizations within the book trade.
General and special information about the Swedish book world may be obtained from

Svenska Bokförläggareföreningen
(The Swedish Publishers' Association)
Kungsholmstorg 13 A
S 112 21 Stockholm

Bibliotekstjänst
(The Library Service Agency)
Tornavägen 9
S 223 63 Lund

Bibliografiska Institutet
(The Bibliographical Institute at the Royal Library in Stockholm)
Kungl. Biblioteket
Humlegården
S 114 46 Stockholm

8 International Membership

The various bodies within the Swedish book trade are members of the corresponding international organizations. The pub-

lishers are members of IPA, the booksellers of ICBA and the antiquarian booksellers of ILAB.
Furthermore there operates in Scandinavia a "Nordic Publishers' Council", founded in 1935 (→ International Section, 4). The Council has 12 members, three from respectively Denmark, Finland, Norway and Sweden.

9 Market Research

There is no institute for regular market research into the Swedish book trade and related matters, but separate aspects are occasionally studied by specialists in this field. An exploration of reading habits by a governmental "Commission on Literature" is at present in progress, but its findings will probably only be published in a few years' time.

10 Books and Young People

About 600 children's books are published each year by nine companies, two of which dedicate themselves entirely to juveniles. Every bookseller has a special department for children's books, and in the big bookshops a special staff is in charge of these books. Information about new children's books is given at special meetings arranged by the publishers before the start of the autumn season. The public gets information about new children's books through reviews and advertisements in the press. During the season the big daily newspapers carry special review pages, and the publishers of juvenile literature issue a joint catalogue.
There are in Sweden 950 public libraries in the cities and about 1,650 school libraries in the country. Often, but not always, the big public libraries have special children's book departments or a "Children's Corner". The librarians also stimulate reading activities in the children's book departments by reading aloud to the children, and arrange dramatic performances and exhibitions of various kinds.
In 1969 the loans of children's books totalled 5,387,841 volumes.
The foundation

Svenska Barnboksinstitutet
(The Swedish Institute for Children's Books)
Tjärhovsgatan 36
S 11621 Stockholm

is a centre for information and scientific research on books for young people. This Foundation, the Memorandum of Association of which is dated 7 December 1965, is sponsored by four bodies: the City of Stockholm, represented by the City Library Board, the Swedish Publishers' Association, the University of Stockholm and the Swedish Association of Juvenile Authors. The nucleus of the Institute is a library of about 10,000 volumes, most of them gifts. This library is a fairly complete collection of children's books published in Sweden, old and new, original as well as translated works, and also includes originals of the translations, and Swedish children's books in translation. There is also a collection of some 400 reference books, original Swedish as well as translated works dealing with children's literature, book illustration, children's reading. Review cuttings, publicity matter, etc. are continually collected, and some twenty magazines dealing with various aspects of children's literature are also available at the Institute.
Sweden is a member of IBBY.

Bibliography

The literature about children's books in Sweden is quite considerable. The following titles are the most important contributions:

G. Bolin, E. von Zweigbergk and M. Örvig, *Barn och Böcker*. (Children and books). 6th rev. ed. Stockholm, Rabén och Sjögren 1966.

G. Klingberg, *Barn och Ungdomslitteraturen.* (Literature for children and young people). Stockholm, Natur och Kultur 1970. 328 pp.

C.-A. Lövgren, *Barn, Böcker och Skola.* (Children, books and school.) Stockholm, Gummerus 1966.

E. von Zweigbergk, *Barnboken i Sverige 1750–1950.* (Children's books in Sweden 1750–1950). Stockholm, Rabén och Sjögren 1965. 520 pp.

11 Training

Svenska Bokhandelsskolan
(The Swedish School for Bookshop Assistants)
Skeppargatan 27
S 11452 Stockholm

founded in 1905, has board members from the "Swedish Publishers' Association", the "Swedish Booksellers' Association" and the "Swedish Union of Bookshop Assistants". Every year this school organizes a basic four weeks' course for young booksellers' employees with one year's practical experience. The training is based on a book called *Bokhandels ABC* (ABC of the book trade). Every two years a higher course of three weeks is organized for employees who have been in the trade for at least five years. This course concentrates on management functions.

Bokhandelns Serviceinstitut
(The Service Institute of Swedish Booksellers)
Skeppargatan 27
S 11452 Stockholm

also organizes courses in business economics within the local sections of the Swedish Booksellers' Association. These courses are meant for business leaders and employees in higher positions. It is a four-day course based on a book called *Företagets ekonomi* (Business economy) by Lars O. Andersson and Margit Gennser. The Institute also arranges sales courses for booksellers, and in order to further the sales of children's books a pilot course was arranged in 1970.

12 Taxes

Books are not exempt from added-value tax, which today amounts to 17.65%. Imported books are subject to taxation, while exported ones are not. Newspapers, publications for members of societies, clubs, etc., and subscriptions to foreign periodicals are free of tax.

In addition to the added-value tax there is a special tax of 4% on printing paper, except for newsprint, and a tax of 4.8% on coated paper.

13 Clearing Houses

The bookseller pays the publisher directly, without any intermediaries. Most booksellers have money on deposit with Seelig & Co., the distribution centre of Swedish bookselling (→ 23), from which payments are made for small lots which have to be paid in cash.

14 Copyright

The term of protection of author's rights prescribed by the Swedish Copyright Act of 30 December 1960 is life plus 50 years. Nordic legislation is uniform in this respect. Certain limitations of copyright apply concerning the use of texts for teaching purposes. The Copyright Act, which also covers artistic, dramatic, musical and cinematographic works, is supplemented by a special Act on Rights in Photographic Pictures of 1960. Sweden is a member of the Berne Convention and adheres to the Universal Copyright Convention./International Section, 14.

Bibliography

a) Periodicals

NIR. Nordisk immateriellt rättsskydd. (Nordic intellectual property protection.) An internordic review.

b) Books

N. Regner (ed.), *The laws of copyright in literature, artistic works and photographs.* Stockholm, Norstedt & Söner 1961.

15 National Bibliography, National Library

There is no general retrospective bibliography of Swedish literature. The period until 1600 is covered by:

I. Collijn, *Sveriges bibliografi intill 1600.* (Bibliography of Sweden until 1600.) 2 vols. Uppsala 1937–38.

The literature of the seventeenth century is listed in:

I. Collijn, *Sveriges bibliografi, 1600-talet.* (Bibliography of Sweden, 17th century.) 2 vols. Uppsala 1942–46.

No bibliography of literature published between 1700 and 1829 exists.

The literature from 1830 and onwards is to be found in

H. Linnström, *Svenskt boklexikon.* (Swedish book dictionary 1830–1965). Stockholm 1867–84. Followed by *Svensk bokkatalog* (Swedish book catalogue, 1866–1950), published in five and ten-year volumes.

Bibliografiska Institutet vid
Kungliga Biblioteket
(The Bibliographic Institute at the
Royal Swedish Library)
Box 5039
S 102 41 Stockholm

publishes and edits *Svensk Bokförteckning* ("Swedish book list") in a weekly catalogue, appearing in the magazine *Svensk Bokhandel* (→ 5). The Institute also publishes quarterly, bi-annual, annual volumes and *Svensk Bokkatalog* ("The Swedish book catalogue") (covering five years), and *Svensk Tidskriftsförteckning* ("Swedish periodicals list") for current periodicals.

Bibliotekstjänst
(Library Service Agency)
S Lund

publishes by subscription "Swedish Newspaper Articles" and "Swedish Magazine Articles".

Other publications: The publishers' annual catalogue of books in print and "Årets böcker" (Books of the Year), a systematized summary catalogue of the books published by the Swedish publishers, issued by the "Swedish Publishers' Association" (→ 4).

16 Book Production

In 1967 Sweden produced 7,218 titles, 1,409 of which were booklets of 48 pages or less.

The leading subjects were:

Subject group	Titles
Fiction	1,311
Economics	637
Natural sciences	631
Technology, industry, communications	601
Philology	558
Children's & juvenile books	504
Social sciences and law	463
Medicine	436
Religion	343
Geography	299

17 Translations

English is the first foreign language taught in Sweden. Pupils start learning English at the age of 10. From ten onwards English is a compulsory language.

Generally there is a selection of English and American books at all important booksellers'. The big bookshops, mainly in the university towns and the big cities have special and well-supplied departments of foreign books which they import themselves. Most booksellers, however, order their foreign books from two import wholesalers:

Importbokhandeln
Gävlegatan 12 A
S 113 30 Stockholm

and

Svensk Bokimport
Agnegatan 34
S 112 29 Stockholm

In 1968 1,460 books, translated from foreign languages, were published in Sweden.

Language of origin	Titles
English	931
German	120
French	114
Danish	82
Norwegian	63
Italian	28
Russian	15
Spanish	13
Other languages	94

There is no complete record of how many books are translated from Swedish into foreign languages, but a tentative number would be 150–200 titles a year (fiction, non-fiction and children's books).

18 Book Clubs

Book clubs were first organized in Sweden in the nineteen forties. The first one—modelled on the German "Büchergilde Gutenberg"—was *Tidens Bokklubb*. Today this club publishes 10 titles a year and has about 20,000 members.

Sweden's largest book club, *Bokklubben Svalan* run by the Albert Bonnier publishing company, has about 100,000 members who are required to buy at least six of the twelve specially printed books—usually hardcover reprints—offered each year.

The *Vår Bok* book club run by the P. A. Norstedt & Söner Publishing Company is organized in roughly the same way as *Svalan* and issues 10 books a year. *Bonniers Book Club* was established in 1970 and has about 60,000 members. Members are required to buy either the club's special quarterly volume, a new publication priced at just under skr 30, or else some other book or books totalling at least this sum and to be chosen from a list offering previously published books at special members' prices.

Bra Böcker is a special book-club company which offers members 6 book parcels a year, every parcel containing 3 books. The club has about 50,000 members.

19 Paperbacks

Swedish paperback publishing began about 1960. Today there are 2,100 titles on the market, from 26 publishing companies. There are about 50 paperback series.

Statistics of paperback publishing:

Subject group (New titles)	1966	1968
Fiction	138	116
Technical books	178	232
Total	316	348

Subject group (New editions)	1966	1968
Fiction	33	89
Technical books	30	69
Total	63	158

Distribution channels	1966	1968
Sales through the booksellers	72.7%	76.4%
Sales by other means	27.3%	23.6%

Most Swedish high-quality paperbacks are sold through the booksellers. From time to time a complete catalogue of paperbacks in print is issued by Seelig & Co. (→ 23). It was last published in the spring of 1970. Seelig & Co. also has a central warehouse for paperbacks.

Bibliography

P. I. Gedin, *Den nya boken. En presentation och analys av pocketboken.* (The new book. Paperbacks: Introduction and analysis.) Stockholm 1966.

Sweden

20 Book Design

Svensk Bokkonst
(Swedish Book Design)
Kungl. Biblioteket
Box 5039
S 10241 Stockholm

is an institution which, since 1933, makes up an honour list of the 25 best-designed books of the preceding year. Originally the jury was nominated by a group of private book-lovers, but since 1939 it is appointed by institutions and organizations connected with books and the graphic trade. The jury also makes a selection of good bindings. The selected books are presented in an annual catalogue, *Svensk Bokkunst* ("Swedish Book Design"). Exhibitions of these are organized at the Royal Library in Stockholm and in provincial libraries, and also at the Frankfurt Book Fair (→ International Section, 20).

Nordisk Bokkonst
(Nordic Book Design)
Kungl. Biblioteket
Box 5039
S 10241 Stockholm

arranges exhibitions in Scandinavia.

21 Publishing

The "Swedish Publishers' Association" (membership 1 January 1970: 78) includes all publishers doing regular business with the booksellers. Further, a great number of institutions issue books under their own imprint, and sometimes books are published by the writer himself. Books of these categories are usually distributed by Seelig & Co. (→ 23).

In 1966 book sales in Sweden totalled skr. 430 million, 50% of which resulted from bookshop sales. 75% of the booksellers' purchases are made from 9 publishers. Apart from these figures Swedish publishing statistics are very incomplete, but a governmental "Commission on Literature", set up in 1969, is at present collecting information for more exhaustive statistics. The only statistical information available today are the following figures of publishers' sales:

Sales up to skr.	50,000	28 publishers
Sales up to skr.	50,000–100,000	5 publishers
Sales up to skr.	100,000–300,000	11 publishers
Sales up to skr.	300,000–750,000	6 publishers
Sales up to skr.	750,000–1,250,000	4 publishers
Sales up to skr.	1,250,000–2,000,000	5 publishers
Sales over skr.	2,000,000	20 publishers

22 Literary Agents

Swedish authors do not employ literary agents but negotiate directly with their publishers. The three literary agencies that do exist act on behalf of foreign publishers, but owing to intensified international communication Swedish publishers increasingly obtain translation rights directly from the country of origin.

23 Wholesale Trade

For the time being there are no private firms or organizations acting as jobbers or wholesale dealers within the Swedish book trade. On the other hand a certain amount of wholesale business is done by

Seelig & Co.
Karlsrogatan 2
S 17120 Solna

the entirely bookseller-owned distribution centre. Seelig & Co. comprises

a) a forwarding department, co-ordinating consignments from different publishers to each bookseller;

b) a distribution department for publishers and other organizations publishing books. 30% of the titles available in Swedish bookshops, i.e. 9,000 titles, are dispatched through Seelig & Co. for about 500 publishers and other organizations publishing books;

c) (since 1970) a complete stock of books in print which serves
1. booksellers needing single copies;
2. the booksellers called secondary booksellers; and, finally,
3. firms without a current account with the publishers.
Through its own 1,200 news stands and 15,000 privately-owned shops

AB Svenska Pressbyrån
(The Swedish Press Bureau)
Strandbergsgatan 61
S 11251 Stockholm

jointly owned by the Swedish press, is responsible for 80% of the sales of single copies of the daily newspapers and 90% of the sales of single copies of magazines. It also distributes books to about 9,000 tobacconists and similar shops and to its 1,200 own stands.
In 1969 sales of books, mainly paperbacks and comic books, through the "Swedish Press Bureau" amounted to skr. 46 million.

24 Retail Trade

For information about the Swedish book trade and its distribution system → 2. In every community where the potential clientele is reasonably large there is at least one fully stocked bookshop. During the last few years the number of retail shops has decreased, but on the other hand many chain stores have set up their own book departments.
The turnover of the 313 members of the "Swedish Booksellers' Association" (→ 4) can be broken down as follows:

under skr.	200,000	86 firms
	200,000–500,000	129 firms
	501,000–1,000,000	67 firms
over skr.	1,000,000	31 firms

Most bookshops also carry stationery and similar articles, music, photographical material, and toys.

26 Mail-Order Bookselling

During the last decades bookselling on the instalment plan has declined in Sweden. The instalment sales departments which were once successfully run by some publishers and important booksellers have been discontinued, or confine their activities to encyclopedias and big handbooks. The turnover from this kind of sales has decreased considerably.
Mail-order sales were never great in Sweden, but a boom may be in prospect in the coming years. Today neither publishers nor booksellers do much business of this kind.

26 Antiquarian Book Trade, Auctions

The main organization for antiquarian booksellers in Sweden is

Svenska Antikvariatföreningen
(The Swedish Antiquarian Booksellers' Association)
c/o Varia-Antikvariatet
Nybrogatan 41
S 114 39 Stockholm

It was founded in 1935 and has 34 members. There are no special laws for the antiquarian book trade in Sweden.
Approximate annual sales figure: about skr. 15 million.
The "Swedish Antiquarian Booksellers' Association" is a member of the "International League of Antiquarian Booksellers" (→ International Section, 26).
Book auctions are held by:

Lunds Bokauktionskammare
S Lund

and

Bokauktionskammaren
Norrtullsgatan 6
S 113 29 Stockholm

There is no special trade press for the antiquarian book world of Sweden.

Sweden

27 Book Imports

The official figures for imports in 1968 are:

Category	1,000 skr.
Books, booklets	33,648
Periodicals	22,261
Picture books for children	2,484
Music	570
Maps	3,671
Total	62,634

The following is a list of the most important countries of origin:

Country	1,000 skr.	Percentage of total
Denmark	8,977	26.7
Netherlands	6,350	18.9
United Kingdom	5,862	17.4
USA	3,537	10.5
Germany (F.R.)	3,366	10.0
Finland	2,084	6.2
Italy	1,668	5.0
Czechoslovakia	1,063	3.2
Norway	1,050	3.1
Switzerland	957	2.8
Poland	874	2.6

For the imports of periodicals, the most important countries of origin were: Denmark, Germany (F.R.), Finland, USA, United Kingdom, Norway, and France.
These official statistics are, however, a rather unreliable basis on which to found a realistic idea of book imports, since imports of original books from different countries and imports of Swedish books printed abroad are lumped together. Denmark, Holland, Finland, Italy, Poland, Czechoslovakia account for a quite extensive production of Swedish books abroad which is why the percentage for these countries is so high.
For importing firms → 17.

28 Book Exports

The official figures for exports in 1968 are:

Category	1,000 skr.
Books, booklets	33,156
Periodicals	16,307
Picture books for children	505
Music	268
Maps	954
Total	51,190

The most import countries of destination for the book exports were:

Country	1,000 skr.	Percentage of total
Finland	9,338	28.2
Denmark	6,020	18.2
Norway	4,457	13.4
USA	2,898	8.7
United Kingdom	1,931	5.8
Germany (F.R.)	1,808	5.4
Switzerland	1,062	3.2
France	756	2.3

The exports of periodicals were mainly directed to the following countries: Finland, Denmark, Norway, Germany (F.R.), United Kingdom, and the Netherlands.

29 Book Fairs

No book fairs are organized in Sweden, but leading Swedish publishers participate in the Frankfurt Book Fair. In 1969 25 Swedish publishing houses participated.

30 Public Relations

Svensk Boktjänst ("Swedish Book Service"), a publicity agency sponsored by the book trade organizations, operated 1941 through 1969. Among other things Svensk Boktjänst was the originator of a national advertising campaign for books and reading, launching the still current slogan "Remember me with a book". It also

issued a joint sales catalogue, a paperback catalogue, the catalogue called Höstens Böcker ("Books of the Autumn") and a small Christmas book list, Julens Bokguide ("Christmas Book Guide").
The organization of the annual Bokens Vecka ("National Book Week") in November was another important activity of Svensk Boktjänst. This great effort in the interest of the book was—and is—organized in collaboration with libraries and adult education institutes all over the country.
In 1970 Svensk Boktjänst was succeeded and its functions taken over by (→ 11)

Bokhandelns Serviceinstitut
(The Service Institute of Swedish Booksellers)
Skeppargatan 27
S 11452 Stockholm

A special feature of the Institute is the organization of special campaigns designed to stimulate booksellers and publishers to greater activity in a certain field. A case in point was the handbook campaign launched a couple of years ago, coordinating the publication of a catalogue and various publicity matter with window displays and advertising on a national scale. Similar drives are made for paperbacks, for the season's new books, for "reading circles", etc. According to the current slogan the reading circle is a means to "read ten books at the price of one".
You may join a reading circle organized by the bookseller, collect a new book at the shop every two weeks and finally keep one of the ten books you have read, or you may organize your own reading circle among friends or colleagues, with the practical assistance of the bookseller. Reading circles play an important role for, especially, autumn sales. The Institute also publishes a popular catalogue for Christmas, listing a selection of books published during the autumn months. This catalogue supplements "Books of the Year" (→ 15) which includes all books published during the year with the exception of textbooks and university literature. It is published by the "Swedish Publishers' Association" (→ 4).

31 Bibliophily

The history of Swedish bibliophily is intimately connected with that of the many large-scale book collectors who have eventually donated their libraries to official institutions.
There are two associations dedicated to the interests of the Swedish bibliophiles:

Föreningen för bokhantverk
(The Association of Book Craft)
The Royal Swedish Library
Humlegården
S 114 46 Stockholm

founded in 1900 in Stockholm. Its purpose is to extend and intensify the interest in book-craft in Sweden. The association organizes lectures and educational visits and supports the institution *Svensk Bokkonst* (Swedish Book Design); it is primarily a society of friends of the Royal Library. The association has 550 members. Each member receives a copy of the year-book of the association, *Biblis,* until now published in 1957, 1958, 1959/60, 1961, 1962, 1963/64, 1965, 1966, 1967, 1968 and 1969.

Sällskapet Bokvännerna
(The Society of Book Lovers)
P.O.B. 5068
S 10242 Stockholm 5

was founded in 1946 in order to provoke and stimulate an interest in book design and the collecting of old and new literature, and to support research and other initiatives in these fields to the best of its ability.
The society brings out the magazine *Bokvännen* (The Book Friend) which is distributed free of charge together with a book gift to each member. There are 2,000 members.

32 Literary Prizes

The *Nobel Prize for Literature* is the most eminent of Swedish literary prizes. Every year since 1901 (with the exception of a few years during the two World Wars) it is awarded by the Swedish Academy on 10 December, the anniversary of Alfred Nobel's death. (International Section, 32).
Every year the Swedish Government makes grants of money to a number of authors and translators of literary merit. In 1970/71 these grants amounted to skr. 800,000.—.
As a compensation for the free loans at the public libraries the Government allocates an annual sum which in 1970/71 totalled skr. 6.6 million. One third of this sum goes directly to the individual authors in proportion to the number of loans of their books, while the remaining sum is paid out as grants of humanitarian aid.
In addition to these governmental awards a great many literary grants and prizes come from other sources. The most important prize ist the *Bellman Prize*, amounting to skr. 30,000,—, awarded every year by the Swedish Academy. Litteraturfrämjandet, the "Association for the Furthering of Swedish Literature", awards the *Big Novel Prize*, worth skr. 25,000,—.
The *Nils Holgersson Plaque* and the *Elsa Beskow Plaque* are given every year by the Association of Swedish Libraries to an author and an artist for, respectively, an outstanding children's book and a particularly well-illustrated book for young people.
A great many grants are made by publishers and newspapers, and prizes are also awarded locally by cities or countries to their own resident authors.

33 The Reviewing of Books

The leading Swedish newspapers review Swedish and, to some extent, foreign literature regularly.
The 10 biggest newspapers are (first half of 1970): "Expressen", "Aftonbladet", "Dagens Nyheter", "Göteborgs-Posten", "Svenska Dagbladet", "Sydsvenska Dagbladet", "Arbetet", "Kvällsposten", "Göteborgs-Tidningen", "Göteborgs Handels- & Sjöfartstidning".
Information about the popular press and the trade press is to be found in *Svensk Annonstaxa* (Swedish Advertising Tariff), 1970, part II, and in the handbook of *Föreningen Svensk Fackpress* (The Association for Swedish Trade Press) and advertising tariff for 1970 with a summary in English.
Important literary magazines are:

Bokrevy
Fack
S 221 01 Lund 1

Bonniers Litterära Magasin
Box 3151
S 103 63 Stockholm 3

Böckernas Värld
Torsgatan 21
S 105 44 Stockholm

Svensk Litteraturtidskrift
c/o Kärnell
Gyllenstiernsgatan 8
S 115 26 Stockholm

34 Graphic Arts

Sveriges Grafiska Industriförbund
(The Swedish Federation of the Graphic Industries)
Hovslagargatan 3
S 111 48 Stockholm

represents its members at *Sveriges Industriförbund* (Federation of Swedish Industries) and attends to common interests.

Svenska Boktryckareföreningen
(The Swedish Federation of Master Printers)
Blasieholmsgatan 4 A
S 111 48 Stockholm

Sveriges Bokbinderiidkareförening
(The Swedish Association of the Bookbinding Industry)
Blasieholmsgatan 4 a
S 111 48 Stockholm

Grafiska Institutet
(The Graphic Institute)
Valhallavägen 141
S 115 31 Stockholm

founded in 1943, provides higher education for the graphic industry.

Grafiskt Forum med Nordisk Boktryckarkonst
(Graphic Forum with Nordic Typography)
Postbox 163 83
S 103 27 Stockholm

11 issues per year.

Switzerland

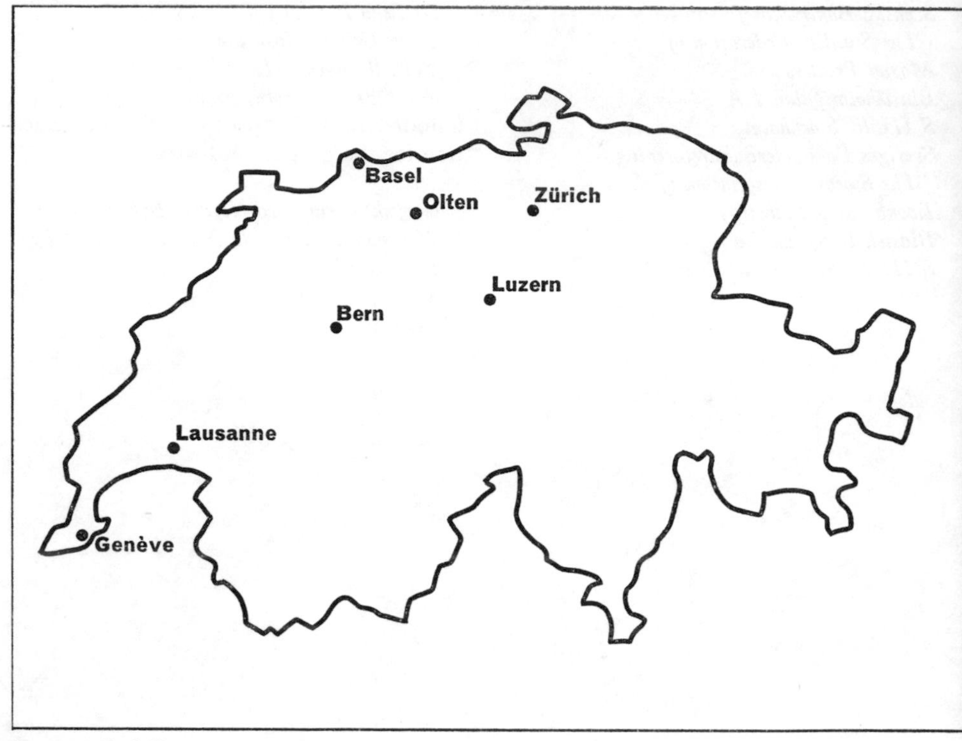

Important Book Centres

1 General Information

Area 41,287 km²
Population 5,945,000 (143.9 per km²)
Capital Bern (166,600)
Largest towns Zürich (438,000); Basel (212,700); Genf (Genève) (175,500); Lausanne (132,000); Winterthur (87,900); St. Gallen (77,400); Luzern (73,000); Biel (66,000); La Chaux-de-Fonds (41,800)
Government Swiss Confederation. The Federal Constitution of 12 September 1848 (revised 29 May 1874) declares Switzerland a Federal State of 22 sovereign cantons
Religion Protestant 36.9%
Roman Catholic 41.5%
Others 21.6%
National languages German, French, Italian, Romansch
Leading foreign language English
Weights and measures Metric system
Currency unit Swiss franc (sfr.)
Education The cantons are responsible for education. Compulsory education (primary and secondary) till 16th birthday. Switzerland has eight universities.
Paper consumption a) Newsprint 17.4 kg per inhabitant (1967)
b) Printing paper (other than newsprint) 34.0 kg per inhabitant (1967)
Membership UNESCO, IPA, ICBA, ILAB

2 Past and Present

Movable type has been used in printing in Switzerland since 1470 (Beromünster). There were 27 presses in the area covered by present-day Switzerland around the year 1500. The early years of book production reached their zenith in the sixteenth and seventeenth centuries. These early printers enjoyed a high standard of education and craftsmanship. At this time a division of work between printer, publisher and bookseller was not usual. No guild membership imposed from above hampered the development of the book trade in those days. The art of printing was not regarded as a trade, but as one of the seven "liberal arts" enjoying numerous privileges. The high cost of production soon led to a division of work. Those who advanced money to the printers became the publishers. In this way a separate profession as publisher developed in the sixteenth century, whilst in the seventeenth printers and paper manufacturers joined the guilds as tradesmen. Thus the printers excluded the publishers and book distributors from the production of books. Book printing, publishing and the book trade spread throughout Switzerland in the seventeenth and eighteenth centuries, but diminished in importance. The causes lay in a rigorous censorship and unfavourable economic factors (customs and taxes, the monetary system, and legal protection). Not till after the foundation of the Swiss Federal State in 1848 did the unrestrained individualism in the book trade give way to professional organization. The "Swiss Booksellers' Association" was founded in 1849, followed in 1866 by the foundation of the "Association of Booksellers and Publishers of French Switzerland". The main efforts of the booksellers' professional organizations are directed to the realization of a liberal marketing system founded on well-trained personnel, resistance to all limitations by the state, such as censorship, customs dues, book taxes and nationalization, the promoting of books and reading, and cooperation with all culturally interested bodies and organizations at home and abroad.

Bibliography

a) Periodicals

Schweizerisches Gutenbergmuseum. (The Swiss Gutenberg Museum). Bern, since 1914.
Periodical for the history of book printing, the graphic arts and newspapers.

→ 31.

3 Retail Prices

According to paragraph 40 of the "Conditions of sale of the Swiss Booksellers' and Publishers' Association", books, maps, atlases and periodicals may only be advertised, offered and sold at the retail prices laid down by the publishers. It is no new idea that the fixed retail price is one of the fundamental prerequisites for the whole book-trade system, and that any deviation from this principle is harmful to the economic and cultural interests of the book-purchasing public.

Thought was already given to this at the beginning of the nineteenth century, when uniform and agreed methods of distribution were being started in the German book trade.

However, considerable obstacles in Switzerland stood in the way of the idea that books, as disseminators of culture and education, should be available everywhere and to all at the same reasonable price: these were lack of a uniform legal protection for the rights of author and publisher—lack of any organization to all booksellers and publishers—a situation that was understandable in the young, liberal society about the mid-nineteenth century, to which liberty to exercise a trade was of supreme importance. The

rivalling economic and legal autonomy of the twenty-five cantons was an obstacle to price-fixing. It was not until the transformation of the Confederation from a federal union to a centralized confederacy in 1848, with uniform monetary and customs systems, assisted by the influence of the Southern German booksellers' organization, that this most unrestrained individualism was partly checked by the founding of the "Swiss Booksellers' Association" in 1849. The Federal Law concerning copyright (1884) completed the circle, thus eliminating price-cutting and pirated editions, and establishing formally the principle of the fixed retail price in bookselling.
The revision of the statutes of the "Swiss Booksellers' and Publishers' Association" in 1888, and their approximation to the statutes of the German "Börsenverein", gave additional strength to price-fixing in Switzerland.
Experience, however, has shown that firm retail prices must always be a necessary and irrevocable principle in the book trade, but that the complete implementation of this principle remains an ideal.
An exclusive book-trade marketing price and a firm retail price are by their nature critically opposed to the aims of the cartel commission of the "Federal Department of Public Economy". The fate of the firm retail price in Switzerland will depend on whether the book trade succeeds in constantly introducing new services in the public interest that will prove the credibility and necessity of this principle in practice.

Bibliography

H. R. Balmer, *Selbstbehauptung des Buchhandels.* (Self-assertion of the book trade). Olten 1960. 32 pp.

W. Röpke, *Der wirtschaftliche Standort des Buchhändlers.* (The economic location of the bookseller). Olten 1959. 25 pp.

4 Organization

After several previous attempts (1842 and 1843), the new Federal Customs Tariff of 1849 provided for a book tax, and this was the direct cause for the foundation of a professional association. The association's statutes valid today date from 1963, the sales regulations from the same year. The booksellers' organizations in Switzerland are divided according to various linguistic and cultural areas, but they cooperate in many fields.

1. *Schweizerischer Buchhändler- und Verlegerverein (SBVV)*
(The Swiss Booksellers' and Publishers' Association),
Bellerivestraße 3
CH 8008 Zürich

The aims of this association are the promotion and cooperation of members among themselves, the representation of their common interests beyond their circle, and cooperation with all organizations engaged in the intellectual and cultural life of Switzerland. Membership is based on the person (honorary member, free member, member). The organs of the association are the meeting of the association, the main meeting of the booksellers' group, the main meeting of the publishers' group, the central board, the directing board of each group, the auditors, the arbitrator, and the local and area associations of Basle, Berne, Luzern, St Gallen, Winterthur, Tessin and Zurich. The supreme organ is the general assembly of the association. In addition to the seven members of the central board and the five members of each group various special commissions assist the executive.
The SBVV cooperates with the "Société des Libraires et Éditeurs de la Suisse romande (SLESR)" ("Association of Booksellers and Publishers in French Switzerland") and the "Vereinigung der Buchantiquare

und Kupferstichhändler der Schweiz (VEBUKU)" ("Association of Swiss Antiquarian Booksellers and Engravers", → 26).
The official journal of the SBVV and SLESR is "The Swiss Book Trade" (→ 5). The SBVV also publishes "The Swiss Book" (→ 15), the bibliographical bulletin of the Swiss National Library—series A twice a month, series B bimonthly—the annual Christmas catalogue "Book 70", the catalogue "Books by Swiss Publishers" published in spring and a catalogue distributed to all households in the German-speaking part of the country, and shares in the publication of the Juveniles book catalogue, "Books for Juveniles".
The following publications also appear at regular intervals:
Adressbuch des Schweizer Buchhandels (The address book of the Swiss book trade), *Verzeichnis der Auslieferungsstellen* (Index of firms representing publishers and distributing their titles to the trade).

2. *Société des Libraires et Éditeurs de la Suisse romande (SLESR),*
(Association of Booksellers and Publishers in French Switzerland)
2 Avenue Agassi
CH 1001 Lausanne

Its statutory aims are essentially the same as those of the SBVV. The organs of the Société are: the general meeting, the governing body, the directing board, the board of appeal and the auditors. The six regional associations of Fribourg, Geneva, Neuchâtel, Valais, Vaud, the French-speaking part of the Bernese Jura are represented in the Société. The statutes of these regional associations must be approved by the governing body of the Société. The official organ of the association is "The Swiss Book Trade" (→ 4). A "Catalogue d'étrennes" ("Christmas catalogue") and a "Catalogue choc" are published annually.

3. The Italian-speaking booksellers and publishers are attached to the SBVV as a local association.

4. *Angestelltenverein des Schweizer Buchhandels (ASB)*
(Employees' Association of the Swiss Book Trade)
CH 3115 Münzingen

In 1883 book-trade employees formed an association with local groups in Basle, Berne, Luzern, Olten, St Gallen and Zurich for the promotion of training and the realization of their economic interests as employees. Since 1919 the ASB has published the journal *Der Buchhändler* ("The Bookseller"). The ASB is associated with the SBVV through the "Paritätische Kommission", which consists of four representatives of the SBVV and four of the ASB. This Commission organizes conferences (in Gwatt till 1966, in Muttenz since 1966), and an annual conference to discuss and criticize new books. It also publishes a series of papers.
Similar interests are promoted in the French-speaking part of the country by the:

5. *Association romande du personnel de la Librairie et de l'Édition (ARPLE)*
(Association of French-speaking Employees in Bookselling and Publishing)
10 Rue du Perron
CH 1200 Genève

It issues the journal *13/12,* which appears six times a year.
Beside the official trade association there are also denominational associations:

6. *Vereinigung katholischer Buchhändler und Verleger der Schweiz (VKBK)*
(Association of Catholic Booksellers and Publishers in Switzerland)
Gallusstr. 20
CH 9001 St. Gallen

The association supports the interests of Catholic booksellers within the SBVV, in the cultural associations, and among the public. The seat of the association is the place of residence of its president.

7. *Verband Evangelischer Buchhändler und Verleger der Schweiz (VEBV)*
(Association of Protestant Booksellers and Publishers in Switzerland)
Badener Str. 69
CH 8026 Zürich

As an outsider organization and in contrast to the SBVV, there is the

8. *Interessengemeinschaft schweizerischer Verleger (ISV)*
(Swiss Publishers' Corporation)
Birmensdorfer Str. 318
Postfach 280
CH 8055 Zürich

founded in 1950. Its aim is to achieve equality of rights in economic matters and the promotion of an independent and qualified profession of publishers.
The corporation's journal was *Edition*, Zurich (from 1950–1970).

Bibliography

Festschrift zum 25jährigen Bestehen der Association romande du personnel de la librairie et de l'édition. (Commemorative publication on the 25th anniversary of the Association of French-speaking employees in bookselling and publishing). Aigle 1967.

V. Gnehm, *Der schweizerische Buchhandel.* (The Swiss book trade). In: Schweiz. Zeitschrift für Volkswirtschaft und Sozialpolitik, vol. 19, 1907.

J. Huber, *Der schweizerische Buchhandel.* (The Swiss book trade). In: N. Reichesberg, Handwörterbuch der schweizerischen Volkswirtschaft, Sozialpolitik und Verwaltung. vol. 1, Berlin–Bern 1901.

Hundert Jahre Schweizerischer Buchhändlerverein 1849–1949. (A century of the Swiss Booksellers' Association). Zürich 1949.

Le Livre d'Or de la librairie et de l'édition romande. (The golden book of bookselling and publishing in French Switzerland). Zürich 1967.

F. Lutz, *Aus der Geschichte des evangelischen Buchhandels in der Schweiz.* (From the history of the Protestant book trade in Switzerland). In: Reformierte Schweiz, vol. 11, Zürich 1944.

Der schweizerische Buchhandlungsgehilfen-Verein. (The Employees' Association of the Swiss Book Trade). Zürich 1908. Short history of the Association, 1883–1908.

5 Trade Press

Considering the small extent of the area of distribution, the function of the trade press is naturally more restricted than in more extensive markets. Nevertheless the "Anzeiger für den Schweizer Buchhandel" (1883–9 and 1890–97) ("The Swiss Book Trade Advertiser")—published as the Swiss "Börsenblatt", (→ Germany, 5)—made a comparatively early appearance. The corresponding foreign trade journals—German, French and Italian—play an additional and important role with those that appear in Switzerland.

Der Schweizer Buchhandel
(The Swiss Book Trade)
Bellerivestraße 3
CH 8008 Zürich

This is the official trade journal and organ of the SBVV (→ 4).
It consists of three parts: editorial, trade informations, advertisements. There is an annual index. Publication is fortnightly. Four special numbers appear during the year: the Easter Number (April), scientific books (June), an export number (October), and a Christmas number (November).
Der Buchhändler (The Bookseller). Official trade journal and organ of the "Angestelltenverein des Schweizer Buchhandels ASB" ("Employees' Association of the Swiss Book Trade", → 4). This consists of an editorial section, official information, local reports, a trade-book corner, and advertisements.—*13/12* → 4.
Edition. Journal of the "Interessengemeinschaft Schweizerischer Verleger" (→ 4).

6 Book-Trade Literature

Book-trade literature as such, dealing with book interests in Switzerland, does rarely exist. Apart from jubilee publications and calendars, present-day problems in the book trade have mostly been discussed in pamphlets (import and export restrictions, turnover tax, fixed retail prices), and in individual essays on book history, prices and copyright: see the bibliography section under individual chapters.

Adressbuch des Schweizer Buchhandels. (Address book of the Swiss book trade) Zürich, SBVV (→ 4).

7 Sources of Information, Address Services

General information on the book trade in Switzerland can be obtained from the secretariats of the various book-trade associations (→ 4):

Schweizerischer Buchhändler- und Verlegerverein
(The Swiss Booksellers' and Publishers' Association)
Bellerivestraße 3
CH 8008 Zürich

Société des Libraires et Éditeurs de la Suisse romande
(Association of Booksellers and Publishers in French Switzerland)
2 Avenue Agassiz
CH 1001 Lausanne

Information on specific matters can be obtained as follows:

Bibliography:
Schweizerische Landesbibliothek
(Swiss National Library)
Hallwylstraße 15
CH 3003 Bern

Technical matters:
Bibliothek der Eidgenössischen Technischen Hochschule
(Library of the Federal Technical University)
Leonhardstraße 13
CH 8006 Zürich

Authors:
Sekretariat des Schweizerischen Schriftstellervereins
(Secretariat of the Society of Swiss Authors)
Kirchgasse 25
CH 8001 Zürich

Book history:
Schweizerisches Gutenbergmuseum
(Swiss Gutenberg Museum)
Gewerbemuseum
Zeughausgasse 2
CH 3000 Bern

Statistics:
Eidgenössisches Statistisches Amt
(Federal Office of Statistics)
Hallwylstraße 15
CH 3003 Bern

Documentation:
Schweizerische Vereinigung für Dokumentation
(Swiss Association for Documentation)
Postfach
CH 3001 Bern

Bibliography

Adressbuch des Schweizer Buchhandels. (Address book of the Swiss book trade). → 4.

Fachbuch für Presse und Werbung. (Manual for the press and advertising). Published under the patronage of the Alliance of Swiss Advertising Advisers, Zürich.

Schweizer Jahrbuch des öffentlichen Lebens. (Swiss yearbook of public life). Ed. H. Reimann. Basel.
This yearbook contains all the addresses of offices and commissions of the Confederation, the Cantons, the parishes, industrial fairs and exhibitions, economic organizations, professional organizations, welfare and social institutions, youth and sport, science and culture, political parties, churches and other communities, international organizations and institutions.
It contains an index of persons and subjects.

8 International Membership

The cultural and geographical situation of Switzerland encourages the exploitation of all possibilities for free exchange in international culture. As a result of this tradition Switzerland is the seat of numerous international, political, cultural and judical organizations.
The Swiss Booksellers' and Publishers' Association (→ 4) also supports the principle of internationalism and liberty in the field of bookselling.
The SBVV is a member of:
the International Publishers' Association (IPA)
the International Community of Booksellers' Associations (ICBA).
The Vereinigung der Buchantiquare und Kupferstichhändler der Schweiz (VEBUKU) (Association of Swiss Antiquarian Booksellers and Dealers in Engravings, → 26), which is closely associated with the book trade, is a member of the International League of Antiquarian Booksellers (ILAB).
Switzerland is a member of Unesco.

9 Market Research

So far systematic, scientific book research does not exist in Switzerland. Neither universities nor private institutions have turned their attention to research into the book trade, book production or reading habits.
The need for this may not have been realized yet on account of the apparent ease with which the language and market areas can be surveyed, and also because of the practical and useful spirit that pervades the Swiss book trade.
In earlier years individual efforts dealt with the problems of book research in so far as they pursued practical aims, but not until 1959 was it decided to begin comprehensive investigations. The aim of this first investigation was "to increase productivity in the Swiss publishing and retail book trade by rationalization of methods within and between firms and on the book market". The inquiries of the Institute for Business Administration were analysed and evaluated in several volumes by the Research Centre for Trade at the Trade College of St Gallen. This publication represents the only scientific work in the field of book research in the narrower sense, apart from individual copyright, historical works (usually theses).
For juvenile book research there is the Johanna Spyri Stiftung (Foundation, → 10).

Bibliography

(W. Gnägi), *Die Rationalisierung im Sortimentsbuchhandel.* (Rationalization in the retail book trade). 2 vols. St. Gallen, Forschungsstelle für den Handel des Institutes für Betriebswissenschaft an der Hochschule St. Gallen für Wirtschaft- und Sozialwissenschaften 1962. 100, 159 pp.
(W. Gnägi), *Die Rationalisierung im Verlagsbuchhandel.* (Rationalization of book publishing). 2 vols. St. Gallen, Forschungsstelle 1963. 187, 250 pp.
E. Schumacher, *Der Leser in unserer Zeit.* (The Reader in our time). Frauenfeld 1963.
H. Weinhold, *Marktforschung für das Buch.* (Market research for books). St. Gallen 1956.
H. Zbinden, *Vom Buchklima unserer Zeit.* (The book climate in our time). Zürich 1953.

10 Books and Young People

It is to the credit of the "Schweizerische Gemeinnützige Gesellschaft" ("Swiss Voluntary Society") and the "Schweizerischer Lehrerverein" ("Swiss Teachers' Organization") that, since 1858, they have influenced the production of books for juveniles through their comments and criticism. With its central and cantonal commissions for juveniles' literature, the Swiss Teachers' Organization has had an important influence on the whole range of published writings for young people. Other influence for the promotion of good books for youth are school and local librarians, the foundation "Pro Juventute", and various religious and private organizations. All these efforts directed to the promotion of good books for children and young people are supported and centralized from the organizational side by the

Schweizerischer Bund für Jugendliteratur
(Swiss Alliance for Youth Literature)
Herzogstrasse 5
CH 3000 Bern

with its cantonal sections.

This overall organization comprises institutions and individual persons interested in the promotion of books for juveniles. The "Schweizerischer Bund für Jugendliteratur" is a part of the International Board on Books for Young People (→ International Section, 10) and publishes book lists like "Das Buch für Dich" ("The book for you"). It also participates in organizing book exhibitions for children and young people and advertising campaigns for juvenile literature.

The

Arbeitsgemeinschaft der Kinder- und Jugendbuchverleger
(Working Group of Publishers of Children's and Young People's Books)
at the Secretariat of the
Schweizerischer Buchhändler- und Verlegerverein
Bellerivestrasse 3
CH 8008 Zürich

deals with the organization of exhibitions and the publication of catalogues and advertising journals for books for children and young people within the framework of the Swiss Booksellers' and Publishers' Association. As part of the Swiss Teachers' Association, the

Jugendschriftenkommission
des Schweizerischen Lehrervereins
(The Commission for Juveniles' Books of the Swiss Teachers' Association)
Ringstrasse 54
CH 8057 Zürich

also looks after exhibitions, publishes the catalogue "Bücher für die Jugend" ("Books for youth"), and controls the "Wanderbüchereien des Schweizerischen Lehrervereins" ("Circulating Libraries of the Swiss Teachers' Association"). Since 1945 the Teachers' Association has donated the "Juvenile Book Prize of the Swiss Teachers' Association".

The

Johanna Spyri-Stiftung
Schweizerisches Jugendbuch Institut
Predigerplatz 18
CH 8001 Zürich

also engages in youth literature research.

The

Schweizerisches Jugendschriftenwerk
(Swiss Reading Material for Youth)
Postfach 8022
CH Zürich

was founded in 1931 within the framework of the "Stiftung Pro Juventute" to combat rubbish and filth in literature. Up to 1970 this institution had published 1,100 titles in German, French, Italian and Romansch.

The

Bureau International d'Éducation
(International Office of Éducation)
Palais Wilson
CH 1211 Genève

is also active in the field of schoolbooks and youth literature.

Bibliography

H. Cornioley, *Notwendigkeit, Aufgaben und Grenzen der Jugendbuchkritik.* (The necessity, task and limits of youth-book criticism). In: Schweizerische Lehrerzeitung, Zürich 1959.

I. Dyhrenfurth, *Geschichte des deutschen Jugendbuches.* (History of German children's literature). 3rd ed. pp. 265ff.: Deutschsprachiges Jugendschrifttum der Schweiz (Swiss juvenile literature in German). Zürich and Freiburg i. Br., Atlantis 1967. 324 pp.

Jugendliteratur. (Youth literature). Sonderheft über die Jugendliteratur in der Schweiz. (Special number on youth literature in Switzerland), 1961, no. 11. München, Juventa 1961.

Jugend und Lektüre. (Youth and reading). Lectures given at the Youth Book Course of the Commission for Youth Literature of the Swiss Teachers' Association in 1956. Zürich 1957.

Schweizerisches Jugendschriftenwerk. (Swiss Reading Material for Youth). Annual reports, since 1931.

Zwanzig Jahre Jugendbuchpreis in der Schweiz. (Twenty years of youth book prizes in Switzerland). Publications of the Swiss Teachers' Association, no. 37. Zürich 1963. 24 pp.

11 Training

The necessity for specialized booksellers' schools has always been recognized in addition to training through practical work in a retail bookshop under the guidance of a trained and experienced bookseller. Three-year specialist courses for the book trade were created in cooperation with the trade schools of the "Schweizerischer Kaufmännischer Verein" ("Swiss Mercantile Society") in Basle and Zurich, in Berne at an independent booksellers' school (since 1920). The various courses proved, however, to be inappropriate. With the cooperation of the "Société des Librairies et Éditeurs de la Suisse Romande" (→ 4) and the "Bundesamt für Industrie, Gewerbe und Arbeit" (BIGA) ("Federal Office for Industry, Trade and Labour") a "Reglement über die Ausbildung und die Lehrabschlußprüfung für die Berufe des Sortiments- und Verlagsbuchhändlers" ("Regulation governing the training and examination of apprentices for the retail and publishing book trade") was created (26 April 1968).

According to this an apprenticeship lasts for three years—two years for those having passed a college or similar school or having a trade diploma, and for trained business clerks. Examination subjects are: the retail trade, publishing, literature, the mother tongue, a first foreign language, correspondence, business practice and law, arithmetic, book-keeping, political and economic science, typewriting. Successful candidates in this examination are awarded the Federal Certificate qualifying them to act as trained booksellers or publishers' employees.

Apart from official training, the education and training of book-trade employees is fostered by the "Paritätische Kommission" (→ 4), by the so-called "Arbeitstagungen" ("Study weekends") in Gwatt (till 1956) and Muttenz (since 1966), and the annual "Buchbesprechungstag" ("Book-reviewing conference").

An inquiry into the working conditions of employees in the Swiss book trade, evaluated by the "Research Centre for Trade" at the University of St Gallen (→ 9), gave the following picture for the year 1964:

Employees with completed book-trade apprenticeship	79%
Employees with commercial apprenticeship	9%
Employees with no particular training	12%

In 1968 there were 639 employees who were members of the ASB (→ 4), of whom 423 were women and 216 men.

Bibliography

Buchhändler, ein Beruf mit Zukunft. (Bookselling, a profession with a future). Zürich 1967.

Reglement über die Ausbildung und Lehrabschlußprüfung für die Berufe des Sortiments- und des Verlagsbuchhändlers. (Regulation governing the training and examination of apprentices for the retail and publishing book trade of 26 April 1968).

Berufe des Buchhandels. (Profession in the book trade). Zürich 1969.

12 Taxes

Ever since the beginning of printing, books in Switzerland have had a privileged position (→ 2). In the course of the centuries this, however, has had to be defended against purely fiscal and bureaucratic thinking. Recently, under the pressure of the war years, books came under economic pressure with a "Warenumsatzsteuer" (WUST) ("turnover tax"), which for a time was openly and then covertly passed on to the purchasers. It was discontinued in 1958.

The traditional attitude, that it is part of the country's cultural policy not to raise taxes or customs duties on books, has meant that books in Switzerland are not subject to tax or customs duties. Switzerland follows the recommendations of UNESCO to implement the principle of the free flow of books.

Bibliography

Gründe und Voraussetzungen für die Aufhebung der Warenumsatzsteuer auf Büchern. (Reasons and prerequisites for the cancellation of the turnover tax on books). Zürich 1955.

Sollen Kultur und Bildung besteuert werden? (Should culture and education be taxed?). Zürich 1967.

13 Clearing Houses

A central clearing house for the book trade does not exist in Switzerland. With the introduction of "Verkehrsnummern" (Decision of the General Assembly of the SBVV in 1967), the creation of a "Abrechnungsstelle für den Schweizer Buchhandel" (Clearing House of the Swiss Book Trade) has been decided. The preparatory work on this is now progressing.

14 Copyright

The idea that copyright is a personal right of the author—as opposed to trade patents—was late in appearing in Switzerland. After regulations on a cantonal basis influenced by French legislation—Geneva (1793), Tessin (1798), Zurich (1832), Basle (1837), Solothurn (1847), Appenzell (1835), Fribourg (1851)—an inter-cantonal agreement came into being at Federal level in 1856. It was not until the Federal Constitution of 1874 was revised in 1884 that a Federal law made provision for copyright on works of literature and art. Present-day law is based on the "Bundesgesetz betr. das Urheberrecht an Werken der Literatur und Kunst vom 7. Dezember 1922, revidiert 1955" ("Federal law concerning copyright on works of literature and art of 7 December 1922, revised in 1955").

Switzerland has joined the following conventions safeguarding copyright internationally:

1. The Berne Convention for the Protection of Works of Literature and Art of 9 September 1886, supplemented in Paris 1896, revised in Berlin 1908, Berne 1914, Rome 1928 and Brussels 1948.
2. The World Copyright Convention of 6 September 1952, Geneva.

The following societies exist in Switzerland to safeguard utilization rights:

Dachgesellschaft der Urheberrechtsnutzer (Swiss Federation of Copyright Users)

Bollwerk 15
CH 3000 Bern

SUISA, Schweizerische Gesellschaft der Urheber und Verleger (Swiss Society of Authors and Publishers)
Bellariastr. 82
CH 8038 Zürich

Mechanlizenz, Schweizerische Gesellschaft für mechanische Urheberrechte (Swiss Society for Rights of Mechanical Reproduction)
Bellariastr. 82
CH 8038 Zürich

Geneva is the seat of the secretariat of the
United International Bureaux for the Protection of Intellectual Property (BIRPI)
32, Chemin des Colombettes
CH 1211 Genève

→ International Section, 14.

Bibliography

E. RÖTHLISBERGER, *Schweizer Urheber- und Verlagsrecht an Werken der Literatur und Kunst.* (Swiss copyright and publishing rights on works of literature and art). 2nd ed. revised by Mentha. Basel 1932. Text of the Copyright Law.

SAENGER, *Das Verhältnis der Berner Konvention zum innerstaatlichen Urheberrecht.* (The Berne Convention and national copyright law). Basel 1940.

STREULI, *Das Urheberrecht der Schweiz.* (Swiss copyright). In: Schweizerische Juristische Kartothek. Genève 1943.

A. TROLLER, *Brennpunkte der Schweizerischen Urheberrechts-Revision.* (The focal points in the revision of Swiss copyright). In: Schweizerischer Juristenverein, Referate und Mitteilungen. 1/1963. Basel 1963.

Periodicals

→ International Section, 14.

15 National Bibliography, National Library

The institution in Switzerland entrusted with the task of systematically collecting the whole national output of printed works is the
Schweizerische Landesbibliothek (Swiss National Library)
Hallwylstr. 15
CH 3003 Bern

It was founded in 1900. As part of its statutory obligations, it has taken over the systematic classification of the country's output of printed works with a bibliographical bulletin which is published in co-operation with the SBVV (→ 4).

This bibliographical bulletin has been appearing under the title *Das Schweizer Buch* ("The Swiss Book"), since 1900, as the successor to the privately printed "Bibliographie der Schweiz" ("Bibliography of Switzerland"), Basle, and shows all works published in Switzerland (individual works, annuals, magazines, geographical maps, printed music and recorded words) plus foreign publications with concern to Switzerland either on account of their author or contents. The "Swiss Book" embraces two series: Series A (half-monthly), containing publications of the book trade, Series B (bi-monthly), containing publications other than those of the book trade. The annual number A 16 is specially devoted to printed music. An index covering both series A and B is published annually, and contains a list of authors and key-words. The Swiss National Library publishes five-year indexes in co-operation with the Austrian National Library in Vienna (→ Austria 15) and the German Library in Frankfurt am Main (→ Germany, F. R., 15).

The most frequently used bibliographical reference work in the Swiss retail book trade is the *Lagerkatalog des Schweizer Buchzentrums, Olten* ("Stock catalogue of the

Swiss Book Centre, Olten"), previously known as the "Schweizerisches Vereinssortiment, Olten"—(using the name of "Swiss Book Centre" already at this period, → 23). This stock catalogue, which first appeared in 1900, and from 1930–40 as a card index, has included an alphabetical catchword and subject index since 1947, and since 1957 informations on the range and year of publication in the case of specialized and scientific works. The stock catalogue contains only those titles in stock.

Bibliography

Fünfzig Jahre Schweizerische Landesbibliothek. (Fifty years of the Swiss National Library), 1895–1945. Bern 1945.

M. GODET, *La Bibliothèque Nationale Suisse, son histoire, ses collections, son nouvel édifice.* (The Swiss National Library, its history, collections and new building). Bern 1932.

16 Book Production

In spite of the four different official languages and, therefore, a restricted market, book production in Switzerland is extensive. In 1967 there was one book per 948 persons.

During the Second World War the planning and production of Swiss publishing improved both in quantity and quality. In the post-war years Switzerland was able to increase its share of the German-speaking and international markets. The main achievements were reached in specialized scientific, art and picture books. The level of book production must, however, be viewed in conjunction with political and economic events. For instance, the years of economic crisis around 1920 and 1930 reveal a considerable decrease in production, whereas the muzzling of free book production in Germany in the thirties and forties led to an increase.

Year	Titles
1920	1,332
1930	2,095
1944	3,831
1948	4,691
1950	3,527
1960	4,817
1962	5,086
1964	4,941
1965	5,202
1966	4,817
1967	5,270
1968	5,213
1969	6,028

The following table shows the distribution according to languages:

Year	German	French	Italian	Romansch	Others
1962	3,463	1,106	72	32	413
1963	3,416	979	75	25	436
1964	3,342	1,041	78	27	453
1965	3,546	996	95	30	535
1966	3,437	837	74	40	429
1967	3,613	1,022	85	—	—
1968	3,531	1,067	88	32	495
1969	3,954	1,361	115	21	577

Switzerland

An analysis of production taken from individual subjects reflects a shifting in readers' interests. Some subjects are quoted as examples (see below).

Bibliography

Jahresbericht der Schweizerischen Landesbibliothek. (Annual report of the Swiss National Library).

Statistisches Jahrbuch der Schweiz. (Statistical year book of Switzerland).

E. VILLARD, *Le livre suisse. Publié par la Communauté d'action en faveur du livre.* (The Swiss Book. Published by the Action Committee to Promote Books). Boudry 1950.

17 Translations

The number of translations in the individual language areas of Switzerland reflects the independence from or influence of other, larger cultural areas. Anglo-Saxon influence on German-speaking Switzerland is evident, whereas French-speaking Switzerland has as much translations from the German. Tessin publishes for the most part books from its own cultural area; the amount of translations is only a small percentage of total production.

In 1967, with a total of 5,270 new titles, 700 books were translated from foreign languages: 25 from classical languages, 671 from European languages and 4 from other languages. The largest share of translations in 1967 is divided among the various languages as follows: English 403, French 113, German 44, Italian 28, Russian 23, Latin 14, Dutch 11, Spanish 10, Norwegian 9, Swedish 9.

Bibliography

Jahresbericht der Schweizerischen Landesbibliothek. (Annual report of the Swiss National Library).

Statistisches Jahrbuch der Schweiz. (Statistical yearbook of Switzerland).

18 Book Clubs

The expansion of Swiss book clubs began in the thirties. Up to that time German

Subject group	1951	1962	1965	1966	1967	1968	1969
Philosophy, psychology	163	158	123	133	134	155	183
Politics	376	48	66	59	—	80	92
Belles-lettres	713	931	808	652	819	808	1079
Literature for juveniles	272	331	333	256	268	288	382
History, folklore	309	232	324	335	348	354	389
Medicine	94	171	229	201	254	266	314
Natural sciences	117	136	179	130	153	167	184

Year	Total of translations	From German	French	English	Italian
1962	745	67	161	350	34
1967	700	44	113	403	28
1968	653	57	108	347	18
1969	973	80	135	610	43

book clubs had worked almost exclusively with branch offices or representatives in Switzerland.
Today there are some 12 book clubs in German- and French-speaking Switzerland. The book clubs' share of total book sales is estimated at 25%. There are altogether about 800,000 members, a fraction of whom have double membership. The acquisition of the books is based for the most part on the obligations connected with membership or through individual sales. Some clubs have modern well equipped shops in the larger towns, and these dispose of up to 50% of the titles offered by the book clubs. The number of titles offered is 800 as a maximum, predominately belles lettres, youth literature, informative books, art books and records. The offers are made through catalogues, regularly appearing magazines, or, in a few cases, through the mail-order system. Some of the book clubs also deliver to the retail trade, to which they grant a small rebate.
The Swiss book clubs are loosely connected through the *Vereinigung der Buchgemeinschaften der Schweiz* ("Association of Swiss Book Clubs"). Book clubs are in general rejected by the retail trade as an undesirable form of competition. Until 1951 Swiss publishers were forbidden to cooperate with the book clubs. The publishing world however, sees in the book clubs a valuable second market and a means of diminishing risks in the case of costly works or new editions. To safeguard the interests of the retail book trade an agreement was concluded between the SBVV (→ 4) and the most important Swiss book clubs in 1956; this governs the ways and means of granting publishing rights with reference to date of publication, nature of presentation and in some way price difference. This agreement was revised on 1969.

Bibliography

Abkommen zwischen dem Schweizerischen Buchhändler- und Verlegerverein (SBVV), Zürich und Ex Libris AG., Zürich, sowie Büchergilde Gutenberg, Zürich, und Schweizerische Volksbuchgemeinde, Luzern, vom 1. Januar 1969. (Agreement between the Swiss Publishers' and Booksellers' Association, Zurich, the Gutenberg Book Guild, Zurich, and the Swiss People's Book Society, Luzern, on 1 January 1969).

19 Paperbacks

After the "Kleine Reihen" ("Small series") and the "Volksausgaben" ("Popular editions"), the paperback, imitating America, has proved a successful form of book production since the Second World War.
With its large editions the paperback in its modern form demands wider markets and can only be planned and distributed by well-organized and large-sized publishing houses.
For this reason only a few pocket-book series have sprung up in Switzerland. Actually there are five paperback series, two of which are devoted to juveniles.

20 Book Design

Greatly increased book production during the war years awakened a sense of aesthetic responsibility for the lay-out of books. For the first time in 1944 the SVBB (→ 4) submitted the production of the previous year to a jury. From the annual awards of the "Best-designed Swiss Books" the publishers' group hope to invigorate standards of quality among publishers and to educate the reading public aesthetically. The jury consists of a member of each of the following institutions: the Swiss Work Alliance, the Association of Swiss Bookbinders, the As-

sociation of Swiss Illustrators, the Swiss Book Printers' Association, the Union of Swiss Typographers, and representatives of book-trade organizations. The books are judged with respect to material, lay-out, printing, binding, dust-cover and general impression. Individual kinds of books have their own particular scale of values: general literature, scientific works and textbooks, books on art and photography, youth literature, bibliophile editions and books that do not pass through the usual trade channels.
A catalogue based on these awards, "The Best-designed Swiss Books", appears annually with illustrations and biographical and typographical notes.

Bibliography

J. Tschichold, *Das schöne Schweizerbuch.* (The well-designed Swiss book). In: Die Welt im Buch der Schweiz, special edition of "Echo". (Journal for Swiss people living abroad). March 1945, pp. 28ff.

21 Publishing

The geographical location of the most important publishing houses in Switzerland has remained the same from the beginning. In most cases these publishing houses have developed from a printing house or a bookshop. A purely publishing firm is rare in Switzerland, even today. The importance and efficiency of publishing firms have varied considerably in the course of the centuries. After a golden age lasting from the sixteenth into the eighteenth century, there was a rapid decline. In the nineteenth century almost all important authors in the literary and scientific fields had their works published in Germany. Political developments in Germany at the beginning of the 1930s led numerous authors to emigrate to Switzerland, thus encouraging a rise in the fortunes of Swiss publishing.

Today 148 publishers and 103 recognized publishers are associated with the SBVV (→ 4). In French Switzerland 60 publishers (35 publishers; 25 bookseller-publishers) belong to the professional association (→ 4). The publishers are distributed among 36 places in Switzerland, the most important being: Zurich (55 publishers and 32 recognized publishers); Basle (22 publishers and 11 recognized publishers); Lausanne (20 publishers); Berne (20 publishers and 7 recognized publishers); Geneva (19 publishers).
The distribution among the language areas is as follows:
102 publishers in German-speaking Switzerland, 50 in French-speaking Switzerland and 1 in Italian-speaking Ticino (Tessin). This does not include recognized publishers.
The size of publishing houses can only be given from the number of employees. The following table includes those associated with the SBVV (→ 4):

Employees	Publishing houses
30 and more	2
20 and more	1
17 and more	5
14 and more	3
13 and more	6
8 and more	10
6 and more	12
4 and more	15
2 and more	35
1 employee and/or owner	59

Structurally Swiss publishing firms are for the most part small businesses with a small production of titles. The mixed publishing houses are in the majority as far as production is concerned.
A movement towards concentration cannot as yet be determined in Swiss publishing.
The most important achievements are to be found among art books, scientific books and multi-coloured picture books.

Apart from the privately organized publishers, schoolbook publishers who are financed out of public funds must be mentioned; they enjoy to some extent a monopoly with respect to their publications.

Bibliography

M. Haupt, *Situation und Aufgabe des Schweizer Verlages.* (Situation and tasks of Swiss publishing houses). In: Schweizer Buchhandel (The Swiss Book Trade), XII, 1954, pp. 310ff.

H. Hauser, *Aspects et rôles des éditeurs suisses en langue française.* (Aspects and role of publishers in French-speaking Switzerland). Nancy 1961.

M. Hürlimann, *Zur Situation des Schweizer Verlages.* (On the position of Swiss publishing). Zürich 1954.

W. Nauer, *Der schweizerische Verlagsbuchhandel.* (The Swiss book-publishing world). 1964.

J. Rast, *Zu den Problemen des Schweizer Verlages.* (On the problems of publishing in Switzerland). Zürich 1966.

22 Literary Agents

In most cases there is little need for literary agents in Swiss publishing firms. Relations between author and publisher are on a basis of personal trust which would be disturbed or complicated by any intermediary. In relations with foreign authors, too, personal contact with the author or original publishing firm is preferred. A real need for a literary agent only arises where the production of a firm becomes difficult to survey in its entirety, so that a division of work becomes a pressing need. Publishing firms of this size are rare in Switzerland, and for this reason literary agents play a very subordinate role in Swiss publishing.

23 Wholesale Trade

In view of the small area involved, the wholesale trade does not play the same part as in larger areas of distribution. The most important wholesale firm of the book trade was therefore not called into being in order to organize distribution, but for the needs of the retail book trade to be able to make purchases of mutual interest on an economic basis.

The

Schweizer Buchzentrum
(Swiss Book Centre)
Amthausquai 23
CH 4600 Olten

formerly known as the "Schweizerisches Vereinssortiment" ("Swiss Cooperative Book Trade Association") from its foundation in 1882 to 1968, has been an association aiming at creating better economic conditions of book purchase for its members. Today the Swiss Book Centre exercises the functions of a Swiss wholesale firm of the book trade with associated publishers' deliveries and an efficient exporting organization. It has 202 members and had a turnover of 21 m Swiss francs in 1967.

A catalogue which appears annually provides information on the stock at the Book Centre—in 1970 it had 35,000 titles (→ 15). In cooperation with the Swiss National Library (→ 15) the Book Centre also publishes the "Schweizerischer Zeitschriften- und Zeitungskatalog" ("Catalogue of Swiss magazines and newspapers").

The

Office du livre SA
(Book House Ltd)
CH 1701 Fribourg

works in a rather different way. It was founded in 1946 and is not only a wholesale firm. The "Office du livre" represents an important number of French and German publishers for Switzerland and has an almost complete range of their productions in stock. A catalogue of its stock (Lagerkatalog—Office du livre) appears annually. The "Office du livre" devotes itself principally to exports, and it produces annually the catalogue "Ouvrages suisses de langue française" ("Swiss books in French" with about 25,000 titles, and a "Schweizerisches Zeitschriftenverzeichnis" ("Index of Swiss Magazines"). The "Office du livre" has a list of 1,800 bookshops as regular customers in 49 countries.

About 130 specialized firms exercise in a modest way a wholesale function with respect to the production of home and foreign publishers. These firms are listed in the *Verzeichnis der Auslieferungsstellen* ("Index of warehousing firms"), latest edition 1968.

Bibliography

H. Helbing, *Das Schweizerische Vereinssortiment Olten 1882–1957*. Festschrift zum 75jährigen Bestehen des Unternehmens. (The Swiss Cooperative Book Trade Association, Olten 1882–1957. Commemorative publication on its 75th anniversary). Olten 1957.

F. Hess, *Die Entstehung der Barsortimente unter der besonderen Berücksichtigung der genossenschaftlich aufgebauten Betriebe*. (The rise of wholesale firms of the book trade, with special reference to firms on a cooperative basis). Olten 1957.

24 Retail Trade

One of the most important problems in the book trade remains the safeguarding of the means of marketing books. The total turnover of books in Switzerland is estimated at 500,000,000 sfr., the turnover in retail bookshops being 300,000,000 sfr. Despite new systems of book distribution, such as book clubs, mail orders and departmental stores, the retail book trade remains the most important channel. In Switzerland there is a dense network of bookselling places (417 retail bookshops and 187 other outlets for the resale of books in 262 towns, etc.).

There is a retail bookshop for every 11,990 inhabitants, but the two most recent federal trade censuses (1955 and 1965) have shown that the number of bookshops has decreased by 20%. Most of the retail bookshops are of a general nature. Specialist bookshops (for medicine, technology, etc.) exist only in large or university towns. The shop is often attached to a printing or publishing firm (27% of Swiss publishing firms own a bookshop).

Book outles are mostly mixed undertakings with their book section attached to the sale of newspapers or stationery, or to a lending library. The bookstall plays a role chiefly at railway stations—there are no station bookshops in Switzerland—and at traffic centres in towns. The sale of books in department stores has only recently had any success, and not every department store keeps books. Pure mail-order bookselling is only beginning to take shape.

The larger centres of the retail book trade are: Zurich (56 retail shops, 19 bookselling outlets); Lausanne (28 retail shops, 6 bookselling outlets); Basle (28 retail shops, 1 bookselling outlet); Berne (21 retail shops, 1 bookselling outlet).

General developments in sales technique and shop decoration have forced the traditionally minded book trade—with 32 of its existing bookshops founded before 1900—to reshape its shops according to modern ideas.

The small and medium-sized shop predominates in the Swiss book trade. This means that the average turnover is small in size and is estimated at 300,000 sfr. The trend towards the large or specialised bookshop cannot be overlooked.

Bibliography

F. Hess, *Die wirtschaftliche Seite des Sortiments*. (The economic side of the retail book trade). Zürich 1943.

W. Röpke, *Der wirtschaftliche Standort des Buchhändlers*. (The economic situation of the bookseller). Olten 1959.

W. RÜEGG, *Der gesellschaftliche Sinn des Buchhändlers.* (The social significance of the bookseller). Olten 1962.

R. SCHINDLER, *Buchhändler, ein Beruf mit Zukunft.* (Bookselling, a profession with a future). Zürich 1967.

E. SUTTER, *Einführung in den Sortimentsbuchhandel.* (Introduction to the retail book trade). 3rd ed. Frauenfeld 1961.

25 Mail-Order Bookselling

The dense network of Swiss bookshops on a relatively small marketing area has left little scope for the mail-order business. Apart from individual cases, where it is being undertaken by bookshops—in some cases incidentally—the mail-order business is usually associated with firms publishing specialized literature (→ 24). Those firms responsible for the mail-order business are placed by the sales regulations in the category of retail booksellers.

26 Antiquarian Book Trade, Auctions

The antiquarian book trade in Switzerland is restricted to a very few firms. Important antiquarian book firms that deal on an international basis and hold auctions with old and costly books are to be found predominantly in French-speaking Switzerland (Geneva, Lausanne, Neuchâtel) and in Basle and Zurich.

The greater part of the antiquarian book trade consists of departments in the larger retail bookshops or deals with second-hand books (remainders). Antiquarian booksellers are members of the *Vereinigung der Buchantiquare und Kupferstichhändler—VEBUKU* ("Association of Antiquarian Booksellers and Dealers in Engravings), which has formed a working group with the SBVV (→ 4) and the SLESR (→ 4). The Association is internationally linked with ILAB (→ International Section, 26). The seat of VEBUKU is always at the business address of its president.

27 Book Imports

Statistics of book imports are based on the official external trade figures for Switzerland. However, these statistics do not give an accurate picture, since dispatches by book post are not included, and books printed abroad but on the accounts of Swiss publishing houses are not distinguished from actual book imports.

The development of total imports of books and magazines in millions of sfr:

1963:	119.4
1964:	138.8
1965:	154.8
1966:	174.5
1967:	197.1
1968:	220.1
1969:	243.5

Book imports from German-speaking countries (in million of sfr.):

Federal Republic of Germany	
1963	69.4 (37.3)
1964	84.2 (44.6)
1965	93.6 (49.4)
1966	110.0 (58.1)
1967	122.6 (63.9)

Austria	
1963	3.4 (2.7)
1964	3.8 (2.9)
1965	4.5 (3.5)
1966	4.5 (3.5)
1967	4.9 (3.3)

German Democratic Republic	
1963	— (0.184)
1964	— (0.407)
1965	— (0.391)
1966	— (0.449)
1967	— (0.567)

Numbers in brackets represent pure book imports without magazines or other productions of the graphical industry.

Switzerland

Book imports from other countries (a selection):

	France	USA	United Kingdom	Italy
1963	41.7 (19.3)	0.4 (1.6)	6.5 (1.9)	11.9 (2.5)
1964	46.8 (22.1)	5.4 (2.5)	9.7 (2.0)	13.1 (2.3)
1965	48.3 (23.0)	8.8 (5.5)	9.6 (1.9)	14.5 (2.5)
1966	51.0 (25.0)	7.2 (3.5)	10.2 (2.0)	16.2 (3.2)
1967	54.0 (26.0)	8.1 (3.5)	11.6 (2.6)	24.2 (8.4)

Numbers in brackets represent pure book imports, excluding magazines or other productions of the printing industry.
As far as imports are concerned, the Federal Republic of Germany is Switzerland's most important trading partner, i. e. in matters of book production Switzerland is one of the Federal Republic's best customers, since she purchases 26.1% of German book exports (1967). The greatly increasing import of books from Italy is due to the rapid growth in the number of Italians working in Switzerland and books printed in Italy for Swiss publishers.

28 Book Exports

The figures for Swiss book exports can be taken from the official statistics for foreign trade. These figures too are only approximate in so far as no distinction is made between the export of books of Swiss origin and those book exports of the printing industry undertaken on behalf of foreign firms. Furthermore the "invisible exports" are missing too, i.e. books produced abroad on behalf of Swiss publishers and sold abroad.
Swiss book exports are affected by the "import compensation tax" of various countries. In addition certain traditional markets have disappeared or greatly decreased (Czechoslovakia, Poland, Hungary, South America). Swiss publishing houses get no export subsidy for their exports. The Federal Republic of Germany is the main customer for Swiss book production (22.2% of the Federal Republic's book imports came from Switzerland in 1967).
Book exports to German-speaking countries (in million of sfr.):

Year	Federal Republic of Germany	Austria	German Democratic Republic
1963	24.6 (19.5)	4.6 (2.5)	— (0.06)
1964	27.7 (22.9)	4.2 (2.12)	— (0.09)
1965	31.8 (24.0)	4.4 (2.1)	— (0.12)
1966	39.9 (25.8)	5.0 (2.2)	— (0.22)
1967	42.0 (26.5)	6.0 (2.4)	— (0.22)
1968	35.6 (28.8)	3.0 (2.2)	— (0.24)
1969	36.8 (29.3)	3.0 (2.4)	— (0.42)

Numbers in brackets represent pure book exports, excluding magazines or other productions of the general printing industry.
Book exports to other countries (a selection):

Year	France	USA	United Kingdom	Italy
1963	23.5 (16.8)	10.9 (6.3)	5.1 (1.9)	5.7 (2.9)
1964	27.8 (20.2)	14.7 (9.0)	5.6 (2.3)	5.5 (3.0)
1965	34.6 (26.3)	18.1 (12.6)	6.2 (2.6)	8.4 (6.2)
1966	45.9 (36.3)	22.7 (16.7)	6.9 (3.3)	5.7 (3.3)
1967	60.0 (48.2)	23.8 (18.6)	12.4 (7.7)	6.7 (3.5)
1968	47.7 (44.1)	18.4 (17.8)	10.5 (9.6)	3.5 (2.8)
1969	47.7 (43.9)	22.4 (21.6)	10.5 (9.4)	3.0 (2.1)

Numbers in brackets represent pure book exports, excluding magazines or other productions of the printing industry.

29 Book Fairs

In Switzerland there are no fairs offering purchasing facilities to the retail book trade. However, publishers and booksellers have always taken part in important All-Swiss exhibitions with representative book exhibitions (National Exhibitions 1914, 1939, 1964, Basle Trade Fair since 1940). Local associations also hold regional and in part original exhibitions to support and

promote Christmas sales (e.g. "Bücherschiff" in Zurich—since 1952).
Youth book exhibitions are also held annually in cooperation with the "Schweizerischer Bund für Jugendliteratur" ("Swiss Alliance for Youth Literature").

30 Public Relations

Only in recent times has the book trade increasingly realized that books do not hold an undisputed position in the public mind, but that from an economic point of view they have to compete with numerous everyday and luxury articles, and that book-reading cannot be taken for granted. For a long time the advertising efforts of the SBVV (→ 4) were devoted to common efforts (pamphlets, catalogues, posters, exhibitions), which are really the province of individual publishers and retail booksellers; but now interest is slowly being awakened in fundamental research into the book market, public relations through press, radio and television, increased association with organizations and associations related with the book trade, and in promoting among booksellers an attitude which is appreciative of the market situation by means of courses and other methods of enlightenment.
This is the purpose of the

Schweizerische Werbestelle für das Buch
(Swiss Centre for Book Promotion)
Bellerivestrasse 3
CH 8008 Zürich

in the SBVV (→ 4).
The Centre organizes and coordinates cooperative advertising and public relations with respect to books in Switzerland. The Centre publishes the Swiss Book News, *Domino*, (19th year of publication in 1970, sales 64–65,000). It is also responsible for the *Schweizerischen Bücherbon* ("Swiss book token"), which can be exchanged in any bookshop throughout Switzerland.

Bibliography

E. Bäschlin and F. Witz, *Buch und Presse.* (Books and the press). Zürich n. d.
Kollektivwerbung für das Buch. (Cooperative book promotion). St. Gallen, Forschungsstelle für den Handel an der Handels-Hochschule St. Gallen.

31 Bibliophily

In Switzerland books for bibliophiles are above all the concern of private associations such as the *Schweizerische Bibliophilen-Gesellschaft* ("Swiss Bibliophiles' Society"), and *Schweizerisches Gutenbergmuseum;* but there are also publishers and printers with bibliophile interests.
The

Schweizerische
Bibliophilen-Gesellschaft
(Swiss Bibliophiles' Society)
Rämipostfach
CH 8024 Zürich

publishes the journal *Librarium* (earlier known as "Stultifera navis"). It also publishes editions for its members. In 1931 the following commemorative publication was issued: "Schweizer Bibliophilen-Gesellschaft, Festschrift zu ihrem zehnjährigen Bestehen 1921–1931". ("Swiss bibliophiles' Society, commemorative publication on its tenth anniversary, 1931").
The "Schweizerisches Gutenbergmuseum" ("Swiss Gutenberg Museum") Society has been responsible since 1914 for the journal

Schweizerisches Gutenbergmuseum
(Swiss Gutenberg Museum)
CH 3000 Bern

This publication is devoted to book-printing, the history of the press, bibliophily and library matters. For information on the museum belonging to this society → Book Museums, p. 64.
The publishing activities of the

Vereinigung der Oltner Bücherfreunde

(Association of Olten Book Friends)
CH 4600 Olten
are to be found in the bibliography "Die 100 V O B Publikationen 1936–1965". ("The 100 publications of the Association of Olten Book Friends, 1936–1965"), which appeared in 1965 in the journal "Der Schweizer Sammler" written by W. Matheson.

Bibliography

F. C. Lonchamp, *Manuel du bibliophile suisse.* (Manual of the Swiss bibliophile). Paris/Lausanne 1922.
→ above, also for periodicals.

32 Literary Prizes

Apart from literary prizes awarded by private foundations, there are those awarded by Federal authorities, cantons and towns. Generally speaking these literary prizes have little influence on the public and, considering the usually small sum of money involved, simply serve as a mark of honour to the writer and artist.
Charles Veillon Prize for novels in German, Lausanne. (Prize for novels in French since 1947 and for Italian since 1948). Donor: Charles Veillon.
Literary prize of the Canton of Zurich.
Emil Bührle Foundation for Swiss Writings, Zurich. Donor: Emil Bührle
Hugo Jacobi Foundation, Prize for New Lyric Writing. Donor: Hugo Jacobi.
Inner-Swiss Foundation's Cultural and Literary Prize (since 1955).
Youth Book Prize of the Swiss Teachers' Associations (since 1943).
Cultural Prize of the town of St Gallen (since 1954).
Art Prize of the town of Basle (since 1948).
Art Prize of the town of Luzern (since 1955).
Art Prize of the town of Olten (since 1963).
Art Prize of the town of Winterthur.
Literary Prize of the town of Berne (since 1939).
Literary Prize of the town of Zurich (since 1930).
Literary Prize of the Canton of Basle-Land. Donor: the Canton of Basle-Land.
Literary Prize of the Canton of Berne. Donor: the Cantonal literary commission of Berne.
Literary Prize of the Canton of Aargau/Aarau. Donor: the Administration of the Canton of Aargau.
The Lions Club Prize, Basle (since 1954).
The Swiss Schiller Foundation, Zurich (since 1905).
The Radio Prize of Switzerland, St Gallen (since 1951).
The Solothurn Art Prize, Solothurn (since 1965).
The Welti Foundation for Drama, Berne (since 1923).
The Georg Fischer Prize, Schaffhausen. Donor: Georg Fischer AG. and the town of Schaffhausen.
The Ulrico Hoeppli Foundation, Zurich. Donor: Ulrico Hoeppli.
The Holderbank Foundation, for the promotion of further training in science and art.
The Foundation of the Swiss National Exhibition, Zurich (since 1939).
The Swiss National Fund for the Promotion of sciences, Berne (since 1952).
The Pro Helvetia Foundation, among others for the promotion of Swiss writing, Zurich.
The Swiss Foundation for Literature, Music and the Graphic Arts, Basle (since 1966).
The Jubilee Fund of the Swiss Banks Association, Zurich (since 1962).
The Conrad Ferdinand Meyer Foundation, Zurich (since 1937). Foundress: Luise Elisabetha Camille Meyer.

33 The Reviewing of Books

The Swiss press is particularly interested in cultural information. Book reviews are published in the cultural section of almost every newspaper ("Neue Zürcher Zeitung", Zurich; "St. Galler Tagblatt", St Gallen e. g.) and magazine. Most advertising in the large dailies is for literature and popular science. Specialized journals are at the disposal of the various sciences; youth books receive support above all through the critical articles on juvenile literature to be found in teachers' journals and those devoted to youth literature.
The following are book newspapers and magazines containing reviews:
(→ 5, 30, 31).

Domino, published by the "Schweizerische Werbestelle für das Buch" (→ 30).

Das Bücherblatt, supported by a working group of Swiss booksellers.

Das neue Buch, a magazine of book advice, published by the "Schweizerischer katholischer Presseverein" ("Swiss Catholic Press Association").

Das Jugendbuch (Youth Books), supplement to the Swiss Teachers' Journal.

Jugendschriftenbeilage (Youth Books Supplement) of the Swiss School. Decisions on new publications by the public and educational libraries.

Bulletin bibliographique (Bibliographical Bulletin), supplement of L'Éducateur (The Educator).

In addition there are juvenile-book supplements to the school-news publications of the cantons of Aargau, Basle, Berne, Solothurn, St Gallen and Zurich.
Both radio and television devote much time to the world of literature. These mass media thus perform a great service to public relations and book promotion.
Of the total broadcasting time on the radio in 1967, 26.8% was devoted to the spoken word, with 4.7% for radio plays, 2.3% for youth programmes and 10.1% for talks and lectures. Of the total television time in 1967, 5.9% was devoted to culture and science, 4.1% to the theatre and 7.3% to youth programmes.

Bibliography

Fachbuch für Presse und Werbung. (Press and promotion manual). Zürich, Verlag Senger-Annoncen.

Handbuch der Reklame (Handbook of advertising).

Schweizerische Werbeagenda. (Swiss advertising agenda).

A. THOMMEN, *Die Schweizer Presse in der modernen Gesellschaft.* (The Swiss press in modern Society). Zürich 1967.

34 Graphic Arts

The over-all organization of the graphic industry is the

Schweizerische Arbeitsgemeinschaft für das Buch
(Swiss Study Group for Promoting Books)
CH 2017 Boudry NE

founded in 1949, which not only includes the professional book trade associations (SBVV, SLESR, → 4), but also the trade organizations of printers, binders, the paper industry and their employees' association.
Among the most important graphic associations in Switzerland are:

Schweizerischer Buchdruckerverein
(The Swiss Book Printers' Association)
Carmenstrasse 6
CH 8030 Zürich

Verein schweizerischer Lithographiebesitzer
(The Association of Swiss Lithographers)
Schlosshaldenstrasse 20
CH 3000 Bern

Vereinigung der Tiefdruckanstalten der Schweiz
(Association of Swiss Photogravure Printing Works)

Effingerstrasse 14
CH 3000 Bern

Verein der Buchbindereibesitzer der Schweiz
(Association of Swiss Bookbinders)
Rue de Saint-Jean 98
CH 1211 Genève

Verband schweizerischer Graphiker
(Association of Swiss Graphic Designers)
Chorgasse 18
CH 8001 Zürich

Schweizerischer Zeitungsverlegerverband
(Association of Swiss Newspaper Publishers)
Röntgenstrasse 16
CH 8005 Zürich

Bibliography

R. Bitterli, *Das Schweizerische Buchbindergewerbe.* Standort und Entwicklungstendenzen. (The Swiss bookbinding trade, its situation and development possibilities). Zürich 1962.

Schweizerischer Buchdruckverein. (The Swiss Book Printers' Association). Beiträge zur Geschichte des Buchdrucks in der Schweiz. (Contributions to the history of book printing in Switzerland). Commemorative publication on the 75th anniversary of the Swiss Printers' Association 1869–1944. Zürich 1944.

H. Strehler, *Das graphische Gewerbe in der Schweiz.* (The printing trade in Switzerland). St Gallen 1944.

35 Miscellaneous

Textbooks

In Switzerland schools come under the authority of the cantons. In the case of the small cantons, with their correspondingly smaller requirements, this makes the acquisition of appropriate educational aids difficult. In view of the competition from the state publishing houses of teaching aids in the larger cantons, the private textbook publisher can only survive after tremendous effort.

Within the framework of the SBVV (→ 4) there is a *Arbeitsgemeinschaft der schweizerischen Schulbuchverleger* ("Working Group of Swiss Textbook Publishers"), which devotes itself to questions and problems of the private production of textbooks.

Swiss textbook publishers are regularly represented at DIDACTA (→ International Section, 29) and at special Unesco conferences devoted to textbooks.

In order to coordinate education and textbooks, the education departments of the cantons maintain the

Zentrale Informationsstelle für Fragen des Schul- und Erziehungswesens
(Central Information Office for Questions of School and Educational Policy)
Palais Wilson
CH 1211 Genève

The Working group mentioned above also has a loose association with the

Bureau International d'Éducation
(International Office of Education)
Palais Wilson
CH 1211 Genève

which is an inter-state organization (→ 10).

Turkey

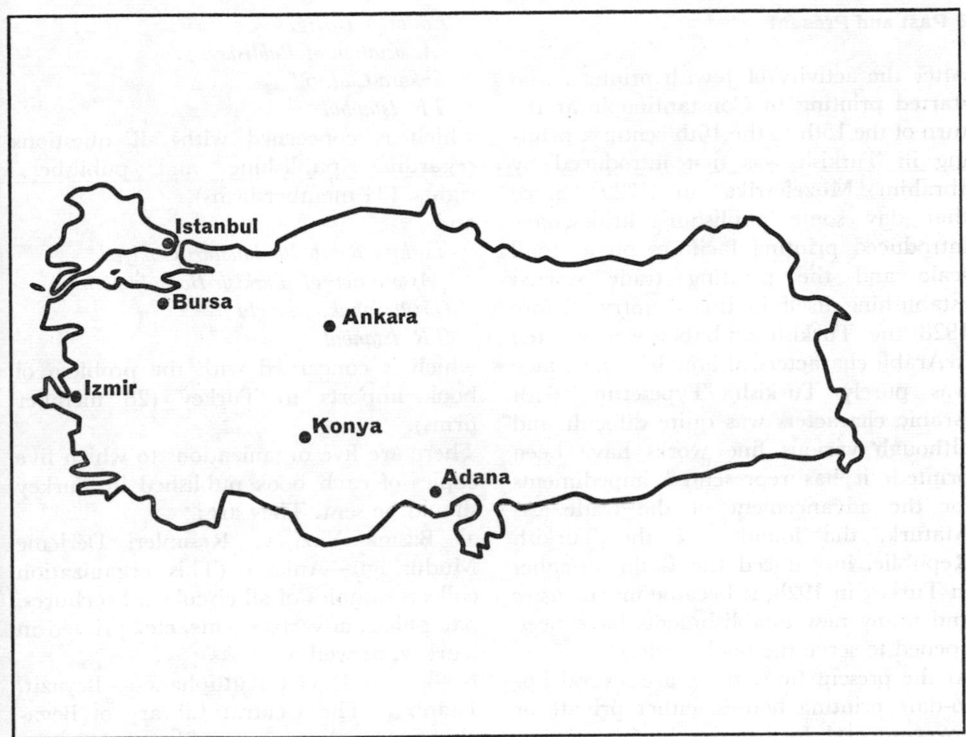

Important Book Centres

1 General Information

Area 780,000 km²
Population 33,203,000 (41.3 per km²)
Capital Ankara (745,000)
Largest towns Istanbul (2,150,000); Ankara (745,000); Izmir (565,000); Adana (330,000); Konya (280,000); Bursa (220,000)
Government The Republic of Turkey is a democratic state with a single central secular power
Religion Muslim 94.9%
Others 5.1%
National language Turkish
Leading foreign languages English, French, German
Weights and measures Metric system
Currency unit Türk Lirasi (TL.)
Education Compulsory: 450,000 students in primary schools; 235,000 students in secondary schools; 148,000 students in higher schools (lycée); 70,000 students in Universities, technical or professional schools
Illiteracy 48%
Paper consumption a) Newsprint 18 kg per inhabitant (1967)
b) Printing paper (other than newsprint) 1.7 kg per inhabitant (1967)
Membership UNESCO, IPA

2 Past and Present

After the activity of Jewish printers, who started printing in Constantinople at the turn of the 15th to the 16th century, printing in Turkish was first introduced by Ibrahim Müzeferrika in 1729. Since that day some publishing firms have introduced printing facilities on a small scale and the printing trade started establishing itself in this country. Before 1928 the Turkish alphabet was written in Arabic characters, although the language was purely Turkish. Typesetting with Arabic characters was quite difficult and although various fine works have been printed, it has represented impediments for the advancement of the trade. As Atatürk, the founder of the Turkish Republic, introduced the Latin alphabet in Turkey in 1928, it became much easier and many new establishments have been opened to serve the book trade.
At the present time, there are several up-to-date printing houses, either private or governmental, for printing books.

Bibliography

J. Baysal (Buğra), *Osmanli türklerinin bastiklari Kitaplar*. Istanbul 1968. 88 pp. Bibliography of Turkish book production from 1729 to 1847. Numerous historical remarks and sources are added. Summary in German.

3 Retail Prices

The prices of books published in Turkey are set by the publishers themselves, with no restriction whatsoever by the government, nor are they bound by laws.

4 Organization

There are two major publishers' and booksellers' associations in existence in Turkey:

Editörler Birliği
(Association of Publishers)
Ankara Cad. 62
TR Istanbul

which is concerned with all questions regarding publishing and publishers' rights. (34 member firms),
and

Türkiye Kitap Ithalatcilari Cemiyeti
(Association of Turkish Book Importers)
Gönül Sokak, Beyoglu
TR Istanbul

which is concerned with the problem of book imports to Turkey (28 member firms).
There are five organizations to which five copies of each book published in Turkey should be sent. They are:
a) Basma Yazi ve Resimleri Derleme Müdürlüğü—Ankara (This organization collects samples of all circulars, brochures, pamphlets, advertisements, etc., printed in Turkey, as well as books);
b) Beyazit Devlet Kütüphanesi—Beyazit, Istanbul (The Central Library of Beyazit);
c) Il Halk Kütüphanesi—Ankara (State Public Library of Ankara);
d) Milli Kütüphane—Ankara (The National Library of Ankara)—also publishes the two major trade papers;
e) Milli Kütüphane—Izmir (Izmir Branch of the National Library).

5 Trade Press

The major trade paper in Turkey is

Türk Bibliografya Dergisi
Namik Kemal Mahallesi
TR Ankara

which is published by the *Milli Kütüphane* ("The National Library", → 15) in Ankara. This quarterly official magazine was published by "Basma Yazi ve Resimleri Derleme Md.", Ankara, a department of "Milli Eğitim Bakanliği" ("The Ministry of Education") up to 1953. With the Law

of the National Library, which went into effect in 1953, the National Library was established and took over the Ministry of Education's publication of this magazine in 1955.
"Milli Kütüphane" publishes also the *Türkiye Makaleler Bibliyografyasi* ("Turkish Bibliography of Editorials and Articles"), which includes all editors and articles printed in newspapers and periodicals in Turkey every quarter. This magazine, as well as the "Türk Bibliyografya Dergisi", uses the Dewey System.
In addition to these two official trade papers there are some private organizations: *Milliyet,* one of the leading newspapers, announces almost all the major book publications of the week, once every week. The major publishers print monthly or quarterly brochures of their publications, which they distribute regularly.
The most important private trade paper is

Kitap Belleten
Elif Kitabevi
Sahaflar Carşisi No. 4
Beyazit
TR Istanbul

This monthly gives all the new publications of the month.
Another of these papers is

Yeni Yayinlar
(New Publications)
Yeni Mahalle
TR Ankara

Some semi-official organizations, such as:
Türk Tarih Kurumu (Association of Turkish History), Ankara;
Türk Dil Kurumu (Association of Turkish Language), Ankara;
Maden Tetkik ve Arama Enstitüsü (Association of Research in Metals), Ankara;
Orta Doğu Teknik Üniversitesi (Technical University of Orta Doğu), Ankara;
Istanbul Üniversitesi (University of Istanbul), Istanbul, have semestrial or annual catalogues consisting of their own publications.

7 Sources of Information, Address Services

Millî Kütüphane
(The National Library)
Namik Kemal Mahallesi
TR Ankara

Amerikan Neşriyati Bürosu
387 Istiklal Cad.
TR Istanbul

8 International Membership

The Turkish publishing world is a member of the "International Publishers' Association" and of UNESCO.

9 Market Research

Although there is no established market research in Turkey for the book trade, one may always apply to:
a) Piyasa Etüd ve Araştirma Merkezi (The Centre of Market Study and Research), Istanbul;
b) Devlet Istatistik Enstitüsü (State Institute of Statistics), Ankara,
for questions in market research for books.

10 Books and Young People

The younger generation constitutes the bulk of consumers for the book market in Turkey, especially in Istanbul, Ankara, Izmir, Adana, Trabzon, and in other major cities in the country.
Their largest demand is for books of "nouvelle vogue" literature, works of a political, social, and economic nature, books on local matters on social and traditional life, political satires.
Lately children's books for the very young are being treated with due attention and this trade is flourishing.

Turkey

11 Training

The main establishment is *Ankara Üniversitesi Kütüphanecilik Okulu* ("Library Section of the University of Ankara")—*Dil ve Tarih-Coğrafya Fakültesi, Ankara,* which has been in existence a number of years and which graduates an average of 100–120 trained personnel yearly. Beside this, there are some private or semi-private establishments which train people to become librarians and competent publishers' staff members, usually for their own needs. But they are too few as yet, and too limited to be named as organs influencing the ratio of trained staff. No general training facilities for publishers and booksellers exist.

12 Taxes

Book printers and dealers are subject to regular trade tax, but there is no special tax on such business. However, authors are exempt from tax up to an income of TL. 10,000 per year as copyright fees, to encourage writing and safeguard their rights.

14 Copyright

Turkey is not a member of the Berne Convention, but there is a prevailing Turkish law concerning copyright. However, there are no really established institutions for copyright. Lately some work is being done on this subject.

15 National Bibliography, National Library

Turkish culture, for nearly 600 years, has shown a great interest in libraries. Since the early days of the Ottoman Empire, the universities and their libraries (which contained many invaluable volumes of great knowledge and wonderful workmanship) were numerous. Now all these libraries have been turned into museums, with their contents exhibited as works of art.

Some of the most prominent of the modern libraries of the Turkish Republic are:

Beyazit Devlet Kütüphanesi
Beyazit Meydani
TR Istanbul

and

Millî Kütüphane
Namik Kemal Mahallesi
TR Ankara

established in 1953 by the "Law of the National Library" and functioning since 1955.

The only national bibliography in the book trade in Turkey is *Türk Bibliografya Dergesi.*

"Türk Bibliografya Dergesi" is an official magazine published quarterly by "Millî Kütüphane Müdürlügü", Ankara ("General Administration Department of the National Library"), and gives the title, author, dimension, subject matter, etc. of all newly published books in the last quarter.

16 Book Production

Most books published in Turkey are paperbacks.

The Turkish Ministry of Education publishes many of the books under its own supervision in larger format paperbacks. Literary translations and novels are usually published in hard-cover form by such publishers as "Altin Kitaplar", "Güven Kitabevi", etc.

In 1967 5,688 titles (books, pamphlets etc.) were published in Turkey. Of those 4,889 were local publications, the rest translations. Of the total, 3,397 titles were published in Istanbul, 1,879 in Ankara, and 412 in the rest of Turkey.

17 Translations

The translations are mostly from the English, French, and German languages, and the publications mostly translated are technical books, works on social sciences, contemporary literature, light romances, and detective novels. Of the 5,688 titles produced in Turkey in 1967, 799 were translations.

19 Paperbacks

Paperbacks constitute, as in almost any other country, the major part of local production. Quality and size are more variable than in other countries. Some of the many paperback publishers and dealers in Turkey are: "Varlik Yayinlari", Istanbul; "De Yayinlari", Istanbul; "Yedi Tepe Yayinlari", Istanbul; "Bilgi Yayinlari", Ankara.

20 Book Design

In the sixteenth, seventeenth, and eighteenth centuries Turkish artists and craftsmen produced some of the best-designed books. Book design, which was one of the main and most widely spread arts of the Ottoman Empire, is, alas, nearly dead now. Today "Doğan Kardeş Yayinlari", producing mostly children's books, publishes the best-designed books in Turkey.

21 Publishing

In 1967 1,363 scientific and technical books were published in Turkey by four different establishments and organizations:

I) Universities:
  a) Ankara Üniversitesi—Ankara
    1) Dil ve Tarih Cografya Fakültesi (Faculty of History, Geography and Languages)—Turkish and general history, Turkish and general geography, arts and history of art, drama, literature
    2) Ziraat Fakültesi (Faculty of Agriculture)
    3) Veteriner Fakültesi (Veterinary Faculty)
    4) Ilâhiyat Fakültesi (Faculty of Theology)
    5) Hukuk Fakültesi (Faculty of Law)
    6) Tip Fakültesi (Faculty of Medicine)
    7) Siyasal Bilgiler Fakültesi (Faculty of Social Sciences)
  b) Orta Dogu Teknik Üniversitesi (Technical University of the Middle East)—Ankara
  c) Istanbul Üniversitesi—Beyazit, Istanbul
    1) Tip Fakültesi (Faculty of Medicine)
    2) Ormancilik Fakültesi (Faculty of Forestry)
    3) Fen Fakültesi (Faculty of Positive Sciences: Physics, Astronomy)
    4) Kimya Fakültesi (Faculty of Chemistry)
    5) Eczacilik Fakültesi (Faculty of Pharmacology)
    6) Hukuk Fakültesi (Faculty of Law)
    7) Ihtisat Fakültesi (Faculty of Economics)
    8) Edebiyat Fakültesi (Faculty of the Arts)
  d) Ege Üniversitesi—Izmir
    1) Ziraat Fakültesi (Faculty of Agriculture)
    2) Tip Fakültesi (Faculty of Medicine)
  e) Karadeniz Üniversitesi—Trabzon (Positive Sciences)
  f) Atatürk Üniversitesi—Erzurum
    1) Ziraat Fakültesi (Faculty of Agriculture)

II) Public institutions established under government care. The names and addresses of some of them are listed below:
  a) Türk Dil Kurumu (Turkish Language Association), Ankara
  b) Türk Tarih Kurumu (Turkish History Association), Ankara
  c) Türk Kültürümü Araştirma Enstitüsü (Association for Research on Turkish Culture), Ankara

III) Institutes of Research established by the Ministeries:
  a) Ormancilik Araştirma Enstitüsü (Institute of Forestry Research), Ankara
  b) Lalahatun Zooteknik Arastirma Enstitüsü

(Lalahatun Institute of Zootechnical Research), Ankara
c) Devlet Istatistik Enstitüsü (Institute of Statistics), Ankara
d) Devlet Planlama Teşkilati (Economic Planning), Ankara

IV) Private organizations:
a) CaglayanKitabevi (technical publications), Tokatlayan Hann, Istiklâl Caddesi, Beyoglu, Istanbul
b) Üniversitesi Kitabevi, Yerebatan Caddesi, Cağaloğlu, Istanbul
c) Ismail Akgün Kitabevi (law), Ankara Caddesi, Vilayet Yani, Cağaloğlu, Istanbul

Literary books are either published by:

I) Millî Egitim Bakanligi (Ministry of Education), who publish a series called "Dünya ve Sark Klasikler" ("World and Oriental Classics").

II) Private publishers:
a) Inkitap ve Aka Kitabevleri, Ankara Caddesi 95, Cağaloğlu, Istanbul (miscellaneous)
b) Ismail Akgün, Kitabevi (law), Ankara Caddesi Vilayet Yani, Cağaloğlu, Istanbul
c) Remzi Kitabevi, Türbedar 20–2, Nuruosmaniye, Istanbul (novels)
d) Hayat Yayinlari, 1001 Direk Sokak 12, Divan yolu, Istanbul (classics, encyclopedias)
e) Bilgi Yayinevi, Sakanya Caddesi, Ankara (literary paperbacks)
f) Arkin Kitabevi, Cağaloğlu, Istanbul (encyclopedias)
g) Avni Anil Yayin Ajansi, Istilâl Caddesi 193–7, Istanbul (musical)
h) Agaoglu Yaymevi, Cağaloğlu, Istanbul
i) Kanaat Kitabevi, Ankara Caddesi, Cağaloğlu, Istanbul (school books, dictionaries)

Most of the 880 literary titles published in 1967 were published by the abovementioned publishers.
Of the 5,688 titles published in Turkey in 1967, 3,397 were published in Istanbul, and 1,897 in Ankara. In Izmir and Konya there are some minor publishers as well.

22 Literary Agents

There are no literary agents in Turkey.

23 Wholesale Trade

Bates Bayicilik Teskilati
Çatalçeşmes 2
Cağaloğlu
TR Istanbul
distributes periodicals, literary works, some technical works.

Okul Kitaplari Ddğitim Ltd. Sti.
Ankara Cad.
Cağaloğlu
TR Istanbul
distributes school books.

Sabri Özakar
Ankara Cad. Vilay et Han
Cağaloğlu
TR Istanbul
distributes periodicals, novels, light literature.

Hür Dağitim
Ankara Cad 15
Cağaloğlu
TR Istanbul
distributes periodicals, papers.

24 Retail Trade

There are over 1,000 retail booksellers in Turkey, but 30% of them sell stationery, office supplies, etc. in addition to books. The greater part of the book trade is situated in Istanbul and Ankara, both as regards the number of titles and copies published per year, and consumption of books.
Most of the rest of the retail book trade is established in the northern and southern regions of Turkey. Some of the major firms are:
"Alman Kitabevi", Istanbul; "Amerikan Neşriyati Bürosu", Istanbul; "Cağlayan Kitabevi", Istanbul; "French-American Kitabevi", Istanbul; "Hachette", Istan-

bul; "Sander Kitabevi", Istanbul; "Tarhan Kitabevi", Ankara.
Some of the big book retailers also import books.

25 Mail-Order Bookselling

Mail order is a comparatively new system in Turkey, although many big companies are beginning to use it. In the book trade there is only "Amerikan Neşriyati Bürosu", the first pioneer and the best-equipped user of the system. Lately some of the larger firms have adapted mail order but their activities are still in an embryonic state as compared to international standards.

26 Antiquarian Book Trade, Auctions

One of the great arts of the Ottoman Empire was producing beautiful handmade books. This art has unfortunately not survived. However, there is still a small group of enthusiasts on the subject. Sales and resales of such items take place mainly in a section of the historical Grand Bazaar in Istanbul. Apart from that, there are some small shops at Babialî, the printing and book-trade centre in Istanbul. But the trade is not wide-spread, and the museums and university libraries absorb most of the old books.

27 Book Imports

The books imported into Turkey are mainly in English, French, and German. These are usually imported directly from the USA, the United Kingdom, France, and Germany. Among the most important book importers are: "Amerikan Neşriyati Bürosu", Istanbul; "Cağlayan Kitabevi", Istanbul; "Hachette", Istanbul; "Sander Kitabevi", Istanbul; "Tarhan Kitabevi", Ankara.

28 Book Exports

There is almost no book exportation from Turkey, although some newspapers and magazines are to be found in European countries where there is an agglomeration of Turkish workers such as in Germany, Belgium, and Holland. Some Turkish-language books have occassionally been exported to Europe in small quantities. There are some small bookshops in Sahaflar Çarşisi, who supply European and American universities ordering books printed in Turkey.
They are usually out-of-print books and old publications.
Some universities and semi-governmental establishments exchange their own publications with those of European and American universities who want to import scientific books published in Turkey.

29 Book Fairs

There are no book fairs in Turkey, with the exception of *Çocuk Kitaplari Sergisi* ("Fair of Children's Books") organized by the Turkish Ministry of Education. Recently some of the major printers and publishers are trying to come together and prepare some book fairs to stimulate the trade, but nothing much has yet been done to this end.

30 Public Relations

The book trade is not sufficiently organized in Turkey to permit any regular public-relations service.

32 Literary Prizes

Some daily newspapers, weekly magazines, and national educational establishments distribute various literary prizes:
Ali Naci Karacan Armagani. This is given by "Milliyet", one of the leading dailies, for

the best literary research work on a different subject every year.
Yunus Nadi Armagani, given by "Cumhuriyet", another important daily, for the best research work.
Türk Dil Kurumu Armagani, donated by "Türk Dil Kurumu" for the best short story, novel, and poem which has made the best use of the Turkish language.
7 Tepe Sür Armagani, distributed by the "7 Tepe Sür Dergisi", a periodical of poetry, for the best poem.
Sait Faik Armagani, awarded for the best short story.

Union of Soviet Socialist Republics-USSR

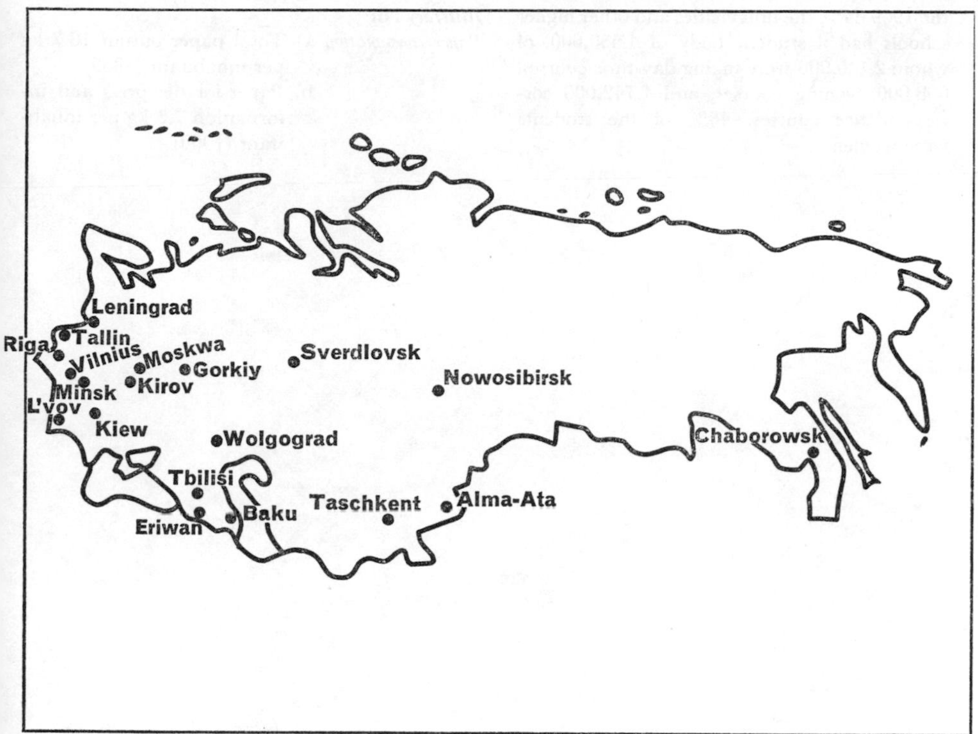

Important Book Centres

1 General Information By *E. Dinerstein*

Area About 22.4 m. km²

Population 241,700,000 (15 per km²)

Capital Moskva (7,061,000)

Largest towns Moskva (7,061,000); Leningrad (3,950,000); Kiev (1,632,000); Tashkent (1,385,000); Baku (1,260,000); Kharkov (1,223,000); Gorky (1,170,000); Novosibirsk (1,161,000); Kuibyshev (1,047,000); Sverdlovsk (1,026,000)

Government The USSR is a socialist state, consisting of 15 Republics (Russian Soviet Federative Socialist Republic, Ukrainian Soviet Socialist Republic, Byelorussian SSR, Uzbek SSR, Kazakh SSR, Georgian SSR, Azerbaijan SSR, Lithuanian SSR, Moldavian SSR, Latvian SSR, Kirghiz SSR, Tajik SSR, Armenian SSR, Turkmen SSR, Estonian SSR). In the USSR all power belongs to the people as represented by the Soviets of the Working People's Deputies. The country's social and state structure is written into the 1936 Constitution

National language There is no state language in the USSR. In accordance with the Constitution, all laws passed by the Supreme Soviet of the USSR are published in the languages of the Union Republics, and judicial proceedings are conducted in the language of the Union or Autonomous Republic (or Autonomous Region). Instruction in the schools is in the native language

Russian is the most widespread language

Leading foreign languages English, German, French

Weights and measures Metric system

Currency unit Ruble (Rbl = 100 Kopeks)

Education Universal compulsory eight-year education. Work is now in progress to introduce universal ten-year education. According to the 1969 data, the universities and other higher schools had a student body of 4,550,000, of whom 2,140,000 were taking day-time courses, 668,000 evening courses, and 1,742,000 correspondence courses. 48% of the students were women

Illiteracy Nil

Paper consumption a) Total paper output 16.7 kg per inhabitant (1969)

b) Paper for the press and information 7.3 kg per inhabitant (1969)

2 Past and Present

By *A. Govorov*

The Lives of the Fathers of the Pechera Monastery in Kiev (1120) contains the first written mention of bookselling in Ancient Russia. We have a knowledge of books in Ancient Russia being made for sale, the prices, and the names of the buyers and sellers, from inscriptions by owners in their books and entries in the chronicles.

The number of manuscript editions in circulation was considerably increased as Moscow gradually came to be the capital of the Russians (15–16th centuries).

Following the start of bookprinting in Moscow (1564) a special institution—Office for Printing—was set up to fix prices and regulate the sale of books. In the 17th century the tsar's Printing House had two bookshops and a "book treasury", which supplied books to departments and monasteries. At the time, printed books were costly and were intended mainly for church services. The people were still extensively using manuscript editions.

In the early 18th century the book trade developed under the impact of Peter the Great's cultural reforms. Together with the opening of civil printing works in St Petersburg (1714) state bookshops were set up. Following the establishment of the Academy of Sciences, a "book chamber" was set up to sell its publications (1728), and it was the first to keep a bibliographical record of book sales, send books by post and sell books on a commission basis.

N. I. Novikov (1744–1818), an outstanding enlightener, first organized the Russian book trade as a special branch of cultural and economic activity. Under his influence, more than 40 private bookshops were set up, stocks appeared, binding contracts were developed and men were trained in the selling of books.

In the first quarter of the 19th century, the book trade was carried on along patriarchal, old merchant lines. Only a few progressive booksellers, like V. A. Plavilshchikov (1768–1824), I. V. Slenin (1789–1839), I. T. Lisenkov (1800–1878) and especially A. F. Smirdin (1794–1857) strove to handle works by progressive scholars and writers.

Russia's book trade in the second half of the 19th century was influenced by the ideas of the revolutionary Narodniks, some of whom, like N. A. Serno-Solovyevich (1834–1866), A. F. Cherenin (1824–1892), and A. A. Cherkesov (1835–1911) set up bookshops as a medium of revolutionary propaganda and democratic enlightenment. Large capitalist enterprises (M. O. Wolff, A. S. Suvorin, P. P. Soykin, "Prosveshcheniye", and others) were set up in that period, and these engaged in a fierce competitive struggle for the book market. A company set up by I. D. Sytin (1851–1934), who started out by selling colourful popular editions, became a world-wide printing, publishing and bookselling concern which in 1913 handled one third of the country's book publishing.

In 1913 Russia had 3,508 retail and small wholesale bookselling enterprises, but more than onehalf of them were in the big cities. Siberia, Central Asia and the Far East remained virtually outside the area of the book trade.

The First and Second Congresses of Russian Booksellers and Publishers (1909 and 1911) made a futile attempt to set the Russian book market in order by introducing a scale of fixed discounts, contractual relations, and a single wholesaling network.

Liberal intellectuals began to open book storehouses under the *zemstvo*—local self-government organs—for the purpose of spreading knowledge among the peasants (1872). Shortly before 1914, consumer co-operatives took up the bookselling trade.

USSR

The first decrees of the Soviet Government (1917) made the main printing facilities the people's property: the largest printing works, publishing houses and storehouses. Tsentropechat, the first Soviet organization for the distribution of printed matter (1918), initiated the free supply of books and periodicals to workers, Red Army men and poor peasants.

After the Civil War, Lenin signed decrees on the resumption of the trade in books (1921). Gosizdat, the largest Soviet publishing house, was given a bookselling apparatus, Torgsector (1922), with the right to control and direct the development of the state, cooperative and private book trade.

As the network of Soviet bookselling enterprises—cooperatives (book societies and book cooperatives), joint-stock companies (Books for the Countryside), and publishing houses (book-marketing offices) was extended and improved in quality, the capitalist bookseller was eased out of the book market.

A single system of Soviet book marketing emerged with the establishment of the Association of State Publishers (OGIZ), called Knigotsentr (1930), and then KOGIZ (1934), the Book-Marketing Association of State Publishers. Bookshops were opened in the areas of the new construction carried out under the five-year plan. The newly organized collective farms received books through an extensive network of bookstalls set up under the political departments of the machine- and tractor stations. Workers and peasants were offered special credit terms and instalment plans for buying books.

During the Great Patriotic War (1941–1945), Soviet book-trading organizations organized the supply of periodicals and books to the Army, the Navy and the partisans in the enemy rear. Workers in the book-marketing organizations worked selflessly, together with the whole Soviet people, making good the losses of the early war years and developing the book trade, especially in areas liberated from the invaders and in the outlying areas to which industrial plants had been moved from the front-line areas and where many new plants had been set up.

After the war, the book trade was restructured to enable it more successfully to meet the tasks of socialist construction. KOGIZ gave way to the Administration for the Book Trade of Glavpoligrafizdat under the USSR Council of Ministers (1949). Local administrations and offices for the sale of books—*knigotorgs*—were set up in the regions, territories and Republics. The reorganization of the book trade was completed with the establishment of *Sojuzkniga,* the All-Union Association of the Book Trade (1958), which is now subordinated to the *Committee for Publishing and the Press under the USSR Council of Ministers* (→ 4). In 1957, book marketing in the countryside was handed over to *Tsentrosoyuz,* the Union of Consumer Cooperative Societies.

The rapid economic and cultural growth in the USSR in the post-war period was reflected in the swift development of the book trade:

	Number of bookshops	Retail sales of books (million rubles)
1952	6,183	183
1959	8,538	359
1968	13,986	508

The structure, forms and methods of the book trade have undergone considerable qualitative changes. Most of the bookshops have been built anew or re-equipped to meet the demands of modern book marketing. Alongside with the establishment of giant universal bookshops, the network of small specialized establishments has been expanded. Books are no longer sold only in shops, more than one third being distributed through book-pedlars, book-vans, mail-order services, etc. The Central Wholesale Bookstore, Europe's largest, was opened in 1962.

The journal *Knižnaja Torgovlja* ("Book Trade", → 5), established in 1948, has been playing a big part in the exchange of experience. There is now a system of secondary and higher education in the book trade (20 specialized secondary schools and 4 institutes → 11). Intensive research into the book trade has been started.

An important factor is the recruiting of the public to take part in the distribution of books, which was started on the initiative of young workers at Leningrad plants in 1959. People's bookshops run by volunteers have been opened in all parts of the country since 1960.

The CPSU Central Committee adopted a special decision in 1960 describing the book trade of the USSR as an important aspect of the communist education of the working people. Together with a number of other Party and Government documents, this decision became a programme for the further development of the Soviet book trade during the construction of communist society.

Bibliography

M. V. Muratov. *Knižnoje delo v Rossii v 19 i 20 vekach.* (The book trade in Russia in the 19th and the 20th centuries. An essay on the history of book publishing and book marketing. 1800–1917.) Moskva–Leningrad 1931.

T. V. Barashkov. *Sovetskaja knižnaja torgovlja. In: 400 let russkogo knigopečatanija 1564–1964. Akademija nauk SSSR. Otdelenie istorii.* (The Soviet book trade). Vol. I. Moskva, Nauka 1964, pp. 494–520.

A. A. Govorov. *Istorija knižnoj torgovli.* (A history of the book trade. A study aid for book trade specialized schools). Moskva, Kniga 1966. 264 pp.

3 Retail Prices

By *V. Markus*

In the USSR, the prices of books are fixed in accordance with a price list for books, albums, music and bindings, approved by the Committee for Publishing and the Press under the USSR Council of Ministers (→ 4). The price list now in force dates from 1 January, 1966 (since then the Committee has made various additions).

The principle of the pricing is to bring prices as close as possible to the socially necessary expenditures of production and circulation, plus a certain profit margin. Retail prices are based on the unit used to measure all textual and illustrative material which is referred to as a publisher's signature and contains 40,000 ems (an em is any letter, figure or space between words). As for illustrations, 3,000 cm^2 of them are equated to 1 publisher's signature. Consequently, the retail price of a book is fixed by multiplying its volume in publisher's signatures by the corresponding price of one publisher's signature, with the addition of the cost of the binding.

The prices of publisher's signatures are differentiated in the price list according to the type of literature (fiction, science, popular science, textbooks, methodological literature, technology and production, reference and other works), and the design (original illustrations, colour printing, higher quality of paper and so on), and also according to the readership for which the edition is intended, so as to make it available to the right category of readers. Some books are sold at less than the cost price (such as primary textbooks), their losses covered by profits from other publications.

In 1968, the price of a 10-signature book (paperback or hard cover) averaged 39 kopeks. It should be borne in mind, moreover, that in the last few years there has been a marked improvement in the design, colour and printing quality of publications. The publishing houses sell their books to booksellers at a 25% discount.

Bibliography

V. A. Markus. *Organizacija i ekonomika izdatel'skogo dela.* (The organization and economics of the publishing business. Textbook for students of Polygraphic Colleges). Moskva, Kniga 1964.

Spravocnik normativnych materialov dla izdatel'skich rabotnikov. (Manual of standards for publishing workers). Compiled by V. A. Markus. 2nd ed. Moskva, Kniga 1969.

Retail price list No. 116a for books, albums, music and bindings. Moskva 1965.—In Russian.

4 Organization

By *A. Marin*

In the Soviet Union, the book trade falls into two categories: wholesale and retail. Bookselling organizations engaged in wholesale operations buy their books from the publishing houses and supply them to retail shops. The latter organize the distribution of literature among the population.

Komitet po pečatj
pri Sovete Ministrov SSSR
(Committee for Publishing and the Press under the USSR Council of Ministers)
ul. Petrovka 26
SU Moskva K. 51

The Committee for Publishing and the Press exercises control over the fulfilment of decisions adopted by the Party and the Government for the book trade. It decides on the size of printings; organizes the distribution of central, republican and local publications, carries out the advertising of books and periodicals; and issues instructions for the guidance of the book trade.

The Committee works out and implements measures to develop new progressive forms of book trading, and encourages the distribution of literature by volunteers; carries out measures for the training and raising of skills among the personnel in the book trade, and determines the need for specialists with a higher and a secondary specialised education. On the basis of proposals submitted by Committees for Publishing and the Press of the Union Republics, it works out plans to develop the book trade throughout the country. The Committee also keeps a statistical record of publications.

The

Vsesojuznoe ob'edinenie Knižnoi
torgovli (Sojuzkniga)
(All-Union Association of the Book Trade)
Lenin Prospekt 15
SU Moskva

of the Committee for Publishing and the Press under the USSR Council of Ministers organizes the collection of orders from book-trading organizations for the printed output of central publishing houses, purchases literature from the latter, and through its "Central Wholesale Book Store" in Moscow and wholesale book stores in other cities forwards it to the Republics and regions (→ 23).

"Soyuzkniga" supplies book-trading organizations with books in accordance with their orders submitted on special order forms under a plan for the output of literature by the publishing houses (→ 6).

"Soyuzkniga" sees to it that all the printed matter produced in the country reaches the categories of readers for whom it is intended, controls the fulfilment of the turnover plan by all organizations subordinate to the "Committee for Publishing and the Press", gives assistance to consumer co-operatives in supplying literature to the rural population, and works to spread knowledge about books and advertise them.

Through *Knigoexport*, an office for the export and import of literature, "Soyuzkniga" fulfils orders from *Meždunarodnaja Kniga* (→ 27, 28) for literature to be sent abroad and buys literature abroad.

"Soyuzkniga" takes part in framing publishers' plans, participates in deciding the size of printings and controls technical standards in printing.

In the Union Republics, the book trade is directed and the work of book-trading organizations coordinated by Committees for Publishing and the Press of the Union Republics, which have their own book-trading administrations.

These administrations buy books from Republican publishing houses and supply them to regional and territorial bookselling organizations, direct the book trade in the Republics, organize the collection of orders for literature issued by the central and Republican publishers, and advertise and spread knowledge about the books they receive.

Regional (territorial) bookselling organizations carry on the book trade in their region (territory).

At present, there are over 5,600 bookshops and 5,300 bookstalls within the system of the "Committee for Publishing and the Press under the USSR Council of Ministers".

In the rural areas, books are sold through shops and kiosks of consumer cooperatives, and the book trade is directed by the *Tsentrosoyuz* of the USSR. In the countryside, books are distributed by 7,800 bookshops and 3,000 bookstalls.

Books are also sold by *Soyuzpečat* of the Ministry of Communications of the USSR, an organization which has within its system almost 200 bookshops and over 26,000 bookstalls.

Literature put out by *Nauka* Publishers is distributed by *Akademkniga*.

Books are also sold by *Transport* Publishers, whose shops and bookstalls sell books mainly on specialized subjects.

In addition to these systems, books are distributed in timber-felling areas by Workers' Supply Administrations, which buy their books directly from the booksellers.

The Literary Fund of the Soviet Writers' Union has a *Writers' Book-Shop* in Moscow, which has a branch in Leningrad. It caters for the needs of writers.

Today, there are almost 15,000 bookshops and more than 34,000 bookstalls over the country.

Bibliography

Spravočnik normativnikh materialov dlya rabotnikov knižnoi torgovli. (Handbook of normative material for bookselling workers). Compiled by A. P. Marin and A. S. Dribinsky. Moskva, Kniga 1970.

Organizacija i technika torgovli knigoj. (The book trade. Organization and techniques). Textbook for specialized schools. Moskva, Kniga 1969. 278 pp.

G. N. Altshil, *Organizacija i technika torgovli knigami.* (The book trade. Organization and technique). Textbook for Cooperative Technical Schools. 2nd ed. Moskva, Kniga 1965.

5 Trade Press

By *V. Osipov*

The monthly journal

Knižnaja Torgovlja
(Book Trade)
Leninskij prospekt
D. 15, Komi. 425
SU Moskva

of the Committee for Publishing and the Press under the Council of Ministers of the USSR, and of the Central Union of the Consumers' Society of the USSR, has been in publication since 1921. From 1921 to

1928 it was called "Bulletin Gosizdata", in 1929–1931 "Na knižnom fronte", in 1932–1935 "Knižny front" and from 1936 to 1940 "Sovetsky knižnik".
Publication of this magazine was suspended during the Great Patriotic War (1941–1945). It resumed publication in 1948 as "Sovetskaya knižnaja torgovlja". Since 1964 it has been called "Knižnaja torgovlja".
The contributors to the journal include the heads of bookselling organizations and publishing houses, staff members of bookshops, scientific workers, volunteer distributors and bibliophiles.
"Knižnaja torgovlja" is a professional journal which carries articles on the history, theory and practice of the book trade. It systematically prints materials to help improve the qualifications of the people working in the book trade, and also reviews professional book-trade literature. Under the headings "Our Friends" and "Abroad" it prints articles and notes on the book trade in foreign countries. Other permanent features are "Lawyer's Advice", "Entertaining Bibliology" and "Chronicle".
It keeps its readers abreast of the work of publishing houses and reviews the more important publications.
It does not print bibliographical information for bookshops. This information is given in special publications sent free of charge to booksellers (→ 24e).
During the past five years the magazine's circulation has doubled, exceeding 20,000 copies. Its size averages 8 publishers' signatures (64 large-format pages). The annual subscription rate is 3 rubles 60 kopeks.
In addition to "Knižnaja torgovlja", articles dealing with the book trade are printed in the critical-bibliographical journal *V mire knig*, the newspaper *Knižnoje obozrenije* and the magazine *Sovetskaja potrebitelskaja kooperatsia.*

Bibliography

V. O. Osipov, *K istorii sovetskoi knigotordovoi pečati.* (On the history of Soviet book trade periodicals). In: Sovetskaja knižnaja torgovlja, 1963, pp. 9–11.

6 Book-Trade Literature

By *V. Osipov*

From 15 to 20 books and pamphlets dealing with the book trade are brought out annually. These include books on the organization and technology of the book trade, on the range of books, on economics and on planning.
Most of these books and brochures are put out by the Publishing House *Kniga* (8/10, Nezhdanova Street, Moskva).

a) Bibliographies

Books and brochures on the book trade are registered in *Knižnaja letopis* ("Book Chronicle") under section "XXX. The Press. Bibliology. Librarianship. Bibliography" and subsection "2. Publishing. Printing. Book Trade. Circulation of Periodicals." The same subsection in the "Chronicle of Magazine Articles" gives a list of articles dealing with the book trade.
In 1969 the "Central Bureau for Scientific and Technological Information and Technological and Economic Research in the Printing and Publishing Industry and the Book Trade" began the publication of *Izdatelskoe delo, knigovedenie, knižnaja torgovlja i gosudarstvennaja bibliografija,* a monthly bibliographical reference containing lists of books, brochures and articles published in the USSR and also abroad.

b) General Surveys and Handbooks

Articles of a scientific character are printed in the yearbook *Kniga. Issledovanija i materialy* (whose issue was started in

1959). Among the articles printed in this almanac (in Russian) are "Book trade in rural localities" by G. N. Altshul, "Some problems of the book trade" by M. F. Arbuzov and "Soviet book-trade bibliography" by V. O. Osipov.

Abstracts and short articles of a scientific character are also printed in the almanac "Book Publishing Bibliology" (which has been in publication since 1968).

Both almanacs are compiled by the "All-Union Book Chamber".

A series of textbooks for book-trade specialized schools have been published in recent years.

L. Y. RABIN AND A. N. LYUBIMOV, *Ekonomika i planirovanie torgovli knigami.* (Book-trade economy and planning.) Moskva, Kniga 1968.

Deals with questions such as the organization and planning of the book trade, planning the circulation of books, labour and wages, circulation costs, trade discounts and so on.

A. A. GOVOROV, *Istorija knižnoj torgovli.* (A history of the book trade). Moskva, Kniga 1966. 264 pp.

Traces the history of the book trade from the earliest times to our days, and deals comprehensively with the history of the written language, book printing and publishing.

V. O. OSIPOV, *Tovarovedenie chudožestvennoj literatury i izdanij po iskusstvu.* (Sale of fiction and art literature). Moskva, Kniga 1968.

Analyses the choice of fiction and art publications and the method of handling this literature in bookshops.

Organizacija i technika torgovli knigoj. (Organization and technology of the book trade). Moskva, Kniga 1969.

This textbook was compiled by a team of authors. It deals with the organizational structure of the book trade in the USSR, with the lay-out and equipment of bookshops, the procedure of ordering books, the wholesale book trade, the display of books and so on.

In addition to these and other textbooks there are lectures and methodological materials on special book-trade subjects published by specialized schools, the "Correspondence Institute of Soviet Trade" and the "Moscow Polygraphic Institute".

Among the books and pamphlets on the book trade the most important are publications which review and summarize experience and offer advice. Some of these publications—individual instructions—are brought out in the form of brochures.

But there also are fundamental publications.

M. F. ARBUZOV, *Propaganda i reklama v knižnoe torgovle.* (Popularization and advertising in the book trade). Moskva, Kniga 1966.

Sums up the experience of dressing show windows, organizing printed advertising, arranging meetings with authors etc.

The alphabetic subject index to

S. E. POLIVANOVSKIJ AND A. T. KAMENECKIJ, *Alfavitno-predmetnyi ukazatal' k "Edinoj scheme klassifikacii literatury v knigotorgovoj seti".* (Literature classification in the book trade). Moskva, Kniga 1968

is widely used by bookshop staffs when indexing and arranging literature.

Books and brochures on the book trade are also printed by republican and regional publishing houses. These are mainly brochures containing instructions, but among them are books dealing comprehensively with the experience of the given republic or region.

For instance

N. N. GREKHOVODOV, *Voprosy organizacii knižnoj torgovli.* (Problems of the organization of the book trade). Alma-Ata, Kazakhstan Publishing House 1965

describes the work of bookselling organizations and enterprises in Kazakhstan.

USSR

7 Sources of Information

→ 4, 15, 27, 28.

9 Market Research

By *I. Monastyrsky*

Most of research and scientific information work in the book trade is conducted by the *All-Union Book Chamber* (→ 15). Besides its functions as a state bibliographical and statistics organization, the "All-Union Book Chamber" (→ 15) is a research establishment. It has a research department which studies the book trade and another concerned with scientific and technological information and technological and economic research in the book trade.

The research department studies the ways and means of improving the book trade (economy and planning), elaborates state standards, instructions and methodological aids designed to help achieve the maximum efficiency in the organization of the book trade.

The scientific-and-technological information and technological-and-economic department studies home and foreign experience in the book trade, builds up a branch reference library of published and unpublished sources of information on the book trade and puts out bibliographies, papers and reviews on the development of the book trade in the USSR and abroad.

Research in the book trade is also conducted by *Soyuzkniga's Department of Sociological Research,* the *Department of Book Science and Bibliography of the Moscow Polygraphic Institute,* and relevant departments in some economic institutes.

Bibliography

P. A. Chuvikov, Main fields of research done by the All-Union Book Chamber. In: Organization of reference service for publishing house personnel, the polygraphic industry, the book trade and state bibliography, Moscow 1969. (Central Bureau of Scientific and Technological Information and Technological and Economic Research in the Polygraphic Industry, Publishing and the Book Trade), pp. 19–21.—In Russian.

V. O. Osipov, Prospective development of research in the book trade, ibid., pp. 55–6.—In Russian.

I. M. Monastyrsky, State and prospects of the system of scientific and technologic information on the polygraphic industry, publishing and the book trade, ibid., pp. 5–19.—In Russian.

10 Books and Young People

By *A. Davtyan*

In the USSR, one book in six is intended for young people. There are now 15 youth periodicals published in Moscow and 8 in the Union Republics. There are also 8 periodicals for children published in Moscow, and 25 in the Union Republics. Thirty-one periodicals from other countries are available in foreign languages.

In 1969 books for children were put out by 10 central and 80 republican and local publishing houses.

Literature for children and young people is published by large specialized publishers: Molodaya Gvardia (Moscow), Molod (Kiev), Esh gvardia (Tashkent), Detskaya Literatura (Moscow), Malysh (Moscow), Vesyolka (Kiev), Gyandjlika (Baku) and Nakaduli (Tbilisi).

The printings of children's literature are constantly growing. In 1968, they were 26% higher than in 1967.

In 1969, a total of 2,473 books for children were issued in a printing of 270.4 million copies in 69 languages of the USSR and foreign languages.

Every year, Detskaya Literatura alone

publishes 55–70 books translated from 40 odd languages of the USSR.
Fiction accounts for 90% of all publications for children and 94% of the total printing. Much attention is also given to works on socio-political and scientific topics, which in 1969 had a printing of 13.8 million copies.
Popular with young readers are the following series: "In the Realm of the Beautiful", "Concise History Library", "Children's Encyclopedia", "School Library", "Golden Library", and "Adventure and Science Fiction Library".
Translations from foreign authors figure prominently in editions of children's literature. In the last 10 years, Detskaya Literatura has issued 500 books by foreign writers.
Soviet books for children have won many awards and medals at international exhibitions and contests (Paris, Brussels and Leipzig).

Bibliography

Pečat SSSR v 1968 godu. (USSR publications in 1968). Statistics. Moskva, Kniga 1969. (→ 16)
Pečat SSSR za 50 let. Stat. očerki. (The press of the USSR for 50 years. Statistical essays). Moskva, Kniga 1967. 199 pp.

11 Training

By *V. Osipov and D. Altshil*

In the Soviet Union the system of professional book-trade education was organized after the Great October Socialist Revolution. Currently it consists of the following links.
Book-trade Schools in Moscow, Leningrad and Kiev training salesmen. For 11 months the trainess study bibliology, the organization and technology of the book trade, the rudiments of accounting, and trade computation. Theoretical study is alternated with work in bookshops. The last five weeks of study are given to an apprenticeship course. Depending on the general education level (eight-year or ten-year schooling) the trainees receive a junior or senior salesman's certificate.
Book-trade *specialized secondary schools* in Moscow, Leningrad, Saratov, Novosibirsk and Kiev. There are also book-trade departments at trade specialized schools in almost all the Union republics.
Book-trade education is given within the system of Consumers' Cooperatives at the *Centrosoyuz School* in Ulyanovsk, and at the corresponding book-trade departments of the cooperative specialized secondary schools in Vinnitsa, Minsk, Alma-Ata, Tselinograd and many other towns.
Trainees enrolling in the specialized school after finishing a ten-year school take a two-year course, and trainees with an eight-year education take a three-year course. During these three years they receive a general secondary education and a secondary professional education.
Compared with trade schools, the specialized secondary schools cover a larger field of training, which includes subjects like the history of the book trade, book-trade economics and planning, book-keeping, fundamentals of civil law, and political economy. Subjects like bibliology (including the principles of publishing and bibliography) and the organization and technology of the book trade are taught more comprehensively than at trade schools. During the term of study the trainees do practical work in bookshops and book-trade depositories. Graduates receive diplomas certifying them as bibliologists.
The specialized secondary schools have day and correspondence departments.
Book-trade experts are trained at four institutions of higher learning. The bibliological department at the *Moscow Polygraphic Institute* offers all three forms of training: day, evening and by correspon-

dence. The *Krupskaya Institute of Culture* in Leningrad and the *Correspondence Institute of Soviet Trade* in Moscow train book-trade experts by correspondence. The *Kharkov Institute of Culture* has a day and a correspondence department.

In addition to a theoretical course, the students of these institutes take a practical course in bookselling enterprises and organizations and in publishing houses.

The curricula of the "Moscow Polygraphic Institute" and the "Institutes of Culture" in Leningrad and Kharkov give priority to the humanities. In addition to special bibliological and economic courses they accord prominence to the history of Soviet and foreign literature, foreign languages and social sciences.

Graduates receive diplomas as bibliologists and bibliographers. At the "Correspondence Institute of Soviet Trade" economic subjects predominate. This institute awards the diploma of book-trade economist. At the "Moscow Polygraphic Institute" the training course (day department —4 years; evening and correspondence departments—5 years) ends with the maintenance of a diploma project. At the other institutes graduates sit for a state examination.

In the system of professional training importance is attached to improving professional qualifications.

Courses designed to improve the qualifications of book-trade personnel operate at the "Moscow Book Trade Specialized Secondary School", the "Krupskaya Institute of Culture" in Leningrad and the "Moscow Polygraphic Institute". Department heads, goods experts, book-keepers, managers and assistant managers of bookshops and others are enrolled in these courses on the recommendation of bookselling enterprises and organizations. At these courses they study the latest methods and current problems of the book trade, attend seminars and meet top-ranking officials of the book trade. At the end of the course they sit for an examination and receive a certificate.

The highest form of book-trade education is the three-year post-graduate course during which the post-graduate is expected to pass examinations and maintain a thesis. This course is offered at the *Book and Bibliography Department of the Moscow Polygraphic Institute*. Theses on the book trade for the degree of "Candidate of Economic Sciences" are also prepared at a number of economic institutes.

Bibliography

M. Pashkov, *Knižnikam-vysšee obrazovanie.* (Higher education for workers in the book trade). In: Knižnaja Torgovlja, 1966, No. 2, pp. 5–6.

M. Arbuzov, *Vysšee professional'noe obrazovanie.* (Higher professional training). In: Knižnaja Torgovlja, 1964, No. 12, pp. 28–30.

D. Oleinik, *Kursy na baze technikuma.* (Courses on the basis of specialized schools). In: Sovetskaja knižnaja torgovlja, 1963, No. 12, pp. 9–10.

A. Porter, *30 let moskovskogo knigotorgovogo technikuma.* (30 years of the Moscow Book Trade Specialized School). In: Sovetskaja knižnaja torgovlja, 1958, No. 5, pp. 38–42.

14 Copyright

By *V. Markus*

In the USSR copyright is regulated by the relevant articles of the Fundamentals of Civil Legislation of the USSR and the Union Republics and the Civil Codes of the Union Republics.

Part IV of the Fundamentals of Civil Legislation says that copyright applies to any scientific, literary or artistic work, regardless of form, purpose or value.

Copyright to works first published on the territory of the USSR, or unpublished but

located on the territory of the USSR in some presentable form, is deemed to belong to the author and his successors in law, regardless of their citizenship; copyright is also deemed to belong to citizens of the USSR and their successors in law to works which are first published or are located in some presentable form on the territory of a foreign country.
Copyright may belong to one person or several persons—co-authors—where the work has been produced jointly. Copyright is recognized as belonging to juridical persons in the instances and within the limits established by the legislation of the USSR and the Union Republics.
The author has the right:
to publish, reproduce and circulate his work under his own name, under an assumed name (pseudonym) or without indication of name (anonymously), by any legal means;
to the integrity of the work (no changes in the text or in the title of the work may be made without the author's consent);
to receive remuneration for the use of his work by other persons (with the exception of the instances expressly provided for by the law).
The author enjoys the copyright for life; it descends by succession in the manner and within the limits established by the legislation of the USSR and the Union Republics.
In the RSFSR, the right of succession is limited to 15 years, a period which begins to run from 1 January of the year of the author's decease. For literary works the heirs are paid 50%, and for all other works, 20% of the remuneration that would have been due to the author.
Copyright to the publication and other use of a work may be compulsorily purchased by the state from the author or his heirs.
Every published work may be translated without the author's consent, provided he is duly notified and provided the meaning and the integrity of the work are retained. The right to receive remuneration for the use of the work in translation belongs to the author of the original in the instances provided for by the law. The translator has the copyright to his translation.
The use of the author's work by other persons is not permitted otherwise than under a contract with the author or his successors in law, except instances specified by law.
Relations between the author and the publishers involving the latter's use of his work are regulated by standard contracts for publication.
The standard contracts for publication provide for the rights and duties of the author and the publishers who enter into contractual relations, the term of the contract, the deadline for the publishers' assessment (approval) of the work and its acceptance for publication, and the publication date. The standard contract lays down the responsibility of the parties and the fines to be paid for breaches of its terms.
The rates at which authors are remunerated are established by the legislation of the USSR and the Union Republics.
In the RSFSR, the rates are as follows:
a) for literary works—by a decision of the RSFSR Council of Ministers No. 530 of 7 April 1960, and No. 620 of 9 September, 1968 (the latter being based on the decision of the USSR Council of Ministers No. 276 of 25 April 1968);
b) for political, scientific, technical, educational and other works—by a decision of the RSFSR Council of Ministers No. 326 of 20 March 1962, and by a decision of the RSFSR Council of Ministers No. 233 of 31 March 1967, "On Authors' Remuneration for Socio-Political Works".
The royalties are established in two forms: for most literary works—per signature, that is, proportional to the size of the

work—for an author's sheet containing 40,000 typographical units, or by line, for verse; by piece-rate (regardless of the size)—mainly for small works.
For most literary and socio-political works the author is paid a remuneration according to the printing. For reprints of all types of works, the author is paid a remuneration as a percentage of the original rate, depending on the number of reissues, on a descending scale.

Bibliography

O. S. Joffe, *Osnovy avtorskogo prava*. (Fundamentals of copyright. Right of authors, inventors and discoverers. Study aid). Moskva, Znanie 1969. 127 pp.

V. G. Kamyšev, *Izdatel'skij dogovor na literaturnye proizvedenija*. (Contract for publication of literary works). Moskva, Jurig. lit. 1969. 144 pp.

D. M. Sutulov, *Avtorskoe pravo. Izdatel'skie dogovorj. Avtorskij gonorar*. (Copyright. Contracts for publication. Author's royalties). 2nd ed. Moskva, Sovetskaja Rossija 1969. 237 pp.

15 National Bibliography, National Library

By *A. Serebrennikov*

The national (state) bibliography of the USSR is centred at the
Vsesojuznaja Knižnaja Palata
(All-Union Book Chamber)
Kremlevskaja/Nab 1/9
SU Moskva
It was first set up as the "Book Chamber of Russia" in Petrograd, but for a number of historical reasons did not become the true centre of state bibliography. Only after a decision by the USSR Government on organizing the country's bibliography, in a decree signed by Lenin, when the "Central Book Chamber of Russia" was set up in Moscow, state (national) bibliography began rapidly to develop. In 1936, the "Central Book Chamber of Russia" was converted into the "All-Union Book Chamber".
Its main aim is to keep a record of the publications appearing on the territory of the USSR and provide information about them through its "chronicles"—periodical bibliographical publications.
This bibliographical record, which ensures a full account of publications printed in the USSR, is based on the arrangement whereby all printing works throughout the country, in pursuance of a government decision, must send in one copy free of charge to the "All-Union Book Chamber" of everything they put out.
In the Union and Autonomous Republics the bibliographical record of printed matter appearing on their territories is kept by their own book chambers.
The "All-Union Book Chamber" has the most extensive system of "chronicles", which are specialized according to the types of publications, and this is reflected in their names: Chronicle of Books, Chronicle of Periodicals of the USSR, Chronicle of Music, Chronicle of Printed Works in the Pictorial Arts, and the Cartographic Chronicle.
Periodicals and serial publications are entered analytically and go into the Chronicles of Magazine Articles, Chronicles of Newspaper Articles, and Chronicles of Reviews.
The *Knižnaja letopis* ("Chronicle of Books") comes in two editions: the main (weekly) edition, and the supplementary (monthly) edition. The main edition is a record of the books and pamphlets intended for circulation at large, and the whole is accumulated in the *Ežegodnik Knigi SSSR* (Annual of Books of the USSR). The supplementary edition contains a record of official, instructional, programme, methodological and information publications.
Detailed information about the bibliographical material is contained in the

annual *Bibliografija sovetskoi bibliografii* ("Bibliography of Soviet bibliography").
A branch of state (national) bibliography in the USSR is the centralized cataloguing of printed publications in Russian, which is carried out by the "All-Union Book Chamber" through the issue of printed cards for books, author's abstracts of dissertations, articles and reviews appearing in magazines, collections and newspapers published in Moscow.
The control copies of printed works which are sent in to the "All-Union Book Chamber" are in permanent stock at its "Soviet Press and Publishing Archives".
The publications of state (national) bibliography of the USSR reflects the state and development of socialist culture, science and technology.

Bibliography

Gosudarstvennaja Bibliografija Sojuza Sovetskich Socialističeskych Respublik. Spravočnik. (State bibliography of the USSR. Manual). Moskva, Kniga 1967. 112 pp.
Gosudarstvennaja bibliografija i statistika pečati v SSSR. (State bibliography and statistics of press and publishing in the USSR). Moskva, All-Union Book Chamber 1960. 28 pp.
→ 6, 24d.

16 Book Production

By *E. Dinerstein*

The Soviet Union is a world leader in book output. Every year it turns out over 75,000 books and pamphlets, with a printing of 1,300 million copies, a daily average of 3,655,000. Almost 91% of the total output and 57% of the printing are new editions.
The USSR has an average of 548 books and pamphlets per 100 population.
Almost 70% of the publications, making up 94% of the total printing, are marked for price and are intended for sale. However, only 38,000 of books and pamphlets are published for broad circulation. This group includes monographs, literary works, textbooks, handbooks, and so on, with a total printing of 1,148.6 million copies.
Of the total issue in 1969, books (of 48 pages and more) constituted 55% of the number of publications and 70% of the copies.
A specific feature of Soviet book publishing is its multinational character. For instance, in 1968 alone, books and pamphlets were published in 61 languages of the USSR and 40 in foreign languages.
Because the publishing business in the Soviet Union has been stable and planned, books for many years now have averaged 10 signatures and 17,000 copies.
Here is a table showing the main content and purpose of publications in 1969:

Subject group	Number of titles	Printing (million copies)
Political and socio-economic works	10,055	202.0
Scientific works	10,374	18.9
Textbooks	7,798	356.1
Technical literature	27,727	187.6
Agricultural literature	5,408	33.3
Fiction	4,744	173.3
Children's literature	2,226	256.5

Bibliography

USSR publications over 50 years. Moskva, Kniga 1967.
Pečat SSSR v 1969 godu. (USSR publications in 1969. Statistics). Moskva, Kniga 1970*.

* *Pečat SSSR* gives detailed statistical information about all aspects of the national book and periodical production, including figures for the Republics, the individual publishing houses, the production within the various publishing systems, etc. "Pečat SSSR" is the most comprehensive statistical survey of a national book and a periodical production.—The Editor.

USSR

17 Translations

By *A. Davtyan*

Translations are a prominent part of the total printed output because Soviet literature is multinational and multilingual.
The USSR is a world leader in the publishing of translations. UNESCO says that the USSR publishes 9 times more translations than the United Kingdom and 4.5 times more than Japan, and 4 times more than the USA.
In 1969, 7,674 books and pamphlets, with a total printing of about 189.5 million copies, were translated from 93 languages into 84 languages. Of these, 2,105 were translated into Russian, and 4,019 into other languages of the USSR.
The works of the world's classics and outstanding scientists are published in the USSR in millions of copies. Thus, in the 50 Soviet years, there have been 89 editions in 8 languages of the works of Darwin, Leibniz, Newton, Pasteur and Einstein.
A prominent part of the translations are the works of Marx, Engels and Lenin. In 1969, the works of Marx and Engels were published in 79 languages: 49 languages of the peoples of the USSR and 30 foreign languages; the works of Lenin were published in 101 languages: 64 of the USSR and 37 foreign languages.
In the last few years there has been a considerable increase in the number of translations of works by African and Asian authors, notably, of India, Burma, Kenya, Cambodia, Angola and Mali.
Most translations fall into the category of political, socio-economic works and fiction. In 1969, political and socio-economic works were put out in 74 languages by 60 central and 168 republican and local publishing houses. Many translations are published in the Union Republics where their share of the total output is steadily increasing.

Bibliography

Pečat SSSR v 1969 godu. (USSR publications in 1969. Statistics). Moskva, Kniga 1970.
Pečat SSSR za 50 let. Stat. očerki. (The press of the USSR for 50 years. Statistical essays). Moskva, Kniga 1967.

18 Book Clubs

By *V. Pletnyov*

Book clubs are among the most effective and promising means of popularizing and distributing literature in the USSR. Most of these clubs, which exist in various forms, rely on bookselling enterprises, and their number is steadily growing.
Bookshop-clubs have appeared in recent years. In 1969 their number had reached 111, of which 86 were in the Russian Federation and the rest in the Ukraine. The Moscow House of Technical Books has been operating as a book club for the past two years. A music-lovers' club has been formed at the Noty Music Shop in Volgograd. Other bookshop-clubs include the Brigantina in Angarsk, Propagandist in Yuzhno-Sakhalinsk, and Poezia and Kobzar in Kharkov, the Ukraine. It may be expected that a large number of bookshops will gradually turn into manifold book-popularizing organizations with a conference hall, a café, a lecture room, a library and premises for exhibitions.
The existing bookshop-clubs have representative councils that regularly draw up plans, and a large number of regular buyers who attend the various functions sponsored by the club. Moreover the bookshop-clubs advertise books directly at factories and offices and run their own cafeterias, where meetings with buyers are arranged. Bookselling enterprises are relying more and more on these clubs to study the demand and comments on published

literature. They have their own staff and the expense of their upkeep is borne entirely by bookshops.
Booklovers' clubs exist also as associations of volunteer booksellers at many state and cooperative bookshops (→ 24b). A distinguished feature of these clubs—there are more than 170 in the towns alone—is that they are set up also at bookshops that do not have as yet special premises and equipment for mass work.
For the manifold nature and content of their work, the voluntary bookshops set up at many hundreds of factories, building projects, scientific organizations, collective and state farms, and institutions of higher learning, and also the many thousands of book cooperatives at secondary schools have long ago become more than simply trade enterprises operated by volunteers. These associations hold literary balls and other evening functions, conduct book lotteries, obtain literature dealing with the specialization of their enterprise, discuss literary works with readers, popularize literature with account for the age and the professional and aesthetic inclinations of readers, conduct literary educational work among children in the schools situated in the vicinity of their enterprises, and so on. As a rule they organize services at their enterprise very efficiently: orders for literature are accepted in advance, these orders are sent to bookshops and when the books are received they are delivered to the workers directly in the workshops and departments or sold through kiosks or from tables conveniently sited on the territory of the enterprise. These bookshop-clubs have the support of the management and public organizations of their enterprises. With the increase in the book output the number of such bookshop-clubs is expected to go up substantially. Hundreds of thousands of regular buyers already fall within the range of the various services offered by these clubs.

20 Book Design

By *E. Goltseva*

The "Committee for Publishing and the Press under the USSR Council of Ministers" (→ 4), together with various unions of writers and artists, arranges various book competitions.
Since 1958, there has been an annual All-Union Design and Printing Competition. This is sponsored by the "Committee for Publishing and the Press under the USSR Council of Ministers" and the "Scientific and Technical Society for Printing and Publication". The competition is held to bring out the country's best publications, and the bodies of workers and enterprises which produced them.
The competition has been gaining in popularity from year to year, with more and more publishing houses and printing works taking part. At the Tenth All-Union Competition in 1969 there were 1,073 publications submitted, of which 238 books and albums and 20 journals were awarded diplomas.
Prominent artists, art critics, editors and specialists in publishing and printing sit on the panel of judges and the Council of the competition. Representatives from Bulgaria, Hungary, the GDR, Mongolia and Poland take part in judging the entries. The publications submitted for the competition are grouped according to the types of literature (socio-political, scientific and technical, fiction, children's, art criticism and so on). Account is taken by the judges of every aspect of design and printing, and ideological and artistic merits, originality of approach, quality of execution, novel features and so on.
Winners are awarded Ivan Fyodorov Diplomas, First and Second Class Diplomas and recognition diplomas.
An All-Union Anniversary Competition was held to mark the Centenary of the

Birth of Lenin. The best Lenin publications were awarded special diplomas.
Books which have won diplomas in all-Union competitions are on show at the Soviet Publishing and Press Pavilion at the USSR Economic Achievement Exhibition. The Book Room of the "Committee for Publishing and the Press" organizes permanent travelling exhibitions of best books which are shown all over the country.
Republican competitions for the best design and printing of books are also staged in the RSFSR, the Ukraine, Byelorussia and other republics. The Baltic and Central Asian Republics have inter-Republican competitions.
Some scientific organizations and unions of writers and artists stage topical competitions for the best book in terms of content. Thus, the All-Union Znanie Society holds annual competitions for the best popular science works. The Writers Union and the Committee for Publishing and the Press under the USSR Council of Ministers arrange all-Union competitions for the best works of fiction for children.

21 Publishing

By *E. Dinerstein*

Russian book printing was started by Ivan Fyodorov, who issued the first dated book, "The Apostle", in Moscow in 1564. Students of the history of Russian book publishing are still trying to trace the authorship of several anonymous publications which had appeared in Moscow before that date.
Moscow printers helped to spread the printing of books in the Ukraine, Byelorussia and Lithuania. They were so successful that one hundred years later, in the mid-17th century, there was a total of 1,000–1,200 copies in print, while spelling books, the Book of Psalms and the prayer-book, intended as study aids, were published in editions of 12,000, 24,000 and even 36,000 copies. In the early 17th century, books were still sold at cost price, but by the mid-century, a margin of 100% was usually added. However, it took some time before book publishing became commercial.
Despite the flourishing of the publishing business in the 1760–80s the prospects for a national book market were only opened up by the Free Printing Act of 1783. By the 20th century, Russia had many companies engaged in publishing and a book trade rivalling the largest companies in Western Europe (M. O. Wolff, A. S. Suvorin, A. F. Marks and I. D. Sytin).
The Great October Socialist Revolution led to the establishment of a new type of publishing house for which profit was not the main aim. For the first time in history, book publishing was organized on state lines, making it possible to exercise purposeful direction of the publishing business and to plan it over a long term.
In August 1963 a special "Committee for Publishing and the Press" (→ 4) was set up under the Council of Ministers of the USSR to provide co-ordination in the publishing industry. Similar committees were set up under the Councils of Ministers of the Union Republics.
The present system of publishing includes, alongside state publishers, publishing houses belonging to the Communist Party, social organizations and the Academy of Sciences of the USSR. In 1969, a total of 233 publishing houses were operating on the territory of the USSR, including 179 within the system of the "Committee for Publishing and the Press under the USSR Council of Ministers", 36 of dual subordination (that is, managed jointly by different departments and Committees), 18 belonging to social organizations, ministries and departments. In addition, various estab-

lishments and educational institutions were also engaged in publishing.
→ 2, 3, 4, 6, 35a.

*Bibliography**

A. I. NAZAROV, *Kniga v sovetskom obščestve.* (Books in Soviet society). Moskva, Nauka 1964.
→ 3, Bibliography.

23 Wholesale Trade

By *A. Marin and D. Altshil*

The leading wholesale organization in the USSR is *Soyuzkniga,* the "All-Union Association of the Book Trade", which, alongside its function of directing the distribution of books throughout the country, has a number of wholesale bookstores, among them the Central Wholesale Bookstore in Moscow, wholesale bookstores in Leningrad and Kalinin, and book-forwarding offices in Minsk, Kharkov and other cities.
"Soyuzkniga" buys all its books from the central publishing houses, under contracts which are concluded annually. At the same time, "Soyuzkniga" concludes contracts with booksellers throughout the country, and under these it supplies literature to wholesale booksellers of Republics, territories and regions within the system of the "Committee for Publishing and the Press under the USSR Council of Ministers" (→ 4), and also wholesale bookstores of consumer cooperatives, the "USSR Ministry of Communications" and the "Akademkniga".
"Soyuzkniga" obtains its books from the publishing houses at a discount of 25%, which is distributed among the bookselling organizations with an eye to the remoteness of the area where they are sited and conditions of work, so that those in outlying areas are allowed a discount of up to 60%, while those closer to major industrial and cultural centres, obtain discounts ranging from 11 to 23%.
Republican, territorial and regional bookselling organizations have their own wholesale bookstores, whose functions include the reception, storage and distribution of literature arriving from "Soyuzkniga's" wholesale bookstores. In addition, they conclude contracts for the supply of literature with Republican, territorial and regional publishing houses. These wholesale bookstores are also allowed a 25% discount by the publishing houses.
Every year, all the publishing houses issue their plans for the output of literature, on the strength of which the bookselling organizations invite buyers to place their orders. The plans are drawn up with the help of those who run the bookstalls, shop assistants, book experts at bookshops and wholesale bookstores and others.
The orders for literature collected from the shops under the plans issued by the central publishing houses are summarized by the regional, territorial and Republican bookselling organizations and submitted to "Soyuzkniga".
"Soyuzkniga" analyses and sums up the submitted orders and passes them on to the publishing houses concerned. "Soyuzkniga" pays for the ordered number of books as soon as these are issued. The publishers have the right to print larger editions of books, and in such instances "Soyuzkniga" accepts the extra copies on a commission basis, with payment as these are sold off. That is also the practice in relations between Republican, territorial and regional publishing houses and the corresponding bookselling organizations.
"Soyuzkniga" wholesale bookstores dispatch books by rail (in containers), by ship, by mail and by plane.
Both the "Soyuzkniga" wholesale book-

* "Pečat SSSR" (→ 16) also contains a list of the annual production of the individual publishing houses.—The Editor.

stores and the Republican, territorial and regional wholesale bookstores allow themselves a reserve when ordering literature from the publishing houses so as to be able to fulfil repeat orders from bookselling organizations. For that purpose, wholesale bookstores have special assortment rooms. The wholesale bookstores supply retailers with the necessary quantities and assortment of books.

At regular intervals they arrange wholesale book fairs at which there is a redistribution of literature and an exchange of editions issued by Republican, regional and territorial publishing houses.

The major wholesale bookstores have been designed and built to individual designs, while the wholesale bookstores of regional bookselling offices are built to type designs.

"Soyuzkniga" has an office for the export and import of literature—*Knigoexport*—which handles the delivery of Soviet publications to foreign countries and buys literature abroad through *Meždunarodnaja Kniga* (→27,28). "Knigoexport" is a wholesale organization and sells imported literature in accordance with orders submitted by bookselling organizations throughout the country.

→ 6, 35a.

Bibliography

A. I. Goldin. The wholesale book trade and the work of book experts. Operation of the wholesale bookstore. In: The book trade. Organziation and techniques. Moskva, Kniga 1969, pp. 211–275.—In Russian.

24 Retail Trade

a) *Bookshops*

By *A. Marin*

Bookshops are now the main enterprises in the sale of literature, handling over 85% of the books sold throughout the country.

There are a total of over 14,000 bookshops in the USSR. Within the system of the "Committee for Publishing and the Press under the USSR Council of Ministers" (→ 4) there are 5,600 and within the consumer co-operative system, 7,800.

The bookshops are active in spreading knowledge about books and strive to meet demand in various branches of knowledge. They have been doing a great deal of work with readers, and are real centres of culture and enlightenment. Most of the bookshops carry a universal assortment of literature.

In the last few years, there have been various changes in the Soviet book trade, involving the introduction of progressive modern techniques in the distribution of books among the population, and differentiated approaches in dealing with different groups of buyers. There has been a spread of specialised bookselling enterprises handling school and teaching aids, political, scientific and technical, agricultural, and other types of literature. Special shops have been set up for the sale of books from the socialist countries and the republics of the USSR, antiquarian and subscription editions. The mail-order service is of great importance in a country like the USSR, with its vast territory and large-scale construction projects. This is handled by shops of the system *Kniga-Pochtoi* ("Book-Parcel Post", → 25).

"Houses of Books", central bookshops in large cities, have become very popular with book-lovers. Among the best known are the Moscow's Dom Knigi, which carries 46,000 titles, the Dom Nauchno-Tekhnicheskoi Knigi ("House of Scientific and Technical Books") in Moscow, in whose nine halls there are 30,000 books in various branches of science, technology, industry and construction, and the Leningrad's Dom Knigi. Most bookshops offer free access to bookshelves, and all accept advance orders for books in print.

A new form of popularizing and disseminating literature—bookshop-clubs—has emerged in recent years (→ 18).
In their work the shops rely on the help of a large body of volunteers, specialists in various fields of science and technology and regular buyers, who do much to popularize and disseminate literature. Many shops have set up public assistance councils.
→ 2, 3, 4, 6, 18, 35a.

Bibliography

A. I. Goldin and V. V. Uspenskaya, Types of shops and their equipment. Receipt and arrangement of printed matter in shops. Sales and services. Management of a bookshop and control over its economic activities. In: The book trade. Organization and techniques. Moskva, Kniga 1969, pp. 21–125, 181–210.—In Russian.

A. N. Ljubimov and L. J. Rabin, *Buchgalterskii učet knižnogo magazina*. (Bookshop accounting). Moskva, Kniga 1966 213 pp.

D. A. Černyi, *Analiz chozjaistvennoi dejatel'nosti knižnogo magazina*. (Analysis of the economic activity of a bookshop. A practical aid). Moskva, Kniga 1966 200 pp.

V. Dobruschin and N. Slucker, *Specializirovannyi knižnyi magasin*. (Specialized bookshop. From practical experience). Moskva, Iskusstvo 1963. 139 pp.

b) *Voluntary Book Trade*

By *V. Pletnyov*

Voluntary book trading is very widespread in the USSR. In 1969 there were 600,000 volunteer distributors of books.
Teams of volunteer popularizers of books are formed at bookshops, factories, educational institutions, collective and state farms and libraries.
Most bookshops have voluntary councils for the dissemination of books, which help to study the requirements of the local population, popularize new literature, hold readers' conferences, arrange meetings with writers and review new literature for the press and radio. Through these councils the bookshops maintain contact with factories, educational institutions and public organizations. The councils play a particularly important role in the period when the annual book-production plans of the different publishing houses are drawn up. In the course of two or three months bookshops frequently have to study and discuss with the buyers and organizations of their districts the plans of from 10 to 50 publishing houses involving several thousand new titles that are to be published in the following year.
At present, in cities alone, there are nearly 2,000 voluntary councils for the dissemination of books at the bookshops, and more than 170 bibliophile clubs (→ 18).
Volunteer booksellers are particularly active at factories, educational institutions, libraries, particularly in rural localities. The volunteer book-popularizer movement is supported by public organizations, by the managements of factories, building projects and collective farms, and by the administration of institutions of higher learning and schools. Almost everywhere the backbone of this movement consists of young workers, young collective farmers, students and schoolchildren—members of the Young Communist League.
The main forms of associations of voluntary booksellers outside the bookshops are shops and bookstalls run on a voluntary basis. There are nearly 7,000 of these. Another form is teams of sellers. Book cooperatives at schools have become widespread chiefly in rural localities. Of the more than 17,000 of these cooperatives in the Soviet Union, approximately 15,000 are in rural localities. Literature is actively

disseminated by many libraries. There are about 18,000 such libraries in rural localities and more than 2,500 in the towns. Besides selling books, all these associations conduct extensive educational work.

Volunteer booksellers are supplied with literature by the nearest state or cooperative bookshop. In order to encourage volunteer book distribution, bookselling enterprises deposit in the account of the associations of YCL organizations 5% of the price of the books sold by them. This money is used for evening functions and conferences and for bonuses to the most active popularizers of books.

Volunteer book trading has assumed large proportions in the Ukraine, Lithuania, Latvia, Estonia, and many regions and Autonomous republics of the Russian Federation.

Tens of millions of books, textbooks and brochures are sold annually by volunteer distributors. They help book lovers to form their own libraries. A movement started in the Ukraine "Books by Lenin to every family" has gained considerable headway. In Lithuania one in ten books is sold by volunteer distributors. Many of the bookshops and bookstalls run by volunteers and the book cooperatives in schools are becoming book clubs.

Bibliography

A. Z. KOMAROVA AND N. V. SAFONOVA, *Obščestvennomu rasprostranitelju knigi*. (Volunteer book distributor. A concise reference book). Moskva, Kniga 1965. 77 pp.

M. F. ARBUZOV, Mass forms of book distribution. In: Book Trade. Organization and techniques. Moskva, Kniga 1969, pp. 154–165. – In Russian.

c) *Library Collectors*

By *A. Marin*

In the USSR there are more than 370,000 libraries with a fund of 2,300 million books. They cater for 115 million readers.

There are 150 library collectors, which regularly supply books to 210,000 libraries in the various departments and organizations.

In 1969 libraries acquired through the library collectors books to the value of 62.8 million rubles.

The library collectors are specialized enterprises of the bookselling organization. They regularly supply books and equipment according to the plans and speciality of the libraries in the different regions (territories or republics).

They are stocked through the booksellers, which give them priority for the purchase of the latest literature on the basis of orders received from libraries and of the approved plan for the delivery of literature.

Their work covers a wide field. They provide libraries with bibliographical consultation and supply them with bibliographies and with literature on library science.

Their main work consists of keeping libraries abreast of the books being published or already brought out by central, republican and local publishing houses and receiving orders for books from them. In addition, they provide libraries with methodological assistance in building up their book funds, for which purpose they compile bibliographical reviews of new books and of books in their own stock and in the stocks of the booksellers, study the demands of libraries by analysing the orders received from them and submit recommendations to the booksellers for the publication or re-publication of the necessary literature.

An important aspect of their work is the organization of exhibitions of books and illustrations on major political events, jubilees and various scientific, technological, literary and art themes, the holding of group and individual consultations, lectures, and meetings with writers, scientists and authors of particular books.

Jointly with republican (territorial or regional) libraries on the basis of orders received from district libraries, the book collectors compile summary orders for books for the rural libraries of the republics (territories or regions), submit these orders to the "Council for the Replenishment of Libraries" and obtain approval for them from the Ministry of Culture of the Union (or Autonomous) republic, from the regional (territorial) department of culture and the Council of Trade Unions. After their approval by these bodies the summary orders are used as documents on the basis of which the given library collector supplies books to libraries.

Bibliography

Y. I. Arest, The work of a library collector. In: Book Trade. Organization and techniques. Moskva, Kniga 1969, pp. 166–180.—In Russian.

d) *Book-Trade Bibliography*

By *V. Osipov*

Russian book-trade bibliography of the 18th and 19th centuries is represented by a large number of book-trade catalogues, many of which retain their importance as bibliographical sources to this day. Before the Revolution book-trade bibliography consisted of scattered publications which did not satisfy the requirements of booksellers. The present system of book-trade bibliography in the USSR began to take shape in the 1920s. At present it is a major component of the book trade and of bibliography as a whole.

Book-trade bibliography is, first and foremost, a system of information on literature awaiting publication. It consists of the annual publication plans of all publishing houses. The plans contain an annotated list of books, posters, music and other printed matter to be published by the given publishing house in the course of the coming year.

The changes and additions in the plans are reported about twice a week in the bulletin *Order Blank* ("To be published soon" section).

The publication plans and the bulletin are sent to all bookshops, which use them when they order books.

For buyers the publishing houses put out prospectuses advertising individual publications (for example, collected works or reference books) and thematic catalogues (for instance, books dealing with the railway transport).

Also part of book-trade bibliography is the system of information on literature that has come off the press. This system exists parallel with state bibliography.

The bulletin "Order Blank" has a section "New Books", which gives a list of books received at the "Central Wholesale Book Trade Depository" and being sent out to booksellers. The weekly newspaper *Knižnoje Obozrenije* carries a column headed "Books of the Week", which contains a partially annotated list of new books available at bookshops. Publishing houses put out annual catalogues of their publications.

Also part of book-trade bibliography is a system of information on literature on sale and available at book depositories. The list of books available at the "Central Wholesale Depository" is published regularly in the section "Books in Stock" in the "Order Blank". Catalogues of books in stock at the "Central Wholesale Depository" are brought out as separate publications. Catalogues are also published of the books available at the regional and republican book depositories. Lists of the books available at these depositories are published in the bulletin "Supply and Demand", which is issued once or twice a week.

The above-mentioned aids of book-trade bibliography are used in the home market. For the foreign market "Meždunarodnaja Kniga" publishes the bulletin "New Books of the USSR" (→ 27, 28).

Bibliography

N. V. Zdobnov, *Sostavlenie knigotorgovych katalogov*. (Compilation of book-trade catalogues). Moskva, Gizlegprom 1933.
V. O. Osipov, Soviet book-trade bibliography. In: Kniga, Vol. 15. Moskva, Kniga 1967.—In Russian.

25 Mail-Order Bookselling

By *A. Marin*

Book-parcel shops and departments have been set up to serve the population in rural localities and out-of-the-way regions that do not have an established network of bookshops of their own. Large sections of the population avail themselves of the services of these enterprises, particularly specialists in various branches of the economy, scientists, students and builders.

The network of these shops and departments has been enlarged in recent years. At present there are over 50 specialized book-parcel shops and nearly 400 departments.

The turnover of the book-parcel trade has grown from 3 million rubles in 1961 to 32 million rubles in 1970.

The turnover of the book-parcel trade accounts for over 8% of the turnover of the entire book retail network operated by the "Committee for Publishing and the Press under the USSR Council of Ministers (→ 4).

The book-parcel turnover of Moskniga, the Moscow City Book Trade Office, exceeded 13 million rubles. Book-parcel enterprises annually receive over 5 million orders by mail from buyers.

An analysis of the letters received by the shops shows that the overwhelming majority of the orders are from individual buyers. Over 90% of the orders received by bookshops sending music and pedagogical and other literature by mail are from individual buyers.

The situation is somewhat different in shops dealing in scientific, technological, building and agricultural literature by mail. There 60–65% of the orders are from individual buyers, and the remaining 35–40% from organizations and offices.

The principal tasks of the book-parcel trade are to provide the largest possible choice in order to satisfy the requirements of out-of-town buyers, attract more buyers, handle orders efficiently and improve advertising and bibliographical work.

The names of regular buyers are entered into card indexes, on the basis of which they are regularly supplied with advertising and bibliographical material.

Bibliography

A. Z. Komarova. *Rabota magasinov i otdelov "Kniga-počtoi"*. (Book-parcel shops and departments). Moskva, Kniga 1964. 56 pp.
Instructions in the work of book-parcel shops and departments. Moskva, Kniga 1968.—In Russian.

26 Antiquarian Book Trade, Auctions

By *S. Puzanov*

Trade in antiquarian books continues the long-established fine tradition of the antiquarian booksellers of pre-revolutionary Russia: Ferapontov, Bolshakovs, Kolchugins, Shibanovs, Fadeyevs, Astapov, Solovyov, Martynov, Klochkov, Nikolayev and others. The antiquarian book trade was conducted mainly in Moscow and St Petersburg, and on an insignificant scale in Kiev, Riga, Tiflis, Saratov, Chernsky Uyezd in Tula Gubernia' Starodub in Chernigov Gubernia and some other places.

At present the antiquarian book trade is handled by the bookselling networks of the "Committee for Publishing and the Press under the Council of Ministers of the USSR" (→ 4), the "Union of Writers of the USSR", the "Academy of Sciences of the USSR" and "Centrosoyuz".

The antiquarian bookselling network of the Committee for Publishing and the Press has more than 200 shops and departments. During the last three years booksellers throughout the Soviet Union have been buying and accepting on commission large numbers of books brought out by Soviet publishing houses in 1947 and later. There are at present more than 2,000 general and specialized bookshops, which purchase old books.

The overall co-ordination and organization of the second-hand book trade is handled by "Soyuzkniga" (→ 4). In 1966 it set up a group for the organization of the antiquarian and commission book trade. "Soyuzkniga" puts out instructions regulating the purchase and acceptance for commission of books from the population, generalizes and disseminates advanced experience of trade in antiquarian books, helps the booksellers to promote and improve the trade in antiquarian books, controls the observance of the instructions and rules for buying and selling books, compiles price-lists for the purchase and sale of antiquarian books and so on.

The principal references in the purchase of books from the population are the catalogue-price-lists approved by the Ministry of Culture in 1960 and published by the "All-Union Book Chamber" (→ 15) in 1961. Brought out in three volumes these catalogues list 8,223 titles.

In the localities the antiquarian book trade is effected by specially trained personnel of the republican, territorial, regional and town bookselling organizations.

In the biggest cultural centre of the country—Moscow—the antiquarian book trade is conducted by *Mosbukkniga*, an independent office affiliated to the city bookselling organization. In Moscow there are specialized antiquarian bookshops: Shop No. 45 (Antikvar) which deals in rare books and pictorial publications; Shop No. 14, which deals in medical literature. In Leningrad Shop No. 10 specializes in scientific, technological and medical literature, and Shop No. 53 specializes in rare books.

The Literary Fund of the Union of Writers of the USSR operates specialized bookshops for writers in Moscow, Leningrad and Kiev. Each of these shops has a large second-hand book department which buys books ordered by the writers.

Nauka, the publishing house of the Academy of Sciences of the USSR, has a book-trade agency—Akademkniga. The shops of Akademkniga (in Moscow and Leningrad) likewise have second-hand book departments.

The book-trade network of "Centrosoyuz" buys from the population books published chiefly after 1947.

Most antiquarian books are sold through the network run by the Committee for Publishing and Printing under the Council of Ministers of the USSR.

Bibliography

P. N. Martynov, *Polveka v mire knig.* (A half-century in the world of books). Leningrad, Nauka 1969. 183 pp.

S. Puzanov, *Organizacija bukinističeskoi torgovli.* (Organization of the antiquarian book trade). In: Knižnaja torgovlja, Moskva, Kniga 1968, No. 2.

P. P. Shibanov, Trade in rare books in Russia. In: The book trade. An aid for booksellers. Ed. by M. V. Muratov and N. T. Nakoryakov. Moskva and Leningrad, Gosizdat 1925, pp. 199–266.—In Russian.

F. Shilov, *Zapiski starogo knižnika.* (Notes of an old bibliophile). Moskva, Kniga 1965. 158 pp.

27 Book Imports
28 Book Exports

a) *General Situation*

The foreign trade business transactions for the export of Soviet literature and the import of foreign publications are conducted on the basis of state monopoly of the USSR through the All-Union Association

V/O Meždunarodnaja Kniga
(The International Book)
G – 200
SU Moskva

which has been in existence ever since 1923. At the present time the "Meždunarodnaja Kniga" is one of the greatest bookselling firms in the world which does export–import business with more than 1,000 bookselling, publishing, musical and philatelic firms in 131 countries on all the continents the world over.

The "Meždunarodnaja Kniga" yearly offers to foreign firms more than 25,000 books with different titles, over 2,000 newspapers and periodicals, more than 1,000 gramophone records and a wide range of postal stamps for collectors.

Soviet books are published in 61 tongues of the peoples of the Soviet Union and in 40 foreign languages (1968). The publication of books in foreign languages is steadily expanding from year to year and now constitutes approximately 28% of the total number of books being exported.

"Meždunarodnaja Kniga" is a wholesale bookselling organization, which has earned itself the reputation of a reputable business partner, both in export and import trade. If so desired by foreign firms, the "Meždunarodnaja Kniga" will also assist in re-publication abroad of the latest works of Soviet authors in the fields of artistic, political, scientific, technical, educational and children's literature.

For this purpose the Association concludes agreements for long-term collaboration as well as for once-only publication of books. Books in Russian and other languages are sent free of charge to foreign publishers with originals or photocopies of the illustrations. In cases requiring it, foreign publishers are provided with prefaces, authors' advice and other material by way of supplements to translations and books to be published.

The "Meždunarodnaja Kniga" accepts orders for books from foreign firms all the year round. The publication of new Soviet books is made known to the readers and booksellers through the medium of advertising bulletins, catalogues and leaflets issued by the Association in various languages of the peoples of the USSR and of foreign countries. Detailed information about the issue of new Soviet books is given in the weekly *Noviye Knigi SSSR* ("New USSR books"). gramophone record fans will find useful information in the monthly catalogue "Soviet long-playing records". Every year, in September at the latest, the catalogue of Soviet newspapers and magazines is published. All the catalogues, bulletins, and leaflets are furnished free of charge.

Books, gramophone records and slides are dispatched to the addresses of the wholesale buyers, as well as newspapers and magazines to the addresses of firms and private subscribers, at the expense of the Association, the daily papers being sent by air-mail using the fastest Soviet and foreign air-line services.

The "Meždunarodnaja Kniga" is a constant participant at international book fairs in Belgrade, Brussels, Frankfurt am Main, Sofia, Warsaw; it takes part in numerous exhibitions of a general character e. g. in Leipzig, Budapest, Plovdive, Izmir, Damascus, Zagreb, Algiers, Cairo; further, the Association always participates in Soviet commercial and industrial exhibitions abroad, offering on show new books, gramophone records, stamps and periodicals. Representatives of the Association give information on the activities of Soviet publishers; they sign contracts for the reprinting of Soviet books as well as for the supply of books and other goods of the Association. More details about the activities of the "Meždunarodnaja Kniga" are contained in the general pamphlet, as well as in other advertising media issued by the Association.

b) *Book Exhibitions*

By *V. Pletnyov*

More and more books are exhibited by Soviet publishers and book-marketing organizations both at international fairs and at various All-Union, Republican and local book expositions and fairs at home (→ 29). The exhibitions are arranged by sections and types of literature and other printed matter, in connection with political and cultural events in the USSR and abroad, and for the dissemination of the latest achievements in science and technology. There are several types of exhibitions: exhibitions showing the achievements of publishing business abroad; exhibitions by publishers and leading printing works, commercial exhibitions from booksellers' stocks, travelling exhibitions, etc.
Every year, the "All-Union Association of the Book Trade" (Soyuzkniga) brings together and sends to various countries of the world more than 200 book exhibitions which are arranged abroad either by the All-Union Association "Meždunarodnaja Kniga" (→ 27, 28) or by the "Union of Soviet Societies for Friendship and Cultural Relations with Foreign Countries".
The Soviet book exhibition at the World Exposition at Montreal, with almost 1,000 different books on display, evoked great interest.
For the International Exposition at Osaka in 1970 the "Committee for Publishing and the Press under the USSR Council of Ministers" (→ 4) has sent almost 2,500 books on various topics.
Every year, the Committee for Publishing and the Press, Soviet publishers and booksellers, together with "Meždunarodnaja Kniga", participate in at least 18 international book fairs (Leipzig, Frankfurt am Main, Plovdiv, Brno, Belgrade, Zagreb, Warsaw and other cities). Apart from arranging an extensive display of books at these fairs, "Meždunarodnaja Kniga" is active in concluding contracts for the export of Soviet publications.
In 1969 alone, almost 10,000 of the latest publications, ranging from scientific monographs to richly illustrated children's books were on display at international fairs and exhibitions in more than 100 countries.

29 Book Fairs

By *A. Marin*

a) *Book Fairs*

All-Union, republican and regional fairs are held for the purpose of redistributing the book stocks of the country's bookselling organizations.
Bookselling organizations which have surplus stocks of republican and regional publications, put them on display at the wholesale fairs.
As a rule, the fairs are used to display samples which enable workers in the state and co-operative book trade, managers of wholesale bookstores, distributing centres for libraries and shops to buy the books they need.
Book fairs help some shops to enlarge their

assortment of literature and others to get rid of surplus book stocks.
At the same time, book fairs are a good form of studying demand for new editions published by republican and regional publishing houses.
At these fairs, conferences and seminars are arranged and a useful exchange of experience takes place on every aspect of the book trade.
The economic effect of these fairs indicates that the redistribution of surplus book stocks helps to enrich the assortment and promotes the successful fulfilment and overfulfilment of planned targets by each bookselling organization.
In 1960, book fairs helped to sell literature worth 2.5 million rubles; in 1969, the figure was well over 12 million.

b) *Exhibitions*

By *V. Pletnyov*

At home, book exhibitions are arranged by the "Committee for Publishing and the Press under the USSR Council of Ministers", Committees for Publishing and the Press in the Union Republics, consumer cooperatives, publishing houses, printing works, booksellers, bookshops, libraries, volunteer distributors of books, special organizing committees for international book exhibitions and other organizations (→ 27, 28).
The international exhibitions arranged by the "Committee for Publishing and the Press under the USSR Council of Ministers" deserve special notice. The first of these was held in Moscow in 1967 to mark 50 years of Soviet power. On display were more than 20,000 books seen by 300,000 visitors. Every day was devoted to a Union Republic or a socialist country. Among its many other activities were large sales of books, an international book competition, and seminars for publishers and printers.
The International Exhibition held in Moscow in 1970 to mark the Centenary of Lenin's Birth was even more impressive. Among its participants were all the publishing houses of the Soviet Union, representing the Union and Autonomous Republics, and publishers from almost 40 foreign countries—socialist, developing and capitalist. The exhibition gave an idea of the many publications of Lenin's vast theoretical legacy, in the USSR and in dozens of countries across the world. The exhibition was a major political and cultural event of international magnitude, with a display of more than 20,000 publications, a special international pavilion of printed masterpieces submitted by the participants for an international competition, an international pavilion of children's books, extensive trading in Soviet and foreign publications, a book lottery and numerous other activities.
The "All-Union Association of the Book Trade" (Soyuzkniga) regularly replenishes its permanent stocks for expositions at home and abroad.

30 Public Relations

By *V. Osipov*

The term "book popularization and advertising" is used in Soviet book-trade literature. On the one hand, it shows that book-trade popularization differs from book popularization at libraries and, on the other, that book advertising markedly differs from trade advertising both in content and many forms and methods.
Diverse forms and methods of popularizing and advertising books are used in the Soviet book trade. They may be classified in the following groups.
Verbal popularization: conversation between salesmen and buyers, meetings with groups of buyers, readers' conferences, meetings with authors and with publishing-

house personnel, reviews of literature. The radio is also included in this category.

Printed advertisements: various catalogues and prospectuses (→ 24e).

Visual means of popularization and advertisement: signboards, show windows in and outside the shop, display of books on tables, counters and stands, book exhibitions in the shop and other premises. Films and television are being used on a growing scale in this category.

Contact between bookselling enterprises and publishing houses and public organizations is an indispensable condition for book popularization and advertising.

Undertakings arranged in the bookshops play a special role in book popularization and advertising. The show-window displays can be: thematic or devoted to new books, to books for some special group of readers, to the works of some one author, or the output of some one publishing house. Recommendations for window displays are published regularly in the magazine "Knižnaja torgovlja" (→ 5).

Catalogues and prospectuses are put out as brochures, leaflets, bookmarks and posters. Advertising bands in which books can be wrapped are put out in large quantities. Jackets help to increase the demand for individual books. This method has made it possible to sell a large number of individual volumes from collected works.

The addresses of regular buyers and organizations interested in specific subjects are entered in a card index and prospectuses and catalogues are sent to them. Parcel-post shops and departments also circulate advertising and bibliographical materials in this manner (→ 25).

Announcements in newspapers and magazines play an exceedingly important role. In the decision "On the state and measures to improve the book trade" adopted by the SSRSU on 31 May 1960, and in the decision "On measures to improve publishing activity and remove the shortcomings in the book trade" passed by the Council of Ministers of the USSR in 1964, it is recommended that newspapers and magazines and also the radio and television should give more attention to advertising new books and set up bibliography and book popularization departments for this purpose.

All republican, territorial and regional bookselling organizations have book popularization and advertising departments. Their work is coordinated and directed by the "Book Popularization Department" of the "Committee for Publishing and the Press of the Council of Ministers of the USSR" (→ 4).

The course of book popularization is given to students of the "Moscow Polygraphic Institute" (→ 11).

Bibliography

M. F. Arbuzov, Book popularization and advertising. In: Book Trade. Organization and techniques. Moskva, Kniga 1969, pp. 126–142.—In Russian.

M. F. Arbuzov, Popularization and advertising in the book trade. Moskva, Kniga 1966.—In Russian.

31 Bibliophily

→ 18, 20, 26.

32 Literary Prizes

By *A. Davtyan*

The USSR has a state system of awards for outstanding literary works, the most important being the *Lenin Prize,* which since 1967 is being awarded once every two years. *State Prizes,* instituted in 1939, are also awarded for outstanding literary works. Since 1967, 10 State Prizes are awarded annually in literature, the arts and architecture.

Annual awards of *Lenin Komsomol Prizes* for literary and artistic works were instituted in May 1967. In addition, the USSR Academy of Sciences awards the *Belinsky Prize* and the *Chernyshevsky Prize* for outstanding works in the history of literature. Special awards are also made by the Journalists' Union of the USSR. The following awards for literary works have been instituted in the Union Republics:

Azerbaijan SSR—Akhundov Prize (1948)
Armenian SSR—State Prizes (1965)
Byelorussian SSR—Yanka Kupala and Yakub Kolas Literary Prizes (1956)
Georgian SSR—Shota Rustaveli Prize (1964) and Georgia Komsomol CC Prizes (1966)
Kazakh SSR—State Prizes in Literature and the Arts (1965)
Kirghiz SSR—Toktogul State Prizes (1965)
Latvian SSR—State Prizes (1957)
Lithuanian SSR—State Prizes (1956)
Moldavian SSR—State Prizes in Literature and the Arts (1965)
RSFSR—Maxim Gorky State Prizes in Literature
Tajik SSR—State Prizes in Literature and the Arts (1959)
Turkmen SSR—Makhtumkuli State Prizes (1966)
Uzbek SSR—Niyazi Republican Prizes (1964)
Ukrainian SSR—Taras Shevchenko Prize (1961)
Estonian SSR—Soviet Estonia Prize (1947)

Some Autonomous Republics also award prizes:

Tatar ASSR—Tukai Prize (1958)
Chuvash ASSR—Konstantin Ivanov Prize and Misha Sespel Prize
Yakut ASSR—Oiunsky Republican Prize (1966)

33 The Reviewing of Books

→ 5.

35 Miscellaneous

Circulation of Periodicals

By *K. Postnov*

Newspapers and magazines are circulated by *Soyuzpečat*, the "Central Board for the Circulation of Periodicals of the Ministry of Communications". Newspapers and magazines are thus sold by a special apparatus, which is independent of the book-distributing system.

Structurally, Soyuzpečat conforms to the administrative divisions existing in the country: from the Central Board for the Circulation of Periodicals in Moscow, through republican, regional and territorial boards and departments for the circulation of periodicals, to Soyuzpečat town and district agencies.

Subordinated directly to Soyuzpečat are the Central Subscriptions Agency, the Central Retail Agency, the Central Agency for Foreign Publications, the Central Advertising and Information Agency and the Central Philatelic Agency.

The following figures illustrate the scale of the work conducted by Soyuzpečat. Its turnover in 1970 exceeded 1,300 million rubles. During the current year the circulation of newspapers and magazines handled by Soyuzpečat agencies has reached 300 million copies, with nearly 80% of the periodicals distributed by subscription.

Subscriptions are accepted by Soyuzpečat agencies, the central post offices, post and telegraph offices, post and telephone stations, branch post offices, postmen and also a large body of volunteer canvassers (more than 1,500,000 persons).

Subscriptions are accepted for a year, six months, three months or one or two months. The subscription rates are given in the catalogues of newspapers and magazines which are published annually by Soyuzpečat in millions of copies and sent to the localities.

For the street sale of newspapers and magazines there are more than 25,000 kiosks and shops and thousands of vending machines.

For the convenience of readers the kiosks at railway stations, airports and hotels work two or three shifts.

In rural localities up-to-date newspapers may be bought at the local post office, from the postman or in the consumers' cooperative shop.

In many towns newspapers and magazines are sold in buses, tramcars and trolleybuses, and also in suburban trains. These sales are handled by drivers, conductors and other non-staff agents of Soyuzpečat. At thousands of factories there are kiosks that function without salesmen or are operated by volunteer salesmen.

The price of daily newspapers—2 and 3 kopeks—is uniform throughout the Soviet Union. The price of magazines ranges from 10 kopeks per copy ("Krestyanka", "Rabotnitsa") to 80 kopeks ("Inostrannaya literatura" and "Novy mir"). The exceptions are "Iskusstvo" (1 ruble 50 kopeks) and "Dekorativnoye iskusstvo SSSR" (1 ruble 20 kopeks), which are richly illustrated with colour reproductions.

Nearly 8,000 (central, republican, territorial, regional, town, district and factory) newspapers are published in the Soviet Union. Moreover, there are branch, Komsomol and Young Pioneer newspapers. The largest of the central newspapers are "Pravda" (9,000,000 copies), "Izvestia" (8,300,000 copies), "Komsomolskaya pravda" (7,700,000 copies), "Selskaya zhizn" (6,600,000 copies), "Trud" (4,100,000 copies), "Sovetskaya Rossiya" (2,900,000 copies) and "Pionerskaya pravda" (9,700,000 copies).

In 1970 the newspaper output was 605 copies per 1,000 of the population. Newspapers are printed in 58 languages.

All branches of the national economy, science, technology and culture have their own magazines. The number of different magazines tops a thousand, and together with publications of the magazine type they total nearly 4,000. These include 120 scientific and 40 popular science magazines, 45 magazines devoted to public education, 21 magazines for women, 22 magazines for young people, and 35 magazines for children.

Magazines are put out in large editions, for example, "Rabotnitsa"—11,200,000 copies, "Zdorovye"—10,000,000 copies, "Krestyanka"—6,100,000, "Murzilka"—5,600,000 copies, "Nauka i zhizn"—3,000,000 and "Ogonyok"—2,000,000.

In 1970 there were 637 copies of magazines per 1,000 of the population. Nearly 3,000 different foreign newspapers and magazines in 30 languages are circulated in the USSR, the best represented being the periodical literature of socialist countries.

Bibliography

K. N. Postnov, Circulation of periodicals. In: Pečat SSSR za 50 let. Stat. očerki. Moskva, Kniga 1967, pp. 156–164.

Central organ for the distribution of newspapers and magazines, including books as a sideline, is
Rasprostranenie Pečatj
(Distribution of Printed Matter)
Ul. Gorkogo 7
SU Moskva K-375
published monthly.—The Editor.

United Kingdom

Important Book Centres

1 General Information

Area 240,869 km²
Population 54,744,000 (= 229.7 per km²)
Capital London (7,949,000)
Largest towns London (7,949,000); Birmingham (1,103,000); Glasgow (1,001,000); Liverpool (722,000); Manchester (638,000); Leeds (509,000); Sheffield (489,000); Edinburgh (472,000); Bristol (431,000); Belfast (407,000)
Government Monarchy, governed by Parliament forming, with the Sovereign, the supreme legislature of the United Kingdom, consisting of the House of Lords (spiritual and temporal) and the House of Commons (elected representatives of counties, cities, etc.).
(1) Education and (2) Police under county and municipal authorities under overall direction of (1) the Department of Education and Science, and (2) Home Office, subject to control of Parliament
Religions Church of England (Protestant) 75.0% (nominal and practising); Roman Catholic 9.8%; Church of Scotland (Presbyterian) 2.0%; Methodist 1.8%; Jews 0.9%; Baptists 0.5%; Other religious groups and dissidents 10.0%
National language English (some Gaelic being spoken in Scotland, and a good deal of Welsh in Wales)
Leading foreign languages French, German
Weights and measures British Imperial System (converting to metric system as from 1972)
Currency unit Pound sterling (£) (became decimalized on 15 February 1971)
Education Compulsory to age 15 (16 from 1972–3). 204,927 (1967–8) full-time students at 44 universities (including 56,301 women, 34,997 post-graduate students.
Illiteracy Nil
Paper consumption a) Newsprint about 25 kg per inhabitant (1967)
b) Printing paper (other than newsprint) about 30 kg per inhabitant (1967)
Membership Unesco, IPA, ICBA, ILAB

2 Past and Present

In Britain, as elsewhere, publishing and bookselling as we know them today began with the advent of printing from movable type. This new technique was introduced in England by William Caxton, who set up his press at the Red Pale in Westminster in 1476, publishing his first work in December that year. Before he died in 1491 he had produced, published and sold almost a hundred works. It is estimated that between 1476 and 1536 two thirds of all the printers in Britain were foreigners. These early printers generally acted as their own editors and booksellers, the separate functions of publishing, printing and bookselling not becoming independent before the end of the eighteenth century. In that time the Stationers' Company, established in 1534 and incorporated in 1557 with powers to supress books that were objectionable for any reason, exercised considerable influence in determining what works should be made available to the public. The powers of the Star Chamber were abolished in 1640, and a Licensing Act introduced in 1662 limited the Company's powers to those of maintaining a register of books licensed to be published. The Company's Register was maintained under the first Copyright Act, the "Statute of Anne", of 1709, but was dropped from legislation in subsequent Acts and no longer has any relevance.

To combat cut-price selling an association of London booksellers was formed in 1848, requiring its members not to sell books below their published prices, but this was held to be illegal by Lord Campbell, and the association was dissolved in 1852. Another association was formed in London in 1890, becoming in 1895 the "Associated Booksellers of Great Britain and Ireland", now know as the *Booksellers' Association of Great Britain and Ireland* (→ 4). A year later, in 1896, the *Publishers' Association* (→ 4) was formed, primarily with the object of maintaining net prices, but nowadays providing extensive information services to its members as well as acting as their spokesman to Government. The two trades and the two Associations have remained quite separate, although there is constant discussion and cooperation between them. Some important booksellers are also publishers, and a number of the largest publishers have bookselling interests; but, in general, the two functions are carried on independently.

Wholesalers play an important part in the British book trade, although there are nowadays only perhaps two who provide a nation-wide coverage. The two largest wholesalers also have extensive chains of retail outlets.

Because they live in a tiny island the British have traditionally been a seafaring race. This led to colonization overseas with, eventually, the establishment of the British Empire. Taking the English language with them, the British created a world-wide need for books in their language, and exports have thus always formed an important part of British book publishing. Although the nature of the former Empire has changed (and for the better), English remains a world-wide language, the book market for which today is shared by Britain with its former "colony", the United States of America. While other former colonies, such as the now giant Commonwealth of Australia, remain important markets for British books, the largest single market for British books is in fact the Continent of Europe.

It is the nature of development that "colonial" markets once dependent for their book supplies upon a metropolitan power become their own source of supply. It is inevitable that, in time, the Anglophone countries of Africa, for example, which currently depend almost exclusively on the UK for their educational book needs, will develop their own publishing industries (with the help of British publishers) and finally produce the books they want for themselves. While at first sight this might seem to indicate the likelihood of a fall in British book exports, the fact is that the new publishing industries will provide a fresh market for British works, acquiring local publishing rights in them and themselves providing new material which British publishers can buy from them to achieve maximum sales. It is not irrelevant that because of the purchase of publication rights the USA provides British publishers with a greater income than any other single country. While, therefore, the physical nature of British publishing may change with the years the future remains full of promise. Nor, in any case, is any country entirely self-sufficient in the matter of books. If "of making many books there is no end", then there certainly will be no end to that exchange of books between nations which is essential to understanding and peace.

Bibliography

J. J. Barnes, *Free trade in books.* A study of the London book trade since 1800. London, Oxford University Press 1964. XIV, 198 pp.

H. S. Bennett, *English books and readers 1475 to 1557.* 2nd ed. London, Cambridge University Press 1969. XIV, 337 pp.

H. S. Bennett, *English books and readers 1558 to 1603.* London, Cambridge University Press 1965. XVIII, 320 pp.

H. S. Bennett, *English books and readers 1603 to 1640.* London, Cambridge University Press 1970. XIV, 253 pp.

C. Clair, *A history of printing in Britain.* London, Cassell 1965. X, 314 pp.

P. M. Handover, *Printing in London from 1476 to modern times.* London, Allen & Unwin 1960.

F. A. Mumby, *Publishing and bookselling.* A history from the earliest times to the present day. 4th ed. London, Cape 1956. 442 pp. (5th ed. Ed. Jan Norrie. Due 1971).
The standard work on this particular field.—pp. 373–415 the best bibliography of publishing and bookselling, compiled by W. Peet.

M. Plant, *The English book trade. An economic history of the making and sale of books.* 2nd ed. London, Allen & Unwin 1965. 500 pp.

3 Retail Prices

A number of London booksellers and publishers made an agreement in 1829 under which any booksellers who sold books below the published price would be refused supplies at trade prices. A 10% discount was permitted to customers paying cash and a 15% discount to clubs and societies. This London Committee was reinforced in 1836 by the formation of a Glasgow Booksellers' Association, but this was disbanded in 1845 as being "conspiratorial and monopolistic". The London book trade introduced fresh regulations in 1848, but these were ruled by Lord Campbell in 1852 to be improper and the booksellers dissolved their society. It was re-formed in 1890 and became the present Booksellers' Association (→ 4) in 1895, the Publishers' Association (→ 4) being formed the following year with the object of preventing the cut-price bookselling that was undermining the trade.

The first net-priced book, "The principles of economics" by Alfred Marshall, the most eminent economist of his day, was published by Macmillan in 1890, and although the author later said that his agreement to the net price had been given on the mistaken assumption that cash customers would be given a discount, the book has remained "net" to this day. Macmillan demonstrated that net prices were lower than prices which had to be set if booksellers were to give discounts off them, and that such prices could be maintained to the trade's and the public's advantage. Other publishers followed Macmillan's example and by 1910 nearly all books other than schoolbooks were being published at net prices under conditions of sale set out in the "Net Book Agreement" to which all members of the "Publishers' Association" subscribed.

In 1962 the Net Book Agreement was found to be "not contrary to the public interest" after a prolonged Hearing by the Restrictive Practices Court under the Restrictive Trade Practices Act, 1956; and publishers' right individually to maintain their prices if they wish was confirmed by the same Court in 1968 under the Resale Prices Act, 1964.

The Standard Conditions of Sale of Net Books (set out in the Agreement) allow booksellers to supply public libraries at a discount of 10%, subject to the grant of a licence by the Publishers' Association, and allow discounts also to be given to book agents and to those buying books in quantity for philanthropic or propagandist reasons. Otherwise net prices have to be observed by booksellers under penalty of law. Probably 80% of all British books are issued at net prices, the rest being schoolbooks issued at "non-net" prices.

Bibliography

R. E. Barker and G. R. Davies (eds.), *Books are different. An account of the defence of the Net Book Agreement.* London, Macmillan 1966. XX, 938 pp.
A classical contribution, dealing with the successful defence of the Net Book Agreement under the Restrictive Trade Practices Act, 1956.

F. Macmillan, *The Net Book Agreement, 1899, and the book war, 1906–1908.* Glasgow, Maclehose 1924.

Price maintenance on an international level → International Section, 3.

4 Organization

The two main organizations representing the two parts of the book trade are:

The Booksellers' Association of Great Britain and Ireland
152 Buckingham Palace Road
GB London S.W. 1

The Publishers' Association
19 Bedford Square
GB London W.C. 1

The former was founded in 1895 and the latter in 1896. Both Associations exist primarily to serve the interests of their members.

The Booksellers' Association has a Library Booksellers' Group, a Schoolbook Suppliers' Group and a Charter Booksellers' Group, each with its own executive committee. The Charter Group was formed in 1963 to set and maintain standards of stock, staff training and service for stockholding booksellers. The Group has some 500 members out of a total Booksellers' Association membership of some 3,000. The Association is governed by an elected Council, most of whom are elected by the regional branches of the Association, with representation according to the number of members of the branch. The President and other Officers of the Council are elected by the membership as a whole.

The "Booksellers' Association" has a wholly owned subsidiary company, *Book Tokens Ltd.* The idea of stimulating the giving of books as presents by means of gift book tokens was conceived by the publisher, Mr Harold Raymond, the company being formed in 1932. The company issues book-token stamps of different values, and these may be affixed by the bookseller who sells them to attractive greetings cards up to the value required. The token stamps may then be exchanged by the recipient of the greetings card for that value in books. The person making the gift pays a small fee for the greetings card over and above the value of the token stamps. The bookseller who sells the stamps buys them from Book Tokens Ltd at a discount of 12½% of their face value, paying for them quarterly as he sells them. The bookseller who exchanges the stamps for a book cashes the stamps with "Book Tokens Ltd", receiving their face value less 12½%. Both booksellers in the transaction thus make equal profits. In its first year of business, Book Tokens Ltd sold stamps to the value of £16,000. Thirty years later, in 1963, booksellers' turnover in book tokens exceeded £920,000. Current sales of book tokens are now well in excess of £1 million a year.

Book Tokens also operate the *Booksellers' Clearing House* (→ 13), and have a further subsidiary company, *Book Trade Improvements Ltd* which, using money supplied by Book Tokens Ltd, and guaranteed by a group of the larger publishers, makes long-term low-interest loans to booksellers who wish to improve their shops.

The Publishers' Association is governed by a Council consisting of a President and two other Officers, and twelve Council members, all elected by the membership as a whole. The Association has a number of Groups concerned with the specialist interests of member firms, such as Education (from 1969 known as the Educational Publishers' Council), Technical and Scientific publishing, Children's books, Medical books, Map publishing, Religious book publishing, Paperback Books, Book Clubs, and General Literature. Each Group elects its own Chairman and Executive Committee.

The Association also has a number of specialist committees concerned with such subjects as Copyright, Obscene Libel, Industrial Training, Export (known as the Book Development Council), Book Production, and Trade Practices. Committees are appointed by the Council.

The Association maintains a Directory of Booksellers, additions to which are made by the Council on the advice of a Joint Advisory Committee on which the Booksellers' Association is represented. The JAC also advises the PA Council on the grant of library licences which entitle public libraries to purchase their books at a 10% discount. The BA is also represented on the PA's Distribution and Methods Committee.

The PA has some 380 publishing firms in membership, representing at least 95% of total book-publishing activity in the UK. The majority of British publishers are situated in London, but there are some 20 important houses in Scotland, mainly in Edinburgh and Glasgow, as well as in Oxford and Cambridge and certain other university centres.

Bibliography

Annual Reports issued each year by the Booksellers' Association and by the Publishers' Association.

Report of the 1948 Book Trade Committee. London, The Booksellers' Association and The Publishers' Association 1954.

F. D. SANDERS (ed.), *British book trade organization. A report on the work of the Joint Committee.* London, Allen & Unwin 1939.

5 Trade Press

The journal of the book trade of the United Kingdom is the

Bookseller
13 Bedford Square
GB London W.C. 1

It is owned and published quite independently of either of the book-trade organizations, although it is used by the trade as the official medium for communicating changes in prices, announcing the publication of new editions, etc. The journal contains a weekly list of new books, as well as information about forthcoming publications, publishers' advertisements and articles of trade interest. Special export editions in spring and autumn contain a comprehensive preview of the season's publishing.

Other journals concerned with the book trade include the following:

British Book News
59 New Oxford Street
GB London W.C. 1

This is published by the British Council for distribution exclusively outside the United Kingdom. It contains independent reviews of some 250 of the best books published each month, bibliographical articles and other articles on book subjects.

The Publisher
79 Limpsfield Road
South Croydon
GB Surrey

This is issued six times a year, with a supplement listing Books of the Month. It incorporates the former journals "Publishers' Circular and Booksellers' Record" and "British Books". It is largely concerned with questions of book production and other problems relating to the publishing industry.

Trade News
10 New Fetter Lane
GB London E.C. 4

This is issued weekly by the wholesale bookseller W. H. Smith. It contains book-trade news, publishers' announcements and special articles, as well as features dealing with newspapers, magazines and stationery.

6 Book-Trade Literature

As each section of this survey of the book trade in the United Kingdom includes the important books dealing with the subjects concerned, it is not necessary here to do more than list the main works dealing with the trade at large.

a) Bibliography

Bibliography in Britain. A classified list of books and articles published in the United Kingdom. Since 1962 annually. Oxford, Oxford Bibliographical Society.

b) General Surveys

R. E. Barker and G. R. Davies (eds.), *Books are different. An account of the defence of the Net Book Agreement.* London, Macmillan 1966. XX, 938 pp.

T. Joy, *The truth about bookselling.* London, Pitman 1964. X, 206 pp.

F. A. Mumby, *Publishing and bookselling. A history from the earliest times to the present day.* 4th ed. London, Cape 1956. 442 pp.

M. Plant, *The English book trade. An economic history of the making and sale of books.* 2nd ed. London, Allen & Unwin 1965. 500 pp.

Sir Stanley Unwin, *The truth about publishing.* 7th ed. London, Allen & Unwin 1960.
The classical work which has been translated into many languages thus securing a lasting international influence upon the attitude towards publishing.

Sir Stanley Unwin, *The truth about a publisher.* London, Allen & Unwin 1960.
The autobiography of Sir Stanley.

c) Handbooks

"*Better Bookselling Series*" on *Accounting* (Fuchs), *Economics* (Bailey), *Library and education supply* (Peacham), *Stock control* (Bartlett), *University bookselling* (Stockham), *Bookselling by mail* (Bartlett). London, Hutchinson, since 1964.

Book Distribution. A handbook for booksellers and publishers on the ordering and distribution of books in the United Kingdom. London, The Publishers' Association 1961.

7 Sources of Information, Address Services

Information about the book trade may be obtained from the Booksellers' Association

(→ 4) and the Publishers' Association (→ 4).
A bibliographical service is provided to its members by the

National Book League
7 Albemarle Street
GB London W. 1

The Publishers' Association operates a mailing service for its members, available to non-members. Current rates available on application. The service covers booksellers, wholesale booksellers, library suppliers and public and university libraries in the United Kingdom.
A comprehensive and finely classified mailing service for United Kingdom libraries and universities has been developed by:

University Mailing Service Ltd

and a similar comprehensive, classified service for the rest of the world by:

Book Development Council

From 1 January 1971 these two services (UMS and BDC) were combined as:

International Book Information Services (IBIS)
New Building
North Circular Road
Neasden
GB London N.W. 10

Prices on application.
Information about libraries in the United Kingdom may be obtained from:

The Library Association
7 Ridgmount Street
Store Street
GB London W.C. 1

8 International Membership

The Booksellers' Association (→ 4) is a member of the "International Community of Booksellers' Associations", and the Publishers' Association (→ 4) is a member of the "International Publishers' Association".
The Antiquarian Booksellers' Association (→ 26) is a member of the "International League of Antiquarian Booksellers".

9 Market Research

The British book trade has done little more than dabble in market research, publishers in general taking the view that it is a waste of money.
Some publishers have commissioned market research for particular purposes of their own, but the results are not available generally.
The Society of Young Publishers (an unofficial society of young people in the publishing industry) have conducted various kinds of research on an amateur basis, but the results have not been useful in a practical sense.
The address of the present Secretary of this organization may be obtained from the Publishers' Association (→ 4).
Dr Peter H. Mann, Lecturer in Sociology at the University of Sheffield, in 1968 completed a social analysis of leisure book reading. Dr Mann outlined his sociological survey at an international conference on book-market research held in London in March 1968.
In the main, British publishers have preferred to concentrate on research into methods of improving distribution, taking the view that unless one can be certain of getting the books to the customer with the minimum delay other kinds of research are unlikely to be profitable. The Publishers' Association, with the cooperation of the Booksellers' Association, has conducted at least three major inquiries into distribution during the past fifteen years; and a further, more intensive, inquiry was begun in 1968. The number of books kept in print by British publishers (something in excess of 250,000 titles) creates its own problems. In 1967 the members of the PA adopted a "Standard Book Numbering System" (since adopted by the USA and other

English-speaking countries, and likely to become the pattern for a world-wide system, → International Section, 35c), and plans are now at an advanced stage for the introduction of "Standard Account Numbers". A substantial proportion of British book publishing turnover is now handled by computer, so that the combination of these two numbering systems should do much to speed deliveries and invoicing.

It must nevertheless be hoped that when British publishers have overcome their delivery problems they will then be able to pay more attention to the other important areas of market research upon which maximum sales depend.

Bibliography

P. H. Mann and J. L. Burgoyne, *Books and reading*. London, A. Deutsch 1969. 104 pp.

P. H. Mann, *Books: buyers and borrowers*. London.
The first two of three progress reports on research programmes supported by the Charter Group of the Booksellers' Association.

Summary of papers given at the "International Conference on Book Market Research", held in London in March 1968. In: Bookseller (→ 5), 30 March and 6 April 1968.

10 Books and Young People

The Children's Book Group of the Publishers' Association is the body of publishers specially concerned with providing a wide range of reading for young people. Frequent contact is maintained with youth librarians and the schools of librarianship. In conjunction with the National Book League the Group stages an annual Children's Book Show, where some three thousand of the latest books, together with classics and other "old favourites", are shown.

National Book League
7 Albemarle Street
GB London W. 1

This body, in addition to giving advice on children's reading to teachers and parents, maintains a reference library of recently published children's books (→ 7 and p. 73).
Annual awards for the best children's books are made by (→ *32*):

The Library Association
7 Ridgmount Street
Store Street
GB London W.C. 1

The
Children's Book Circle
Secretary, Miss Margaret Clark
c/o Bodley Head
9 Bow Street
GB London W. C. 2

is an informal group of children's book editors, which meets about seven times a year and provides a forum for discussion with those working in other fields concerned with children's books.
About four years ago a

Joint Committee on Children's Books
c/o The Publishers' Association
19 Bedford Square
GB London W.C. 1

was set up, on which are represented authors, publishers, booksellers, school librarians and youth librarians in public libraries, the National Book League and the BBC.
→ 32

Journals concerned with books for young people include:

Growing Point
Ashton Manor
Ashton
GB Northamptonshire

Books for your Children
Belvedere
100 Church Lane East
Aldershot
GB Hampshire

United Kingdom

Junior Bookshelf
Marsh Hall
Thurstonland
Huddersfield
GB Yorkshire

Children's Book News
140 Kensington Church Street
GB London W. 8

11 Training

In general, bookselling and publishing as we know them today have in Britain been largely amateur. There have been no minimum qualifications required for anyone to start a bookselling business or a publishing business, and new entrants to the trade have generally been taught by being placed alongside others doing the work until they were capable of doing it themselves. British book-trade training today, however, is happily more scientific. It is still open to anyone to set up in business as a bookseller or publisher (if he has the money, or can borrow it, and can find suitable premises), but those who wish to advance in their chosen profession will nowadays generally seek to undergo one or more of the various courses of training open to them.

The Booksellers' Association (→ 4) has for many years conducted a correspondence course, leading to a Diploma in Bookselling, and has from time to time organized specialist seminars for senior booksellers. Since the advent of the BA Charter Booksellers' Group this specialist training has been intensified so that the BA currently run residential courses in basic bookselling, middle management, as well as courses for "training the trainers". There has always been, and still is, a marked degree of training within individual bookshops.

The BA has also produced a "Work Book" for new entrants to bookselling, listing the essential textbooks for their career, the main sources of information and the accepted practices of the trade. The "Work Book" amounts to an intensive questionnaire designed to show the new entrant (and his employer!) whether or not he requires training.

In 1967, 157 bookselling firms sent a total of 279 students to residential courses (109 basic, 83 middle management, 87 management).

In 1969 there were the following number of students: senior management 20, middle management 41, basic 59, training techniques 25, children's bookselling 12; and there were 352 candidates for Diploma examinations.

While a number of publishers have provided individual training programmes for newcomers to the industry (and more especially for potential executive directors), coordinated training was begun by the Publishers' Association (→ 4) only in 1960, when the first book-production course, organized in consultation with the Book Production Managers' Group (an informal society of publishers' senior production managers), began as a course of evening classes.

The advent of the Industrial Training Act of 1964 lent new stimulus to book-trade training, and the PA currently runs a day-release course on book production, as well as a preliminary (general) course for those who have been in the industry for two or three years. It is currently developing a number of specialist courses, including ones covering editorial work, sales and marketing, distribution and warehouse management. A course in top management for likely executive directors is planned to start shortly. Most of the specialist courses will be residential, but some will be on a day-release basis. Evening classes are no longer considered a suitable medium for teaching those employed in work during the day.

Under the Industrial Training Act each industry in the UK is brought under an Industrial Training Board. An Industrial Training Board for the Printing and Publishing Industry was set up during 1968. It possesses (like the other Boards) legal powers to impose a levy on all employers to cover the costs of training, and to make grants to cover those costs when they are actually incurred. In other words, employers now have to pay the cost of training whether or not they give their staff training advantages. They will get their money back (and possibly with interest) only if they do provide training facilities.
Both the "Booksellers' Association" and the "Publishers' Association" have a full-time Training Officer on their staffs.

Bibliography

I. Babbidge, *Beginning in bookselling*. London, Deutsch 1965.

C. Bingley, *Book publishing practice*. London, Crosby Lockwood 1966.

J. Hyams, *Careers in bookselling*. London, Hutchinson 1968.—'Better Bookselling' series.

T. Joy, *The truth about bookselling*. London, Pitman 1964.

P. Unwin, *Book publishing as a career*. London, Hamish Hamilton 1965.

Sir Stanley Unwin, *The truth about publishing*. 7th ed. London, George Allen & Unwin 1960.

12 Taxes

There are no taxes on books in the United Kingdom. Nor are there any import or export duties on them. Books are one of the few commodities exempt from purchase tax.
There are, however, import duties and domestic taxes on articles, such as gramophone records and tape-recordings, which are increasingly sold together with books to supplement their contents. Pre-recorded tapes, for example, used in language teaching, were made subject to a 50% purchase tax in April 1968.
It is possible that the United Kingdom may before long introduce a value-added tax. It is impossible to forecast whether it will prove possible to gain exemption for books (as was done in the case of purchase tax even in the crucial war days of 1940), but it is not unreasonable to expect that even if books cannot escape altogether there would at least be a 50% reduction for books on educational and cultural grounds. A value-added tax system would almost certainly provide for the payment of a rebate to exporters, and since British publishers export about 50% of their total product such a rebate would provide some relief.

Bibliography

G. McAllister, *The book crisis*. London, Faber & Faber (for the "National Committee for the Defence of Books") 1940.

13 Clearing Houses

The Booksellers' Association (→ 4) in 1948 set up the *Booksellers' Clearing House (BCH)*, operated by their totally owned company:
Book Tokens Ltd
152 Buckingham Palace Road
GB London S. W. 1
Those members of the BA who wish may send BCH a monthly cheque for all their accounts with publishers, BCH then analysing the payments and sending single cheques to individual publishers on behalf of all those booksellers choosing to pay that way. The Publishers' Association (→ 4) has been represented on the Committee which controls BCH since 1950, and a publisher has served on the Board of Book Tokens Ltd since 1964.
The *Publishers' Accounts Clearing House (PACH)* was set up in 1958 by the

United Kingdom

British Publishers' Guild Ltd
182 High Holborn
GB London W. C. 1
to facilitate the supply of and payments for single copy orders, and is currently operated as a simplified ordering and accounting service by:
Publishers' Accounts Clearing House
Book Centre Ltd
North Circular Road
Neasden
GB London N. W. 10
Under this system, the bookseller completes a multi-copy order form, carbon copies of which are used severally as an address label, advice note and invoice. Book Centre Ltd also operates an *Overseas Booksellers' Clearing House* which aims to do for overseas booksellers what BCH does for UK booksellers.

Bibliography

T. Joy, *The truth about bookselling*. London, Pitman 1964.

14 Copyright

The current copyright law of the United Kingdom is the Copyright Act, 1956. This Act repealed all previous copyright enactments with the exception of Section 15 of the Copyright Act, 1911, which deals exclusively with the deposit of copies with certain privileged libraries and has nothing to do with copyright.

The Act provides protection to original works for the lifetime of their author and fifty years thereafter or, where the work is first published posthumously, for fifty years from first publication. The protection of the Act extends to works first published in any country which is party to an international copyright convention of which the UK is a signatory, and also to works the author of which is a national of any such country regardless of where that work is first published.

The United Kingdom became party to the "Universal Copyright Convention (UCC)" on 27 September 1957. It acceded to the Brussels (1948) Text of the "Berne Convention" on 15 December 1957. The UK has neither signed nor acceded to the Stockholm Act of revision of July 1967, believing that the "Protocol Regarding Developing Countries", which is an integral part of that Act, would undermine international copyright. (Latest development of this problem → International Section, 14).

The Copyright Act, 1956, covers all literary, dramatic, musical and artistic works. It includes certain exemptions in respect of the photocopying by libraries of single copies of articles from periodicals and short extracts from other copyright works. There are also certain limitations in respect of educational use of copyright works.

Bibliography

R. E. Barker, *The revised Berne Convention. The Stockholm Act 1967*. London, The Publishers' Association 1967.
This was followed by several other concise reports on international governmental discussions leading towards the removal of the Stockholm Protocol Regarding Developing Countries culminating with *International copyright: a formula emerges*. London, The Publishers' Association 1970.

R. E. Barker, *Photocopying practices in the United Kingdom*. London, Faber & Faber 1970. 104 pp.
p. 103: bibliography.

P. F. Carter-Ruck and E. P. Skone James, *Copyright. Modern law and practice*. London, Faber & Faber 1965.

Copinger and E. P. Skone James, *Copyright*. 10th ed. London, Sweet & Maxwell 1965.

R. F. Whale, *The Stockholm Act. Protocol regarding Developing Countries*. London, British Copyright Council 1968.

15 National Bibliography, National Library

The most comprehensive bibliography of books published in the United Kingdom is:

Whitaker's Cumulative Book List
J. Whitaker & Sons Ltd
13 Bedford Square
GB London W. C. 1

cumulated quarterly into an annual volume, alphabetically by author and title and with subject guides. Whitaker also publish annually *British Books in Print,* which lists over 200,000 titles. Originally published under the title of "The Reference Catalogue of Current Literature", this comprehensive bibliography was first published in 1874. "British Books in Print" contains a comprehensive bibliography of books dealing with publishing and bookselling.

A more detailed bibliography, widely used by librarians, is:

British National Bibliography
The Council of the British National Bibliography Ltd
7 Rathbone Place
GB London W. C. 1

which is also cumulated quarterly with an annual volume of all British books recorded during the year, arranged by subjects under their "Dewey Decimal Classifications", with an author and title index.

The oldest British bibliography, first published in 1836, although no longer predominant, is:

The English Catalogue of Books
The Publishers' Circular Ltd
79 Limpsfield Road
South Croydon
GB Surrey

This, issued annually, contains an author list and subject and title indexes, covering maps and atlases and paperbacks as well as other books.

Whitaker also publish twice annually a bibliography of *British Paperbacks in Print,* listing more than 25,000 titles, classified by subjects and with author and title indexes. They also issue a reference catalogue of *Technical Books in Print,* listing some 13,500 technical titles, classified under subjects and with author and title indexes.

The National Library of the United Kingdom is that of the

British Museum
GB London W. C. 1

dating from 1753. The

National Central Library
Store Street
GB London W. C. 1

is the national centre for the inter-loan of books throughout the British Isles, and a similar function for scientific and technical books is performed by the

National Lending Library for Science and Technology
GB Boston Spa, Yorkshire

There is also a

National Reference Library of Science and Invention
25 Southampton Buildings
GB London W. C. 2

which is part of the "Department of Printed Books of the British Museum".

The counterpart to the British Museum library in Scotland is the

National Library of Scotland
George IV Bridge
GB Edinburgh 1

and the Welsh equivalent is the

National Library of Wales
GB Aberystwyth

There is also a

Scottish Central Library
Lawnmarket
GB Edinburgh 1

An inquiry into the present functions and future status of the national libraries was published in 1969 by the Dainton Committee.

United Kingdom

Bibliography

Report of the National Libraries Committee. London, Her Majesty's Stationery Office 1969.

16 Book Production

The richness of English literature and the world-wide use of the English language has made British book production particularly prolific. Some 32,000 titles are now published annually in the United Kingdom, and British publishers maintain in print something approaching a quarter of a million titles.

Comparisons with other countries are difficult to make because the count is not always made on the same basis. The USSR publishes the greatest number of titles, but Russian statistics count separately those many titles that may be published in several of the 80 or more languages of the Soviet Union. US title output currently exceeds that of the UK, but the basis of the American count was altered a few years ago to bring in publications that had previously been excluded. The British count excludes books and pamphlets priced at less than $2^1/_2$ p and excludes the vast majority of Government publications. No UK statistics are published on the UNESCO definition of a book as a publication of 49 pages or more. But the $2^1/_2$ p price level used by J. Whitaker & Sons Ltd, who produce the statistics, has been used since well before World War II and its significance today is miniature, so that the following statistics more or less conform to the UNESCO standard.

In 1969 32,393 titles were published in the UK, including 9,106 new editions and reprints, 1,476 translations and 108 limited editions. The number of new titles was 27,703.

The following are the numbers of titles published in the principal classifications, together with their percentage of the total:

Subject group	Titles	Percentage of total production
Fiction	4,405	13.6
Children's books	2,456	7.6
Political science and economy	2,441	7.5
School textbooks	1,821	5.6
History	1,555	4.8
Medical sciences	1,241	3.8
Religion and theology	1,164	3.6
Literature	1,128	3.5
Engineering	1,045	3.2
Art	911	2.8
Education	911	2.8
Biography	850	2.6

Bibliography

Bookseller, 3 January 1970. London, J. Whitaker.

17 Translations

The 32,393 titles published in 1969 included 1,476 translations from other languages. Considering the size of the UK book production, translations form a relatively small part, representing only 4.5% of the total. Translations are made predominantly from French, German, Italian and Spanish, with the main emphasis on literary works; but a great many titles are also translated from the Russian, particularly in the fields of science and technology. There are also some translations from Scandinavian languages and from the classical languages, amounting to less than a tenth of the total.

The following are the number of titles published in the main classifications in 1969:

Subject group	Titles	Percentage of total
Fiction	208	14.0
Religion and theology	123	8.3
Children's books	119	8.0
Art	107	7.2
History	77	5.2
Political science economy	72	4.9
Poetry	68	4.6
Biography	63	4.3

As will be seen from the other chapters in this work, and from UNESCO's *Index Translationum,* English is the richest source of translation throughout the world.

In 1969 the Publishers' Association set up a National Clearing House to assist those in the developing countries who found difficulty, for whatever reason, in securing licences for translation or reprint rights in British copyright works.

Bibliography

Bookseller, 3 January 1970. London, J. Whitaker.

18 Book Clubs

Book Clubs, as we know them today, began in Britain in the middle of the 1930s. Book clubs with a political emphasis were among the first to be formed, the "Left Book Club" (established by Victor Gollancz during the Spanish Civil War) possibly being the best known. Two of the major general book clubs, "The Book Club" (W. & G. Foyle Ltd) and "World Books" (The Reprint Society) are still among the major clubs today although the "Companion Book Club" (Odhams Press) formed after the war now has the largest membership.

There are at present some 30 book clubs in the United Kingdom, including two religious book clubs. There are no longer any political book clubs in existence.

Regulations for the conduct of book clubs were introduced in 1939, being revised a number of times since. The regulations provide that no book-club edition may be published sooner than twelve months after first trade publication, save in the case of a religious or political book club registered as such, where publication may take place simultaneously. New "Regulations" introduced in September 1968 now permit the publication of book-club editions simultaneous with first trade publication, subject to a proviso that the price of the book-club edition shall not be more than 25% less than that of the trade edition and subject, also, to certain provisions in respect of premium offers.

The 30 or so book-clubs currently operating generally offer one choice and one alternate choice each month, although sometimes two alternates are offered. The cost per volume is generally between 30 p and 35 p. The new simultaneous book clubs generally offer one choice and three alternate choices each month, with bargain premium offers to attract new members.

19 Paperbacks

Although paper-bound books were published in Britain from the end of the 19th century, they first appeared in the series in which they are now recognized in 1936 when "Penguin Books" issued their first twelve titles. Six were fiction and six were non-fiction covering a wide field of knowledge. The pattern set then has been accentuated over the years so that in April 1967 out of 25,039 titles published in paperback form only 5,450 were fiction. The 1969/70 Winter edition of "Paperbacks in Print" (→ 15) listed 37,539 titles, of which 6,451 were fiction. It is estimated that some 3,700 titles were published in paperbacks in 1970, of which about one sixth were fiction.

The paperback of today has completely replaced the cheap (hard-bound) edition that before the war distinguished the lists of such literary publishers as Jonathan Cape (his "Florin Books", costing two shillings, were an excellent example).

The post-war era has seen the advent and flowering of the "quality" or "egg-head" paperback, presenting in paper-bound form books which previously were thought to have a limited high-price public but have now found a larger public at a median price level.

Paperback books may now be obtained from more than 400 publishers in the UK, but only a proportion of these are series of paperbacks originally published in the UK. The number of British publishers issuing paperback editions is about 300, but the number of these issuing sizeable series of paperbacks is less than 20. The output is nevertheless considerable and fiction, although not predominant in terms of titles, is undoubtedly predominant in terms of total sales.

A development in recent years of considerable promise is the establishment in schools of "book agencies" which stock and sell paperback books to the students and staff. There are now more than 300 such agencies in the UK and it may confidently be expected that the number will increase enormously during the next five years. This development is regarded by publishers as most important for the inculcation of the book-buying habit. More importantly, it is welcomed by teachers as a means of intensifying education.

"Penguin Books", paramountly, have established a very high level of design for British paperback books.

Bibliography

D. Flower, *The paperback. Its past, present and future.* London, Arborfield 1940.

J. E. Morpurgo, *Paperbacks across frontiers.* London, Bowater Paper Corp. Ltd and the National Book League (*c.* 1954).

F. A. Mumby, *Publishing and bookselling. A history from the earliest times to the present day.* 4th ed. London, Cape 1956.

Paperbacks in Print. London, J. Whitaker, twice yearly.

M. Plant, *The English book trade. An economic history of the making and sale of books.* 2nd ed. London, Allen & Unwin 1965.

20 Book Design

With notable (and even internationally outstanding) exceptions, British book design before World War II was most noticeable by its absence. Historically, even before the time of William Morris, Britain had set high standards of book design, but these were observed only by a minority. General standards of design were (odd though it may seem) considerably improved by the paper economies necessitated by World War II. Shortage of materials forced upon publishers economy of design and thus a greater purity. Today British books hold their own with those of any other country.

It is only in the past twenty years, however, that British publishers have concerned themselves to any marked degree in seeking distinctions of merit for book design. For some years now the National Book League (→ 7) has organized an annual exhibition of British books chosen for the quality of their design by a panel of experts. This selection has been made, however, more upon the basis of the suitability of the presentation for the content, rather than for beauty alone. British publishers have thus not chosen to compete for distinctions of merit in the field of "beautiful books" because they take the view that such books should be beautiful because of their nature and that real distinction in design rests more in the appositeness of design to content. On this basis the NBL's panel of experts has annually selected a hundred or more books of which some 50 have been chosen, for the international exhibit at the "Frankfurt Book Fair" and elsewhere.

The NBL also organizes a periodic selection of textbooks whose design is outstandingly fitting for their purpose.

Bibliography

British Book Design and *British Textbook Design.* London, National Book League, annual catalogues.

K. Day (ed.), *Book typography 1915–1965.* London, Benn 1966.

S. Morison, *Four Centuries of fine printing.* London, Benn 1960.

S. Morison and K. Day, *The typographic book 1450–1935.* London, Benn 1963.

H. Williamson, *Methods of book design.* London, Oxford University Press 1966.

21 Publishing

Publishing in Britain began as in most European countries at the seats of the ancient universities. Today the majority of British publishers are located in London, although there are important publishing centres in Edinburgh and Glasgow, as well as in Oxford and Cambridge and the other university towns. More than 300 of the 350 members of the Publishers' Association (→ 4) are located in London.

The total turnover of British publishers in 1969 (at trade prices) was about £ 140 million, of which about £ 67 million was from exports (47,2%). These figures relate to book publishing alone, and do not include periodical or newspaper publishing.

Although a number of publishers are taking part in an "interfirm comparison", which will enable them to measure their economic success against their competitors, no statistics have been published which enable any analysis to be made of the size of the various firms or their profitability.

J. Whitaker & Sons Ltd (13 Bedford Square, London W. C. 1), in their *Publishers in the United Kingdom and their Addresses* (published annually), list almost 2,100 firms and organizations which publish books; but the majority of these are organizations which publish only yearbooks or local guides and are not publishers in the general trade sense. The 380 members of the Publishers' Association (→ 4) are reckoned to cover about 95% of total publishing turnover in the UK. Some 40 British publishers issue more than 100 titles a year, and about 6 publish in excess of 200 titles a year each.

It is probable that about 75% of the total turnover of British publishers may be attributed to about 50 publishing houses, and that 50% results from the activities of the fifteen largest. This serves merely to underline the importance of the small publishing house in the production of the variety of books for which British publishers are renowned.

Various censuses taken by the British Government have produced figures to indicate the size of British publishing houses, their consumption of paper and printing, and various other statistics; but these figures are virtually useless in so far as the book-publishing industry is concerned because they confuse printing with publishing.

(→ 2, 4, 5 and 6).

22 Literary Agents

Literary agents play an important part in the British publishing scene. Most best-selling authors, whether British or American, are represented by an agent and many new authors prefer to ask an agent to handle their work rather than submit it themselves direct to individual publishers. These remarks apply, however, almost exclusively to the fields of creative writing, primarily fiction.

Educational publishers nearly always deal direct with authors, as do publishers of scientific and technical works. A majority of children's book authors also deal direct with their publishers.

There are some 80 literary agents operating in the United Kingdom. A number of them specialize in dramatic rights, newspaper and periodical serial rights, and in the placing of translations. Many British publishers also act as agents for their authors in these fields.

United Kingdom

Bibliography

Cassell's Directory of Publishing. 6th ed. London, Cassell 1970.

Writers' & Artists' Yearbook. London, A. & C. Black, annually.

23 Wholesale Trade

Wholesale bookselling, as an isolated activity, has not been particularly successful in the United Kingdom. Until shortly after World War II the famous wholesale booksellers Simpkin Marshall Ltd filled a valuable role in British book distribution, particularly within the United Kingdom; but that company had to go into liquidation in 1955 because it could no longer operate profitably. British publishers have traditionally (and, in the writer's view, mistakenly) kept their prices to the lowest possible level so that it has been virtually impossible for them to allow an adequate margin for wholesale traders. Retailers, to get the terms they felt they must have, have generally purchased direct from publishers, save possibly in the case of uneconomic orders which are not necessarily attractive to wholesalers.

The two largest wholesalers in the UK today both control extensive chains of bookshops, one of them controlling the largest chain in the country. There are, in addition, some 200 other wholesalers, mainly small and concerned predominantly with paperback books and other popular lines.

Wholesale distributors play an important part in the field of periodicals and newspapers, but those are not the concern of this book. Some wholesale booksellers in the UK also conduct valuable export business.

Bibliography

Directory of Book Wholesalers. London, The Publishers' Association 1966.

24 Retail Trade

Because of the size of their output British publishers regard booksellers as indispensable for the maximization of sales. While some books can be sold effectively by direct mail promotion, and school textbooks are sold mainly by the publishers' effectiveness in bringing them to the attention of schoolteachers, the vast majority of other books can be sold only if they are stocked by booksellers or if booksellers exist who are willing to order them specially for customers. The Net Book Agreement case (→ 3) was fought and won on the principle that the existence of stockholding booksellers was essential to the satisfactory service of the public. No bookseller can stock all books in print, but he renders a considerable service to the public if he stocks and displays a wide selection of books available and provides an obtain-to-order service. The Charter Booksellers Group of the Booksellers' Association (→ 4) exists to maintain and improve the standards of bookselling, but even those booksellers who are not members of that Group may nevertheless contribute significantly to publishers' effective distribution. The suburban newsagent who maintains a small stock of paperback books relevant to his customers' needs, performs an important service. Thus, although there are only some 3,000 booksellers in membership of the Booksellers' Association (and they undoubtedly account for a substantial part of total turnover in the UK) some 12,000 names and addresses are listed in the *Directory of Booksellers* maintained by the Publishers' Association.

The Booksellers' Association's membership includes wholesale booksellers as well as retail booksellers, and also specialist booksellers such as those serving universities, education authorities and libraries.

Inevitably the greatest numbers of bookshops are to be found in the largest towns, with London at the top of the list. But since the British Isles are quite small there is no great significance in listing the numbers of bookshops in individual towns. These can readily be determined by reference to the PA "Directory".

From time to time economic surveys of retail bookselling have been conducted by Chalmers, Impey & Co., the Accountants for the Booksellers' Association, beginning with the period 1948–52 and being repeated in 1958 and 1959. More recently the same firm has conducted similar surveys for the BA Charter Booksellers' Group, the sixth and most recent being that covering the year 1969. This analysed total book sales in excess of £31 million, which represents about two fifths of total home sales. The report shows booksellers' gross margins in that year to be 25.9% compared with 26.9% in 1968 and 25.7% in 1967. With the 1969 gross profit at 25.9% and expenses at 22.3%, the average trading profit was 3.6% compared with 2.8% in 1968 and 5.7% in 1967. Larger booksellers with a turnover between £50,000 and £100,000 showed an improved gross margin of 0.9% compared with 1968.

The 1966 survey revealed that among the booksellers having the largest turnover only those who were part of a chain of bookshops (and not independent) operated in cities having a population of less than 100,000. Only one independent bookseller in the category of the second largest operated in a city of between 50,000 and 100,000 inhabitants.

Bibliography

I. Babbidge, *Beginning in bookselling*. London, Deutsch 1965.

H. E. Bailey, *Economics of bookselling*. London, Hutchinson 1965.

R. E. Barker and G. R. Davies, *Books are different. An account of the defence of the Net Book Agreement*. London, Macmillan 1966.

G. R. Bartlett, *Stock control in bookselling*. London, Hutchinson 1965.

F. T. Bell and F. S. Smith, *Library bookselling*. London, Deutsch 1966.

Charter Bookselling, 1967. (Reviewing the year 1966). London, The Booksellers' Association 1967.

Directory of Booksellers in the United Kingdom. London, The Publishers' Association 1968.

N. Fuchs, *Accounting for booksellers*. London, Hutchinson 1965.

T. Joy, *The truth about bookselling*. London, Pitman 1964.

Better Bookselling (series), see Bibliography → 6.

25 Mail-Order Bookselling

Direct selling by mail promotion has long been practised by a few publishers of specialized works, but it has developed in a general way only in the past few years. A number of bookselling organizations now promote individual titles by direct mail with considerable success. Expensive books lend themselves best to this kind of promotion since it is generally recognized as being more expensive than selling through bookshops. Sets of books (such as the collected works of a renowned author, even including authors whose works are no longer copyright) have shown themselves particularly suited to this kind of promotion.

Bibliography

G. R. Bartlett, *Bookselling by mail*. London, Hutchinson 1965.

26 Antiquarian Book Trade, Auctions

It is necessary to distinguish between the trade in second-hand books and antiquarian books. Many booksellers whose main business is the sale of new books also have a small department (or even a few shelves) devoted to second-hand books. These, in the main, are books whose owners no longer have any use for them, so that they have sold them for what they will fetch. There is a particularly valuable market in second-hand university and other text-books. Antiquarian books, on the other hand, are books having a particular value because of their rarity, and booksellers dealing in such books need highly specialized knowledge if they are to be successful.

Second-hand booksellers as defined above will generally be in membership of:

The Booksellers' Association of
Great Britain and Ireland
152 Buckingham Palace Road
GB London S.W. 1

and antiquarian booksellers will more generally be in membership of:

The Antiquarian Booksellers' Association
29 Revell Road
Kingston-upon-Thames
GB Surrey

Apart from purchasing unwanted books from customers for resale, second-hand booksellers also buy publishers' remainders, which they offer as bargains. Their individual purchases may sometimes coincidentally include a book with rarity value, and such books generally find their way into the antiquarian trade.

The antiquarian booksellers purchase and sell collections and also individual books. The *Antiquarian Book Fair*, held at the National Book League (→ 7) annually, has established itself as one of the most important events of the antiquarian booksellers' year. Some antiquarian booksellers used to form a ring at the major book sales, each member of the ring bidding low so that the books could be purchased at "knock-out" prices; but the "knock-out" system (thanks largely to the vigour with which it was fought by the famous Oxford bookseller, Sir Basil Blackwell) was ended by law some years ago and no longer operates. The present standards of antiquarian bookselling in the UK are of the highest level.

The first book auction to be held in London is said to have begun on 31 October 1676, and sales have been held frequently ever since. The main three auction houses are in London, and in 1963 their total book sales were £786,921. In 1966, Sotheby's alone achieved a total of £1,746,224, holding 38 sales during the year. Sales in subsequent years have proved less rewarding, possibly because there has been less of value to offer for sale.

The special journal of the antiquarian book trade is

Clique
83 Holden Rd.
GB London N 12

This weekly offers, apart from the extensive sections for books wanted and offered, interesting editorial matter including official information about the activities of the Antiquarian Booksellers' Association.

Bibliography

Book Auction Records. Annually. Seventh general index. Farnham, Surrey, Henry Stevens, Son & Stiles 1966.

Book Prices Current, 1887–1903, and intermittently to volume 63, 1948–52. London, H. F. & G. Witherby 1957.

J. Lawler, *Book auctions in England.* London 1898.

27 Book Imports

Book imports into the United Kingdom increased dramatically in the eleven years between 1958 and 1969. The official statistics are:

Category	1958 Value £ m	1969 Value £ m
Printed Books	3.7	19.9
Newspapers and periodicals	1.2	4.6
Other printed matter	2.0	18.2
Total	6.9	42.7

The official statistics exclude any imports by post, so that the actual value of imports is rather higher than indicated. In 1952 it would probably have been correct to increase the book import figure by 50% but the under-estimate for 1969 is probably no more than 10%, or even less. The reason for this—which is also the reason for the significant increase in imports—is that British publishers nowadays print far more books abroad than they used to do.

The main countries from which books were imported into the UK in 1969 were:

Country	Value £ m	Percentage of total
USA	9.3	46.7
Italy	2.2	11.1
Netherlands	1.7	8.5
Switzerland	1.2	6.0
Germany (Federal Republic)	0.7	3.5
Hong Kong	0.5	2.5
Czechoslovakia	0.5	2.5
Other foreign countries	2.6	13.1
British Commonwealth countries	1.2	6.0

These figures show clearly that the UK's main book supplier abroad is the other large English-language publishing country, the USA. A majority of the books imported from the USA are imported in bulk for exclusive distribution by British publishers or agents throughout the British market at home and overseas. A preponderance of all other book imports are also of complete editions, generally printed abroad on the publishers' behalf.

The foregoing figures for book imports do not include children's picture books which in 1969 were imported to a total value of £1.8 million, half of them being imported from the Netherlands and thus, once again, indicating a print import.

There are no import duties on books imported into the United Kingdom. The UK is a signatory of the "Florence Agreement" on the importation of educational, scientific and cultural materials.

Bibliography

Trade figures. London, Her Majesty's Stationery Office, monthly and annually.

Printing and publishing exports and imports in 1969. London, National Economic Development Office 1970.

28 Book Exports

In relation to its size (and in some sense absolutely) the British publishing industry is the largest book exporter in the world. The USA alone nowadays reports larger earnings abroad than the UK, but British books are generally cheaper and the probability is that in terms of numbers of volumes exported UK book exports exceed those of the USA. To avoid contention, however, let it be said merely that British book exports are substantial, amounting to £67 million a year, and accounting for 47.2% of publishers' total turnover. In 1939 British book exports totalled £ 3.2 million and represented 30% of the total. Exports more than doubled between 1961 and 1969.

Official export statistics for 1969 were:

Category	Amount £ m
Printed books	42.6
Newspapers and periodicals	13.9
Other printed matter	24.5
Total	81.0

These figures, like the official figures for imports, exclude books sent through the post. It is estimated that, so far as books are concerned, the figures should be at least doubled to compensate for this fact, since a substantial part of British book exports is sent by bulk post. The Government nowadays collects *actual* figures of export turnover from all publishers. The last complete year for which figures are currently available is 1969, when the actual total export turnover of British publishers was 67.2 million. The PA's accountants prepare a territorial analysis of exports, the official statistics being misleading in this respect also. The following are the principal countries to which British publishers exported in 1968 (the last year for which the trade's actual figures are available):

Country	Amount £ m	Percentage of total
USA	11.4	18.4
Australia	9.6	15.6
Germany (Federal Republic)	3.0	4.9
Canada	2.8	4.5
New Zealand	2.5	4.1
West Africa	2.5	4.1
Eastern Africa	2.2	3.5
India	2.1	3.4
Netherlands	2.0	3.2
Sweden	1.5	2.4
West Indies	1.4	2.3
France	1.3	2.1
Japan	1.2	1.9

The above statistics include British publishers' earnings from the sale of rights, as well as from the sale of physical books. This is particularly important in relation to the figure for the USA, where rights may account for as much as a third of the total. Australia remains Britain's largest book-export market in terms of books as such. It should also be remarked that Western Europe as a whole in 1968 provided an income of £14.8 million, more than any other area of the world.

The "official" statistics for the export of British newspapers and periodicals show that in 1969 their export total was £13.9 million, or slightly less than the previous year's book earnings in Europe alone.

Wholesale export booksellers account for about 8% of total book exports and retail export booksellers about 5% of the total.

The British Government introduced an export rebate on 26 October 1964. This initially entitled British publishers to receive 2% of the value of their physical exports, subsequently increased to 2.25%, although subject to tax which reduced the actual benefit to about 1.2%. This rebate was cancelled, however, on 31 March 1968 because of the UK's economic difficulties.

The Export Division of the Publishers' Association, the

Book Development Council Ltd
19 Bedford Square
GB London W.C. 1

is active in the fields of research and promotion for book exports, initiating a number of book exhibitions each year, generally in collaboration with the "British Council".

The exhibitions department of the

British Council
Book Exhibitions Department
Albion House
59 New Oxford Street
GB London W.C. 1

mounts more than a hundred book exhibitions a year, the largest of which (consisting of more than 3,000 titles) is the national British exhibit at the "Frankfurt Book Fair".

Bibliography

Bookseller. London, J. Whitaker & Sons, weekly. Frequent articles on book exports.

A. T. G. Pocock, *Export. The next ten years.* A paper delivered to the Society of Bookmen on 4 April 1963. London, The Publishers' Association 1963.

29 Book Fairs

There are no regular international book fairs held in the United Kingdom. A "World Book Fair" was held in London in 1964, and enjoyed considerable success although it was somewhat expensive because it was primarily designed to display books to the general public rather than to the trade alone. It is probable that other international exhibitions will be organized in the future, but the likelihood is that they will have more trade emphasis.

Numerous book exhibitions are held in the United Kingdom each year, many of them being organized by the

National Book League
7 Albemarle Street
GB London W. 1

A number of specialist exhibitions, such as those for schoolteachers in specialized subjects, technical books, and so on, are organized by the various specialist Groups of the Publishers' Association (→ 4).

Additionally, the National Book League occasionally arranges international exhibitions as, for example, of children's books. These are not, however, of the dimensions of international fairs akin to the "Frankfurt Book Fair", or those held elsewhere.

30 Public Relations

A number of organizations in the British book trade are concerned with publicity and public relations. The Publishers' Association has a Book Promotion Officer (who is also the Press Officer) on its staff, who works in conjunction with a special Publicity Committee and is primarily concerned with securing press publicity for Association activities and generally to try to present a good "image" of the trade to the world at large. Constant contact is also maintained with the BBC and other broadcasting organizations.

The Charter Booksellers' Group of the BA also have an active Publicity Sub-committee, consisting of both booksellers and publishers. The Committee has been responsible for the production of a number of poster kits and was instrumental in encouraging Dr Mann to carry out his sociological survey into leisure reading (→ 9).

An unofficial group of young men and women, the Society of Young Publishers (→ 9), are also active in the field of publicity, having produced many series of attractive posters, as well as organizing a book "float" in London's Lord Mayor's Show in 1967. Publicity ideas are also discussed by the *Publishers' Publicity Circle*, a luncheon club of publishers' publicity men and women.

Important public relations work is also done by the

National Book League
7 Albemarle Street
GB London W. 1

which has a large public membership as well as many book-trade members.

In 1964 the two trade associations, together with the National Book League, the Society of Authors and the Library Association, formed a "Joint Committee" to organize Britain's first *National Library Week*. This took place in 1966 and was repeated in 1967. A third NLW took place in March 1969. This Week follows the US pattern, relying heavily upon local committees of bookmen and businessmen and women all over the country to organize exhibitions, competitions, readings, performances, and so on. There are also a number of national competitions and events designed to attract publicity.

Book Tokens (→ 4).

The first National Book Week is to take place in 1972.

Bibliography

S. Hyde, *Sales on a shoestring*. London, Deutsch 1956.

D. Ogilvy, *Confessions of an advertising man*. London, Longmans, Green 1964.

United Kingdom

31 Bibliophily

There are numerous reading circles and literary debating societies in Britain, but most of them are local and generally informal. The one body which unites most book-lovers is the

National Book League
7 Albemarle Street
GB London W. 1

Founded in 1925 as the National Book Council, the League's aim is to foster the growth of a wider and more discriminating interest in books. Its membership exceeds 10,000. The NBL issues Readers' Guides on many subjects and organizes numerous book exhibitions during the year, as well as providing lectures at its headquarters. There are a number of societies concerned with the art of book production (such as the "Wynkyn de Worde Society") but as their only address is generally that of the Honorary Secretary for the time being, it would not be useful to list them.

Outstanding among the societies concerned with bibliography is:

The Bibliographical Society
c/o The British Academy
Burlington Gardens
GB London W. 1

Founded in 1892, this Society is concerned with gathering and distributing information on all subjects connected with bibliography. It has an excellent bibliographical library and encourages research in bibliography. Important papers on the subject are read at meetings held at the headquarters. BS publishes

The Library
Oxford University Press
Ely House, 37 Dover Street
GB London W. 1

Mention should also be made of:

Books Across the Sea
c/o The English-Speaking Union
Dartmouth House, 37 Charles Street
GB London W. 1

Founded during World War II, this society is now amalgamated with the English-Speaking Union, and encourages the exchange of new books published on both sides of the Atlantic. It has committees in Australia, New Zealand, India and Canada.

An outstanding journal for book collectors is

The Book Collector
58 Frith Street
GB London W. 1

32 Literary Prizes

There are more than 40 literary prizes and awards offered in the United Kingdom each year, but most of them are small and do not carry the publicity value of the top French literary prizes.

The following are among the more important literary prizes offered in Britain:

James Tait Black Memorial Prizes (one for the best biography and one for the best novel each year)
Booker Prize for Fiction (a high prize for the best novel by a British Commonwealth, Irish or South African author each year)
Winston Spencer Churchill Literary Award (for any aspect of history of the English-speaking peoples) (Cassell)
Geoffrey Faber Memorial Prize (alternately for a novel and a volume of verse) (Faber and Faber)
Guardian Fiction Prize (The Guardian)
Hawthornden Prize (imaginative prose or verse by an author under 41 years)
Richard Hillary Memorial Prize (prose or poetry)
Library Association Carnegie Medal (for a children's book) (The Library Association)
Library Association Kate Greenaway Medal (for a children's book illustration) (The Library Association)
Somerset Maugham Trust Fund (for authors under 35 years: to travel)
John Llewelyn Rhys Memorial Prize (for a

literary work) (Mr Rhys and the National Book League)
Scott-Moncrieff Prize (for the best translation from French) (Society of Authors)
W. H. Smith & Son Annual Literary Award (for the most outstanding contribution to literature) (W. H. Smith & Son Ltd)
Yorkshire Post Book of the Year (for fiction and non-fiction) (Yorkshire Post)

Bibliography

Cassell's Directory of Publishing. 5th edn. London, Cassell 1968.
Writers' & Artists' Yearbook. London, A. & C. Black. Annually.

33 The Reviewing of Books

Being a fairly small country, the United Kingdom has been blessed with a truly national press, so that reviews in the main national newspapers and magazines are read throughout the entire country. The same, broadly speaking, applies to radio and television transmissions.
The following are the main weekly book-review media:
The Times Literary Supplement,
The Times Educational Supplement,
The Sunday Times,
The Observer,
The Sunday Telegraph,
The Spectator,
The New Statesman,
The Listener.
The following daily papers carry book-review columns at least once a week:
The Times,
The Financial Times,
The Daily Telegraph,
The Guardian,
The Evening Standard.
All the above papers are published in London. Important reviews are also published outside London by the following newspapers:
The Scotsman (Glasgow),
The Birmingham Mail (Birmingham),
The Yorkshire Post (Leeds).
Specialist weekly publications concerned more or less exclusively with book reviews include: *Books and Bookmen* (incorporating *John O'London's Weekly*).
Other weekly papers that include book reviews (all in London) are:
The Economist,
Punch,
Queen,
Nova,
Illustrated London News,
Tribune,
The Teacher,
Teacher's World,
Education.

Bibliography

Willing's Press Guide. London, James Willings Ltd. Annually.

34 Graphic Arts

There is in the United Kingdom no single institution concerned with the graphic arts. The following institutions are, however, concerned with the maintenance of standards in this field:

Society of Graphic Artists
195 Piccadilly
GB London W. 1

The Society of Industrial Artists
and Designers
7 Woburn Square
GB London W.C. 1

There are also a number of private luncheon clubs (such as the Wynkyn de Worde Society and the Double Crown Club) that are concerned with graphic standards, and the "National Book League" (→ 20) organizes the selection of best-designed books.

35 Miscellaneous

There are two features of particular significance which have not been covered by this brief review of British publishing. The first concerns the economic pattern of the publishing industry, and the second the forward march of publishing in company with technological development.

a) Economic Pattern of Publishing

In the years following World War II a number of publishing companies grouped themselves together with a view to sharing the cost of certain common services, such as invoicing and warehousing. Even before the War, the great cooperative warehouse of Book Centre Ltd (→ 13) was established, and today has more than 60 publishers in its membership. In the past decade, however, there has been an increasing tendency for publishing houses to merge their publishing interests completely or, in some cases, larger publishing houses have "taken over" some smaller ones. Given a business of a certain size it is clearly economic to use certain physical services (such as warehousing and invoicing) to full capacity, so that the addition of one or two smaller publishing houses to a publishing group can be done profitably to all concerned. The amalgamation of editorial policies, however, presents greater difficulties. Authors tend to form allegiances with their individual editors, and it is in the nature of book publishing that the list created by an individual tends to have more character than one collected together by a number of people. Where a team of editors is small enough a list may still have that homogeneity which spells character, and this is particularly important in the field of creative writing. Thus it is that the small publisher still occupies an important part in the British publishing scene, even though he may nowadays be surrounded by a number of giants.

This individuality of approach is less important in the fields of technology and science where, inevitably, Board policy is bound to rely upon the advice of numerous experts, both within and outside the publishing house. It seems probable that the amalgamation of firms in the scientific and technical and educational fields will continue, but that the small publisher in the field of creative writing will always have his place.

b) Audio and Visual Supplements

The second notable feature of recent years is the development of audio and visual supplements to books. Tape-recordings, gramophone records, film loops and "programmes" are increasingly becoming a feature of the British book publishing scene as elsewhere. And now audio-visual cassettes.
Microform publishing (by 35 mm. and 16 mm. film rolls and cassettes, microcards and microfiche) have for some years been used for reprinting out-of-print works required by libraries. Such forms are now beginning to be used for original publications, and the probability is that in future many works—and particularly learned journals—will be published simultaneously in printed form and microform (probably microfiche). Publishers have to keep abreast of these developments if they are to retain their position as the entrepreneurs of the printed word.

c) Standard Book Numbering

Standard Book Numbers (SBNs) were devised under the sponsorship of the Publishers' Association by Professor F. G. Foster in 1966, at that time of the London School of Economics. The object of SBNs is to simplify book ordering and speed supply, as well as enabling computerized records to isolate individual book titles for the endless variety of statistics which computers can produce. SBNs may prove to be invaluable in the calculation of authors' earnings from the Public Lending Right (a royalty on public library use of books, which the UK hopes to have in the near future), and even for assessing payments for photocopying.

Professor Foster's proposed system was adopted by the PA in 1967. It requires a nine-figure standard, with a prefix number, identifying the publisher, and the remaining digits (less one, for the check digit—see below) identifying the title, followed by a check digit which confirms that the preceding numerals are accurately reproduced by dividing the number (beginning by a pair of digits and then progressively) by 11 ("modulus 11") so that, with the addition of the check digit, the SBN is scanned by "modulus 11" and works out exactly with nothing left over. The "check digit" is, of course, designed solely to verify that the SBN is reproduced accurately. If the modulus 11 does not check out, the computer rejects the SBN as inaccurate. The following SBN will illustrate the principle:

949999 01 6

The publisher using this SBN would require a new prefix or to start numbering afresh after publishing 99 books. Publishers issuing larger numbers of titles are allocated shorter prefix numbers, allowing for more *title* numbers, such as:

571 09243 8 and so on.

In 1969 this British initiative was taken up by the British Standards Institute, and then the International Standards Organization, so that there are now International Standard Book Numbers (ISBNs), the SBN being preceded by a single digit representing the national, regional, or linguistic identification. Publications in the English language are identified by the ISBN prefix "0" because the UK were the originators of the system.

→ International Section, 35c.

Bibliography

Standard Book Numbering. London, The Standard Book Numbering Agency Ltd 1968.

Yugoslavia

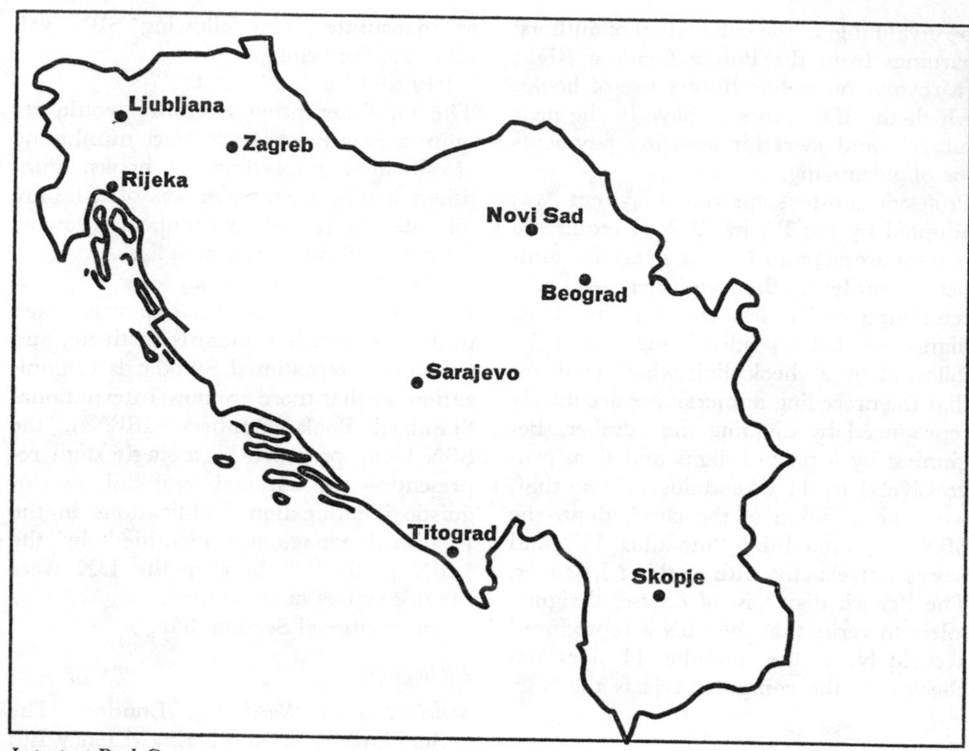

Important Book Centres

1 General Information

Area 255,804 km²

Population 20,351,000 (estimate for 1969) (78 per km²)

Capital Beograd (697,000)

Capitals Republic of Serbia (8.2 m): Beograd (697,000); Republic of Croatia (4.4 m): Zagreb (503,000); Republic of Slovenia (1.7 m): Ljubljana (182,000); Republic of Bosnia and Herzegovina (3.8 m): Sarajevo (227,000); Republic of Macedonia (1.6 m): Skopje (228,000); Montenegro (0.5 m): Titograd (42,000)

Other large towns Novi-Sad (126,000); Rijeka (116,000); Split (114,000); Niš (98,000); Maribor (94,000); Osijek (84,000); Subotica (78,000)

Government A Federation of six Socialist Federal Republics with their own parliaments and governments. Their work is unified by a common Federal Parliament and Government; the Federal Government is responsible for the army and foreign policy

Religion Orthodox (pravoslavni)
Roman Catholic
Mohammedan
Protestant
others, including unattached and not-declared

National languages Serbo-Croat, Slovene and Macedonian; the national minorities have the right to use their mother tongue generally and in state and administrative affairs

Main foreign languages English, German, French, Russian

Weights and measures Metric system

Currency unit Dinar (din)

Education Compulsory: elementary, middle higher. Elementary comprises 8 years, middle 4–6 years, higher (university) 4–6 years; there are also intermediate stages. In 1966–67 2,921,607 pupils attended elementary school, 731,493 middle school, and 206,923 students were at university

Illiteracy approx. 19.7%. Individual republics: Serbia 21.9; Croatia 12.1; Slovenia 1.8; Bosnia and Herzegovina 32.5; Macedonia 24.5; Montenegro 21.7

Paper consumption a) Newsprint 3.9 kg per inhabitant (1968)
b) Printing paper (other than newsprint) 4.8 kg (1968)

Membership UNESCO

2 Past and Present

Yugoslavia is one of those countries to which the art of book printing came very early. Only 37 years after Johann Gutenberg of Mainz discovered the art of printing with movable metal letters, the first printing and publishing house was founded (1482) in Kosinj, at that time an important Croatian cultural and religious centre. It was at the same time the first printing works in the world with glagolitic letters. Of its numerous works the "Missal of Kosinj" has been preserved. It is dated 22 February 1483, is printed in two colours, a splendid work of 438 pages, and is regarded as the original South-Slavonic edition. Another work that is known to have been printed here is the "Breviary of Kosinj" from the year 1491; only one copy has survived and is now in the Library of San Marco in Venice. After the defeat of the Croatian army at Krbava (1493), and due to the advancing Turks, this printing work was moved to the cathedral city of Senj, and after a time to Rijeka, where, after 1531, every trace of it is lost.

At the end of the fifteenth and in the first half of the sixteenth centuries a comparatively large number of printing works were started in monasteries to further the religious and national propaganda of the Orthodox Church in Cetinje (1494), Rujno (1537), Gračanica (1539), Mileševo (1544), Beograd (1522), Mrkšina Crkva (1562). All of these works used Cyrillic letters.

The first book-printing work in Zagreb, the capital of Croatia, was founded by Hermagora Kraft in 1527. By a resolution of the Provincial Diet of Croatia on 11 December 1694, Pavao Ritter Vitezović founded the "Zemaljska tiskara" (Provincial Printing Works) in Zagreb, one of the first official printing works in the world. Many of the works from this press have been preserved.

Yugoslavia

The first press to be built in Ljubljana, the capital of present-day Slovenia, appeared in 1575. The large number of incunabula proves, however, that before that time there existed a lively traffic in books in this area of Yugoslavia, especially in the west (Croatia and Slovenia).

In the early centuries printers were, as in other countries, publishers and booksellers too, and that continued in several variations till the middle of the nineteenth century. From 1762 onwards the bookshop of Franjo Zeramscheg existed independently of a printing workshop.

The first booksellers dealing in Serbian books worked in Venice (sixteenth century) and Vienna and Budim (seventeenth century).

In 1832 Grigorij Vozarević founded a bookbinding and selling firm in Belgrade, and from that time there was a rapid development in the book trade in Serbia; by 1903 there were already 128 booksellers and at the outbreak of the First World War more than 200. On the territory of present-day Serbia there were 312 booksellers in 1935, more than half of which (162) were in Belgrade.

In Slovenia Janz Mandelc opened the first bookshop to his printing works in 1575, and from then onwards, apart from occasional hitches, the book trade developed very favourably in this part of the present-day republic, so that today the network of bookshops is thickest there.

Bibliography

Z. Kulundžić, *Kosinj, die Wiege der Buchdruckerkunst im Slawischen Süden.* (Kosinj, the cradle of the art of printing in the Slavonic south). In: Gutenberg Jahrbuch 1964. Mainz 1964.

Z. Kulundžić, *Gutenberg und sein Werk im slawischen Süden.* (Gutenberg and his work in the Slavonic south). Mainz 1968.

M. Breyer, *Der kroatische Buchhandel.* (The Croatian book trade). Leipzig 1910.

S. Novaković, *Srpska knjiga, njeni prodavci i čitaoci u XIX veku.* (The Serbian book, its sellers and readers in the 19th century). Beograd 1900.

V. Klaić, *Knjižarstvo u Hrvata.* (The book trade in Croatia). Zagreb 1922.

3 Retail Price

Till 1945 private publishing firms alone fixed the prices. They were guided by the principles and conditions of free trade. From 1945 to 1950 the price of a book was officially determined in accordance with all the costing factors, fees, rebates and taxes. Today the publisher freely and independently fixes the prices of his books. In principle the prices are firm, but publishers have the right to increase or lower the price of books already on the market. Reductions of up to 90% can also be made in sales. Even though there are no legal restrictions in this matter, publishers do try to keep to the original retail price.

4 Organization

The book trade was already being organized in 1918, though not very thoroughly. From 1945 onwards this matter was dealt with systematically. The organizations existing in the individual republics are now brought together in a coordinating association:

Udruženje izdavača i knjižara Jugoslavije
(Association of Yugoslavian Publishers and Booksellers)
Ulica Kneza Miloša 25/I
YU Beograd

5 Trade Press

The oldest Yugoslavian book-trade paper is "Knjižarski glasnik" ("Book Trade Messenger"). It first appeared in Novi Sad in 1908. Later (in 1922) the trade paper of the booksellers in Belgrade appeared under this heading. In Zagreb two trade papers began to appear, one in 1923, "Knjižarski vjesnik" ("Book-Trade

News"), the other in 1925, "Knjižarstvo" ("Book Trade"). The journal "Narodna knjiga" ("People's Book") appeared in Zagreb between 1948 and 1950.
The monthly journal *Knjiga i svet* ("The Book and the World") has been appearing since 1958, and is published by the "Association of Yugoslavian Publishers and Booksellers" (→ 4).

6 Book-Trade Literature

In this respect Yugoslavia is still dependent on foreign publications, but there does exist a series of smaller books and journals in the national languages.
→ 2.

7 Sources of Information, Address Services

All information referring to the book and publishing trades can be obtained from:

Udruženje izdavača i knjižara Jugoslavije
(Association of Yugoslavian Publishers and Booksellers)
Ulica Kneza Miloša 25/I
YU Beograd

Information of a specialist nature can be obtained from:

Jugoslavenski bibliografski institut
(Yugoslavian Bibliographical Institute)
Terazije 26
YU Beograd
(for contemporary editions and periodicals)

Jugoslavenski leksikografski zavod
(Yugoslavian Lexicographical Institute)
Strosmayerov trg 4
YU Zagreb
(this Institute edits and publishes the bibliography of Yugoslavian periodicals from their first appearance, i.e. from the eighteenth century to the year 1945).

Narodna biblioteka Srbije
(Serbian National Library)
Knez Mihajlova 56
YU Beograd

Nacionalna i sveučilišna biblioteka
(National University Library)
Marulićev trg 21
YU Zagreb

Narodna i univerzitetna biblioteka
(National and University Library)
Turjaska 1
YU Ljubljana

Narodna knjižnica Bosne i Hercegovine
(National Library of Bosnia and Herzegovina)
Obala Vojvode Stepe 42
YU Sarajevo

Narodna i univerzitetska biblioteka S.R.M.
(National and University Library of the Socialist Republic of Macedonia)
Dimitri Vlahova 49
YU Skopje

Centralna narodna biblioteka
(Central National Library)
Njegoševa 100
YU Cetinje

Addresses of publishing houses and bookshops →29 (Catalogue of the International Belgrade Book Fair).

8 International Membership

Through the "Association of Yugoslavian Publishers and Booksellers" (→4) links are maintained with similar institutions throughout the world; individual publishers too have direct contact with the Association and thus stimulate the development of business connections with many lands.
In addition, "Udruženje" (→ 4) is a permanent exhibitor at the Frankfurt Book Fair. Yugoslavia is also represented from time to time at many other international gatherings of a similar nature, as e.g. in Leipzig, Warsaw, Bologna and other towns where publishers exhibit individually or collectively.

Yugoslavia

9 Market Research

This is carried out by individual publishing houses, but preparations are being made for this to be done by a separate institution.

10 Books and Young People

Yugoslavia can boast a great tradition in this field. It goes back to the time before 1918, when Yugoslavia had not yet gained its independence.
More and more attention has been paid to books for youth in recent years and the matter is being dealt with in greater depth and more scientifically. A number of meetings and conferences have been held and works specially dealing with the subject have appeared. Many publishing firms in Yugoslavia are concerned with the appearance of this type of literature, and there are also firms specializing in this field:" Mlado pokolenje" ("Young Generation"), Belgrade; "Naša djeca" ("Our Children"), Zagreb; "Mladost" ("Youth"), Zagreb; "Mladinska knjiga" ("Youth Books"), Ljubljana; "Detska radost" ("Children's pleasure"), Skopje; "Svjetlost" ("Light"), Sarajevo.

11 Training

Training for the book trade is provided in special departments of the commercial schools, which pupils attend after completing their eight years of elementary education. School attendance, which runs parallel with practical experience in bookshops, lasts three or four years. These schools also provide instruction for higher qualifications, and apart from this more and more young people with a university education—especially students of Slavonic languages, comparative literature and the history of art—are today entering the book trade.
In future the requirements for studying for the trade will be a secondary school education plus a course of six or twelve months.

12 Taxes

Yugoslavian publishers enjoy various privileges and tax reliefs as compared with other branches of the economy, since books are not merely regarded as goods, but also as an instrument in social progress.

14 Copyright

In the part of Yugoslavia which was formerly part of the Austro-Hungarian Empire—i.e. present-day Croatia, Slovenia, Bosnia, Herzegovina and the northern part of Serbia—protection of copyright was first regulated by the Imperial Charter of 11 October 1846, and later by the copyright laws of 26 April 1884 and 26 December 1895. The first Yugoslavian law to protect authors' rights was published in the Kingdom of Yugoslavia on 26 December 1929; the new law was published in the Socialist Republic of Yugoslavia on 25 May 1946. This was succeeded by a new version on 20 July 1968.
This law protects the work of all native authors, whether a work appears at home or abroad or whatever its form of expression may be, e.g. books, essays, speeches, drama, musical or choreographical works, pantomimes, sculptures, pictures: in a word, any work springing from a creative act; to these must be added translations and re-casting of works when done with the author's permission.
Copyright is concerned in the first place with protecting the moral right of the author, the integrity of his works against any damage or change and the prevention of the publishing of a work without the express consent of its author. No consent is necessary for the publication of the

works of deceased authors, but the material rights are guaranteed to their heirs. These have a right to fees for fifty years after the author's death.

By a decree of the Presidium of the Popular Assembly dated 23 June 1951 Yugoslavia joined the "Berne Convention" in the form of the revised text of the Conference of Brussels 1948.

Bibliography

B. Eisner, *O autorskom pravu.* (On copyright). Zagreb 1949.

J. Schuman, *Komentar zakona o zaštiti autorskog prava i medunarodnih propisa.* (Commentary of the law of copyright and the international regulations). Beograd 1935.

V. Spaić, *Autorsko pravo.* (Copyright). Sarajevo 1957.

J. Stempihar, *Autorsko pravo.* (Copyright). Ljubljana 1960.

M. Stojanović, *Izdavački ugovor.* Zakonodavstvo, teorija i praksa. (Publishing contract. Legislation, theory and practice). Beograd 1967.

15 National Bibliography, National Library

A complete Yugoslavian bibliography is being created. At present only fragments have been published. For example, the beginning of Croatian—and therefore, Yugoslavian—printed books has been treated in the work "Glagoljaška stamparija XV–XVI stoljeća" ("Glagolitic printing in the XVth and XVIth centuries") by Z. Kulundžić (Senj 1966). Among Serbian bibliographies mention should be made of "Srpska bibliografija XVIII veka" ("Serbian bibliography of the XVIIIth century") by G. Mihajlović (Beograd 1964). It forms the beginning of the "Serbian retrospective bibliography" which is now being published. A similar bibliography for Croatian books is being worked out at present in Zagreb. The most thorough work of all is being done on a bibliography of Slovenian books, the fundamental work being the "Slovenska bibliografija" ("Slovenian bibliography") by F. Simonič. It deals with books from 1550 to 1900. The period from 1945 onwards is being systematically edited and published, and by 1964 eighteen volumes had appeared under the title "Slovenska bibliografija" ("Slovenian bibliography"). There are also a number of fragmentary works, for the most part obsolete.

Retrospective bibliographical material from 1945 to 1967 is in process of printing and should have appeared by the end of 1969. This will be a work of twenty volumes with about 100,000 bibliographical units which will include all Yugoslavian books that have appeared in socialist Yugoslavia in the time mentioned. The "Jugoslavenski leksikografski zavod" ("Yugoslavian Lexicographical Institute"), Zagreb, publishes a special bibliography from 1768 onwards under the title "Bibliografija rasprava, članaka i književnih radova" ("Bibliography of treatises, essays and literary works").

Books and periodicals from 1945 onwards are systematically dealt with by the *Jugoslavenski bibliografski institut* ("Yugoslavian Bibliographical Institute"), *Belgrade* (→ 7). It publishes the series *Bibliografija Jugoslavije* ("Bibliography of Yugoslavia"), which is in three parts: 1) sociology, 2) natural and applied science, 3) philology, art, sports, literature and music. In addition, the "Udruženje izdavača i knjižara Jugoslavije" (→ 4) publishes a bibliography intended for the book market. It is part of the publication *Knjiga i svet* ("The Book and the World"), which has been appearing since 1958. The Slovenes publish their monthly journal intended for the book trade in Ljubljana:

Knjiga (The Book)
Mestni trg 26
YU Ljubljana

For national bibliographical centres → 7.

Yugoslavia

16 Book Production

In recent times book production has increased from year to year:

1948	3,413
1950	4,371
1952	5,184
1957	5,768
1962	5,637
1964	8,019
1967	9,226

A detailed picture of 1967 is given in the following table, worked out according to types of literature, and includes also the number of editions.

9,226 titles appeared in 1967. Arranged according to the various republics they were as follows:

Serbia	4,711
Croatia	1,759
Slovenia	1,321
Bosnia and Herzegovina	723
Macedonia	652
Montenegro	60

The number of published titles in 1967 arranged according to important subjects was as follows:

Subject group	Titles
Belles-lettres	2,774
Economics	764
Education	691
Technology	414
Law	325
Politics	320
Philology	297
Medicine	281
Trade, communications	250
Art	231

The average edition in 1967 comprised 9,908 copies.

17 Translations

Translation work is very extensive throughout the country. In this respect Yugoslavia stands high on the list compared with other countries.

The following table shows the relationship of native to foreign authors:

Year	All titles	Native authors	Foreign authors
1962	5,637	4,787	850
1963	6,400	5,343	1,057
1964	8,019	6.773	1,246
1965	7,980	6,651	1,329
1966	7,768	6,446	1,322
1967	9,226	7,560	1,666
Editions in thousands			
1962	39,667	33,968	5,699
1963	45,722	36,181	9,541
1964	54,284	42,716	11,568
1965	59,417	45,667	13,750
1966	56,988	43,489	13,499
1967	69,001	50,657	18,326

18 Book Clubs

The publication of books for members of a particular group of readers is an old-standing tradition in Yugoslavia. A series of societies and clubs for this purpose already existed in the nineteenth century and publishers sent the book direct to members, thus ensuring a favourable purchasing price. The firm of "Matica srpska", which is still active in Novi Sad was founded in 1826; the firm of "Matica hrvatska", founded in 1839, still exists in Zagreb, and "Slovenska matica", founded in 1864, in Ljubljana. The "Društvo svetog Jeronima" ("Society of St Jerome") published books for Croatian peasants. The firm, which was founded in 1867, was in the hands of the Catholic Church. By 1945 it had a wide sphere of activity, and between 1868 and 1945 more than 700 titles with more than 11 m copies had appeared on every conceivable subject. During that time a whole series of similar societies was at work, including the "Družba svetego Mohorja" ("Society of St Mohor") in Celovac, founded in 1860 and later moved to Celje, where it is still operating. This society already had 20,000 members in 1872, 80,000 in 1891, 90,000 in 1918; but in 1940 the number fell to 45,000. From its foundation until the present day the society produced 25 m copies, serving mainly the religious-minded members of the population. The firm is still in production today under the name "Mohorjeva Druzba".

In Yugoslavia today there is a whole series of clubs tied to various publishing firms, as for example "Mladost" ("Youth") in Zagreb with about 120,000 members, and "Prosveta" ("Education") in Belgrade, but these clubs are not like those in other countries.

The first book club similar to those found abroad was formed in Zagreb at the end of 1968 and is called the "Klub prijatelja poezije" ("Club of Poetry Lovers").

19 Paperbacks

Small-sized books, which because of their lay-out and large editions are particularly cheap and intended for the broad mass of the population, have existed for many years in Yugoslavia. The publishers in Mostar, Paher and Kisić, for example, started the "Mala biblioteka" ("Small library") in 1899, which existed till 1910 and in that time produced 185 titles. Later, and under the same title, up to ten such series appeared in Belgrade, Zagreb, Dubrovnik and Sarajevo. The "Džepna biblioteka" ("Pocketbook library") appeared in Zagreb in 1933, and there existed and still exists a whole series of similar editions under various names.

Today a number of paperback series are being published, the most successful being "Reč i misao" ("Word and Thought") of the Belgrade publishers "Rad" ("Work") with 126 titles to date, and the "Dzepna biblioteka" ("Pocketbook library") by the Sarajevo publishers "Svjetlost" ("Light"), with 70 titles to date.

20 Book Design

Books as works of art can be found in Yugoslavia at a very early date. The oldest South-Slavonic printed book, the Glagolitic "Missal of Kosinj" (1483) is a masterpiece, as is also the fine "Crnojević Psalter" in Cirilica (1494). During the centuries there have appeared a great many books whose contents and lay-out would do credit to the greatest nations. Since 1962 awards for the best-designed books have been made by the "Poslovno udruženje izdavačkih poduzeća i organizacija" ("Business Association of Publishers and Publishing Organizations"). The titles of books receiving these awards are made known every year at the "International Book Fair" in Belgrade.

21 Publishing

There are 63 publishing houses in the six republics. They are members of "Udruženje" (→ 4). Outside this association there are numerous enterprises and organizations concerned with publishing as well as a certain number of newspaper publishers who also publish books. Since private persons also have the right to publish their works themselves, it is estimated that about 50% of the published books are published outside the 63 registered publishing houses.

A list of all publishing houses together with their addresses, information on their activities and other important data can be found in the *Katalog medunarodnog sajma knjiga* ("Catalogue of the International Book Fair", Belgrade,—annually).

Yugoslavia

The regional distribution of the registered publishing houses is as follows:
→ 16.

Serbia	26
Croatia	21
Slovenia	7
Bosnia and Herzegovina	3
Macedonia	4
Montenegro	2

22 Literary Agents

In Yugoslavia there never have been intermediaries between author and publisher to do this work as a legalized activity, and today, bearing in mind the social order existing in the country, such an activity would be incompatible with the principles of socialism.

24 Retail Trade

A high percentage of the many first-class Yugoslavian bookshops is owned by publishing houses.
The total number of bookshops is over 800 of which most are situated as follows:

Serbia	204
Croatia	104
Slovenia	26
Bosnia and Herzegovina	61
Macedonia	22
Montenegro	3

Addresses could be found in *Katalog XV medunarodnog sajma knjiga* ("Catalogue of the International Book Fair"), pp. 3–40, Beograd 1970.
The combination publishing/bookselling also involves wholesale activities and travelling agents. Instalment buying is popular.

25 Mail-Order Bookselling

This is very widespread. It is estimated that in this way up to 50%—and in individual cases up to 90%—of some editions are sold. "Jugoslavenski leksikografski zavod" ("The Yugoslavian Lexographical Institute") for example, sells all its production in this way.

26 Antiquarian Book Trade, Auctions

Compared with former times, the second-hand book trade has visibly decreased in recent years. Whereas up to 1945 a large number of small second-hand bookshops existed, today only a few larger ones are to be found in the major towns, and these are mainly firms working on a commission basis.
The largest second-hand bookshops are the following:

Antiquariat Matica hrvatska
Ilica 62
YU Zagreb

Antiquariat Cankarjeve založbe
Mesni trg 25
YU Ljubljana

Antiquariat Srpske književne zadruge
Marsala Tita 19
YU Beograd

Antiquariat Matice srpske
Maticina 1
YU Novi Sad

Antiquariat Svjetlost
Zrinskoga 6
YU Sarajevo

27 Book Imports

The reciprocal arrangements in matters concerning the printed word between Yugoslavia and other countries in and beyond Europe are extraordinarily active.

Imports are characterized by their great variety, which is only to be expected in view of the dynamic developments in science, education, technology and sociology. Particular mention must be made of the import of periodicals, which are a permanent aid in the work of many institutions. The import of books and magazines has been liberalized; it is therefore not surprising that imports rose from about US$ 1 m in 1963 to about US$ 3 m in 1968. Included in this are the imports for national minorities and their schools.

The foreign trade in books and periodicals is handled by specialized firms which in turn are mostly connected with the publishing and bookselling activities of certain firms.

The official foreign-trade statistics of Yugoslavia show the following results for book imports in 1967:

Category	Amount din.
Books in national languages	3,074,941
Books in foreign languages	10,014,662
Picture books	1,754,773
Total	14,834,376

Within the category "Books in foreign languages" the leading countries of origin were: Germany (Federal Republic) (1.3 m); Hungary (1.3 m.); USSR (1.2 m); United Kingdom (1.1 m), and USA (1.0 m).

28 Book Exports

Although the languages spoken in Yugoslavia are not international, the export of Yugoslavian books continues to rise. Coproductions with foreign firms contribute much to this, but also the high quality of the work of the graphic industry of the country, especially its gravure and offset printing. In 1967 exports amounted to almost US$ 3 m.

In 1967 the foreign trade statistics of Yugoslavia gave the following information about book exports:

Category	Amount din.
Books in national languages	268,320
Books in foreign languages	14,713,539
Picture books	268,320
Total	15,250,179

The leading receiving countries for books in foreign languages were: Hungary (2.4 m); USA (2.3 m); Germany (Federal Republic) (1.8 m); United Kingdom (1.7 m); and Germany (Democratic Republic) (1.7 m).

29 Book Fairs

The

International Belgrade Book Fair
P.O.B. 883
YU Beograd

held for the last 13 years in Belgrade, (the first was held in Zagreb in 1957), provides the greatest display for the book trade in Yugoslavia. This book fair has increased in range from year to year in the number of exhibitors from at home and abroad, in area, and in the number of books displayed. At the 14th book fair in 1969, 45,000 titles were displayed on 800 stalls. Besides the 76 Yugoslavian firms there were also 68 exhibitors from 18 countries of Europe, Asia and America.

A detailed catalogue is published for each book fair. The catalogue for 1968 contains 1,595 pages and is divided into five parts. The first part contains all the essential information about Yugoslavian publishing firms, foreign exhibitors and a list of all Yugoslavian newspapers and magazines. The second is a list of all Yugoslavian bookshops arranged under republics and towns, with addresses and detailed information about their activities. The third part consists of a bibliographical index of book offers arranged alphabetically according to publishers and authors. The fourth part contains all books according to the name of the author without reference to the publisher. The fifth part is an alphabetical list of books arranged according to title, with the additional information of author and publisher. This catalogue, which is revised every year, is therefore a complete reference book containing bibliographical information on all publications appearing at the time on the book market. The publishers of this catalogue are: "Udruženje izdavača i knjižara Jugoslavije" (→ 4).

30 Public Relations

Information on books published, especially the most important, is disseminated through advertisements in newspapers and magazines, posters and the dispatch of prospectuses, etc. The more important books are reviewed on radio and television and in newspapers and magazines. When the collected works of M. P. Miškina appeared at the end of 1968, a festival was organized at his birthplace, and his works were handed over to the book trade. At the same time a monument to him was unveiled and a memorial room opened in the neighbouring town of Koprivnica.
The search is continually going on for new ways of awakening the public's interest in books. Thematic exhibitions by publishers are also being organized.

31 Bibliophily

This has never been found to any large extent in Yugoslavia and was limited to a few individuals; however, it is possible to trace bibliophily back to the Middle Ages. This is proved by many handwritten codices and finely embellished editions. The names of individuals, particularly Croatian and Slovenian noblemen and wealthy citizens, have an honoured place in this field of culture too.

In 1905 the journal "Hrvatski bibliofil" ("The Croatian Bibliophile") appeared in Zagreb.
In 1967

Naučno i kulturno društvo Kosinj
(The Kosinj Cultural and Scientific Society)
Buconjićeva 19
YU Zagreb II

was founded for research into and the popularization of old and comparatively old Croatian and Southern Slavonic books.

32 Literary Prizes

There are a number of prizes for literary and scientific works in Yugoslavia, and this tradition goes back to the previous century (e.g. the prize of Count I. N. Drašković). Today these prizes are awarded by individual associations, republics, towns and by some publishers: "Mladost" in Zagreb, "Matica srpska" and "Forum" in Novi Sad etc. Some of the larger newspapers and periodicals must also be mentioned, e.g. "Vjesnik" in Zagreb, "NIN" in Belgrade, and "Hid" in Novi Sad. The most coveted is the "AVNOJ *Prize*", founded in 1967 and awarded for masterpieces or for a life's work in literature, art or social activities.

33 The Reviewing of Books

This work is for the most part undertaken by a number of periodicals intended mainly for the book trade. The most important are:

Knjiga i svet
(The Book and the World)
Ulica Kneza Miloša 25/I
YU Beograd

and

Knjiga
(Book)
Mestni trg 26
YU Ljubljana

Annex

Annex 1: International Book Production, 1968

(*Source: Unesco Statistical Yearbook, 1968. Paris 1969*).

Country	*Titles*
Afghanistan	172 (1966)
Albania	502 (1965)
Algeria	258
Argentina	3,645
Australia	2,339
Austria	4,987
Belgium	3,888
Bhutan	1 (1966)
Bulgaria	3,754
Burma	2,141 (1966)
Burundi	17 (1966)
Cambodia	358
Cameroon	30 (1966)
Canada	3,782
Central African Republic	23
Ceylon	1,534
Chile	1,556
China	
a) Peoples' Republic	(?)
b) Republic (Taiwan)	2,252
Colombia	709 (1965)
Costa Rica	237
Cuba	748
Cyprus	207
Czechoslovakia	8,079
Denmark	4,895
El Salvador	27
Finland	5,485
France	19,021
Gabon	10 (1965)
Germany	
a) Federal Republic	29,524
b) German Democratic Republic	5,312
Ghana	233
Greece	1,241
Guatemala	335 (1966)
Guinea	8 (1966)
Haiti	18
Hong Kong	1,003
Hungary	5,301
Iceland	637 (1966)
India	10,617
Iran	1,231
Iraq	485 (1966)
Ireland	233
Israel	1,471 (1966)
Italy	8,215
Ivory Coast	50
Jamaica	78
Japan	30,027
Jordan	162
Kenya	162
Korea	
a) Republic of	3,464 (1966)
b) Peoples' Democratic Republic	(?)
Kuwait	153
Laos	14
Lebanon	427
Liberia	11 (1966)
Libya	86
Luxembourg	200
Madagascar	154
Malawi	14 (1966)
Malaysia	483
Maldive Islands	24 (1965)
Malta	65
Mauritius and deps.	50
Mexico	4,558 (1966)
Monaco	114
Mozambique	149
Netherlands	11,262
New Zealand	850
Nigeria	778
Norway	3,276
Pakistan	3,312
Peru	985 (1966)
Philippines	726 (1966)
Poland	9,694
Portugal	5,522
Romania	6,085
Sierra Leone	73
Singapore	322
Somalia	17 (1965)
South Africa	2,641
Spain	19,380
Sweden	7,218
Switzerland	6,041

Syria	87	(1966)
Tunisia	250	
Turkey	5,688	
United Arab Republic	1,819	(1966)
United Kingdom	29,564	
United States of America	58,877	
Uruguay	341	
USSR	74,081	
Viet-Nam		
a) Republic of	713	
b) Peoples' Democratic Republic	(?)	
Yugoslavia	9,226	
Zambia	39	(1965)

Annex 2: Translations, 1968

(Source: Index translationum, 21. Paris, Unesco 1970.)

Country	*Number of Translations (Titles)*
Albania	137
Andorra	8
Australia	22
Austria	319
Belgium	931
Bolivia	2
Bulgaria	561
Burma	56
Burundi	0
Cameroon	16
Canada	80
Ceylon	89
Chad	1
Chile	5
China	
a) Peoples' Republic	?
b) Republic (Taiwan)	238
Colombia	1
Czechoslovakia	1,750
Denmark	1,419
Ecuador	1
Finland	749
France	2,035
Germany (FRG + GDR)	3,026
Guatemala	7
Guinea	2
Guyana	1
Holy See	9
Hungary	1,043
Iceland	164
India	854
Iraq	13
Ireland	17
Israel	406
Italy	1,688
Ivory Coast	2
Japan	2,145
Kenya	2
Lebanon	32
Mexico	393
Netherlands	1,942
New Zealand	3
Nigeria	2

Norway	858
Pakistan	95
Poland	924
Portugal	383
Romania	812
South Africa	161
Spain	2,538
Sudan	2
Sweden	1,479
Switzerland	680
Syria	27
Turkey	715
United Arab Republic	219
United Kingdom	631
United States of America	2,182
USSR	3,607
Venezuela	8
Viet-Nam	
a) Republic of	23
b) Peoples' Democratic Republic	?
Yugoslavia	1,294

Annex 3: UNESCO Florence Agreement

Agreement on the Importation of Educational, Scientific and Cultural Materials

Preamble

The contracting States,
Considering that the free exchange of ideas and knowledge and, in general, the widest possible dissemination of the diverse forms of self-expression used by civilizations are vitally important both for intellectual progress and international understanding, and consequently for the maintenance of world peace;
Considering that this interchange is accomplished primarily by means of books, publications and educational, scientific and cultural materials;
Considering that the Constitution of the United Nations Educational, Scientific and Cultural Organization urges cooperation between nations in all branches of intellectual activity, including 'the exchange of publications, objects of artistic and scientific interest and other materials of information' and provides further that the Organization shall 'collaborate in the work of advancing the mutual knowledge and understanding of peoples, through all means of mass communication and to that end recommend such international agreements as may be necessary to promote the free flow of ideas by word and image';
Recognize that these aims will be effectively furthered by an international agreement facilitating the free flow of books, publications and educational, scientific and cultural materials; and
Have, therefore, agreed to the following provisions:

Article I

1. The contracting States undertake not to apply customs duties or other charges on, or in connection with, the importation of:

(a) Books, publications and documents, listed in Annex A to this Agreement;
(b) Educational, scientific and cultural materials, listed in Annexes B, C, D and E to this Agreement;
which are the products of another contracting State, subject to the conditions laid down in those annexes.
2. The provisions of paragraph 1 of this article shall not prevent any contracting State from levying on imported materials:
(a) Internal taxes or any other internal charges of any kind, imposed at the time of importation or subsequently, not exceeding those applied directly or indirectly to like domestic products;
(b) Fees and charges, other than customs duties, imposed by governmental authorities on, or in connection with, importation, limited in amount to the approximate cost of the services rendered, and representing neither an indirect protection to domestic products nor a taxation of imports for revenue purposes.

Article II

1. The contracting States undertake to grant the necessary licences and/or foreign exchange for the importation of the following articles:
(a) Books and publications consigned to public libraries and collections and to the libraries and collections of public educational, research or cultural institutions;
(b) Official government publications, that is, official, parliamentary and administrative documents published in their country of origin;
(c) Books and publications of the United Nations or any of its Specialized Agencies;
(d) Books and publications received by the United Nations Educational, Scientific and Cultural Organization and distributed free of charge by it or under its supervision;
(e) Publications intended to promote tourist travel outside the country of importation, sent and distributed free of charge;
(f) Articles for the blind:
(i) Books, publications and documents of all kinds in raised characters for the blind;
(ii) Other articles specially designed for the educational, scientific or cultural advancement of the blind, which are imported directly by institutions or organizations concerned with the welfare of the blind, approved by the competent authorities of the importing country for the purpose of duty-free entry of these types of articles.
2. The contracting States which at any time apply quantitative restrictions and exchange control measures undertake to grant, as far as possible, foreign exchange and licences necessary for the importation of other educational, scientific or cultural materials, and particularly the materials referred to in the annexes to this Agreement.

Article III

1. The contracting States undertake to give every possible facility to the importation of educational, scientific or cultural materials, which are imported exclusively for showing at a public exhibition approved by the competent authorities of the importing country and for subsequent re-exportation. These facilities shall include the granting of the necessary licences and exemption from customs duties and internal taxes and charges of all kinds payable on importation, other than fees and charges corresponding to the approximate cost of services rendered.
2. Nothing in this article shall prevent the authorities of an importing country from taking such steps as may be necessary to ensure that the materials in question shall be re-exported at the close of their exhibition.

Article IV

The contracting States undertake that they will as far as possible:
(a) Continue their common efforts to promote by every means the free circu-

lation of educational, scientific or cultural materials, and abolish or reduce any restrictions to that free circulation which are not referred to in this Agreement;
(b) Simplify the administrative procedure governing the importation of educational, scientific or cultural materials:
(c) Facilitate the expeditious and safe customs clearance of educational, scientific or cultural materials.

Article V

Nothing in this Agreement shall affect the right of contracting States to take measures, in conformity with their legislation to prohibit or limit the importation, or the circulation after importation, of articles on grounds relating directly to national security, public order or public morals.

Article VI

This Agreement shall not modify or affect the laws and regulations of any contracting State or any of its international treaties, conventions, agreements or proclamations, with respect to copyright, trade marks or patents.

Article VII

Subject to the provisions of any previous conventions to which the contracting States may have subscribed for the settlement of disputes, the contracting States undertake to have recourse to negotiation or conciliation, with a view to settlement of any disputes regarding the interpretation or the application of this Agreement.

Article VIII

In case of a dispute between contracting States relating to the educational, scientific or cultural character of imported materials, the interested Parties may, by common agreement, refer it to the Director-General of the United Nations Educational, Scientific and Cultural Organization for an advisory opinion.

Article IX

1. This Agreement, of which the English and French texts are equally authentic, shall bear today's date and remain open for signature by all Member States of the United Nations Educational, Scientific and Cultural Organization, all Member States of the United Nations and any non-member State to which an invitation may have been addressed by the Executive Board of the United Nations Educational, Scientific and Cultural Organization.
2. The Agreement shall be ratified on behalf of the signatory States in accordance with their respective constitutional procedure.
3. The instruments of ratification shall be deposited with the Secretary-General of the United Nations.

Article X

The States referred to in paragraph 1 of Article IX may accept this Agreement from 22 November 1950. Acceptance shall become effective on the deposit of a formal instrument with the Secretary-General of the United Nations.

Article XI

This Agreement shall come into force on the date on which the Secretary-General of the United Nations receives instruments of ratification or acceptance from 10 States.

Article XII

1. The States Parties to this Agreement on the date of its coming into force shall each take all the necessary measures for its fully effective operation within a period of six months after that date.
2. For States which may deposit their instruments of ratification or acceptance after the date of the Agreement coming into force, these measures shall be taken

within a period of three months from the date of deposit.

3. Within one month of the expiration of the periods mentioned in paragraphs 1 and 2 of this article, the contracting States to this Agreement shall submit a report to the United Nations Educational, Scientific and Cultural Organization of the measures which they have taken for such fully effective operation.

4. The United Nations Educational, Scientific and Cultural Organization shall transmit this report to all signatory States to this Agreement and to the International Trade Organization (provisionally, to its Interim Commission).

Article XIII

Any contracting State may, at the time of signature or the deposit of its instrument of ratification or acceptance, or at any time thereafter, declare by notification addressed to the Secretary-General of the United Nations that this Agreement shall extend to all or any of the territories for the conduct of whose foreign relations that contracting State is responsible.

Article XIV

1. Two years after the date of the coming into force of this Agreement, any contracting State may, on its own behalf or on behalf of any of the territories for the conduct of whose foreign relations that contracting State is responsible, denounce this Agreement by an instrument in writing deposited with the Secretary-General of the United Nations.

2. The denunciation shall take effect one year after the receipt of the instrument of denunciation.

Article XV

The Secretary-General of the United Nations shall inform the States referred to in paragraph 1 of Article IX, as well as the United Nations Educational, Scientific and Cultural Organization, and the International Trade Organization (provisionally, its Interim Commission), of the deposit of all the instruments of ratification and acceptance provided for in Articles IX and X, as well as of the notifications and denunciations provided for respectively in Articles XIII and XIV.

Article XVI

At the request of one-third of the contracting States to this Agreement, the Director-General of the United Nations Educational, Scientific and Cultural Organization shall place on the agenda of the next session of the General Conference of that Organization, the question of convoking a meeting for the revision of this Agreement.

Article XVII

Annexes A, B, C, D and E, as well as the Protocol annexed to this Agreement are hereby made an integral part of this Agreement.

Article XVIII

1. In accordance with Article 102 of the Charter of the United Nations, this Agreement shall be registered by the Secretary-General of the United Nations on the date of its coming into force.

2. In faith whereof the undersigned, duly authorized, have signed this Agreement on behalf of their respective governments.

Done at Lake Success, New York, this twenty-second day of November one thousand nine hundred and fifty in a single copy, which shall remain deposited in the archives of the United Nations, and certified true copies of which shall be delivered to all the States referred to in paragraph 1 of Article IX, as well as to the United Nations Educational, Scientific and Cultural Organization and to the International Trade Organization (provisionally, to its Interim Commission).

Annex 4: Book-Trade Answer Code

By kind permission of Book Centre, London

1	RP/Shortly	Reprinting shortly
10	RP/ND	Reprinting — no date
11	RP/UC	Reprint under consideration
1**	RP/MONTH	Reprinting and the number of the month it is expected, e.g. 106 = Reprinting June
2	BDG/Shortly	Binding — expected shortly
20	BDG/ND	Binding — no date
2**	BDG/MONTH	Binding and the number of the month it is expected
3	NE/Shortly	New edition expected shortly
30	NE/ND	New edition — no date
33	NE/UC	New edition under consideration
3**	NE/MONTH	New edition and the number of the month it is expected
4	NP/Shortly	Not published — expected shortly
40	NP/ND	Not published — no date
4**	NP/MONTH	Not published and the number of the month it is expected
5	O/O Germany	On order from Germany
6	T.O.P.	Temporarily out of print
7	O/O USA	On order from the USA
8	OTO USA	Only to order from USA
9	Shortly	Expected shortly

Annex 5a: Berne Union Member Countries*

As of January 1, 1970

Argentina
Australia
Austria
Belgium
Brazil P
Bulgaria R
Cameroon P
Canada R
Ceylon R, P
Congo (Brazzaville) P
Congo (Kinshasa)
Cyprus R, P
Czechoslovakia R
Dahomey
Denmark P
Finland
France P
Gabon
Germany:
a) FRG P
b) GDR ST
Greece
Holy See P
Hungary R, P
Iceland R
India P
Ireland
Israel P
Italy P
Ivory Coast P
Japan R
Lebanon R, P
Liechtenstein P
Luxembourg P
Madagascar
Mali
Malta R
Mexico P
Monaco P
Morocco P
Netherlands R, P
New Zealand R
Niger
Norway
Pakistan ST
Philippines
Poland R
Portugal
Romania ST
Senegal ST, P
South Africa
Spain P
Sweden P
Switzerland P
Thailand B
Tunisia P
Turkey
United Kingdom P
Upper Volta
Uruguay
Yugoslavia P

* *Countries not followed by a letter have ratified the Brussels version of the Revised Berne Convention. An R indicates that they have signed the Rome version, and a B the Berlin version. The German Democratic Republic, Pakistan, Romania and Senegal have ratified the Stockholm version, including protocol for developing countries; this is indicated by ST.*
A P indicates that the country has signed the Paris version (24 July, 1971) of the international conventions.

Annex 5b: Universal Copyright Convention, Accessions and Ratifications

As of January 1, 1970

Country	*Effective Date*
Andorra	September 16, 1955
Argentina	February 13, 1958
Australia	May 1, 1969
Austria	July 2, 1957
Belgium	August 31, 1960
Brazil P	August 31, 1960
Cambodia	September 16, 1955
Canada	August 10, 1962
Chile	September 16, 1955
Costa Rica P	September 16, 1955
Cuba	June 18, 1957
Czechoslovakia	January 6, 1960
Denmark P	February 9, 1962
Ecuador	June 5, 1957
Finland	April 16, 1963
France P	January 14, 1956
Germany, Federal Republic P	September 16, 1955
Ghana	August 22, 1962
Greece	August 24, 1963
Guatemala P	October 28, 1964
Haiti	September 16, 1955
Holy See P	October 5, 1955
Iceland	December 18, 1956
India P	January 21, 1958
Ireland	January 20, 1959
Israel P	September 16, 1955
Italy P	January 24, 1957
Japan	April 28, 1956
Kenya P	September 7, 1966
Laos	September 16, 1955
Lebanon P	October 17, 1959
Liberia P	July 27, 1956
Liechtenstein P	January 22, 1959
Luxembourg	October 15, 1955
Malawi	October 26, 1965
Malta	November 19, 1968
Mexico P	May 12, 1957
Monaco P	September 16, 1955
Netherlands P	June 22, 1967
New Zealand	September 11, 1964
Nicaragua	August 16, 1961
Nigeria	February 14, 1962
Norway	January 23, 1963
Pakistan	September 16, 1955
Panama	October 17, 1962
Paraguay	March 11, 1962
Peru	October 16, 1963
Philippines	November 19, 1955
Portugal	December 25, 1956
Spain P	September 16, 1955
Sweden P	July 1, 1961
Switzerland P	March 30, 1956
Tunisia P	June 19, 1969
United Kingdom P	September 27, 1957
United States of America P	September 16, 1955
Venezuela	September 30, 1966
Yugoslavia P	May 11, 1966
Zambia	June 1, 1965

A P indicates that the country has signed the Paris version (24 July, 1971) of the international copyright conventions. This is also true for Hungary and Mauritius.